KHIRBAT ISKANDAR
FINAL REPORT ON THE EARLY BRONZE IV
AREA C "GATEWAY" AND CEMETERIES

AMERICAN SCHOOLS OF ORIENTAL RESEARCH ARCHEOLOGICAL REPORTS

Kevin M. McGeough, Editor

Number 14

Khirbat Iskandar

Final Report on the Early Bronze IV Area C "Gateway" and Cemeteries

ARCHAEOLOGICAL EXPEDITION TO KHIRBAT ISKANDAR
AND ITS ENVIRONS, JORDAN

VOLUME ONE

KHIRBAT ISKANDAR

FINAL REPORT ON THE EARLY BRONZE IV AREA C "GATEWAY" AND CEMETERIES

Edited by

SUZANNE RICHARD, JESSE C. LONG, JR.,
PAUL S. HOLDORF, AND GLEN PETERMAN

With contributions by

CARLOS E. CORDOVA, JAMES D. D'ANGELO, SUSAN ELLIS, JEANETTE FORSEN,
YUVAL GOREN, MARY C. METZGER, YORKE M. ROWAN, AND LYNN WELTON

AMERICAN SCHOOLS OF ORIENTAL RESEARCH • BOSTON, MA

Khirbat Iskandar

Final Report on the Early Bronze IV Area C "Gateway" and Cemeteries

edited by

Suzanne Richard, Jesse C. Long, Jr., Paul S. Holdorf, and Glen Peterman

The American Schools of Oriental Research © 2010

ISBN 978-0-89757-082-4

Library of Congress Cataloging-in-Publication Data

Khirbat Iskandar : final report on the early bronze IV Area C gateway and cemeteries /
      edited by Suzanne Richard ... [et al.] ; with contributions by Carlos E. Cordova
      ... [et al.].
      p. cm. -- (Archaeological expedition to Khirbat Iskandar and its environs, Jordan ;
        v. 1) (American Schools of Oriental Research archeological reports ; no. 14)
  Includes bibliographical references and index.
  ISBN 978-0-89757-082-4 (hardcover : alk. paper)
 1. Khirbet Iskander (Jordan) 2. Excavations (Archaeology)--Jordan--Khirbet Iskander.
      3. Bronze age--Jordan--Khirbet Iskander. I. Richard, Suzanne
  DS154.9.K48K55 2010
  939'.4601--dc22
                  2009043984

Printed in the United States of America on acid-free paper.

Contents

List of Illustrations

TEXT FIGURES

List of Tables

Preface

The Expedition to Khirbat Iskandar and its Environs from its inception has been affiliated with the American Schools of Oriental Research (ASOR) and the American Center of Oriental Research in Amman (ACOR), and we are indebted to them for their continued support. The Department of Antiquities of Jordan has graciously granted the expedition a permit to excavate since 1981, and we are indeed grateful for the opportunity to work in the great country of Jordan, excavating a truly unique site for the Early Bronze IV Period (hereafter EB IV).

The Expedition to Khirbat Iskandar and its Environs became a reality in 1980 when Dr. Adnan Hadidi, Director General of the Department of Antiquities, granted a permit to Suzanne Richard to excavate. In this regard, it is most appropriate to acknowledge the role of the late Dr. James A. Sauer, Director of ACOR at that time. As a fresh, young Ph.D hoping to find a site related to the area of her dissertation—culture change at the end of the third millennium BCE—she approached Jim for advice. He immediately suggested the EB IV site of Khirbat Iskandar as a nice little project and was extremely supportive in discussions with Dr. Hadidi. A special note of thanks must go to Mr. Peter Parr, who graciously conceded his permit to the site of Khirbat Iskandar, thus facilitating the entire matter.

That "little project," whose early research objectives were to spend a few seasons investigating whether or not the EB IV remains at Khirbat Iskandar reflected a sedentary or pastoral nomadic population, has grown into a major long-term interdisciplinary operation. Needless to say, the objectives have changed since then, as the breadth and nature of EB IV occupation on the mound became clear, and as the preceding urban settlement began to emerge. Indeed, it is likely that the site may have been occupied throughout the Early Bronze Age, ca. 3600–2000 BCE. Current work focuses on exposing the EB II/III settlements in Area

B, as well as a probable EB I stratum. The expedition has expanded its research objectives beyond illuminating sedentism in the EB IV period to investigating the enigmatic transition from urban to rural lifeways, as well as charting the urbanization process at the site.

This volume represents the final report on the Area C "Gateway" and the EB IV Cemeteries in the vicinity of the site, both excavations of which occurred in the Phase 1 seasons (1981, 1982, 1984 and 1987) reported on in this volume. Since that time, some additional work to check the stratigraphy in Area C was done in 2004 and 2007, and three seasons of restoration and consolidation took place in 1998, 2006, and 2008. The results of the regional survey conducted during Phase 1 will appear in a future volume, along with recently completed exploration and excavation of the remaining megalithic features in the vicinity of the site. With the completion of Vol. 1 of the Khirbat Iskandar Expedition Series, we turn our attention to preparing the EB IV materials in Area B for publication.

Originally, the intent was to publish this volume as a final report on the Area C excavations only. However, as work progressed on the cemeteries, including the drafting and study of pottery, we expanded the scope of the volume. We believe that the addition of the cemetery materials, which allow for tell/tomb comparative analysis, enhances our view of the occupants of the site, their social organization, and their burial ritual. There are few sites that can offer both a stratified sequence of EB IV multi-phase occupation and associated burial remains. Bâb adh-Dhrâ' is another such site.

Throughout this volume, we will be referring often to Bâb adh-Dhrâ'. One reason for the delay in finalizing this volume was the decision to adopt their classification system in the midst of our own quantitative studies of the Area C ceramics. Since one of the main goals was to present the stratified ceramic typology of Khirbat Iskandar as a template for the Central Transjordanian Plateau in EB IV, it seemed imperative to strive for a cross-comparative study with a kindred site, whose stratigraphy and ceramic classification set the standard as a model for the southeastern Dead Sea Plain. After numerous attempts to correlate two different systems, the decision was made to adopt their system, although it caused a delay in the completion of this volume. However, we believe that the valuable correlations between the quantified ceramic studies at both sites represent a first step towards developing an objective typological sequence for the EB IV period, one based not on tomb deposits or one-period sites, but one tied firmly to stratigraphy. For ease in comparative analysis of the two sites, this volume attempts to follow a format similar to that of the Bâb adh-Dhrâ' publications.

A Personal Note from the PI

It is not always the case that the subject of a dissertation becomes one's life work. However, this is just the case with principal investigator and co-director, Suzanne Richard, and co-director, Jesse C. Long, Jr., and their dissertations (Richard 1978; Long 1988). On a personal note, Suzanne Richard would like to mention that in the first major season (1982), there was a Drew University graduate student in the trenches; that student is a co-editor of this volume, Jesse C. Long, Jr., who was a square supervisor in Area A that year. He caught the bug for archaeology, eventually writing his dissertation on Khirbat Iskandar and the Early Bronze IV Period to complete his Ph.D at Drew University. His excellent dissertation demonstrated the important role sedentism played in EB IV Palestine-Transjordan and the complex nature of adaptation in the period. Co-editor Long never excavated in Area C during Phase 1 operations at the site. Rather, he joined the project as Assistant Director in 1994, and soon immersed himself in the stratigraphy of

Area C to prepare the final report, which is found in Chapter 3. He quickly became co-director and has been an invaluable colleague, and best friend, since that time.

Also, it is impossible to express how essential co-editor Paul Holdorf has been and continues to be to the expedition since 1994. As the Information Specialist, Paul has single-handedly brought the expedition into the computer age and continues to curate the data. Truly, this publication became a reality because of Paul's control of the database and, in particular, his quantitative analysis, upon which the typo-chronological study rests. He has been involved with every aspect of the project and of this volume, but it is his great friendship and support for which I am exceedingly grateful.

It is quite apropos that Glen Peterman, another archaeology student from Drew University and later from the University of Arizona, should be a full partner in bringing the Area C excavation to publication: as the Area C supervisor in 1982, he discovered the gate! His GIS work in the Wâdi al-Wâla region and research on the EB IV period has been an invaluable resource throughout this volume. It is, to a great extent, his work on the cemeteries, including the restoration and drafting of the pottery assemblage that drove the decision to expand this volume. His drafting of all the plates has ensured their very highest standard, while his editing skills have greatly enhanced this volume. I value his friendship greatly.

I personally owe a great debt of gratitude to Jesse, Paul, and Glen for helping me to publish the important results of the Khirbat Iskandar Excavations. The team looks forward to continued excavation at the site and to the appearance of Volume 2 in a time frame far shorter than that for the present volume.

The Editors
July, 2009

Acknowledgments

Phase 1 operations at the site, that is, the 1981, 1982, 1984, and 1987 seasons, were made possible by a number of granting agencies, universities, and many private donors. The pilot season in 1981 became a reality when The Endowment for Biblical Research provided the seed money. The Endowment also granted Glen Peterman research moneys in 1985 that enabled him to restore and draft the ceramic assemblage from the cemeteries. The Endowment has also provided much-needed travel moneys for a number of Khirbat Iskandar participants over the years. We are grateful for all of their support.

Major funding for the 1982 and 1987 seasons came from two matching grants from the National Endowment for the Humanities (NEH No. RO-203886-82 and No. RO-21166-86). We are extremely appreciative of their support. Richard and Long would also like to acknowledge their respective NEH/ACOR fellowships in 1984 and 1995, which allowed them to work on the Khirbat Iskandar materials. A recent CAORC fellowship (2008) allowed Suzanne Richard to finalize this volume for submission to the ASOR Publication Committee.

We extend thanks to the consortium of schools in Phase 1, Drew University, Upsala University, and Seton Hall University, that supported the expedition during part or all of that period. A special note of thanks goes to our current consortium — Gannon University, Lubbock Christian University, and McMurry University — whose support throughout Phase 2 has enabled a pilot season in 1994, full-scale excavations in 1997, 2000, 2004, and 2007, and three restoration seasons in 1998, 2006, and 2008. In addition, grants from the Harris Foundation (2000, 2006) and the Heritage Foundation (2007) made it possible to resurvey and remap Khirbat Iskandar with state-of-the-art GPS equipment. We thank them all.

We would also like to recognize the following corporate and private donors for their financial support: Exxon Corporation, Sonetic Corporation, Johnson & Johnson, Marlin and Sarah White, Suzanne von Lengerke, Dennis and Carolyn Buss, Herbert B. Huffmon, Roger S. Boraas, Sylvia Hnat, June Curtis, Molly Ellsworth, MaryAnn Kaub, Les Morgan, Bill Libby, Paul and Lois Holdorf, James D'Angelo, Suzanne Richard, Glen Peterman, and The Friends of Khirbat Iskandar. A special thanks goes to Dickinson College (Glen Peterman) and to The Collins Institute for Archaeological Research at Gannon University (Suzanne Richard), as well as to Lubbock Christian University (Jesse C. Long, Jr.), Paul Holdorf, and Suzanne Richard for their donations to cover the publication subvention fee.

Co-editor Richard would particularly like to acknowledge grants from the Gannon University Faculty Research Committee in 2000, 2002, 2004, and 2007, for the expedition, as well as for research and publication. Richard would also like to express a debt of gratitude for the great support from Dean Timothy M. Downs for The Collins Institute for Archaeological Research at Gannon University, which since 2004 has helped to underwrite the costs of the excavation and costs of post-excavation research.

She wishes to acknowledge especially Marlin and Sarah White, whose continued help, advice, organizing skills, accounting skills, hard work, and dedication enabled the success of the Phase 1 operations, as well as the 1994, 1997 and 2000 seasons. It is impossible to express how integral they were to the expedition. Their friendship over the years has been steady and strong.

Finally, a special note of thanks goes to Roger S. Boraas for his help directing the 1982 and 1984 field operations, his astute guidance, for the use of a field manual he devised for the Tall Hesban excavations, and, in general, good friendship through the years. Although not officially associated with the expedition, William G. Dever has been a great supporter of the Khirbat Iskandar Expedition from the beginning, and a special note of appreciation goes to him for his wise counsel, encouragement, and help over the years. To Herb Huffmon, for his support of the project during the Drew University years and thereafter, a special note of thanks is in order.

The editors would especially like to thank the past Directors of ACOR, the late Dr. James Sauer, Dr. David McCreery, Dr. Bert DeVries, and Dr. Pierre Bikai, as well as current Director, Dr. Barbara Porter, all of whom smoothed the way through so many of both the mundane and the serious matters involved with directing a dig in a foreign country. And special thanks goes to Dr. Adnan Hadidi, Dr. Ghazi Bisheh, and Dr. Fawwaz al-Khraysheh, past and current Director Generals of the Department of Antiquities, Jordan, who have over the years been extremely supportive of the expedition. We would like to voice our appreciation for the staff at the Wâdi al-Wâla Agricultural Station for help throughout the years, especially Abdulmagid Bashabsheh who, as Director, was of exceptional help to the project in so many ways. We would like to acknowledge the al-Kawamleh family from Dhiban for their friendship and help from the beginning of the project.

A long-term project such as this one inevitably required much revising of the work, as newer technology and techniques became known; we have already mentioned in the Preface the multiple revisions in the classification system. Thus, we would like to recognize the work of a number of people who helped at various stages in the work-up of the Khirbat Iskandar materials, from cutting sherds to drawing, to organizing and reorganizing materials, from data entry to restoration. We express gratitude to Dr. Linda Galate, Sarah White, Carolyn Buss, Paul Holdorf, and Lois Holdorf. For work in The Collins Institute at Gannon University, a distinctive note of thanks to Ross Miceli, Drew Saxton, Sue Pennock Bailey, Tina Curtis, Tricia Close, Michele Seaman, Rick Rohaly, and Lisa Coleman. And, to Gannon University colleague, Elizabeth Kons, many thanks for help reading an earlier draft of this volume.

We are especially grateful to Fawwaz Ishakat, who has resurveyed the site and provided us with an up-to-date and accurate map of the site and vicinity to GPS accuracy. We appreciate all of their time and effort spent on this project. Thanks to Sarah White, who drew the Cemetery and Area C objects from 1984 and 1987 and to Cindy Winrow Mathewson for drawing the 1982 objects. Glen Peterman produced all the final figures in this volume (pottery, tombs, objects), except for the figures in chapter 3, which were drawn and finalized by Jesse Long. Michael Miller deserves a great deal of thanks for finalizing the topographic maps of the site and region (based on Fawwaz Ishakat's maps), aided in this endeavor by James D'Angelo and Glen Peterman. Rikke Wulff Krabbenhøft created the GPS map of EB IV sites, aided by Ronnie Rama. The majority of the photos published here are the work of Kevin Klein (1982) and Edyth Skinner (1984 and 1987), and her students Dick Hermann, Stephen Neigh, and Linda Travisano (1987). And a special thanks to Drew Saxton for his work finalizing the digitized photos, especially the artifacts, and to Michele Seaman, both of whose work in the Collins Institute has helped immensely to bring this volume to publication.

A special note of acknowledgement is due to the directors of our kindred Early Bronze Age site of Bâb adh-Dhrâ'. We thank Tom Schaub for his good colleagueship in sharing materials with us, for working closely with and facilitating the work of Paul Holdorf on the quantified ceramic study. We would also like to acknowledge the late Walt Rast, who was a gracious and supportive colleague always. Another colleague we would like to acknowledge is Larry Herr, who graciously allowed us to use the Madaba Plains Project Manual for the expedition (Herr and Christopherson 1998). We would also like to acknowledge the good colleagueship of Stanley Klassen for advising us on technological aspects of the ceramic collection. We would like to thank all those contributors whose articles appear in this volume, and the many square and field supervisors (listed in Chapter 1) whose great work and documentation form the basis for this final report.

Finally, to the ASOR publication staff, Joe Greene and Kevin McGeough, and Susanne Wilhelm at The David Brown Book Company, a deeply felt thank you for their incredible help in making this volume a reality.

Chapter 1

Introduction

by Suzanne Richard

The original intent of the expedition's pilot season in 1981 was to test certain hypotheses set forth in the author's dissertation concerning culture change at the end of the third millennium BCE in the southern Levant (Richard 1978). That work had posited the importance of sedentary adaptive strategies in the Early Bronze IV (EB IV) period (ca. 2300–2000 BCE), along with strong continuities of Early Bronze Age tradition following the collapse of urbanism at the end of EB III, ca. 2350/2300 BCE. Informing that study was the new evidence for EB IV sedentism beginning to emerge in Jordan at such sites as Iktanu (Prag 1974), Adir (Cleveland 1960), 'Ara'ir (Olavárri 1965; 1969), and Bâb adh-Dhrâ' (Rast and Schaub 1978), as well as earlier work at Khirbat Iskandar (Parr 1960). Because scholars considered the period to be a "dark age" or "nomadic interlude" having no links to the preceding or succeeding urban eras, this new evidence for a sedentary population was a watershed for EB IV studies (Dever 1973).

Since then, excavation in Jordan, especially, has affirmed an important agrarian component (see map, fig. 1.1). These sites include: Tall al-Hayyât (Falconer et al. 2006), Tall Abu an-Ni'aj (Falconer and Magness-Gardiner 1989), Tall Umm Hammad (Helms 1986), Dhahrat Umm al-Marar (Falconer, Fall, and Jones 1998; 2007), Khirbat al-Batrawy (Nigro 2006), Tall al-Hammam (Prag 1991), ar-Rahil and other Wâdi al-Yâbis sites (Palumbo, Mabry, and Kuijt 1990), Khirbat Hamra Ifdan (Adams 2000), Tall al-'Umayri (Mitchel 1989), as well as continued excavations at Iktanu (Prag 1991), Bâb adh-Dhrâ' (Rast and Schaub 2003), and current excavations at Khirbat Iskandar (see figs. 1.3–1.4). Although pastoral nomadism is the more popular model to explain subsistence in Cisjordan, a sedentary component to the population existed there as well, including tell sites, such as Jericho, Hazor, Megiddo, Beth Yerah, Rosh ha-Niqra (see chap. 16). When combined, the newly discovered sedentary and the well-documented pastoral-nomadic populations provide a more balanced perspective on the peoples of the rural EB IV period. The work reported on in this volume affirms the trend to incorporate an important sedentary component within the EB IV population.

Indeed, as this report on the Khirbat Iskandar excavations will make clear, rural complexity existed in the EB IV period. In fact, due to its well-preserved and substantial remains and "urban-like" characteristics—reuse of fortifications, an impressive "store-

1

FIG. 1.1   *Map of major EB IV sites in the southern Levant mentioned in the text (prepared by R. Wulff Krabbenhøft and R. Rama).*

room" in Area B, and a "gateway" in Area C—the site appears to continue sedentary traditions from the earlier fortified town settlement now emerging in the excavations in Area B (see topographic map, fig. 1.2). Those excavations, along with exploration of the vicinity of Khirbat Iskandar, largely inform our interpretation of the Area C remains in this volume (see an isometric view of the Phase 3 gate in fig. 1.6 and proposed reconstruction in fig. 1.7).

The objectives of this final excavation report are to: 1) set forth the evidence for three EB IV strati-graphical phases in Area C, showing the development of a domestic area into a public "gateway;" 2) provide the evidence for the EB IV tombs excavated in the vicinity of the site (see fig. 9.1); and 3) present the results of a quantitative ceramic study of tell and tomb corpora, including correlations with Bâb adh-Dhrâ'.

As this final report will show, Area C's multiple phases offer an excellent opportunity to chart the recovery, change, growth, and final demise of the EB IV sedentists, as viewed in the history of the gate area. The stratified sequence at Khirbat Iskandar also provides some critically needed chronological pegs for the period, especially for ceramic typology. This volume will also show that distinctions exist in and between the various cemeteries, and that the grave goods correspond to the traditions of sedentists, undoubtedly the occupants of the site. The quantitative study illuminated a three-phase typo-chronological sequence in Area C. When compared quantitatively with the ceramic corpus from the cemeteries, the Area C phasing allowed for a seriation and relative dating of the tombs. A quantitative comparison with the EB IV assemblage of Bâb adh-Dhrâʿ illuminated important correlations between the two sites, thus providing a link in phases between sites of the Transjordanian Central Plateau and Southern Dead Sea Plain in the EB IV period.

OVERVIEW OF THE EARLY BRONZE AGE IN THE SOUTHERN LEVANT

Traditionally, the Early Bronze Age (ca. 3600–2000 BCE) has been seen as an era comprising an EB I proto-urban phase (ca. 3600–3100 BCE), followed by an urban EB II–III period (ca. 3100–2300 BCE), which ended in a period of collapse in EB IV (ca. 2300–2000 BCE). In light of the primary urban states in neighboring Mesopotamia and Egypt, and especially the late-third-millennium-BCE First Intermediate Period in Egypt, the above scenario for the southern Levantine EBA has been an acceptable cultural-historical reconstruction for years. Yet, diversity of opinion has existed over whether urbanism was derivative or indigenous or a combination of external and internal forces; whether it was "small-scale" or a unique regional trajectory. Equally controversial are the causes for the eclipse of urbanism (or town life) at the end of EB III and for the subsequent non-urban (or rural) EB IV period. Past scholarship has wrestled with all of these issues, as the numerous surveys of the period attest (Hennessy 1967; Lapp 1970; Amiran 1970; Wright

1971; de Vaux 1971; Kempinski 1978; Kenyon 1979; Rast 1980; Ross 1980; Ben-Tor 1982; Richard 1987a; 2003; Prag 2001; Joffe 1993; Greenberg 2002). If there is a consensus, it is that the fortified towns/cities of the southern Levant do not meet the criteria for urbanism attested in the highly complex societies in neighboring countries.

Recently, newer approaches question whether the EB II–III period in the southern Levant is urban, arguing instead for a non-elite, non-hierarchical (such as non-urban) political organization, that is, heterarchy (Philip 2001; 2008; Savage, Falconer, and Harrison 2007). These latter scholars interpret the organizational strategies of the EB II–III as reflecting a decentralized village (rural) kinship society, more in line with heterarchy rather than hierarchy, especially as regards Transjordan. For a survey of the Early Bronze Age in light of current trends, see Richard (2009).

Although this volume concerns the EB IV period at Khirbat Iskandar, as mentioned above, the interpretation of the site hinges upon the view that "urban-like" traditions continue in the post-EB III period. Whether the large, fortified towns of EB II–III represent hierarchical or heterarchical strategies, the level of complexity at Khirbat Iskandar in the EB IV is certainly more reflective of antecedent "tell" occupation than of the sedentarization of pastoral nomads. A recent view sees "urban-like" traditions in the period as well, but suggests a derivation from Syrian tradition (Prag 2009). The concern in this volume is to explain the extraordinary (for the EB IV period) features at the site in the context of continuity and change at the EB III/IV transition in the southern Levant.

OVERVIEW OF THE EARLY BRONZE III/IV TRANSITION

The destruction and/or abandonment of every walled site in the southern Levant occurred by the end of the EB III period, a phenomenon interconnecting the region with widespread collapse in the Near East (Dalfes, Kukla and Weiss 1997). Although the latter reference posits climate change as the major factor (and see the discussion on climate in Chapters 2 and 16 of this volume), scholars have proposed a variety of internal and/or external causes to explain the still enigmatic EB III/IV transition in the southern Levant. Highlighting invasion, scholars have cited Amorite nomadic incursions and/or Egyptian military campaigns. A series of internal events, such as disruption of trade, over-crowding of sites, and reduced agricultural product are also possible factors, perhaps set in motion by invasion or climate degradation (and see the Early Bronze Age surveys cited above). This volume presupposes multilinear regional trajectories of collapse throughout the southern Levant (for several scenarios, see Dever 1989; Greenberg 2002; Richard and Long 2009), as well as varied responses and recoveries in the subsequent EB IV period. For a development of the collapse and recovery trajectory peculiar to the Khirbat Iskandar region, see Chapters 2 and 16. Although the present chapter highlights some of the areas of scholarly disagreement (below), for a thorough discussion of the issues, as well as a review of theoretical constructs postulated to explain the EB III/IV transition, see the convenient summaries in Richard (1987a; 2003) and Long (2003).

One of the period's still outstanding issues is terminology. Today, scholars tend either to favor the term "EB IV," or a form of Intermediate terminology. At one time (Dever 1980; Richard 1980; 1987a), these two terms were distinctive of two conceptual approaches. Those favoring strong continuities with Early Bronze Age tradition following collapse, generally used the term EB IV; those preferring to emphasize disjunction and dramatic change (at the beginning and end) generally applied some form of the Intermediate terminology. Such is not the case today, as scholars using the Intermediate terminology can just as likely emphasize continuities with both Early Bronze and Middle Bronze Age traditions, while emphasizing dramatic change and population incursions (see most recently Prag 2009).

It was W. F. Albright who first recognized the new period at the end of the third millennium BCE on the basis of pottery picked up from the site of Bâb adh-Dhrâ' (1924). His student, G. Ernest Wright, later introduced the term EB IV in his masterful analysis and phasing of third-millennium-

BCE sites, calling it "the last gasp" of Early Bronze Age tradition (1937). The confusion began when Albright differentiated EB IV pottery as earlier than his Stratum H–I horizon at Tel Beit Mirsim (1949; 1962), which he termed Middle Bronze I (MB I). Since the latter site's pottery came to define the phase, the term MB I became popular in the literature (Dever 1970). However, when Transjordanian pottery began to emerge from excavations at Bâb adh-Dhrâ' and other sites, Dever recognized it as an earlier horizon of Stratum H–I pottery and revitalized the combined term EB IV–MB I (1973). Ultimately, despite regional differences, the homogeneity of the various pottery traditions was evident, and the term EB IV was applied to the entire period (Dever 1980).

A dichotomy in terminology really began with Kathleen Kenyon in 1960. Based on her excavations of 346 shaft tombs and ephemeral occupation on the mound at Jericho, she adopted the term, Intermediate Early Bronze–Middle Bronze (EB–MB), arguing for a complete break at the beginning and end of the period. In 1966, Paul Lapp introduced the variant term, Intermediate Bronze Age (IBA), which has gained adherents, although both versions are in use today. This volume will utilize EB IV terminology in the traditional sense that strong continuities exist with antecedent Early Bronze Age tradition, of which it is "the last gasp." For a recent evaluation of the tortuous history and attendant ambiguity of late-third-millennium-BCE terminology, see now Parr (2009).

Another issue (related to terminology) that still defies resolution today is the conceptualization of the period; that is, whether it is more sedentary or pastoral-nomadic, whether cultural change is greater than cultural continuity, and whether the change is due to movements of peoples or to cultural diffusion. The engine of change is often seen as emanating from the northern Levant, in Syria, during Ebla's apogee (2400–2100 BCE). This was a period characterized by an immensely popular and widespread corrugated pottery assemblage, whose influences on the local EB IV ceramic corpus are evident, although usually of a hybrid and provincial quality, except for the rare import (and see Ch. 4). Although a backwater in this period, the southern Levant shares broad cultural traditions with Syria in metals and tombs, as well as pottery, again, provincial in comparison. The question is, are these the same broad cultural influences connecting the north and south throughout the Early Bronze Age, or is the situation in the EB IV radically different and explained only by movements of peoples, like the Amorites?

Kenyon connected the EB–MB peoples with movements of Amorite nomads who are documented in late-third and early-second-millennium-BCE texts in Mesopotamia (Kenyon, Bottéro, and Posener 1971). In this view, the Amorites swept into the southern Levant, destroyed the cities, and precipitated a 300-year period of nomadism. This view came under immediate criticism, for a variety of reasons. For example, there were new insights on the subsistence strategies of pastoral nomads (see Dever 1971; 1989; 1992) in the literature, and new scholarly approaches that emphasized internal, not external change (see Richard 1980; 1987a). More recently, there has been a swing back somewhat to revitalize theories of movements of peoples from Syria to explain cultural similarities (Prag 2009).

This volume stresses indigenous recovery at Khirbat Iskandar through adaptation and change, the latter probably due to a combination of factors and influences, both internal and external. The waxing and waning of urban and rural periods is a well-documented phenomenon in the ancient Near East. The EB IV period, with its many similarities to the pre-urban EB I period (shaft tombs, pottery corpus, village/cemetery contiguity, etc.) appears to be one of those rural intervals. New insights concerning ruralism and investigations of rural Bronze Age communities have helped to illuminate the continuities and changes in the late third millennium BCE. It is the rural communities that led to the renascent reurbanized Middle Bronze Age around 2000 BCE (see most recently Falconer et al. 2006).

Thus, this volume interprets the EB IV period as a typical rural period that incorporates both sedentary and pastoral-nomadic populations. As discussed in detail elsewhere (Richard and Long 2009; Richard 2009), there appear to be regional emphases on one or the other subsistence strategy throughout the southern Levant. For example, in the hundreds of small settlements in the marginal region of the Negev, the model of pastoral nomadism may be more applicable than elsewhere, especially Transjordan, where multiphase agrarian settlement is well attested.

The view from Khirbat Iskandar clearly reflects the agrarian component of the EB IV population and illuminates strong ties with antecedent Early Bronze Age traditions. These two datasets, derived from excavation and detailed in this volume, influence the view of the Early Bronze Age maintained in and informing this work. That view finds the Early Bronze Age as one continuous tradition ebbing and flowing over 1600 years (3600–2000 BCE). There is a great deal of evidence from sites in Jordan for continuity from EB I to EB IV, including the abundant data from the Faynan for metal production (Hauptmann 2007). Regardless of the debate over urbanism, there is a clear development from village (EB I) to the towns/cities of EB II/III, followed by devolution in EB IV to a rural society. Further, although a topic beyond the parameters of this volume, the growing list of connections with the succeeding Middle Bronze Age (Richard 2006; Greenberg 2002; Falconer et al. 2006) is germane to the recovery and reorganization strategies discernible in the three phases in Area C. As alluded to above, it is the EB IV agrarian settlements that helped the regeneration of urbanism at the beginning of the Middle Bronze Age.

HISTORY OF EXPLORATION AT KHIRBAT ISKANDAR

Earlier Work

The location of Khirbat Iskandar (fig. 1.1) on the north bank of the Wâdi al-Wâla is at a major crossing point of the main north–south highway running through Jordan (for the geo-environmental setting of the site, see Ch. 2). The number of early travelers/explorers who commented on the site suggests that it was a clear landmark (figs. 1.3–1.5). Charles Irby and James Mangles (1823: 463), while picnicking near the "Wady Wale," observed large standing

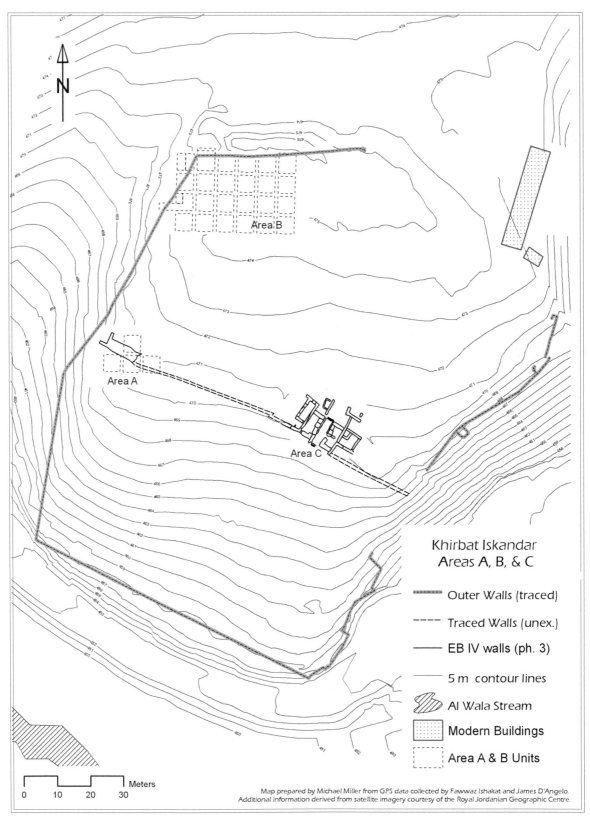

FIG. 1.2   *Topographic Map of Khirbat Iskandar (prepared by M. Miller).*

FIG. 1.3 *Photo of Khirbat Iskandar and its vicinity from the South.*

stones (menhirs) on both sides of the stream. They compared them with ancient boundary-stones mentioned in the Bible. Passing by the site on his journey through Moab, Conrad Schick paid more attention to detail, probably because he was an architect by profession. He described the site of "Skander" as covered with ruins and defended by walls and a fosse; to the east, he noted scattered house remains, megalithic structures (probably circle-of-stone features), and standing stones, which were probably menhirs (1879: 189–90). Alois Musil surmised that the whole area was like an ancient cult place (1907: 111–12). Brünnow and von Domaszewski simply refer to "Skander" as a formless ruin heap on a mountain chain (1904: 28). Interestingly, Burckhardt described the ruins in the Wale on the summit of a lower ridge of mountains as a "small castle" (1822: 370). This was, apparently, a reference to the site of Khirbat Iskandar (and see Brünnow and von Domaszewski 1904: 28). It was not, however, until Nelson Glueck's visit in 1936 that any real effort to document the site occurred (1939: 127–29).

Glueck depicted a well-fortified site surrounded by a thick perimeter wall with square towers at the corners and at intervals, as well as an east–west fortification wall that bisected the site roughly in the middle (fig. 1.5). From his observations, it is clear that the best-preserved remains were at the northwest corner (Area B), and his east–west wall (the "Glueck" wall) is equivalent to the line connecting Areas A and C (fig. 1.2). His exploration of the area revealed "EB IV–MB I" sherds to the north, west, and east of the site, and across the wâdi to the south.

The current expedition has affirmed these original observations by Glueck, making it likely that the "site" comprised a much larger area than the 2.7 ha tell might suggest. Since the eastern sector of the "site," which Glueck described as being between wadis to the east, was of a similar size, Khirbat Iskandar would be closer to 5.0 ha or more. In fact, he noted that cultural remains, primarily of a cultic nature, were evident even beyond the easternmost of the wadis (Area E, ca. 1.5 ha). There was also occupation on the small

FIG. 1.4   *Photo of Khirbat Iskandar and its vicinity from the Southeast.*

plain to the north of the site (0.5 ha). Considering all these elements, including evidence for menhirs to the south, it is estimated that in antiquity the combined area of Khirbat Iskandar was at least 8 ha, if not larger. Unfortunately, given the olive groves covering most of the eastern sector, the extent of domestic remains there is irretrievable. The current expedition has observed and excavated only cultic remains, including tombs in Area E. Because of Glueck's work, Khirbat Iskandar became a site known as an important EB IV settlement.

It was not until later that actual excavation took place, conducted by Peter Parr (1956: 81; 1960: 28–33). Like Glueck, Parr also noted that the site appeared to consist of two distinct parts, both of which had either domestic walls and/or fortifications (1956). In a trench on the eastern brow of the tell (Trench I), excavation to bedrock (3 m) revealed three major strata (periods) with multiple sub-phases. The lowest level (Period 1) revealed primarily a stone fortification some 2.30 m in width, originally built against a carved-out escarpment of

about 2 m in height. Unfortunately, erosion had washed away all contemporary occupation levels, but the few pieces of pottery associated with and sealing it were dated to the Late Chalcolithic/EB I period. Period 2, characterized by streaky grey and yellow layers partially overlain by mudbrick debris, seemed to represent occupation (courtyard) debris (1960: 129). Pottery from the streaky layers included Late Chalcolithic, EB I, and later materials, indicated by a pinch-lapped ledge-handle and a red burnished stump-base (Parr 1960: 132).

After a gap, the Period 3(i) occupants constructed a major fortification, if the 2 m deep and 3 m wide foundation trench is any indication. Very little of the wall remained, but there was evidence for several rebuilds. In Period 3(ii), there was a building that incorporated some of the Phase 3(i) wall, but whose cobbled pavement sealed the earlier foundation trench. In the middle of the pavement, there was a stone socket for roof support. Interestingly, one remaining wall measured 1.5 m high and 0.75 m wide, much like the uppermost Phase 3 walls

FIG. 1.5 *Photo showing "outlines of Khirbat Iskandar on n. side of Wadi Wala"* (Explorations in Eastern Palestine III [AASOR 18–19, 1937–39, p. 125, fig. 47]; *Courtesy of the Semitic Museum, Harvard University, ASOR Nelson Glueck Archive, Neg. 1936 #140*).

preserved at the east end of Area C (and in Area A) of the current expedition. In Trench II at the northeast corner, where bedrock was not reached, parallel Period 2 streaky materials and Phase 3 architecture came to light. However, here the upper phase included three to four phases of occupation and the latest structure measured some 9.5 × 7.5 m in dimension, again with 0.75-m-wide walls (Parr 1960: 129–30). The Period 3 pottery dated to EB IV (Parr 1960: 132–33). The parallels between Parr's work and the stratigraphy of Area C thus concern primarily Period 3 data. The earlier Periods 1–2 will tie in with future publication of the pre-EB IV stratigraphy in Area B.

The Current Expedition

Phase 1 Excavations (1981–1987)

The original research objective of the 1981 pilot season was to test the alternating hypotheses of seasonal vs. permanent occupation on the mound. This research agenda seemed compelling, given

the accepted model of the time (pastoral nomadism) and the newly emerging agrarian sector in the EB IV. As substantial evidence of continuous occupation was uncovered in 1981, it became clear that a research design formulated to explore sedentary adaptive strategies in the EB IV would be appropriate for this new project. Integral to this research design, as well, was the then debated issue of whether the cultural assemblage of the EB IV peoples represented local or external (such as Syrian) ancestry.

Thus, the major questions developed for the 1982 season were: 1) What were the extent and nature of sedentism at the site, and 2) Did the material culture indicate a shared cultural tradition with the local Early Bronze Age, or did it manifest foreign (Syrian) origin? Moreover, to contextualize these concerns, the broader question posed was: What role did Khirbat Iskandar play in a larger regional setting? In order to answer all of these questions, work focused on horizontal exposure in three major areas, A, B, C (see fig. 1.2), and on a preliminary regional survey. This strategy enabled a sampling of occupational and organizational patterns across the mound, recovery of a wide range of material culture, and a contextualizing of the site within the region. For a survey of these seasons of excavation, see below.

The stunning remains (for the EB IV period) uncovered in the 1982 season, including fortifications in Area B and what appeared to be a gate structure in Area C with connecting wall to the Area A interval tower, led to refinements in the research design for the 1984 and 1987 seasons. The primary objective of the project, thereafter, was to determine the level of social complexity attainable by the occupants of Khirbat Iskandar, one of a minority of EB IV settlements discovered on a previously occupied tell site. Secondarily, a continuing objective was to determine the degree of continuity or change with Early Bronze Age traditions. By the end of the 1987 season, it was evident that Khirbat Iskandar was a major EB IV site, perhaps a regional center. The combined data pointed to an unusually high level of complexity for a pastoral-nomadic or even a rural period. It seemed likely that some keen insights about human adaptability at the crossroads of change would eventuate from the wealth of data retrieved from the site.

In the 1984 and 1987 seasons, through the fortuitous, albeit unfortunate, act of bulldozing, cemeteries to the east, west, and across the wâdi to the south came to the attention of the survey team. The search for tombs before this had been unsuccessful. This new evidence added to the datasets available for contextualizing the occupants of Khirbat Iskandar, for example, their associated ritual customs and extent of their exploitation of the vicinity. The number of EB IV sites with contiguous cemeteries being few, excavation would afford the opportunity to compare tell and tomb material remains.

Throughout the Phase 1 operations, the project achieved its objectives by recovery of architectural, ceramic, lithic and other objects, faunal, botanical remains, and human skeletal remains, as well as regional site survey. All of these data, except for the regional site survey and the ongoing botanical study of the site, appear in this volume. This volume also includes a geomorphological and environmental study carried out during Phase 2 operations.

Phase 2 Excavations (1994–present)

Although this volume reports only on the Phase 1 excavations in Area C (except for later probes) and the cemeteries, it is obvious that later excavations and discoveries at the site influence the general interpretations presented in this volume. As detailed below, the discovery of a pre-EB IV settlement on the mound necessarily has entailed new, refined objectives and research questions throughout the Phase 2 operations. Yet, the underlying rationale for excavation has remained to elucidate fully the sedentary character of the EB IV population, with a view toward offering an alternative view to the prevailing model of pastoral nomadism, one that resonates with current scholarship on the topic of social complexity in a rural setting.

Briefly, in light of the EB II/III fortified town settlement on the mound, as well as a probable EB I stratum, the project defined several additional objectives: a) to investigate the still enigmatic transition to a rural society in EB IV, and b) to understand the rise and collapse of the walled site of Khirbat Iskandar. In addition, in light of the fierce pace of agricultural development near the site, the documentation, excavation, and exploration of the cultic features (menhirs, circles-of-stone) remaining from Nelson Glueck's visit became a pressing goal of the expedition. To meet the objectives of these expanded research goals, the expedition in Phase 2 has concentrated on the site and immediate surroundings of Khirbat Iskandar. The cultic features investigated, considered together with the cemetery remains, enhance our view and our interpretation of the Area C and cemetery remains reported on in this volume.

FIELD SEASONS AT KHIRBAT ISKANDAR

This section surveys the major discoveries at the site in Phase 1. It is a general narrative about each season's work. A short summary of the Phase 2 excavations, presented to offer a broader lens from which to view the Area C and cemetery remains, will follow.

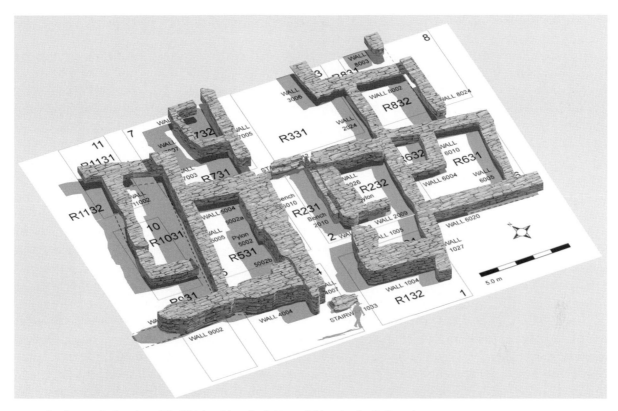

FIG. 1.6   *Isometric drawing of the Khirbat Iskandar "gateway" (drawing by R. Rama).*

Phase 1 Summary

1981 Season

The purpose of this short pilot season was to reconnoiter the site in its immediate vicinity and probe the stratigraphy of the mound (Richard 1982). After mapping the site and preparing it for an excavation grid of 5 × 5 m squares, the staff conducted a random surface sampling by collecting all sherds and artifacts within a specified radius at randomly chosen grid points across the entire site. This survey, along with a study of surface remains, confirmed Glueck's observations that substantial architecture and occupation were present at the northwest corner of the mound; likewise, a continuous series of wall lines appeared to confirm his identification of an east–west wall line bisecting

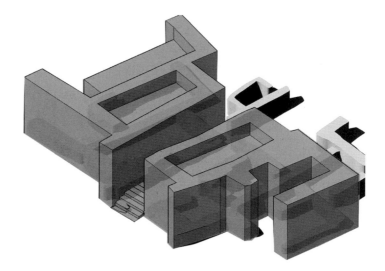

FIG. 1.7   *Isometric reconstruction of the Khirbat Iskandar "gateway" (drawing by R. Rama).*

the site. Considering all these factors, the team opened Probe A at the southwest and Probe B at the northwest corners, both 4 × 4 m squares.

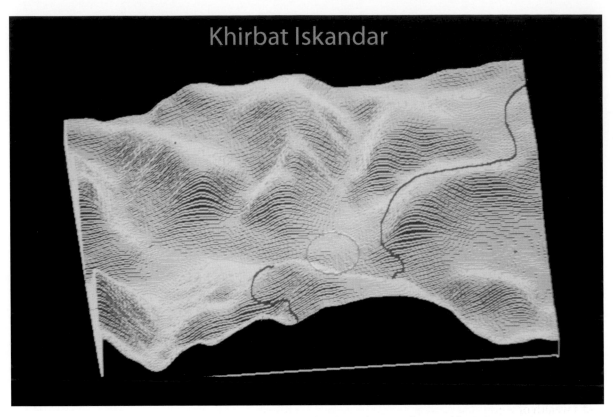

FIG. 1.8   *Digital elevation isometric representation of Khirbat Iskandar and vicinity (prepared by G. Peterman).*

Both probes uncovered multiple phases of EB IV architecture. In Probe A, the edge of a square tower associated with a 1.25–1.50 m high east–west wall appeared along with EB IV pottery, including a restorable EB IV holemouth cooking pot (Richard 1982: fig. 4:2, pl. 90). Probe B produced a portion of a well-built domestic structure including a two-phase tabun. The probe also uncovered a restorable necked cooking pot (Richard 1982: fig. 4:3, pl. 91) and a "teapot" with a small wavy handle and painted decoration (Richard 1982: fig. 4:1, pl. 89). Although this short season precluded a stratigraphic section to bedrock, it was already evident that Khirbat Iskandar's multiple phases and substantial architecture showed little evidence that they were the remains of seasonal pastoral nomads.

1982 Season

Work took place in three areas on the mound, with squares numbered sequentially in the order in which they were opened (Richard 1983; Richard and Boraas 1984). We expanded Probes A and B into 5 × 5 m squares and opened three contiguous squares in each (now Areas A and B). At the southeastern corner, where there was an outline of an apparent gate, we opened partial squares aligned with the eastern half of the presumed passageway and flanking building. Thus began the excavation of the remarkable structures in Area C that are the primary focus of this volume. Work uncovered monumental-like architecture, part of a bench, and a segment of a well-laid plaster surface.

Greater exposure in Area A revealed more of Glueck's east–west wall and the tower, as well as earlier EB IV structures. In Area B, the domestic character of the upper EB IV settlement was coming into focus, along with good indications of Early Bronze Age continuities in architecture and material culture. The northern and western fortifications began to emerge at the edges of squares in which excavation was uncovering EB IV domestic architecture. In addition, a preliminary regional survey began with the objective to check Glueck's site survey within a five-km radius of the site. The survey reconfirmed seven of the sites noted by Glueck and added eight more. Except for EB IV sherds found at Khirbet Abu Khirqeh and near a circle-of-stone feature (el-'Asi), both some two km to the west, the sites yielded mostly Iron Age and Roman/Byzantine pottery.

1984 Season

A major goal this season was to expand Area C to expose the expected western half of the "gateway" and contiguous structures and activity areas (Richard and Boraas 1988). Juxtaposed rooms, found on either side of a plastered passageway, along with benches and steps, appeared to confirm the nature of the complex. In Area B, three new squares exposed more of what was evidently a significant neighborhood of interconnected houses in Phase A, some with multiple rooms. Excavation below a Phase A surface revealed destruction debris and a wealth of whole and restorable vessels within the outer fortification line. The discovery of what appeared to be a "storeroom" (Phase B) disclosed a new view of EB IV complexity. This new evidence, along with an imported painted "caliciform" cup fragment found in what appeared to be a foundation trench for the northwest tower, suggested an EB IV date for the fortifications. Finally, the survey team redirected their efforts to exploring and excavating tombs uncovered by bulldozing activities in the area. Work took place in Area E to the east of the tell, as well as across the Wâdi al-Wâla (Area D). The latter area became the focus of a salvage operation sponsored by the Department of Antiquities following the excavation season. The Area D tombs are a primary focus of this publication.

1987 Season

The expedition fielded a major season with a large staff in 1987, factors that enabled considerable progress toward achieving a significant horizontal exposure of the Phase A settlement in Area B (Richard 1988; 1989; 1990; 1991). Also, additional lateral exposure of the Phase B "storeroom" helped

us to recover more restorable pottery (mostly large storage jars), as well as to reveal exceptional architectural features, such as a bench room, a well-hewn stone bin, and pillar bases. All of these discoveries were pertinent to addressing a major research question posed about the level of social complexity attainable at the site in EB IV. By the end of the season, a section through the fortifications had revealed a series of buttresses between an outer stone wall and an inner collapsed mudbrick and stone wall.

Hoping to understand the east–west ("Glueck") wall, additional excavation took place in Area A, along with surface tracing of a line of interconnected structures to the east as far as Area C. This work revealed that the only point of ingress in the "Glueck" wall was the Area C "gateway." Endeavoring to uncover if a stratified link existed between the Area A tower and the outer curtain wall on the western perimeter, the team excavated a small probe. Although there was a suggestion of linkage, the results were inconclusive due to heavy erosion at that edge of the mound. The objective to excavate more tombs was successful, as work progressed in Cemeteries E, D, H, and J.

Finally, in light of the decision to preserve the gate, the major objectives set for Area C in 1987 were to concentrate on lateral exposure of the uppermost phase, but to investigate the constructional history of the gate through a series of probes. The team met both objectives, the results of which form the basis for this final report.

Phase 2 Summary

1997 Season

Following a hiatus in excavation, a short study season took place in 1994 (Richard and Long 1995a–b) in order to develop strategies specific to addressing unresolved issues and questions following the 1987 season in Area B. These strategies, carried out in 1997, focused on investigating the construction history of the two fortification systems and excavating more of the remarkable Phase B "storeroom," which appeared to be a complex of rooms (Richard and Long 1998). The excavation of interior surfaces associated with the fortifications made it clear that the founding of the Area B fortifications dated to an earlier stratum on the mound, whose pottery was termed EB II/III. Notably, however, because of more exposure toward the east, there appeared a third room to the Phase B "storeroom," the eastern-most wall of which abutted the outer fortifications. This was the first solid evidence of the reuse of the fortifications in the EB IV period. Finally, the excavation of some additional probes took place in Area C to clarify certain stratigraphical issues. The following year, 1998, a four-week season of restoration and preservation of the Area C "gateway" took place (Long and Libby 1999), followed by more consolidation in 2006 and 2008.

2000, 2004, and 2007 Seasons

With the definitive evidence for a major pre-EB IV settlement on the mound, the expedition modified and refined its objectives and overall research design. Having made significant progress toward illuminating rural complexity at Khirbat Iskandar in EB IV, the project refocused its efforts to shed light on the particular trajectory of settlement on the mound throughout the Early Bronze Age. The expedition's publications offer an alternative view on the EB IV, as well as detail the work carried out in these three seasons (Richard 2002; Richard and Long 2000; 2006; 2007a–b; Richard, Long, and Libby 2001; 2004; 2005; 2007; 2008).

In broad outline, the following summary highlights the major strata and phases (not sub-phases) in Area B, as we know it today, from the latest to the earliest.

Stratum I – EB IV: There are two major phases. Phase A represents an EB IV domestic neighborhood, constructed immediately above the destruction layer of the Phase B settlement. Subsequent to the Phase A settlement, the site lay abandoned, except for what appears to be some Iron Age presence on the mound. Phase B is an EB IV settlement of a very different character, including what appears to be a public area with "storeroom" within the northern fortifications. Phase B was constructed above (and partially within) a major destruction level belonging to an earlier occupational stratum

on the mound. Recent work has affirmed additional stratigraphic links between the EB IV and the western perimeter wall (Richard, Long, and Libby 2007; 2008).

Stratum II – EB II/III: Phase C clearly represents an earlier occupational stratum comprising multiple sub-phases, including a destruction level and two occupational phases of an urban settlement. We await the results of additional radiometric (C14) analysis to provide dates. Thus far, the view of Phase C is of a series of rooms within the northern fortifications, including a large room with pillar base and much restorable pottery and carbonized grain; a well-preserved structural wall with doorway connected with a room to the south, where a considerable number of ground stone objects and restorable vessels were found. Phase C surfaces, linked to the tower, clearly affirm a founding in Phase C. Still in question is the construction phase of the inner mudbrick wall line.

Stratum III – EB I/II: Another destruction level separates Phase C from newly emerging Phase D. The latter is a little-known occupational stratum whose features include a curvilinear stone and mudbrick structure in association with a stone pier, discovered lying below the Phase C western perimeter defensive line. Somewhat limited ceramics appear to be early in date, perhaps EB I, although diagnostics are lacking. It is also not yet known how Phase D relates to earlier materials discovered north and below the level of the Phase C tower.

Future excavation with further exposure of the occupational area and an expanded assemblage of diagnostic sherds may necessitate revision to the tentative phasing outlined above.

METHODOLOGY, RECORDING SYSTEM, AND GUIDE TO THE VOLUME

As an American Schools of Oriental Research (ASOR) affiliated expedition from its inception, this project has used the methods and principles of excavation approved by ASOR's Committee on Archaeological Policy. The latter is a peer-review panel that has approved the Khirbat Iskandar Expedition's proposals annually for affiliation, excavation, and publication. Although refinements to the recording system have occurred intermittently, from the onset of the project the expedition has followed the accepted methods and procedures practiced by American excavators, such as those detailed in the Gezer Manual (Dever and Lance 1978).

In 1982, when Roger Boraas joined the staff, and for most of Phase 1, the project adopted the manual for excavation and recording that he had developed for the Tall Hesban Excavations. It was the practice at Tall Hesban to use the term Area, rather than Field, which explains the use of the former term to identify the separate excavation sites at Khirbat Iskandar and in the vicinity. Later, a combined documentation system of diary and locus sheet became the norm. In Phase 2, some major changes occurred when the project adopted the revised manual and recording system of Tall al-'Umayri, created to enable and facilitate computerized data entry.

Locus

The locus system used at Khirbat Iskandar is the basic unit of excavation for any three-dimensional context, whether wall, soil layer, pit, or other such feature. In each Area, there are multiple squares, each of which has its unique sequential list of loci and associated sequential list of buckets/pails. For example, C01010 refers to Area C, Square 1, Locus 10; C01.14 refers to Area C, Square 1, Pail 14. The pail information is essential, since it is uniquely configured with both "Area" and "Square" and since all associated materials, ceramic, lithics, objects, soil, bones, botanical remains, sieved materials, etc. would be similarly identified as C01.14.

In this volume, the only loci presented are those considered to be primary or sealed loci. Chapter 5 discusses the procedure further, including an introduction to methods applied in ceramic sampling, classification, as well as the quantitative analysis. The objective to present a quantitative typo-chronological ceramic study of the EB IV ceramic assemblage at Khirbat Iskandar made it essential to rely solely on primary and sealed loci. For a complete list of these loci, see Appendix B. The list of loci derives from a relational Access database, all keyed to the Area/Square/Locus (e.g., C01010).

With regard to the Cemetery materials, which make up the second half of this volume, please find a complete introduction in Chapter 9. However, as above, the tomb loci are the key to the relational database. Although the concept of primary loci is not relevant to the tomb material—all the tomb materials are included in this volume—the numbering system is equivalent; e.g., D02013 refers to Cemetery/Area D, Tomb 2, Locus 13; and D02.15 refers to Cemetery/Area D, Tomb 2, pail 15.

Pottery

As mentioned in the Preface, the classification utilized in this volume is that developed for the Bâb adh-Dhrâ' cemeteries and town site (Schaub and Rast 1989: 4–9; Rast and Schaub 2003, especially the Preface in Part 2) with some modifications. For the specific usage in this volume, see Chapters 4–5, and 12.

Following the methods defined in the field manuals mentioned above, square supervisors maintained records and lists of all pottery buckets and associated material culture excavated. Logs compiled by the pottery registrar and other specialists provided a second control over the materials as they underwent processing, including counting of diagnostics and non-diagnostics, and registration. The practice from the beginning has been to save all the diagnostics, a good sample of body sherds, and, of course, all restorable pottery. As discussed in Chapter 5, drawings made of cut diagnostics and of restored vessels were at a scale of 1:1. To complete the process, scanning and computerized drawings of all pottery selected for publication took place to enable the production of the computer-generated figures and plates presented in this volume.

For ease of comparative analysis, the drafting procedures used for the Area C and cemetery assemblages are identical. The scale used is 1:4, the section appears on the right, and diagonal lines indicate red slip. There are three separate series of ceramic illustrations contained in this volume: Specific Types in Chapter 4 (Area C) and Chapter 12 (cemeteries), complete tomb assemblages in

FIG. 1.9   *Staff photo, 1981 season.*

Chapters 10 and 11, and the complete Area C assemblage from the primary loci in the Appendix A plates. In order to facilitate use of the collection in Appendix A, the pottery is arranged by Phase, Square, Locus. Whenever possible, this arrangement also maintains the order of classification categories, that is, restricted vessels, necked jars, and bowls. Facing tables include all the relevant information. The presentation of the cemetery pottery is in sequential pail order for each tomb. The "Specific Types" arrangement is by classification code (see Appendices D–E).

Topographic Map

The map included in this volume supersedes all earlier topographic maps published of the site and its vicinity. This map is the result of a thorough re-survey of the site, completed through differentially corrected GPS survey data. The placement of the excavation grid and other features on the mound is now highly accurate. The vicinity map derives from the latest images available from the Royal Jordanian Geographic Center.

The Volume

This volume is primarily an excavation report. It is a final report on the stratigraphy and associated material culture in Area C and on the EB IV cemeteries and their assemblages. It is not *the* final report on the people who occupied Khirbat Iskandar in the EB IV period. That report remains to be written from the broader perspective of the complete cultural record/stratigraphic profile of the EB IV period on the mound, not to say, the cultural record of the entire occupational history of the site. Nevertheless, the materials in this volume, considered in the context of the significant database of materials summarized above, do present a tantalizingly new picture of EB IV peoples.

In the aftermath of the collapse of cities and general abandonment of tells ca. 2300/2350 BCE, the Khirbat Iskandar tell shows a history in the EB IV period of recovery, change, growth, and final abandonment. The three stratigraphic phases in Area C and associated ceramic assemblages reflect this occupational pattern. The data witness to re-organization strategies of some complexity in the EB IV period: a "storeroom" complex reusing the

FIG. 1.10 *Staff photo, 1982 season.*

fortifications in Area B, the transformation of a domestic area into a public "gateway" in Area C. The site of Khirbat Iskandar provides a view of EB IV peoples not hitherto attested in the southern Levant. The settlement and assemblages display the remnants of Early Bronze Age tradition; the contiguous cemeteries with their domestic repertoire establish a strong link between the tell and the tombs, and the customs of the living and the dead.

In summary, the picture emerging from the collective data is of a community maintaining antecedent "urban-like" traditions in the midst of change. The continued excavations at the site will aim to clarify the precise relation between the EB IV occupants and the preceding urbanites. As the project now turns its full attention to the publication of the EB IV settlements in Area B, the hypotheses of this volume, especially the quantified ceramic study, will surely be put to the test.

Staff

The following section lists the project members who were participants in Phase 1, during which time virtually all of the work in Area C and the cemeteries was completed.

1981 (fig. 1.9)

Suzanne Richard (director/ceramist), James D'Angelo (photographer/surveyor), Donald H. Wimmer (square supervisor), Suzanne V. Kane (square supervisor), Gail D'Angelo (pottery registrar), Ghazi Bisheh (excavator), Brian Bloom (excavator), Omar Unis (Department of Antiquities Representative), Abu Arif (cook).

1982 (fig. 1.10)

Suzanne Richard (director/ceramist), Roger Boraas (field director), Kevin Klein (photographer/surveyor), Cindy Winrow Matheson (artist), JoAnn Long (nurse, pottery registrar), Marlin White (camp manager), Frank L. Koucky (geological consultant), Gerald Mattingly (Survey Leader); area supervisors: Sue Kane, Glen Peterman, Andrew Dearman, James D'Angelo; square supervisors: Terry Brensinger, Jesse C. Long, Jr., Caroline Susan Spark, Herbert B. Huffmon, Stephen, Pamela Mattingly (survey); volunteers: Kathleen Fonseca, Mary Czyzewski, John L. DeGisi, Stephen Reid, Randall C. Bailey, Bonnie Wistoff, Mary Ann Kaub, Hala Hyassat, Salam H. Hijjawi, Shahir Abu-Alghanan, Abid Abdulrehim

FIG. 1.11 *Staff photo, 1984 season.*

FIG. 1.12 *Staff photo, 1987 season.*

Saleh; Shahir Abu-Alghanan (Dept. of Antiquities representative), Abu Samir (cook).

1984 (fig. 1.11)

Suzanne Richard (director/ceramist), Roger Boraas (field director), Robert Suder (architect/surveyor),

Edyth Skinner (photographer), Peter Warnock (palaeobotanist), Andrew Dearman (area supervisor), Jonathan Elias (area supervisor), Jeannette Ohlson Forsen (object registrar/square supervisor), James D'Angelo (tomb supervisor/survey), Nan Broder (pottery registrar), Marlin White (camp manager), Sarah White (artist), Luis Lanese (consultant in magnetometry); square supervisors: Herbert Huffmon, Mary Louise Mussell, Ann Ross, MaryAnn Kaub, Gary R. Grisdale, Stirling Dorrance, Tom Reid, Jack Livingston, Stephen Taylor, Will Agee, Rozanna Pfeiffer, Bill Hammond; Hussein Qandil (Dept. of Antiquities representative); Abu Arif (cook).

1987 (fig. 1.12)

Suzanne Richard (director/ceramist), Jeannette Ohlsen Forsen (assistant field director), Edyth Skinner (photographer), Marlin White (camp manage), Sarah White (artist), Robert Suder (architect/surveyor), Nan Broder (pottery registrar), Peter Warnock (paleobotanist), Mary Metzger (paleozoologist), Reinder Neef (paleobotanist), Mary Louise Mussel (area supervisor), Jonathan Mabry (area supervisor), Gaetano Palumbo (director of cemetery operations and survey), Nigel Sadler (area supervisor), Kathy Gruspier (osteologist/tomb excavator), Grant Mullen (osteologist/tomb excavator), James D'Angelo (tomb supervisor/survey); square supervisors: Arthur O. Hellander, Harriet Saxe, Aline Carr, H. Dianne Rowan, Jodie Benton, Sarah Collins, Jon Seligman; Carol J. Vogler, Rozanna Pfeiffer, Shona Cox, Elizabeth Ledingham; Volunteers: Daniele Russoniello, David I. Connolly, Clarice Tomassini, Constantino Sarnelli, Marilia Poli, Sanjay Nanda, Emma Jane Reilly, Suzanne Gallagher, Scott Broeder, and photographer assistants: Linda Travisano, Dirk Herrmann, and Stephen Neigh; Tayseer Atiyyat (Dept of Antiquities representative), Abu Arif (cook).

During the 1981–87 seasons, the expedition hired many local laborers, from seven in the first season to thirty-five in the major seasons. Many of the workers came from the vicinity of the Wâdi al-Wâla, but also from Dhiban to the south and even Madaba to the north.

Chapter 2

Khirbat Iskandar and its Modern and Ancient Environment

by Carlos E. Cordova and Jesse C. Long, Jr.

The site of Khirbat Iskandar (map reference Palestinian Grid: 2233.1072)[1] lies 24 km south of the town of Madaba and some 400 m west of the al-Wâla bridge, the place where the King's Highway crosses Wâdi al-Wâla. The site is located in the territory of northern Moab,[2] a "mountain tableland" (Aharoni 1979: 36) designated in the biblical text as *hammisor* (e.g., Josh 13:9, 16, 17). This region is bordered on the south by the Wâdi al-Mujib, on the west by an escarpment overlooking the Rift Valley, and on the east by the Eastern Desert. The northern boundary is less well defined,[3] but may be set roughly at the Wâdi Hisban, where the land begins to rise gradually northward to the hills of Gilead (Smith [1933] 1966: 353; Baly 1974: 226–27, 229; Aharoni 1979: 36).

ENVIRONMENT

Geology and Topography

The stratigraphy of this region is composed of calcareous formations of the Belqa and 'Ajlun series, which are resting on "Nubian sandstone," with outcroppings of basalt from volcanic activity.[4] At the western edge of the plateau, sedimentary units are cut by the wadis and perennial streams that flow into the Dead Sea Rift below (Aharoni 1979: 36; Orni and Efrat 1971: 110–11; Burdon 1959: 1–4, 9–14). In northern Moab, the level of the plateau is cut by two major wâdi systems, the Wâdi Zerqa Ma'in and the Wâdi al-Wâla, beside which lies Khirbat Iskandar. Wâdi al-Wâla is part of a geo-hydrographic system that includes Wâdi ath-Thamad and its tributaries, whose headwaters are on the fringes of the desert. Before reaching Khirbat Iskandar, the wâdi flows in a gorge, incising the Cretaceous limestone. In the area of Khirbat Iskandar, the wâdi widens and receives more tributaries from the Madaba and Dhiban Plateau. About 2 km west of the site, the Wâla enters into Wâdi Heidan and joins Wâdi al-Mujib, just before breaking the escarpment at Bâb al-Mujib (Naval Intelligence 1943: 414–15).

The flow of the Wâla follows an east–west zone of structural weakness in the vicinity of Khirbat Iskandar (Bender 1975: pls. 1; 3). Sedimentary rock of the Belqa series is cut by the wâdi as it flows across the plateau. Downstream from Iskandar, the wâdi dissects 'Ajlun series deposits before cutting the sandstone deposits that lie underneath. In the immediate vicinity of Iskandar, Belqa basal chalk,

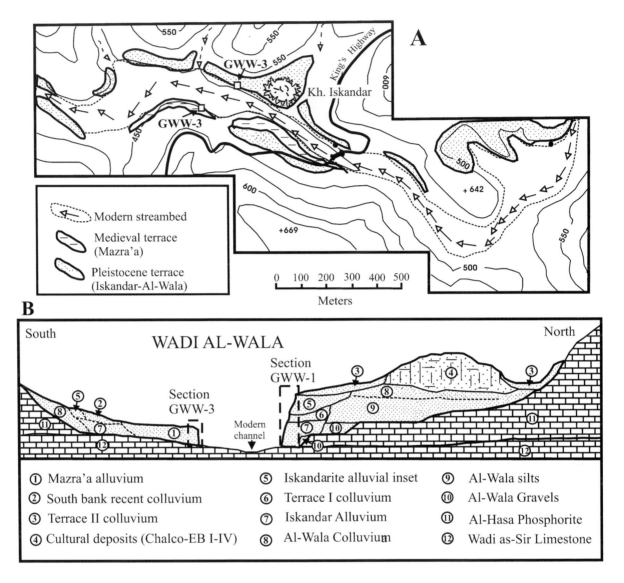

Modern streambed

Medieval terrace
(Mazra'a)

Pleistocene terrace
(Iskandar-Al-Wala)

0   100 200 300 400 500

Meters

B

South   North

WADI AL-WALA

Section
GWW-1

Section
GWW-3

Modern
channel

① Mazra'a alluvium   ⑤ Iskandarite alluvial inset   ⑨ Al-Wala silts

② South bank recent colluvium   ⑥ Terrace I colluvium   ⑩ Al-Wala Gravels

③ Terrace II colluvium   ⑦ Iskandar Alluvium   ⑪ Al-Hasa Phosphorite

④ Cultural deposits (Chalco-EB I-IV) ⑧ Al-Wala Colluvium   ⑫ Wadi as-Sir Limestone

FIG. 2.1   (A) Fluvial and colluvial morphological features in Wâdi al-Wâla. (B) Cross-section of Wâdi al-Wâla with main stratigraphic units.

flint, upper limestone, chalk, and phosphate dominate, although some older material may appear
in the wâdi bottom (see Burdon 1959; Quennell
1955: Sheet 2). Approximately 2.4 km east of the
Madaba–Karak highway, still in Belqa sediments
and in line with the block fault, the Wâdi al-Wâla
becomes a perennial stream, the 'Ain al-Wâla
(Ras al-Wâla) being its primary source (Naval
Intelligence 1943: 414–15).

Khirbat Iskandar is situated on the northern
bank of Wâdi al-Wâla as it makes its way in a
west–northwesterly direction before turning

southwest at a point approximately 3 km northwest
of Barza. In the area of Iskandar, Wâdi al-Wâla
flows through a narrow valley that is less than 1
km wide (fig. 2.1A); however, north–south cutting
wâdis further extend the expanse of the canyon.
The plateau just north of the site has an elevation
of 653 m, while the wâdi bed runs at ca. 450 m
above sea level. The highest point on the mound,
near its northwest corner, is at a level of 484.46 m,
but gently descends to a level of 478.46 m before
falling off to the wâdi below.

At its southern extremity, the mound rises at least 20 m above the surrounding surface. The tell sits atop a mantle of colluvium that covers a fluvial terrace of late Pleistocene alluvial and colluvial deposits (fig. 2.1B). A younger stage of colluvial deposit marks post-occupational degradation of the mound and helps form the present shape of the tell. The underlying deposits that make up the alluvial terrace include silts, gravels, and coarse materials that form a sequence of flood, streambank, and channel facies, all predating the settlement at Iskandar. From the wâdi bottom and narrow flood plain, the terrace rises abruptly and forms a steep bank below the mound. On the south bank of the wâdi, the rise is less severe, and the deposits are younger than those on the northern bank. The units that are contemporaneous with the occupation of the site are contained in an alluvial inset, named here Iskandarite Alluvium, which will be a topic of further discussion in this chapter.

The tell proper covers an expanse of ca. 2.7 ha, although it is clear from previous and current work that the site of Khirbat Iskandar in antiquity was far greater (see Ch. 1). The western, southern, and eastern slopes of the mound fall off abruptly to the surrounding terrain. On the west, the mound is set off from a hill by a small depression. To the south, the tell is cut by the bank of the Wâla (see above), while the eastern grade is cut by a small north–south wâdi (Wâdi Iskandar) that joins the Wâla below. In the north, the slope is a gentler drop to a wide plain that fans out to the foot of the hills beyond. Nelson Glueck (1939: 127) described the site as

"…a large, low, completely destroyed mound, with its s. side reaching to the very edge of the n. bank of the Wâdī el-Wâlā, which at this point has been sliced away straight and steep by the continuously flowing stream in the wâdī. The ruins are located partly between and partly beyond two small wudyân, which coming from the north join the Wâdī el-Wâlā. The w. section of the ruins seems to be most important."

For the most part, the western section of the mound is all that remains. The area east of the site appears to have been eroded since Glueck's day and is also now under cultivation. The current expedition has excavated cemeteries and megalithic features in Area E, just beyond the easternmost of the wudyân.

The settlement of Khirbat Iskandar must have been strategically located at a major crossing for transportation across the Wâdi al-Wâla. While the canyon does not provide quite the obstruction that does the Wâdi al-Mujib to the south, it represents, nevertheless, an obstacle for north–south transport. In addition, the Wâdi itself does not provide an easy route of transportation or communication, so east–west contact was on either side of the canyon. Today, a modern highway crosses the valley south and east of the site. This highway follows closely the *via nova Traiana* of Roman times and presumably the King's Highway of biblical fame.

Climate

The highlands and mountainous regions of Transjordan (including northern Moab) have a sub-Mediterranean climate that is characterized by winter rains and summer drought.[5] From May until October the land is dry, while the months of November through April generally encompass the rainy season. The heaviest rains occur in January and February, although the rainfall regime is variable (Shehadeh 1985: 30–31; Al-Eisawi 1985: 45; Bender 1974: 11). On average, the climate is similar to the uplands of Cisjordan; however, the rainy season in Transjordan starts later, and there is less rainfall and more variability (Naval Intelligence 1943: 421, 424; Baly 1974: 61). The differences are a result, in part, of a "rain shadow" created by the action of the prevailing westerlies on a topography that is dominated by the Rift Valley and adjacent highlands (Shehadeh 1985: 30; Zohary 1973: 25). As with rainfall amounts, there also may be considerable variation in temperature values from year to year (Al-Eisawi 1985: 45–46).

The average annual temperature at Khirbat Iskandar is between 18 and 20° C, with an annual range (defined by Shehadeh [1985: 32] as the "difference between the average minimum temperature in the coldest month and the average maximum temperature in the hottest month") of 29°C and a mean daily range of 12–14°C (Shehadeh 1985: 32, figs. 6–7; *Climatic Atlas of Jordan* 1971: 49). The minimum average temperature of the coldest month is 4.6°C, while the average maximum temperature in the hottest month is 33.7°C (Al-Eisawi 1985: 47, table 1). Rainfall in the summer months is nearly nonexistent, but because of the perennial stream of the Wâla, the valley still supports lush vegetation. In the spring, greater rainfall results in a dense growth of grasses, weeds, and wild flowers that covers both the plateau and the Wâla basin. The average annual precipitation is, however, only between 200 and 300 mm a year (*Climatic*

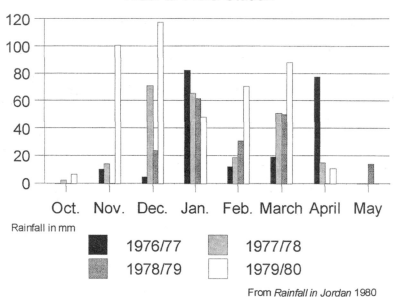

FIG. 2.2   *Average Monthly Rainfall in Wâdi al-Wâla Station, 1976–1980. Source:* Rainfall in Jordan 1980.

Atlas of Jordan 1971: 11; Ashbel 1967: 1; Bender 1974: 10). From 1961/62 to 1979/80 (excepting the year 1963/64), rainfall at the Wâdi al-Wâla meteorological station (just across the wâdi from the site) had an annual average of 257.23 mm (*Rainfall in Jordan* 1980; see also Al-Eisawi 1985: 47, table 1). In the interval of 1937/38 to 1979/80 (excepting the year 1966/67), Dhiban, roughly 7 km south of Iskandar, recorded an average rainfall amount of 276.75 mm (*Rainfall in Jordan* 1980). The lower rainfall amounts, as compared with other areas, are surely related to the region's topography that is distinguished by the Rift Valley and the Wâla and Mujib drainage systems.[6]

The rainfall of the region is also characterized by wide variability (Shehadeh 1985: 30–31). In the rainy year of 1944/45, for example, the Khirbat Iskandar area received between 400 and 500 mm of rainfall, but only between 100 and 200 mm in 1946/47 (Amiran et al. 1970: IV/2 C, IV/2 D). Rainfall totals for the Wâla station for 1976/77 to 1979/80 were recorded at 205.8, 237.1, 179.5, and 440.8 mm. From 1954/55 to 1979/80, the lowest

recorded annual total was 103 mm in 1954/55; the highest annual total was 450 mm in 1973/74. In the period of time between 1937/38 and 1979/80, Dhiban recorded a minimum rainfall amount in 1957/58 of 102 mm and a maximum rainfall amount in 1951/52 of 490 mm (*Rainfall in Jordan* 1980). Figure 2.2 reflects the year-to-year variability in more recent times.

Nevertheless, even in years of marginal rainfall, the inhabitants of the settlement at Khirbat Iskandar may have had an adequate supply of water available in Wâdi al-Wâla. The wâdi drains the plain around Madaba and Jiza, a catchment of ca. 2,050 sq km. While almost eighty percent of the catchment has an annual rainfall average of below 300 mm, 1,700 sq km of the catchment lie above Khirbat Iskandar (Ionides 1939: 131, table 14; figs. 5, 9; McDonald 1965: II-4). There is perennial baseflow in the Wâla at Iskandar, and flood flows at the Wâdi al-Wâla Bridge, right at the site, have been estimated to be about 41 million cubic meters of water annually (McDonald 1965: II-1, 4–6, 8). A reconnaissance survey has also identified evidence of a spring on the eastern slopes of the tell. The spring, now dry, suggests that the water table was higher during Early Bronze Age settlement at the site (Koucky 1982). This supports the view that water was in ample supply.

Vegetation

The region of Cisjordan-Transjordan (including northern Moab) is situated at the crossroads of four vegetation zones: the Mediterranean, Saharo-Arabian, Irano-Turanian, and Sudanian territories (Zohary 1973: 67–68, fig. 22). All four zones have representatives east of the Dead Sea, and Khirbat Iskandar is located at the junction of two of these plant communities. A Mediterranean zone appears north and south of the area. A zone of Irano-Turanian vegetation defines the vicinity of the site, where the Wâla basin represents one of the parts of Transjordan where the Mediterranean zone is interrupted by wâdis flowing into the Rift (Zohary 1966: Map 1; 1973: 67–68, fig. 22; 1962: 112–15; Feinbrun and Zohary 1955; Al-Eisawi 1985: 50–52). Zohary describes this zone as one of "Irano-Turanian dwarf shrub steppes on western escarpments of Transjordan" (1962: 115). The Mediterranean region usually occurs in areas with a mean annual rainfall over 300 mm; Irano-Turanian regions usually have rainfall amounts over 150 mm (Al-Eisawi 1985: 50–51). In conditions that support Irano-Turanian Steppe zones, shrubs and bushes dominate with grasses and annuals and bulbous plants that flower briefly in the spring (Baly 1974: 80; Al-Eisawi 1985: 51). The actual make-up of this vegetation, though, may vary with its relationship to Mediterranean areas. Steppe vegetation west of the plateau is influenced by the tropical conditions of the Rift Valley, while the eastern steppe regions are influenced by the desert conditions to the east (Al-Eisawi 1985: 54).[7]

The influence of human activity on the natural vegetation has been especially pronounced in the Middle East. Mankind's primary impact on the environment seems to have been the extermination of flora. Clearing land for cultivation and overgrazing have been particularly significant factors in the loss of plant cover, as well as soil, to such an extent that erosion has marred much of the landscape (Beaumont 1985: 294; Zohary 1962: 208–9). One should, therefore, assume that both the landscape and vegetation of the Iskandar catchment have through the course of the settlement's history been affected by human agency. The intrusion of Irano-Turanian vegetation on the Mediterranean zone may even have been aided by human interference (Zohary 1962: 209). The course of ecological changes and adaptation in the Wâdi al-Wâla should, then, be viewed not only in terms of how humans adapted to the conditions of their environment but also in terms of how they affected and changed it. From this perspective, human strategies of adaptation were ones that also led to periodic migration and/or extinction.

Soils

The soils along the course of the Wâdi al-Wâla depression are sandy and gravelly. Transported Terra Rosa and Rendzinas border the Iskandar region to the north (Feinbrun and Zohary 1955: 7–12). Bender (1974: 187–89) categorizes the soils of the wâdi basin as Yellow Mediterranean with Red Mediterranean soils (known also as *terra rosa*) not far away.[8] Yellow Mediterranean soils are found between highland and steppe regions and along the slopes that fall off to the Rift Valley and its tributaries, of which the Wâdi al-Wâla is one (Burdon 1959: 20). These yellow soils are derived from loess-like sediments, calcareous rocks and basalts (Bender 1974: 189), while Terra Rosa soils come from the hard limestone and dolomites of Upper Cretaceous rocks (and some Eocene rocks) and in this area also from basalt and sandstone (Zohary 1962: 10; Burdon 1959: 20). Transported red soils in the lowlands and mountain valleys have properties in common with alluvial-colluvial soils (Zohary 1962: 10).

Yellow Mediterranean soils are generally confined to areas with annual rainfall between 250 to 350 mm, and Red Mediterranean soils to areas above 350 mm (Burdon 1959: 20). In flat-lying areas, the Red Mediterranean soils are suited for cereals, tomatoes, melons, and tobacco. In hilly areas, the red soils may grow grapes, olives, certain fruits, and forests. Yellow Mediterranean soils are good for the production of cereals employing dry farming. With irrigation, they may allow more intensive cultivation (Bender 1974: 189; Zohary 1962: 10–11).

Around Khirbat Iskandar, the steep slopes of the hillsides and similar inclines in the valley are primarily of limestone. Here soils may not have developed due to the high slope angle or, if there was a thin mantle of soil, it may have been removed by a combination of surface runoff and gravitational processes. The removal of these soils may be forming the colluvial deposits on the terrace of the wâdi.

The predominately yellow soils on the more level areas of the catchment today support intensive agriculture. This is due in large part to the continuous supply of water that is available and pumped from the Wâdi al-Wâla (see below). A government agricultural farm now oversees cultivation in the immediate vicinity of the site. Fields north of the site on the west slopes of the Wâdi Iskandar have extensive field plowing and terracing. On the east slopes of the wadi are found orchards and fields with grape vineyards, olive groves, and deep plowing for field crops. West of Khirbat Iskandar lies a hill that is terraced for olive trees. A few fig trees sprinkle this area. Across the wâdi to the south, a large field is also worked as a part of the farm.

The occupational history of the area supports the interpretation that the valley has through the course of its history been agriculturally productive. While a preliminary survey of the catchment did not locate datable Early Bronze Age agricultural installations, substantial evidence of settlement especially during the Iron Age and Roman/Byzantine periods was evidenced. The survey located three mills in the immediate environs of the site that may date as early as the Roman/Byzantine period, underscoring the productivity of the Wâdi al-Wâla region.

Geoarchaeological Interpretation of Alluvial Deposits in Wâdi al-Wâla

In the Wâdi al-Wâla area, alluvial accumulation occurs due to the widening of the channel and the reduction of the gradient that follows the hard limestone of the Wâdi as-Sir limestone. In the area of Khirbat Iskandar, just south of the Wâdi al-Wâla bridge, there is a set of deposits that contain a sequence of four Quaternary alluvial units (fig. 2.1B). The alluvial units of Wâdi al-Wâla have been previously described and named by Cordova (1999a; 1999b; 2000). The oldest alluvial units are the Al-Wâla Gravel and the Al-Wâla Silt, both of Pleistocene age. Their ages are uncertain, since there are no absolute dates. Its stratigraphic position, and the development of carbonate nodules, suggests that its age is likely older than 18,000 BP. The next unit is the Iskandarite alluvium, which has two dates (Cal 15,000–15,085 BCE [Beta 134556] at the bottom and Cal 14,120–12,765 [Beta 142335]). The unit consists of silts at the bottom and silts and gravel on top. The bottom half has a well-developed soil and a series of cumulic soils. The top half has a large concentration of angular and subangular gravel and a large concentration of lithic materials. On the erosive surface on the Iskandarite alluvium lies a silt deposit named here "Iskandarite Alluvial Inset," because its age is very close to the nearby site of Khirbat Iskandar. The date obtained from a small piece of charcoal is Cal 3105–2880 BCE (Beta 133945). The deposit contains Chalcolithic sherds and pieces of charcoal. A rock structure that seems to be a wall or possibly a shallow well intrudes this deposit and part of the underlying Iskandar Alluviuum (see fig. 2.5 below).

A terrace on the southern bank of the wâdi exposes the historic Mazra'a alluvium, which has been dated to 1190 ± 50 BP (Cal CE 705 to 980 [Beta-121656]). The Mazra'a alluvium at GWW-3 is a three-meter sequence of deposition of several silt-loam units separated by short stable period. The latter is evidenced by a paleosol and a mat of organic material. At the very top of the sequence, there is evidence of a wetland soil with snails, and apparently high organic matter content. Below this soil, the sequence shows mottling, indicating a high water table at some point. This deposit suggests the evidence of a floodplain environment that had short times of stability, during which there was the formation of a flood meadow, which culminated with the formation of a wetland.

THE EARLY BRONZE AGE LANDSCAPES IN TRANSJORDAN

The transformation of vegetation in much of the Middle East introduces the issue of the Early Bronze Age environment. A consensus has formed that conditions were more lush in the past than at present. Forests, in particular, were more common (see, for example, Mattingly 1980: 64–65; Harlan 1981, 163; Isserlin 1955: 87–88). Bender (1974: 11) allows that the highlands of Jordan were probably all wooded before the early historical periods and suggests that deforestation began then with copper smelting. In Cisjordan, deforestation (due to human activity) probably did not begin until the Bronze Age (Currid 1984: 7). At Jericho, Early Bronze Age faunal remains indicate a variety of habitats including woodland (Fargo 1979: 24), and there is also evidence of clearing just before and during the Early Bronze Age with the spread of agriculture and pastoralism (Western 1971: 38). During EB III, the environment of Tell el-Hesi also appears to have been partially wooded (Fargo 1979: 23). Denis Baly (1985: 21), following Kenyon (1979: 114), dates increased deforestation in the region to ca. 2600 BCE, which he correlates with the widespread use of bronze tools. Clason and Clutton-Brock (1982: 146) argue that clearing began as early as the Natufian and Neolithic periods and write that "desertification in the region as a whole has been escalated by human interference with the environment and that this process was begun much earlier than is often claimed" (147). Some studies maintain that the major impact occurred when a second wave of agricultural innovations, coincident with the proliferation of urban centers, produced intensive forms of agriculture during the third and second millennium (Miller 1991; Fall, Lines, and Falconer 1998).

Michael Rowton (1967: 276–77) assembled a body of cuneiform texts that indicate most of the forests in the mountainous regions of Western Asia survived until the end of the Bronze Age and beyond, and has argued that the process of deforestation was a gradual one. In a similar fashion, G. H. Wilcox (1974: 132) contends that the present state of vegetation in Eastern Anatolia was not reached until Late Medieval times and perhaps not until the nineteenth century.[9] In Cisjordan, analysis of the spatial distribution of populations from the Chalcolithic through the Middle Bronze Age in the Central Coastal Plain suggests that deforestation due to human activity must have occurred in later periods (Gophna, Liphschitz, and Lev-Yadun 1986). Descriptions of Jordan by nineteenth-century travelers indicate that the region at that time was more verdant. Legend even has it that the Turks in the early twentieth century felled the forests of the southern highlands in order to fuel the Medina-to-Mecca railroad, but this is unlikely (Harlan 1985: 12–28). In this context, Harlan concludes that "whether the highlands [of southern Jordan] were in woodland or grassland in Early Bronze Age times, the vegetational cover must have been better than the present one" (1981: 163).

The existence of a pristine forest on the plateau north of Khirbat Iskandar is based in the fact that this area today receives more than 300 mm of rain a year and has relict red Mediterranean soils, which suggests that in pre-agricultural times the area may have supported pine-oak Mediterranean woodlands. As a matter of fact, the region has been classified as "Mediterranean non-forest vegetation" (Al-Eisawi 1985). Using Geographic Information Systems, the Madaba Plains Project created a model to explain the gradual removal of the forest and soil loss as farmed areas and sedentary population grew (Christopherson and Guertin 1995).

Regions with a cool steppe climate (BS in the Köppen classification), like Khirbat Iskandar, have difficulties with erosion and desertification (Shehadeh 1985: 35). The presence of gazelle[10] in stratified levels at Iskandar probably indicates that the flora in EB IV was more abundant. There is, however, some indication that vegetation in the region of Bâb adh-Dhrâ' during the Early Bronze Age was similar to the present (McCreery 1980: 150; see below). Even though human activity, and perhaps changes in climate, must have had an impact on the natural environment, it is unlikely that the ancient verdure was completely different from that of today (see Mattingly 1980: 69). After analyzing the vegetational history of the Eastern Mediterranean and Near East, van Zeist and Bottema (1982: 289) conclude that by 2000 BCE the "present-day distribution of forest and steppe had established itself in a broad outline."

Although there has been a consensus that climate during the Early Bronze Age was more humid than today, this has been a matter of speculation. It was not until the 1990s that more thorough studies provided evidence to support this assumption; however, it seems that despite enhanced moisture, there were short spans of drought (Weiss 2000; Issar 2003). Evidence for high humidity levels comes from different sources, mainly from Dead Sea Levels (Frumkin et al. 1991; Frumkin and Elitzur 2000), and alluvial sediments (Donahue, Peer and Schaub 1997). Indirect data also come from pollen diagrams in Lake Kinneret (Baruch 1990), Lake Hula (Baruch and Bottema 1999), and Birkat Ram (Schwab et al. 2004), which are discussed more comprehensively in the next section; however, the strongest and most detailed evidence comes from paleo-rainfall levels reconstructed from stable isotopes in Soreq Cave (Bar-Matthews, Ayalon, and Kaufman 1998).

The levels of the Dead Sea rose presumably due to increased precipitation, as indicated by isotopic data (fig. 2.3). Nonetheless, by 4000 years BP the levels had dropped to the point that the southern basin, which is the shallowest part of the lake, dried out. This drop in levels contributed to a drop of the base levels of all the streams emptying into the Dead Sea. This was one of the causes of floodplain erosion in Wâdi Numayra and Wâdi Karak (Donahue, Peer, and Schaub 1997).

Rapid aggradation and increased alluviation in the Nahal Lachish also suggest conditions of flooding in EB IV that may be related to fluctuating rainfall patterns, although the implications of

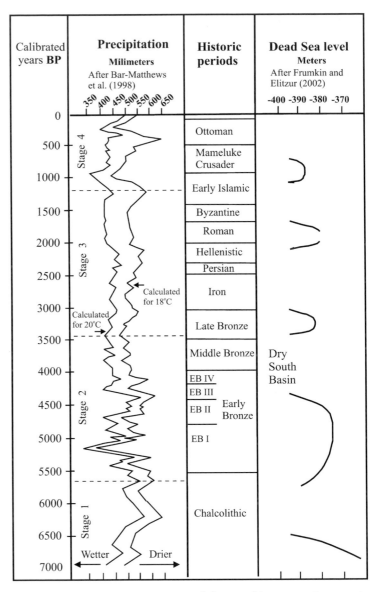

FIG. 2.3 *Precipitation reconstructed from stable oxygen isotopes in speleothems of Soreq Cave (after Bar-Matthews et al. 1998) and Dead Sea lake levels (Frumkin and Elitzur 2002).*

these data for the past climate are unclear (Rosen 1986a: 56–58; 1986b: 62–74; 1989: 252; see Mabry 1992: 129). Sediments in the Nahal Lachish near Tel Erani also appear to indicate a different environment at the Chalcolithic–Early Bronze transition (Rosen 1991: 192–96; see Mabry 1992: 130). The formation of alluvial terraces at Tell el-Hesi has been interpreted to indicate wetter conditions in the Early Bronze Age with dryer conditions in the latter stages of formation, also in the Early Bronze Age (Fargo 1979: 25–27).[11] In contrast, weathering patterns on stones from archaeological contexts in Cisjordan suggest that while the Neolithic appears to have been wetter than present conditions, since the Chalcolithic period the climate has been about the same. Of particular interest is analysis of rock samples from two EB IV settlements in the Negev, permitting the inference that conditions then were similar to the present (Danin 1985: 36, 41). For Central Moab, Mattingly concluded it is "likely that the intimate connection between sites and water sources, the general continuity of crops raised in this area, and the adaptability of human culture tend to diminish the chances that climatic change had a severe impact on EBA Moab" (1980: 68–69).

Another two important issues discussed for decades with regard to climate in the Early Bronze Age is whether the Early Bronze IV climate was drier, and whether this influenced the decline of settlement. These issues sparked a series of discussions and disagreements published by Dalfes et al. (1997); however, oxygen isotopes from Soreq cave provide evidence of a sudden and sharp decline in moisture during this period (fig. 2.3).

Before the results of paleo-rainfall reconstructed from oxygen isotopes were available, Rosen (1989) hypothesized that the most plausible explanation for climate change was change in settlement patterns. This hypothesis is supported by Mabry's (1992) study of settlement pattern change in the Jordan Valley. Offering the first comprehensive treatment of climate in the EB IV, Rosen concluded that the available data (i.e., isotope studies, paleolimnology, palynology, and geomorphology) suggest a wet period in the Early Bronze Age that was followed by a time of severe desiccation around 2400 BCE (1989: 247–53). The data are augmented by her own research in the Erani Terrace of south central Israel and the Nahal Lachish (1989: 251–52; see 1986a; 1986b; 1991). Particularly intriguing, though, is her thesis that changing settlement patterns from wâdi courses were based primarily on lower rainfall amounts and a decreased water table. In EB IV, settlements were moved to higher elevations, where there was more rainfall, and to sources of perennial water supply. Although this portrait fits the EB IV settlement at Khirbat

Iskandar, with its location on the perennial Wâdi al-Wâla, the site appears to have been occupied throughout the Early Bronze Age. Settlements in the more arid regions, like the Negev, were located near springs. Rosen argues that the Early Bronze Age urban adaptive response was less able to accommodate climatic changes because of a "less developed hydraulic technology" (1989: 253–54).[12] To be sure, however, she does not see climate as the only factor in the decline at the end of the Early Bronze Age. Disruption in trade and other socio-economic variables must have also been at work (254).

While Rosen's construct (1989) best explains the available evidence, her declining water table thesis must be tested, and there are other ways to construe the evidence. Goldberg and Bar-Yosef (1982) see a period of increased humidity in the EB IV (see above). With the nature of the data for climate in the Early Bronze Age as they now are, the only reasonable conclusion to draw is that there are no sure answers (as Mattingly 1980: 65, n. 117). There is evidence to suggest conditions were wetter in the southern Levant in the Early Bronze Age with declining precipitation toward the end of the millennium, but the data are contradictory.

The preceding discussion has also demonstrated the inherent pitfalls in reconstructing past climates, which are pronounced in dealing with climates in the Middle East (see Butzer [1975] 1981: 389). Hopkins' observation provides a good summary: "Evidence for significant climatic variations in the ancient Near East is diverse, multiform, of varying quality and applicability, and, above all, widely open to competing interpretations" (1985: 101). Perhaps the most significant obstacle for determining climate in the Holocene, however, is that climatic change as represented by paleobotanical and faunal data is subject to the noises of human impact on the environment (see van Zeist 1985: 201; Hopkins 1985: 106). Rosen (1989: 248–50) demonstrates sensitivity to this issue, but it is not clear that the human factor can be easily defined.

The amount of data produced, and the inconsistency between data from different sources and regions is an additional problem to the different schools of interpretation of the data. One claims that climate in the Levant has not changed significantly in the last 5000 years, and the other cannot reach a consensus (Finkelstein 1995). For this reason, some geographers have worked on models in which climate change plays a limited role in the rise and decline of civilization. After analyzing several sources of both paleoclimatic and archaeological information from regions spanning between Turkey and Egypt, and Greece and Iran, Butzer (1996) came to the conclusion that the collapse of the Bronze Age civilization at the end of the third millennium BCE was due to political instability that affected the early world economy in a domino fashion. His model proposes that Cisjordan was reduced to a subsistence economy, right after Egypt spiraled into decentralized chaos, at the same time that Akkad was not able to generate capital, leading to a collapse of the Near Eastern political system. In this context, climate may have only played a secondary role, simply incrementing the stress on an already deteriorated economy (see Rosen 1995 for a more local model).

Nevertheless, if conditions were more humid in the Early Bronze Age, as the data appear to indicate, by EB IV, if not before, the climate had approached that of today. Further, the lack of overwhelming evidence for climatic change and the continuity in Early Bronze floral assemblages with the present strongly suggest that, while climate may well have been a factor in the decline of Early Bronze urbanism, there is no clear evidence to suggest that it was the major reason for that decline. The EB IV environment at Khirbat Iskandar appears to have been not unlike the conditions of today.

Agricultural Landscapes

The Chalcolithic and the Early Bronze Ages are part of the Middle Holocene, which is known by high rainfall variability (Stage 1 in oxygen isotope curve, fig. 2.3). Nonetheless, the amount of rain was relatively higher compared with modern times. This increased moisture implied a more permanent stream flow in wâdis, even in those that today are intermittent or perennial. Recharge of springs would be higher, which would provide not only more permanent sources of water for local popula-

tions, but also maintain high water table in wâdis.

From the early days of archaeological research in the southern Levant, archaeologists noticed the recurrent proximity of most Early Bronze Age sites to streams (Albright 1925). Observations of such patterns have already been mentioned by numerous geoarchaeological studies (Rosen 1986a; Mabry 1992; Donahue 1985; 1988; Donahue, Peer and Schaub 1997; Cordova et al. 2005). The explanation to this pattern was often that the Early Bronze towns depended on flood irrigation (Mabry 1992); however, no evidence of irrigation structures have been found, although Mabry (1992) reports some sort of floodplain dams near Tall al-Handaqûq (N). Betts (1991) also reports some structures thought to be irrigation installations in Chalcolithic–Early Bronze sites in the wâdis near the site of Jawa on the basaltic plateau of northwest Jordan (Helms 1981; Betts 1991).

In the particular case of Khirbat Iskandar, it seems that the proximity of the site to a watered floodplain was one of the main reasons for the location of the site. This is probably why the destruction of the floodplain by erosion (see following section) was a decisive factor in keeping the site unsettled in post-Early Bronze periods (Cordova 2007).

The events leading to the destruction of the floodplain containing a rich soil, named here the Iskandarite Soil, was studied through geoarchaeological research along a stretch of Wâdi al-Wâla. The reconstruction of the events that led to the destruction of the rich floodplain soil is depicted in figure 2.4. Using the remains of the Iskandarite Soil and the morphology of the valley, it is estimated that the floodplain was about 9 ka ha in area (Cordova 2007).

The causes of floodplain erosion are unclear, but they seem to be related to a drop in water table, which may be related to aridization. Proof of the high water table comes from a stone structure indicative of a water well found in the floodplain and evidence of a well on the site (fig. 2.5). This could be interpreted as a proxy for paleolevels of the water table, which at the time seem to have been relatively close to the surface, probably a meter or even less.

The Agricultural Landscapes around Khirbat Iskandar

The Iskandarite alluvium is of great importance because it is contemporaneous with the Early Bronze Age settlement at Khirbat Iskandar. The Iskandarite soils, which developed on the Iskandarite alluvium, present a silt loam texture and a relatively high content of organic matter. It is also abundant in pores and overall presents characteristics of a fertile soil. The lamination of silts in the non-weathered and non-plowed part of the profile suggests that the deposit formed under continuous episodes of low-energy flooding. As mentioned above, the soil presents an organic horizon, which consists of cavities (pores and root marks) filled with clay and silt. The presence of worm casts suggests also that organic activity in the soil is intense.

The pollen grains extracted from a sample of this soil also reveal interesting aspects about the agricultural use of the Iskandarite floodplain soil (fig. 2.6). While pollen of most plants that exist around the site are present in the sample, the numbers of olive tree pollen are considerable, even compared with today's numbers. The presence of cereal pollen suggests also that wheat and barley were cultivated in the floodplain or in its vicinity; however, the amount of olive tree pollen suggests that this was probably the main agricultural activity in the floodplain. Still, a systematic and thorough counting of pollen grains in more samples is needed to support these preliminary results.

Further confirmation of the cultivation of the floodplain near the site comes from palaebotanical analysis, from which preliminary results indicate the following cultivated plants: olive (*Olea euro-*

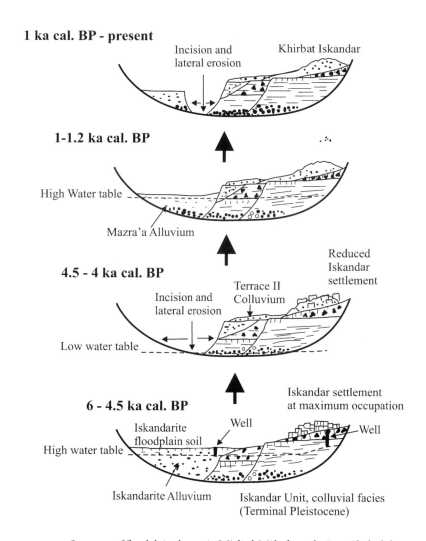

FIG. 2.4 *Sequence of floodplain change in Wâdi al-Wâla from the Late Chalcolithic to the present.*

paea), six-row barley (*Hordeum vulgare*), lentil (*Lens culinaris*), as well as chick pea (*Cicer arietinum*), pea (*Pisum sativum*), grape (*Vitis vinifera*), and fig (*Ficus carica*). It is not certain whether fig was cultivated or gathered; apparently pistachio nuts were gathered in the wild (Neef 1990).

The extraordinary amount of olive wood samples from Khirbat Iskandar, as well as olive-stone remains, supports the view that settled agriculturalists cultivated the fertile soils in the vicinity of Iskandar in the EB IV period. Tracing the development of olive culture in Jordan, Neef notes that irrigated olive orchards at Iskandar, as well as at Khirbat Zaraqun, Bâb adh-Dhrâ', and Numayra, demonstrate that olive cultivation was

FIG. 2.5   *Photo of section showing the Iskandarite Alluvium and the remains of a well dug into the Iskandarite floodplain. Associated material and radiocarbon dates suggest that the structure was built during the Early Bronze period.*

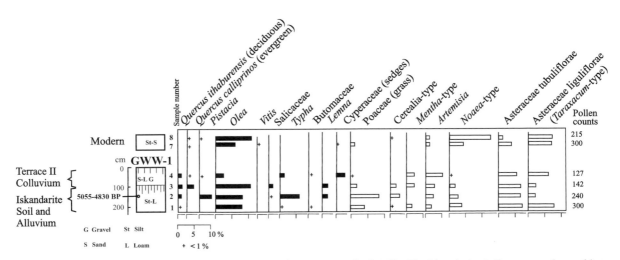

FIG. 2.6   *Pollen assemblages from the Early Bronze Age deposits in Wâdi al-Wâla. The Iskandarite Soil corresponds roughly to the Late Chalcolithic, EB I, and EB II Phases. The Terrace Colluvium II accumulated during EB III or EB IV phases.*

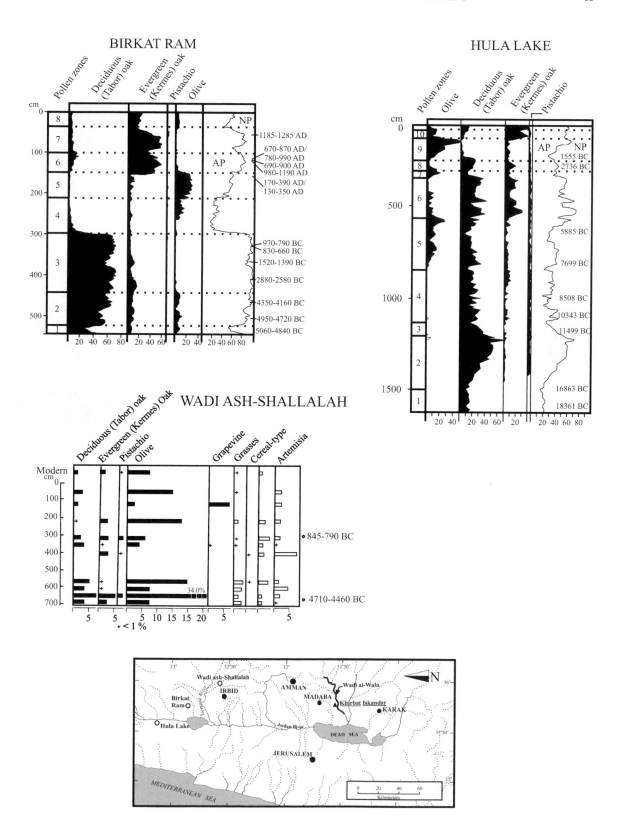

FIG. 2.7   *Summaries of regional pollen diagrams with calendar dates from Birkat Ram (Schwab et al. 2004), Wâdi ash-Shallalah (Cordova 2007), and Hula (Baruch and Bottema 1999).*

"firmly established" in the Early Bronze Age (1990: 304; and see tables 2–3). Regional pollen diagrams also support the widespread presence of olive pollen (fig. 2.7).

The two main peaks of olive pollen in the region appear to coincide with the Early Bronze Age and the "Hellenistic/Roman/Byzantine" period. The diagrams also show how as olive tree pollen increase, pollen of other trees decrease. This demonstrates also how olive cultivation took over space formerly occupied by forests.

At one location on the exposure of the Iskandarite soil, there is a stone structure built into the soil. The feature is about 1.65 m tall and about 0.75–1 m wide. It seems that this is a small well built into the soil; however, no similar structures are seen in the exposures or reported in similar locations elsewhere in Jordan.

Looking at the overall geomorphological and chronological context of the Iskandarite alluvium, it is evident that the floodplain did not exist very long. Today, the remains of this deposit are fragmentary. This suggests that the floodplain was carved in and eroded by intense flash floods. This phenomenon may have started around the turn of the third to second millennium BCE, and may suggest a rapid shift to drier conditions. Looking at the descriptions of similar Early Bronze sites and their environs in other localities of Jordan (Mabry 1992; Donahue 1985; 1988), the Shephelah region (Rosen 1986b; 1989), and the Negev (Cohen and Dever 1980), it seems that the relation between Early Bronze sites and floodplains was very strong; however, more research is needed to date the events of soil farming and floodplain destruction by erosion.

CONCLUSIONS

Local and regional paleoclimatic records show that the time spanning the Chalcolithic and Early Bronze Age periods witnessed high variability and sudden change. The Chalcolithic, the EB I, and the EB II were for the most part wet. The EB III saw some fluctuations in precipitation and some colluvial accumulation on floodplains; however, the EB IV seems to coincide with a decline in precipitation. This dry event may have contributed to the collapse of Early Bronze Age towns. Nonetheless, the evidence, or lack thereof, seems to lead to discussions of whether or not climate change was the main cause. Evidence of change in streams in the southern Levant shows a lowering of the water table and erosion of the floodplains. This phenomenon could be linked to the drying event, but it could also be related to other factors, such as deterioration of the catchment areas by human activities. Alternative explanations are the frequency of tectonic changes due to earthquakes and the drop of the Dead Sea Level, which constitutes the base level of most streams studied thus far.

Preliminary geoarchaeological data from the alluvial deposits of Wâdi al-Wâla indicate that there was a large floodplain with wetlands perhaps as late as the Early Bronze Age. Environmental changes led by climatic shifts, among other factors, contributed to a change in stream flow regime that eroded the floodplain. Once the fertile floodplain soils were missing, the wâdi became unattractive. This probably explains why the site was never re-settled after EB IV. If this is a widespread phenomenon in the region, then it will have to be considered as one of the reasons for Early Bronze Age collapse, as suggested by Richard some time ago (1980).

Pollen analysis from the sediments of Wâdi al-Wâla indicates that cereals were cultivated on the floodplain. The presence of aquatic plant pollen suggests that irrigation was possible, or at least that the floodplain was wet for some time. Large amounts of pollen for the Chalcolithic and Early Bronze Age deposits correlate with large amounts found in regional records of pollen and macro-botanical remains.

NOTES

1   PGE: 223.300; PGN: 107.200; UTME: 7631; UTMN: 34948. See Palumbo 1994, *JADIS* no. 2210.001.

2   Yohanan Aharoni (1979: 39) divides Moab into two sectors that are bisected by the Wâdi al-Mujib. The Central Moab Survey, how-

ever, separates Moab into three regions: 1) Northern Moab, the area north of the Mujib; 2) Central Moab, from the Mujib to Karak; and 3) Southern Moab, from Karak to the Wâdi al-Hasa (Mattingly 1980: 44). In both systems of classification Khirbat Iskandar falls into the geographical region of Northern Moab.

3 Orni and Efrat (1971: 111–12), e.g., suggest that there is no clear boundary between the regions of Ammon and Moab and that the two should be considered one geographic area.

4 For a more detailed breakdown of the geological makeup of Northern Moab, see Bender 1974 and 1975.

5 For more detailed treatments of the climate of Jordan, see Shehadeh 1985, Bender 1974, and Ferguson and Hudson 1986.

6 On the basis of rainfall averages and temperature extremes, Al-Eisawi (1985: 49, fig. 6, p. 50) describes the area of the Wâdi Wâla station as having a semi-arid Mediterranean bioclimate of the warm variety. In the Köppen system of classification the Khirbat Iskandar catchment falls into the category of a Cool Steppe Climate (Shehadeh 1985: 33, fig. 11, p. 35).

7 For a more detailed description of both Mediterranean and Irano-Turanian vegetation, see Zohary 1973; 1962; Feinbrun and Zohary 1955; Al-Eisawi 1985.

8 Dawud M. Al-Eisawi (1985: 46, 51, 54) separates the Red and Yellow Mediterranean (roughly equal to Terra Rosa and Rendzina) from the loess and calcareous soils of Irano-Turanian regions and indicates that the latter are less fertile, although Irano-Turanian vegetation does vary "according to the soil and other climatic differences depending on its location with respect to the Mediterranean region." The Khirbat Iskandar region lies at the confluence of the Mediterranean and Irano-Turanian zones and supports Irano-Turanian vegetation in the vicinity of the site.

Soil classification in this volume follows Bender (1974), Burdon (1959), and Moorman

(1959) in terms generally used in the literature of the region. For a similar approach, see Lacelle (1986). For the more recent systems of classification see *Soil Survey Staff* 1975 and the *Food and Agriculture Organization of the United Nations Soil Map of the World* [1974] 1990.

Red Mediterranean soils correlate to Calcic Rhodoxeralfs in the current American system and Chromic Luvisols in the United Nations system. Yellow Mediterranean Soils are similar in the newer classifications to Red Mediterranean Soils but may correspond to Typic Camborthids in the American system and Calcic Yermosols in the United Nations system (Lacelle 1986: 45–48; see *Soil Survey Staff* 1975; *Food and Agriculture Organization of the United Nations Soil Map of the World* [1974] 1990).

9 William C. Brice (1978: 143) argues that recent changes in the flora of Anatolia must be ascribed to human interaction with the environment, but over the course of the Holocene such changes must have been, for the most part, the result of alterations in climate (see below).

10 The issue of change in the fauna of the region is not addressed here *per se*. One should assume that humans have also affected the faunal assemblage, and that with any significant change in vegetation there was an accompanying impact on animal life.

11 There are many factors that may have been involved in the formation of the alluvial deposits at sites like Lachish and Tell el-Hesi (see Butzer 1978: 9).

12 From his analysis of Tall al-Handaqûq (N) and alluvial deposits in the Jordan Valley, Mabry (1992: 315) believes that during the Early Bronze Age a cycle of wâdi downcutting eroded "channel-bottom checkdams," preventing diversion of water for storage at that site. He sees this as the major reason for the abandonment of Tall al-Handaqûq (N) and other valley sites in the mid-third millennium BCE.

Chapter 3

The Stratigraphy of Area C

by Jesse C. Long, Jr.

The stratigraphy of Area C represents three major architectural phases of occupation with some sub-phases (for the location of Area C on the mound, see fig. 1.2). The sub-phases are primarily architectural, but include several surfaces. These material remains date to Early Bronze IV, with perhaps some early EB III–IV ceramic material in Phase 1 (see Ch. 4). Earlier loci, probably representing EB II/III material remains, were exposed in the C8 extension during the 2007 season of excavation. Since the building complex in Phase 3 represents a unique Early Bronze IV "gateway," the expedition decided to preserve the structure and limit the excavation of earlier phases. The following outline will highlight key loci for differentiating the stratigraphic relationships of the features exposed in Area C (for plans of the architectural features, see figs. 3.1; 3.11; and 3.26).[1]

PHASE 1

Overview

While lateral exposure of Phase 1 is limited, this phase is important for understanding the stratigraphic sequence of EB IV occupation in Area C. EB IV ceramic forms from an early stage of typological development (see Ch. 4) characterize this level of occupation. Phase 1 loci were identified in squares C1, C6, and C8 (and adjacent balks), representing parts of at least four rooms (Rooms 111, 611, 612, 811; see fig. 3.2).

C6 Building

The C6 building (Rooms 611, 612) is the most substantial structure exposed in Phase 1. Well-built, two-row walls were preserved to a height of four courses. Walls 6025, 6026, and 6034 of this building form a room 3.0 m in width, the northern perimeter of which remains unexposed. All of these Phase 1 walls were founded on Surface 6033 (477.09). This compacted earth surface sloped gradually from northwest to southeast and contained pottery that dates to Early Bronze IV. Soil Layers 6029, 6030, and 6032 overlie Surface 6033 and are characterized by an even distribution of sherds, flints, and bone chips with rubble, deposited sometime after the C6 building went out of use. Surface 6019 (top level = 477.14, bottom level = 477.09) sealed this layer. North–south Wall 6037, exposed in the C6 west balk, may be associated with the same complex

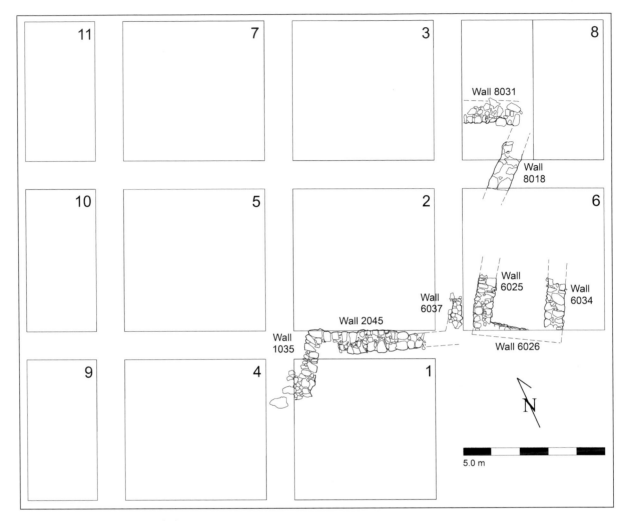

FIG. 3.1 *Phase 1 architectural plan.*

and Surface 6033, although founding levels for this wall were not reached (figs. 3.1–3.2).

Overriding surfaces and structures seal the loci of this phase in C6. Phase 2 Surfaces 6016 and 6018 and associated features (see below) overlie the walls of Phase 1 Room 611. In figure 3.3, north–south Wall 6025 appears beneath Phase 2 Table 6013. In figure 3.4, Wall 6025 is shown running under Wall 6004 of Phase 3 Bin 632 (cf. figs. 3.5; 3.19). Subsidiary Section C6-1 (fig. 3.6) represents a north–south cut from 6013 to 6014, showing the relationships between Phase 1 Wall 6025 and overlying Phase 2 Surfaces 6016, 6018. Major Phase 3 north–south Wall 2024 also rides over Phase 1 Wall 6037 (at 476.79).

Phase 1 Remains in C8

In an effort to expose additional Phase 1 material, in the 2004 season excavation in C8 resumed in a 1.5 × 2.5 m probe, which was expanded to 3 × 2.5 m in 2007. From Phase 1, Wall 8018 was exposed, running on a north–south axis in line with Wall 6025 to the south (figs. 3.1–3.2). In 1987, Wall 6025 was discovered to run beneath Phase 3 Wall 6004 to the north. The upper courses of Wall 8018 and Wall 6025 may represent the same building in Phase 1.

In 2007, the four upper courses of Wall 8018 were observed to be more narrow than the two lower courses, suggesting reuse in an upper phase. When a similar phenomenon was observed in Area

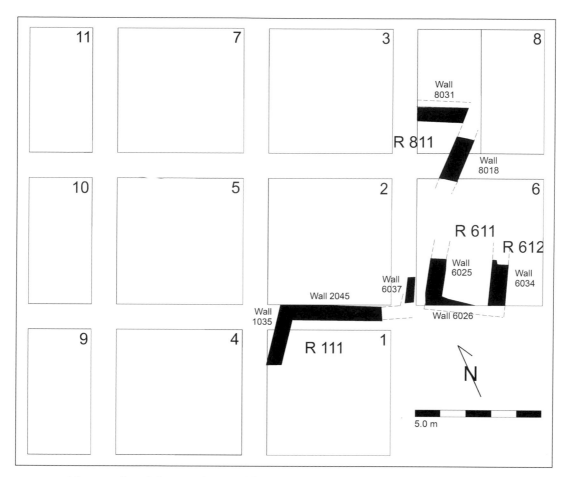

FIG. 3.2 *Schematic plan of Phase 1 architectural features.*

B (EB IV walls constructed on more substantial EB II/III walls), Wall 8018 was divided into 8018B (Phase 1) and 8018A (pre Phase 1; figs. 3.7–3.8). Uncontaminated loci associated with 8018B (Ash Layer 8019 and Surfaces 8020, 8022) contain early EB IV pottery. Wall 8018A and associated loci (Post-occupational Loci 8038, 8039, 8040, and Surface 8041 [476.00–476.05 m]) represent the only pre-EB IV loci exposed in Area C. The limited number of diagnostic sherds, however, precludes more precise placement of loci within the Early Bronze Age sequence.

Room 111

Further west in C1 and C2, Walls 1035 and 2045 form the corner of Room 111 (figs. 3.9–3.10).[2] Secure occupational surfaces associated with these features were not exposed. Although the area excavated

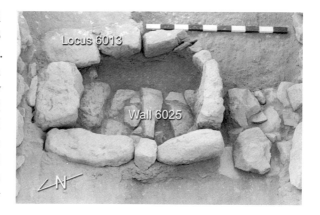

FIG. 3.3 *Phase 2 Industrial Feature 6013 above Phase 1 Wall 6025.*

from Phase 1 is limited, the associated material remains suggest a domestic function. The ceramic study, in particular, evidences a typical domestic assemblage (see Chs. 4–5); however, limited lateral

FIG. 3.4 *Phase 1 Wall 6025 running beneath Phase 3 Bin 632.*

FIG. 3.5 *Square C6 looking southwest. Phase 1 walls lie exposed below Phase 3 structures in the southern half of the square.*

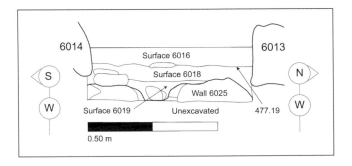

FIG. 3.6 *C6-1 subsidiary section sketch (looking west) between Industrial Features 6013 and 6014.*

exposure precludes drawing hard and fast conclusions about this phase.

PHASE 2

Overview

Although still limited, Phase 2 features were uncovered in eight of the eleven squares excavated in Area C (fig. 3.11). The exposed Phase 2 remains include a well-preserved broadroom that appears to represent domestic occupation. A workshop area with worktables and knapping debitage was uncovered in Square C6. Two sub-phases (2A and 2B) are apparent from the architectural remains, especially in Squares C2, C3, and C6.

Central Broadroom (Room 521)

Phase 2A

The most complete building exposed in Phase 2 (Room 521; fig. 3.12) evidences sub-phases. Foundation levels (Phase 2A) of the building were exposed at the base of Walls 3013 (Surface 3034, 477.68 m) and 5013 (Surface 2037 at 477.55 m). Ensuing surfaces at higher levels (for example, 2040 at 478.04–478.14 m; fig. 3.13) represent an additional sub-phase (Phase 2B). Later, Phase 3 construction covers Phase 2B collapse debris.

Clarifying these relationships, a major north–south cut down the center of the Phase 3 "gateway" reveals Phase 3A Surface 5011 above Phase 2 Wall 2039 and related loci (figs. 3.10; 3.13). Figure 3.14 shows the steps of the "gateway" to the north running over Wall 2039. Major Surface 2037 serves as the foundation layer for Phase 2A east–west Wall 5013 and runs up to Phase 1 Wall 1035 (figs. 3.10; 3.13). Phase 2B corresponds with the reuse of Room

521 architectural features before a reorganization of the structures in the area as a "gateway" in Phase 3 (see below).

Wall 2039 of Room 521 does not bond with the northern boundary of the room (Wall 3013), suggesting that it may not have been part of the original building. Since Walls 2039 and 3013 were founded at the same level, their abutment may indicate some alteration of Room 521 in Phase 2A; however, excavation did not delineate additional use surfaces. Both Wall 3013 and Wall 2039 are incorporated in Phase 2A (see figs. 3.11–3.12).

There is some evidence to suggest that the central broadroom extended further to the east. Broadroom house Walls 5013 and 3013 continue beyond the eastern boundary formed by Wall 2039. Both 5013 and 3013 end abruptly 1.0–2.0 m east of Wall 2039. Wall 5013 ends with what appears to be a purposeful, finished face. The Phase 3 extension to the wall (2009) does not obscure Wall 5013's original form. On the other hand, Wall 3013 ends in an irregular stub, suggesting it may have been breached (see figs. 3.11–3.12; 3.26).

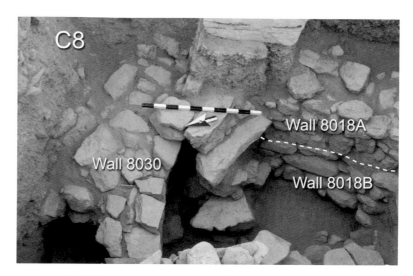

FIG. 3.7 *C8 Walls 8018A, 8018B, and 8030, looking east.*

Phase 2B

Apparently, there was only one period of occupation before some major alterations to Phase 2A structures in Room 521. Founding Surface 3034 is the only surface associated with Wall 3013 in Phase 2A. Sometime later, the area to the north appears to have been raised with fill to a level of ca. 478.10. Soil Layers 3025, 3027, 3028, and 3032 represent this reconstruction as Phase 2B (figs. 3.13; 3.15).

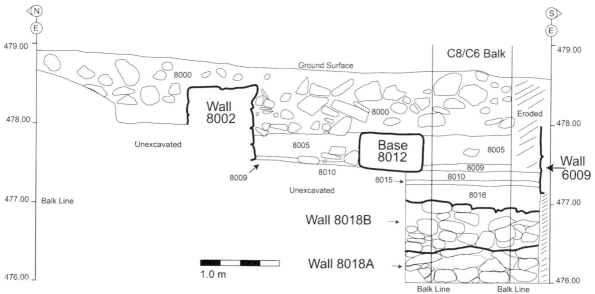

FIG. 3.8 *C8 east balk.*

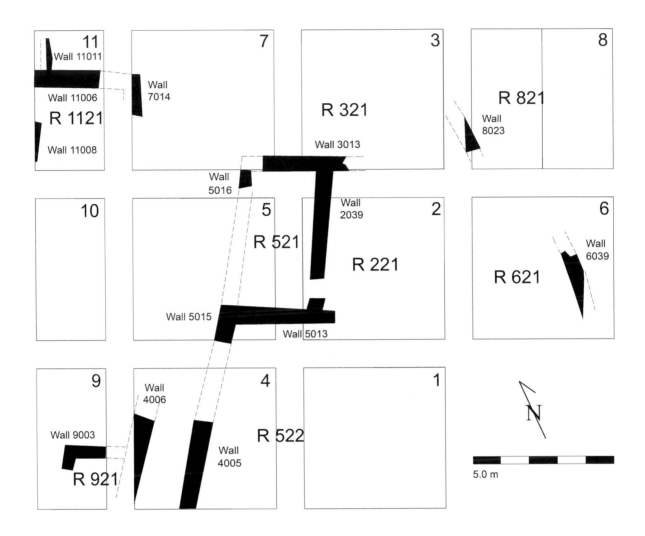

FIG. 3.12 *Schematic plan of Phase 2 architectural features.*

alternating layer of mudbrick and stone as part of the construction of Wall 2039; however, Probe 2051 (0.5 × 0.5 m, south of Wall 3013) disclosed that Wall 2039 was constructed of stone at the founding level of Wall 3013, with which it abuts. The mudbrick with facing (2041/2042) may represent a Phase 2B reuse of Wall 2039 after the wall had been cut down. Because of the decision to preserve as much as possible of the Phase 3 "gateway," the limited exposure of these Phase 2B loci precludes precise interpretation, especially in terms of the function of this mudbrick layer.[3] Nevertheless, the mudbrick and stone facing indicates a sub-phase in Phase 2, sandwiched between the foundation of Room 521 and the reorientation of the area in Phase 3.

Phase 2 Remains in C4

To the south in Square C4, Phase 2 was exposed in Walls 4005 and 4006. Wall 4004 of the Phase 3 gate complex overlies Walls 4005 and 4006 and secures their placement in Phase 2.[4] Phase 3 Pavement 4009/5009 also appears to cover these loci to the north (fig. 3.18). At the end of the 1987 season, Phase 2 Walls 5015 and 5016 were identified running north–south beneath Phase 3 Pylon 5002. Probes in the 1997 season further clarified these features. Wall 5016 forms a corner with Wall 3013 of Phase 2 Room 521; Wall 5015 in the south bonds with Wall 5013 of the same building and continues underneath 5002 to the north. By interpolation,

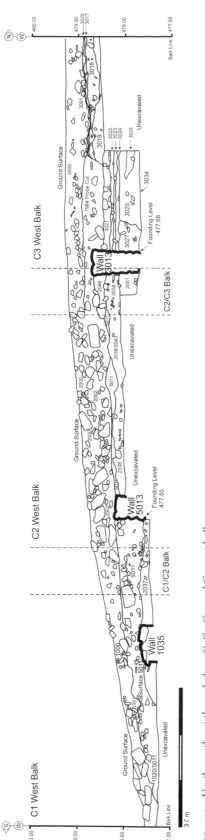

FIG. 3.13 *North–south cut through Area C: C1, C2, and C3 west balks.*

FIG. 3.14 *North–south Wall 2039 with overlying Phase 3 Stairway 5012.*

the line of these loci suggests that they form the western boundary of Room 521 (fig. 3.12). Phase 2 Wall 4005 may form part of this building beneath the Phase 3 gate, but only further exposure could affirm this interpretation.

Phase 2 Remains in C6

Workshop Area

Important evidence for Phase 2 occupation in the eastern sector of the field was uncovered in the stratigraphic sequence of Square C6. In this square, flint debitage was found in association with the Phase 1 room, and particularly in association with worktables in Phase 2, immediately above. Additional evidence for a workshop came to light in Phase 3. The best evidence came from Phase 2: two stone and mudbrick platforms (6012 and 6013),

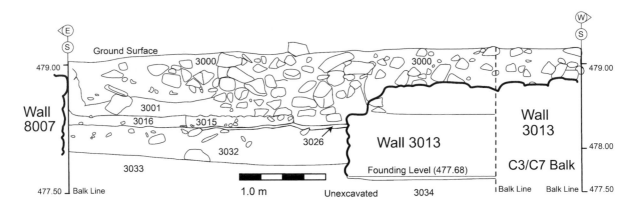

FIG. 3.15 *C3 south balk.*

a bin (6014), a stone table (6028), and occupational surfaces that contained significant quantities of flint debitage.

This workshop area overlies Phase 1 construction (see figs. 3.19–3.20 for the superposition of three phases in C6). In C6, Phase 2 features override and seal Phase 1 walls and surfaces as follows: Work Table 6013 over Wall 6025, Work Table 6012 over Surface 6018, and Wall 6005 over Wall 6039. These phases were dramatically brought to light as Work Table 6013 was dismantled. Phase 1 Wall 6025 emerged in excavation directly below this feature (see figs. 3.3–3.5, where Phase 1 structures appear beneath Phase 3 structures).

Initially, Platforms 6012 and 6013, Bin 6014, Stone Table 6028, and Bin Room 632 were thought to be contemporaneous in Phase 3; however, the evidence does not support the field reading. The platforms and bin were constructed in Phase 2 on Surface 6018 (lower level 477.14 to upper level 477.19 m). Overriding Surface 6016 appears to be an additional use surface associated with these features. Section 6013–6014 (fig. 3.6) shows Platform 6013 and Surfaces 6018 and 6016 above Phase 1 Wall 6025 (see also fig. 3.3). Surface 6027 (top level 477.34–40), as the next use surface in C6, and Table 6028 are key loci that go with Phase 3 use of the area, after Platforms 6012 and 6013 went out of use. Bin Room 632 was also constructed in Phase 3, the last period of occupational use of the building. It appears that in Phase 2 curvilinear Wall

FIG. 3.16 *Wall 2039 with Surface 2040 and overlying Debris Layer 2043 to the west, looking north.*

6039 bounded a number of work features, such as the two stone worktables and the bin. The fact that the western Wall 2024 lies over Phase 1 Wall 6037 may indicate that this area was a courtyard.

FIG. 3.17 *Debris Layer 2030 in Room 521, looking northwest.*

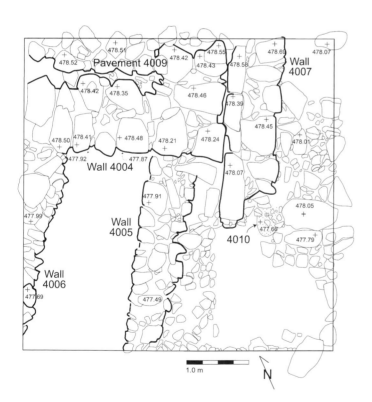

FIG. 3.18 *Square C4, with Phase 2 Walls 4005 and 4006 running underneath Phase 3 Wall 4004.*

Phases

Several lines of evidence help clarify Phase 3 in C6. The data indicate that Bin Room 632 (figs. 3.4–3.5) was constructed after Phase 2 use of Features 6012 and 6013, since Wall 6004 of the bin was founded above Phase 2 surfaces. An east–west cut across the square (fig. 3.21) shows Surface 6016, which was in use with Platforms 6012 and 6013, below Phase 3 Wall 6004 and Table 6028. Bench/Bin 6014 (top level 477.59) was apparently built in phase 2 and may have been reused in Phase 3 (fig. 3.22). Northwest–southeast running Wall 6039 was constructed in Phase 2 on the east (figs. 3.11–3.12; 3.19). Surface 6027 covered these features in Phase 3.

Cleanup of debris between seasons and removal of wall collapse apparently dug into and through Surface 6027 in the southern half of the square, which also may have been partially eroded in antiquity. In figure 3.23, Surface 6027 can be seen with bin Wall 6010 in the back-

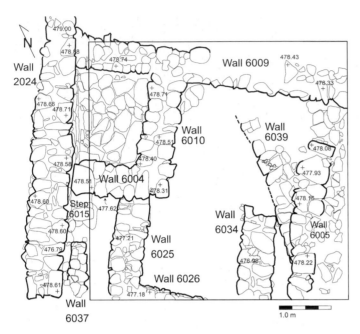

FIG. 3.19 *Square C6, with Phase 1, 2, and 3 architectural features.*

FIG. 3.20 *Phases in Square C6.*

ground. Table 6028 is in the foreground; two work stones appear on the surface. In comparison, figure 3.24 shows Room 631 with Table 6028 at the end of the season, after a portion of Surface 6027 was removed. Phase 2 Surface 6016 appears in the photograph (to the west and south), while Table 6028 rests on what remains of Surface 6027. The same view is reflected in the C6 east–west cut (fig. 3.21), where Surface 6016 emerges well below Table 6028 and underlying Surface 6027, which sealed Phase 2 material in Phase 3.

Phase 2 Remains in C8

In the 2004/2007 C8 Probe, Phase 2 Wall 8023 surfaced just inside the west balk (see figs. 3.11–3.12; 3.25). Lying below Phase 3 Wall 2024 and above Phase 1 Wall 8031, Wall 8023 corresponds with Phase 2 features discovered elsewhere in Area C. The founding surface for Wall 8023, however, was impossible to trace. Since Wall 8023 was encased in Fill Layer 8016 and was cut on the north by Pit 8035, the founding surface for Wall 8023 was probably a casualty of construction activities related to Phase 3, which included a foundation trench for Wall 6009 (see below).

Room 1121

At the northwest corner of Area C, Phase 2 construction was identified immediately below the Phase 3 monumental building evidenced in Rooms 931, 1031, and 1131 (see fig. 3.27). In the course of delineating the founding levels of the Phase 3 structure, Room 1121 surfaced in the bonded corner formed by Walls 7014 and 11006 (figs. 3.11–3.12). Due to limited depth and exposure, sub-phases were not delineated in this Phase 2 structure.

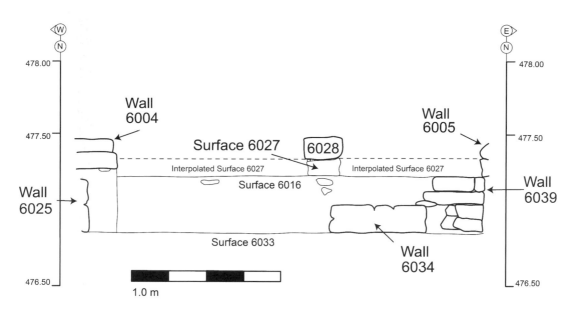

FIG. 3.21 *C6-2 east–west subsidiary balk.*

FIG. 3.22 *Bin 6014 with Industrial Features 6012 and 6013 in the foreground, looking west.*

PHASE 3

Overview

There was an alteration in plan and in function for Area C in Phase 3 (cf. figs. 3.11–3.12; 3.26–3.28). The Phase 2 central broadroom (Room 521) was replaced with construction that almost completely covered the earlier building. From Room 521, only Wall 5013 was reused. In the northwest corner of the area, Rooms 1132 and 1031, as part of a larger structure, were erected above Phase 2 architecture with a different alignment and on a more substantial scale. All of these alterations correspond to a change in the function of the area (especially in Squares C2, 3, 5, 6), from material remains that are consistent with domestic and workshop uses to a public "gateway."

Realignment in Squares C9, C10, and C11

Realignment occurs in squares C9, C10, and C11. Room 1121 was covered with walls on an altered plan (northeast to southwest vs. north to south). Phase 3 Room 1132 is on a different angle (a 16° shift) than underlying Phase 2 Room 1121 (figs. 3.29–3.32).

Bonded into the same construction, the Phase 3 walls (11001, 7003, 5005, and 9002) are also more substantial than underlying structures. For example, Wall 9002 has a width of 0.97 m, and Wall 11001 was measured at 0.65 to 0.80 m. Underlying Phase 2 Wall 11006 has a width of only 0.60–0.62 m. In addition, Wall 5005 on the east stretches 9.0 m in length, further indicating the substantial nature of this Phase 3 construction. Interior Walls 10001 and 10003 delineate a large multi-roomed building (see figs. 3.26–3.27).[5] Even more important to understanding the larger settlement in this phase, the east–west enclosure wall observed by Glueck to run across the mound (dubbed by us the "Glueck" wall) is bonded to this building as Wall 9002. The continuation of the "Glueck" wall to the west suggests that the new construction was incorporated into a larger town plan. Projected wall lines, traced on the surface, appear to connect the Phase 3 construction in Area C with an outer defensive wall found at the northwest corner of the mound (Area B; see fig. 1.2), demonstrating the reuse of the original EB II–III outer fortifications in EB IV.

North of the "Glueck" wall, Phase 3 north–south Wall 9004 abuts this wall and with it forms a small bin (fig. 3.33). On either side of Wall 9004, Paved Surface 9005 (on the east, 478.24) and Surface 9006 (on the west, 478.15) were exposed. South of the "Glueck" wall, Phase 3 Surface 9007 (477.69) appears between Walls 9002 and 9003. Surface 9008 (477.58) was exposed within the Wall 9003 corner, which appears to have been founded in Phase 2. Wall 9003 may have intersected Wall 4006 in Phase 2 (figs. 3.11–3.12; 3.34).

FIG. 3.23 *Phase 3 Surface 6027, looking west.*

FIG. 3.24 *Table 6028 on what remains of Surface 6027, looking north.*

Phase 3A "Gateway"

East of Room 1031, north–south "Gateway" 231 emerged with associated Rooms 531, 232, and 131 (figs. 3.26–3.27). Room 531 shares a common wall with Room 1031. East–west Walls 5004 and 4004 abut Wall 5005 forming the north and south boundaries of the room. The inner faces of these two walls are 6 m apart. On the eastern side of Room 531, Square Pylon 5002 stood between two framed doorways (later blocked by 5002a and

FIG. 3.25 *Square C8 at the end of the 2007 season, with Phase 2 Wall 8023 sandwiched between Phase 3 Wall 2024 and Phase 1 Wall 8031.*

5002b in Phase 3B, fig. 3.28). East–west Wall 4004 also abuts north–south Wall 4007 on the east and overrides Phase 2 Walls 4005 and 4006 (fig. 3.18). Wall 5004 seals Phase 2 north–south Wall 5015/5016 of Room 521 (see fig. 3.11), further clarifying the stratigraphic relationships of the features exposed in this area.

Room 531

Room 531 is demarcated by Walls 5004, 5005, 4004, 4007, and Pylon 5002 (figs. 3.26–3.28).

FIG. 3.26 *Phase 3 architectural plan.*

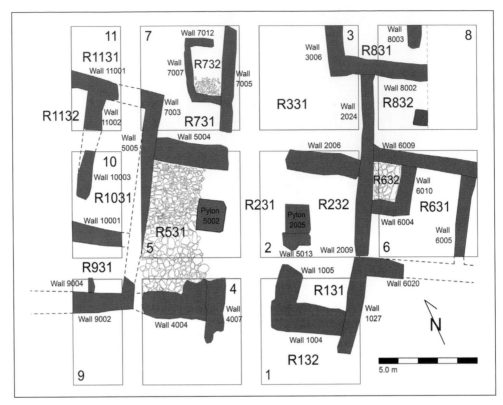

FIG. 3.27 *Schematic plan of Phase 3A architectural features.*

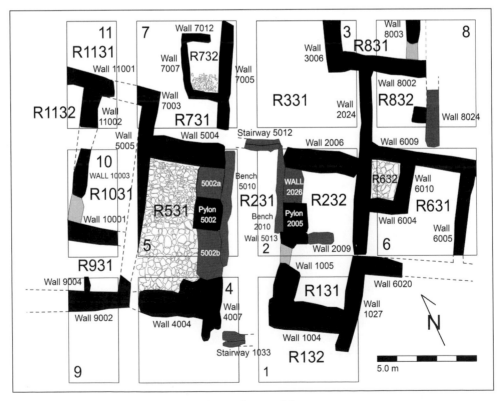

FIG. 3.28 *Schematic plan of Phase 3B and 3C architectural features.*

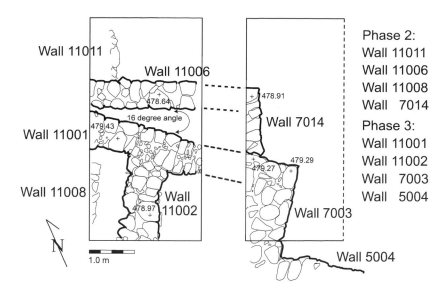

FIG. 3.29 *Squares C7 and C11, with Phase 2 features running underneath Phase 3 features.*

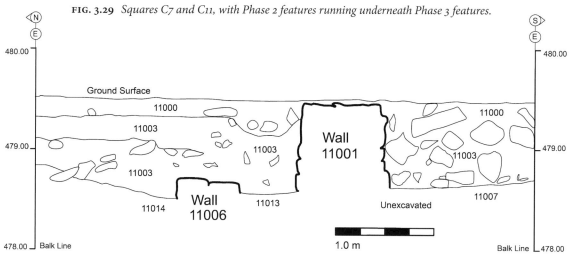

FIG. 3.30 *C11 east balk.*

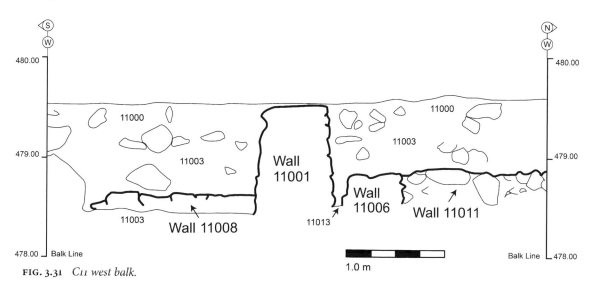

FIG. 3.31 *C11 west balk.*

Pavement 5009/4009 (478.74–478.51) runs up to the interior faces of these features. In 1987, a probe south of Pylon 5002 through Block 5002b demonstrated that Pavement 4009 extended underneath 5002b into what must have been a doorway in Phase 3A. North of Pylon 5002, a similar doorway is posited for the space blocked by 5002a. Pavement 5009 in the north of Room 531 is of smaller stones, generally set on end. In the south, Pavement 4009 is formed by larger, flat-lying stones (figs. 3.35–3.36). The line of demarcation between the two pavements follows the south face of Pylon 5002. With its flat-lying stones, Pavement 4009 may have been laid over Phase 2 debris, filling a rectangular room beneath.[6] Both doorways appear to have been blocked in Phase 3B (Blocks 5002a, 5002b; fig. 3.28).

Room 232/131

On the eastern side of the "gateway," Room 131/232 is essentially symmetrical to Room 531 on the west (figs. 3.26–3.27). East–west Walls 1004 and 2006 of this companion room both abut Wall 2024. North–south Wall 1005 bonds with Wall 1004, matching the "L" shape created by Walls 4004 and 4007. Central Pylon 2005, adjacent to the "gateway," parallels the construction of the chamber on the west in Pylon 5002; however, the east room was not paved. Pylon 2005 was framed on its southern face by Phase 2 Wall 5013, forming a doorway into Room 131 with Wall 1005.

Wall 1004 was constructed on Surface 1010 (477.787), exposed in the area south of the "gateway." To the north in Room 131, Surface 2018 (479.049–479.339) emerged as the room's latest occupational layer, characterized by granular bits of charcoal, olive-sized pieces of flint, bone, and flat-lying sherds (fig. 3.37). Below this surface, Loci 2022 and 2023 served as makeup for 2018, with an underlying layer of rock and debris (Locus 2025). This layer of debris overlay the first use surface of Room 131/232 (Phase 3), Surface 2029a (478.20), below which lay the destruction layer (2030, 478.00) of Phase 2 Room 521.

FIG. 3.32 *Square C11 looking southeast. Wall 11006 of Phase 2 Room 1121 appears in the foreground, north of Phase 3 Rooms 1031 and 1132.*

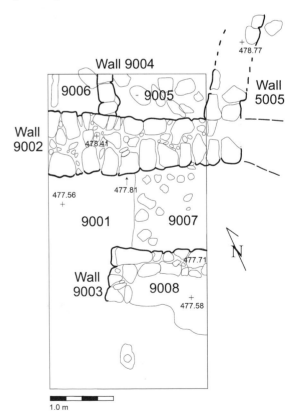

FIG. 3.33 *Square C9.*

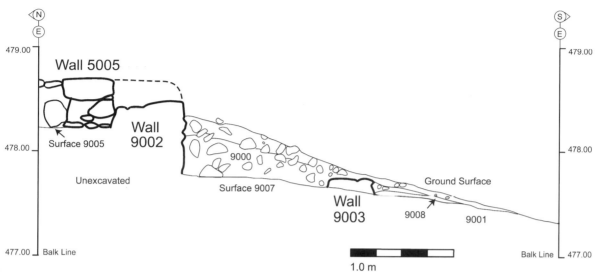

FIG. 3.34 *C9 east balk.*

FIG. 3.35 *Paved Surfaces 4009 and 5009 from above. The doorway framed by Pylon 5002 can be seen in the lower right hand corner of the photograph.*

Phases

To enable the construction of this complex, Phase 2 Room 521 was dismantled. Wall 5013 was trimmed down between the east and west gate chambers to create the passageway between. Pylon 2005 was constructed up against Wall 5013. Thus, only a portion of east–west Wall 5013, east of the passageway, was reused. At some point (in Phase 3B; see below), Stub Wall 2009 was added to extend 5013 into the east guardroom (figs. 3.26–3.28). Surface 5011 (sloping to the south, 478.425–478.275) paved the "gateway" atop the earlier structure (fig. 3.13). This thick surface covered Phase 2 Wall 5013 and rode over Phase 2 Wall 2039 and the overlying Phase 2B material. In figures 3.38–3.39, Surface 5011 covers Phase 2 Wall 5013 and continues down the slope.[7] Below 5011, compacted dirt Surface 2038 (478.31–478.28), with plaster scattered throughout, represents the earliest surface in Room 231 (fig. 3.13). This locus also served as makeup for Surface 5011.

FIG. 3.36   *Room 531 with Paved Surfaces 5009 and 4009, looking south.*

FIG. 3.37   *Surface 2018, looking northwest.*

FIG. 3.38 *Gate Surface 5011 from above.*

Courtyard 331

North of Phase 2 Wall 3013, a courtyard was exposed (Room 331) with several surfaces and soil layers, not all of which appeared through the square. The area to the north of the "gateway," where there must have been increased traffic, evidenced more deposition than in the courtyard to the east.[8] North of Room 232, hard-packed Surface 3017/7015 (478.75–80), on which were flat-lying sherds, emerged as the latest surface associated with the "gateway" (fig. 3.13). Layers 3018 (478.67) and 3019 (478.55) served as makeup below this locus. Representing the major use-layer of the courtyard, Cobbled Pavement 3021 (478.29) underlies these loci and parallels Cobbled Pavement 3015 (478.41) to the east (fig. 3.15).[9] Apparently, only a small area just north and east of the entrance to the interior of the site was cobbled. Surface 3016 (478.41) extends from 3015 further to the east without cobbles. Below, in and rising over Cobbled Pavement 3021 (478.29), appeared Ash Layer 3022 (478.27). Associated cooking pot forms and other domestic wares with faunal remains suggest that in Phase 3A there was a courtyard hearth in the cobbled surface.

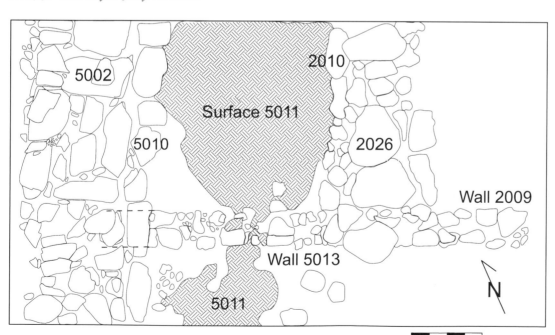

FIG. 3.39 *Gate Surface 5011 running over Phase 2 Wall 5013.*   1.0 m

FIG. 3.40 *East–west Wall 3013 exposed in N–S cut through Area C.*

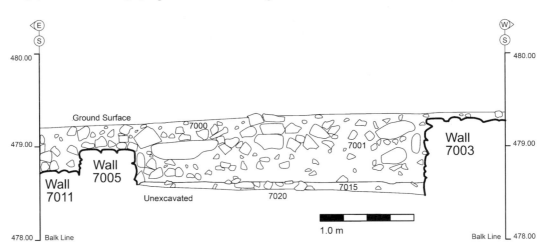

FIG. 3.41 *C7 south balk.*

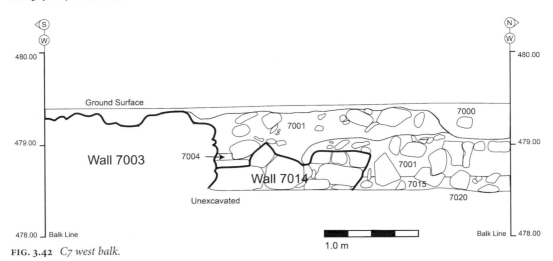

FIG. 3.42 *C7 west balk.*

Below Pavement 3021 and Ash Layer 3022, Layer 3023 served as makeup for the Phase 3 construction. Phase 2B Surface 3024/3026 (478.20–24) underlies Cobbled Pavement 3015/3017 and slopes up to Wall 2021 to the south (figs. 3.13; 3.15).

Phase 3 Remains in C7

In C7, north–south Wall 7005 cut across the area north of the "gateway" and with Wall 5004 formed a doorway. This wall also ran over the northwest corner of Phase 2 Room 521, further clarifying the stratigraphy of the area (figs. 3.26–3.27). Abutting the west face of 7005, Wall 7007 with Wall 7012 formed a bin (Room 732; fig. 3.40). In the southern half of the 2 × 2 m chamber lies stone Pavement 7016 (478.56). Hard packed Surface 7017 (478.65) in the north ran up to that pavement and the interior faces of the walls of the bin, which may have been mud-plastered. Walls 7003, 5004, 7005, and 7007 were all founded on Surface 7020 at 478.64. This ties major Wall 7005 and the accompanying bin to the same phase as the gate complex (Phase 3; see figs. 3.26–3.28; 3.40–3.43).[10] Hard-packed Surface 7015 overlies 7020 over much of the square. At a level of 478.75–478.65, Surface 7015 corresponds with Surface 3017 (478.80), linking the exposed

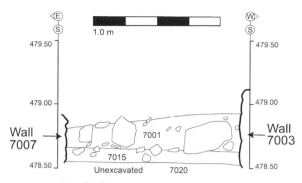

FIG. 3.43 *C7 subsidiary section.*

areas in C7 and C3. Surface 7020 corresponds with Cobbled Pavements 3015 (478.46) and 3021 (478.29; cf. figs. 3.13; 3.15).[11]

Phase 3 Remains in C6

In the southeast corner of Area C, Room 631 enclosed Bin Room 632. This top-loading bin (Walls 6009, 6010, 6004) with a cobbled surface (6022, 477.34) corresponds with the Phase 3 reorientation of Area C. Just to the east of the bin, Table 6028 was exposed in this phase. A couple of stone tools were found nearby (fig. 3.23). With associated Surface 6027, Table 6028 and Bin Room 632 (fig. 3.44) covered the underlying Phase 2 work area,

FIG. 3.44 *Phase 3 Bin 632, Table 6028, and Surface 6027, looking north.*

where tables and a significant amount of flint debitage indicate flint knapping.[12] The lack of debitage in Phase 3 Surface 6027, along with the addition of Bin 632, suggests a change in function for the room. Step 6015 (fig. 3.19) was set at the construction of the bin, running through and on either side of Wall 6004 at its juncture with Wall 2024.

Phase 3 Remains in C8

In C8 to the north, Phase 3 preconstruction excavation cut into Phase 2 features. A founding/use surface for Phase 2 Wall 8023 was difficult to trace, apparently as a result of Phase 3 building activities. Fill 8016 surrounded Wall 8023, and Pit 8035 cut through this Phase 2 feature to the north (figs. 3.25; 3.45). To the south, Wall 8023, without a clear ending face, did not continue south to the balk, suggesting that it was robbed (fig. 3.46).

In addition, because of the natural slope of the mound in this area, Wall 6009 appears to have been constructed with a foundation trench. The C8 Extension south balk (fig. 3.47) shows Wall 6009 embedded in Fill Layer 8016 (on an uneven line, without a clear founding surface), below Locus 8015, the founding layer for Phase 3 Wall 2024 (at 477.34–37). In fact, a composite photo of Walls 8002, 2024, and 6009 (fig. 3.48), with images (taken from inside the square) of the three Phase 3 walls in C8 spliced together, brings out the stepped construction of wall foundations to deal with the slope of the mound to the south. This further highlights the extent of Phase 3 construction.

Above Fill 8016, Phase 3 walls were set in Layer 8015. Overlying 8015, Surfaces 8010 (477.54) and 8009 (477.64) were deposited as use surfaces for Room 832. Pillar Base 8012 was set on Surface 8010, indicating that the room was roofed.[13] Surface 8009 (top level 477.64) evidences the buildup of occupation debris above Surface 8010 and in association with the large pillar base (fig. 3.8). In Surface 8009, flint debitage, stone objects, and floral and faunal remains

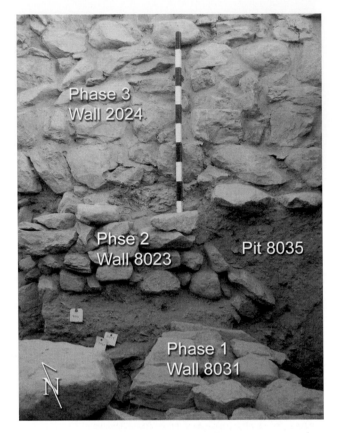

FIG. 3.45 *Phase 2 Wall 8023, sandwiched between Phase 3 Wall 2024 and Phase 1 Wall 8031.*

FIG. 3.46 *C8 extension, looking west.*

were recorded. The amount of debitage (261 flakes in four bags) suggests a function for this room that is similar to Phase 2 in C6 to the south.

Phase 3B

Phase 3B in the "Gateway"

Modifications were made across the area in Phase 3B. Sometime following the reorientation of the area, the gate complex received both alterations and a few additions. In the "gateway," the two doorways into Room 531 on the west and the north door of Room 232 on the east were blocked (Blocks 5002a, 5002b, and Block 2026; see figs. 3.26; 3.28; 3.49). These doorways were blocked prior to the addition of Benches 2010 and 5010 along both sides of the "gateway." Bench 2010 on the east does not extend as far south as 5010 on the west, leaving the south doorway into Room 131 open.

Probably at the time these blocks were added, east–west Wall 5013 was extended into Room 232/131 as Wall 2009, framing a 1 m doorway with north–south Wall 2024 (figs. 3.13; 3.39; 3.50–3.51). At the north end of the passageway, two rows of steps (5012) were set atop Surface 5011 (fig. 3.14). Soil and rubble (2046) made up the space between the steps and the remaining courses of Phase 2A Wall 3013. Also, two rows of steps (Locus 1033) were set atop Surface 5011 at the southern end of the passageway (figs. 3.26; 3.28).

In Room 232, Surface 2018 represents the last occupational surface within the confines of Room 232/131 in what must be a sub-phase in Phase 3 (figs. 3.37; 3.50–3.51). As the first surface of Room 232/131, Surface 2029A corresponds with the initial reorientation of the area following the destruction of Phase 2 Room

521. The debris layer below Surface 2029A (Locus 2030) indicates significant burning and destruction at the end of Phase 2 (fig. 3.17).

As for the "gateway" itself (Room 231), Locus 2038 (= 2012, 2050) appears to be makeup for Surface 5011 (fig. 3.13). With the limited exposure of surfaces and related loci below the final phase of the complex, it is unclear how Surface 2038 related to other features and, in general, what the "gateway" looked like before the alterations in Phase 3B. Surface 5011 functioned as the "gateway" surface through the construction of the complex in Phase 3A and the time of alterations in Phase 3B.

Phase 3B in C8

In Square C8, Fill 8005 was deposited to cover Pillar Base 8012 (see figs. 3.8; 3.52) and raised the floor of the room to the level of Surface 8011 (478.10) in Room 831, to the north of Wall 8002. Lying above Surface 8011, Surface 8008 (478.37) appears to have been associated with Block 8013 (below), although

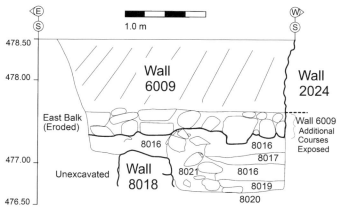

FIG. 3.47 *C8 extension South Balk.*

FIG. 3.48 *C8 "composite" photograph of Walls 6009, 2024, and 8002.*

there was limited exposure of surfaces, and founding levels were not reached for the walls in Room 831. Also in Phase 3B, Wall 8024 (coming to light in 2004, after the erosion of the east balk exposed this feature) was added above and just to the east of Pillar Base 8012 (fig. 3.53).

Phase 3C Blockages

A north–south distribution of stones (Locus 2015) south of Wall 2009 may represent a block of the doorway between 2009 and Wall 1005 (fig. 3.51). Additional Phase 3C blockages were exposed in Room 831 with Block 8013 and in Room 1031 with Blocks 10001A and 11002A. Blockages were also added to Pillar Wall 6005 (fig. 3.54), forming a solid wall with parallels elsewhere on the mound. In Squares B7 and B11, pillared walls were blocked to form solid wall construction that typifies the final Early Bronze IV phase at Iskandar.

SUMMARY AND INTERPRETATION

This section's purpose is to summarize the stratigraphic report in terms of settlement plan, rooms, and activity areas in each phase, utilizing data from throughout this volume. For details, see the ceramic and quantitative studies (Chs. 4–5), specialist reports on faunal remains and objects (Chs. 7–8), and see the final overall conclusions in Chapter 16 and comparative study.

Phase 1 Settlement

Due to limited excavation, it is difficult to interpret the Phase 1 architectural plan; however, the partial rooms sealed below the Phase 2 settlement appear to be typical Early Bronze Age (probably broad-room) domestic structures

FIG. 3.49 *Block 2026, looking east. Bench 2010 appears below the meter stick.*

FIG. 3.50 *Wall 2009 with Phase 3B Surface 2018.*

FIG. 3.51 *Block 2015 with Phase 3B Surfaces 2016 and 2018, looking north.*

(fig. 3.1–3.2). The best evidence comes from the well-constructed 3-m-wide building in Area C6. It may link with newly discovered Area C8 wall 8018 to the north, and Surfaces 6033/6038 may be contemporary with Surfaces 8020/8022; however, this is speculative since the preserved remains of Phase 3 architectural features in the northern half of Area C6 block our view. The partial house remains to the west may indicate a similar arrangement of connected walls. Nevertheless, in the super-position of Phases 1–2 architecture, and in their similar orientation (north–northeast by south–southwest), continuity is apparent. The substantial wall remains excavated in a 5 × 2.5 m area (C8) in association with large pavers, along with the clear reuse of pre-EB IV Wall 8018A, parallels recent findings in Square B19a in Area B.

The quantitative ceramic study revealed an abundance of early EB IV forms with clear Early Bronze Age antecedents, suggesting a transitional phase. It is only in Phase 2 when the diagnostic EB IV incising/rilling becomes characteristic. The material cultural remains

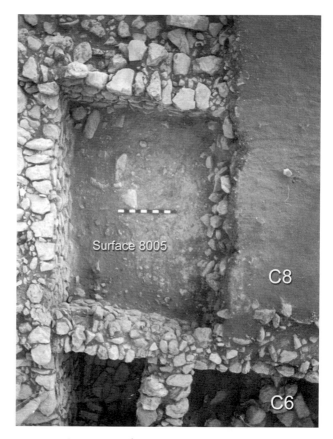

FIG. 3.52 *Square C8 and Locus 8005, from above.*

FIG. 3.53 *Wall 8024, exposed by erosion following the 1987 season.*

FIG. 3.54 *Wall 6005 beyond Bin 632, looking east.*

from Surfaces 6033 and 6038 included remains of food preparation (cooking pots), storage (holemouth jar), and serving (platter bowl) vessels, along with a total of 90 pieces of lithic debitage (R611). Chipped-stone debris becomes more abundant in Areas C6 and C8 in the following phases.

Phase 2 Settlement

Again, the partial excavation of this settlement makes interpretation of the settlement plan conjectural (see figs. 3.11–3.12), although, like Phase 1, it is a domestic area. As exposed, it appears that a series of interconnected buildings, aligned north–northeast by south–southwest, made up several rows of domestic structures separated by a lane, given the space between parallel Walls 4005–4006. Sandwiched between Phases 1 and 3 walls, the two wall fragments on the east (8023 and 6039) are somewhat enigmatic, although Wall 6039 may have served as a boundary wall to a courtyard for workshop activities. Limited exploration of the westernmost rooms (1121, 921) renders analysis difficult except to say that they are broadrooms, the former with an entrance in the corner, the latter yielding a significant number of domestic vessels.

What is clear is the phasing of this settlement: it overlies and seals Phase 1 and, at the same time, is sealed by the architecture and surfaces of Phase 3 above. For example, Phase 2 founding Surface 2037 seals Wall 1035; Phase 2 Wall 6039 grazes the

corner of Phase 1 Wall 6034; and, Phase 2 Wall 8023 overlies Phase 1 Wall 8031. From above, Phase 3 Wall 2024 overlies Phase 2 Wall 8023; Phase 3 plaster surface (2015) seals the Phase 2 destruction level and the broadroom house; and Phase 3 Wall 6005 overlies Phase 2 Wall 6030. Elsewhere, there is a clear superposition of Phase 3 over Phase 2 structures at the northwest (Wall 11001 over Wall 11011) and southwest (Walls 9002/4004 over Walls 4006/4005).

Central Area (R521/R221)

From the central area, there is a building with an Early Bronze Age broadroom, whose doorway is at the corner (as with R1121). The eastern area (R221) was a roofed room, based on the remains of beams, pottery, and general destruction debris found on (Phase 2B) Surface 2030 (=Surface 2040 in R521). The truncation of Walls 3013/5013, apparently a consequence of building activities in Phase 3, obscures the extent of this room. In comparison with other broadroom houses in Area C and at the site generally (e.g., R1031 in Phase 3), R521 is somewhat unusual in that Wall 2039 is a mudbrick construction with stone facing. Although all of the walls (3013/5013/5016 and 2039a/b) have the same founding level (Phase 2A Surfaces 3034/2037), only Wall 2039 abuts. It is an interior wall dividing R521 from R221. Whether Wall 2039, apparently cut down in Phase 2B (Surface 2040), was an interior wall or bench at that time is unclear. Despite only partial excavation, the central complex itself included considerable material remains, which reveal the typical domestic activities that took place there.

In Room 221, there was evidence for spinning (a limestone spindle whorl, A148), short and long-term storage (3 holemouth jars, 3 storejars), food preparation and serving (1 cooking pot, 9 platter bowls, 4 large bowls, 3 small bowls, 3 "teapots"), and a special usage vessel (1 holemouth basin). In R521, limited excavation uncovered a typical domestic assemblage of 1 large bowl, 3 cooking pots, 7 platter bowls, and 2 storejars. Probable courtyard Room 321 just to the north yielded 1 holemouth jar, 3 platter bowls, and 2 "teapots." Similar domestic activities are not evident in Room R921, where there were no cooking pots, only two serving dishes (1 platter bowl and 1 cup), five storejars, and two "teapots."

The Eastern Area: R621

The area east of the broad-room structure was evidently a courtyard, enclosed by fragmentary Wall 6039 and used for specialized work activities. This is indicated by the contiguity of two work platforms and a bench/platform. The two rounded worktables 6012 and 6013 were, like Wall 2039, constructed of stone and mudbrick. Associated Surfaces 6018, 6016, 6019, and 6036 yielded unusual quantities of flint debitage (257 flakes), along with associated objects: 2 handstones (A306/A337), 1 hammerstone (A305), a Type B pierced stone (A311), a terracotta lid or stopper (A307), and a ceramic spindle whorl (A424). That this courtyard was a multi-purpose area seems clear from the evidence of cooking (5 cooking pots), serving (5 platter bowls, 1 large bowl, 3 small bowls, 3 "teapots"), and storage (2 storejars, 2 holemouth jars, 1 holemouth bowl), and a lamp fragment.. The debitage from primary and non-primary loci combined implies that a specialized workshop of flint knapping was a major activity (see Ch. 8).

Phase 3 Settlement: the "Gateway"

The preserved and restored Phase 3 "gateway" (Long and Libby 1999) offers the greatest lateral exposure in Area C, and a view of society not encountered elsewhere in the period as yet. Both the plan and the monumentality (at least for the EB IV period) of the "gateway" complex, which presupposes a public function, distinguish it from the type of domestic remains described for the Phases 1–2 settlements. The complex also included specialized rooms for agricultural processing and/or storage, as well as workshop activities. Yet, the ceramic assemblage includes a similar range of pottery found in association with the domestic contexts of the earlier settlements (see Ch. 5). Thus, it is apparent that a variety of activities took place in the Area C "gateway," including the preparation, serving, and storing of food. These findings support the mixed economy and reduced level of specialization that is the hallmark of the rural EB IV period.

Phases

Bonded walls (9002–5005) and associated surfaces demonstrate the contemporaneous construction of the gate and east–west wall at the beginning of Phase 3. Wall 9002 overrides Phase 2 Wall 4006 (for the superposition of Phase 3 over Phase 2 architecture and features, see above). The essential elements of the "gateway" and contiguous structures were erected in Phase 3A, when a simple single entryway existed juxtaposed by rooms with a central pylon (see fig. 3.27). It is difficult to say how long after construction, but, at some point within Phase 3, alterations took place. The Phase 3B architectural changes included: blockages, against which benches were set on either side of the plaster passageway; the addition of stairways; and the subdivision of the eastern structure. Moreover, multiple surfaces in R131/R232/R331 and the addition of a pavement in the northern half of R531 also provide evidence for this sub phase. An ephemeral phase (3C) in which doorways were blocked in R831, R131, and R1031 (also observed in Area B) suggests an intent of the occupants to return; however, the site lay abandoned until the Iron Age, for which there is some evidence of occupation. A description of the Phase 3B plan of rooms/assemblages follows.

Entryway/Room 231

Room 231, with its well-made thick (0.30 m in places) plaster surface, was evidently in use throughout Phase 3. The 9 × 2.5 m passageway, flanked by two rooms of monumental construction, was the focus of the complex, enabling traffic to and from the upper site. The monumental (1-m-wide, boulder) construction of the two rooms contrasts with the 0.60–0.80 m wide (small to medium cobble) walls against which they abut. The erection of benches suggests some modification in function in Phase 3B to include, apparently, a communal gathering place. The nicely cut stone benches and stairs are a sign of extra care taken in the gate construction. The eastern bench ends near the doorway to R131, but the western bench extends further. Steps at the south and north formalized the function of the passageway. Stairway 5012 led up to a higher level of courtyard surface in R331, and there is a step down into R731. The few sherds discovered in the entire passageway (2 platter bowls, 1 basin, and 1 storejar) suggest that activities relating to food preparation did not take place there and/or that the plaster surface was swept regularly. Presumably, these few sherds and the 71 pieces of debitage are refuse from the activities in or traffic through the "gateway."

Eastern Gate Area Rooms R131/232

In the eastern building, modifications in Phase 3B include the addition of Wall 2009 against Wall 5013, which effectively closed off the northern room (R232) from the southern (R131), leaving a small doorway. R232, therefore, was not at this time immediately accessible from the passageway. Plaster Surface 2018 was the final use surface, separated from earlier Phase 3A Surface 2029A by makeup layers and a layer of rock and debris. The upper surface contained serving vessels (1 jar, 1 "teapot," 1 platter bowl) and two cooking pots, plus a handstone fragment (A083). Except for a lamp fragment, R131 was devoid of materials. The pottery indicates

some limited domestic activity of cooking and eating taking place in the room.

Western Gate Area, Rooms 531/1031/931/1132

The lack of materials from Room 531 is not surprising, given its well-made pavement, which was, apparently, swept clean regularly. There are two distinctly different pavements in the room, small cobbles set on edge at the north, larger, flat pavers at the south. A probe revealed that blockage Wall 5002b covered the southern pavement, suggesting the latter's purpose was to seal earlier Phase 2 levels. It is likely that the Phase 3B alterations included the addition of the northern pavement. The purpose of this nicely paved room, for which there is no apparent entrance (unless there was a higher doorway at the edge of the final step), and few material remains, is beyond our grasp. Limited excavation further to the west revealed the outlines of a large (10-m-long), well-built, multi-roomed structure (R1031/R931), overlying Phase 2 features at the north and south (see above). As seen elsewhere, the broadroom house includes a doorway at the corner. This is a substantial EB IV building, but now superseded in size by a multi-roomed building ca. 13 m long with five doorways recently found in Area B (Richard and Long 2007).

Courtyard R331

Considering the relative sterility of the courtyard surfaces, it seems plausible to consider R331 as an extension of the passageway to the upper site. Hard-packed Surface 3017, with 3 flat-lying sherds, was the latest surface associated with the Phase 3B entryway. There was surprisingly limited refuse: serving (6 platter bowls, 1 large bowl), storage (1 holemouth jar, 1 storejar, 1 jug), and cooking (1 cooking pot) vessels; there was 1 object (A432 flakes). In Phase 3A, the original surface was a cobbled one, based on patches of small stones in several areas.

R731/R732

At the northwest, there was an area of specialized activities. R732, a well-constructed one-course, one-row room, had a doorway at the north, not immediately accessible from the entryway/courtyard. A well-preserved compacted (plaster) surface (7017= 7015 in R731) led to an area of pavement at the south end, on which sat two cooking pots. Remains of plaster on the walls at the south end indicate additional care in the construction of this room. Bin R732 seems associated with exterior area R731 (Surfaces 7015 and 7020), which contained the largest assemblage of ceramics found in Area C (27 platter bowls, 2 cups, 9 large bowls, 3 small bowls, 1 jug, 3 "teapots," 3 special purpose basins, 1 lamp, and 3 cooking pots), as well as 46 flakes, a handstone (A361), and a hammerstone (A378). Whether this combined courtyard/bin area was for storage, a kitchen, or a specialized area for processing of agricultural product (4 basins), its assemblage is significantly different from elsewhere in the complex.

Eastern Gate Area (R631)

The contiguity of top-loading paved bin (R632), monumental (1.5 × 0.40 × 0.20 m) stone slab table 6028, three stone benches (6028a–c), and a reuse of Bench 6014 within one small room, argues against a domestic residential area. Unfortunately, erosion and topsoil disturbance left only patches of plaster Surface 6027 in the north. There was, thus, no evidence of surface buildup here, as in Area C8 to the north; however, Surface 6027 did yield a handstone (A350), basalt pestle (A360), and polishing stone (A351) in association with Worktable 6028 and Benches 6028a–c). The contiguity of Bin R632 with the worktable suggests that related activities took place there. Steps integrated into Wall 6004 indicate a purposeful use intended for Bin R632

at construction. It was a storage bin whose high walls (1.25 m) and lack of entrance necessitated access from above, hence the steps. Unfortunately, its fill was debris and rockfall. Lack of plaster on the interior of the bin would appear to militate against its use as a granary, although possibly it was for storage of food/liquid containers, or other materials (equipment?) used in connection with the worktable. We surmise that lithic workshop activities continued in this area from Phase 2. Further support comes from significant evidence for such activities just to the north, in Area C8.

R832/R831

Phases 3A–B surfaces were found in this area. On Surface 8010, massive stone 8012 (0.73 × 0.71 × 0.36 m) apparently served as the central pillar base for the roofed room (R832), although it is not impossible that it was a stone worktable. Use Surface 8009 yielded 261 flakes of flint debitage. Phase 3B Surface 8005a covered pillar base 8012, at which time Wall 8024 (fragmentary and in the balk) may have been erected. Interestingly, Phase 3B Surface 8008 in R831 to the north yielded 249 lithic flakes. The combined evidence makes this area a good candidate for a lithic workshop (see Ch. 8). Again, the material culture indicates that along with specialized lithic activities, cooking and serving took place in the two rooms. In R831, excavation uncovered one cooking pot, three platter bowls, one cup, one jug and two "teapots," as well as two hammerstones (A425/A426). In R832, there was a similar assemblage (1 cooking pot, 5 platter bowls, 1 small bowl, 1 jug, 2 cups, and 1 storejar), along with the only grinding slab (A367) found in Area C.

NOTES

1 For a descripiton of other loci, see Appendix B.
2 In figs. 3.9–3.10, Wall 1035 can be seen west and below Wall 1004 in the north–south cut through the gate.
3 Mudbrick Layer 2049, which lies above Loci 2041 and 2042 and below Step 2044 (fig. 3.16), may correspond with this sub-phasing, al-

though, without more exposure, articulating the exact sequencing of loci is difficult.
4 In Square C1, south of Wall 1004, a companion to Wall 4004 in the gate complex, underlying Phase 2 architectural features were not found. Phase 2 Surface 1016 was exposed as a compact beaten earth layer that underlies Surface 1010

on which Phase 3 Wall 1004 was constructed. Surface 1019 underlies Surface 1016.

5   Surfaces associated with this building have been identified in Plaster Surface 10002 (north of 10001 at 478.58) and Beaten Earth Surface 11007 (in the corner formed by 11001 and 11002 on the east at 478.66). Because of limited exposure in these "half-squares" (C9–11), however, the material remains are insuficient to say anything definite about the function of these areas.

6   The desire to preserve this room as part of the "gateway" precluded extensive excavation. A 1998 probe in the area of the south doorway uncovered Phase 2 Wall 5016 (above).

7   Figs. 3.38–3.39 also reflect the erosion of Surface 5011 in antiquity, above and around underlying Phase 2 Wall 5013.

8   The difference in deposition can be seen by comparing the C3 West and South Balks (figs. 3.13; 3.15).

9   In terms of phasing, this pavement also corresponds with plaster Surface 7020, north of Room 531 in Room 731.

10   The C7 Subsidiary Section (fig. 3.43), representing a cut between Walls 7003 and 7007, demonstrates that these features were constructed on Surface 7020.

11   Differences in levels may be explained by the unevenness of the courtyard area and the natural slope of the mound.

12   See above for a more detailed discussion of the Phase 2 workshop area and a delineation of Phase 2 and Phase 3 features in Square C6.

13   The location of 8012 in what appears to be the center of Room 832 suggests a function as a pillar base, although a worktable of some sort is not out of the question. For a parallel, see the similar base in Room 2440 at Arad (Ruth Amiran and Ornit Ilan, *Arad II* [1996], Plate 38, ph. 2; Plate 39, ph. 1 and ph. 2).

Chapter 4

The Area C Early Bronze IV
Ceramic Assemblage

by Suzanne Richard

This chapter will focus on the typology of specific EB IV vessels from Area C, relying heavily on the quantitative analysis of the ceramic assemblage found in Chapter 5. The classification is based on form/size to determine basic types—59 Tell Code Basic Form non-random sorted categories—which, in combination with rim, allowed for the classification of 96 specific types, detailed in outline form below. The basic (four-digit) form code includes the vessel type (e.g., spouted vessel within the restricted form), size, and contour description, the latter varying for different form categories (see Ch. 5 for a detailed discussion). This basic form system is a modification of the whole vessel classification used for the cemetery assemblage (Ch. 12).

The rationale for the original classification system for the Bâb adh-Dhrâ' tombs was, essentially, that form/size are the best criteria for objectively determining functional categories, which can then facilitate comparative studies with other sites (for details, see Schaub and Rast 1989: 4–9). That rationale drives the town classification system as well, although, obviously, modifications were necessary for a collection consisting almost exclusively of sherds (for details, see Rast and Schaub 2003:

preface in part 2). As mentioned elsewhere, the classification employed in this study, with some modifications, is based on that originally devised for the Bâb adh-Dhrâ' ceramic corpus.

The rim type is a very important component of the classification. Although rim identification introduces subjectivity into the system, it allows for the resultant typology of specific types, in this case, the specific EB IV ceramic types in Area C at Khirbat Iskandar. Other variables included in the quantified study were handles, decorative elements, and surface treatments. In some cases, these proved to be significant to a type. The specific types (or type series/typology) is an invaluable catalogue of the distinctive attributes and attribute clusters of the corpus, a catalogue that engenders fruitful cross-comparisons with the cemetery pottery and sequence comparisons with other sites.

Thus, through a combined analysis of the statistical patterning of these variables in relation to well-known and well-established EB IV types, the typology is both objective and accessible for comparison with other sites. The basic form types are: cooking pots, holemouth jars/bowls, spouted vessels ("teapots"), storejars, jugs, platter bowls, bowls, cups, and lamps. The specific types combine

incising/grooving) is added to the combed ware, the percentage is 43 percent overall. Besides these, eight percent of vessels have some type of applied molding (for example, thumb-impressed, piecrust). The percentage of red slip and red slip/burnishing is also quite high: 54.2 percent (198/365) of vessels were slipped on the exterior or interior or both, 50.4 percent (184/365) were burnished, and 48.8 percent (178/365) were slipped *and* burnished. Except for a virtual absence of overall body combing in Area C, the surface treatment of vessels at the site compares favorably with that at Bâb adh-Dhrâ' (Rast and Schaub 2003: 427).

SPECIFIC EB IV TELL TYPES

Figures 4.1–4.4 illustrate virtually all the basic form types that, when combined with rim, present the specific EB IV type series identified from Area C at Khirbat Iskandar. The relevant data for each appear in the facing descriptive page. The benefit of parsing the corpus into such quantifiable size/form and size/form/rim types is to grasp the overall distribution of major and minor vessel groups at the site for comparison between tell and tomb and with other sites. Those who wish to analyze the pottery by locus have access to all the pottery utilized in the quantitative study (Appendix A).

The outline presents the classification in the following manner: EB IV functional types (for example, spouted vessels), subsumed under the primary form (Restricted, Necked Jar, and Bowl) and size (Very large, Large, Medium, Small) categories, further broken down into contour (for example, open/closed) and/or rim types. After each rim type the number of examples is listed in parentheses, followed by the specific code for the rim. Generally, the four-digit form code is included after size.

As an example, within the Restricted (essentially "holemouth") category, there are three main form/functional types in Area C: storejars, cooking pots, and spouted vessels. These break down into size category and rim type. Thus, within the Restricted (Holemouth Jar) category, there is one Large (4060) Spouted Vessel with direct (squared) rim (I[1].C.1.a), rim type 10. For a complete list of the specific types in this chapter (and Ch. 12), see the corpus in Appendix I. All of the code descriptions used for Khirbat Iskandar vessels are detailed in Appendices D and E.

I(1). Restricted (Holemouth Jar) Forms

A. Storejars (12 ex.)

1. Very Large (4000) storejars with direct rim (2 ex.): 10
2. Large (3010) storejars with bulbous direct rim (1 ex.): 18d
3. Large (4010) storejars with interior lip direct rim (1 ex.): 17
4. Medium (4020) storejars (7 ex.)
   a. direct rim (5 ex.): 10, 11, 12
   b. interior lip direct rim (1 ex.): 17
   c. bulbous direct rim (1 ex.): 18d
5. Small (4030) storejars, with interior lip direct rim (1 ex.): 17

B. Cooking Pots (36 ex.)

1. Large (4010C) cooking pots (4 ex.)
   a. direct rim (1 ex.): 10
   b. interior lip direct rim (1 ex): 17
   c. bulbous direct rim (2 ex.): 18d
2. Medium (4020C) cooking pots (30 ex.)
   a. direct rim (14 ex.): 10, 11, 12
   b. interior lip direct rim (7 ex.): 17
   c. bulbous direct rim (9 ex.): 18, 18b, 18d
3. Small (4030C) cooking pots, with interior lip direct rim (2 ex.): 17

C. Spouted Vessels ("teapots") (31 ex.)

1. Large (4060) spouted vessels (11 ex.)
   a. direct rim (3 ex.): 10, 11
   b. interior lip direct rim (1 ex.): 17
   c. bulbous direct rim (2 ex.): 18a, 18d
   d. turned-up rim (3 ex.): 41, 42
   e. flared ("necked") rim (2 ex.): 61, 65
2. Medium (4067) spouted vessels (17 ex.)
   a. direct rim (2 ex.): 10, 11
   b. beveled direct rim (2 ex.): 13
   c. turned-up rim (12 ex.): 41, 42
   d. flared ("necked") rim (1 ex.): 65

3. Small spouted vessels (4072) (3 ex.)
    a.   direct rim (1 ex.): 11
    b.   turned-up rim (2 ex.): 41, 45

Holemouth Jars

Basic Forms: The holemouth jars in Area C fall into three major categories: cooking pots, storejars, and spouted vessels or "teapots." Whereas they all share virtually the same range of simple, elaborated (interior lip; beveled) or bulbous direct rim types, it is only the "teapot" that illustrates more variety, in particular, the turned-up rim. Even with a limited number of holemouth jars, preferences vary somewhat: bulbous or squared rim for cooking pots, squared or elaborate rim for storejars, and a turned-up rim for "teapots." Except for the one storejar pithos, in all three categories there was a similar size range from large to medium to small. The preference, however, was for the medium size, as at Bâb adh-Dhrâ'. The prevalence of simple direct rims at Khirbat Iskandar may relate to the statistical evidence at Bâb adh-Dhrâ', which found an increase in simple direct rims through the Early Bronze Age into the EB IV (Rast and Schaub 2003: 32). These three restricted categories occur in the tombs, although as expected in ritual contexts, cooking pots and storejars were rare. By use of rim diameter comparisons with the tell, the quantitative study observed a preference for the medium form in the tombs as well.

A. Storejars

Fabrics, Tempers, Surface Treatment: As usual, discriminating between holemouth cooking pots and holemouth jars is sometimes difficult, given similar rim types. Based on ware (unblackened, finer), temper (no calcite), and decoration (four had red slip, rills, pattern combing or stabs), there were 12 holemouth storejars in Area C.

Specific Types: The typical Early Bronze Age holemouth storage jar is well represented in the range of direct rim types, although the bulbous type is the least popular. The preferred type was the simple direct, usually squared (fig. 4.1:1, 6) rim, although rounded and tapered types also appear. Also popular was a more elaborated rim, characteristically having an interior lip (fig. 4.1:4), which may appear as a flange (fig. 4.1:2). The latter is a more popular rim on jars/cooking pots elsewhere, for example, in north Transjordan at Tall Umm Hammad (Helms 1986: fig. 19) and in central and southern Cisjordan at Be'er Resisim (Cohen and Dever 1980: fig. 17: 23–28).

The number of storejars at Khirbat Iskandar (12 ex.) and Bâb adh-Dhrâ' (12 ex.) is relatively small, but both sites show comparable types, a popular size range of medium (14–20 cm), and a preference for a simple direct rim. In the cemeteries, there was one medium-sized storejar with thumb-indented bulbous rim found in Tomb D9 (see Ch. 12). Overall, the storejar form does not offer any significant typological or chronological indicators. Absent one in Phase 1 and two in Phase 3, all holemouth storejars occur in Phase 2, correlating with a clear domestic housing function, as indicated by the central broadroom house (see Chs. 3 and 16).

B. Cooking Pots

Fabrics, Tempers, Surface Treatment: Cooking pots are usually easily identifiable by their ware and temper; all have soot, calcite, and significant quantities of tempering agents, including wadi gravel. Technological studies of ware found a high correspondence between the holemouth cooking pot and calcite as a tempering agent in contradistinction to the necked or holemouth bowl cooking pot (Sauders 2001).

Specific Types: The cooking pot category with 36 examples provides a better sample with which to compare rim type popularity and size preferences among holemouth jar vessels. Similar to the storejar, there are few large (4) and small (2) examples. The medium size (4020C), ca. 14–20 cm in diameter, is the most popular. The simple direct and elaborated rims remain popular (fig. 4.1:3, 7), but there are, proportionately, many more bulbous (11) rims (fig. 4.1:5), showing perhaps a more dominant Early Bronze Age tradition in the cooking pot form. Although there are more examples at Khirbat

FIG. 4.1   *Area C specific type series: Restricted (holemouth) vessels.*

#	Form	Ph	Locus	Type	FormHaRiBa	Size	Description	Ref
1	Holemouth Jar	2	C03034	Storejar	4000.00.10.00	Large	Storejar with direct (squared) rim	pl. 9:20
2	Holemouth Jar	2	C02030	Storejar	4010.00.17.00	Large	Storejar with direct (interior lip) rim	pl. 6:3
3	Cooking Pot	3	C06021	Cooking Pot	4020C.00.17.00	Medium	Cooking pot with direct (bulbous) rim	pl. 13:3
4	Holemouth Jar	1	C06033	Storejar	4030.00.17.00	Small	Storejar with direct (interior lip) rim	pl. 14:18
5	Cooking Pot	1	C06029	Cooking Pot	4010C.00.18d.00	Large	Cooking pot with direct (bulbous) rim	pl. 13:14
6	Holemouth Jar	2	C01036	Storejar	4020.00.10.00	Medium	Storejar with direct (squared) rim	pl. 3:13
7	Holemouth Jar	2	C03024	Cooking Pot	4030C.00.17.00	Small	Cooking pot with direct (interior lip) rim	pl. 9:14
8	Holemouth Jar	3	C02033	Spouted Vessel	4060.00.10.00	Large	"Teapot" with direct (squared) rim	pl. 6:8
9	Holemouth Jar	2	C09001	Spouted Vessel	4060.00.61.00	Large	"Teapot" with lightly flared (rounded) rim	pl. 20:9
10	Holemouth Jar	3	C02025	Spouted Vessel	4067.00.10.00	Medium	"Teapot" with direct (squared) rim	pl. 4:20
11	Holemouth Jar	2	C02030	Spouted Vessel	4072.00.41.00	Small	"Teapot" with turned-up (rounded) rim	pl. 5:23
12	Holemouth Jar	2	C06016	Spouted Vessel	4072.00.11.00	Small	"Teapot" with direct (rounded) rim	pl. 12:5
13	Holemouth Bowl	2	C02037	Storejar	4046.00.18a.00	Medium	Storejar with direct (bulbous) rim; molding	pl. 7:3
14	Holemouth Bowl	2	C01016	Storejar	4050.00.12.00	Medium Small	Storejar with direct (tapered) rim	pl. 1:12
15	Holemouth Bowl	3	C07015	Cooking Pot	4040C.00.12.00	Large	Cooking pot, straight-sided, with direct (tapered) rim	pl. 17:16
16	Holemouth Bowl	3	C03016	Cooking Pot	4050C.00.11.00	Medium Small	Cooking pot with direct (rounded) rim	pl. 8:5
17	Holemouth Bowl	2	C05014	Spouted Vessel	4040.00.71.00	Large	Spouted basin with thickened (flat) rim	pl. 11:16
18	Holemouth Bowl	1	C06032	Storejar	4050.00.12.00	Medium Small	Storejar with direct (tapered) rim, molding	pl. 14:16
19	Deep Bowl	2	C01016	Basin	4080.00.71.00	Very Large	Basin with thickened (flat) piecrust rim	pl. 1:14
20	Deep Bowl	2	C06016	Basin	4080.00.10.00	Very Large	Basin with thickened/swollen direct (squared) rim	pl. 12:4

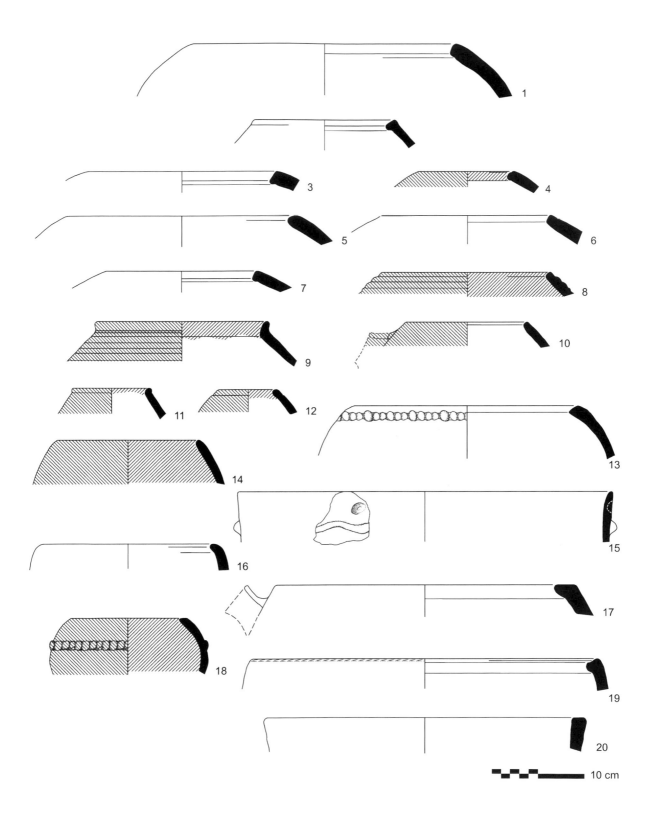

FIG. 4.1 *Area C specific type series: Restricted (holemouth) vessels.*

Iskandar (36) than at Bâb adh-Dhrâ' (25), both as-semblages share a preference for a medium-size cooking pot and the same rim types, including a prevalence of bulbous rims.

The quantitative analysis indicates that the decrease of bulbous rims from Phase 1 to Phase 2 is significant, while the more elaborated (in-ner lip) direct rim increases significantly (see Ch. 5). Additionally, there is a statistically significant chronological evolution from holemouth (Phase 1), to necked (Phase 2), to holemouth bowl (Phase 3) cooking pots at Khirbat Iskandar (see discussion below). This typo-chronological sequence correlates with Bâb adh-Dhrâ' (Schaub and Rast 2003: 431–32), although the latest type, the holemouth bowl, is not found there. For an illustration of a complete holemouth cooking pot at Khirbat Iskandar, see Richard (1982: fig. 4.2; pl. 90). What the corpus lacks is also of interest: cooking pots with "flanged" rim mentioned above, molding at or just below the rim, or the unusual groove-rim and folded-over cooking pot rims found at Be'er Resisim in the Negev (Cohen and Dever 1981: fig. 11:18–19, 20–24). However, one example at that site (fig. 18:16) provides a striking parallel for a storejar rim found in Area C (pl. 19:19), although considered EB III on ware.

C. Spouted Vessels ("Teapots")

Fabrics, Tempers, and Surface Treatment: Despite similar direct rim types, "teapots" are generally distinguishable from holemouth storejars by their finer, thinner ware and decoration, although, in the absence of a spout, one cannot always be certain. In Area C, there are 22 red-slipped and/or burnished "teapots," of which 15 also have rills and another seven have only rills, or varieties of combing and/or stab marks.

Specific Types: Based on the tomb types (fig. 12.1), it would seem reasonable to assume that both global and squat "teapots" are extant in Area C, and that the latter were more characteristic. The feature distinguishing the "teapot" from the other holemouths is its most popular rim type: the turned-up rim (17/31). In profile the rim can have a slight upturn (fig. 4.1:11), a "flared neck" (fig. 4.1:9) as discussed further below, and beveled rim approaching a flange (pl. 10:9). Even a simple, incised, rim can approximate the slightly everted profile (4.1:8). But, overall, there are few simple direct rims, two bulbous and one interior lip type, differentiating the "teapot" from preferences noted in the other holemouth categories, except for the popularity of the medium size (17/31).

Similar evidence from Bâb adh-Dhrâ for the popularity of a medium "teapot" with upturned rim offers good support for distinguishing this variety as the most characteristic EB IV "teapot" type at both sites (also in the tombs, but see Ch. 12). Although few examples have survived, it is likely that there were knobs or, less often, a vestigial ledge handle on the "teapots." Both the tombs and Area B (Richard 2000: fig. 2) witness to such attachments on "teapots." There is even a parallel in the tombs (fig. 10.8:2) for the one lug-handled "teapot" found in Area C (pl. 2:3).

Notably, the quantitative analysis concluded that the spouted vessel was a relatively conservative vessel form, the only significant change being an increase in rim diameter from Phase 2 to Phase 3, and a slight trend noted in the appearance in Phase 3 of the beveled direct (#13) rim. Having to do more with function, probably, there was an interesting pairing observed of small and large spouted vessels in both the tombs and in the rooms of Area C, and also at Bâb adh-Dhrâ' (see Ch. 5 for details).

There is one category of spouted vessel with "flared" rim (60s code; fig. 4.1:9) that is included in the restricted holemouth jar category for ease of comparison with what is called the "taller rim flared teapots" at Bâb adh-Dhrâ' (Rast and Schaub 2003: 433). However, this subtype has affinities with the "necked" cooking pots (below) and may in the future prove to be a separate category. The four examples at Khirbat Iskandar come from Phases 2–3, precisely when the "necked" cooking pots begin to supersede the "holemouth" type.

I(2). Restricted (Holemouth Bowl) Forms

A. Storejars (4 ex.)

1. Medium (4046) storejars, with bulbous direct rim (1 ex.): 18a
2. Medium-small (4050) storejars, with direct rim (3 ex.): 12

B. Cooking Pots (3 ex.)

1. Large (4040C) straight-sided cooking pots (steam holes) with direct rim (2 ex.): 11, 12
2. Medium-small (4050C) cooking pots, with direct rim (1 ex.): 11

C. Spouted Vessels (1 ex.)

1. Large (4040) spouted vessels (basin), with thickened flat rim (1 ex.): 71

D. Basins (4080) (14 ex.)

1. Thickened rim (10 ex.)
   a. flat (4 ex.): 70, 71
   b. rolled (3 ex.): 73
   c. knob (3 ex.): 91
2. Thickened/swollen direct rim (4 ex.): 10

Holemouth Bowls

Basic Forms: The holemouth bowl category comprises the same basic forms—storejar, cooking pot, spouted vessels—as the holemouth jar category, but it primarily describes the deep basin or vat form (4080). The criteria for distinguishing the cooking pot from storejar were similar to those detailed above for holemouth jars, regarding ware, fabric, and surface treatment. With the basin form and spouted vessel (vat) removed, it is clear that the holemouth bowl variant of the storejar and cooking pot is clearly the less favored (7 ex.) at Khirbat Iskandar in EB IV (none in the tombs). When the two late cooking pots (straight-sided holemouth bowls with steam holes) are also removed, there are really only four storejars and one cooking pot, as compared with 11 and 36, respectively, in the ho-

lemouth jar category. Three storejars are medium–small (18–12 cm) and one is medium (24–20 cm). These are somewhat different size ranges from the holemouth bowl types. The situation at Bâb adh-Dhrâʿ is similar in that the holemouth bowl form is not particularly well attested (even in the basin category).

A. Storejars

Specific Types: All three examples are in Phase 2 and have either bulbous (fig. 4.1:13) or simple direct (fig. 4.1:14, 18) rims, two with molding. They may be differentiated from the holemouth variety by virtue of a steep wall contour. Presumably, holemouth jars and holemouth bowls had different functional purposes.

B. Cooking Pots

Specific Types: In clear Phase 3 stratified contexts, two "straight-sided" cooking pots with steam holes and sinuous molding came to light, along with another two in Phase 3 non-primary loci. They all have diameters of 40 cm or more (fig. 4.1:15; pl. 4:4). Although the stance of the former is somewhat uncertain, it appears to be of a type similar to one found at ʿAraʿir (Olávarri 1969: fig. 5:12), where they are said to be common (255). Although the date of the ʿAraʿir cooking pot and examples found at other sites in EB IV contexts (Tel Beit Mirsim H–I) were originally questioned, it is now clear that the well-known Middle Bronze IIA (MB IIA) cooking pot type originated late in the EB IV period. The two Khirbat Iskandar examples are of the type (Cf A.2) classified by Cole as an early form with vestigial "steam holes," intermediate between the type with fully pierced holes and those when even vestigial holes were abandoned (1984: 61–62; fig. 16). There was a third holemouth bowl cooking pot, also in Phase 3, but it was closer to the holemouth jar form (pl. 8:4).

C. Spouted Vessels

Specific Types: There is one example of a spouted vessel, which shares many of the characteristics of the basin category with its large diameter (32 cm), thick walls, coarse ware, and thickened flat rim (below).

D. Basins

Specific Types: There is an extraordinary number of basins or vats in Area C (30), all of which share similar characteristics, such as thick walls, coarse ware, thickened rims, decoration, large size, and deep wall profile: 14 are holemouth bowls, the other 13 are deep bowls (see below). These basins are in the 40–50 cm diameter range, only a few being smaller, around 30–34 cm. Although no two are alike, a consistent feature is a thickened rim, even thickened direct rims. The types includes flat (fig. 4.1:19; pl. 6:20), rolled (pl. 17:11–12), and knob (pls. 10:16; 14:5) rims, and "swollen" direct rims (fig. 4.1:20). At Bâb adh-Dhrâ' there are good parallels with thickened rims (Rast and Schaub 2003: pls. 129:10; 131:56), although only the latter is actually called a vat.

Only general trends were noticeable in the quantitative study; thickened flat (#70 or #71, fig. 4.1:19) rims appear to die out in Phase 2. There is molding or a "piecrust" rim (fig. 4.1:19; Rast and Schaub 2003: pl. 131:56; Helms 1986: fig. 17:8–9) on seven examples, a feature also characteristic of the deep bowl basins (below). Given the relatively small number of holemouth storage jars discovered in Area C, the storage function of the basins must be considered, although the type, often interpreted as evidence for olive oil production, may have other special purposes.

On the basis of a whole example from Khirbat Iskandar (Richard 2000: fig. 31), a basin over 50 cm in diameter and almost half a meter high, calculated at a capacity of 57 liters, it is probable that both vertical and horizontal bands were added to reinforce these huge vessels. Such reinforced molding/bands are a tradition reminiscent of EB III vats whose diameters range from 40–80 cm with a height of 50–70 cm, for example, at Khirbat Hamra Ifdan (Adams 2000: fig. 21.10:5–6).

II. Necked Vessels
(Pithoi, Large to Medium-Small, Small)

A. Storejars (40 ex.)

1. Pithoi, with curved-out neck (6 ex.)
   a. tall neck (3110), with flared rim (2 ex.): 64, 65
   b. tall neck, everted (4114), with flared rim (2 ex.): 63
   c. short neck, flared (4119)
      i. direct rim (1 ex.): 10
      ii. flared rim (1 ex.): 63
2. Large to medium-large mouthed storejars, with tall neck (14 ex.)
   a. angled-out (4122)
      i. direct rim (1 ex.): 11
      ii. flared rim (1 ex.): 61
   b. curved-out, everted (4120/4124/4140/4149)
      i. flared rim (11 ex.): 60, 61, 62, 63
      ii. thickened outside rim (1 ex.): 81
3. Medium-small mouthed, with tall, wide neck (13 ex.)
   a. cylindrical (4221)
      i. direct rim (3 ex.): 11
      ii. flared rim (1 ex.): 62
   b. curved-out, everted (4224) with flared rim (8 ex.): 61, 62, 63
   c. curved-out, flared (4232), with flared rim (1 ex.) 61
4. Small-mouthed storejars (7 ex.)
   a. tall neck cylindrical (4260/4261), with direct rim (2 ex.): 11, 12
   b. tall neck, curved-out, everted (4264), with flared rim (3 ex.): 61, 62
   c. tall neck, curved-out, flared (4272), with flared rim (1 ex.): 61
   d. short, wide neck (4281), with flared rim (1 ex.): 61

B. Cooking pots with short neck (14 ex.)

1. Pithoi, curved-out neck (4119C), with flared piecrust rim (3 ex.): 60, 65
2. Large cooking pots (10 ex.)
   a. everted neck (4129C)

i.   with flared/angled piecrust rim (2 ex.): 62, 41
ii. with flared rim (1 ex): 61
b.   inflected neck (4139C)
     i.   with flared piecrust rim (5 ex): 61, 60
     ii. with flared rim (2 ex.): 61
3. Medium-large, everted neck (4175C), with angled-rim (1 ex.): 41

C. Wide-mouthed Jugs/Pitchers/Juglets, with tall neck (6 ex.)

1. Large (4400) jugs, with flared rim (1 ex.): 61
2. Medium-large (4420) jugs, with flared rim (1 ex.): 62
3. Medium-large (4422) flask-pitchers, cylindrical neck (4 ex.)
   a.   flared rim (3 ex.): 60, 61
   b.   direct rim (1 ex): 11

Necked Vessels

Fabrics, Tempers, and Surface Treatments: Unlike necked vessels in the tombs, slip and burnish seem rare in Area C, but the small size of many rim fragments may be the reason. There was one example of applied molding, a decoration not attested on necked vessels in the tombs. The two corpora, however, share the decorative technique of incision. Nearly half of the necked jars (23 of 53 analyzed), especially the larger ones, have gray inclusions. This includes all five pithoi analyzed, five out of 14 large and medium–large vessels, but only four of 20 medium–small and small-necked jars, pointing to possible distinctions in tempering agents for smaller and thinner vessels.

Basic Forms: Necked vessels on the tell fall into three major categories: storejars, cooking pots, and pitchers or jugs/juglets. Aside from the clearly identifiable cooking pots, necked vessels are the most difficult to classify as a result of fragmentary rims and/or missing shoulder joins. Despite a disparity in corpus size (49 in Area C, 116 at Bâb adh-Dhrâ'), the size categories at the latter site are representative of those at Khirbat Iskandar in Area C. Both have pithoi (30–22 cm), large (21–16 cm),

two medium size ranges (15–12 cm and 12–9 cm), and small (8 cm or 8–7 cm) size vessels. Yet, there is variability between the two. For example, form codes 4141, 4142, 4144 are missing from Area C, while at other times interpolations for the Area C assemblage (4122) were necessary (4121 at Bâb adh-Dhrâ'). Variability in the classification is greater in the Necked category than in the Restricted or Bowl categories.

When compared with the mouth diameter ranges in the tombs, the Area C necked vessels were comparable, except for the largest sizes being absent from the tombs, as indicated earlier. Although mouth diameter does not necessarily equate with jar size, overall the Area C corpus matches the range of necked types found in Area B and in the tombs, including ledge-handled and handleless storejar vessels. That the ledge-handle jar was popular in Area C is fairly clear (see pls. 21–22).

As regards the basic form classification, within the size ranges, the most important variables in determining distinct types were the following attributes: neck height/width (tall, short, wide), contour (cylindrical, angled, curved-out: everted or flared), and, especially, whether the neck join was a corner or inflected point. Admittedly, given fragmentary rims the assessment was more of an educated guess at times. The terminology followed here for all "curved-out" necks is that "flared" refers to a continuous curve (for example. fig. 4.2:9), while "everted" describes a sharper, more angular curve (for example. fig. 4.2:5). "Cylindrical" is a term used for necks that tend to be vertically straight (for example. fig. 4.2:19), whereas "angled" refers to a non-vertically straight neck (pl. 6:7). Note that in the tombs, the terminology is somewhat different (following the Bâb adh-Dhrâ' tomb classification) in that the term "flared" is used for most of the necks, which are further broken down by inflected (curved-out) or corner (everted) point, as above. Generally, the rims of tomb and tell can be correlated by the latter terms.

Fig. 4.2 *Area C specific type series: Necked vessels.*

#	Form	Ph	Locus	Type	FormHaRiBa	Size	Description	Ref
1	Necked Jar	1	C06030	Necked Storejar	3110.00.65.00	Pithoi	Storejar with sharply flared (squared) rim	pl. 14:6
2	Necked Jar	3	C07015	Necked Storejar	4114.00.63.00	Pithoi	Storejar with sharply flared (squared) rim	pl. 15:25
3	Necked Jar	2	C02030	Necked Storejar	4119.00.63.00	Pithoi	Storejar with sharply flared (squared) rim	pl. 5:22
4	Necked Jar	2	C09001	Necked Storejar	4122.00.11.00	Large	Storejar with direct (rounded) rim	pl. 20:6
5	Necked Jar	2	C09001	Necked Storejar	4124.00.63.00	Large	Storejar with sharply flared (squared) rim; band combing	pl. 20:3
6	Necked Jar	1	C06030	Necked Storejar	4149.00.61.00	Medium Large	Storejar with lightly flared (rounded) rim	pl. 14:2
7	Necked Jar	3	C07015	Necked Storejar	4221.00.62.00	Medium Small	Storejar with lightly flared (tapered) rim	pl. 15:21
8	Necked Jar	1	C06030	Necked Storejar	4224.00.62.00	Medium Small	Storejar with lightly flared (tapered) rim	pl. 14:1
9	Necked Jar	3	C07020	Necked Storejar	4232.00.61.00	Medium Small	Storejar with lightly flared (rounded) rim	pl. 18:6
10	Necked Jar	3	C01010	Cooking Pot	4119C.00.65.00	Pithoi	Cooking pot with sharply flared (squared) piecrust rim	pl. 1:2
11	Necked Jar	1	C01021	Cooking Pot	4139C.00.60.00	Large	Cooking pot with lightly flared (squared) piecrust rim	pl. 2:6
12	Necked Jar	2	C05014	Cooking Pot	4139C.00.62.00	Large	Cooking pot with lightly flared (tapered) piecrust rim	pl. 11:10
13	Necked Jar	3	C07015	Cooking Pot	4129C.00.41.00	Large	Cooking pot with angled (rounded) piecrust rim	pl. 15:24
14	Necked Jar	2	C05014	Necked Storejar	4261.00.12.00	Small	Storejar with cylindrical neck, direct (tapered) rim	pl. 11:8
15	Necked Jar	2	C01036	Necked Storejar	4264.00.61.00	Small	Storejar with lightly flared (rounded) rim	pl. 3:5
16	Necked Jar	2	C02030	Necked Storejar	4272.00.61.00	Small	Storejar with lightly flared (rounded) rim	pl. 5:19
17	Necked Jar	1	C06035	Necked Storejar	4281.00.61.00	Small	Storejar, wide neck, with lightly flared (rounded) rim	pl. 14:24
18	Jug	3	C07015	Jug	4400.22.61.00	Large	One-Handled Jug with lightly flared (rounded) rim	pl. 15:17
19	Jug	3	C08005a	Jug	4420.00.62.00	Medium Large	Jug with lightly flared (tapered) rim	pl. 19:2
20	Jug	2	C05014	Flask Pitcher	4422.00.60.00	Medium Large	Flask Pitcher with lightly flared (squared) rim	pl. 11:7

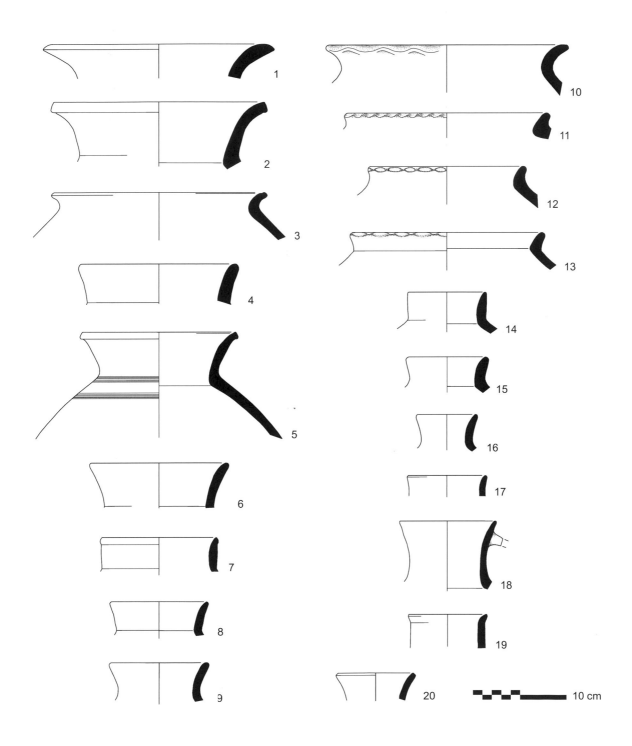

FIG. 4.2 *Area C specific type series: Necked vessels.*

A. Storejars

Basic Forms: Essentially, except for three short-necked examples, all of the storejars are tall wide-necked vessel types (in the tombs also). Necks are everted, flared, cylindrical, or angled in that decreasing order of popularity, as in the tombs also. Most rims are worked, even if only with a slight flare near the lip. As for chronological indicators, the quantitative study found necked jars with simple direct rim to be significant in Phase 2, while a curved-out, flared rim was significant in Phase 3. Generally, though, in the absence of whole forms, the chronological usefulness of rim fragments seems limited, except in a few cases.

Specific Types – Pithoi: Aside from two clear EB III sharply flared rims in Phase 1 (3110, fig. 4.2:1; pl. 14:7), there are only four rims in the 22–30 cm range. Two of these, from Phase 3, are the well-known EB IV ovoid storejar type with tall, everted neck and sharply flared (#63) rim that tapers down (4114, fig. 4.2:2) or appears as a flange (pl. 4:11). Both are broken just below the neck join, but typically this vessel type has either band combing (as the slightly smaller fig. 4.2:5) or molding of some sort, as found in the Area B "storeroom" (Richard 2000: fig. 3:2–3 with everted rim). The two others illustrate short-necked flared (4119) storejar types (fig. 4.2:3), with inflected curve and squared rim, a storejar type that seems to continue an Early Bronze Age tradition. All have gray inclusions.

Specific Types – Large to medium-large mouthed storejars: There are 14 examples (all with black inclusions), almost exclusively of one type: the everted-neck storejar with flared rim, discussed above under pithoi. Only two examples represent a second type, the angled-out neck (fig. 4.2:4 and pl. 6:7). Of the latter two examples, the former is the only example of a simple direct rim, the latter having a slight flare at the tip. The rim types noted among everted necks range from a slight flare (pl. 14:2) to the more elaborated rim types discussed above, either tapered or flanged (fig. 4.2:5; pl. 19:17). Also noted are rims with interior groove (pl. 12:3) and thickened-outside rounded rim (pl. 20:5). Thus,

the range is from simple to elaborated, the latter paralleling the well-known "flanged" rim curved necks of central and southern Cisjordan, for example, at Jebel Qaʿaqir (Gitin 1975: fig. 1:1–4, 6). Elsewhere on the mound, in Area B, these storejars often include band combing, stabs, or molding (Richard 2000: fig. 3). Parallels with the corpus at Bâb adh-Dhrâʿ are evident, with the notable exception of the specialized tetrafoil rimmed jar (4180) and few examples of the "flanged" types found in Khirbat Iskandar.

Specific Types – Medium–small to small-mouthed storejars: The diameter range of the 20 medium–small (12–9 cm) and small-mouthed (8–7 cm) storejars may generally be compared with the tall, wide-neck storejars in the tombs, the majority of which range from 12–7 cm in diameter (only five are somewhat smaller). The three main neck types are everted (fig. 4.2:8, 15), flared (fig. 4.2:9, 16), and cylindrical (fig. 4.2:7) in both size categories. Only one short, wide-neck form came to light (pl. 14:24). Rims are mostly flared, but several direct rims are attested (pl. 11:8), as well as the thickened-outside (flanged) type (pls. 10:7; 12:18). The medium–small necked jars link up closely with the tombs and with Bâb adh-Dhrâʿ, except for a popular vessel at the latter site, the jar with sloping shoulder (4240), which is unattested to date (see Rast and Schaub 2003: fig. 13.6:11).

Among the seven small-mouthed jars, the rim types are predictably simpler, usually direct (fig. 4.2:14) or slightly flared rims (fig. 4:2:15–17) within the three major contour types mentioned above (also one example of a short, wide-neck vessel). The fragmentary nature of these jars renders it impossible to determine if they parallel the small and miniature vessels in the cemeteries, or whether the latter are, in fact, unique tomb offerings. Even in comparison with the several small-to-miniature vessels found in Area B (Richard 2000: fig. 2:1–3), the tomb vessels at both Khirbat Iskandar and Bâb adh-Dhrâʿ are somewhat distinctive (see discussion in Ch. 12).

B. Cooking pots

Basic Forms: The necked cooking pots are immediately recognizable by their short, wide necks, cooking-pot ware, soot, and characteristic piecrust rim (all but four examples). The vessel diameters indicate three size categories: pithoi (30–22 cm), large (21–16 cm), and medium–large (15–12 cm) cooking pots, although there is only one of the last category. Most (10/14) are large, while at Bâb adh-Dhrâ' most are in the medium–large category (several in a large size). The fabric color is primarily reddish brown or red. The majority (9/14) has gray inclusions, and unlike holemouth jar cooking pots, none has crystalline inclusions. This suggests the technology for producing them changed with cooking pot shapes.

Specific Types: There are two distinguishable types; the more popular has a flared neck (fig. 4.2:10–12), while the other has an everted neck (fig. 4.2:13). It is not clear whether the difference is essential to the form, since all of these short wide-necked cooking pots look remarkably similar. More obvious, in fact, and a criterion considered in the classification, is the presence or absence of a piecrust rim. Only four do not have piecrust rims (pls. 5:20; 12:19; 18:1–2), and there are only three everted-neck examples (fig. 4.2:13; pls. 11:10; 18:1). The rim types are mostly slightly flared (#60–61), but one is sharply flared (#65). The preference is clearly for the curved-out neck with flared rim, the only type found at Bâb adh-Dhrâ'.

It is now clear that in the EB IV period, the necked cooking pot (a Syrian tradition) and the local holemouth cooking pots were in use contemporaneously. A study at Bâb adh-Dhrâ' found that the holemouth cooking pots in EB IV had reduced in size, in overall median mouth (to around 16 cm), from previous periods at the site, while the necked cooking pots included a larger size with diameters of 24, 25, and 30 cm (Rast and Schaub 2003: 31–33). The new, larger, cooking pot type with neck raises questions about changing function and/or behavior or influences. The correlation of larger cooking pots with increasingly larger platters (see below) is also suggestive of some basic underlying changes.

It is worth repeating the statistically significant data concerning the necked cooking pot, which in Phase 2 supersedes the holemouth cooking pot in popularity, a phenomenon corroborated by the Bâb adh-Dhrâ' study. For an example of a complete, necked cooking pot from Khirbat Iskandar, see Richard 1982, fig. 4.3; pl. 90.

C. Wide-mouthed jugs / pitchers / juglets

Basic Forms: Based on ware, thin walls, and shape of upper necks, and including comparative analysis with the tomb assemblage, there are six vessels classified as wide-mouthed jugs/pitchers/juglets, ranging from large to medium–large.

Specific Types: Despite fragmentary evidence and an overlap in form with the small storejars, it appears that the Area C corpus witnesses to the two major types defined in the tombs: tall-necked, one-handled jugs (fig. 4.2:18, 19) and the "flask-pitcher" (fig. 4.2:20). The number of jugs and pitchers in the tombs, as well as those attested in the Area B "storeroom" (Richard 2000: fig. 1), provide the parallels. Of the half dozen fairly certain examples on the tell, only one had a handle. There were only three such vessels classified at Bâb adh-Dhrâ'.

III. Bowls, Platters, Cups, Lamps

Basic Forms: Of the three broad form categories, Restricted, Necked, and Bowl, it is the Bowl form that comprises the greatest range of distinct classes of vessel types. Thus, it seemed appropriate to situate this general section before, not after the outline, as was the practice previously. Additionally, here the outline is presented in three parts, followed by discussion. In this general Bowl category, the major specific types are deep bowls (including basins), platters, medium–small bowls, small bowls/cups, and lamps. As typical of most EB IV sites in the mid-to-southern region of the country, the bowl (particularly platter bowl) is the best-attested vessel type at Khirbat Iskandar. It is no surprise that the strongest statistical evidence for positing three ceramic phases at the site hinges to a great extent on the platter-bowl category. Fabrics, tempers and surface treatment will be included under each specific bowl category. The size ranges (large, medium–large, and medium) and contour types (open, closed, angled) match the Bâb adh-Dhrâ' corpus remarkably well.

A. Large, Medium–Large to Medium Deep Bowls (39 ex.)

1. Open (24 ex.)
    a. Basins (13 ex.)
        i. with thickened rim (4520L/4530ML)
            a. flat (9 ex.): 70, 71
            b. turned-down (2 ex.): 75
            c. knob (1 ex.): 91
        ii. with thickened/swollen direct rim (1 ex.): 10
    b. Incurved, rilled rim (4530ML/4570M) bowls, with direct rim (10 ex.): 10, 11, 19
    c. Splayed-side (angled) (4546ML) bowls, with direct rim (1 ex.): 11
2. Lightly closed (11 ex.)
    a. Beveled direct rim (4500L) bowls (4 ex): 76
    b. Shouldered bowls, (4510ML) with beveled direct rim (5 ex): 10, 13
    c. Carinated bowls (4560M), with direct rim (2 ex): 11

Bowls

A. Deep Bowls: Large, Medium–Large to Medium

Basic Forms: The deep bowls in Area C can be separated into two general categories of open (24) and lightly closed (11) forms. The open forms comprise three distinct types: large to medium–large basins with steep sides, medium–large and medium incurved bowls, and the medium–large splayed-sided (angled) bowls, the last a typical Early Bronze Age bowl with simple rim found in Phase 2. The lightly closed forms divide into three recognizable types: the large beveled-rim bowls, the medium–large shouldered bowls, and the medium-sized carinated bowls.

1. Open Deep Bowls

Specific Types: The basin is a major type in the deep-bowl category, 11 of which are in the large (4520) and three in the medium–large (4530) size ranges. When combined with the holemouth bowl (4080) variety, the basin constitutes a major functional vessel category in Area C with a total of 27 examples. Both share virtually identical characteristics: thick walls, coarse ware, thickened rims, as well as a few direct swollen rims, and decoration, usually a piecrust rim or molding. They share the same rim types: flat (fig. 4.3:1), turned-down (fig. 4.3:2; pl. 3.8), knob (pl. 1.6), or direct swollen (pl. 13.15). Decoration is more essential to the deep bowl category: eight with piecrust rim, two with molding, and one with rilling. The fabric colors shade to the gray, dark gray and pinkish gray (4/13), or light brown, reddish brown or light reddish brown (5/13). Only four are slipped, of which three are also burnished. The fact that relatively few basins occur in Phase 3 (7/27), as compared with Phase 2 (17/27), may reflect functional changes coeval with the transition from a domestic residential area to a more public "gateway."

The quantitative study illuminated several chronological trends in deep bowls (including the related holemouth basins). There was a significant decrease in simple direct rims from Phase 1 to Phase 2. Likewise, the thickened flat rims (#70–71) show an interesting sequence, one example each in Phases 1 and 3, the rest in Phase 2. Statistically, there is a significant increase from Phase 1 to Phase 2 and decrease from Phase 2 to Phase 3 in these rims (and see a similar finding in platter bowls, below). A comparison with Bâb adh-Dhrâ' revealed a similar sequence of simple direct to thickened inside rims (see Ch. 5). Although called deep bowls at the latter site, the parallels with the Area C thickened and direct swollen rims are numerous (see fig. 4.1), including outsized examples of 50 cm. The Bâb adh-Dhrâ' statistical study offers insight into this category: there is a higher percentage of very large, large, and medium–large bowls in EB IV than in the previous EB II–III strata (Rast and Schaub 2003: 434). For a comparable range of basins, see the large and medium-sized basins discovered in a domestic (cave) context at Jebel Qaʻaqir (Gitin 1975: fig. 2:10–16; p. 53*).

Specific Types – Incurved, rilled-rim bowls: The well-known EB IV simple incurved bowl with characteristic rilled shoulder is primarily a medium (4570) bowl, although there are three in a medium–large size (4530). The wares are usually in pink or pinkish gray fabric colors, all ten are red-slipped, and, with the exception of one example, burnished as well. These popular, hemispherical bowls have a direct rounded (fig. 4.3:9), squared (fig. 4.3:5) or thinned (pl. 17.1) rim, and a surface treatment of 1–3 rills. The form can be high-shouldered or carinated, particularly with a thinned rim. Here too, a general trend sees the simple direct (rounded) rims decrease significantly from Phase 2 to Phase 3. This is a popular bowl form at Bâb adh-Dhrâʻ as well (Rast and Schaub 2003: fig. 13.5:2, 3, 5), which in the 4530 code includes basins just as at Khirbat Iskandar (see fig. 13.5:2 and parallels cited there). As discussed in Chapter 12, rather than the incurved rilled-rim bowl in the medium–large to medium size, the preferred variety in the tombs appears to be a lightly closed, even carinated form (fig. 10.12:8–9), more characteristic of the 4560 version on the tell (below).

Specific Types – Splayed-sided (angled) bowls: Only one example of this category of bowl came to light (fig. 4.3:6) on the tell (none in the tombs). This apparent Early Bronze Age remnant bowl, with its distinctive straight, angled walls is better known, but also not popular, at Bâb adh-Dhrâʻ.

2. Lightly Closed Bowls

Specific Types – The beveled-rim bowl: This large-size bowl with beveled rim (#76) is distinguishable from the turned-down thickened rim bowls (#75) by virtue of manufacturing technique. The rim is not folded over; rather, it generally thickens at the top and is then beveled. Characteristics associated with the bowl are a high-shouldered and/or carinated profile, red slip and burnish, and incision, in particular wavy combing. Although there are only four examples of this large (4500) deep bowl (fig.

4.3:3; pl. 17:5–8), the type reappears in the platter bowl (4620) category (below), and correlates with the 4503/4539 series (also with wavy incision) in the tombs. Unlike the platters, though, fabric colors are reddish gray, red and light red. The fact that the 4500 bowls are all Phase 3 is statistically significant. Thus, it is possible to identify this particular vessel as a diagnostic typological form for the latest phase in Area C. The type was noted in non-primary loci (T. Schaub, personal communication) at Bâb adh-Dhrâʻ, and there is one similar example of a 4500 bowl with beveled outside rim (#14) (Rast and Schaub 2003: pl. 135:10).

Specific Types – Shouldered bowls: Related to the above category is the medium–large shouldered bowl (4510) with characteristic beveled rim (#13), although one example has a related type of squared (#10) rim. Three of the bowls (pls. 4:10; 11:5; 14:14) illustrate a worked shoulder, while the other two (fig. 4.3:4; pl. 7:1) show a sharp carination. Several early examples of the type can be noted at Tall Umm Hammad (Helms 1986: fig. 17: 1, 3–4), and see an example at Jebel Qaʻaqir (Gitin 1975: fig. 3:23). The form occurs in the platter bowl category as well (4660). Four of the five bowls exhibit red slip and burnish. Two have reddish brown, and two have light red core colors. The shouldered bowls do not appear in the tombs and are not evident at Bâb adh-Dhrâʻ.

Specific Types – Carinated/incurved bowl: This lightly closed bowl type with simple direct (rounded) rim is similar to the open incurved rilled-rim bowls above. Although there were only two examples in primary loci (fig. 4.3:7–8), almost exact parallels are present in the tombs (4568), affirming that a carinated profile is essential to the form.

B. Very Large to Large to Medium Shallow Platter Bowls (145 ex.)

1. Very large (4600) open platter bowls, with thickened rim (14 ex.)
   a. turned-down (10 ex.): 75
   b. rolled (2 ex.): 73, 74
   c. knob (1 ex.): 91
   d. flat (1 ex.): 71

Basic Forms: The platter bowls in Area C parallel the size ranges observed at Bâb adh-Dhrâʿ: very large (40+ cm), large (39–30 cm), and medium (29–17 cm). The platter bowl category is the largest (145 ex.) in the assemblage, as is the case at Bâb adh-Dhrâʿ (272 ex.). In the Bâb adh-Dhrâʿ platter bowl classification, unlike the deep bowls, there is no separation of open from lightly closed vessels. At Khirbat Iskandar, a small group of lightly closed platter bowls with the distinctive beveled rim has proved to be of statistical significance. To highlight the specific type, the outline singles out open from lightly closed platter bowls (as in the tombs), although for the purposes of cross-comparative analysis here, the basic form codes at Bâb adh-Dhrâʿ are maintained. As the above outline indicates, the three size ranges, for the most part, share similar rims: turned-down, rolled, knob, flat. The only exceptions are the beveled rim and "other" rims, which do not occur in the very large size range.

As detailed in the quantitative study, the platter bowl assemblage revealed significant phase-to-phase distinctions: 1) size increases, 2) evolution of types from rolled and flat rim to turned-down and beveled, 3) richness variances between Phase 2 and Phase 3. Correlations with Bâb adh-Dhrâʿ confirm the typo-chronological significance of the platter bowl evolution of types (Schaub 2000; Richard and Holdorf 2000), which is the foundation for the typo-chronology proposed in this volume. This sequence likewise formed the basis for a seriation of the tombs. For discussion of the Bâb adh-Dhrâʿ data, see Rast and Schaub (2003: 436–40) and for Area C and the Tombs, see Chapter 5.

1–2, 4. Very Large, Large, Medium
Open Platter Bowls

Specific Types – Turned-down rim: Perhaps the best-known category of EB IV bowl, the shallow platter bowl with thickened inside rim is characteristic of sites in the mid-to-southern regions of the country. The "fossil type," "turned-down" rim is primarily found in the large (4620) category (52 ex.), but there were also ten examples in the very large (4600) and 12 in the medium (4660) categories. These frequencies mirror the Bâb adh-Dhrâʿ evi-

dence. Their increase from Phase 1 to Phase 2 and from Phase 2 to Phase 3 is statistically significant. Virtually all red-slipped and burnished, half the assemblage (37/74) exhibits deep-grooved rilling (as at Bâb adh-Dhrâʿ). Originally, the number of rills (or lack thereof) and the degree to which the rim was pushed down, either bulbous (figs. 4.3:10; 4.4:2) or flattened (pl. 4:8), were considered possible diagnostic features; however, only a particular beveled rim (#76) proved to be a statistically significant diagnostic in Phase 3 (below). There are virtually no turned-down rims in Phase 1 at either Khirbat Iskandar or the earliest EB IV phase at Bâb adh-Dhrâʿ.

Specific Types – Rolled/pointed rim: These distinctive platters all have a rim that curves from the shoulder and thickens inside at various angles, either in a rolled (rounded) rim (fig. 4.3:11) or a rolled pointed rim (figs. 4.3:12; 4.4:3). Of 36 examples, only two are in the very large (4600) range; the type is virtually always red-slipped and burnished and, except in two rare cases, never has rilling. As with the turned-down rim frequencies and characteristics of surface treatment, the rolled rim platter bowl matches the Bâb adh-Dhrâʿ evidence well. The type is diagnostic for Phase 1, and there is a significant decrease from Phase 2 to Phase 3 (the rolled pointed rim dies out in Phase 2). This well-known Early Bronze Age platter bowl predominates in Phase 1, decreases in Phase 2, and is virtually non-existent in Phase 3, all changes of which have a high statistical significance (Ch. 5).

Specific Types – Knob rim: This distinctive rim (#91) continues the well-known EB III knob rim tradition. There are only five examples on the tell and none in the tombs. As a variant of the thickened rim platter bowls, the term knob describes a variety of rims distinguished by internal/external thickening resulting in a hammer knob, or bulbous rim (pls. 5:14; 14:17). Examples on the tell are all red-slipped and burnished and occur in all three size ranges, but it is mostly a medium form.

Specific Types – Flat rim: Another well-known Early Bronze Age type, the flat-rim platter bowl shows a sequence similar to the rolled-rim platter bowls, namely, a significant decrease from Phase 1 to Phase 2 and virtual absence in Phase 3 (fig. 4.3:13; pl. 18:4). Of the nine examples of flat rims, eight are red-slipped and burnished, but only four are rilled.

Specific Types – Other: Finally, a few examples of Early Bronze Age platter bowl types (all Phase 2) may be mentioned: inverted rim (pls. 1:7; 9:17), angled or straight-walled with direct rim (pl. 2:14), triangular rim (pl. 1:16), and the upturned rim (pl. 2:18) platter bowls. These are all red-slipped and burnished. Bâb adh-Dhrâ' likewise has examples of these types, which were not found in the tombs at either site.

3, 5. Large and Medium Lightly Closed Platter Bowls

Specific Types – Beveled rim: The combination of characteristic upright, carinated, or lightly closed walls (similar to the parallel large deep bowl categories 4500/4510) and thickened beveled (#76) rim were variables suggestive of a distinct type within the 4620 large category. These platter bowls (fig. 4.4:1; pls. 4:18; 15:14, 16; 16:1–2, 4; 20:10) have all the characteristics mentioned above for the beveled rim deep bowls: a shouldered look, either a rilled or wavy incision, two have cream slip and burnish, and a particular type of thickened rim that broadens toward the top and is then beveled (#76), not pushed down (as #75). Its statistical significance has been mentioned several times, but bears repeating: it appears only in Phase 3 and provides a good gauge for late contexts. There are several in the tombs. An equivalent late form appears at Bâb adh-Dhrâ' in the medium (4660) range (below).

Specific Types – Shouldered/carinated platter bowl: This particular medium size (4660) platter bowl, which is closely related to the thickened beveled rim platter bowl above and the 4510/4560 deep bowl types, exhibits a type of carinated or worked upper shoulder that also sets it apart from the open platter bowls. The rim is beveled (#13), but there are

slight variants, exemplified by one squared (#10) and one tapered (#2) platter bowl. Even the sharply carinated type, singled out in the lightly closed deep bowl category, has identical parallels in this category (pls. 6:16; 9:15; 15:7; 19:13). The other three vessels display a high-shouldered appearance (fig. 4.4:4; pls. 2:4; 4:14). This platter bowl/rim combination trends with rim #76 and is significant for Phase 3. Most (6/8) have a pink core and six are slipped and burnished. At Bâb adh-Dhrâ' there are a number of these medium-size platter bowls (some of which appear lightly closed), almost all of which have a square or beveled rim, often on the exterior (Rast and Schaub 2003: fig. 13.5:8; pl. 114:15–16).

C. Medium-Small to Small, Deep Bowls and Lamps (28 ex.)

1. Medium–Small Bowls (10 ex.)
   a. Open (3 ex.)
      i. Deep cup-bowls (4710), with direct rim (2 ex.): 10, 11
      ii. Cup-bowls medium depth (4740), with direct rim (1 ex.): 11
   b. Lightly closed (7 ex.)
      i. Deep cup-bowls (4700), with direct rim (2 ex): 11
      ii. Cyma-profiled (carinated) (4730) bowls (5 ex): 42, 62
2. Small Bowls (Cups) (13 ex.)
   a. Open (6 ex.)
      i. Incurved cups (4770), with direct rim (5 ex.): 11, 12, 19
      ii. Incurved cups (3749), with inverted rim (1 ex.): 32
   b. Lightly closed (7 ex.)
      i. Incurved cups (4756), with direct rim (3 ex.): 11
      ii. Cyma-profiled cups (4760), with flared rim (4 ex): 62
3. Four-Spouted Lamps (5 ex.)
   a. Small four-spouted lamps (4855), with direct (rounded) rim (5 ex.): 10, 12

Medium–Small to Small Deep Bowls and Lamps

Basic Forms: The bowls in this category essentially divide into medium–small cup-bowls, small bowls (cups), and shallow bowls (lamps). The repertoire of forms is virtually identical to that found at Bâb adh-Dhrâʿ, and size ranges are very close. In the medium–small deep category, there are open and lightly closed examples, ranging from 16–6 cm (16–9 cm at Bâb adh-Dhrâʿ); a medium depth type—the cyma-profile/carinated bowl—has a size range (18–10 cm) somewhat broader than at Bâb adh-Dhrâʿ (16–12 cm, but examples in the 20–17 range are found). Both sites also have an open form of medium–small bowl of medium depth.

As for the small bowls (cups), the size range of 11–6 cm matches well the Bâb adh-Dhrâʿ range of 11–7 cm, in both the lightly closed and open forms. Missing from Area C is the votive cup form (Rast and Schaub 2003: fig. 13:5: 16–17), a form that was missing from the tombs as well. Otherwise, despite the disparity in frequencies between the two assemblages—25 examples in Area C, 127 examples at Bâb adh-Dhrâʿ—there is a good correlation of types. Both sites attest the small saucer or lamp form (16 cm), although, again, Area C has five in primary contexts and Bâb adh-Dhrâʿ has 29 examples. Presumably the differences stem from the popularity of these categories in a cultic context at Bâb adh-Dhrâʿ (Area XVI).

1. Medium–Small Bowls

Fabric, Tempers, and Surface Treatment: Of ten examples, eight are combed and nine are slipped and burnished.

Specific Types: There are two categories of open and lightly closed bowls, in each of which there are both deep and medium depth kinds of bowls. The specific types are deep cup-bowls, cyma-profile (carinated) cups, and a medium depth cup-bowl. The closed (4700) and open (4710) deep cup-bowls with direct rim are essentially smaller versions of the medium-sized hemispherical bowls discussed earlier (fig. 4.3:5, 9). Like the latter, the smaller bowls tend to have an incised line below the rim

that suggests a "bead" rim (fig. 4.4:7; pl. 12: 1–2), although one example has a knob instead (fig. 4.4:5). Only one example of an open medium-depth bowl (4740) was noted (fig. 4.4:9). There are examples in the tombs, and at Bâb adh-Dhrâʿ similar types occur (Rast and Schaub 2003: pls. 115:12; 116:1; fig. 13.5:9–10, 13).

The cyma-profiled bowl (fig. 4.4:8) has a characteristic everted rim (#42), but one example of a flared rim (#62) also occurs (pl. 15:23). These bowls are exemplars of a well-made and fine type of pottery found at the site (and in the tombs). A delicate band combing decorates three of these bowls (fig. 4.4:8; pls. 5:5; 15:3), along with slip and burnish on two. The quantitative study has found that cyma-profiled bowls (and cups) are a statistically significant diagnostic for Phase 3 (see chap. 5). The numerous examples found at Bâb adh-Dhrâʿ are primarily from Field XVI, the cultic area (Rast and Schaub 2003: 442). The form is often considered a forerunner of the "carinated-bowl" tradition, illuminating continuity with the succeeding Middle Bronze Age.

2. Small Bowls: Cups

Fabric, Tempers, and Surface Treatment: Virtually all (11/13) are slipped and burnished, three of which also show a combed decoration.

Specific Types: As above, there are two categories of open and lightly closed cups: a simple open cup with direct rim (fig. 4.4:12), a lightly closed cup (fig. 4.4:10), and a cyma-profiled cup (fig. 4.4:11). These cups generally appear as smaller versions of the medium–small bowls discussed above. The only other cup found was an EB III votive-type of bowl (pl. 19:22) with inverted rim. That cup seems to be of a genre similar to an EB III example at Bâb adh-Dhrâʿ (Rast and Schaub 2003: fig. 11.12:20), and becomes a popular form in the Middle Bronze Age. The cyma-profiled (carinated) cups mirror the larger variety in slip, burnish, fine ware, combed decoration, and their diagnostic significance for Phase 3 (fig. 4.4:11). It is the cyma-profiled cup that occurs in the tombs and is found at Bâb adh-Dhrâʿ. The one unusual cup discovered in Area C is a small

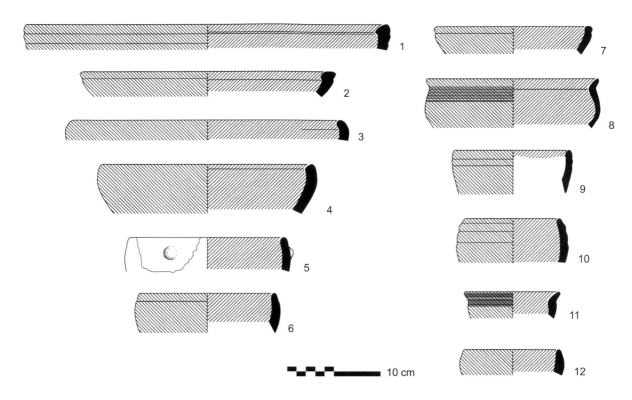

FIG. 4.4   *Area C specific type series: Platter bowls, small bowls and cups.*

#	Form	Ph	Locus	Type	FormHaRiBa	Size	Description	Ref
1	Platter Bowl	3	C03017	Lightly closed	4620.00.76.00	Large	Platter bowl with thickened (beveled) rim	pl. 8:7
2	Platter Bowl	3	C08009	Open	4660.00.75.00	Medium	Platter Bowl with thickened (pushed-down) rim	pl. 19:15
3	Platter Bowl	2	C01036	Closed	4660.00.73.00	Medium	Platter Bowl with thickened (rolled) rim	pl. 2:16
4	Platter Bowl	3	C07015	Lightly closed	4660.00.13.00	Medium	Platter bowl, shouldered with direct (beveled) rim	pl. 15:5
5	Deep Bowl	2	C06019	Lightly closed Cup-Bowl	4700.00.11.00	Medium Small	Cup-bowl with direct (rounded) rim; knob	pl. 12:12
6	Deep Bowl	2	C06016	Open Cup-Bowl	4710.00.11.00	Medium Small	Cup-bowl with direct (rounded) rim	pl. 12:2
7	Deep Bowl	3	C07015	Open Cup-Bowl	4710.00.10.00	Medium Small	Cup-bowl with direct (squared) rim	pl. 15:4
8	Deep Bowl	3	C02022	Lightly closed Cup-Bowl	4730.00.42.00	Medium Small	Cyma-profiled bowl with everted rim	pl. 4:7
9	Deep Bowl	2	C06018	Open Cup-Bowl	4740.00.11.00	Medium Small	Cup-bowl with direct (rounded) rim	pl. 12:8
10	Deep Bowl	2	C02030	Lightly closed Cup	4756.00.11.00	Small	Incurved cup with direct (rounded) rim	pl. 5:4
11	Deep Bowl	3	C07015	Lightly closed Cup	4760.00.62.00	Small	Cyma-profiled cup with flared rim	pl. 15:1
12	Deep Bowl	2	C02030	Open Cup	4770.00.12.00	Small	Incurved cup with direct (rounded) rim	pl. 5:3

fragment of a cup exhibiting a fine and almost cor-rugated ware similar to well-known exemplars in Cisjordan (pl. 19:3).

3. Lamps

Specific Types – Four-Spouted Lamps: Although five lamp fragments were found in primary loci in Area C, only the one draftable fragment is illus-trated (pl. 17:17), a typical flat-based lamp with fully flanged spouts. There were ten other examples in non-primary loci. There were 18 lamps at Bâb adh-Dhrâʿ, most (15) came from Field XVI, the cultic area. A number of examples in Area B witness to the type at Khirbat Iskandar. For a full discussion of the lamp types known from Khirbat Iskandar, see Chapter 12.

Handles (35 ex.)

A. Loop Handles (3 ex)
   1.   Strap handle (2 ex.): 20a, 22
   2.   Round handle (1 ex.): 20b
B. Lug/Ear Handles (6 ex.)
   1.   Functional lug (2 ex.) 40a
   2.   Pierced ear handle (4 ex.): 40b, 44
C. Ledge Handles (26 ex.)
   1.   Wavy ledge handle (3 ex.): 14
   2.   Envelope ledge handle (15 ex.)
        a.   with spaced flaps (7 ex.): 16a
        b.   with spaced flaps (pinch-lapped (4 ex.): 16b
        c.   folded (overlapping) flaps (4 ex.): 16c
   3.   Vestigial (8 ex.)
        a.   envelope (pinch-lapped) profile (5 ex.): 17a
        b.   thumb-indented (scalloped) (3 ex.): 17b

Basic Forms: The 35 handles found in Area C com-prise loop, lug, and ledge handles, only three of which are attached to vessels. Many of the ledge handles are functional, which, at first glance, ap-pears to contrast with the tomb assemblage in which there were only a few vestigial ledge handles. However, the absence of large storejars in the tombs is undoubtedly the reason for that disparity, since

it is these vessels on the site that normally include functional ledge handles (Richard 2000: fig. 3). The Bâb adh-Dhrâʿ corpus is strikingly similar in terms of numbers of handles, range, and popularity of types (Rast and Schaub 2003: 442–43). Despite the relatively small number of ledge handles, the quantitative analysis discerned several significant trends.

Specific Types – Loop Handle: Of the very few loop handles found in Area C, there were two strap han-dles (pls. 15:17, attached below the rim; 22:12) and one rounded in section (pl. 22:9). Representatives of both types occur in the tombs as well as in Area B (Richard 2000: fig. 1).

Specific Types – Lug/Ear Handle: These handles appear in two clear varieties, one functional (pl. 22:19), while the other "ear" handle type is pierced, presumably through which to thread a string (pls. 2:3; 22:11). These are also attested in the tombs and in Area B (Richard 2000: fig. 1).

Specific Types – Ledge Handle: The most popular handle type in Area C is the ledge handle. In order to shed light on a typo-chronological sequence, if any, the Bâb adh-Dhrâʿ handle classification from the tombs was somewhat refined. Essentially, the ledge handle series divides into wavy (pl. 21:8), envelope (pl. 21:1), and vestigial types (pl. 21:11–12). There were only three wavy handles in the collec-tion.

Envelope handles fall, generally, into two broad categories in EB IV, those with spaces between flaps and those without spaces. At Iktanu, Prag observed that the former predominated in Phase 1 and the latter in Phase 2 (1974: 78). Given different manufac-turing techniques applied, that is, pinching or fold-ing, the typology of ledge handles presented here includes three categories: folded envelope handles with spaces (#16a; pl. 22:16), pinch-lapped envelope handles with spaces (#16b; pl. 22:18), and folded (overlapping) envelope handles (#16c; pl. 21:1). At Bâb adh-Dhrâʿ, only one folded envelope (without spaces) handle was found (four at Khirbat Iskandar). Both sites had a number of envelope ledge handles with spaces (pinched lapped), as well as vestigial handles. That the types overlap is clear from the Area B "storeroom" (Richard 2000, fig. 3).

As for vestigial handles, they divide nicely into miniature envelope handles (#17a; pl. 21:11) and miniature thumb-indented or scalloped handles (#17b; pls. 21:2, with trickle paint). A third type, the vestigial handle slashed, occurs in the tombs (fig. 10.18:1) but not on the tell at Khirbat Iskandar.

The quantified study found that the true envelope ledge handle (#16c) was diagnostic for Phase 1 and the vestigial scalloped form for Phase 2. The pinch-lapped envelope handle (handle with spaces between flaps) was the most popular form in Area C and clearly lasted till the end of the period.

Spouts

A. Short Spout (3 ex) S1A
B. Long Spout (1 ex.) S1B

Specific Types: The very few spouts recovered on the tell illustrate the two well-known types of knife-cut spouts: the short, wide spout whose lower wall generally is longer than the upper wall (pl. 21:9), and the narrower and longer spout (pl. 22:17). On the basis of the Area B "storeroom" materials (Richard 2000: fig. 2: 7, 11–13), as well as the tombs, it is evident that the shorter variety is the preferred type (see Ch. 12).

EB IV PHASES 1–3 DIAGNOSTICS AT KHIRBAT ISKANDAR

The following discussion is a summary of the various diagnostics among the specific types mentioned in this chapter. The intent is to group the relevant diagnostics by phase (figs. 4.5–7), as derived from the quantitative analysis. These diagnostics have varying ranges of statistical significance (see Ch. 5 for details, especially conclusions). To illustrate a general diagnostic, several examples are presented.

Diagnostics by Phase

Phase 1 (Figure 4.5)

1. Holemouth jar cooking pot with bulbous direct rim. Also, holemouth jar cooking pots, gener-

ally, are diagnostic.
2. Necked jar cooking pot with flaring, squared rim.
3. Platter bowl with thickened flat rim. Also, small size platter bowls are, generally, diagnostic.
4. Platter bowl with thickened rolled rim.
5. Platter bowl with thickened rolled and pointed rim.
6. Large bowl with simple direct rim (example 1). Also, large to medium bowls with simple direct rim are, generally, diagnostic.
7. Medium–large bowl with simple direct rim (example 2).
8. Medium–large bowl with simple direct rim (example 3).
9. Medium bowl with simple direct rim (example 4).
10. Small incurved bowl (cup) lightly closed.
11. Envelope ledge handle with folded/overlapping flaps.

Phase 2 (Figure 4.6)

1. Holemouth jar cooking pot with interior lip direct rim.
2. Necked jar cooking pot with lightly flared (rounded) rim. Necked jar cooking pots are, generally, diagnostic.
3. Platter bowl with thickened turned-down rim. Large size platters and richness (variety) in platter bowl rims are, generally, diagnostic. Large–medium bowls with thickened inside rims are, generally, diagnostic.
4. Medium–large bowl with thickened turned-down rim (example 1).
5. Medium–large bowl with thickened flat rim (example 2).
6. Basin-bowls with thickened flat rim. Large holemouth bowl (spouted vessel) with thickened flat rim (example 1).
7. Basin-bowl with thickened flat rim (example 2).
8. Medium–small to small bowl with simple direct rim. Small bowl (cup) with tapered direct rim (example 1).
9. Medium–small to small bowl with rounded direct rim (example 2).

FIG. 4.6   *Area C Phase 2 diagnostics.*

#	FORM	TYPE	SIZE	DESCRIPTION	REF
1	Holemouth Jar	Cooking Pot	Small	Cooking pot with direct (interior lip) rim	pl. 9:14
2	Necked Jar	Cooking Pot	Large	Cooking pot with lightly flared (tapered) piecrust rim	pl. 11:10
3	Platter Bowl	Open	Large	Platter bowl with thickened (turned-down) rim	pl. 5:12
4	Deep Bowl	Basin	Medium Large	Basin with thickened (turned-down) piecrust rim	pl. 5:16
5	Deep Bowl	Basin	Medium Large	Basin with thickened (flat) piecrust rim	pl. 3:4
6	Holemouth Bowl	Spouted Vessel	Large	Spouted basin with thickened (flat) rim	pl. 11:16
7	Deep Bowl	Basin	Very Large	Basin with thickened (flat) piecrust rim	pl. 3:11
8	Deep Bowl	Open Cup	Small	Incurved cup with direct (rounded) rim	pl. 5:3
9	Deep Bowl	Open	Medium	Incurved, rilled-rim bowl with direct (rounded) rim	pl. 1:11
10	Deep Bowl	Lightly closed Cup	Small	Incurved cup with direct (rounded) rim	pl. 5:4
11	Necked Jar	Necked Storejar	Small	Storejar with clylindrical neck, direct (tapered) rim	pl. 11:8
12				Vestigial ledge handle, thumb-indentations/scalloped	pl. 21:4

jar to Phase 3 holemouth bowl (straight-sided) to be statistically significant. Within the Restricted category, holemouth jar cooking pots vary little between Phases 2–3, the notable trend being fewer rounded (bulbous) rims and more squared or beveled rims. Conversely, the holemouth bowl (straight-sided) cooking pot only appears in Phase 3. Thus, in the Restricted cooking pot category, figure 4.8:1–3 illustrates types diagnostic for each phase: Phase 1 holemouth jar with bulbous (rounded) direct rim; Phase 2 holemouth jar with interior lip direct rim; Phase 3 holemouth straight-sided (steam holes) bowl.

The necked jar cooking pot sequence (virtually all with piecrust rim) is clear: Phase 1 flaring, squared rim; Phase 2 flaring, rounded rim; Phase 3 everted/angled-rim (fig. 4.8:7–9).

Spouted Vessels ("teapots")

The only slight (not significant) statistical trend is for a beveled rim in Phase 3 (fig. 4.8:6*). Phase 1 direct (rounded) rim (fig. 4.8:4**) and Phase 2 popular upturned rim (fig. 4.8:5**) are inferred trends only.

Necked Storejars

Simple direct rims and curved-out flared rims were diagnostics for Phases 2 and 3, respectively. Thus, the sequence posited is: Phase 1 slightly flared rounded rim (an inferred trend fig. 4.8:10**), Phase 2 simple direct rim (fig. 4.8:11), and Phase 3 curved-out, flared rim (fig. 4.8:12).

Basin-Bowls (Large to Medium Bowls)

A general trend for large to medium bowls shows simple direct rims in Phase 1 and thickened inside flat rims in Phase 2, thus suggesting the following sequence: Phase 1 basin-bowl with direct swollen rim (fig. 4.8:13), Phase 2 basin-bowl with thickened inside, flat rim (fig. 4.8:14), and Phase 3 large bowl with direct swollen rim (an inferred trend based on a general decrease in thickened inside flat rims (fig. 4.8:15**).

Large to Medium Bowls

A possible sequence of large to medium bowls (non-basin) relies on the Phase 1 general trend mentioned above, and the statistically significant beveled-rim bowl of Phase 3. Thus, the pos-

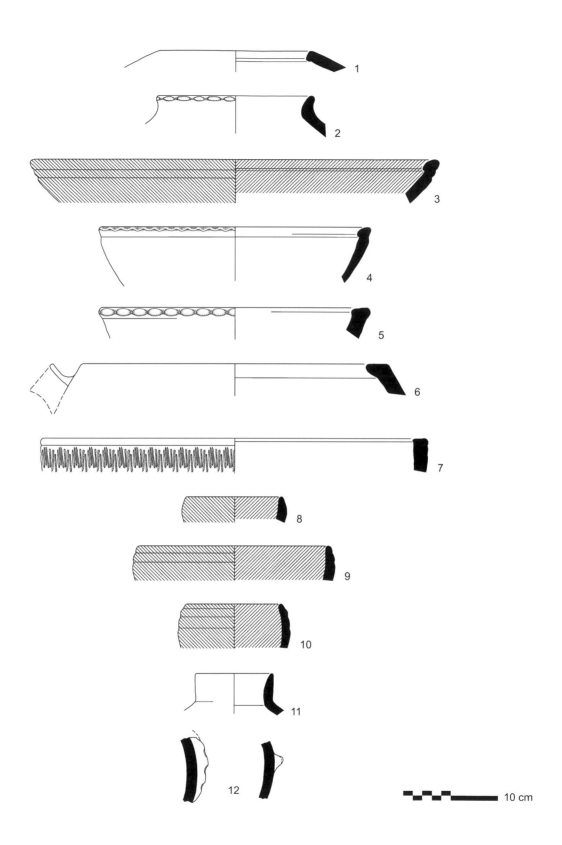

FIG. 4.6 *Area C Phase 2 diagnostics.*

FIG. 4.8   *Area C: Suggested typo-chronology Phases 1–3; Restricted, necked, basins.*

#	FORM	TYPE	SIZE	DESCRIPTION	REF
1	Cooking Pot	Cooking Pot	Large	Cooking pot with direct (bulbous) rim	pl. 13:14
2	Holemouth Jar	Cooking Pot	Small	Cooking pot with direct (interior lip) rim	pl. 9:14
3	Holemouth Bowl	Cooking Pot	Large	Cooking pot, straight-sided, with direct (tapered) rim	pl. 17:16
4**	Holemouth Bowl	Spouted Vessel	Medium	"Teapot" with direct (rounded) rim	pl. 19:20
5**	Holemouth Jar	Spouted Vessel	Medium	"Teapot" with turned-up (rounded) rim	pl. 12:20
6*	Holemouth Jar	Spouted Vessel	Medium	"Teapot" with direct (beveled) rim	pl. 17:13
7	Necked Jar	Cooking Pot	Large	Cooking pot with lightly flared (squared) piecrust rim	pl. 2:6
8	Necked Jar	Cooking Pot	Large	Cooking pot with lightly flared (tapered) piecrust rim	pl. 11:10
9	Necked Jar	Cooking Pot	Large	Cooking pot with angled (rounded) piecrust rim	pl. 15:24
10**	Necked Jar	Necked Storejar	Medium Large	Storejar with lightly flared (rounded) rim	pl. 14:2
11	Necked Jar	Necked Storejar	Small	Storejar with cylindrical neck, direct (tapered) rim	pl. 11:8
12	Necked Jar	Necked Storejar	Pithoi	Storejar with sharply flared (squared) rim	pl. 15:25
13	Deep Bowl	Basin	Medium Large	Basin with thickened/swollen direct (squared) rim	pl. 13:15
14	Deep Bowl	Basin	Very Large	Basin with thickened (flat) piecrust rim	pl. 3:11
15**	Deep Bowl	Basin	Very Large	Basin with thickened/swollen direct (squared) rim	pl. 17:10

Not a significant statistical trend (*). Suggested diagnostic, based on inferred trends only (**). This also applies to figs. 4.9–4.10.

4.9:13–15 offers a possible Phase 1 EB III-type platter bowl as prototype for two distinctive varieties of turned-down rim (bulbous and flattened), the latter of which possibly serving as antecedent to the diagnostic beveled rim platter bowl of Phase 3.

Thus, the sequence posited is: Phase 1 platter bowl with hammer rim, an inferred trend (fig. 4.9:13**), Phase 2 examples of platter bowls with turned-down bulbous (fig. 4.9:14a) and flattened (fig. 4.9:14b) rim, and Phase 3 platter bowl with turned-down bulbous rim (fig. 4.9:15a) and Phase 3 platter bowl with beveled rim (fig. 4.9:15b).

Medium-Small to Small Bowls

Figure 4.10:1–3 essentially illustrates a sequence similar to that of the medium bowls (above), although this category includes the statistically significant cyma-profiled bowl in Phase 3. Thus,

the sequence posited is: Phases 1 and 2 bowls with direct rim and Phase 3 carinated, (cyma-profiled) bowl.

Small Bowls (Cups)

Figure 4.10:4–6 illustrates a Phases 1 and 2 sequence of diagnostic incurved small bowls with simple direct (rounded) rim and a Phase 3 carinated (cyma-profiled) cup, a sequence paralleling the previous category of medium–small to small bowls.

Ledge Handles

Phase 1 envelope ledge handle with folded/overlapping flaps (fig. 4.10:7); Phase 2 vestigial ledge handle with scalloped edge (fig. 4.10:8); Phase 3 envelope ledge handle with spaces between flaps, not a statistically significant trend (fig. 4.10:9*).

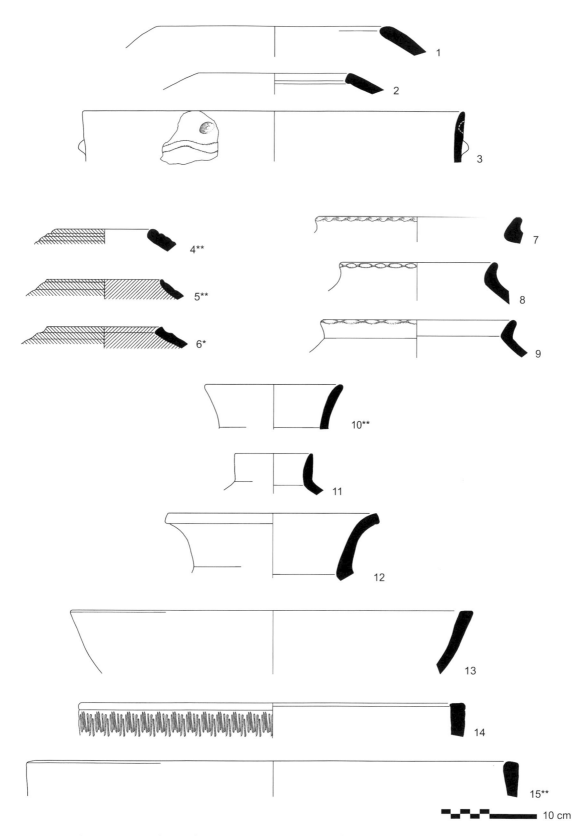

FIG. 4.8   *Area C: Suggested typo-chronology Phases 1–3; Restricted, necked, basins.*

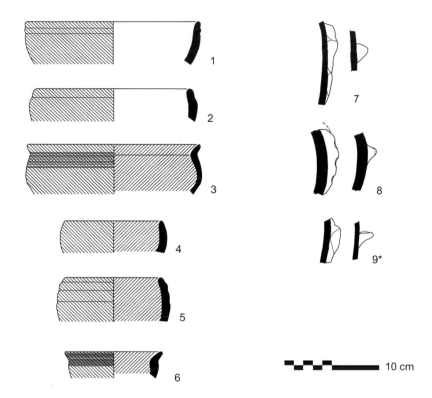

FIG. 4.10 *Area C: Suggested typo-chronology Phases 1–3; Bowls, cups, and ledge handles.*

#	FORM	TYPE	SIZE	DESCRIPTION	REF
1**	Deep Bowl	Open	Medium	Incurved, rilled-rim bowl with direct (rounded) rim	pl. 13:27
2	Deep Bowl	Lightly closed Cup-Bowl	Medium Small	Cup-bowl with direct (rounded) rim	pl. 12:1
3	Deep Bowl	Lightly closed Cup-Bowl	Medium Small	Cyma-profiled bowl with everted rim	pl. 4:7
4	Deep Bowl	Lightly closed Cup	Small	Incurved cup with direct (rounded) rim	pl. 13:5
5	Deep Bowl	Lightly closed Cup	Small	Incurved cup with direct (rounded) rim	pl. 5:4
6	Deep Bowl	Lightly closed Cup	Small	Cyma-profiled cup with flared rim	pl. 15:1
7				Envelope ledge handle with folded/overlapping flaps	pl. 21:1
8				Vestigial ledge handle, thumb-indentations/scalloped	pl. 21:4
9**				Envelope ledge handle with spaced flaps	pl. 21:6

of ceramics and phases. As Holdorf concisely states the correlations in his conclusions to Chapter 5:

> "According to the excavators of Bâb adh-Dhrâ', Field X, Phase A = Field XVI, Phase B (Rast and Schaub 2003: 440). Considering all of the above-mentioned phase to phase similarities and differences in the ceramic corpora of the two sites, the present study suggests that Area C Phase 1 corresponds with Field X Phase C, Area C Phase 2 corresponds with Field X Phase B, and Area C Phase 3 corresponds with Field X Phase A/ Field XVI Phase B."

From the point of view of the Bâb adh-Dhrâ' evidence, the best links are between the first and third phases at both sites (Rast and Schaub 2003: 448). We are in broad agreement that 'Ara'ir VIB = Bâb adh-Dhrâ' Stratum 1C = Phase 1 at Khirbat Iskandar, and that 'Ara'ir VIA = Bâb adh-Dhrâ' Stratum 1A = Phase 3 at Khirbat Iskandar (448); likewise, there are parallels at 'Ara'ir for virtually every vessel form at Khirbat Iskandar, as at Bâb adh-Dhrâ' (446). Indeed, as the list of parallels attests (fig. 4:11), Khirbat Iskandar and Bâb adh-Dhrâ' (table 13.7) share virtually the same comparanda. The two sites embody a regional interrelatedness in ceramics. As Palumbo has noted (1990), the most common southern Transjordanian characteristics are red slip and the rilled turned-down (his inverted) platter bowl, neither of which occurs north of the Zarqa' River (1990: 103). Thus, except for the earlier phase at Iktanu (see below), the cogent parallels to the Khirbat Iskandar assemblage come from the Karak Plateau and the Dead Sea Plain region, where the red slip tradition continues through the period, particularly at Adir, 'Ara'ir, Khirbat Hamra Ifdan, as well as at Bâb adh-Dhrâ'.

That said, given the typo-chronological diagnostics at Khirbat Iskandar and correlation with Bâb adh-Dhrâ', more precise cross-sequencing is possible with other sites. For instance, 'Ara'ir VIB clearly overlaps Phase 2 at Khirbat Iskandar, when the "necked cooking pots with piecrust rim" and the rilled repertoire (the "fossil type" "turned-down rim" platters especially) combine statistically to herald the change from Phase 1 (see types in

Olávarri 1969: figs. 1:8–22; 2:12–17). This overlap recedes when one removes the earliest platter types in Stratum VIB (fig. 1:1–7, p. 235) and the pottery found in "les couches les plus profondes et les plus anciennes d'occupation..." (fig. 3:6–10), which Olávarri himself describes as transitional between EB III and EB IV (p. 234). It is highly probable that there is an earlier, transitional phase at 'Ara'ir, the characteristics of which match more closely those of Phase 1 at Khirbat Iskandar and Phase 1C at Bâb adh-Dhrâ'.

Due to evident mixing of ceramic forms at the site of Adir, it is more difficult to tie that site to the chronology at Khirbat Iskandar, although parallels to virtually each type can be cited (Cleveland 1960: figs. 13–15). On the basis of Albright's observation concerning the development of the ledge handle from wavy (Phase C) to envelope (Phase B) to vestigial (Phase A), along with the range of pottery from early to late, it is likely that a sequence similar to that reconstructed for 'Ara'ir existed there.

Further south, in the Faynan, the pottery sequence at Khirbat Hamra Ifdan exemplifies the continuation of Early Bronze Age tradition (Adams 2000), a conceptualization of the late third millennium BCE advanced throughout this volume. The late EB III pottery in Phase 5b, especially the large storejars with everted necks, secondarily luted on (fig. 21:4), as well as the hemispherical bowls (fig. 21.7:4–6), and early four-spouted lamps (fig. 21.6:4–6) are clear forerunners of the subsequent EB IV exemplars. The dominant red-slipped and burnished tradition continues into Phase 6, along with the addition of band-combed EB IV pottery (fig. 21.9:7–10). The medium and small hemispherical bowls discussed in this chapter are dead-ringers for those at Khirbat Hamra Ifdan. In Phase 5b, the simple, direct rims of holemouths (fig. 21.9:1–6) and the range of inverted (or rolled) platter bowls (fig. 21.8:1–7, and compare Phase 6 examples 8–12) also hearken the characteristics noted in Phase 1 vessels at Khirbat Iskandar.

For a good range of parallels in southern Transjordan see the pottery from the site surveys of Adir, 'Ara'ir, Feqeiqes, Humeimat North-West, al-Lajjun, and Khirbat Umm es-Sedeirah (Palumbo 1990: figs. 55–58). Also, note the close parallels at

Early Bronze Age. Studies show that south Syria and north Transjordan/Cisjordan exhibit parallel traditions throughout the Early Bronze Age (Braemer and Echallier 2000: 403), including the EB IV period (p. 406–9). An analysis of pottery forms illuminates the commingling of northern and southern Levantine vessel types. Of particular interest, there are examples of goblets (or the "caliciform" ware), which, similar to their attestation elsewhere in the southern Levant, are representative of the latest Syrian EB IV incised and painted forms (409; fig. 22.3:18–19). These goblets occur alongside Syrian made "teapots" of fine ware (fig. 22.3:20–21), analogous to their well-known presence in northern Cisjordan, for example, at Qedesh (see Tadmor 1978) and Megiddo (Guy 1938: pls. 10: 5; 11: 26–33).

The authors conclude that the modern border regions of the southern Homs plain, north Jordan Plateau, and upper Jordan Valley across to the Lebanese Beqa'a were all integrated into one ceramic cultural area during the entire Early Bronze Age (Braemer and Echallier 2000: 409). In fact, petrographic evidence affirms more southerly ties, attested by Syrian storage jars at the newly excavated site of 'Ein el-Helu in the northern Jezreel Valley (Covello-Poran 2009: 18). The excavator suggests that these vessels possibly reached the site via coastal or Jordan Valley trade routes along which are found a network of villages (p. 18). Prior to excavation in the borderlands, the discernment of the general area of Hama as the closest source for parallels to the imported wares and the "caliciform" traditions had been noted (Dever 1971; Prag 1974; Mazzoni 1985).

The presence of Syrian vessels in the southern Levant raises an issue introduced in Chapter 1 concerning the mode of transmission for Syrian and/or Syrian-inspired traditions in the local EB IV corpus. Was it through trade, general contact between kindred regions/peoples, or an influx of new peoples? Numerous earlier studies attempted to deal with this subject, suggesting either more or fewer influences from Syria (Dever 1971; 1980; Richard 1978; 1980; Prag 1974). For a history of the evolution from external to local change as mechanisms for explaining Syrian influences on the ceramic

repertoire, see Bunimovitz and Greenberg (2006). For new efforts to understand Syrian influence on the south, see a study on the "caliciform" ware and the ideology of drinking and feasting for the EB IV period (Bunimovitz and Greenberg 2004). For a renewed study and emphasis on Syrian prototypes for the EB IV period see Prag (2009).

Throughout this work, the emphasis has been on continuity of local Early Bronze Age forms, which begin to show a hybrid quality in Phase 2 with the adaptation of the well-known Syrian EB IV "caliciform" tradition, including a preponderance of the decorative technique of incising (rilling). This horizon of pottery stretches throughout greater Syria-Mesopotamia (Mazzoni 1985). In the southern Levant, the tradition is primarily imitative, having little connection with the finely tempered, thin, and wheel-made pottery known from Syria. It is only the presence of actual Syrian vessels in the north (discussed above) that reflects the extension of the true "caliciform" tradition into the southern Levant. These contacts, with the rare exception, do not extend south of Megiddo. Palumbo notes that this absence in the south probably indicates no active trade networks with communities in Syria (Palumbo 2008: 252). We would modify this statement somewhat to say that some trade is evident in metals and probably other products, but, clearly, the contiguity of settlement at the boundaries of the northern and southern Levant facilitated contact. The close proximity of the numerous EB IV regions may be sufficient explanation for spread of the new vogue—the rilled wares—to the south. In sum, we are in agreement with the assessment of the EB IV Bâb adh-Dhrâ' assemblage that there are "pattern shifts," but they are not significant enough to support a new population (Rast and Schaub 2003: 448).

Families

Finally, this study of EB IV ceramics would not be complete without mention of the well-known classification framework that comprehends the period's ceramics into chronological, but overlapping regional families (Dever 1971; 1973; 1980). The subdivision of the EB IV into seven geographical-typological families recognized and emphasized the regional nature of the period. The families comprise the following regions: Northern (N); North-Central (NC); Jericho/Jordan Valley (J); Southern (S); Central Hills (CH); Coastal (C); and Transjordan (TR). Dever later accepted the new Amman-Zarqaʾ (A-Z) family. For our purposes, his insights that Family TR (the red-slipped and rilled tradition) chronologically preceded Family S still resonate with some of the observations made ear-

lier about these two regions. As the current quantified typo-chronological study is anchored in the stratigraphic profile of the site of Khirbat Iskandar, we have not referenced the Families in this volume. However, there is still much insight to be gained about the EB IV by utilizing the Family conceptualization, since it highlights the distinguishing characteristics of the various regions (and see an application of the family typology to the Area B "storeroom" assemblage in Richard 2000).

TABLE 4.1   *List of Parallels for Area C Ceramic Corpus.*

Fig.	#	Form	Rim	Parallels
4.1	1	4000	10	Bâb adh-Dhrâʿ: Rast and Schaub (2003): fig. 13.4:1
	2	4010	17	Bâb adh-Dhrâʿ: Rast and Schaub (2003): fig. 13.4:4; Iktanu: Prag (1974): fig. 3:18; Tall Umm Hammad: Helms (1986): fig. 19:9, 11
	3	4020C	17	Bâb adh-Dhrâʿ: Rast and Schaub (2003): fig. 13.4:4; Kh. Iskandar: Richard and Boraas (1984): fig. 18:3; ar-Rahil: Palumbo (1990): fig. 52:3; Tall Umm Hammad: Helms (1986): fig. 19:3–5
	4	4030	17	Bâb adh-Dhrâʿ: Rast and Schaub (2003): fig. 13.4:4
	5	4010C	18d	Bâb adh-Dhrâʿ: Rast and Schaub (2003): fig. 13.4:1, 3
	6	4020	10	Iktanu: Prag (1974): fig. 6:6
	7	4030C	17	Khirbat al-Batrawy: Nigro (2006): pl. IV:A.1/4 A.1/3; Tall al-Hayyât: Falconer et al. (2006): fig. 4.1:1; Bâb adh-Dhrâʿ: Rast and Schaub (2003): fig. 13.4:4; Tall Umm Hammad: Helms (1986): fig. 19:3–5
	8	4060	10	Bâb adh-Dhrâʿ: Rast and Schaub(2003): fig. 13.4:8; ʿAraʿir: Olávarri (1969): fig. 5:5; Adir: Palumbo (1990): fig. 58:1; Kh. Iskandar: Richard and Boraas (1984): fig. 18:29; Richard (2000): fig. 2:7, 11; Abu Irshareibeh: MacDonald (1992): pl. 14:9
	9	4060	61	Bâb adh-Dhrâʿ: Rast and Schaub (2003): pls. 110:1, 2; 115:10
	10	4067	10	Bâb adh-Dhrâʿ: Rast and Schaub (2003): fig. 13.4:8; Kh. Iskandar: Richard and Boraas (1988): fig. 19:7–9
	11	4072	41	Bâb adh-Dhrâʿ: Rast and Schaub (2003): fig. 13.4:10
	12	4072	11	Bâb adh-Dhrâʿ: Rast and Schaub (2003): pl. 131:4
	13	4046	18a	Tall Umm Hammad: Helms (1986): fig. 19:6; Bâb adh-Dhrâʿ: Rast and Schaub (2003): fig. 13.4:6
	14, 18	4050	12	Bâb adh-Dhrâʿ: Rast and Schaub (2003): pl. 132:12

Chapter 5

Quantitative Analysis of the Early Bronze IV Tell and Tomb Ceramic Assemblages

by Paul S. Holdorf

This chapter details a wealth of data based on a statistical analysis of the ceramic assemblages within each of three stratified phases in Area C, and of the ceramic assemblages from the tombs published in this volume. Moreover, collaboration with the staff of Bâb adh-Dhrâ‘, which ultimately included the adoption of their classification system (see Chs. 1 and 4), allowed for a comparative quantified study of their tomb and tell assemblages in order to identify key shared trends and to identify corresponding phases. That combined study provides a first attempt at a correlation of EB IV phasing from central and southern Transjordan, strengthening its usefulness as a template for comparison with other regional assemblages. As the EB IV period is known for its regionalized settlement, multiple ceramic families, and rare stratified occupation, the ceramic phasing presented here, hopefully, will be a valuable tool for scholars in the field.

The Area C excavations included eleven squares (three half squares) that yielded EB IV diagnostics from 56 primary loci. These contiguous squares had the same types of activities and yielded data corroborated by that for platter bowls, cooking pots, and bowls from Bâb adh-Dhrâ‘. Although these squares encompass only 1–2 percent of the site, the future publication of Area B, which includes specialized areas such as the "storeroom" and possible cultic areas, will add more than twice as much reported EB IV area of the site. The statistics-driven inferences in this chapter are hypotheses that await testing and refinement by the Area B analysis, which will probably also prompt new hypotheses.

A major objective of the study was to determine if statistically significant differences in the Phases 1–3 ceramics in Area C reflect typo-chronological phasing. First, it was necessary to conduct a sample selection procedure and analysis of the distribution of ceramic forms from the tell to assess whether or not the sample is representative. Then, through various statistical methods listed below, the study concluded that three different ceramic assemblages matched the three stratigraphic phases in Area C. The ceramics differ significantly on form and size, form and rim, and other characteristics. These findings, when compared with the ceramic phasing at Bâb adh-Dhrâ‘, illuminate important correlates.

This chapter also includes a statistical analysis of the distribution of ceramics in the excavated tombs, again utilizing the Bâb adh-Dhrâ‘ classification system with some refinement. The major objectives were to compare the cemetery corpus with the three stratified ceramic phases from the tell, and to highlight contrasts and similarities between the assemblages of the two main cemeteries (D and E). Using the significant differences in the tell phases and other tools, it was possible to determine the likely sequence of tombs in all the cemeteries together with Bâb adh-Dhrâ' Tombs A52 and A54.

STATISTICAL METHOD

The study used standard statistical tools that are described most fully by Drennan (1996) and Sinopoli (1991), supplemented with another tool for testing apparent differences in *variety/richness* (Kaufman 1998; and see Rice 1987: 202–3). The tools revealed statistically significant inter-phase differences on the following: a) *quantitative* measurements, such as rim diameter; b) *qualitative* data, such as the frequency (presence/absence) of a form and form/rim combination; c) *variety/richness,* such as the number of different form/rim combinations. The results were then compared with the patterns observed in the Khirbat Iskandar tombs and those found at Bâb adh-Dhrâ' in an attempt to match phases at both sites. For the tombs, and the pottery types in the tombs, the study applied the WinBasp (the Windows version of the Bonn Archaeological Software Package) program. WinBasp employs matching pairs of specific types to predict the most likely order in which the tombs were laid down, as well as of the type production sequence.

THE CLASSIFICATION

Specifically, this chapter a) focuses on changes in platter bowl types and the similar changes at Bâb adh-Dhrâ', b) covers the changes in cooking pot, "teapot," basin, and cup types, c) compares the richness of platter bowl types, and d) describes changes in ware and decoration.

The Area C assemblage of 365 rim diagnostics consists of 62 from Phase 1, 149 from Phase 2, and 154 from Phase 3. Phase 1 has the smallest assemblage due to limited exposure; nevertheless,

as discussed below, there are sufficient numbers to do a quantitative study. The classification is based on form/size, which—in combination with rim—allowed for the classification of specific types. Although some preliminary studies of ware families are also included in this analysis at this time, it is not possible to be definitive about correlations between ware families in relation to the typology. The Bâb adh-Dhrâ' study was more complete in this respect. Ongoing technological studies of the Khirbat Iskandar pottery will be included in future publications (but see the petrographic study in Ch. 6).

Almost every percentage distribution of the classifications within the form categories changes from phase to phase. Many of the differences in the assemblages statistically can be attributable to random fluctuations caused by sampling methodology. Therefore, a ceramic phase is not defined as one that has different percentage distributions of types from the assemblage that precedes or follows it. Rather, a ceramic phase is defined as one in which there are *statistically* significant differences in the proportions or richness of the types between it and the "phase" that adjoins it. Such significant differences appeared on both sides (i.e., between Phases 1 and 2, and between Phases 2 and 3) in forms that account for a majority of the total assemblage of 365 vessels.

As detailed below, there are significant typological differences among the 145 platter bowls, 57 bowls, and 53 cooking pots, which together represent over two-thirds of the total assemblage. In addition, there are significant differences either between Phases 1 and 2, or between Phases 2 and 3, in other types. The only major form that does not display a statistically significant difference anywhere is the remarkably stable "teapot." Through statistical analysis, this study was able to discern a series of diagnostics for each phase. They are the main datasets used to distinguish the typo-chronological sequence presented in this volume (see also Ch. 4).

Given the fact that only a limited portion of the site is included in the study, it is, however, important to be mindful that "artifacts are originally cluster samples representing spatial contexts" (Rice

1987: 290). The study includes two preliminary steps designed to determine if clusters in spatial contexts may skew the results. The first step was to look *inter*-phase to see if there was evidence in the ceramic assemblage that suggests a fundamental change in the activities in Area C from phase to phase.[1] The second step was to look *intra*-phase to determine if the separate loci in the phases appear to reflect the overall differences in vessel distributions.

Following a discussion of collection and selection strategies, the chapter divides into three major sections: Tell Assemblage, Cemetery Corpus, and Comparison with Bâb adh-Dhrâ'. Within each section, and for each major ceramic category, there is a summary of the major conclusions followed by the specific statistical data. The latter are included in an effort to make all the raw data from which conclusions are drawn accessible to the reader.

COLLECTION AND SELECTION

All potsherds excavated in Area C were washed, counted, and read in the field. All diagnostic sherds were saved and registered along with a sampling of body sherds. In the case of possible restoration, all sherds were kept. All the pottery in the tombs was saved for restoration and then drawn at a scale of 1:1. There were only a few whole vessels found in the tombs. Non-restorable diagnostics from tell and tomb were also cut and drawn at a 1:1 scale.

Given the objectives of the statistical study to determine if typological phasing exists in Area C, the final selection for analysis included diagnostics from primary loci (surfaces/makeup) only in Phase 3 and Phase 2. Because the Phase 2 structures and surfaces sealed the Phase 1 settlement, and because there was limited exposure in Phase 1, all rim diagnostics from the latter phase were included in the study. The Phase 1 materials yielded a few pre-EB IV sherds.

Every attempt was made to exclude all rims from potentially contaminated or mixed buckets, and all likely joins (i.e., all multiple diagnostic sherds that connected, or were probably from the same vessel). In a few cases it was clear that separate appendages, such as spouts and handles, could not go with

any rim diagnostic from the same locus. They are included in the counts for the limited purpose of assessing the inter- and intra-phase distributions of basic forms (see below).

Similar procedures were used for the tomb pottery, except that all 249 restored EB IV vessels from 16 tombs are included. To avoid duplication in the statistical study of the tombs, only base sherds that clearly did not match rims in tombs were included in this study (20 other bases were excluded from the quantitative study).

CLASSIFICATION SYSTEMS: TOMBS AND TELL

The Khirbat Iskandar tell and tomb classification system is the same as that used for the Bâb adh-Dhrâ' town (Rast and Schaub 2003) and cemetery (Schaub and Rast 1989) vessel forms. The tomb classification system, based on whole vessels, is the more detailed (10-digit) version. Date, shape, size, and proportion determine the first four digits of the tomb vessel code. The first digit represents the time period in the Early Bronze Age. This volume covers almost exclusively EB IV vessels for which the first digit is "4." There are only four earlier vessels in Phase 1 whose first digit is "3," which signifies EB III. The second digit describes the general form group, e.g., restricted, necked, or bowl forms. For example, platter bowls are assigned a "6." Generally, platter bowls are at least 17 cm wide and have an H/M (height/rim diameter) ratio of 0.35 or less. The third digit is for size. For example, a 462_ platter bowl is classified "large," and is generally 25–30 cm wide with a capacity of 1,800–2,900 ccs. The fourth digit is for contour types, proportion, and geometric shape. As an example, a 4623 platter bowl has a flat base, walls curved upright and a B/M (base/rim diameter) ratio between 0.40 and 0.54. The following three sets of two digits separated by periods signify, respectively, handle type, rim shape, and base shape and join. Thus, 4623.00.75.13 would indicate that the above platter bowl has no handle, has a thickened inside turned-down rim, and a flat base with corner point between wall and base, and a convex juncture with the wall.

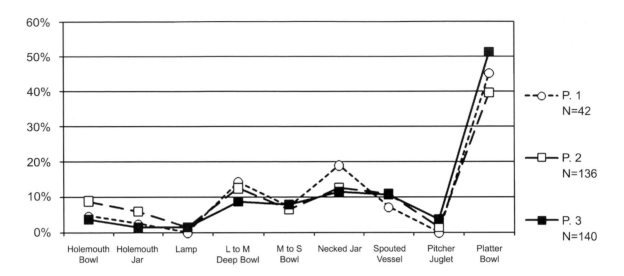

FIG. 5.1 *Inter-phase distribution of forms, cooking pots excluded.*

All of the code descriptions used for Khirbat Iskandar vessels are detailed in Appendices D and E. Since some Khirbat Iskandar tomb and town vessels have no equivalent at Bâb adh-Dhrâʿ, it was necessary to interpolate some of the four-digit vessel codes. For example, since there are so many larger spouted vessels in the Khirbat Iskandar tombs that are not found at Bâb adh-Dhrâʿ, a new code, 4036, was added for "large," 21+ cm wide spouted vessels. Such interpolated and added codes are noted in the Appendices.

Appendix D sets forth the necessarily less detailed four-digit code system for tell vessels diagnosed, with rare exception, from rim sherds. The Bâb adh-Dhrâʿ numerical system used here is the following: first digit equals date/stratum, second digit represents the structural form, third digit is for size, and the fourth digit allows for special characteristics of vessels. Thus, 4620 would indicate an EB IV platter bowl, large with shallow, flat base; or 4119 would be an EB IV necked jar, with pithoi-mouth, and short neck, curved-out (flared).

Given the two corpora—whole vessels in the tombs, sherds on the tell—the classification system varies somewhat at points. Some of the size ranges for the tell are different from those for tomb vessels; for example, a "large" platter bowl on the tell has a rim diameter of 30–39 cm, while in the tombs the diameter would be 25–30 cm. Also, the method for

determining the size categories of spouted vessels changes. In the tombs the maximum diameter is usually known, since the vessels typically are whole or restored. For the tell, since the maximum diameter usually is unknown, rim diameter ("M") is used instead. Accordingly, all of the comparative studies use actual rim diameters.

TELL ASSEMBLAGE

Inter-Phase Distribution of Forms

The percentage of cooking pots fell from 32 percent (20/62) in Phase 1 to about 10 percent (17/152[2]) in Phase 2, and remained there (16/157[3]) in Phase 3. This difference in distribution probably reflects an increased diversity of functional areas, such as the Phases 2 and 3 workshop areas in the eastern sector, and the Phase 3 construction of two bins and an entryway (see Ch. 3). Accordingly, it is preferable to consider the cooking pots separately (see below).[4] When all 53 cooking pots are excluded, the distribution of forms among the three phases is sufficiently similar so as to render statistical comparisons reasonable (fig. 5.1).

Intra-Phase Distribution of Forms

Although there is some un-evenness in the intra-phase distribution of forms, the largest categories, platter bowls (145), bowls, (58), cooking pots (53), and necked jars (40), are broadly distributed. There are 56 loci that yielded one or more vessels, 14 in Phase 1, 14 in Phase 2, and 28 in Phase 3. Platter bowls are present in all but two of the 34 loci with three or more vessels: Locus 6029 in Phase 1 and Locus 6016 in Phase 2, both of which yielded substantial quantities of flakes debitage. Bowls and cooking pots are present in all nine loci with ten or more vessels. Necked jars are present in all of the same nine loci except for 2037. One Phase 2 locus, 9001, with nine vessels and no cooking pots, has an unusual distribution that includes five large necked jars and two spouted vessels and thus probably represents a storeroom context.

What is most uneven about the intra-phase distributions is the *concentration* of vessels on two surfaces. Phase 3 Locus 7015 has 55 vessels, about 4.5 per square meter. Of the vessels found in Phase 3, this locus has all three of the very large holemouth bowl deep basins—each with a rim diameter of 50 cm—and 13 of the 21 deep bowls, but only three of the 16 cooking pots. Because Room 732, a specialized bin area, is contiguous with outer Room 731, the ceramic assemblage of Locus 7015 in the latter was probably used for agricultural processing, not domestic habitation. Phase 2 Locus 2030 has 27 vessels, about 3.6 per square meter. They include a holemouth bowl deep basin (54 cm rim diameter), seven of the 29 deep bowls in Phase 2, including one with a 46 cm rim diameter, and only one cooking pot. Because these concentrated areas probably were or could have been used for specialized purposes, the particular characteristics of their vessel assemblages were scrutinized separately. Any instances in which their assemblages could possibly skew the overall phase-to-phase averages or percentages[5] are pointed out below.

TABLE 5.1 *Distribution of Area C platter bowls in size categories.*

FORM	DESCRIPTION	P. 1	P. 2	P. 3
4660	platter bowl: M (29–17) shallow, flat base	11	17	15
4620	platter bowl: L (39–30) shallow, flat base	8	32	48
4600	platter bowl: VL, wide (40+) shallow, flat base		5	9
	TOTAL	19	54	72

TABLE 5.2 *Area C platter bowl rim diameter averages and ranges.*

	P. 1	P. 2	P. 3	ALL
MEAN	28.7	32.3	32.9	32.2
MEDIAN	28	32	32	32
RANGE	22–38	20–50	22–44	20–50

Platter Bowls

As the largest and best-known category at Khirbat Iskandar and Bâb adh-Dhrâ', the platter bowl is the primary indicator of inter-phase differentiation. There are significant differences between the three phases in the platter bowl category: 1) size increases; 2) evolution of types from rolled and flattened rim, to turned-down and beveled rim; 3) decreasing richness distinction between Phases 2 and 3.

Size Increases

All of the town platter bowls are shallow with a flat base, but distribute to the higher size ranges through the successive phases (table 5.1). The rim diameter averages and ranges bear this out (table 5.2).

Figure 5.2 illustrates that the Phase 2 platter bowls are more evenly distributed across the size ranges, and that the distribution for Phase 3 has two pronounced peaks, one at 28–32 cm, and the other at 36–38 cm, which together total 49 platter bowls. This emerging bi-modal distribution in Phase 3 may suggest increased standardization.

An analysis of the variance ("ANOVA") shows that the Phase 1 to Phase 2 increase in platter bowl sizes is highly significant.[6] The 3.6 cm increase in mean rim diameter represents nearly a 50 percent increase in average capacity, from about 3.2 to 4.7 l,[7] indicating, possibly, an increase in family size, or dietary changes.

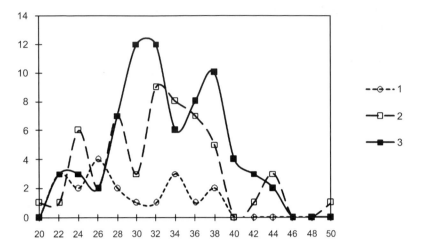

FIG. 5.2   *Size distribution of platter bowls.*

Evolution of Types

More than 80 percent of each phase's platter bowls have rims that are thickened inside, but the shapes change significantly through the phases (fig. 5.3). Chi-square tests confirm that the increases in turned-down (#75) rims (see fig. 4.3:10) are highly statistically significant both between Phase 1 and Phase 2,[8] and between Phase 2 and Phase 3.[9] Platter bowls with turned-down rims are widely distributed in 33 different loci. The Phase 1 to Phase 2 decrease in the combination of rolled and rolled and pointed (#73 and #74)

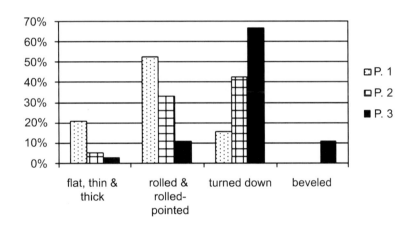

FIG. 5.3   *Rim shape changes of platter bowls.*

rims (see figs. 4.4:3 and 4.3:12) is significant,[10] as is the further decrease from Phase 2 to Phase 3.[11] The Phase 1 to Phase 2 decrease in the combination of flat, thin and flat, thickened (#70 and #71) rims (see fig. 4.3:13 and pl. 18:4), from four of 19 to three of 54, is significant.[12] The Phase 3 increase in, and first appearance of thickened inside beveled (#76) rims (see fig. 4.4:1) is highly significant.[13] Of the eight platter bowls with #76 rims, five are in Locus 7015, and all eight are within the two Phase 3 rim diameter peaks. Six of the nine platter bowls in Locus 2030 have turned-down (#75) rims. The eight platter bowls with simple direct rims are widely dispersed throughout all three phases and have rim diameters ranging from 20 cm up to only 28 cm. Of these eight platter bowls, the proportions with

direct beveled (#13) rims (see fig. 4.4:4) increase significantly from Phase 2 to Phase 3, from one of three to four of four.[14]

Richness

Of equal importance are changes in the assemblage richness from Phase 2 to Phase 3. Phase 2 has 13 different types among its 54 platter bowls. Phase 1, with 19 platter bowls, has seven different types, and Phase 3, with 72 platter bowls, has only seven types (table 5.3). The raw richness[15] index numbers are shown in Table 5.4. The decrease in richness between Phase 2 and Phase 3 is statistically significant,[16] and may indicate a decrease in trade, or increasing standardization, possibly a result of shifting from household to more centralized pottery production. The bi-modal distribution of Phase 3 sizes supports the latter inference.

Rilling

In Phase 1, nine of 19 platter bowls have rilling; in Phase 2, 24 of 54 have rilling; and 47 of 72 are rilled in Phase 3. But rilling is not a diag nostic feature by itself, since nearly all rilling is associated with turned-down (#75) or beveled (#76) rims.

Cooking Pots

In the classification, cooking pots are indicated by the addition of a "C" just after the four-digit code for form to distinguish them from other restricted holemouth bowls, jars and necked jars. As with the platter bowls, there are significant inter-phase differences (see table 5.5 and fig. 5.4). The most significant change is in the evolution of cook-ing pot types from holemouth jar (see fig. 4.1:5) to necked jar (see fig. 4.2:12) to holemouth bowl (see fig. 4.1:15) forms through three phases. Between Phase 1 and Phase 2, holemouth jar cooking pots decrease significantly while necked jar cooking pots increase significantly.[17] Holemouth bowl forms, including the straight-sided type with steam holes, make their first appearance in Phase 3, a significant increase.[18]

Significant differences have also been noted in rim type. For example, although all of the holemouth jar cooking pots are classified as hav-ing simple direct (10 series) rims, there are dis-tinctions within that broad classification. From Phase 1 to Phase 2, those with interior lip (#17) rims (see fig. 4.1:7) increase significantly from 1 of 18 to 5 of 9,[19] and those with bulbous (#18) rims (see fig. 4.1:5) decrease significantly from 9 of 18 to 2 of 9.[20] Table 5.6 shows that all nine

TABLE 5.3 *Area C platter bowls by rim code.*

Code	Description	P. 1	P. 2	P. 3
10	simple-direct: squared		1	
11	simple-direct: rounded		1	
12	simple-direct: tapered	1		
13	simple-direct: beveled, inside		1	4
31	inverted: rounded, same thickness		1	
32	inverted: tapered, same thickness		1	
33	inverted: triangular, short		1	
51	curved-in or upright: rounded		1	
52	curved-in or upright: tapered		1	
70	thickened inside: flat, thin	3	3	1
71	thickened inside: flat, thick	1		1
73	thickened inside: rolled	7	12	8
74	thickened inside: rolled and pointed	3	6	
75	thickened inside: turned down	3	23	48
76	thickened inside: beveled			8
91	thickened, in and out: rounded-knob	1	2	2
	TOTAL	19	54	72

TABLE 5.4 *Richness of Area C platter bowl rims.*

	P. 1	P. 2	P. 3
Vessels	19	54	72
Categories	7	13	7
Richness	1.606	1.769	0.825

TABLE 5.5 *Area C cooking pot types.*

	P. 1	P. 2	P. 3
holemouth jar	18	9	9
necked jar	2	7	5
holemouth bowl	0	0	3
TOTAL	20	16	17

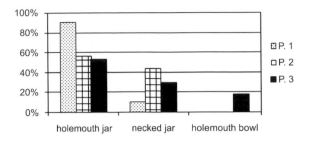

FIG. 5.4   *Area C cooking pot types.*

TABLE 5.6 *Area C necked jar cooking pot rims.*

	P. 1	P. 2	P. 3
60-curved-out: lightly flared, squared	2	2	1
61-curved-out: lightly flared, rounded	0	4	1
62-curved-out: lightly flared, tapered	0	1	0
65-curved-out: sharply flared, tapered	0	0	1
41-everted/angled: slight angle, rounded	0	0	2
TOTAL	2	7	5

TABLE 5.7 *Rim diameters of Area C spouted vessels.*

	P. 1	P. 2	P. 3
MEAN	11.7	12.5	15.7
MEDIAN	11	12	15
RANGE	10–14	6–22	12–22

necked jar cooking pots in Phase 1 and Phase 2 are curved-out and lightly flared, but both of those in Phase 1 have squared (#60) rims (see pl. 2:6) while only two of the seven in Phase 2 have squared rims, a significant decrease.[21] The general category of curved-out, flared (60 series) rims decreases significantly from Phase 2, seven of seven, to Phase 3, three of five.[22] And everted/angled-rims (see fig. 4.2:13) make their first appearance (2) in Phase 3, a significant increase.[23]

The rim diameters of Phase 2 holemouth jar cooking pots range from only 11–16 cm, while the ranges in Phase 1 and Phase 3 are both 14–24 cm.

Bowls (Large to Medium Deep "L–M")

Of the distinctions noted among L–M (4500 series) bowls, the most important appear to relate to changing rim types. Notably, there is a decrease in simple direct rims and an increase in rims that are thickened inside. For example, bowls with simple direct (10 series) rims decrease significantly from Phase 1 (5/6) to Phase 2 (8/17), and those with thickened inside (70 series) rims increase significantly from Phase 1 (1/6) to Phase 2 (9/17).[24] As in the platter bowl category, the beveled-rim bowl (#76) appears only in Phase 3 (see fig. 4.3:3). It has a narrow 32–36 cm rim diameter range, which suggests a specialized function. The increase from none in Phase 2 to four in Phase 3 is significant,[25] but this difference should be treated with caution because all four are in Locus 7015.

The thickened inside rim increases significantly on large (32+ cm) and medium–large (31–22 cm) open bowls (4520, 4530 and 4546) from Phase 1 (1/3) to Phase 2 (9/11).[26] Also, as a group, basin-bowls (4520/4530), together with holemouth bowl

basins (4080/4040), with thickened inside, flat (#70 and #71) rims (see fig. 4.1:17) decrease significantly from Phase 2 (12/18) to Phase 3 (1/7).[27]

Bowls (Medium to Small, Deep or Medium Depth "M–S")

For M–S (4700 series) bowls, simple direct (10 series) rims decrease significantly from Phase 2 (7/9) to Phase 3 (4/11).[28] And the proportion of those with simple direct, rounded (#11) rims (see fig. 4.4:6) decreases significantly from Phase 2 (6/9) to Phase 3 (0/11).[29] Of particular interest are the statistics for the cyma-profiled (carinated) bowl, which increases significantly from Phases 2 to 3. Specifically, the number of M–S bowls with carinated walls (see fig. 4.4:11) increases from Phase 2 (2/9) to Phase 3 (7/11).[30] All three of the M–S bowls in Phase 1 are incurved basic forms (see pl. 13:5); only three of the nine in Phase 2 are incurved, a significant decrease.[31]

Necked Jars (excluding Cooking Pots)

This category is less easily analyzed because rim diameter generally does not correlate well with capacity. Either maximum diameter or height correlates better, but whole or restorable vessels are necessary to determine this, and none were found in Area C. The sherd collection includes necked jar rim diameters ranging from as small as six or eight cm, to as large as 22 or 24 cm for all of the phases, if the two EB III pithoi in Phase 1 are included. There is a significant decrease in simple direct (10 series) rims from Phase 2 (5/17) to Phase 3 (1/16),[32] and a significant increase in curved-out, flared rims (60 series) from Phase 2 (11/17) to Phase 3 (15/16).[33]

Spouted Vessels

The rim diameters of spouted vessels ("teapots") increase significantly from Phases 2 to 3 (table 5.7).[34] This is primarily because Phase 3 does not have any spouted vessels smaller than 12 cm. Although none of 14 Phase 2, and two of 14 Phase 3 spouted vessels have a beveled (#13) simple direct rim, unlike the beveled-rim platter bowls and deep bowls, this increase is not significant.[35] Interestingly, spouted vessels are almost always accompanied by necked jars, and spouted vessels display a large-small pairing pattern (see, especially, Loci 2030, 2033, 5010, 5014, 6019, 7015, 8008 and 9001). The pairing of spouted vessels may indicate different product contained in each, or, if the same product, perhaps separate vessels were used for different people. They also may have been used for pouring at different stages of an agricultural purification process, for example, olive oil production.

Ledge Handles

The ledge handles from primary loci are shown on Plates 21 and 22 and quantified in Table 5.8.[36] There is a significant decrease in (#16c) envelope ledge handles with folded/ overlapping flaps (see pl. 22:10) from Phase 1 (3/3) to Phase 2 (1/13).[37] Also

TABLE 5.8 *Area C ledge handles.*

CODE	DESCRIPTION	P.1	P.2	P.3
14	Wavy ledge handle	0	1	2
16a	Envelope ledge handle with spaced flaps	0	3	4
16b	Envelope ledge handle with spaced flaps (clear pinching)	0	2	2
16c	Envelope ledge handle with folded/overlapping flaps	3	1	0
17a	Vestigial ledge handle, envelope/pinch-lapped profile	0	3	2
17b	Vestigial ledge handle, thumb-indentations/scalloped	0	3	0
	TOTAL	3	13	10

significant is the decrease in (#17b) vestigial ledge handles with scalloped edge (see pl. 21:2) from Phase 2 (3/13) to Phase 3 (0/10).[38]

Ware

The bulk of the fabric (core) colors of Area C vessels are pink (35%), light reddish brown (12%), light red (9%), red (9%), gray (7%), and pinkish gray (7%)[39] (see table 5.9). The fabric colors of Area C cooking pots are quite different, dominated by red (27%), and reddish brown (20%). Pink represents only 10%. There are few differences among the phases when cooking pots are removed, although there is a decrease in pink ware from Phase 1 to Phase 2, which is attributable to the higher number of Phase 1 necked jars with pink ware. This observation suggests probable continuous use of the same clay sources throughout EB IV, or that firing technology did not change. The distributions by phase of fabric colors among the other forms do not vary much from the overall distribution in figure 5.5. A comparison with Bâb adh-Dhrâʿ shows that the clay sources or technology used there is clearly different, given that 88% of Stratum I vessels there have core colors of reddish yellow, reddish brown, or light red.[40]

CONCLUSIONS:
STATISTICAL DIAGNOSTICS
FOR EB IV PHASES 1–3

The diagnostics designated with a capital letter listed below have a confidence level [41] of 95 percent or higher, and represent the most important diagnostics (or diagnostic characteristics). Those with 90–95 percent confidence levels are indicated numerically. The third level of diagnostics (indicated in lower alphabetic case) indicates those with lower confidence levels, 80–90 percent.

Phase 1

A. Holemouth jar cooking pot (98.0%)
    a. Holemouth jar cooking pot with simple direct (bulbous) rim (83.3%)
    b. Necked jar cooking pot with flaring, squared rim (83.3%)
B. Small size platter bowls (97.7%)
  1. Platter bowl with flat rim (93.0%)
    a. Platter bowl with rolled or rolled and pointed rim (86.3%)
    b. Large–medium bowl with simple direct rim (85.6%)
  2. Small bowl (cup) with incurved sides, lightly closed (90.9%)
C. Envelope ledge handle with folded/overlapping flaps (99.3%)

Phase 2

A. Holemouth jar cooking pot with simple direct (interior lip) rim (99.2%)
B. Necked jar cooking pot (98.0%)
    a. Necked jar cooking pot with curved-out and lightly flared rim (84.8%)
C. Large size platter bowls (97.7%)
D. Platter bowl with turned-down rim (96.4%)
  1. Large variety of platter bowl rims (91.9%)
    a. Large–Medium bowl with thickened inside rim (85.6%)
E. Basin-bowls with thickened inside flat rim (97.3%)
  1. Medium-small bowl with simple direct rim (92.0%)

F. Medium-small bowl with simple direct (rounded rim) (99.8%)
    a. Necked jar with simple direct rim (89.9%)
    b. Vestigial ledge handle with scalloped edge (83.9%)

Phase 3

    a. Holemouth bowl cooking pot (87.5%)
    b. Necked jar cooking pot with everted/angled-rim (84.8%)
A. Platter bowl with turned-down rim (99.3%)
B. Platter bowl with beveled rim (98.9%)
    a. Platter bowl with simple direct, beveled rim (85.7%)
  1. Small variety of platter bowl rims (91.9%)
C. Large-medium bowl with thickened inside beveled rim (97.9%)
  1. Medium-small bowl with carinated walls (cyma-profiled) (93.6%)
D. Necked jar with curved-out, flared rim (95%)

Phase 1 Assemblage

Most platter bowl rims are rolled, some are flat, and even fewer are turned-down. None is a very large size (40+ cm). Nearly all cooking pots are holemouth jars, half of which have simple direct (bulbous) rims. The necked cooking pots have flaring, squared rims. Nearly all large–medium bowls have simple direct rims. All of the medium–small bowls are incurved. The ledge handles are envelope with folded/overlapping flaps.

Phase 2 Assemblage

There is a large variety of platter bowl rims; nearly half are turned-down, fewer are rolled, and almost none is flat. Almost half of the cooking pots are necked jars, all with curved-out, flared rims, and half of the holemouths have simple direct (interior lip) rims. Only half of large–medium bowls have simple direct rims; the other half have rims that are thickened inside. Most medium–small bowls have simple direct, rounded rims, and a few are cyma-profiled. A third of the necked jars have simple direct rims. Some of the ledge handles are vestigial with scalloped edge.

Phase 3 Assemblage

Only a few platter bowls are medium size (< 29 cm). There is a limited variety of rims; a sizable majority is turned-down, fewer are rolled, and there are almost no rolled or flat thickened inside rims. A new thickened inside rim appears: the beveled rim. Holemouth bowl (straight-sided) cooking pots are also unique. Some necked jar cooking pots have everted/angled-rims. The thickened inside beveled rim also appears uniquely among large–medium bowls. Less than half of medium–small bowls have simple direct rims, and more than half are cyma-profiled. Nearly all of the necked jars have curved-out, flared rims.

TOMB ASSEMBLAGE

Introduction and Summary Conclusions

By means of a few comparative figures and charts, it is possible to: 1) summarily illustrate the similarities and the differences between the tell and tomb corpora; 2) highlight differentiation between Cemeteries D and E; 3) illustrate the results of the seriation of the tombs, including a tell and tomb correlation. The quantified study of Restricted, Necked, and Bowl types (size/shape/rim and ware) reveals significant correspondences

TABLE 5.9 *Munsell codes and colors.*

MUNSELL	COLOR	MUNSELL	COLOR
10R4/6	red	5YR6/2	pinkish gray
10R4/8	red	5YR6/3	light reddish brown
10R5/6	red	5YR6/4	light reddish brown
10R5/8	red	5YR7/2	pinkish gray
10R6/6	light red	5YR7/3	pink
10R6/8	light red	5YR7/4	pink
10YR5/1	gray	5YR8/3	pink
10YR6/1	gray	5YR8/4	pink
2.5Y5/0	gray	7.5R4/6	red
2.5Y6/0	gray	7.5R4/8	red
2.5YR4/6	red	7.5R5/0	gray
2.5YR4/8	red	7.5R5/6	red
2.5YR5/0	gray	7.5R5/8	red
2.5YR5/6	red	7.5R6/0	gray
2.5YR5/8	red	7.5R6/6	light red
2.5YR6/0	gray	7.5R6/8	light red
2.5YR6/4	light reddish brown	7.5YR5/0	gray
2.5YR6/6	light red	7.5YR6/0	gray
2.5YR6/8	light red	7.5YR6/2	pinkish gray
5Y5/1	gray	7.5YR7/2	pinkish gray
5Y6/1	gray	7.5YR7/4	pink
5YR5/1	gray	7.5YR8/4	pink
5YR6/1	gray		

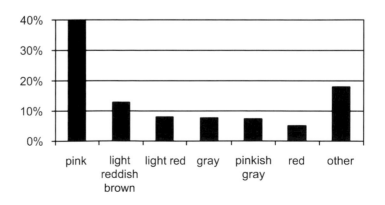

FIG. 5.5 *Overall distribution of fabric colors.*

TABLE 5.10 *Distribution of forms in tombs.*

	D2	D3	D4	D9	D10	E3	E9	E10	E14	H3	TOTAL
Lamp	7	8	0	1	3	0	2	0	1	3	25
L-M bowl	4	3	1	3	0	0	0	0	1	1	13
M-S bowl	7	0	0	1	0	2	3	3	1	0	17
Necked jar	20	13	6	6	2	0	3	3	3	2	58
Spouted vessel	6	4	2	2	0	1	1	1	0	0	17
Wide mouth jar/jug/let	3	3	0	2	0	1	0	0	0	0	9
Platter bowl	38	21	8	11	3	2	4	4	1	2	94
TOTAL	85	52	17	26	8	6	13	11	7	8	

TABLE 5.11 *Distribution of forms in Cemeteries D and E.*

CEMETERY		LAMP	L–M BOWL	M–S BOWL	NECKED JAR	SPOUTED VESSEL	PITCHER JUGLET	PLATTER BOWL	TOTAL
D	No.	20	11	8	47	14	9	88	197
	%	10%	6%	4%	24%	7%	5%	45%	
E	No.	3	1	9	9	3	1	11	37
	%	8%	3%	24%	24%	8%	3%	30%	

between tell and tombs in all but a few categories. Based primarily, but not solely, on the statistically significant inter-phase changes in platter bowls on the tell (correlated with Bâb adh-Dhrâʿ phases), it is possible to seriate the tombs.

Shared characteristics of tell and tomb include: spouted vessels, medium and small necked store-jars, pitchers and jugs, open and closed deep bowls and platter bowls, medium and small bowls, cups, and lamps. Additional support for shared tell and tomb traditions is found in the presence of two cooking pots and one holemouth jar.

As for contrasts, there are no necked cooking pots, pithoi, or large necked storejars in the tombs; also missing are holemouth bowls, such as the straight-sided and other holemouth bowl cooking pots, and spouted vats/basins. Notably, the tomb assemblages are lacking functional ledge handles as well as the distinctive piecrust-rim vessels (usually necked cooking pots/basins/bowls) from the tell. There are also distinctions in distribution. For example, the tombs have fewer L–M deep bowls, many more lamps, more medium to small to miniature necked jars, and pitcher/juglets; and rim diameters for platters range somewhat larger on the tell.

Considering all of the above, one could plausibly infer that the major distinction between the tell and tomb assemblages is, except for a few outliers, the lack of long-term storage and/or food preparation/or processing/industrial (i.e. olive oil production) equipment in the tombs. The tomb assemblages thus generally comprise serving dishes, small bowls (cups) for drinking, and short-term storage vessels, specialized containers ("teapots"/miniatures for unguents or other precious commodities), and lamps for lighting. As Table 12.1 (Ch. 12) illustrates, when cooking pots are removed from the assemblages, the profiles of tell and tombs are remarkably similar.

Inter-Tomb Distribution of Forms

There are 249 EB IV vessels in the 16 tombs, including the Cemetery D test pit. Each of the 13 tombs with three or more vessels had one or more platter bowls. The distribution in the ten tombs with five or more vessels, exclusive of the two cooking pots and one holemouth jar, is shown in Table 5.10. With the exception of E3, all of these tombs had necked jars, suggesting they also were an important part of ceramic gift assemblages.

There are only two cooking pots in the tombs, both in E10. As mentioned above, when cooking pots are removed from the assemblages the profile is similar to the tell, except that the tombs have no holemouth bowls, fewer L–M deep bowls, and many more lamps, necked jars, and pitcher/juglets. See below for a discussion of the necked jars. Notably, the primarily domestic context of Phase 1 on the tell has a higher proportion of necked jars than the more industrial contexts in Phases 2 and 3 (see fig. 5.1). The fact that cooking pots are rare and L–M deep bowls are infrequent in the tombs suggests that food preparation/processing was not part of burial ritual gifts, whereas the greater number of lamps probably indicates both a utilitarian and/or ritual function in burial interment.

COMPARISON OF CEMETERIES D AND E

The number of tombs with pottery excavated in both cemeteries is not equivalent, yet their ceramic distributions, as shown in Table 5.11, are highly informative. Summarily, the quantified ceramic study shows that differentiation between Cemeteries D and E is apparent. For example, in Cemetery E there was a trend toward smaller bowls. In Cemetery D larger family-sized platter bowls were more characteristic.

The vessels in all eight tombs of Cemetery D and all four tombs of Cemetery E distribute as found in Table 5.11. Cemetery E has a significantly higher proportion of M–S bowls (24% versus 4%)[42] and a significantly lower proportion of platter bowls (30% versus 45%).[43] This suggests that M–S Bowls were substituted for platter bowls in Cemetery E. Actually, Cemetery E's proportions of these forms are comparable to those of Field XVI at Bâb adh-Dhrâ', the cultic area (see table 5.15).

A significantly higher proportion of Cemetery E vessels (other than the two cooking pots), 12 of 37, have reddish-yellow core colors as compared to only ten of the 189 in Cemetery D available for a reading.[44] This points to different clay sources or firing techniques. Moreover, only ten of 37 Cemetery E vessels have interior or exterior red slip. In Cemetery D a significantly higher proportion (133 of 197) is slipped.[45] Cemetery D also has a significantly higher proportion of burnished vessels (79 of 197), as compared with only seven of 37 in Cemetery E.[46] Since slip and burnish can reduce the permeability of vessels (see Rice 1987: 230–32), it is possible that the vessels of Cemetery E were not intended to store liquids for any substantial period of time.

As for platter bowls, the proportions of thickened inside rims (70 series), and turned-down (#75) rims are similar among the 88 Cemetery D and 11 Cemetery E Platter Bowls. Cemetery D has 66 thickened inside rims of which 50 are turned-down. Cemetery E has nine thickened inside rims of which seven are turned-down. The rim diameter ranges are similar, but the averages are not. Cemetery E ranges from 17–42 cm, with a median of 22.5 cm and mean of 24.3 cm. Cemetery D ranges from 18–46 cm, with a median of 31 cm and a significantly higher mean of 31.2 cm.[47] The following section presents the data in each category.

Platter Bowls

There were 104 sufficiently complete vessels in the tombs to determine that they were platter bowls. Of the 96 with rims, 73 are in the four tombs with the largest assemblages; they are clearly "life-size," that is, not miniatures, correlating well with Area C. The overall mean rim diameter is 30.9 cm, and the means range from 25.7 to 34.7 cm in the four largest tombs, as shown in Table 5.12. From the changes in

TABLE 5.12 *Four tombs with largest assemblages of platter bowls.*

		RIM DIAMETERS		RIM CODE #				RICHNESS		BEST PHASE MATCH
	No.	MEAN	TWO PEAKS	75	73, 74	70, 71	76	TYPES	INDEX	
D2	38	30.7	No	58%	16%	0%	3%	10	1.62	2
D3	16	34.7	Yes	75%	6%	0%	0%	5	1.25	3
D4	8	31.4		63%	13%	0%	0%	3	1.06	2
D9	11	25.7		55%	27%	9%	0%	4	1.21	1–2

the mean platter bowl rim diameter, rim type percentages, and richness from tomb to tomb, it is possible to infer several things: tomb D3 was used during Phase 3 and tomb D2 during Phase 2, although the one #76 (thickened inside beveled) rim in tomb D2 suggests reuse or continued use during Phase 3 (see table 5.12). Tomb D9 appears to have been used earlier, probably during Phases 1 and 2. Tomb D4 has characteristics of both Phase 2 and Phase 3 (see below).

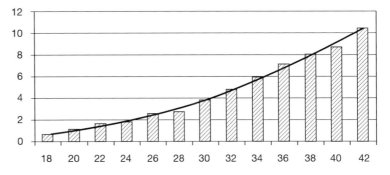

FIG. 5.6 *Estimated capacities of tomb platter bowls.*

The rim diameters of 10 of the 16 platter bowls in D3 are in the same ranges of a two-peak distribution as Phase 3 in Area C (fig. 5.2), which is additional evidence it was used during that phase; namely, first peak of 28–32 cm (figs. 10.11:2, 4, 5, 8; 10.12:1), and second peak of 36–38 cm (figs. 10.11:7; 10.12:3–6).

The pattern of estimated capacities of the fully measurable tomb platter bowls shows that differences in average rim diameter are not trivial. Beginning at 30 cm, the average capacity trend is an increase of about 1 liter for each 2-cm increase in rim diameter (fig. 5.6).

Bowls (L–M)

Tomb D2 has the most L–M bowls, four that are evenly split between simple direct and thickened inside. This is close to the ratio in Phase 2 on the tell. Tomb D4 may have spanned Phases 2 and 3 because it has a bowl that is the only one in the

tombs with a beveled (#76) rim, found on the tell only in Phase 3.

Bowls (M–S)

In Tomb D2 three of the seven M–S bowls have carinated walls, again consistent with Phase 2. Each of the four tombs in Cemetery E has at least one M–S bowl with carinated walls.

Necked Jars

There are 36 necked jars with rims in the tombs. It appears that, unlike platter bowls, they are smaller than "life-size." This is an important distinction between the tell and the tombs. The range of necked jar rim diameters in the tombs is 4.5–12.0 cm, and the mean is 8.8 cm. The capacity range of the four completely drawn necked jars with rim diameters close to this mean is between 0.5 and 1.4 l. In Area C the mean rim diameter of the 40 necked jars is 14.2 cm. The capacity range of the five whole or restored necked jars from the Area B "storeroom" of Khirbat Iskandar with rim diameters close to this mean range between 8.5 and 25.5 l.[48] But these include some with tall, narrow necks[49] of which there are none in the tombs (and none that can be confirmed as such in Area C). In all events, necked jars may have had different purposes. Some, particularly the smaller ones, may have been used for serving or short-term storage, and the larger ones for processing or long-term storage.

Four of the 15 necked jars in D2 have simple direct rims, and 11 have curved-out, flaring rims; both ratios are close to those in Phase 2 of the tell.

Spouted Vessels

The spouted vessels or "teapots" appear to be smaller than those found on the tell. The range of spouted vessel rim diameters in the tombs is 6–12 cm, most are 8 or 9 cm, for which the capacity range is 0.65–1.8 l. But only six of the 18 spouted vessels in the tombs are sufficiently complete to estimate capacity. An example of a small-rimmed (9.5 cm), large capacity, incomplete spouted vessel is in Tomb D3 (fig. 10.13:14). The estimated capacity of the smaller necked jar just to the left of it (fig. 10.13:10) is 6.2 l. In Area C the mean rim diameter of the 31 spouted vessels is 13.9 cm. The capacity range of the three spouted vessels from the "storeroom" that have rim diameters of ten or more cm is 4.5–7.3 l.

When there is more than one in a tomb, spouted vessels come in pairs, one large and one small, as observed on the tell also. There are three large-small pairs in D2 (fig. 10.8:1–6), two in D3 (fig. 10.13:11–14), one in D4 (fig.10.18:1–2), and perhaps one in D9 (fig. 10.23:18–19), although the larger one in D4 is not as large as some in D2 and D3. They might have been intended for dispensing different liquids, or the same liquids to different people; however, given the disturbed nature of the tomb remains, it is impossible to connect individual burials with specific ceramic tomb gifts.

Notably, all of the holemouth jar spouted vessels in the tombs and in the Area B "storeroom" have a common design characteristic that makes them ideal decanters. Each of the 12 in the tombs, drawn with a complete spout attached, and each of the four in the "storeroom" (Richard 2000: fig. 2:11; Richard and Boraas 1987: fig.19: 7–9) has a rim that is level with the bottom of its spout outlet. It could be filled up to the brim of its rim without starting to pour. If filled or nearly filled, it would start pouring at the slightest tilting of the vessel toward the spouted side. As a serving vessel, it could be used for dispensing water, beer or wine. It would also work well for olive oil processing because it would concentrate the lighter oil in the narrowing top part of the vessel above the heavier water and precipitate layers, and the oil could be poured out slowly, with only light to moderate tipping and little disturbance of the lower layers.

Holemouth Bowls

There are no holemouth bowls in the tombs. Whatever they (mostly basins) were used for on the tell was not something needed for serving or other purposes in the tombs.

TOMB SERIATION:
TOMB TO PHASE CORRELATION

A seriation program originally designed for tombs, WinBasp,[50] was applied to test the sequence suggested by the platter bowls, bowls, and necked jars. The Table 5.13 seriation includes 147 of the Khirbat Iskandar vessels from 11 tombs, and 50 of the Bâb adh-Dhrâ' vessels from EB IV Tombs A52 and A54. It uses frequency associations between all of the specific types found in more than one tomb where the tomb has as few as two different types. An early attempt, using a combination of form and rim types, split the assemblages into too many different combinations to yield a sufficient number of connections. Using only the 35 form numbers, which describe the basic shapes and sizes of the vessels, but include no rim type data, yields a stable seriation. The results here followed the sequence of best tomb matches, based on platter bowl rims, from Phase 1 to Phase 3 (see table 5.12) with D9 being seventh, D4 eighth, D2 ninth, and D3 eleventh of the thirteen tombs. The three medium (23–17 cm) platter bowl classifications

TABLE 5.13 *WinBasp seriation of Khirbat Iskandar and Bâb adh-Dhrâ' tombs.*
Input correlation: 0.1594, output correlation: 0.6750, % variance 20.065.

		1 J1	2 A52	3 A54	4 E3	5 D5	6 E10	7 D9	8 D4	9 D2	10 E9	11 D3	12 D10	13 E14	Total
1	4769		2	1											3
2	4798		1	1											2
3	4252		2	2											4
4	4422	1	7	4	1	1		1		2					17
5	4272		2	2			2			2		1			9
6	4066		5	3	1		1	1	2	2	1	2			18
7	4262		4				1	1	1	3					10
8	4626		2							2					4
9	4665		1			1		3		1					6
10	4421	1	1					1		1		1			5
11	4667				1					1					2
12	4232		1									1			2
13	4666		1		1					2	1				5
14	4281		1							2					3
15	4766		1				1			2	1				5
16	4222		1	1					5	6					13
17	4645							2		2					4
18	4605		1	1		1				6	1	4			14
19	4612								1	1					2
20	4625			1					1	1			2		5
21	4659								1	2					3
22	4071							1		1		1			3
23	4762						1	1		2	1			1	6
24	4765									1	1				2
25	4606								1	2		1			4
26	4142									4		1			5
27	4036									3		1			4
28	4857			1						5	2	4	3		15
29	4623									1		1			2
30	4602									1		1			2
31	4231									1		1			2
32	4856							1		2		3		1	7
33	4568									1		2			3
34	4141									2				1	3
35	4538									1		1		1	3
	Total	2	33	17	4	3	6	12	12	65	8	26	5	4	197

(4665, 4666 and 4667) are all in the first third of the form seriation, and all four of the very large (31+ cm) platter bowl classifications (4602, 4605, 4606 and 4612) are in the latter half. This mirrors the shift in size distributions through the phases in Area C (see table 5.1). Not surprisingly, M–S bowls with closed, curved walls (4766; 4769) are in the early half of the sequence, and those with carinated walls (4762; 4765) do not appear until the last third. The seriations enable the following additional inferences:

1. Since D2 has 31 of the 35 types, this tomb probably covers much of EB IV.

2. Cemeteries D and E were in use during most, if not all, of EB IV.

3. Interments in Tombs E14 and D10 took place during Phase 3.

4. Spouted vessels are not part of the tomb tradition in late EB IV. The only two sizeable Khirbat Iskandar tomb assemblages in the seriation that lack them (see table 5.10) are D10 and E14, the last two in the seriation. Both Bâb adh-Dhrâʿ tombs have spouted vessels.

5. Bâb adh-Dhrâʿ Tombs A52 and A54 are early EB IV. This is consistent with the observation that only four of their 13 platter bowls have thickened inside, turned-down (#75) rims. The excavators reached the same conclusion by noting the absence of the distinctive larger lamps and everted rim bowls of the cultic Field XVI (Rast and Schaub 2003:446).

6. Necked jars increase in size from early to late. All three of the small necked jar forms (4262; 4272; 4281) are in the first half of the form seriation, and both large necked jar forms (4141; 4142) are in the last third.

7. Necked jars with tall, wide neck, mid-range tangent, global to rounded (4141; 4231) do not appear until nearly the end of the sequence.

There is less evidence for sequencing the other tombs. Tomb H3 has eight vessels, but provides little information except for the presence of two platter bowls with turned-down (#75) rims, and the absence of spouted vessels, both of which point to Phase 3. Tomb D7 has only platter bowls, but two of three have thickened inside, turned-down

TABLE 5.14 *EB IV tomb–tell phase correspondence.*

Seriation	Tomb	P. 1				P. 2			P. 3		
1	J1	×	×	×							
2	A52	×	×	×	×						
3	A54	×	×	×	×	×					
4	E3	×	×	×	×						
5	D5	×	×	×	×						
6	E10					×	×	×	×		
7	D9		×	×	×	×					
	D7					×	×	×			
8	D4					×	×	×	×		
9	D2			×	×	×	×	×			
10	E9					×	×	×	×		
11	D3								×	×	×
12	D10								×	×	×
13	E14								×	×	×
	H3								×	×	×

(#75) rims, and none of the three corresponds with the two rim diameter peaks of Phase 3, which suggests correspondence with Phase 2. Tomb E10 has a platter bowl with a thickened inside, beveled (#76) rim, which suggests use continued into Phase 3. Considering all of the above, the most likely tomb-phase correspondence is set forth in Table 5.14. (Tombs D1, D testpit and H2 have only one vessel each, none of which points to a phase.)

COMPARISONS WITH EB IV (STRATUM I) ASSEMBLAGES AT BÂB ADH-DHRÂʿ

The comparative analysis with Bâb adh-Dhrâʿ includes both Field XVI (the cultic area) and Field X, the village outside the city walls. Because the former context is a specialized area, an initial comparison with Khirbat Iskandar Area C is made separately for Field XVI and Field X. With the six Field XVI, 25 Field X, and 53 Area C cooking pots removed, the ceramic distributions at Bâb adh-Dhrâʿ, compared with Khirbat Iskandar Area C, are those found in Table 5.15. While there are some differences between the distributions in Field

X and Area C, their profiles are closer than either is to Field XVI.

The general characteristics of the assemblage in Field XVI include the following: there are no holemouth bowls (similar to the tombs at both sites); smaller bowl forms are much more numerous than in Field X and Area C (perhaps indicating the need for individual servings in a cultic context); there is a higher proportion of lamps than found in Field X or Area C; there is a proportionate higher percentage of fine ware (Rast and Schaub 2003: 443). As for the characteristics in Field X, there are: proportionately fewer holemouth bowls; fewer L–M deep bowls and spouted vessels (suggesting less intensive processing activity than in Area C); more M–S bowls than in Area C. What follows is a statistical analysis of ceramic categories at Bâb adh-Dhrâ' with reference to Area C, starting in each case with a comparison between Area C and Field X.

Platter Bowls

Like Area C, more than 70 percent of the platter bowls in Field X have thickened inside (70 series) rims. As noted by Rast and Schaub (2003: 439–40), the sequence of platter bowls at Bâb adh-Dhrâ' shows the flat and rolled rim platter bowls are superseded by the turned-down thickened rims. This general sequence correlates well with the platter bowl sequence in Area C, although the latter is more gradual (compare fig. 5.3 with fig. 5.7). There is also a good match up for the earliest phases at both sites in the platter bowl distributions of Phase C of Field X and Phase 1 of Area C; namely, in Field X, 26 of 45 platter bowls have either #73 or #74 rims (thickened inside: rolled or rolled and pointed), and have a mean rim diameter about 2 cm less than those in the next phase, much like Phase 1 in Area C (see table 5.16).

TABLE 5.15 *Distribution of forms at Bâb adh-Dhrâ' and Khirbat Iskandar.*

	FIELD XVI		FIELD X		AREA C	
	No.	%	No.	%	No.	%
holemouth bowl	0	0%	11	4%	19	6%
holemouth jar	4	1%	13	4%	11	3%
lamp	15	5%	3	1%	4	1%
L-M bowl	21	6%	24	8%	35	11%
M-S bowl	83	26%	42	14%	23	7%
small shallow bowl	38	12%	2	1%	0	0%
necked jar	61	19%	46	15%	41	13%
spouted vessel	6	2%	17	5%	33	10%
pitcher/juglet	1	0%	3	1%	7	2%
platter bowl	95	29%	150	48%	145	46%
TOTAL	324	100%	311	100%	318	100%

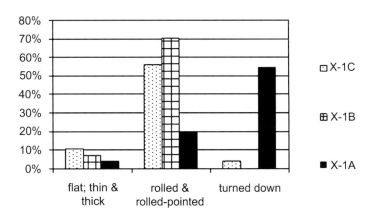

FIG. 5.7   *Rim shape changes of platter bowls in Bâb adh-Drâ' Field X.*

Finally, like the platter bowls in Phase 3 of Area C, the platter bowls of Phase A of Field X show a decrease in richness, down from an index of 1.54 in Phase B to 1.03 in Phase A. In Phase A there are no large platter bowls with #76 (thickened inside, beveled) rims, but there are three medium platter bowls with rim shapes identified as simple direct, beveled (#13) that are similar to those of Area C #76 rims (Rast and Schaub 2003: pl. 130:12, 22, 23).

The mean rim diameters of Field X Phase B and Phase A platter bowls are 2–3 cm less those of Area C Phases 2 and 3 (compare tables 5.16 and

TABLE 5.16 *Field X platter bowl rim diameter averages and ranges.*

	P. C	P. B	P. A
mean	28.8	30.7	30.5
median	30	31	33
range	18–50	20–44	18–50

5.2), representing an estimated average capacity difference of 1.0–1.5 l.

For Bâb adh-Dhrâ', the excavators concluded that a stratigraphic correspondence exists between Phase B of Field XVI and Phase A of Field X, in part because 94 percent of the examples of turned-down (#75) rims are in the two field-phases (Rast and Schaub 2003: 440). Seventy-five of the 155 platter bowls in this "concatenated phase" have #75 rims (Rast and Schaub 2003: table 13.5), and rolled and rolled pointed rims virtually disappear, making it a good match for either Phase 2 or Phase 3 of Area C.

Cooking Pots

At Bâb adh-Dhrâ', like Area C, there is a typo-chronological trend from holemouth to necked jar cooking pots; namely, all 13 of the cooking pots in the earliest level, Phase C of Field X, are hole-mouths (of which nine have simple direct bulbous rims); Phase B has one holemouth jar cooking pot and seven necked jar cooking pots; and in the latest level, Phase A has one holemouth jar and six necked jar cooking pots (compare with table 5.5). Unlike in the Khirbat Iskandar assemblage, there are no holemouth bowl cooking pots in Phase A, which suggests that it may have ended earlier than Area C Phase 3.

Surprisingly, five of the six cooking pots in the other part of the concatenated phase (Field XVI, Phase B) are *holemouth* jars (the sixth is a spouted vessel). This counter-trend could be attributable either to the different nature of the food to be prepared or to the observance of an earlier tradition for cooking pot forms.

L–M Bowls

Although nearly all L–M bowls at Bâb adh-Dhrâ' have simple direct rims, thickened inside rims (2) do not appear until late, in the concatenated Field XVI, Phase B. This is consistent with the Area C trend from simple direct to thickened inside rims.

M–S Bowls

As in Area C, the cyma-profiled (carinated) M–S bowl first appears late, only in the concatenated Phase B of Field XVI. This is consistent with the Area C trend to increasing cyma-profiled (carinated) M–S bowls, especially in Phase 3.

Necked Jars (excluding Cooking Pots)

Unlike Area C, there is no increase from early to late in necked jars with curved-out, flared (60 series) rims in Field X. In Phase A, *none* of the 25 necked jars has a curved-out rim. The concatenated Field X-A/Field XVI-B has only a minority of 18 of the 83 total necked jars with curved-out rims. By contrast, most Area C Phase 3 necked jars have curved-out rims.

Spouted Vessels

Large-small "teapot" pairings found in Area C also appear in Field X at Bâb adh-Dhrâ': Phase C, Field 3, Locus 57 (pl. 124:08, 12), Phase A, Field 1, Locus 27 (pl. 131:1, 3–4), and Phase A, Field 2, Locus 1 (pl. 131:36–38).

Phase-to-Phase Correlation

According to the excavators of Bâb adh-Dhrâ', Field X, Phase A equals Field XVI, Phase B (Rast and Schaub 2003: 440). Considering all of the above-mentioned phase-to-phase similarities and differences in the ceramic corpora of the two sites, the present study suggests that Area C Phase 1 corresponds with Field X Phase C, Area C Phase 2 corresponds with Field X Phase B, and Area C Phase 3 corresponds with Field X Phase A/Field XVI Phase B.

NOTES

1 Magness-Gardiner and Falconer detected significant intra- and inter-phase differences in the distributions of cooking, storage, or serving vessels in temple interiors, temple courtyards, or domestic areas in the Middle Bronze Age village of Tall al-Hayyât (Magness-Gardiner and Falconer 1994).

2 Added to the 149 rim diagnostics in Phase 2 are one spouted vessel for a lug handle (pl. 22.5), and two lamps for fragments too small to draw (Locus C01036, Reg. C01.40.08, and Locus C06019, Reg. C06.37.04).

3 Added to the 154 rim diagnostics are one spouted vessel for a spout (pl. 21:9), one jug for a functional lug handle (pl. 22:19), and one lamp for a fragment too small to draw (Locus C03016, Reg. C03.63.07/08).

4 For example, if cooking pots were included, the percentage of Phase 1 holemouth jars would be much higher (32%).

5 See Magness-Gardiner and Falconer 1994.

6 $F = 5.36$, $p = 0.023$. (The presence of an "F" indicates an ANOVA.)

7 Estimated from trend line in fig. 5.6.

8 $X^2 = 4.403$, $p = 0.036$. (The presence of an "X^2" symbol indicates a chi-squared test.)

9 $X^2 = 7.271$, $p = 0.007$.

10 $X^2 = 2.414$, $p = 0.137$.

11 $X^2 = 9.305$, $p = 0.002$.

12 $P = 0.070$. (The absence of an "X^2" and an "F" indicates a Fisher's Exact Test.)

13 $X^2 = 6.407$, $p = 0.011$.

14 $P = 0.143$.

15 Menhinick Index: number of categories, divided by the square root of the number in the sample.

16 $F = 3.476$, $p = 0.081$.

17 $X^2 = 5.400$, $p = 0.020$.

18 $P = 0.125$.

19 $P = 0.008$.

20 $P = 0.167$.

21 $P = 0.167$.

22 $P = 0.152$.

23 $P = 0.152$.

24 $P = 0.144$.

25 $P = 0.021$.

26 $P = 0.176$.

27 $P = 0.027$.

28 $P = 0.080$.

29 $P = 0.002$.

30 $X^2 = 3.430$, $p = 0.064$.

31 $P = 0.091$.

32 $P = 0.101$.

33 $X^2 = 2.695$, $p = 0.101$.

34 $F = 4.225$, $p = 0.054$.

35 $P = 0.241$.

36 One #17a is added to the Phase 2 numbers for the one handle attached to the platter bowl (pl. 14:8).

37 $P = 0.007$.

38 $P = 0.161$.

39 Robert R. Sauders (Sauders 2001: 49) made all of the Area C readings on fresh breaks under a Sylvania 75 watt / 120 volt, double life "Softwhite" incandescent bulb.

40 Rast and Schaub 2003: 426, fig. 13.1.

41 Confidence levels equal, in each case, 100 percent *minus* the probability ("p") that the observed difference is due to the vagaries of sampling. The latter figure is expressed in the endnotes as a portion of 1.000. That portion is converted to a percentage before it is subtracted from 100%. For example, if $p = 0.015$ this would convert to 1.5 percent and, subtracted from 100 percent, would equal 98.5 percent.

42 $X^2 = 18.985$, $p < 0.001$.

43 $X^2 = 2.849$, $p = 0.091$.

44 $X^2 = 25.941$, $p < 0.001$.

45 $X^2 = 21.484$, $p < 0.001$.

46 $X^2 = 6.013$, $p = 0.014$.

47 $F = 5.160$, $p = 0.025$.

48 These wide variations are attributable to the fact that the *maximum* diameter (width), or even the *height*, is a much better predictor of capacity than rim diameter. Unfortunately, rim diameter is the only measurement available for necked jars in Area C. Nevertheless, rim diameters correlate somewhat with capacities.

49 A correlation between height of neck and capacity has been noted for tall, narrow necked jars in an EB IV tomb context (Gitin 1975).

50 WinBasp Version 5.43, © The Unkelbach Valley Software Works 2007.

Chapter 6

Ceramic Technology and Provenance at Khirbat Iskandar

by Yuval Goren

INTRODUCTION AND FOCUS

This chapter presents the results of a petrographic study of representative pottery samples from the site of Khirbat Iskandar. Petrographic examinations of thin sections from over sixty vessels, representing the principal wares at the site, form the basis of this analysis. The objective of the study was to understand the nature of the local pottery production and to distinguish local from imported wares. By using mineralogical and geological considerations, together with the existing database of petrographic fabric groups of pottery assemblages from other southern Levantine Early Bronze Age III–IV (EB III– IV) sites, it was possible to suggest the provenience of imported vessels. The latter could then be used to reconstruct the nature of the intra-site relations of Khirbat Iskandar with other sites.

Utilizing a petrographic analysis of pottery, the author attempted to determine the internal relations and centers of gravity of the major EB IV sites in southern and central Israel and southern Jordan (Goren 1996). The results indicated that while nearly all of the pottery from Nahal Refaim, a major site in the vicinity of present-day Jerusalem, was

locally produced, the situation in the contemporary desert sites of the central Negev was completely different. Among the latter, only Har Yeruham contained evidences for local ceramic production, as indicated both by the archaeological data and the petrographic results, and the products of its workshop showed very limited distribution.

Within the study area, the majority of the pottery from the other major sites, En Ziq, Be'er Resisim, Nahal Nissana, Har Sayyad, and Mashabei Sade, derived primarily from three external sources: west-central Jordan (namely the area to the east of the Dead Sea Rift Valley), southwest Jordan (the eastern 'Arabah Valley), and the Judean Mountains. Minor amounts of pottery originated from the northern Negev (the Beer-Sheva and/or Arad Valleys) and, presumably, from the southern Negev. Only one vessel from Be'er Resisim was an import from the northern area of the Beth-Shean Valley in northern Israel. On the other hand, vessels from EB IV sites in northern Israel, such as Tel 'Amal (Goren 1991b) and 'Ein el-Helu (Covello-Paran 1999: 74–75) yielded no southern wares.

The main conclusion of the study was that it is very likely that the areas east of the Jordan Rift Valley, especially to the east of the Dead Sea and the 'Arabah Valleys, greatly influenced the central Negev sites socio-economically. In particular, the exploitation of copper in the Faynan area and its assumed trade with Egypt during the epoch of the First Intermediate Period seemed to be the most significant trigger (Goren 1996). Another outcome of the study was the recognition of the continuity of some earlier Early Bronze Age ceramic technological traditions in some of the typical wares versus the introduction of entirely new ones in others. This was interpreted as reflecting a longer sequence for some of the Negev EB IV sites than previously thought, ranging throughout the EB III–IV sequence, and a shorter sequence of only EB IV occupation in others.

The reports of the excavations at Khirbat Hamra Ifdan (Levy and Adams 2001; Levy, Adams, and Najjar 2001; Levy et al. 2001; 2002), published shortly after the above study, affirmed the conclusions. The site, which yielded massive EB III–IV copper production activity, in combination with the occupation levels at Barqa al-Hetiye (Adams 2003), demonstrated that this area of the southern 'Arabah was populated in EB III, unlike the picture suggested by the excavators of the Negev sites. With this new data in mind, it was possible (as predicted) to link the south Jordanian fabric groups of the previous study (Goren 1996) with this specific area and, naturally, with the copper production centers.

The examination of the pottery from the EB IV sites along the overland route between Egypt and the Levant on the northern Sinai coast (Oren and Yekutieli 1990, petrographically examined by Goren), demonstrated that the south Jordanian fabric groups appeared there also. However, they did not appear in sites in central Cisjordan, including Nahal Refaim (Goren 1996), Jebel Qa'aqir (Glass, in London 1985) and Manhat (examined by Goren, as yet unpublished), as well as the surveyed sites in the Samaria Highlands (examined by Goren, as yet unpublished). This absence indicates that central Cisjordan was outside the confines of the copper-based economic system. At the same time, however, the presence in the Central Negev sites of significant levels of the "Moza clay - dolomitic sand" fabric group of the Judean Mountains witnesses contact between the Central Hill Country with the desert area of the central Negev.

In summary, the previous study and the more restricted examinations that followed indicate a complex social and economic system interrelating the areas of central and southern Cisjordan and southern Transjordan (Goren 1996). This picture is by far more complex than can be explained by nomadic, pastoral, or rural subsistence patterns, as assigned to the EB IV inhabitants by some earlier scholars (such as Albright 1962; Amiran 1960; 1969; Cohen 1986; 1992; Dever 1973; 1980; 1985a–b; 1992; 1995; Falconer 1987; Finkelstein 1991; Kochavi 1967).

The main goal of the present study was to investigate how the site of Khirbat Iskandar—located in west-central Jordan east of the Dead Sea, and being as yet the sole settlement to feature some urban features in the period (Richard 1987a–b; Richard and Boraas 1988)—related to this complex social and economic framework. It was necessary to examine its ceramic assemblage by the same analytical tools in order to complement the previous work and to test further the nature of interrelationships in central and southern Jordan and Israel.

THE GEOLOGICAL SETTING OF THE SITE AND ITS ENVIRONMENT

Khirbat Iskandar is located on the plateau on the northern bank of Wâdi al-Wâla, between Dhiban in the south and Madaba in the north. The local geology and pedology at the exploitable area around the site include a rather limited choice of available raw materials that might be used for pottery production. These include some of the local soils and clay formations that expose within a range of about 5–10 km of the site.

The source of information for the local soil types includes the soil maps of the National Soil Map and Land Use Project (NSMLUP), conducted by the Ministry of Agriculture of The Hashemite Kingdom of Jordan, the Royal Jordanian Geographic Centre, and Huntings Technical Service (1989–1995). The soil region of Khirbat Iskandar covers the entire area of the northern highlands dissected limestone plateau of Jordan, extending from the Yarmouk

River in the north to Wâdi al-Wâla in the south. The entire region is typical of the Mediterranean sub-humid climatic zone, with a range in precipitation between 250 mm and 500 mm. The region contains a wide range of soil types, reflecting the range of physical characteristics. Xerochrepts and chromoxererts are the major soils with the typical subgroup predominantly in the western half of the region and calcixerollic in the eastern half. Lithic subgroups occur on the shallow eroded areas of the steeper slopes and, in particular, on the hilltops and upper slopes from which most of the residual soils have been eroded. Soils of this region are mainly clay and considered the most rainfed productive soils in Jordan.

The local lithology around the site consists of a set of geological formations belonging to the Belqa Group (Bender 1974; Al Hunjul 1985). These formations are the Wâdi Umm Ghudran, the Amman Silicified Limestone, the Al-Hisa Phosphorite, and the Muwaqqar Chalk-Marl Formations. The bulk sediments of this group comprise chalk, dolomite, silicified and marly limestone, flint, phosphorite, and marl. These will be discussed in more detail below.

METHOD

The petrographic examination of the pottery assemblage from Khirbat Iskandar was carried out after receiving a selection of samples of representative wares from the excavators. The samples were chosen on the basis of both the typology of the vessels and their raw materials as seen under a magnifying glass. After the preparation of the thin sections, they were examined under a petrographic (polarizing) Zeiss Axiolab-Pol microscope at magnifications ranging between 50× and 400× (a detailed inventory of the thin sections is presented in Appendix G).

During the petrographic analysis, the samples were divided into petrographic fabric groups. A fabric group encompasses vessels sharing similar petrographic affinities in both clay and temper. The quality of raw materials alone, regardless of variables such as typology, chronology, and geographic location of the site, determines this classification.

Therefore, it may serve as an independent technical criterion for a comparative assortment of ceramic assemblages. In previous studies, it was possible to define many fabric groups and to correlate them with specific lithological environments (Goren, Finkelstein and Naʿaman 2004, with more references therein). These are fabrics bearing typical attributes that allow for a reasonable assessment of their geographical origin, and thus may be used for provenance studies. Given the limited number of fabric groups traced in the pottery assemblage under discussion, it was possible to determine their provenance on the basis of these comparisons and on the typical lithological "fingerprint" of each one of them.

RESULTS

The examined vessels divide into several fabric groups according to their petrographic properties. By their dominance and lithological properties, the two main fabrics most likely represent the local products at the site of Khirbat Iskandar. The other fabrics, based on their lithology and on the data obtained from other contemporary assemblages studied by the author, probably reflect other production areas.

Khirbat Iskandar Fabric Group A: Marly Matrix with Calcareous, Flint, and Phosphorite Inclusions

The matrix (fig. 6.1) is characterized by calcareous clay, sometimes silty and usually very rich in opaque minerals; the latter were identified as iron oxides (usually hematite or "limonite"). The matrix is often optically active with apparent zoning, exhibiting striated b-fabric. In other cases the matrix is rich in fine, fibrous carbonate crystals, sometimes exhibiting weak optical orientation. Well-sorted, sparsely distributed silty quartz appears in many cases.

The inclusions contain sand-sized rock fragments, all pointing to the Santonian-Campanian or Maastrichtian lithological environment of the Belqa Group. These include chalk, replacement flint with common styloliths, often with silicified phosphorite. Calcitic phosphorite also occurs, including phosphatic ooids and occasional fossil fish bone fragments. In many cases, dolomite rhombs also appear.

Based on its lithological, mineralogical, and palaeontological affinities, this fabric group is identified as marl of or clay with an inclusion assemblage, all derived from the Amman Silicified Limestone and the Al-Hisa Phosphorite Formation of the Belqa Group in Jordan. Therefore, the immediate vicinity of Khirbat Iskandar is highly likely the source of this fabric. This is mainly attested by the various facies of the phosphorite, flint, and chalk that are represented by the inclusion assemblage. The late Campanian to probably early Maastrichtian Al-Hisa Phosphorite Formation consists of phosphorite beds with intercalations of marl, chalky marl, limestone, flint, and oyster-coquinal layers (Barjous 1992: 31–41; Shinaq and Bandel 1998) and can be easily distinguished from the underlying Amman Silicified Limestone Formation, which is generally composed of hard, massive flints and silicified limestone beds. The upwards, gradual disappearance of phosphate and flint beds and the domination of massive marl, chalky marl, and marly limestones differentiate the upper part of the formation from the overlying Muwaqqar Chalk-Marl Formation.

Inspection and thin-section investigation of Al-Hisa Phosphorite Formation have identified two primary microfacies, described from bottom to top as phosphatized skeletal-pack-rudstone (made up of brown, very well-rounded, well-sorted, spherical to ovoid-shaped, phosphatized skeletal bones, shark teeth and peloids, aggregate grains, reworked black phosphatized lithoclasts, and echinoderm bioclasts) and bioclastic foraminiferal gastropod-floatstone (composed of brown, very well-rounded, well-sorted, spherical-shaped, phosphatized peloids, foraminifera, gastropods, brachiopods, isolated echinoderm remains, reworked black phosphatized lithoclasts, phosphatized skeletal bones, shark teeth and scales, and laminoid-fenestral fabrics [birdseyes-structures]) (Shinaq et al. 2006).

A belt of Upper Cretaceous–Eocene phosphorite province extends from Syria and Iraq through Cisjordan and Transjordan to North Africa, up

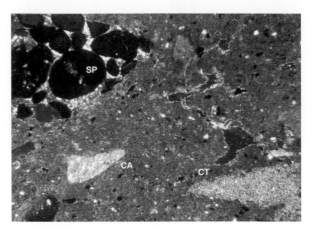

FIG. 6.1   *Khirbat Iskandar Fabric Group A: marly matrix with calcareous, flint, and phosphorite inclusions. SP: silicified phosphorite, CT: flint, CA: calcite. Crossed polarizers, field length: 1.5 mm.*

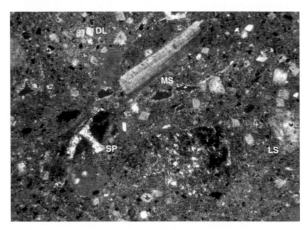

FIG. 6.2   *Khirbat Iskandar Fabric Group B: marly matrix with dolomite inclusions. DL: dolomite rhombs, MS: mollusk shell fragment, SP: silicified phosphorite, LS: limestone. Crossed polarizers, field length: 1.5 mm.*

FIG. 6.3   *Khirbat Iskandar Fabric Group C: marly matrix with crushed calcite inclusions. Crossed polarizers, field length: 1.5 mm.*

to Togo and Senegal. The beds are remarkably similar in texture and constitution across the whole province. Within southern Cisjordan, these upper Campanian layers form the uppermost member of the Mishash Formation. The equivalent Transjordanian phosphorites are commonly considered as Maastrichtian, yet on the basis of palaeontological studies there is a marked similarity between the faunal assemblage in the Cisjordan and Transjordanian phosphorites. On the other hand, many of the above components, which typify the Transjordanian section of the entire group, do not exist in the geological section west of the Rift Valley. This includes, for example, the dolomite-rich and the oyster-coquinal layers. Therefore, the local Transjordanian provenance of this fabric group is evident, and the entire group should be considered local to the general area of Khirbat Iskandar.

Phosphate is of major economic importance and ranks very high in terms of gross annual tonnage and volume of world trade, since it is widely used as fertilizer. In Transjordan, phosphorite outcrops are distributed in six major zones: near Rusayfa, in Al-Hisa, in Sweileh, around Qatrana, near Maʻan, and near Eshidiya. In Cisjordan, two main large concentrations exist; the larger one in terms of economic value is situated in the northeastern Negev, along the Oron-Efʻe, ʻZin, and Haʻzera synclines, and in the southern and central Judean Desert. On archaeological grounds, the Transjordanian origin should be favored, since no significant Early Bronze Age sites exist in the Cisjordan regions mentioned here. Moreover, in the Central Negev sites this fabric group has not been observed.

Khirbat Iskandar Fabric Group B: Marly Matrix with Dolomite Inclusions

This fabric group (fig. 6.2) is closely related to fabric group A, but the inclusions are dominated by dolomite rhombs. The other inclusion types also resemble those of fabric group A. It is apparently derived from the same lithostratigraphic unit, but from the marl units found in contact with the dolomitic component of the Mawaqqar Chalk-Marl Formation. Therefore, the separation between fabric groups A and B is merely technical.

Khirbat Iskandar Fabric Group C: Marly Matrix with Crushed Calcite Inclusions

In this fabric group (fig. 6.3), the matrix is calcareous (marly) as above. However, the inclusion assemblage is formed mainly by pure calcite particles with the addition of some limestone and voids resulting from the presence of vegetal matter. The calcite crystals are clear, exhibit typical twinning and zoning features, and split by their cleavage plains, indicating that the craftsman intentionally crushed them prior to their mixture in the paste. The process of mining the mineral, usually from naturally-occurring veins in limestone, carefully crushing it, and mixing it in the matrix was most likely more elaborate and time-consuming than the use of the more available wâdi sand, commonly used in antiquity as temper.

The use of calcite as temper is known to increase the thermal-shock resistance of the clay body and reduce its porosity. This is due to the rather similar expansion rates of calcite and clay. Pure calcite is superior to limestone (formed mainly of calcite) because it decarbonates at higher temperatures and thus is more resistant to heating. For these reasons, crushed calcite is common as tempering material of cooking pots and holemouth jars from the Early Bronze Age I to the end of the Iron Age, when it is replaced by other tempers. Indeed, the vessels in the Khirbat Iskandar assemblage that belong to this fabric group include a cooking pot and a holemouth jar.

Khirbat Iskandar Fabric Group D: Lower Cretaceous Shales

This fabric (fig. 6.4) is characterized by the use of argillaceous, ferruginous, shale-rich clay, or fine non-calcareous, homogenous clay with clear optical orientation under the microscope. The first type is usually accompanied by relatively high contents of silt and typical ferruginous ooliths (spherical to elliptical bodies, 0.25 to 2.00 mm in diameter, which have concentric or radial structures). Some ooliths are developed around quartz grains; others have no internal structure. In most of the thin-sections, quartz sand appears, usually as

Khirbat Iskandar Fabric Group F: Marly Matrix with Calcareous and Basaltic Sand

There is only one example of this fabric (fig. 6.6) represented in the Khirbat Iskandar pottery examined: sample no. 60 (storage jar). Its characteristics are a marly clay rich in foraminifera and tempered with sand containing alkali-olivine basalt, limestone, and chalk. This fabric group dominates ceramic assemblages of the central Jordan valley, including Munhata (Goren 1992), Sha'ar Ha-Golan(Goren 1991a), and, in the EB IV period, the ceramic assemblage of Tel 'Amal (Goren 1991b). For the reasons explained by Goren and Fischer (1999), the provenience of fabric group F should be the central Jordan Valley, between Beth-Shean and Wâdi az-Zarqa'. This is the only area where one can find all the components discussed above.

DISCUSSION AND CONCLUSIONS

The results of the petrographic study of the selected vessels from Khirbat Iskandar indicate that the major part of the ceramic assemblage is of local production. Imported pottery was limited to the neighboring areas of the Jordan Rift Valley, especially the Dead Sea basin. It is significant that the single vessel found to be a northern import belongs to the Jezreel–Beth Shean valleys group, representing a family of vessels bearing clear earlier Early Bronze Age stylistic affinities. Within the examined assemblage, there was not a single vessel found to belong to any of the known fabric groups attributed to the Central Hill Country of Cisjordan, the Shephelah, the Northern Negev, or the 'Arabah Valley (Goren 1996). The only possible exception to this observation is the group of holemouth jars belonging to Khirbat Iskandar fabric group E. The latter's provenance, attributed to the 'Uvda Valley area up to now, could also derive from some parts of central and southern Transjordan, for the reasons explained above.

As far as pottery exchange is concerned, the developing picture appears to depict a separation of Khirbat Iskandar from the areas west of the Jordan or south of the Dead Sea, including the copper-rich area of Faynan. The last point is significant, because the excavations at Khirbat Hamra Ifdan and Barqa al-Hetiye both underscore continuous EB III–IV occupation in the Faynan. If pottery transportation indeed indicates direct contacts between sites, then we may infer that the two regions developed independently throughout this sequence, having no direct economic contacts. Since the development of Khirbat Hamra Ifdan can be related directly and primarily with the mining and production of copper, it suggests that Khirbat Iskandar had little if anything to do with this economic activity during that time. In terms of ceramic provenance, while the intersite connections of the Faynan area seem to orient westwards, towards the Central Negev highlands and the overland route of Northern Sinai, the intersite relations of Khirbat Iskandar do not extend westward beyond the range of the Jordan Rift Valley, but they do extend northwards to some extent.

The main conclusion to draw from the results of the present study is that the EB IV economy characteristically manifests localized processes primarily. In the Mediterranean sub-humid climatic zones of the southern Levant, there was a phase of ruralism and localized material culture traditions both at the dawn and decline of Early Bronze Age urbanization. In the arid zones of Cisjordan and Transjordan, however, the decline of the urban centers was followed by societies that relied strongly on copper production together with pastoral modes of subsistence. In this respect, it would be justified to distinguish a "southern" from a "northern" development of EB I–III cultures into the EB IV period, as they appear to reflect different socio-economic occurrences.

Chapter 7

Faunal Remains from Area C

by Mary C. Metzger

The Khirbat Iskandar Excavations have focused on the EB IV period, following the disruption in urban settlement patterns that took place at the close of EB III. The results of the Area C excavations, along with other work on the mound, have affirmed that permanent sedentary settlements existed in the EB IV period. Combined with numerous other permanent sites in Jordan, the Khirbat Iskandar evidence qualifies past studies that emphasized pastoral nomadism for the period, at the expense of the sedentary element. The role of faunal analysis at Khirbat Iskandar is to provide a profile of subsistence strategies of this long-lived EB IV community.

The expedition recovered over 1,000 animal bones, teeth, and bone fragments in Area C (see Appendix G for a complete inventory). Of these, slightly over 300 could be identified as to species and anatomical element. The species represented are: sheep (*Ovis aries*), goat (*Capra hircus*), cattle (*Bos taurus*), pig (*Sus scrofa*), and equid, probably domestic donkey (*Equus asinus*). One bird bone represents the rock dove (*Columba livia*), which is native to the region. The sheep/goat cohort represented about 92% of the total (284 bones). A subset of this sheep/goat assemblage, used to consider carcass distribution patterns, totaled 250 specimens. Bones from within this total were considered to determine survivorship patterns. Within this subset of bones, it was possible to identify six as sheep and eight as goat.

Faunal remains were most numerous in Phases 2 and 3, whereas in Phase 1 they were less abundant. Although the small number of bones in Phase 1 may be due to the small area exposed, it also may reflect a carcass deposition pattern that shifted over time. For a list of the numbers within the sheep/goat cohort and cattle and pig assemblages by chronological phase, see Table 7.1.

SHEEP/GOAT ASSEMBLAGE

Carcass Distribution

Sheep/goat bones, teeth, and bone fragments at the site represent primary butchering. The presence of many bones with low meat utility, such as mandibles and teeth, metapodials, carpals, and tarsals, suggests this pattern. Other elements, such as humerii and femurii, represent meat-rich portions. There is no indication of secondary butchering, in which consumers prepare specific cuts acquired

TABLE 7.1 *List of Phase 1–3 faunal species distribution at Khirbat Iskandar.*

	P. 1	P. 2	P. 3
Sheep/Goat	31	124	129
Cattle	1	14	9
Pig	1	3	2
Equid	0	0	2

from the producer. Table 7.2 illustrates the sheep/goat carcass distribution pattern.

Survivorship

A subset of the Area C collection, used to consider sheep/goat survivorship, totaled 131 specimens. Table 7.3 lists the slaughter schedules based on bone fusion rates, calculated according to Silver (1969). Given the sample size of Phases 2–3, it is possible to draw firm conclusions about survivorship. Sheep and goats reach maturity at about two years. The Phase 2 and Phase 3 sheep/goat cohort shows the greatest kill-off at about age 2 to 2 ½ years. Tooth wear patterns also suggest this conclusion.

These data are consistent with a strategy to maximize herd security and offtake of meat (Payne 1973; Horwitz 1989), while maintaining older animals for reproductive purposes and for furnishing wool and hair (Redding 1981; Payne 1973).

Sheep and goat husbandry predominated at Khirbat Iskandar, but these animals existed alongside cattle and, to a small extent, pigs. Cattle were probably used for traction with dairying a secondary benefit. Pigs, usually slaughtered before age two, supplied a meat resource.

ENVIRONMENTAL CONSIDERATIONS

Khirbat Iskandar has an average annual precipitation between 200 and 300 mm per year (*Climatic Atlas of Jordan* 1971: 11; Bender 1974: 10; and see Ch. 2). This was sufficient to support sheep and goat herding, but insufficient to support pig husbandry on any significant scale. This accords with the record at the Early Bronze site of Bâb adh-Dhrâ'

TABLE 7.2 *List of sheep/goat carcass distribution at Khirbat Iskandar.*

	P. 1	P. 2	P. 3
Cranium	0	12	11
Mandibles + Teeth	2	16	13
Scapulae + Humerii	0	17	24
Radii + Ulnae	2	15	5
Atlas + Axis	0	1	1
Metapodials	4	9	7
Carpals + Tarsals	2	10	15
Innominate	4	14	20
Femurii + Tibiae	8	8	17
Phalanges	7	4	2
Total	29	106	115

TABLE 7.3 *List of ovi-caprid Phases 1–3 survivorship patterns at Khirbat Iskandar.*

Phase 1			
Age at fusion	Total	No. Fused	% Fused
6–10 months	3	2	67
12–16	4	4	100
18–28	2	2	100
30–36	1	1	100
36–42	3	0	0

Phase 2			
Age at fusion	Total	No. Fused	% Fused
6–10 months	30	26	87
12–16	10	9	90
18–28	7	5	71
30–36	12	6	50
36–42	5	1	20

Phase 3			
Age at fusion	Total	No. Fused	% Fused
6–10 months	22	20	91
12–16	6	6	100
18–28	12	7	58
30–36	8	7	87
36–42	6	1	17

(Finnegan 1978; 1981) and the environmentally similar location of Early Bronze Age Arad (Lernau 1978). Whereas swine husbandry would have been challenging at Iskandar, the EB IV–MBII site of Tall al-Hayyât in the Jordan Valley, which is along the 350 mm isohyet, demonstrated greater reliance on pigs (Falconer et al. 2006).

CONCLUSIONS

The people who lived at Khirbat Iskandar pursued an animal husbandry strategy that focused on sheep and goats. The faunal deposition suggests that the basis of the husbandry strategy was maximizing sheep and goat herd security while maintaining protein offtake. Cattle and pigs were also part of the subsistence pattern in Phases 2 and 3. While environmental conditions probably limited pig husbandry, vegetative conditions permitted the development of a stable agricultural regime. In general, the faunal remains from Area C indicate a successful agricultural system that supported the community.

Chapter 8

Ground Stone and Small Artifacts from Area C

by Jeannette Forsen and Yorke M. Rowan

This chapter describes the ground stone artifacts and small finds recovered from Area C at Khirbat Iskandar. A total of 45 artifacts is included in this study, representing artifacts derived from contexts dated to the Early Bronze IV (EB IV) period. Ground stone artifacts number 26; there are 9 chipped stone artifacts, while the remaining ten artifacts are ceramic, glass, and metal. Included in the original 126 artifact numbers registered in Area C, 69 were bags of lithic flakes/debitage (ca. 1400 pieces), 37 were ground stone, chipped stone, or small finds, and 20 were discarded in the field. This is a relatively small assemblage of objects, and thus our primary effort focuses on artifact description, comparison to similar examples from sites of comparable age, and discussion of their potential relevance to interpretation of the area's function.

Ground stone artifacts are defined as those in which abrasive wear is the primary feature of the final lithic reduction process, whether a by-product of use or manufacture. Various scholars have pointed out that ground stone is a general term that does not always accurately depict the broad array of material culture typically included in this class (Adams 2002: 1; Rowan and Ebeling 2008: 2;

Runnels 1981: 218; Schneider 1993: 5; Wright 1991: 4). Distinctions between ground stone and chipped stone artifacts are not always clear-cut, and both technologies share some attributes (Wright 1993: 93). Many ground stone artifacts were first roughly shaped by chipping, establishing the general morphology of the desired product, which may or may not be further reduced or shaped through intentional grinding and wear from use. Our descriptive terms and typology largely follow that of Wright (1992a; 1992b). See figures 8.1–8.2 for illustrations.

GROUND STONE OBJECTS

Grinding Slabs (N=1)

Only one grinding slab fragment was found in Area C. Grinding slabs, frequently termed "querns" or "saddle querns," are essentially roughly shaped stone slabs. These are the lower, stationary stones utilized as surfaces upon which grains and other materials were placed for crushing and grinding. Wright (1993: 94–95) distinguishes between two types: "grinding slabs," which exhibit lateral grinding striae, and "querns" that exhibit elliptical grinding striae. The specimen from Khirbat

at Bâb adh-Dhrâʿ (Rast and Schaub 2003: fig. 21.1.7).

KI Reg. No. A076. Provenance: Area C.2.18 – L.2017. Flint. Dimension: Dia. 6.0 cm. (fig. 8.7).

KI Reg. No. A077. Provenance: Area C.2.18 – L.2017. Flint. Dimension: Dia. 6.3–6.8 (fig. 8.7).

KI Reg. No. A177. Provenance: Area C.6.16 – L.6002. Flint. Dimension: Dia. 6.2–7.1 cm. Pecked. Frag-ment. (figs. 8.1:3; 8.8).

KI Reg. No. A305. Provenance: Area C.6.38 – L.6016. Flint. Dimension: Dia. 7.3 cm. Slightly flattened faces. Fragment. (fig. 8:9).

KI Reg. No. A378. Provenance: Area C.7.21 – L.7015. Flint. Dimension: Dia. 7.6 cm. Fragment. (fig. 8:10).

KI Reg. No. A426. Provenance: Area C.8.18 – L.8003. Flint. Dimension: Dia. 6.6–6.8 cm. Slightly flattened faces. Fragment. (fig. 8:11).

FIG. 8.6   *Photo of handstone A350.*

FIG. 8.7   *Photo of hammerstones A076 and A077.*

Stone-Mortar Vessels (N=3)

Three mortars were found in Area C. These three vessels represent different sub-types. The first (A197) is a pebble mortar fragment, with a hemispherical hollow ground into a roughly shaped blank. The second (A443) is a fragment of a large heavy limestone mortar with a hemispherical concavity ground into a rectangular slab. Other examples of these heavy immobile mortars remain *in situ* at the site as part of the architectural components. The third, made of basalt (A329), is a fragment of a wide, shallow, round mortar similar to a crude platter or basin. For comparison with Early Bronze Age types of mortars at Bâb adh-Dhrâʿ, see the discussion in Lee (2003: 625, 629–30) and see the EB IV mortars from Iktanu (Prag 1991: fig. 2). For late Early Bronze Age examples at Tall al-ʿUmayri, see Platt 2000: fig. 8.2:6–9).

KI Reg. No. A197. Provenance: Area C.6.8 – L. 6002. Limestone. Dimensions: L: 5.6, W: 3.6, T: 3.1 cm. Concavity Dia. 10 cm, depth 5 cm. Concavity ground into roughly shaped black. Flat exterior base (fig. 8.12).

KI Reg. No. A329. Provenance: Area C.7.8 – L.7006. Basalt. Dimensions: L: 12.8, W: 7.1, T: 4.8 cm. Concavity Dia. 8 cm, depth 2 cm. Flat base, round shape, interior surface smoothed (figs. 8.1:5; 8:13).

KI Reg. No. A443. Provenance: Area C.10.1– L.10001. Limestone. Dimensions: L: 24.6, W: 13.3, T: 7.7 cm. Concavity Dia. 4.5 cm (figs. 8.1:4; 8.14).

FIG. 8.8   *Photo of hammerstone A177.*

FIG. 8.9   *Photo of hammerstone A305.*

FIG. 8.10   *Photo of hammerstone A378.*

FIG. 8.11   *Photo of hammerstone A426.*

Pestles (N=1)

One basalt pestle fragment was found in Area C. This appears to be a fragment of a cylindrical shape, with a damaged proximal end. Similar pestles are illustrated from Early Bronze Age contexts at Arad (Amiran et al. 1978: pl. 80:12), En Shadud (Braun 1985: figs. 37.9; 38:4, 5), Jawa (Helms 1991: fig. 193:691–93), Tall Umm Hammad (O'Tool 1992: fig. 283:26), Jericho (Dorrell 1983: fig. 230:6), Bâb adh-Dhrâʿ (Lee 2003: fig. 21.1:1–2), and Tall al-ʿUmayri (Platt 2000: fig. 8.2:13).

KI Reg. No. A360. Provenance: Area C.6.49 – L.6027. Basalt. Dimensions: L: 7, Dia. 4.4 cm (max.) (figs. 8.1:6; 8.15).

Grooved Stone (N=1)

This is a simple basalt grinding slab with a groove (4 cm in length) on the working surface.

KI Reg. No. A400. Provenance: Area C.7.27 – L.7021. Basalt. Dimensions: L: 9.8, W: 7.9, T: 7.5 cm (fig. 8.16).

Pierced Stones: Types A–C (N=6)

Although perforated stone rings are fairly common from prehistoric and protohistoric sites, their functions are far from understood. In particular, the larger perforated cobbles are of enigmatic function and often referred to as "digging stick weights" or "dibble stick weights." Some smaller examples are clearly spindle whorls based on their size, weight, and symmetric balance, but others would not serve as spindle whorls. These larger or cruder examples are sometimes termed "loom weights," but could also serve as flywheels or weights for other purposes. Smaller examples are illustrated from many sites, including ʿAi (Callaway 1980: fig. 84, pls. 94:11, 15, 16;

FIG. 8.12 *Photo of mortar A197.*

FIG. 8.13 *Photo of mortar A329.*

FIG. 8.14 *Photo of stone mortar A443.*

FIG. 8.15 *Photo of pestle A360.*

FIG. 8.16 *Photo of grooved stone A400.*

FIG. 8.17 *Photo of pierced stone A019.*

FIG. 8.18 *Photo of pierced stone A339.*

FIG. 8.19 *Photo of pierced stone A331.*

bifacial concavities that do not pierce the blank. Three examples are basalt, two of limestone, and the sixth material was unidentified. These artifacts are separated into three types: A, B, and C.

Type A

Type A consists of stones with a relatively well-centered perforation, bifacially drilled. Type A stones have a central perforation ranging in diameter between approximately 16–20 mm, with an average diameter of 18 mm. The function of Type A artifacts is unclear; the smaller of the two (A019) may have served as a flywheel weight for a drill. The other (A339) is smoothed and polished, particularly on the narrow interior of the bi-conical perforation.

KI Reg. No. A019. Provenance: Area C.1.1 – L.1001. Limestone. Dimensions: L: 17.1, W: 11.9, T: 8.1 cm. Hole Dia. 1.6 cm. Half fragment (fig. 8.17).

KI Reg. No. A339. Provenance: Area C.7.10– L.7006. Basalt. Dimensions: L: 10.8, W: 8.1, T: 5 cm. Hole Dia. 2.0 cm. Fragment (fig. 8.18).

140: 19), Arad (Amiran et al. 1978: pl. 76:7–27), Azor (Shamir 1999: fig. 17:1–2), En Shadud (Braun 1985: fig. 38:1, 3), Jawa (Helms 1991: figs. 196:704–8; 197:709–11, 713), Me'ona (Shamir 1996a), 'Ein Assawir (Rowan 2006), Qiryat 'Ata (Rowan 2003), Tall al-Handaqûq (N) (Mabry 1989: figs. 12:7; 14:3), Tall Umm Hammad (O'Tool 1991: fig. 283:9–10), Tall al-'Umayri (Platt 2000: fig. 8.3:16), and Bâb adh-Dhrâ' (Lee 2003: figs. 21.1:10; 21.2:1). Larger examples are also known from Arad (Amiran et al. 1978: pl. 77:12–23), 'Ein Assawir (Rowan 2006), Tall al-Handaqûq (N) (Mabry 1989: fig. 14:4), the Tel Halif Terrace "Silo Site" (Alon and Yekutieli 1995: fig. 26:5), and Bâb adh-Dhrâ' (Lee 2003: figs. 21.1:12; 21.2:2).

For the examples from Khirbat Iskandar, this category includes perforated stones, whether through drilling or pecking, as well as stones with

Type B

Type B consists of discs with bifacially pecked concavities that do not pierce the stone. It is unclear whether this type represents artifacts incompletely perforated, or performed some other function, such as hand rests on top of bow drills (Dorrell 1983: 562, fig. 231:4). The presence of very similar types of artifacts at a variety of sites such as Gilat (Rowan et al. 2006), Tel Jemmeh, Abu Matar (Commenge n.d.), and some of the Golan Chalcolithic sites (Epstein 1998: pl. 43:13–19), however, suggests similar functions rather than unfinished tools.

KI Reg. No. A311. Provenance: Area C.6.35 – L.6019. Limestone. Dimensions: Dia. 11.6, T: 3.8 cm (fig. 8.1:7).

FIG. 8.20 *Photo of pierced stone A075.*

FIG. 8.21 *Photo of macehead A156.*

FIG. 8.22 *Photo of carnelian pendant A404.*

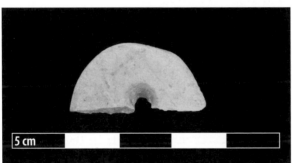

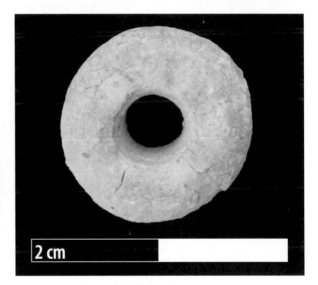

FIG. 8.23 *Photo of spindle whorl A148.*

FIG. 8.24 *Photo of spindle whorl A289.*

FIG. 8.25 *Photo of spindle whorl A034.*

FIG. 8.26 *Photo of spindle whorl A081.*

KI Reg. No. A331. Provenance: Area C.8.7 – L.8000. Basalt. Dimensions: Dia. 7.6, T: 4.3 cm. Half fragment (fig. 8.19).

Type C

Type C is a roughly shaped or irregular stone blank with a perforation that is not well centered. Similar types of roughly shaped, irregular stones with haphazard perforations are commonly recovered from late prehistoric and proto-historic sites, including Chalcolithic sites in the Golan (Epstein 1998: pl. 42:9–16) and Tel Jemmeh (author Rowan's note). The disinterest in creating a centered perforation suggests that these stones probably served in some capacity as weights, perhaps for loom weights, roof thatching, or as agricultural implements.

KI Reg. No. A075. Provenance: Area C.2.22 – L.2020. Dimensions: L: 5.2, W: 4.8 cm. (fig. 8.20).

Macehead (N=1)

A fragment of a macehead was found on the site surface. Made of hard white limestone, the fragment appears to represent a typical spheroidal, or possibly piriform shape. Note that a calcite macehead was a surface find in Field XVI at Bâb adh-Dhrâʿ (Rast and Schaub 2003: 332, Reg. #1602).

KI Reg. No. A156. Surface find. Limestone. Dimensions: L: 5.5, W: 3, T: 3 cm. Hole Dia. 1 cm. Fragment (figs. 8.2:6; 8.21).

Personal Ornaments: Pendant (N=1)

This is a small carnelian pendant (A404) in the shape of a lotus. The pierced end has a diameter of about 3 mm, while the bulbous section has a diameter of about 5 mm. This is similar to those from Megiddo, at least one of which is dated to the LB II (Guy and Engberg 1938: 178, pls. 95:27; 100:18a–b; 132:10), and from Tel Jemmeh (author Rowan's note). An additional lotus-shaped pendant (or amulet) made of jasper was found at the more recent excavations at Megiddo and is dated to the Middle Bronze to Iron Age (Sass 2000: 392, fig. 12.29:18).

KI Reg. No. A404. Provenance: Area C.6.54 – L. 6031. Carnelian. Dimensions: L: 1.5, W: 0.5 cm (figs. 8.1:9; 8.22).

Spindle Whorls (N=5)

Five spindle whorls were found in Area C, two of stone and three of ceramic. The stone spindle whorls are similar in exterior diameter, although one has a significantly larger perforation. Similar to an example found during the City of David excavations (Shamir 1996b: pl. 12:4, fig. 22:16), the more carefully worked (A289) of the two stone spindle whorls was manufactured from an Echinoid fossil (*pedina*). This was drilled relatively straight through, probably from one side. The other example (A148) is a fragment of a relatively thin, flat limestone whorl, drilled bifacially.

KI Reg. No. A148. Provenance: Area C.2.43 – L.2030. Limestone. Dimensions: Dia. 3.4, T: 0.8 cm. Fragment (figs. 8.1:10; 8.23).

KI Reg. No. A289. Provenance: Area C.2.60 – L.2035. *Pedina* fossil (limestone). Dimensions: Dia. 3, T: 1.3 cm. Complete (figs. 8.1:8; 8.24).

Two (A34, A81) of the three ceramic spindle whorls are smaller than the stone spindle whorls. The third (A424) is larger in diameter than the two stone spindle whorls (above). There is an example of an EB IV ceramic spindle whorl at Bâb adh-Dhrâʿ (Rast and Schaub 2003: fig. 20.16.d).

KI Reg. No. A034. Provenance: Area C.2.6 – L.2002. Ceramic. Dimensions: Dia. 2.1, T: 1 cm. Fragment, straight perforation (fig. 8.25).

KI Reg. No. A081. Provenance: Area C.3.4 – L.3002. Ceramic. Dimensions: Dia. 2.1, T: 1.1 cm. Fragment, bifacial perforation (fig. 8.26).

KI Reg. No. A424. Provenance: Area C.6.61 – L.6036. Ceramic. Dimensions: Dia. 4.3, T: 1.4 cm. Fragment, bifacial perforation (figs. 8.1:11; 8.27).

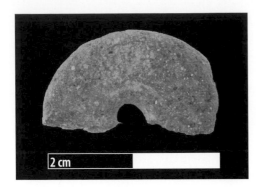

FIG. 8.27 *Photo of spindle whorl A424a.*

FIG. 8.28 *Photo of terracotta object A140.*

FIG. 8.29 *Photo of ceramic lid A307.*

FIG. 8.32 *Photo of necklace A143.*

FIG. 8.30 *Photo of metal pin A206.*

FIG. 8.31 *Photo of metal object A405.*

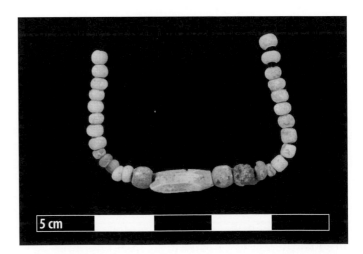

FIG. 8.33 *Photo of necklace A145.*

TERRACOTTA OBJECTS (N=3)

Bowl Fragment

KI Reg. No. A140. Provenance: Area C.5.3 – L.5000. Ceramic. Dimensions: L: 7.4, W: 4.1, T: 3 cm. Leg of a bowl. Cylindrical hand-molded piece of pottery with one rounded end. Reddish yellow paint (fig. 8.28).

Burnishing Tool

KI Reg. No. A190. Provenance: Area C.3.34 – L.3007. Ceramic. Dimensions. L: 2.4, W: 2.1, T: 1.1 cm. Burnishing tool. Light reddish-brown ware with a dark gray slip. Highly polished convex working surface.

KI Reg. No. A307. Provenance: Area C.6.38 – L.6016. Ceramic. Dimensions: L: 11.1, W: 9.9, T: 1.5 cm. Lid. Oval in plan, slightly chipped (fig. 8.29).

METAL OBJECTS (N=2)

Only two metal objects were recorded from Area C, and they are both probably of copper. No chemical analysis has been conducted, so this is uncertain. For the one object, a pin fragment, see discussion and parallels in Chapter 13.

Pin

KI Reg. No. A206. Provenance: Area C.8.2 – L. 8002. Metal. Dimensions: Dia. 0.4, L: 2.6 cm. Fragment, both ends missing (figs. 8.1:12; 8.30).

Unidentified

KI Reg. No. A405. Provenance: Area C.7.7. – L.7009. Metal. Dimensions: L: 1.7, W: 1.2 cm. Lump of unspecified metal, probably slag (fig. 8.31).

GLASS OBJECTS (N=2)

All the beads in the necklace are modern and originate from a Bedouin grave.

Necklaces

KI Reg. No. A143. Provenance: Area C.5.5 – L.5003. Glass. Dimensions: Dia. range from 0.2 to 0.5 cm. Three purple, four white, one green, one off-white, one grey, one chevron, 1.5 cm long and 0.4 cm in dia. (fig. 8.32).

KI Reg. No. A145. Provenance: Area C.5.7 – L. 5006. Glass. Dimensions: Dia. range from 0.2 to 0.5. Twelve purple, two white, two pale red, one off-white, one green. (fig. 8.33).

CHIPPED FLINT ARTIFACTS TOOLS (N=13) AND DEBITAGE (N=6)
(examined at Gannon University)

Although the majority of flint artifacts recovered during the excavations of Area C were not available for examination,[1] some summary observations may be made.

Although few debitage pieces (four flakes, two chunks) were available for direct examination, photographs and hand illustrations indicate that debitage included standard flaking technology typical of late Early Bronze contexts. Tool types included retouched flakes, utilized flakes, a fragment of a possible sickle, and a Canaanean sickle blade. Two retouched flakes (A026) have bilateral dorsal retouch, and both appear to be simple flake borers or perforators. However, the tips are broken, and so the original morphology cannot be ascertained definitively. Another inverse, bilaterally retouched flake (A065), with dorsal retouch on the distal end, may have been intended as a sickle, but has no sickle sheen (gloss). One retouched flake (A021) with inverse bilateral retouch converging on the distal end appears to be heavily water-rolled and may represent an intrusive earlier tool. One convergent, leaf-shaped flake (A022) may have edge damage that does not appear to be intentional retouch.

Two blades were examined, although the illustrations (fig. 8.2:1–2, 5) indicate more were recovered than examined for this analysis. For instance, a medial blade segment (A189) appears to be retouched on at least one lateral edge (fig. 8.2:2). Another complete blade (A149; fig. 8.2:1) has ventral retouch along one lateral edge. One blade (A064) is heavily retouched bilaterally, and measures 51 × 22 × 7 mm (fig. 8.2:5). An additional piece (A043; fig. 8.2:3) is triangular in shape, with natural limestone backing and light serration along the dorsally retouched edge. The wide end is dorsally truncated. Another blade (A045; fig. 8.2:4) is a Canaanean sickle blade with clear sickle sheen on the edge. This piece, measuring 64 × 29 × 7 mm, falls within the standard range of Canaanean blade widths (Rosen 1989: fig. 3), exhibits a trapezoidal cross-section, and has only ventral edge retouch. There is no backing retouch, and both ends are snapped. Comparisons with EB IV blades, including sickle blades and retouched flakes, can be found at Tall Umm Hammad (Betts 1992: 126–31 and figs. 280–81) and Bâb adh-Dhrâ' (McConaughy 2003: figs. 16.2.h; 16.9.a, c, h; Rast and Schaub 2003: fig. 12.9:8).

CONTEXT AND DISCUSSION

Based on the limited number of artifacts available, augmenting the stratigraphic discussion and interpretation of spatial dynamics is difficult. Nevertheless, the assemblage of debitage, ground stone, and other small objects can supplement field observations. Perhaps Surface 8009 in Phase 3, represented by the high density of debitage in association, represents the clearest function of an area. The recovery of plentiful debitage elements (N=261), as well as on Surface 8008 (N=249), indicate that flint tool production or rejuvenation occurred in association with other features supporting the interpretation of a workshop area. In Phase 2, Surfaces 6018, 6019, and 6016 also contained unusual quantities of flint debitage (257 flakes), along with associated stone worktables and other materials such as two handstones (A306/A337), one hammerstone (A305), and a Type B pierced stone (A311).

NOTE

1   Note that the many bags of flakes/debitage were stored at ACOR following Phase 1 operations in 1987. After a lengthy hiatus, Richard and Long returned to excavate in 1994 and discovered that in the interim, probably during ACOR's move to new facilities, the materials were unfortunately either misplaced or lost. Other objects not available for present study are either with the Department of Antiquities or displayed in several exhibits elsewhere in the United States.

Chapter 9

The Early Bronze IV Cemeteries at Khirbat Iskandar

by Suzanne Richard, Glen Peterman, and James J. D'Angelo

The discovery of EB IV cemeteries in the immediate vicinity of the site of Khirbat Iskandar—to the south, east, and west—reveals the extent to which the inhabitants exploited their natural environment (fig. 9.1). That exploitation is far more extensive in light of recent exploration and excavation. Although not included in the present volume, it is relevant to note that excavation of a "high place" on the summit of the hill (Umm al-Idhâm) behind the site to the north took place in 2004 and 2007. Further work occurred to the east of the site (Area E) in the area of the above-ground megalithic structures originally observed by Glueck. Although the megalithic structures and other cultic features will be presented in a future volume, it is worth noting the apparent 360° cultic landscape surrounding the site of Khirbat Iskandar, which seems to evoke a watchful symbolism over the site and the living (see conclusions Ch. 16).

This chapter provides a general introduction to the cemeteries investigated in 1984 and 1987; for detailed analysis, see Chapters 10–11. The publication of the cemeteries in a volume focused primarily on the EB IV settlement in Area C offers an opportunity for a comparative study of stratified tell and ritual tomb material culture. Indeed, the quantified study has elucidated interesting comparisons and contrasts between the tell and the tombs, as well as specifically between Cemeteries D and E (see Ch. 5).

The quantified ceramic study has proven to be critical regarding interpretation of the cemeteries, given the poor state of preservation of the burial remains, generally, in virtually all of the tombs excavated. In the absence of undisturbed contexts, inferences about the original interment practice, whether primary or secondary, are speculative at best. It is possible that burial tradition at the site reflects a pattern of primary interment followed by secondary reorganization of the remains during the deposition of subsequent individuals. The best evidence for this tradition comes from Tomb E9 (see Ch. 11). The majority of the tombs excavated, however, give the appearance of disarticulated secondary burials. Thus, inferences about burial customs derive primarily from the quantified study of the ceramics (Ch. 12), the skeletal remains (Ch. 14), and the artifacts (Ch. 13), along with tomb morphology (Ch. 10–11). All combined, these data offer interesting and compelling information about the occupants of Khirbat Iskandar and those interred in the cemeteries.

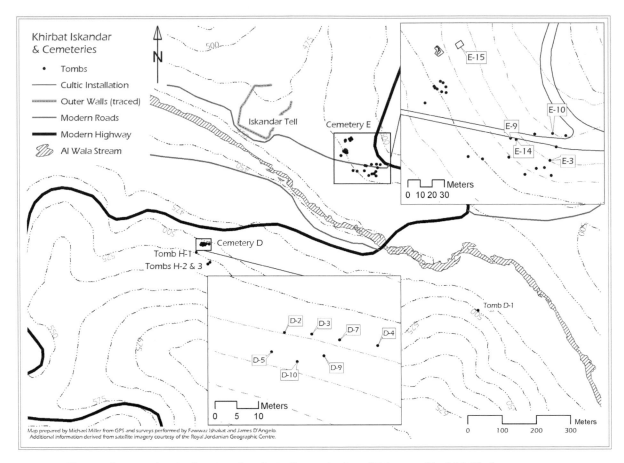

FIG. 9.1   *Topographic map showing location of tombs in Cemeteries D and E (prepared by M. Miller).*

CEMETERIES

Area E

Area E is the designation for what Nelson Glueck called the "tremendous ancient cemetery" in an area as large as the site itself, located "between two *wudyân* to the east or slightly beyond the eastern of the two *wudyân*" (1939: 128; and see Ch. 1, fig. 1.5). His inference about a burial ground derives from the above-ground megalithic structures he observed, such as "circles-of-stone," rectangular stone structures, and numerous menhirs. The current expedition has affirmed his insight. In 1984 and 1987, road cuts and/or farmers plowing in preparation for the planting of olive trees exposed tombs in this area. In light of agricultural development, particularly expanding olive tree orchards and cash crop cultivation that is gradually encompassing the

vicinity of the tell, the project has focused on the survey, exploration, and excavation of the remaining features in the area.

Apparently, because of the geological formation of the eastern ridge, Cemetery E (fig. 9.1) included a variety of tomb types. The breccia flow between Umm al-Idhâm and this ridge is in sharp contrast to the stratified layers of marl, flint, limestone, and chalk on Jabal as-Sultaniya, the hillside across the wâdi to the south, where those layers were more conducive to the cutting of classic shaft and chamber tombs. Due to the breccia formation, the below-ground condition in Cemetery E is a honeycomb of partially natural, partially cut chambers of some irregularity: caves, small chambers, shaft tombs, or combined shaft/cave. The only example of a multiple chambered tomb is in this cemetery. Although original primary burial is not out of the question (see Ch. 14), the cemetery appears to contain multiple disarticulated secondary burials. Cemeteries D and E share a number of characteristics, yet, there are distinctions between the two as well, as will be shown. Of the six EB IV tombs explored or excavated in Cemetery E (Ch. 11), two were sterile shaft tombs.

Area J

Some 350–450 m west of the site, beyond a small north–south wâdi, the survey team in 1987 located several tombs exposed as the result of a bulldozer road cut. Designated Area J, the cemetery contained evidence for burial in the EB IV (Tomb J1) and EB IB (Tombs J2–3) periods. Only the former is included in this volume (Ch. 10). The latter—briefly reported on previously (Richard 1990)—and other EB I materials from the site await analysis and publication in a future volume. A return to full excavations at the site (1997) after a long hiatus, as well as additional survey of the area in 2004, revealed extensive damage to that hillside by the further widening and construction of a roadway. Thus, the extent of this cemetery is now probably beyond our grasp. At most, we can say that it appears that the cemetery was utilized over a lengthy period of time. In addition to the EB I and EB IV burials, there are numerous caves, which may have been used during the Early Bronze Age. A sherd collection indicates that some of the caves were in use as late as the Roman Period, not a surprise, since the site of Roman Iskandar lies less than one km to the west at the bend of the wâdi.

Jabal as-Sultaniya: Areas D, H, and F

The main area of investigation was Area D, located almost directly opposite the site of Khirbat Iskandar, south of the wâdi on the hillside of the mountain known locally as Jabal as-Sultaniya. Other areas explored on that hillside were Areas H and F. Chapter 10 details the work on Jabal as-Sultaniya.

The survey team undertook archaeological exploration of this hillside (fig. 9.1) following the bulldozing of an access road / firebreak by personnel from the Wâdi al-Wâla agricultural station. Left exposed by the cut was Tomb D1, an empty

single-chamber shaft tomb at the east end of Jabal as-Sultaniya. This was the first evidence of tombs in the vicinity. Further exploration thereafter uncovered four additional single-chamber shaft tombs exposed by the same bulldozing activity to the west (Cemetery D refers to the tombs at this end of the hillside). A salvage excavation of those four tombs (D2 through D5) was conducted following the regular season in 1984 by Suzanne Richard of the Khirbat Iskandar Excavations and Hussein Qandil of the Department of Antiquities.

The tombs were mapped in the 1987 season, when excavation of additional tombs in the area took place. The survey team that season, directed by Gaetano Palumbo, explored the entire hillside and excavated Tombs D7, D9, and D10. His team also uncovered another tomb, D6, lying to the west of D4. However, upon investigation work was suspended when it became clear that the road cut had totally destroyed the shaft. Moreover, the chamber was completely filled with roof collapse. In another instance, the excavation of potential Tomb D8 began when the team discovered evidence thought to be a capstone. Unfortunately, work in this area ceased as well when the big slab of stone proved to be lying on bedrock.

Based on the two clear rows of tombs excavated, as well as survey across the hillside, it is likely that Cemetery D could have some ten or more rows of shaft tombs dug every 5–6 m apart into the horizontal alternating layers of soft marl and limestone of the slope (fig. 9.1). Because the shafts were filled in antiquity by the local rock, it is difficult to detect the outlines of the filled shafts. Compounding this situation are the reforestation efforts of the agricultural station. The hillside is heavily overgrown, and places where the pine seedlings failed to root have left the area pockmarked by planting holes and depressions. It seems likely that many planting pits were inadvertently dug into presumed "natural depressions" in the ground where the earth may have been softer, which, in actuality, were the upper portions of tomb shafts. Thus, a substantial part of the cemetery is now inaccessible where the trees were successful. Moreover, given the reforestation project and accompanying terracing of the hillside, bedrock now is found 25 to 50 cm below the surface, so that it is not possible to recognize the presence of shafts by surface survey only.

On the same hillside, the survey team also uncovered another cemetery, designated Area H. In an area dotted with caves, there was evidence of usage in the EB IV period, including the reuse of natural caves with associated shafts. Two caves were excavated (H2 and H3). The regional survey team likewise made several probes some 300 m west of and above the Area D tombs, on a hill flank above the road to Dhiban. Termed Area F, this hillside showed promise of being an extension of the cemetery in Area D; however, several probes revealed only depressions rather than tomb shafts. Although the team discontinued the survey in order to concentrate on the excavation of Area D, it is possible that further effort there would have located tombs.

COMPARISON OF CEMETERIES

Despite the fact that all of the tombs were either disturbed and/or robbed, thus mitigating any definitive conclusions about burial ritual, they nevertheless offer a wealth of information suggesting variability and distinctions among the cemeteries. Although the number of tombs uncovered in Areas D–E is not equivalent, a quantitative study of the two ceramic assemblages has provided important information concerning their ceramic distributions, which probably would remain statistically constant if more tombs were found (see Ch. 5).

Judging from the regular spacing between tombs, Area D is a well-planned cemetery. The orientation of the tombs varies at a 30° angle toward the east. Perhaps dozens of tombs are still to be found under the terraces of the pine forest, as well as below the road cut. The variation in tomb orientation probably means that the tombs were cut all-year-round. This is the only cemetery in the vicinity of the site where there is some regularity to tombs, compared to those in Areas H and E, and perhaps in J. For these and other distinctions elaborated elsewhere (Chs. 10–12, and see conclusions in Ch. 16), we have concluded that the Area D hillside was the major cemetery in the vicinity of Khirbat Iskandar during the EB IV period.

Whether Area H is a separate cemetery or a part of one vast cemetery on Jabal as-Sultaniya, the combination natural cave/shaft tombs distinguishes it from Area D, but connects it to Cemetery E in terms of the use or modification of caves. The natural terrain at that location on the hillside may have driven the choice of tomb type, yet, one cannot discount the possibility of cultural differentiation.

Given the location of Area E contiguous to the site itself, and considering the array of "cultic" features Glueck observed there, it seems reasonable to hypothesize that the cemetery may contain interments of individuals or families of differentiated status. Support for that hypothesis derives from the quantitative ceramic study, which illuminated a number of interesting distinctions about the grave goods in Cemetery E (see below and Ch. 5). This is also the only cemetery in which possible evidence for primary burial came to light (see Ch. 10). The megalithic aboveground stone structures (including an open-air sanctuary) and menhirs suggest differentiation of those interred belowground, from the general burial ground posited to be Cemetery D, across the wâdi to the south. This hypothesis gains strength when work across the tell is considered, especially the evidence recovered in Area B, suggesting unequal access to resources. Some preliminary observations and tentative conclusions about the landscape symbolized by the various features in the vicinity of the site are discussed in Chapter 16.

A Sequence of Tombs in Relation to Area C

Through a quantitative ceramic study of tomb assemblages based on the stratified sequence of pottery from Area C, a seriation of the tombs was possible. The study of 142 vessels from the Khirbat Iskandar tombs and 51 vessels from Bâb adh-Dhrâ' Tombs A52 and A54 combined provides an overlapping sequence of tombs from early to late in the period. The 35 specific form/size classifications utilized in this study yielded a stable seriation showing that: 1) Cemeteries D and E appear to have been in active use throughout Phases 1–3 in Area C, 2) the Cemetery H assemblage correlated with Phase 3, and 3) the Bâb adh-Dhrâ' Tombs A52/54 matched

Phase 1 at Khirbat Iskandar with some overlap in early Phase 2 (see detailed analysis in Ch. 5).

Statistical Ceramic Comparison between Cemeteries D and E

What we may glean from the quantified ceramic study is that differentiation between Cemeteries D and E is apparent. In Cemetery E, the distribution of platters and medium–small bowls shows characteristics of Field XVI, the cultic area at Bâb adh-Dhrâʿ. There are distinctions pointing to different clay sources in Cemeteries D and E, as well as different preferences for use of slip/burnish. Moreover, Cemetery E had a more limited number of vessels per interment (mean = 7), there was no evidence for phasing or reuse in the tombs, and there was evidence for architectural additions to Cemetery E in the form of lintels. In Cemetery D, larger platters were more characteristic, as well as less well-fired ware, more vessels per interment (mean=12), and a reuse of these probable extended family tombs .

Comparison of Tell and Tomb

Finally, the patterning and variations discerned in a comparison of tell and tomb support the conclusion that, unexpectedly, ceramic traditions of the living were remarkably similar to those of the dead at Khirbat Iskandar in EB IV. For example, the tombs contain such domestic categories of ceramics as cooking pots, spouted vessels ("teapots"), storage vessels (including a holemouth jar), and serving dishes (such as platter bowls, bowls, cups, and lamps for lighting). The primary distinction appears to be one of size in some categories, as well as a preference for certain types, for example, small bowls, small to miniature necked vessels, jugs, and many more lamps.

As elaborated in Chapters 4, 5, and 16, the major categories absent in the tombs are, except for a few outliers, long-term storage and/or food preparation/or processing/industrial (i.e., olive oil manufacturing) equipment. Conversely, there is nothing in the tombs that is not found on the tell, the possible rare exceptions being the lamp or miniature vessel. The observation of variability in burial assemblages, combined with distinctions in tomb type and cemetery location, suggests some social stratification at the site. Concerning burial custom, despite some distinctions noted above, the domestic character symbolized in the gifting rituals for the dead at Khirbat Iskandar is striking (and see Ch. 16 for details).

Chapter 10

Excavation of the Area D, H and J Cemeteries

by Glen Peterman and Suzanne Richard

Cemeteries D and H are located across from the site of Khirbat Iskandar to the south on the hillside known as Jabal as-Sultaniya, and Cemetery J lies on a ridge to the west of the site (see figs. 1.4 and 9.1). For more information and a general summary of these cemeteries, see Chapter 9. All of the preserved shaft tombs excavated in these cemeteries were of the round shaft, single chamber type. The chambers varied from square to oblong or irregular. The interments all appeared to be secondary disarticulated burials. However, since all tombs located thus far were robbed/reused in antiquity and/or damaged from heavy roof collapse and water damage, it is not impossible that some of the tombs originally held articulated burials. There is evidence for flooding in the tombs on the basis of a type of plaster-like substance, possibly caliche caused by lime-laden water seepage, found in shafts and chambers, sometimes encasing pottery. This substance also affected the skeletal remains, which were in a state of poor preservation (see Ch. 14). All the tombs contained roof collapse, rock fall, and silt reaching nearly to the top of the chamber. The chamber floors were 50–75 cm below the lowest extent of the shaft. Few whole vessels survived the disturbance in the tombs.

CEMETERY AREA D

Although all of the Cemetery D tombs have round shafts, their chamber plans vary. Four of the tombs (D2–4, D9) have square or squarish chambers. Survey leader G. Palumbo noted in his field summary that round shafts and square chambers are features not found elsewhere in the southern Levant. He also suggested that the "Outsize Tombs" at Jericho were the closest parallels, yet there the shaft is always square, while the chamber can also be round (Kenyon 1960). Even the dimensions at Khirbat Iskandar (over 3 m in length and width) compare favorably with Jericho's "Outsize Tombs." Despite similarities in architectural plan, these tombs contain a ceramic assemblage that is dissimilar to the usual repertoire of the "Outsize Tombs." Whereas at Khirbat Iskandar the typical assemblage includes four-spouted lamps, platter bowls, bowls, cups, jars, "teapots," and juglets with long neck, at Jericho the usual grouping would be several ledge handled jars, amphoriskoi, and "teapots."

Nearly all of the pottery was broken and also scattered across the chamber. Given the fragmentary and non-restorable nature of many vessels, the confusion of sherd material in the tombs, and

FIG. 10.3 *Pottery from Tomb D2.*

#	BUCKET	LOCUS	AP	FormHaRiBa	VESSEL	M	CAP	DESCRIPTION
1	D02.21.31	D02013		4762.45.42.00	Bowl	4.5	79	5YR5/1 gray; 10R6/6 red; some sm. white incl.; well fired; handmade.
2	D02.28.54	D02013		4762.00.41.00	Bowl	6.9	131	5YR7/4 pink; 10R5/6 red; few sm. white incl.; med. fired; handmade.
3	D02.16	D02014	AP287	4765.00.60.13	Bowl	10.25	277	5YR6/4 light reddish brown; burnished ext. & int. 10R5/8 red; few sm. white incl.; med. fired; handmade.
4	D02.29	D02013	AP293	4766.00.11.00	Bowl	8.8		5YR5/6 yellowish red; 10R5/6; few sm. white & black incl., few lg. incl.; poorly fired; handmade.
5	D02 NR 7	D02		4766.00.10.00	Bowl	10		7.5YR6/4 light brown; (burnished?) ext. 2.5YR 6/6 light red; poor–med. fired.
6	D02.16.31	D02013		4740.00.11.00	Bowl	11.8		5YR7/4 pink; 10R5/6 red; some med. white incl.; poor–med. fired.
7	D02.31.4	D02013	AP284	4749.00.12.13	Bowl	12.2	294	5YR7/3 pink; burnished ext. 2.5YR6/8 light red–5YR6/6 reddish yellow; very few sm. white and few basalt incl.; med. fired.
8	D02.29.98	D02013		4666.51.73.13	Platter	19	739	2.5YR6/6 light red; 10R5/6 red; few med. white incl.; poorly fired, soft.
9	D02.25.3	D02013		4665.00.74.13	Platter	20	994	7.5YR8/2 pinkish white; burnished int. & ext. 10R5/6 red; few sm. black & white incl.; well fired; handmade.
10	D02.21.88	D02013	AP257	4667.00.10.30	Platter	20		5YR7/3 pink; burnished ext. & int. 10R5/6 red; few sm. white incl.; med. fired.
11	D02	D02013	AP297	4659.00.19.13	Platter	20	1,361	7.5YR8/2 pinkish white; burnished ext. 10R6/6 light red, burnished int. 2.5YR6/6 light red; some white and many med. black incl.; well fired, handmade.
12	D02b	D02013–D02014	AP295	4659.00.11.13	Platter	22.2	1,411	2.5YR6/8 light red; burnished (?) int. 2.5YR6/6 light red; many lg. white gravel & flint; poorly fired through but friable; handmade.
13	D02.29.1	D02013	AP292	4666.51.73.13	Platter	23.8	1,867	5YR7/4–7/6 pink–reddish yellow; burnished ext. (concentric pattern), burnished int. (radial pattern) 10R6/6 light red–2.5YR6/6 light red; few white incl.; well fired; handmade slow wheel finished.
14	D02.24.8	D02013		4645.00.42.11	Platter	22	1,711	7.5YR8/2 pinkish white; burnished ext. & int. 2.5YR6 light red; few sm. black incl.; med. fired.
15	D02.17.2	D02013		4645.00.74.13	Platter	23	1,515	7.5YR8/2 pinkish white; burnished ext. & int. 10R6/6 light red; many sm. black incl., some lg. grits; med.–well fired; handmade.
16	D02.14.18	D02014		4660.00.11.00	Platter	22		7.5YR8/2 pinkish white; 5YR6/6 reddish yellow, burnished int. 5YR6/6 reddish yellow; well fired, wheel finished.
17	D02.11.8a	D02011		4640.00.10.00	Platter	26		7.5YR8/4 pink; burnished ext. & int. 2.5YR6/6 light red.
18	D02.19.8	D02013–D02015	AP290	4623.00.72.10	Platter	25.5	2,772	7.5YR7/4 pink; burnished ext. & int. 10R5/8 red; many sm. & med. white & gray incl.; occasional wadi gravel; med. fired; handmade, wheel-finished.
19	D02.15.2–5	D02013		4626.00.75.13	Platter	26	2,422	5YR7/4 pink; burnished int. & ext. 10R5/6 red; med. fired; handmade.
20	D02.19.1	D02014		4626.00.75.13	Platter	27	2,620	5YR8/3 pink; burnished int. & ext. 10R6/6 light red; some med. & lg. gravel; well-fired; handmade.
21	D02.21.91	D02013–D02014	AP303	4625.00.75.15	Platter	25.2	2,011	7.5YR8/2 pinkish white; burnished ext. & int. 10R6/6 light red; many sm. white incl.; med.–well fired, handmade, slow-wheel finished (?).
22	D02.16.8	D02014		4620.00.11.00	Platter	27		7.5YR8/4 pink; few traces of burnish(?) 10R5/6 red; many sm. & med. black & white incl.; poorly fired.

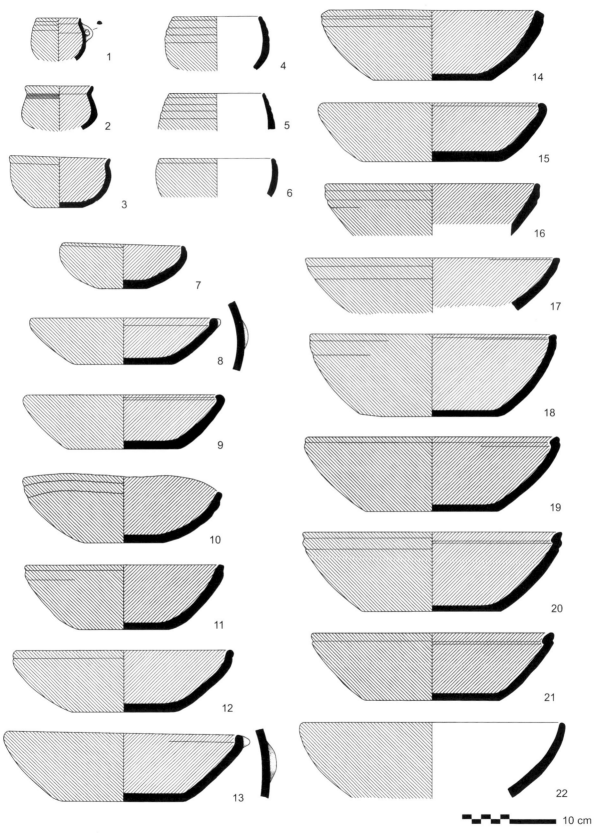

FIG. 10.3 *Pottery from Tomb D2.*

FIG. 10.5 *Pottery from Tomb D2.*

#	BUCKET	LOCUS	AP	FORMHARIBA	VESSEL	M	CAP	DESCRIPTION
1	D02.22.1–4	D02013		4605.00.75.15	Platter	38	8,325	5YR7/4 pink; burnished ext. & int. 10R6/6–5/6 light red–red; many sm. & med. white inclusions; med. fired.
2	D02.24.7	D02013		4605.00.75.13	Platter	40	8,703	7.5YR7/4 pink; burnished ext. & int.; 10R6/6–5/6 light red–red; many med. black & white inclusions; well fired; handmade, slow-wheel finished.
3	D02.21.101	D02013		4602.00.13.00	Platter	42		5YR7/4 pink; burnished ext. & int.; 10R5/6 red; many sm. & med. black inclusions; well fired; handmade.
4	D02.28.8	D02013		4600.00.75.00	Platter	32		7.5YR8/4 pink; burnished ext & int.; 2.5YR5/6 red; some sm. black inclusions; poorly fired.
5	D02.25.2	D02013		4600.00.75.00	Platter	31		5YR7/3 pink; burnished ext & int.; 10R5/6 red; some med. & lg. black & white inclusions; med. fired.
6	D02.31.8	D02014		4600.00.75.00	Platter	34.5		5YR8/3 pink; burnished ext & int.; 10R5/6 red; few sm. & med. black inclusions; well fired; handmade.
7	D02.16.11	D02014		4600.00.75.00	Platter	34		7.5YR8/2 pinkish white; burnished ext & int.; 10R6/6 light red; many sm. white & black inclusions; poorly fired.
8	D02 NR #2	D02		4600.00.75.00	Platter	40		5YR8/3 pink; burnished ext. & int.; 10R4/4-5/6 weak red–red.

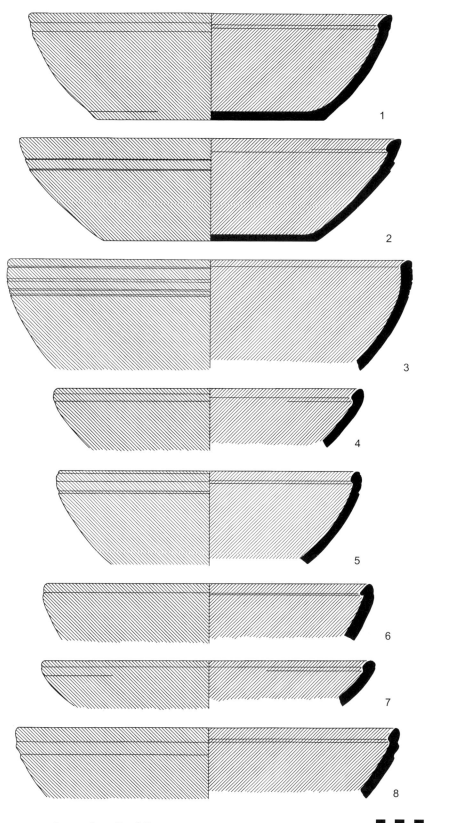

FIG. 10.5 *Pottery from Tomb D2.*

10 cm

FIG. 10.6 *Pottery from Tomb D2.*

#	BUCKET	LOCUS	AP	FORMHARIBA	VESSEL	M	CAP	DESCRIPTION
1	D02.11.8b	D02011		4600.00.75.00	Platter	40		5YR7/3 pink; burnished ext. & int.; 10R6/4–5/6 pale red–red; some sm. black & white incl.; med. fired.
2	D02.25.27	D02013		4600.00.11.00	Platter	40		7.5YR8/2 pinkish white; 5YR7/4 pink; many sm. & med. white inclusions; well fired.
3	D02.22.5	D02013		4600.00.75.00	Platter	40		5YR7/4 pink; burnished ext. & int.; 10R6/6–5/6 light red–red; many sm. & med. white & gray inclusions; med. fired; handmade.
4	D02.33.8	D02013		4600.00.75.00	Platter	42		5YR7/3 pink; burnished ext. & int.; 2.5YR6/4 light reddish brown; many sm. & med. black inclusions; poorly fired.
5	D02.18	D02013		4600.00.75.00	Platter	44		5YR7/3 pink; 2.5 YR6/6 light red; very many sm. white inclusions; med. fired; handmade.
6	D02.26	D02013	AP256	4568.51.11.13	Bowl	20.8	1,720	10R6/6 light red; burnished ext.; 10R5/6 red, 10R5/6 red; many sm. white inclusions; med.–well fired.
7	D02.25.1	D02013		4538.00.73.00	Bowl	29		5YR7/4 pink; burnished ext & int. 10R6/4 pale red; many sm. & med. white inclusions; well fired.
8	D02.29a	D02013–D02015	AP291	4518.00.13.13	Bowl	29.8	4,650	7.5YR6/6 reddish yellow; ext. & int.; 5YR6/6 reddish yellow; many sm. & med. black & white inclusions occasional lg. white inclusions; med. fired; handmade, wheel-finished rim.
9	D02.16.1	D02014		4531.00.75.00	Bowl	33		7.5YR8/2 pinkish white; burnished ext & int.; 10R6/6 light red; med. fired.
10	D02.14.41	D02014		4422.00.61.00	Jug	7		7.5YR7/4 pink.
11	D02.24.11	D02013		4422.00.60.00	Jug	9		7.5YR8/2 pinkish white.
12	D02.31.23	D02014–D02015		4421.23.61.00	Jug	7		7.5YR8/2 pinkish gray; 10R5/6 red; some sm. white inclusions; poor-med. fired; handmade.

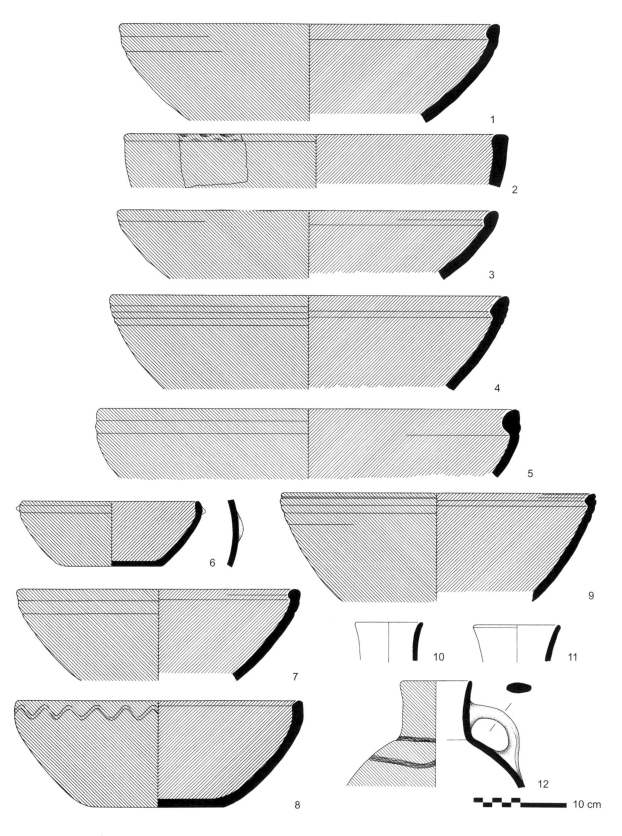

FIG. 10.6 *Pottery from Tomb D2.*

FIG. 10.7 *Pottery from Tomb D2.*

#	BUCKET	LOCUS	AP	FormHaRiBa	Vessel	M	Cap	DESCRIPTION
1	D02.NR 13	D03		4281.00.12.13	Jar			7.5YR7/4 pink; 2.5YR6/6 light red; some med. gravel, poorly fired.
2	D02.14	D02013–D02014	289	4281.54.61.13	Jar	4.5	301	2.5YR6/6 light red; burnished ext.; 10R6/8 light red; many sm. white incl.; well fired; handmade.
3	D02 NR 14a	D02		4272.00.10.00	Jar	8		7.5YR8/2 pinkish yellow; 2.5YR5/4 reddish brown.
4	D02.31.2	D02014		4272.00.00.11	Jar	9.5		5YR7/6 reddish yellow; burnished ext.; 2.5YR6/6 light red; many sm. black & white inclusions; poor-med. fired, friable.
5	D02.23.23	D02013		4262.00.61.00	Jar	7		7.5YR8/2 pinkish white; 2.5YR6/6 light red; many sm. white inclusions; poorly fired; soft.
6	D02.23.2	D02013		4262.54.61.11	Jar	6.4	529	7.5YR8/2 pinkish white; burnished ext. & int. rim; 10R6/6 light red; some sm. white inclusions, some lg. gravel; poorly fired.
7	D02.23.17	D02013–D02014	298	4262.54.61.13	Jar	8	632	5YR7/4 pink; 10R6/6 light red; some lg. white inclusions; poorly fired, friable; handmade.
8	D2.24.19	D02013		4222.00.00.00	Jar	6		5YR7/4 pink; 10R6/6 light red; some sm. white inclusions; poorly fired, friable; handmade.
9	D02.14–21	D02013–D02014	294	4231.54.60.13	Jar	7.7	1,177	7.5YR8/4 pink; 5YR7/6 reddish yellow; many sm. white inclusions; poorly fired; hand-finished rim.
10	D02.31.41	D02014–D02015		4222.54.61.00	Jar	8.7		7.5YR8/2 pinkish white; 10R6/4 pale red; few sm. white inclusions, well fired.
11	D02.30.7	D02013		4222.00.11.00	Jar	7.5		5YR7/3 pink; burnished ext.; 2.5YR5/4 reddish brown; many med. & sm. black incl.; poorly fired, friable.
12	D02.14.25	D02013		4222.54.00.00	Jar	9		5YR7/3 pink; 10R6/6 red.
13	D02.28.53	D02013	255	4222.00.60.13	Jar	9.2	1,361	7.5YR7/2 pinkish gray–7/4 pink; possible burnishing marks; many sm.–med. black incl.; well fired.
14	D02.12-29	D02012–D02015	285	4142.54.11.13	Jar	9.9	4,768	7.5YR8/4–7/4 pink; 10R6/6 light red; many sm. white, med. black incl., extremely pitted; well fired; handmade.
15	D02.25.62	D02013		4222.00.62.00	Jar	10		2.5YR4/0 red; 2.5 YR5/6 red.
16	D02.24.19	D02013		4142.00.00.00	Jar			5YR7/4 pink; burnished; 10R6/6 light red; some med. black & white inclusions; med. fired; no evidence of fluted neck.
17	D02.07.1	D02007		4142.00.60.00	Jar	11		7.5YR7/2 pinkish gray–7/4 pink; many sm. & med. white incl.; well fired; handmade, wheel finished rim.
18	D02 NR 6	D02		4142.54.00.00	Jar	8.8		7.5YR7/2 pinkish gray; burnished 5YR5/6 yellowish red; many med. white incl.; med.–well fired.
19	D02a	D02013–D02015	296	4141.54.61.13	Jar		11.4 4,096	7.5YR7/4 pink - 6/4 light brown; burnished ext., 10R5/5 red; some sm. white & black inclusions; well fired, handmade, wheel-finished rim.
20	D02.25.12	D02013		4141.54.62.13	Jar		10.3 3,266	5YR5/1 gray; 10R5/6 red; some med. white incl.; well fired; hand fluted-rim (?).

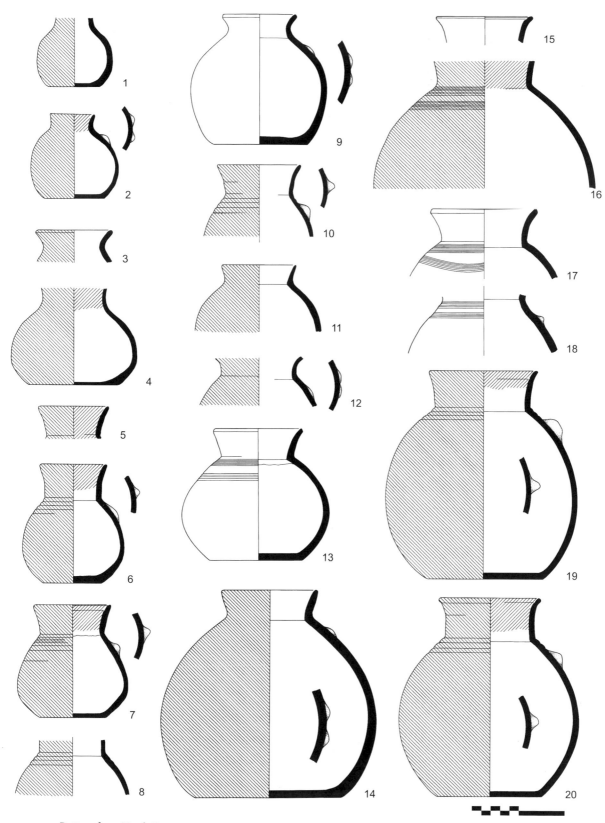

FIG. 10.7 *Pottery from Tomb D2.*

FIG. 10.8 *Pottery from Tomb D2.*

#	Bucket	Locus	AP	FormHaRiBa	Vessel	M	Cap	Description
1	D02.26.2–6	D02013		4071.00.41.13	Teapot	9.1	655	7.5YR8/4 pink; 5YR7/4–7/6 pink–reddish yellow; few sm. white inclusions; med. fired; handmade.
2	D02.26.7	D02013		4066.44.41.00	Teapot	7		5YR7/3 pink; burnished ext.; 2.5YR6/6 light red; many sm. black & white inclusions; poor to med. fired.
3	D02.30.3	D02013		4066.00.11.00	Teapot	9		7.5YR7/4 pink; burnished ext.; 5YR5/6 yellowish red; some med. black incl.; med. fired.
4	D02.12.4	D02012		4036.00.41.00	Teapot	9.5		7.5YR7/3 pink; burnished ext. 5YR6/8 reddish yellow; many sm. & med. white inclusions & gravel; well fired.
5	D02.21 et al	D02013		4036.54.42.00	Teapot	9.5		5YR7/4 pink; burnished ext. 10R5/6–4/4 red–weak red; some med. gravel; med. fired; handmade.
6	D02.29.16	D02013		4036.54.11.00	Teapot	11		2.5YR6/6 light red; some sm. black & white inclusions; med. fired.
7	D02.16.29	D02014		Base.00.00.13				2.5YR6/6 light red; 2.5YR6/6 light red; many small white incl.; poorly fired; handmade.
8	D02.29.2	D02013		Base.00.00.13				7.5YR8/4–7/4 pink; 10R6/6 light red; some small white incl.; friable, poorly fired; handmade.
9	D02.29.35	D02013		Base.00.00.15				7.5 YR7/4 pink; burnished 2.5 YR5/6 red; some small black inclusions, well fired.
10	D02.30.1	D02013		Base.00.00.13				7.5YR6/4 light brown; burnished ext. 2.5YR5/6 red–5YR5/6 yellowish red; many small and medium black inclusions, few medium white inclusions; medium fired.
11	D02.31.26	D02014–D02015		Base.00.00.13				2.5YR7/6; burnished ext.; 2.5YR6/6 light red; many medium black and white inclusions; medium fired; handmade.
12	D02 NR 9	D02		Base.00.00.15				5 YR7/4 pink; exterior burnished; 2.5 YR6/6 light red; many small black inclusions; medium fired.
13	D02.23.1	D02013		Base.00.00.13				7.5YR7/3 pink; burnished ext.; 7.5YR5/6 strong brown; many small and medium gravel; medium fired; handmade.
14	D02 NR 4	D02		Base.00.00.13				5 YR7/4 pink; burnished ext.; 10R6/4 pale red; many medium inclusions, well fired.
15	D02.22.7	D02013–D02015	302	4857.00.12.15	Lamp	16.5		7.5YR8/2 pinkish white; 5YR5/6 yellowish red; many sm. white & few med. white inclusions; well fired; handmade.
16	D02.23.82	D02013	300	4857.00.12.15	Lamp	17		7.5YR8/2 pinkish white; some med. white & black inclusions; med. fired, handmade.
17	D02.28.1	D02013	283	4857.00.11.16	Lamp	16		2.5YR6/6 light red; gritty, lg. black & white inclusions; soft/poorly fired; handmade.

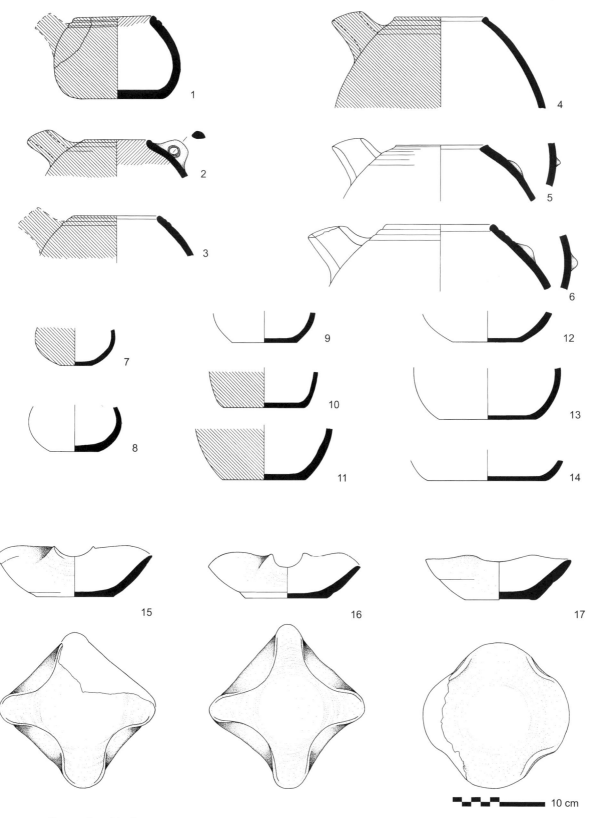

FIG. 10.8 *Pottery from Tomb D2.*

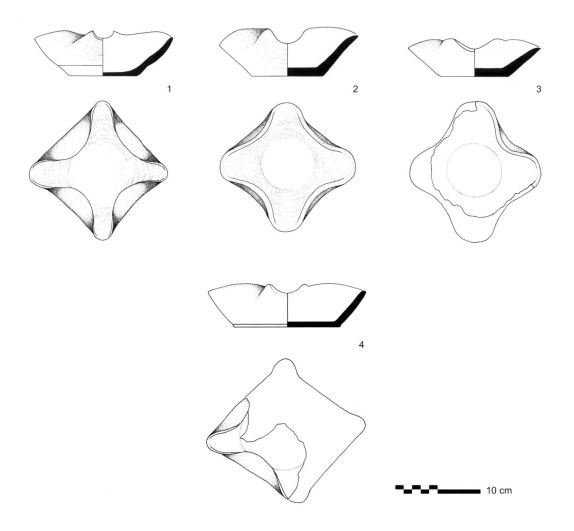

FIG. 10.9 *Pottery from Tomb D2.*

#	BUCKET	LOCUS	AP	FORMHARIBA	VESSEL	M	CAP	DESCRIPTION
1	D02.29.4	D02013	299	4857.00.11.15	Lamp	16.5		7.5YR7/2 pinkish gray; many sm. & med. (white and few black) inclusions; well fired; handmade.
2	D02.25	D02013	259	4857.00.61.11	Lamp	16		7.5YR8/2–7/2 pinkish white–pinkish gray; many sm. black and few white inclusions; poor-med.-well fired; handmade; all four spouts burned.
3	D02.28.7,20	D02013		4856.00.12.14	Lamp	15		5YR7/4 some sm. black & white inclusions; poorly fired.
4	D02.19.47	D02014		4856.00.00.15	Lamp	19		7.5YR8/4 many sm. black & white incl., some lg. gravel; poor-med. fired.

were packed to seal the entrance. On the northern and eastern perimeter of the shaft a plaster-like material was encountered that was difficult to penetrate. It was probably caliche, although it could have been a crude mortar as found in the shaft of Tomb A54 at Bâb adh-Dhrâ' (above). The plaster-like material was also found around the blocking stone. As excavation continued, it soon became apparent that there was a second (earlier) blocking stone (2005) lying slightly on edge on the shaft surface. Under it lay restorable pottery and disarticulated bones, apparently the final burial remains of the earlier phase (L. 2010; bucket no. 10). The pottery was found within a highly compacted layer mixed with caliche, making excavation extremely difficult.

Given the second capstone, it is evident that reuse of the tomb occurred, if the quantity of grave goods is any indication. The sequence seems to be that the lower capstone was pushed aside during a re-entry into the tomb, after which an upper, smaller capstone was put into place along with cobbles and small boulders to block the entrance before the shaft was filled with soil and stones.

The chamber of D2 was marked by a heavy layer of roof collapse, stone, and very dark soil as high as 0.30 m below the roof of the chamber, which was a little less than 2 m above the floor. Below this overburden, but within a locus of debris and rock, there was a layer of grave goods, including fragmentary ceramics and skeletal materials visible in the western half of the tomb and at the rear. Work started at the bench on the west, then continued in a section of the western half of the chamber. It was clear that there were remains mixed throughout a 0.30 m layer of soil and lying right on the bedrock. In places, there appeared to be a demarcation between upper and lower deposits; unfortunately, throughout most of the chamber the disarray rendered it impossible to separate the two, for at times ceramic fragments in the upper layer intruded into the lower deposit and vice versa. There were virtually no discernable interments or patterns indicating undisturbed burial deposits; rather, the remains lay mixed and scattered in a continuous deposit across the chamber, heavier in the center and along the back wall opposite the opening. Only in one area was

there a concentrated pile of bones, smashed pottery, and two fragmentary skulls.

The lower layer of deposits found lying on the bedrock contained fewer remains of ceramics and bone, and was located primarily at the back of the tomb chamber (bucket nos. 23–25), opposite the entrance, although a smattering of bone remains was found along the eastern side of the chamber (bucket nos. 26–28, 30–31). Fragments of pottery were found in a lower layer on the bench (Bucket nos. 21–22, 32) and in a small area near the shaft (bucket no. 33). These remains, as well as the assemblage found under blocking stone 2005, represent what probably was an earlier use phase of Tomb D2.

That the quantitative analysis of the ceramic assemblage yielded no distinguishing characteristics in the two layers is not surprising, given the restoration of "upper" with "lower" level pottery. Nonetheless, the pottery ranged from early to late (see Ch. 5).

Tomb D2 Objects (metal untested)

A270: Fragment of metal pin (copper?) (D2.10).
A268: Broken dagger with four (originally six) rivets (copper?) (D2.19).
A269: Tip of awl/pin (copper?) (D2.24).
A271: Fragment pin (copper?) (D2.14).

Tomb D2 Human/Animal Remains

Many fragments give an MNI of three adults and one juvenile; infant *capra/ovis* remains.

Tomb D3

Although the northern half of the upper part of the shaft of D3 (figs. 10.10–15) was destroyed, the edge at its lower extent was still visible. Thus, it was possible to obtain a plan of the dimension of the lower shaft. A type of plaster lined the bottom of the shaft and covered a number of cobble-sized stones, which blocked the opening to the chamber. There was no intact capstone at the entrance. The squarish burial chamber was 4 × 5.25 m, and, like D2, contained a small alcove-like structure along its western edge, but in this case there was no bench.

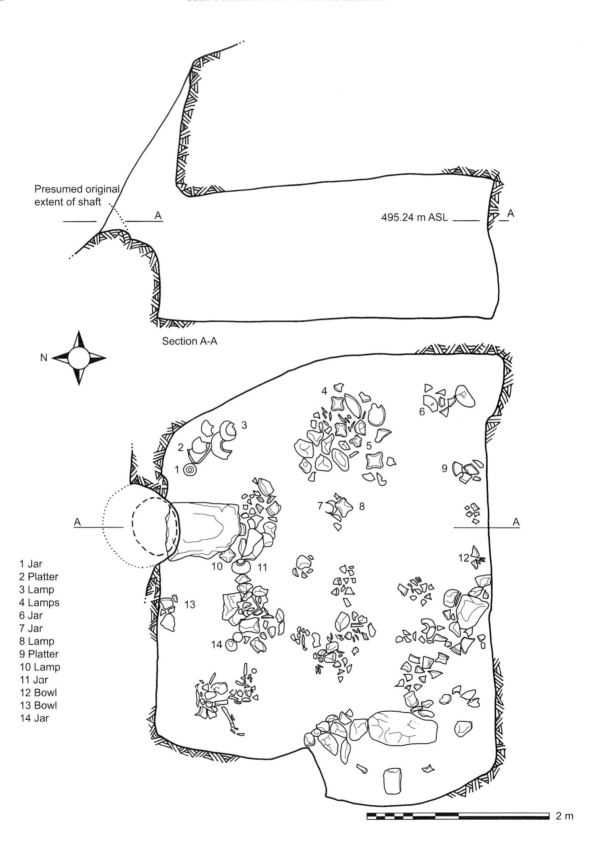

Presumed original
extent of shaft

495.24 m ASL

A   A

Section A-A

N

A   A

1 Jar
2 Platter
3 Lamp
4 Lamps
6 Jar
7 Jar
8 Lamp
9 Platter
10 Lamp
11 Jar
12 Bowl
13 Bowl
14 Jar

2 m

FIG. 10.10   *Plan and Section of Tomb D3.*

Excavation

As with D2, a granular soil with huwwar chips (probably from the original cutting of the tomb) was encountered in the shaft, beneath which was a layer of compacted soil and pottery fragments. Like D2, the chamber of D3 contained an over-burden virtually up to the ceiling. Excavation of this overburden—a matrix of granular soil and limestone chips, but compacted—began on the west side. Removal of this debris (ca. 1 m) revealed a level of heavy rock fall, probably roof collapse, toward the back of the chamber. The eastern half of the chamber was then brought down to the same level of rock fall. Below the rock fall lay another debris layer, within which was found the missing capstone, just south of the shaft. Presumably, it had fallen in at the time of the latest interment(s), and there was no effort made to re-block the entryway with it; instead, cobbles were used along with the plaster. Clearance of the fill layer, some rock fall, and huwwar chips revealed the burial layer.

In contrast to D2, this tomb provided evidence for segregated burials and associated grave goods. Several whole vessels (three jars and seven nearly complete or complete lamps) survived the roof collapse, however, pottery fragments from single vessels were found scattered about different parts of the chamber. The "alcove" in the western portion of the chamber contained a mass of crumbly, reddish-black ceramic fragments resembling tabun ware, seemingly smashed on a fairly high mound of dirt, which ran north south. The fragments could have been cooking-pot ware, given the discovery of two cooking pots in Tomb E10 (fig. 11.7:12–13).

The ceramic fragments and vessels in the northern portion of the tomb, particularly along the sides of the chamber and resting on bedrock near the entrance, were difficult to remove, as they appeared embedded into the surface. Apparently, slow seepage of water through the limestone created a tough, thick layer of caliche, which cemented some grave goods to the bedrock of the chamber. There were only two non-ceramic objects recovered.

Tomb D3 Objects (metal untested)

A285:   Flint blade (D3.01).
A272:   Fragment (copper?) pin (D3.23).

Tomb D3 Human/Animal Remains

Many fragments give an MNI of two adult individuals and one young adult; infant *capra/ovis* remains.

Tomb D4

This tomb (figs. 10.16–18) suffered the greatest damage to its shaft when the access road was bulldozed, and only a small portion of the southern perimeter of the shaft was preserved, showing a diameter of ca. 0.50 m. Removal of bulldozer debris revealed the chamber entrance, which was not blocked by a capstone. The chamber itself was square (almost 4 × 4m). Of all the tombs in Cemetery D, Tomb D4 has the largest chamber and the smallest shaft.

Excavation

As with the other tombs discussed, D4 had also suffered roof collapse and debris filled the tomb virtually to the chamber roof. Removal of the over-burden from the tomb revealed the capstone, which was found leaning upright inside the chamber just below the entrance. Its base rested on a soil layer in which was found a scatter of smashed pottery across the tomb. Unlike Tombs D2 and D3, there were relatively few remains in this extremely large and well-cut tomb. There seemed to be a concentration opposite the entrance in the middle of the tomb, but elsewhere there were simply individual pieces of broken pottery scattered. As in D3, upon clearance of the northern half of the chamber, near the entrance, there was pottery embedded in the bedrock and covered with caliche. The only discernible interments were found along the wall to the east of the entrance, where a skull and some bone remains were found, and along the western edge, where there was also a fairly intact skull along with several long bones and restorable pottery. A copper pin fragment was the only non-ceramic

FIG. 10.11   *Pottery from Tomb D3.*

#	BUCKET	LOCUS	AP	FORMHARIBA	VESSEL	M	CAP	DESCRIPTION
1	D03.21.1–8	D03017		4623.00.72.13	Platter	26	2,804	7.5YR7/2–7/4 pinkish gray–pink; ext. & int. burnished; some lg. black gravel; well fired.
2	D03.03.55	D03004		4620.00.14.00	Platter	30.5		5YR8/3 pink. Impressions on rim.
3	D03.16.17	D03014		4606.00.75.13	Platter	33	5,400	2.5YR6/6 light red; 2.5YR5/8 red.
4	D03.16.1	D03014		4605.00.75.11	Platter	29	3,611	7.5YR7/4 pink; ext & int. burnished 5YR6/6 reddish yellow.
5	D03.20.2	D03017		4605.00.75.00	Platter	30		7.5YR8/2 pinkish white; ext & int. burnished 10R6/6-5/8 light red–red.
6	D03.03.22	D03004		4605.00.75.00	Platter	34		5YR7/4 pink; ext & int. burnished 10R5/6 red.
7	D03.20a	D03017		4605.00.75.11	Platter	38	9,280	5YR7/3 pink; ext & int. burnished 10R6/6 light red; ovoid.
8	D03.19.1	D03016		4603.00.74.13	Platter	32	5,219	7.5YR7/4 pink; 2.5YR5/6 red.
9	D03.16.2	D03014		4602.00.13.00	Platter	46		5YR6/4 light reddish brown; 2.5YR6/6 light red.

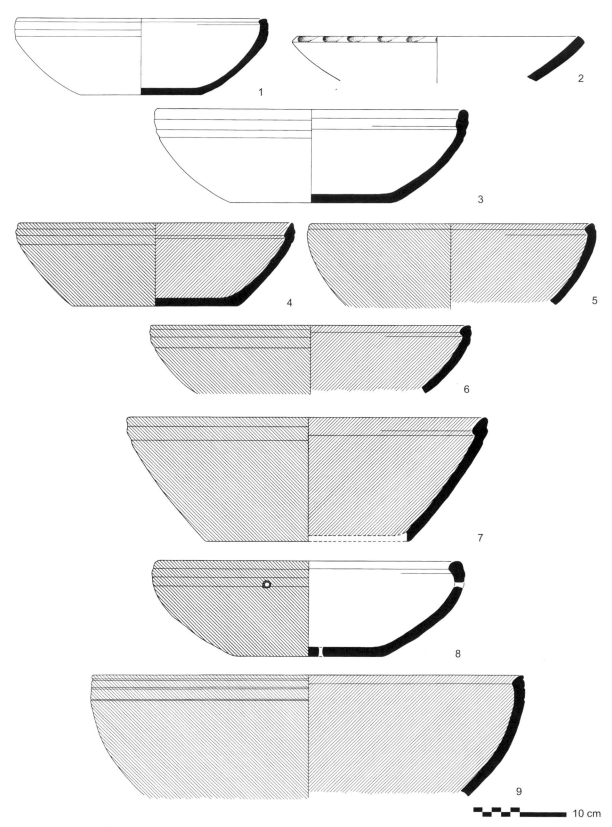

FIG. 10.11   *Pottery from Tomb D3.*

FIG. 10.12   *Pottery from Tomb D3.*

#	BUCKET	LOCUS	AP	FORMHARIBA	VESSEL	M	CAP	DESCRIPTION
1	D03.23.23	D03018		4600.00.75.00	Platter	31		5YR7/4 pink; ext & int. burnished 10R5/8 red.
2	D03.22	D03017		4600.00.75.00	Platter	34		2.5YR6/4 light reddish brown.
3	D03.24.10	D03019		4600.00.75.00	Platter	38		5YR7/4 pink; ext & int. burnished 10R5/6 red.
4	D03.24a	D03019		4600.00.75.00	Platter	37		7.5YR7/2 pinkish gray; ext & int. burnished; 10R5/6-4/6 yellowish red; many med. black inclusions, well fired.
5	D03.24.b	D03019		4600.00.75.00	Platter	38		7.5YR7/2 pinkish gray; ext & int. burnished 10R4/4 weak red; many sm., med., & lg. black inclusions, poorly fired.
6	D03.24c	D03019		4600.00.75.00	Platter	38		5YR7/4 pink; ext & int. burnished 10R5/6 red.
7	D03.21.4	D03017		4600.00.75.00	Platter	40		7.5YR7/4 pink; 2.5 YR6/6 light red.
8	D03.24.1–6	D03019	276	4568.00.11.13	Bowl	21	1,733	5YR7/4 pink; concentric burnishing 10R5/6-4/5 red; many sm. white inclusions, med. firing.
9	D03.21.11	D03017	282	4568.51.10.13	Bowl	21.3	1,921	5YR8/3-7/3 pink; concentric burnishing 10R6/8-5/8 light red–red; some sm. med. black inclusions; poor-med. firing.
10	D03.23.17	D03018		4538.00.73.13	Bowl	29.5	4,402	5YR7/4 pink; ext & int. burnished 10R6/6 light red.

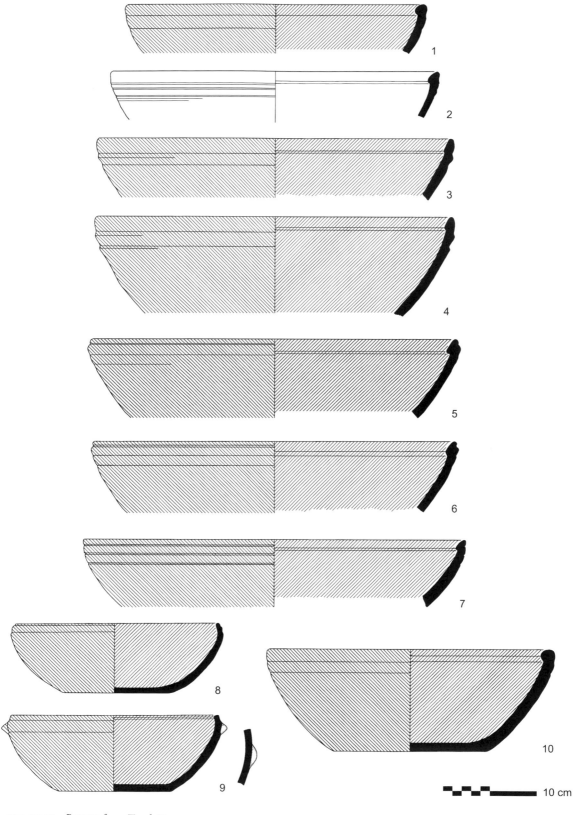

FIG. 10.12   *Pottery from Tomb D3.*

FIG. 10.13 *Pottery from Tomb D3.*

#	BUCKET	LOCUS	AP	FORMHARIBA	VESSEL	M	CAP	DESCRIPTION
1	D03.20.17	D03017, D03018, D03020	288	4443.22.61.15	Jug	3	192	2.5YR5/6; 7.5YR7/4 pink–2.5 YR5/6 red; many lg. gravel, black & white incl.; med. fired.
2	D03.21.20	D03017		4443.23.00.00	Jug			5YR7/4 pink; 10R6/6 light red; handmade.
3	D03.03.48	D03004		4421.22.61.00	Jug	10		5YR7/6 reddish yellow; med. fired.
4	D03.25.1	D03020		4272.00.11.00	Jar	5.2		7.5YR8/2 pinkish white; 5YR6/6 -5/6 reddish yellow–yellowish red.
5	D03.10	D03016		4271.00.61.00	Jar	8.25		7.5YR7/4 pink; 10R5/6 red; wheel finished; well fired.
6	D03.10.10	D03016	261	4271.54.61.13	Jar	7.3	599	5YR7/3-7/4 pink; burnished ext. 10R4/4-4/6 weak red–red; some sm. black & white inclusions; poorly fired; soft; handmade.
7	D03.23.26a	D03018		4220.54.00.00	Jar	7		close rills/combed.
8	D03.07	D03014	265	4232.54.12.13	Jar	7.7	1,588	5YR7/4- 10R6/4 pink–pale red; 10R6/6-5/6 light red–red; many med. white inclusions; poor-med. fired.
9	D03.09.30–15	D03015	266	4231.54.60.13	Jar	11.1	2,148	7.5YR7/2-7/4 pinkish gray–pink; ext. burnished 5YR6/4–5/4 light reddish brown–reddish brown; few sm. white and lg. black inclusions; handmade body, wheel-finished rim; poor-med. fired.
10	D03.19-20	D03016–D03018	286	4142.54.60.13	Jar	10.8	6,248	5YR7/4 pink; 10R6/6–5/6 light red–red; many sm. & med. white incl.; med.-well fired.
11	D03.20	D03017	279	4071.54.11.13	Teapot	6	592	7.5YR7/4 pink ext. burnish 10R5/6 red–7.5YR7/4 pink; many sm. black & white inclusions, some lg. gravel; well fired; extremely pitted.
12	D03.20.10–12	D03017		4066.17b.11.13	Teapot	7.8	1,179	10YR9/2 white; burnished ext. 5YR6/6-5/6 reddish-yellow–yellowish red; med. fired.
13	D03.21.13	D03017		4066.54.42.00	Teapot	10		5YR7/3 pink; burnished ext. 5YR6/6 reddish yellow; well fired.
14	D03.17	D03015		4036.00.42.00	Teapot	9.5		7.5YR6/2-6/4 pinkish gray–light brown, burnished ext. 2.5YR5/6 red–5YR5/6 yellowish red; med. fired.
15	D03.24.20	D03019		Base.00.00.13				5YR6/6 reddish yellow; burnished exterior 2.5YR6/6 reddish yellow; many large gravel; medium-well fired.
16	D03.23.33	D03018		Base.00.00.13				10YR7/3 very pale brown; 2.5YR6/6 light red.
17	D03.16.20	D03014		4260.00.00.13	Jar			5YR7/4 pink.
18	D03.03.1	D03015		4220.00.00.30	Jar			5YR7/4 pink; 2.5YR6/6 light red.
19	D03:24.19	D03019		Base.00.00.30				2.5YR7/2 pinkish gray; 2.5YR6/6 light red.
20	D03.21.17	D03018		4220.00.00.13	Jar			7.5YR8/2 pinkish white; ext. burnished.

FIG. 10.13   *Pottery from Tomb D3.*

FIG. 10.14 *Pottery from Tomb D3.*

#	Bucket	Locus	AP	FormHaRiBa	Vessel	M	Cap	Description
1	D03:23.26	D03018		Base.00.00.13				2.5YR6/4 light reddish brown; some small black inclusions; well fired.
2	D03.03.27	D03015		Base.00.00.13				2.5 YR6/6 light red; 10R6/6 light red.
3	D03.21.10	D03018		4220.00.00.10	Jar			2.5YR5/6 red; ext. surface 5YR6/6 reddish yellow.
4	D03.23.8	D03018		4220.00.00.13	Jar			2.5YR 6/6 light red; ext. surface 5YR7/4–7/6 pink–reddish yellow.
5	D03:21.3	D03018		4220.00.00.13	Jar			5YR6/4 light reddish brown; burnished ext. surface 5YR7/4 pink.
6	D03.22a	D03018		4600.00.00.13	Platter			
7	D03.03.12	D03015		4600.00.00.11	Platter			
8	D03.24	D03019		4600.00.00.11	Platter			
9	D03.23.05	D03018		4600.00.00.11	Platter			
10	D03.23	D03018		4600.00.00.11	Platter			
11	D03.10.3	D03016	281	4851.00.11.20	Lamp	14.5		2.5YR6/6 light red; few sm. white inclusions; poorly fired/friable.
12	D03.08.1	D03015	280	4857.00.12.13	Lamp	14.5		10YR6/6 brownish yellow; few med. white inclusions; well fired; one spout burned.
13	D03.15	D03018	262	4857.00.12.11	Lamp	16		7.5YR7/2 pinkish gray; trace of red slip on spout 2.5YR6/6 red; some sm. black & white inclusions; well fired; one spout burned.

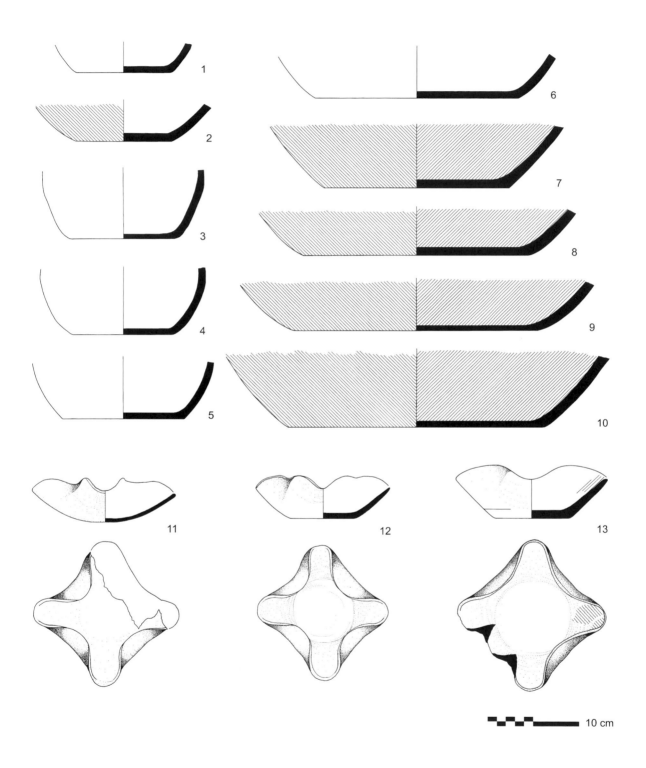

FIG. 10.14   *Pottery from Tomb D3.*

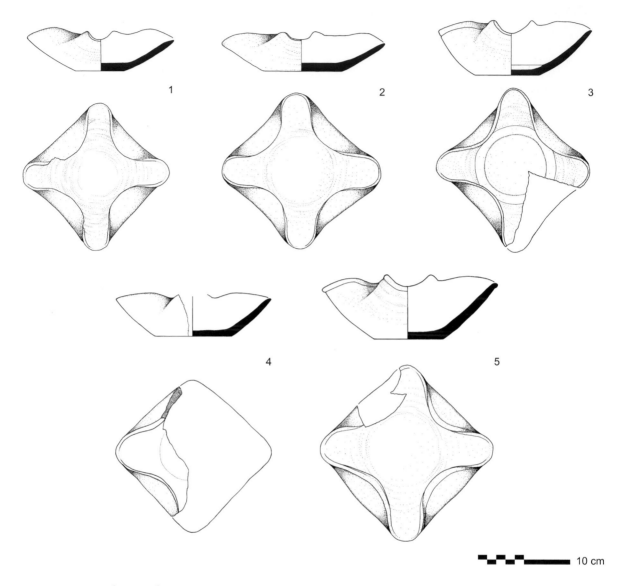

10 cm

FIG. 10.15 *Pottery from Tomb D3.*

#	Bucket	Locus	AP	FormHaRiBa	Vessel	M	Cap	Description
1	D03.12	D03017	264	4856.00.12.11	Lamp	16.3		2.5YR6/6 light red; some sm. white inclusions; well fired; one spout burned.
2	D03.11	D03017	263	4857.00.12.11	Lamp	17		7.5YR8/2–7/4 pinkish white–pink; some sm. white & black incl.; med. fired; one spout burned.
3	D03.23.29	D03018, D03019	301	4856.00.12.13	Lamp	16.5		7.5YR8/2 pinkish white; some sm. white inclusions; well fired.
4	D03.21.39	D03018		4857.00.12.13	Lamp	17		5YR7/4
5	D03.14	D03017	260	4856.00.62.13	Lamp	19		7.5YR7/4 pink; small black and a few sm. white incl.; medium-well fired; all four spouts burned.

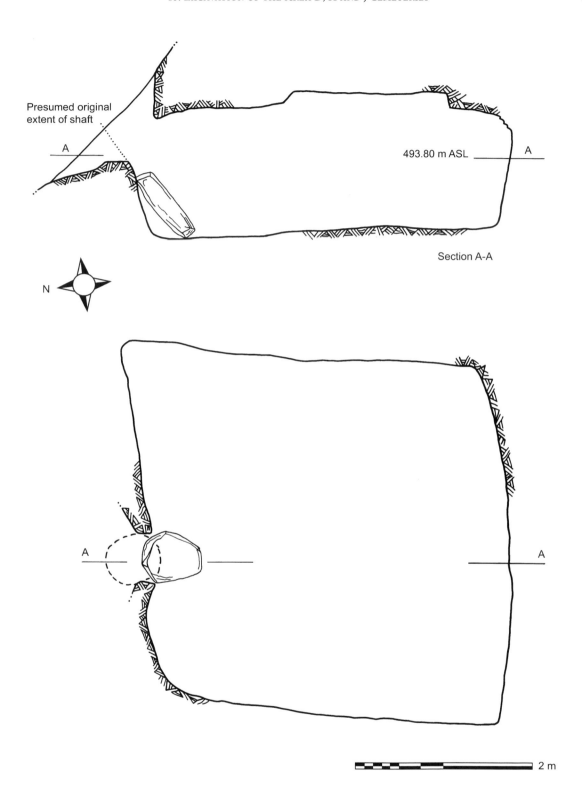

Presumed original extent of shaft

493.80 m ASL

Section A-A

N

2 m

FIG. 10.16 *Plan and Section of Tomb D4.*

FIG. 10.17 *Pottery from Tomb D4.*

#	Bucket	Locus	AP	FormHaRiBa	Vessel	M	Cap	Description
1	D04.20	D04005	278	4668.51.10.13	Platter	19.9	1,156	5YR7/3; burnished ext & int. 10R5/4–5/6 weak red–red; many med. black & white inclusions; well fired.
2	D04.25	D04005	275	4659.00.10.30	Platter	23	1,728	10YR7/3 very pale brown; burnished ext & int. 5YR6/6-2.5YR5/6 red–yellowish red; many med. black & white inclusions; poor-med. fired.
3	D04.05.2	D04005		4625.00.73.13	Platter	24	2,008	10YR8/2 white; burnished ext & int. 2.5YR5/6 -5YR7/6, red–reddish yellow.
4	D04.05.1	D04005		4606.00.75.13	Platter	36	6,226	5YR8/4-7/4 pink; burnished ext & int. 10R6/6–2.5YR6/6 light red.
5	D04.07.5	D04005		4612.00.75.11	Platter	37	6,645	5YR6/6 reddish yellow, ext. & int. burnished 2.5YR5/6 red.
6	D04.08.10	D04006		4600.00.75.00	Platter	31		5YR7/6 reddish yellow; burnished ext & int. 5YR6/6 reddish yellow.
7	D04.09.12	D04006		4600.00.75.00	Platter	40		7.5YR9/2-9/4 pinkish white–pink; burnished ext & int. 7.5YR5/5–10R5/6 brown–weak red.
8	D04.09.5	D04006		4600.00.75.00	Platter	40		7.5YR7/4 pink; burnished ext. & int. 10R5/6 red; handmade.
9	D04.08.1,6	D04006		4503.00.76.00	Bowl	33		7.5YR7/2-7/4 pinkish gray–pink; burnished ext & int. 5YR5/6-6/6 yellowish red–reddish yellow.
10	D04.05.18	D04005		4960.00.62.00	Misc.	3.8		5YR8/3-7/4 pink.
11	D04.05.23	D04005		4262.00.62.00	Jar	7		7.5YR8/2 pinkish white; 5YR7/4 pink.
12	D04.09.23	D04005		4222.00.61.00	Jar	9		2.5YR6/8 light red.
13	D04.08.27	D04005		4222.00.62.00	Jar	12		5YR7/3-7/4 pink.
14	D04.05.14,25	D04005		4222.00.60.00	Jar	12		7.5YR8/4 pink; 10R5/6 red.
15	D04.10.1	D04006		4222.00.11.00	Jar	10		7.5YR7/4 pink.
16	D04.04.8	D04005		4222.00.00.30	Jar			5YR7/4 pink.

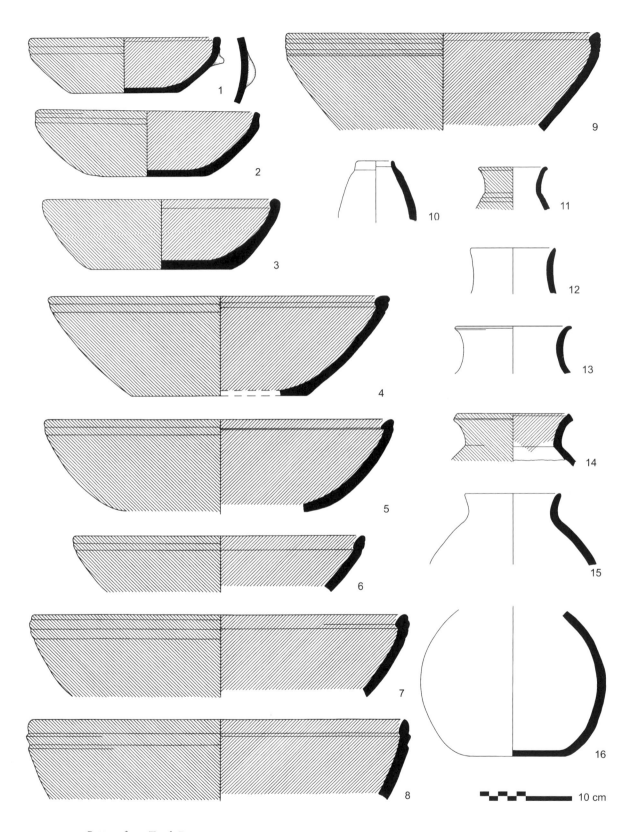

FIG. 10.17 *Pottery from Tomb D4.*

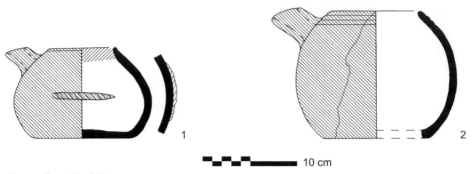

FIG. 10.18 *Pottery from Tomb D4.*

#	BUCKET	LOCUS	AP	FORMHARIBA	VESSEL	M	CAP	DESCRIPTION
1	D04.04.5,7	D04005	277	4066.18.41.10	Teapot	7	846	7.5YR7/2–7/4 pinkish gray–pink; 5YR5/6 yellow-ish red; many sm. white incl.; well fired; handmade.
2	D04.11	D04006		4066.00.11.13	Teapot	9	1,809	7.5YR8/4–7/4 pink; ext. burnished 5YR7/6–6/6 reddish yellow.

object recovered, along with 18 vessels. The bad preservation and scatter of the skeletal remains, and general disturbance of the tomb suggest that robbing of this tomb had occurred.

Tomb D4 Object (metal untested)

A273:   Fragment (copper?) pin (D4.02)

Tomb D4 Human/Animal Remains

Many fragments give an MNI of two adult individuals; infant *capra/ovis* remains.

Tomb D5

Tomb D5 (figs. 10.19–20), located a few meters up-slope of D2 and the bulldozed road, was excavated in the hope that there would be an undisturbed chamber. The shaft was complete, being nearly 1.75 m in depth, and marked by the absence of pottery in the rocky debris which filled it. There was no blocking stone. Unfortunately, the chamber was nearly filled with rubble and soil debris from partial roof collapse. Once the overburden was removed, it became obvious that this tomb had been cleared out. On the floor was one small EB IV pitcher and a few bones, all that was left to provide evidence that

it had been used at all. Tomb D5 had a somewhat irregular, almost oblong plan, roughly 2.75 × 1.85 m, showing some similarity to Tomb D10 (also on the upper row).

Tomb D5 Human/Animal Remains

The seven bone fragments provided an MNI of one adult.

Tomb D6

In the interim between the 1984 and 1987 seasons, a widening of the bulldozed road cut had occurred, revealing another shaft tomb exposed about 6.8 meters west of D4. The mostly destroyed tomb was noted, but not excavated.

Tomb D7

Tomb D7 (fig. 10.21) represents a tomb that had suffered massive destruction. Bulldozing of the road sliced off the upper half of the tomb, which obliterated evidence of an entry shaft. What remained took on the appearance of an ill-defined pit. The chamber was not fully delineated, and the shaft not found. An architectural plan was not prepared. The ceiling of the chamber had collapsed and was found underneath a 1.3 m thick layer of debris and spoil shoved in by the bulldozer. Removal of the ceiling collapse revealed a thin layer of smashed ceramics, plus eroded and crushed human bones and a spacer bead.

Tomb D7 Object

A286:   Bone spacer bead (D7.01).

Tomb D7 Human/Animal Remains

The fragmentary remains indicate an MNI of one adult.

Tomb D8

After a brief reconnaissance of Area D in 1987 to identify additional potential tomb locations, the designation D8 was assigned to a flat limestone slab (0.75 × 0.75 m) lying in a slight depression in the ground.

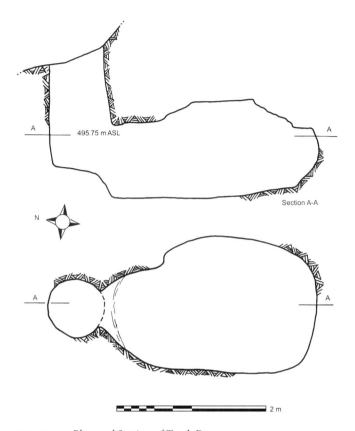

FIG. 10.19   *Plan and Section of Tomb D5.*

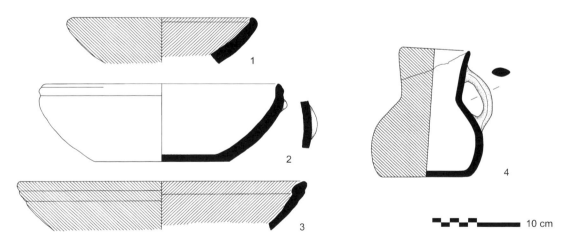

FIG. 10.20   *Pottery from Tomb D5.*

#	Bucket	Locus	AP	FormHaRiBa	Vessel	M	Cap	Description
1	D05.01.3	D05003		4665.00.73.00	Platter	20		7.5YR7/4 pink; vestigial slip 2.YR5/6 red; some gravel.
2	D05.01.1	D05003		4628.51.12.13	Platter	26	3,000	7.5YR7/4 pink; well fired, sm.–med. gravel.
3	D05.01.2	D05003		4605.00.75.00	Platter	32		7.5YR7/4 pink; 2.5YR5/6 red; well-fired, sm.–med. gravel.
4	D05.01	D05003	267	4422.23.11.13	Jug	6.6	742	5YR6/4 light reddish brown; ext. burnished 10YR5/6 red, many white and some black incl., well-fired.

FIG. 10.23 *Pottery from Tomb D9.*

#	BUCKET	LOCUS	AP	FORMHARIBA	VESSEL	M	CAP	DESCRIPTION
1	D09.18.1	D09005		4762.00.62.13	Bowl	6	176	5YR8/4 pink; 2.5YR4/6 red; friable, core, sm. white & black inclusions. Local to KI.
2	D09.22.1	D09007		4665.00.73.10	Platter	18		7.5YR7/4 pink; 10R4/8 red; well fired, sm.–med. gravel, white inclusions.
3	D09.01.3	D09001		4665.00.11.00	Platter	18		7.5YR7/4 pink; well fired, sm. gravel; white incl.
4	D09.10.1	D09006		4664.00.71.13	Platter	20	907	7.5YR7/4 pink; 2.5YR4/8 red; well fired, sm. gravel.
5	D09.06.1	D09004		4665.00.73.15	Platter	22	1,278	7.5YR8/4 pink, 2.5YR5/6 red; well fired. Local to KI.
6	D09.11	D09006		4645.00.73.11	Platter	23	1,501	7.5YR7/4 pink; some sm.–med. limestone & gravel.
7	D09.04.3	D09002		4645.00.75.13	Platter	24	1,871	7.5YR8/2 pinkish white; sm.–med. gravel, well fired.
8	D09.24.1	D09007		4620.00.75.00	Platter	28		5YR8/4 pink (light core); well fired, 10R4/8 red, sm. gravel, limestone.
9	D09.01.4	D09001		4620.00.75.00	Platter	30		7.5YR7/4 pink; 5YR5/6 yellowish red; well-fired, some gravel.
10	D09.17.6	D09004		4600.00.75.00	Platter	32		7.5YR8/2 pinkish white; 2.5YR5/6 red; well fired sm.–med. gravel.
11	D09.06.2	D09004		4600.00.75.00	Platter	32		7.5YR7/4 pink; 2.5YR6/6 light red; well fired, mend hole; sm.–med. gravel, some limestone.
12	D09.01.8	D09001		4600.00.75.00	Platter	36		2.5YR5/6 red; 2.5YR5/6 red.
13	D09.05.3	D09003		4560.00.75.00	Bowl	22		7.5YR7/4 pink; 2.5YR6/6 light red; well fired; sm.–med. gravel; grog.
14	D09.15.9	D09007		4422.23.61.00	Jug	5		5YR6/8 red-yellow; 25YR4/6 red; well fired, sm.–med. gravel.
15	D09.16.3	D09007		4421.22.12.00	Jug	10		7.5YR6/4 light brown; 2.5YR4/6 red; soft; much sm.–med. gravel. Local to KI.
16	D09.27.1	D09007		4262.00.61.13	Jar	8	505	7.5YR6/4 light brown, well fired, sm. white inclusions, few sm. gravel. Local to KI.
17	D09.21.1	D09007		4220.00.62.00	Jar	10		10YR6/4 light yellowish brown; 2.5YR4/8 red, well fired, sm. gravel. Local to KI.
18	D09.17.1	D09004		4071.54.41.00	Teapot	8		7.5YR7/4 pink; 2.5YR5/6 light red, well fired, sm. gravel. Local to KI.
19	D09.26.2 et al.	D09007		4066.00.41.00	Teapot	9		7.5YR5/4 brown; 2.5YR5/6 red; sm.–med. gravel, med. fired.
20	D09.01.9	D09001		4020.00.18.00	Jar	20		7.5YR7/4 pink; well-fired; many sm. gravel.

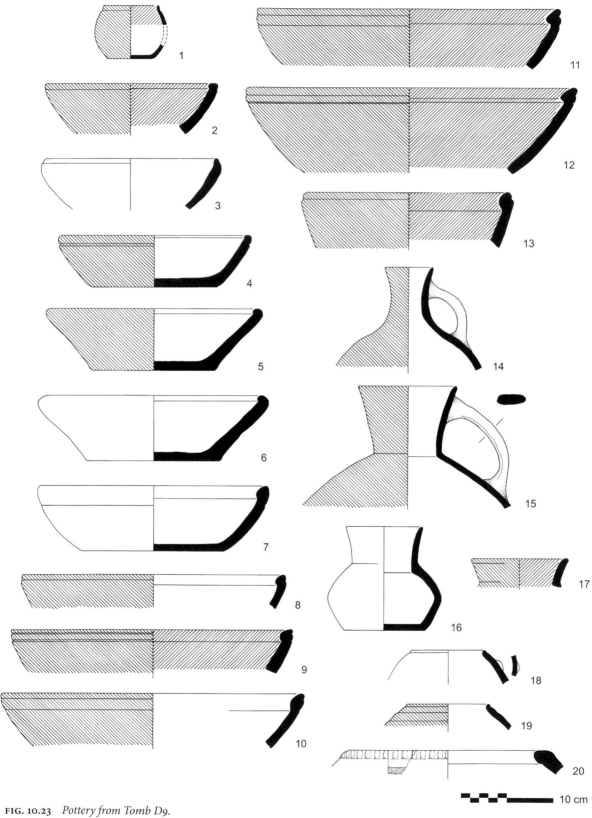

FIG. 10.23 *Pottery from Tomb D9.*

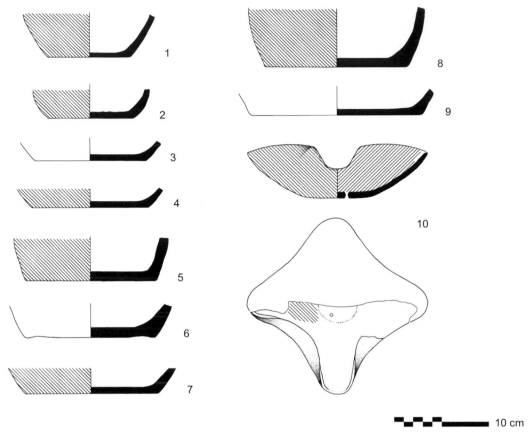

10 cm

FIG. 10.24 *Pottery from Tomb D9.*

#	BUCKET	LOCUS	AP	FORMHARIBA	VESSEL	M	CAP	DESCRIPTION
1	D09.04.2	D09002		Base.00.00.13				7.5 YR8/2 pinkish white vest. ext. slip 5 YR6/6 red–yellow; many sm.–med. gravel.
2	D09.09.1	D09006		4220.00.00.13	Jar			7.5YR7/4 pink; 2.5YR4/8 red; many sm. gravel.
3	D09.05.4	D09003		4560.00.00.13	Bowl			5YR6/4 light reddish brown; 2.5YR6/6 light red; well fired; sm.–med. white & black inclusions.
4	D09.01.7	D09001		4560.00.00.13	Bowl			5YR6/4 light red brown; slip ext 2.5YR5/8 red; sm.–lg. wadi gravel; limestone.
5	D09.02.1	D09002		Base.00.00.11				7/5YR8/2 pinkish white; 10R light red; well fired; sm.–med. black inclusions.
6	D09.04.10	D09002		4220.00.00.14	Jar			7.5YR5/4 brown; well fired, sm. gravel.
7	D09.20.1x	D09007		Base.00.00.13				
8	D09.28.15	D09002		4140.00.00.13	Jar			10YR6/4 light yellowish brown; 5YR5/6 red; much gravel, white inclusions.
9	D09.20.1	D09007		4140.00.00.30	Jar			7.5YR7/4 pink; well fired; sm.–med. gravel.
10	D09.09.11	D09006		4856.00.00.13	Lamp		17.5	5YR8/4 pink (light core); well fired, 10R4/8 red, sm. gravel, limestone.

Tomb D9 Objects

A328:   Flint flake (D9.09).
A355:   Carnelian bead (D9.24).

Tomb D9 Human/Animal Remains

Poorly preserved bone indicated an MNI of one adult and one juvenile.

Tomb D10

Above the road cut, some 6 m west of and aligned with Tomb D9, a test trench revealed the shaft of Tomb D10 (figs. 10.25–26). This tomb is the smallest found in Cemetery D. Its shape is irregular (almost egg-shaped) like that of Tomb D5, which is slightly larger. Both of these tombs are located in the upper ledge of the cemetery dug so far, and they are the only ones in this cemetery having a very irregular shape. The shaft of Tomb D10 was round and relatively small (a diameter of 0.90 m), but almost 2 m in depth. The chamber was ca. 2.25 × 1.85 m. Tomb D10 was robbed in antiquity, but contrary to other tombs in the area, nothing was found in the shaft except for a carnelian bead and a small piece of bone.

Excavation

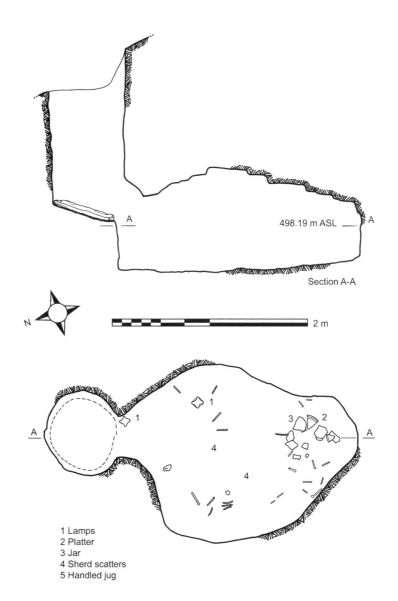

498.19 m ASL

Section A-A

N

2 m

A

A

1 Lamps
2 Platter
3 Jar
4 Sherd scatters
5 Handled jug

FIG. 10.25   *Plan and Section of Tomb D10.*

The upper part of the shaft included loose soil and rocks, below which there was a layer of flint and limestone having the hardness of concrete—a bedrock-like consistency—making excavation extremely difficult. Below this concreted material, at ca. 0.95 m in depth, the team encountered a "floor" of flat stones, well-cemented to the surrounding hard-packed flint and huwwar. Below this "floor," there was a much looser soil and rock matrix, which proved to be covering a large blocking stone, removed from its original position at the entrance. Three large stones obstructed the entrance to the chamber. Removal of this obstruction revealed a layer of roof fall (huwwar chips and stones) atop a 0.40 m light brown layer of soil. Several fragments of pottery and broken bones lay scattered all over the tomb on top of this layer.

Dispersed within, on top, and throughout this layer were sherds from individual vessels and broken bones. A complete lamp lay in front of the entrance in the middle of this layer. The grave goods found in D10, along with its peculiar shape may have originally pointed to some distinctions with the other tombs and interments found in

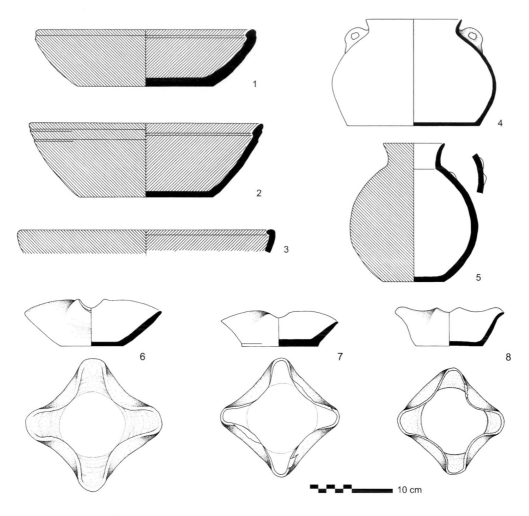

FIG. 10.26 *Pottery from Tomb D10.*

#	Bucket	Locus	AP	FormHaRiBa	Vessel	M	Cap	Description
1	D10.02.1–2 et al.	D10003		4625.00.75.13	Platter	26	2,106	7.5YR7/4 pink; 10R5/6 red; med fired, sm.–med. gravel.
2	D10.02.41–45	D10003		4625.00.75.13	Platter	28	3,388	7.5YR7/4 reddish yellow; 2.25YR5/8 red; well fired; sm.–med. gravel.
3	D10.04.3	D10003		4600.00.73.00	Platter	31		7.5YR6/6 reddish yellow; 5YR6/6 reddish yellow; sm.–med. limestone.
4	D10.04.27 et al.	D10003		4211.45.11.15		12	2,582	7.5YR7/6 reddish yellow; core; poorly fired; med.–lg. gravel, some lg.
5	D10.04.36	D10003		4221.54.61.13	Jar	7	1,474	7.5YR8/2 pinkish white; neck 5YR6/6 red; well fired, sm. gravel.
6	D10.08	D10003	322	4857.00.12.11	Lamp	16		7.5YR6/4 light brown; well fired; many sm.–med.–lg. limestone.
7	D10.09.1	D10003		4857.00.12.15	Lamp	14		7.5YR6/6 reddish yellow; well fired, sm.–med. gravel.
8	D10.10	D10003	323	4857.00.12.11	Lamp	13		5YR6/6 reddish yellow; well fired; sm.–lg. gravel limestone.

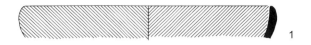

FIG. 10.27 *Pottery from Tomb D Test Pit.*

 10 cm

#	Bucket	Locus	AP	FormHaRiBa	Vessel	M	Cap	Description
1	Dtestpit.1			4620.00.11.00	Platter		26	5YR5/8 yellowish red; 10R5/6 red; well fired; sm.–med. gravel.

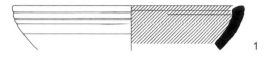

FIG. 10.28 *Pottery from Tomb H2.*

10 cm

#	Bucket	Locus	AP	FormHaRiBa	Vessel	M	Cap	Description
1	H02.01.2			4660.00.75.00	Platter		20	7.5YR7/4 pink; vestigial slip int. 5YR6/6 reddish yellow; many white inclusions; few gravel "grainy."

Cemetery D, for example, square tombs D9 and D10.

Tomb D10 Objects

A354: Carnelian bead (D10.01).
A408: Carnelian bead (D10.07).
A409: Carnelian bead (D10.07).
A403: Five fragments of black stone bead (D10.04).
A407: Black stone bead (D10.07).
A401: Black stone bead (D10.02).
A402: Black stone bead (D10.02).

Tomb D10 Human/Animal Remains

Highly fragmented remains are indicative of an MNI of one younger adult and one juvenile.

Tomb D Test Pit

In the search for shaft tombs, a test pit was excavated in which one EB IV vessel was found. This excavation was abandoned and the precise location was not marked on the map as a "tomb."

CEMETERY H

This Cemetery is upslope and to the east of the Cemetery D shaft tombs. It was an area of natural caves, some of which showed evidence of modification into cave/shaft tombs. Tomb H3 showed some evidence of excavation of bedrock that may have been a shaft. A survey of the area found EB IV sherds in front of Cave H2. Exploration of a road cut on the hill flank (H1) uncovered some EB IV remains as well. It was difficult to estimate the size of this cemetery because of lack of more complete information. There were several small caves in the area that could have been used as burial places, but erosion, roof collapse, and robbing were serious obstacles for the understanding of burial practices in this area.

Square H1

In the road cut on the hill flank, an EB IV loop handle and a basalt grinding stone were found. These are probable evidence of a tomb in this vicinity.

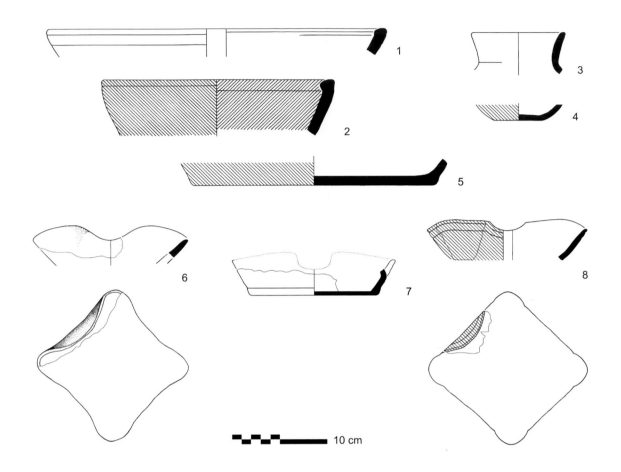

FIG. 10.29 *Pottery from Tomb H3.*

#	BUCKET	LOCUS	AP	FORMHARIBA	VESSEL	M	CAP	DESCRIPTION
1	H03.01.2	H03001		4600.00.75.00	Platter	40		7.5YR7/4 pink; vestigial slip int 5YR6/6 reddish yellow; many white inclusions; few gravel "grainy."
2	H03.03.1	H03004		4570.00.75.00	Bowl	24		5YR8/4 pink; 2.5YR85/8 red; many sm.-med. gravel; well fired.
3	H03.01.1	H03001		4230.00.11.00	Jar	9.5		7.5YR7/4 pink; well fired, sm.-med. white/black inclusions.
4	H03.04.1	H03004		4260.00.00.13	Jar			7.5YR7/4 pink; 2.5YR5/6 red; friable; many is.
5	H03.02.1	H03003		4600.00.00.15	Platter			7.5YR8/4 pink; 5YR6/6 reddish yellow; well fired; sm. bl/white inclusions.
6	H03.05.1	H03004		4850.00.00.00	Lamp	16		7.5YR7/4 pink; well fired; fine temper.
7	H03.05.5	H03004		4850.00.00.15	Lamp			5YR6/4 light reddish brown, black core; med. fired; some gravel.
8	H03.03.7	H03004		4850.00.00.00	Lamp	16.5		7.5YR8/4 pink; 10R5/8 red; rilled ext.; much gravel, white ls.

FIG. 10.30 *Pottery from Tomb J1.*

#	Bucket	Locus	AP	FormHaRiBa	Vessel	M	Cap	Description
1	J01.02	J01001	312	4422.23.61.13	Jug	5	347	strap-handled, squat; with flaring neck; ext. burnish.
2	J01.01	J01001	311	4421.21.61.13	Jug	5	2,298	squat with strap handle; orange ware; one-half rim preserved.

Cave H2

It is possible that this cave was a tomb, since in the rubble in front of the cave, which was used by local people as a rubbish pit, there were EB IV sherds (fig. 10.28). Given the condition of the cave, the decision was made to not excavate it.

Cave/Shaft Tomb H3

Tomb H3 was probably a shaft tomb that used an already existing cave modified for burial use (fig. 10.29). A trench was opened in this cave to test the presence of EB IV burials in the area. Human bones and EB IV pottery sherds in an extremely decayed condition were found sitting directly on bedrock, under a heavy layer of roof collapse and soil deposits. The cave had clearly been used as a rubbish pit. The trench cutting in H3 began about 1.50 m in length and 1.50m in width outside of the cave and continued for 1 m into the cave.

The area just in front of the entrance to the cave appeared to be cut and modified, and perhaps enlarged. At the entrance of the cave, a layer with many stones was exposed, some of them in line suggesting an entrance blocking, the date of which could not be determined. Excavation exposed a flat stone, possibly the blocking stone to the entrance. The cave appeared to be around 5 × 4 m, a vast chamber, filled almost to the roof. The EB IV sherds come from the area immediately outside the entrance, where there is some evidence of excavation of bedrock for a shaft. A burial on Floor 3004/bedrock was found to be badly damaged because of roof collapse and probably reuse or robbing. There were incomplete pottery vessels, along with the disintegrating and smashed bones. Due to the level of collapse, the decision was made to abandon the excavation of this cave.

H3 Objects

A294: Shell pendant (H3.03).

H3 Human/Animal Remains

The very few bone fragments suggest an MNI of one adult.

FIG. 10.31 *Photo of Tomb J1.*

CEMETERY J

Tomb J1

Following a report about a vessel found in a "tomb" cut by a bulldozer, the survey team investigated the area, which is on the hillside some 450–550 m west of the tell. What remained of the tomb (figs. 10.30–31) was a niche or perhaps the back of a chamber of a shaft tomb. It was a small chamber, about 0.73 m in diameter, 0.64 m deep, and about 0.70 m high. Two whole vessels were found in a thin layer of soil just above bedrock, one juglet and one jug, on their side, surrounded by disarticulated human bones.

J1 Objects

A366a–b: Two black stone pendant beads (J1.01).

J1 Human/Animal Remains

The remains suggested an MNI of two juveniles, one approximately 5–7 years and the other 11–13 years.

Chapter 11

Excavation of the Area E Cemetery

by James J. D'Angelo

The area immediately east of the main mound, which Glueck (1939: 128) had referred to as "another fully as large, located between two small parallel *wudyân,*" was first examined in 1981 and 1982 by means of informal pedestrian survey (see figs. 1.5 and 9.1). The area was, at the time, under cultivation, about equally divided between groves and open fields. The southern-most portion of this area, nearest the Wâdi al-Wâla, had been developed as part of a government agricultural station, and was seen to be greatly disturbed due to construction activities that included buildings, septic tanks, and roads. Although not a systematic survey, no architectural or other stone features were observed in either of these locales, nor were any concentrations of ceramics observed. In fact, the sherd density appeared to be markedly sparse as compared to the mound itself. No attempt at collection was made.

Beginning in 1984, a more systematic survey and mapping effort, as well as excavations, began in the area that Glueck described as extending "somewhat beyond the eastern of the two *wudyân,*" and where he reported possible "foundation remains of houses, menhir-circles, and large standing or fallen menhirs" (1939: 128). It is in that eastern

area where there is an alluvial deposit of limestone breccia. Weathering of the breccia caused the formation of irregular cavities and crannies, some of which were later opportunistically utilized for use in burials. Excavation of nine of the breccia concavities in 1984 resulted in the discovery of five sterile chambers (E4–8); one feature with two small, connected chambers, silt and ash layers, but no cultural materials (E1); a small cavity with one adult femur but no cultural material (E2); and two chambers (E3 and E9) with skeletal and artifactual remains.

Sometime prior to the 1987 season, road construction connecting the Dhiban Highway with Barza (Roman Iskandar) to the west at the bend of the wâdi bisected Area E, exposing three additional shaft/chamber tombs of which two were sterile (E12 and E13) and one contained a burial (E10). These and two additional burials (E11 and E14) were excavated in 1987.

What follows is a discussion of the EB IV burials excavated in Cemetery E in 1984 and 1987: E3, E9, E10, and E14. Non-EB IV materials, as found in E11, will appear in a future volume. Other features explored and/or excavated in Area E in recent seasons, such as, "circles-of-stone," menhirs, "open-air

209

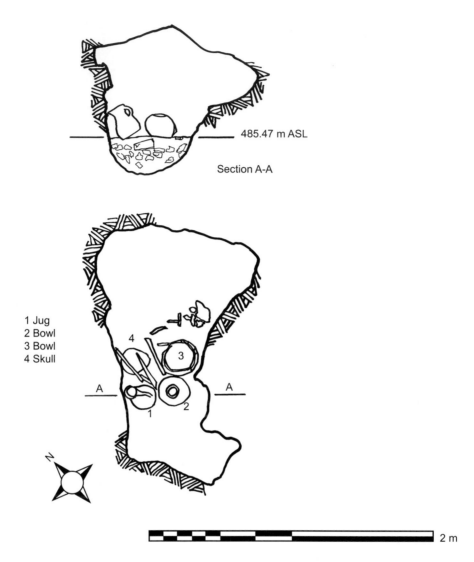

FIG. 11.1   *Plan and section of Tomb E3.*

sanctuaries," as well as a cultic installation on the ridge behind the site, will also appear in a future volume.

THE TOMBS

Tomb E3

Tomb E3 (figs. 11.1–11.3) was a small, irregular chamber containing an undisturbed, disarticulated double burial. When first seen, the opening was about 0.30 m high, obscured by vegetation. Small or smaller openings like this were common in Area E, and only an attempt at excavation established whether there was an actual cavity large enough to contain a burial. This small cavity contained two skulls, one slightly larger than the other, carefully placed on either side of a bone pile with the remaining bones placed between and over them. The skulls, both juvenile individuals, faced the rear of the chamber so that they were facing east. Across the opening of the chamber were three upright, whole EB IV vessels. There was a prepared surface of small stones (Locus 3003) under the burial and vessels. The irregular chamber measured, after excavation, approximately 0.50 m wide by 1 m deep by 0.70 m in height.

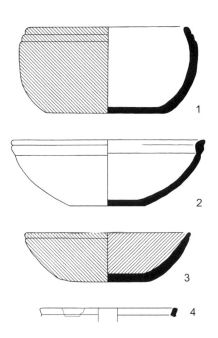
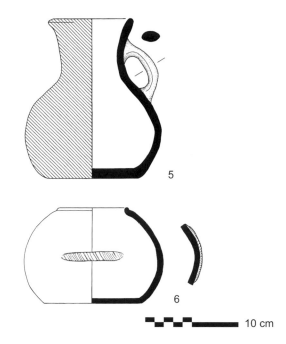

FIG. 11.2 *Pottery from Tomb E3.*

#	BUCKET	LOCUS	AP	FORMHARIBA	VESSEL	M	CAP	DESCRIPTION
1	E03.02	E03003	216	4705.00.11.13	Bowl	16	1,638	7.5YR /4 pink; burnished ext. 5YR7/4 pink.
2	E03.02.1	E03003		4667.00.75.13	Platter	20	1,179	5YR7/6 reddish yellow, well fired, fine temper.
3	E03.04	E03003	217	4666.00.19.30	Platter	17	585	single rill. 5YR7/3 pink; burnished ext. & int. 10R 4/6 red.
4	E03.02.04	E03003		4730.00.62.00	Bowl	13.6		7.5YR7/4 pink; poorly fired, med.–lg. gravel.
5	E03.03	E03003	228	4422.23.62.13	Jug	8.5	1,058	5YR7/4 pink; burnished ext. 5YR5/8 yellowish red.
6	E03.01.1	E03003		4066.18.41.13	Teapot	7	1,022	5YR6/6 reddish yellow; friable; many gravel.

Excavation

A 1 × 2 m probe in front of the cavity opening uncovered the edges of a "pit" at a depth of only 0.10 m. Fortunately, the pit was large enough at the opening to serve as a transverse control section before actual excavation of the interior portion of the cavity. Altogether, there were three distinct soil loci (3001–3003) excavated within the pit, each peeled back into the chamber. The first two levels were sterile and consisted of 0.20 m of loose, dry, silty loam, with small flint and limestone inclusions, becoming more consolidated with depth. The

third level, ca. 0.15–0.20 m, was a moist, compact, reddish clay loam with pebble-sized inclusions. It is this level within the chamber that contained the burial and grave goods. Given the confined space, excavation of the burial and soil as one locus (equals Locus 3003) was necessary. There was decomposed bone throughout the matrix.

Apparently, the bed of cobbles and small stones (Locus 3006) under the burial was intended to level the bottom of the chamber. This locus of stone was confined to the chamber. In the pit, the compact clay loam of Locus 3003 continued to the bottom, where one sherd and one small cobble

FIG. 11.3 *Photo of Tomb E3.*

were recovered. The fact that no blocking stone or other stones were found suggests that the burial may have originally been covered with soil, with additional soil and gravel penetrating the cavity from a crack that ran over the top of the chamber. Since soil Locus 3003 is the same inside and outside the chamber, it is probable that it was deposited as one event, either at the time of the interment or naturally, over time.

Tomb E3 Objects

A171:   Flint fragment (E3.04).
A178:   Flint fragment (E3.01).
A185:   Fragment of flint blade (E3.01).

Tomb E3 Human/Animal Remains

On the basis of crania and other bone fragments, there were two juveniles, one approximately 7–9 years and the other 3–4 years.

Tomb E9

This tomb and E14 are two chamber tombs sharing a common shaft. Tomb E9 (figs. 11.4–11.6) contained three interments, although bones and pottery were scattered over the chamber floor. Of all the tombs excavated at Khirbat Iskandar, the fairly well segregated interments in Tomb E9, as well as the number of skeletal remains (3266), including the only evidence of vertebral bodies found, offer the best evidence for the suggestion that burial tradition at the site possibly reflects a pattern of primary interment followed by secondary reorganization of the remains during the deposition of subsequent individuals (see study of skeletal remains in Ch. 14). Nevertheless, the positions of the large platter bowl fragments and turned over lamps, plus a fragment of copper, suggest that the disturbance was likely due to looting as well as roof fall. The ovoid chamber measured 2.5 m in diameter with an estimated height of the domed chamber of 1.5 m. The chamber's entrance

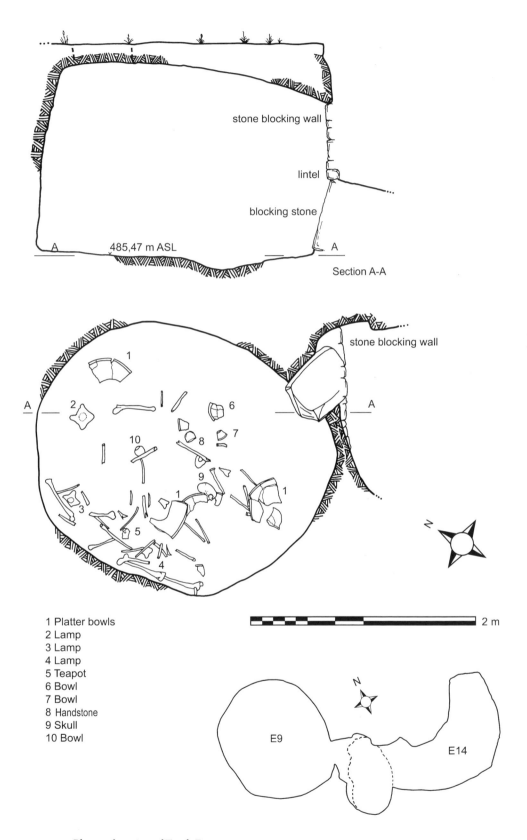

Section A-A

1 Platter bowls
2 Lamp
3 Lamp
4 Lamp
5 Teapot
6 Bowl
7 Bowl
8 Handstone
9 Skull
10 Bowl

2 m

FIG. 11.4 *Plan and section of Tomb E9.*

FIG. 11.5 *Pottery from Tomb E9.*

#	BUCKET	LOCUS	AP	FORMHARIBA	VESSEL	M	CAP	DESCRIPTION
1	E09.06	E09008	254	4766.00.12.30	Bowl	7.2	237	2.5YR4/0 dark grey, ext. surface 7.5YR6/4–5/0 light brown–gray, large white sand or flint inclusions, roughly handmade, burned.
2	E09.06.10X	E09008		4762.00.62.13	Bowl	8	227	7.5YR7/4 pink; vest. slip ext 5 YR6/6 red–yellow; few small ls; very fine temper.
3	E09.06.10	E09008		4765.00.42.00	Bowl	10		5YR7/4 pink; burnished ext. 10R6/4–5YR7/3 light yellowish red–pink.
4	E09.02.1	E09005		4660.00.75.00	Platter	20		10YR8/3 very pale brown; grooves, core, white/black inclusions.
5	E09.06.11	E09008		4660.00.75.00	Platter	22		7.5YR7/4 pink; few white/black inclusions, probably ls.
6	E09.05	E09007–E09008	253	4666.51.75.13	Platter	23	1,705	5YR5/6 yellowish red. burnished ext. & int. 2.5YR5/8 red, few limestone inclusions, medium fired.
7	E09.08	E09008, E09010	248	4605.00.75.13	Platter	42	10,429	2.5YR6/8 - 10R6/8 light red; burnished ext. & int. 10R6/8 light red.
8	E09.06.16	E09008	252	4066.00.61.00	Teapot	8		7.5YR7/2 pinkish gray; burnished ext. 10R6/6/-5/6 red. Many large–small limestone inclusions. Many medium–small basalt inclusitons. Well-fired.
9	E09.08.3	E09010		4260.00.00.13	Jar			5YR8/4 pink, handmade.
10	E09.02.2	E09005		4220.00.00.13	Jar			7.5YR6/4 light brown; well fired; core; fine temper.
11	E09.08.4	E08008, E09010		4220.00.00.13	Jar			"white ware" 7.5YR8/2 pinkish-white; much limestone, few sm. gravel; poorly fired.
12	E09.03.1	E09002	250	4857.00.11.13	Lamp	18.8		7.5YR7/4 pink. One spout burned.
13	E09.04	E09006	249	4857.00.12.13	Lamp	17		5YR7/6 reddish yellow.

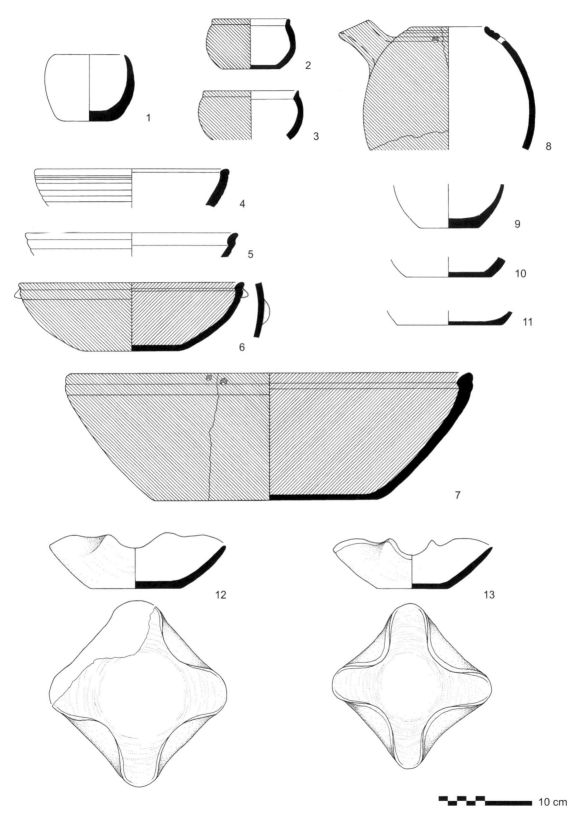

FIG. 11.5 *Pottery from Tomb E9.*

FIG. 11.6 *Photo of Tomb E9.*

had collapsed but originally included a blocking stone, lintel, and small wall.

Examination of the surrounding rock, especially after full excavation of the shaft and discovery of the adjacent tomb E14, made it clear that the chamber of E9 underwent modification from a natural opening in the breccia to effect the appearance of a traditional dome-shaped chamber. Support for this hypothesis comes from the east side of the chamber, where the construction of a rock wall filled in a gaping hole in the breccia. The wall incorporated a stone lintel to create an entrance that could then be blocked with a blocking stone. Thus, although this tomb represents an opportunistic use of natural cavities common to Cemetery E, it is apparent that there was considerable effort expended to create a more traditional shaft tomb.

Excavation

As in case of Tomb E3 (above), a small opening obscured by vegetation was the first indication of

the tomb. After enlarging the hole, the excavation of a 1 × 1 m sounding to approximately 2 m below the surface encountered a complete, overturned EB IV lamp. This was then covered with soil to protect it while excavation continued on the soil and roof fall that filled the chamber. A lateral excavation proceeded across the top of the fill to a row of cobbles on the east side of the chamber, presumed to be the entrance. This strategy actually located the collapsed entrance/shaft, which was partially excavated in order to obtain better access to the interior of the chamber.

Contents of the shaft fill included EB IV pottery, bone, and a lithic blade. Working from the collapsed entrance/shaft into the chamber, the blocking stone with its base apparently still *in situ* was found to have fallen back into the shaft. There was also a lintel stone fallen into the chamber, along with some of the large cobbles from the blocking wall. Whether the poor preservation of the shaft/entrance of the tomb was due to robbers or to bulldozing, there was little evidence within the one burial level for reuse of the tomb. Under a fill of alternating layers of soil and roof collapse (Locus 9001), the disturbed and disarticulated burial loci came to light essentially in one layer lying on bedrock.

Tomb E9 Objects (metal untested)

A205A: Flint blade fragment (E9.01).
A247:   Basalt handstone fragment (E9.05).
A246:   Pin shaft fragment (copper?) (E9.10.)
A445:   Bone needle fragment (E9).

E9 Human/Animal Remains

Of 3266 bone fragments, there is a suggested MNI of 3 adult individuals.

Tomb E10

A bulldozer cut had exposed the south side of E10 (fig. 11.7) causing the roof to collapse as additional material was pushed into the chamber. Cut out of the breccia, as Tomb E9, this chamber was, however, more than 4 m in diameter and its original height was probably over 2 m. Tomb E10 also gave the appearance of being an opportunistically utilized cavity altered to give the appearance of a shaft tomb with ovoid chamber. The badly preserved tomb contained the disturbed but articulated and very fragmentary burial of a young adult male, as well as EB IV pottery. Fear of roof collapse necessitated abandonment at midpoint of the excavation.

Excavation

Clearance of the tomb debris began at the opening on the south side of the chamber caused by the bulldozer. This opening was near the top of the chamber, so that most of the chamber was actually below and north of the bulldozed road. Excavation began on the topsoil and two debris layers that radiated out and down from the opening, creating a steep slope of approximately 30°. The two debris layers contained EB IV sherds and some bone; at the bottom of the lower layer (Locus 10004); a grinding stone was recovered in the northeast quadrant.

A north–south section through the center of Locus 10004 revealed a very hard compacted surface (10005) in the east, on which the blocking stone rested. The 0.60 × 0.70 m stone was in an upright position, but lying on its side. In the south, directly under the road cut, the remains of the shaft appeared, in which there were fragments of EB IV bowls and platter at the bottom. Continued removal of Locus 10004 revealed an articulated burial (10006) in a semi-flexed position with its legs in the chamber and the skull in the shaft. This skeleton did not lie on compacted surface 10005, but rather was on top of a layer of cobble-sized rocks and gravelly soil, part of the roof fall matrix encountered across the chamber, including a large boulder. A scatter of EB IV sherds was recovered under the boulder and on the floor of the chamber.

The interment is problematic because it was in the chamber fill, not on the chamber floor, and the skull was in the shaft. It seems evident that it was not a formal interment as further suggested by the absence of funerary offerings directly associated with it. More likely, the death was accidental and occurred when the individual broke into the tomb and tried to get out after a catastrophic roof collapse. Early abandonment of this operation precluded the excavation of more of Locus 10005, the chamber surface, on which additional skeletal remains presumably lay.

Tomb E10 Objects

A406: Limestone handstone fragment (E10.03).

Tomb E10 Human/Animal Remains

Burial of unknown date; one adolescent individual of indeterminate sex, aged approximately 12–15 years.

Tomb E14

In the 1987 season, work continued in the badly preserved Tomb E9 shaft and chamber entrance (above). Once completely cleared, it was evident that the irregular shaft opened on the east into

FIG. 11.7 *Pottery from Tomb E10.*

#	Bucket	Locus	AP	FormHaRiBa	Vessel	M	Cap	Description
1	E10.01.07	E10001		4762.00.62.00	Bowl	8		7.5YR7/6 reddish yellow; delicate; well fired; much sm. limestone; some sm. black inclusions.
2	E10.08.1	E10010		4766.44.12.00	Bowl	10		7.5YR7/4 pink; band combed; well fired; some med.–lg. gravel.
3	E10.05.02	E10002		4764.00.62.00	Bowl	10		10YR7/3 very pale brown; band combed; well fired; fine tempered.
4	E10.01.04	E10001		4640.00.76.00	Platter	24		7.5YR7/4 pink; well fired; much limestone; some med. gravel.
5	E10.01.02	E10001		4640.00.75.00	Platter	24		5YR7/6 reddish yellow; well fired; many sm.–med. gravel.
6	E10.01.05	E10001		4620.00.73.00	Platter	30		7.5YR7/4 pink; vestigial slip ext. 2.5YR6/6 light red; well fired; sm.–med. gravel.
7	E10.08.02	E10010		4600.00.75.00	Platter	36		5YR6/6 reddish yellow; light core; much sm.–med. gravel & limestone; well fired.
8	E10.01.06	E10001		4272.00.61.00	Jar	6		7.5YR7/6 reddish yellow; 2.5 YR4/6 red; well fired; sm.–med. gravel.
9	E10.04.03	E10004		4272.00.11.00	Jar	8		5YR7/4 pink; well fired; fine temper.
10	E10.04.04	E10004		4262.54.00.00	Jar			10YR7/3 very pale brown; well fired, many sm. black inclusions.
11	E10.04.02	E10004		4066.00.11.00	Teapot	12		5YR7/4 pink; med.–lg. limestone.
12	E10.01.1	E10001		4020C.00.10.00	Cooking Pot	20		7.5YR7/2 pinkish gray; blackened; limestone inclusions and grog.
13	E10.04.1	E10004		4020C.00.11.00	Cooking Pot	18		10YR6/4 very pale brown; blackened, much sm.–med. gravel.
14	E10.01.03	E10001		Base.00.00.13				7.5YR8/2 pinkish white; well fired; sm.–med. gravel.
15	E10.05.01	E10002		Base.00.00.13				10YR8/4 very pale brown; well fired; fine temper.

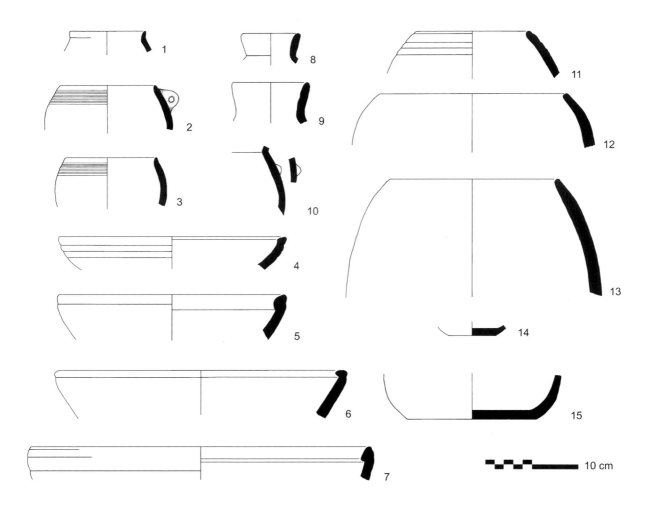

FIG. 11.7 *Pottery from Tomb E10.*

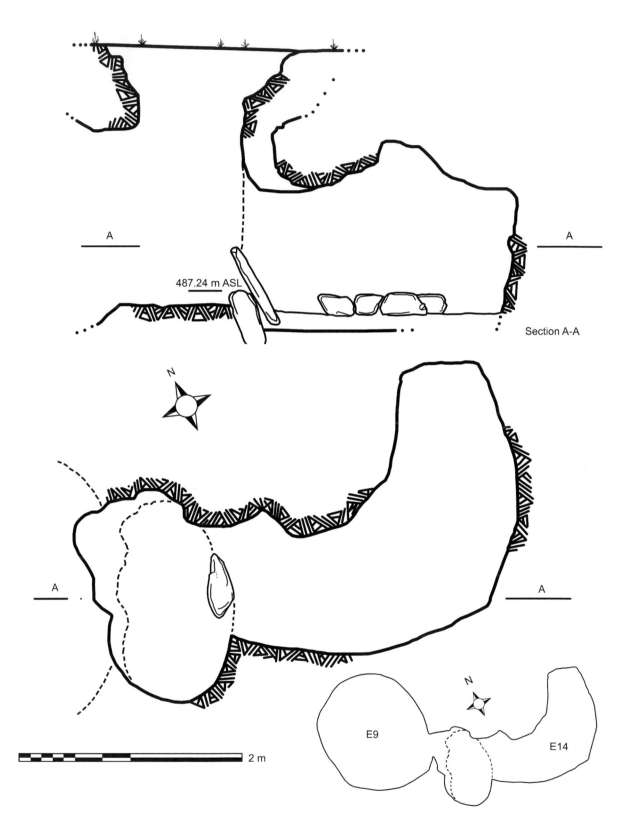

Section A-A

487.24 m ASL

E9   E14

2 m

FIG. 11.8 *Plan and section of Tomb E14.*

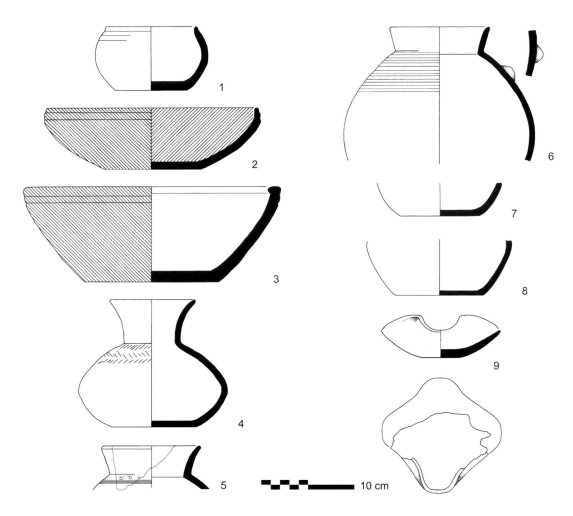

FIG. 11.9 *Pottery from Tomb E14.*

#	Bucket	Locus	AP	FormHaRiBa	Vessel	M	Cap	Description
1	E14.04.10,13 et al.	E14002		4762.00.62.13	Bowl	10	442	5YR6/8 reddish yellow; core; friable; much sm.–lg. limestone/gravel.
2	E14.02-03 et al.	E14002		4669.00.10.13	Platter	22	1,476	7.5YR7/6 reddish yellow; dark core; sm.–med. bl/white inclusions; well fired.
3	E14.01-02-05.1-2 et al.	E14001, E14002		4538.00.73.13	Bowl	26	2,977	5YR7/6 reddish yellow; 2.5YR5/8 red; well fired; sm.–med. limestone/gravel.
4	E14.02.15	E14002		4225.00.61.30	Jar	9	1,017	5YR7/6 reddish yellow; herringbone design; well fired; sm.–med. gravel.
5	E14.01.9–16	E14001, E14002		4220.00.10.00	Jar	10		5YR7/4 pink, sm.–med. white/black incl.; well fired.
6	E14.04.01	E14002		4141.54.61.00	Jar	10		7.5YR5/6 yellowish red & well fired; sm.–med. limestone & gravel.
7	E14.02.22	E14002		Base.00.00.13				5YR7/6 reddish yellow; well fired; sm.–med. gravel.
8	E14.03.1-3	E14002		Base.00.00.13				7.5YR6/4 light brown; med. Fired; mostly limestone; some gravel.
9	E14.02.10	E14002		4856.00.12.20	Lamp	12.5		7.5YR6/6 reddish yellow; well fired; sm.–med. white/black inclusions.

a second chamber (figs. 11.8–11.9). The shaft fill contained several sherds of a small EB IV platter bowl and two bone fragments. The E14 chamber was also of irregular shape, although there was also evidence for alteration of a natural cavity into a shaft tomb with a dome-shaped chamber. However, unlike E9, there was apparently no effort made to carve out a more typically ovoid shape. Had the south and east sides been carved out further to achieve an ovoid shape, the diameter of the tomb would have been more than 2 m. The height was at least 1.5 m. In distinction to E9, there was no lintel or rock wall at the entrance; however, the blocking stone, whose dimensions were 0.90 × 0.50 m, gives an idea of the size of the original opening. The latter showed signs of enlargement, possibly by robbers attempting to gain access over the top of the dislocated blocking stone. There were bones and pottery scattered over the chamber floor.

Excavation

Apart from some roof fall, most of the debris (14001) in the chamber appeared to come from the refilling of the shaft. Unlike E9, whose debris (almost to the top of the chamber) had penetrated through a hole in the roof, the debris in E14 sloped up towards the entrance to the chamber, leaving relatively little overburden to remove. Upon removal of the overburden, small bone and sherd fragments appeared just inside the entrance. A probe a few centimeters into this layer (14002) encountered restorable pottery. A second probe into Locus 14002 at the opposite (east) end of the chamber also encountered bone and pottery, demonstrating a distribution of cultural and skeletal remains across the entire tomb. Locus 14002 proved to be a 0.10 m soil level containing bone and pottery, overlying Surface 14005. A large flat stone, leaning into the shaft somewhat, rested on this surface. Behind it there was another large block of stone. It is not certain if these were two blocking stones or, paralleling Tomb E9, a blocking stone and lintel. Unfortunately, threatening conditions of collapse forced the abandonment of work in this tomb. It is likely that the chamber floor (and earlier interments) had not been reached.

Tomb E14 Human/Animal Remains

Of 238 bone fragments, only 4 were identifiable, suggesting an MNI of one adult of unknown age.

Chapter 12

Ceramic Assemblage of the Early Bronze IV Cemeteries

by Suzanne Richard and Glen Peterman

This chapter focuses on the typology of specific EB IV tomb vessels, relying heavily on the quantitative analysis of the ceramic assemblage found in Chapter 5. In parallel fashion to Chapter 4, the classification is based on form/size to determine basic types—46 Tomb Code Basic Form non-random sorted categories– which, in combination with rim, allowed for the classification of 47 specific types, detailed in outline form below. As with the Area C sherd study, other variables included in the quantified study were handles, decorative elements, and surface treatments. The resultant specific types (or type series/typology) is an invaluable catalogue of the distinctive attributes and attribute clusters of the corpus, a catalogue that engenders fruitful cross- comparisons with the tell pottery and seriation studies with other sites. The cemetery system is a classification based on whole vessels, a variation of the classification of the sherd collection from Area C. For a general discussion and relation to the original Bâb adh-Dhrâ' classification system, see the introduction in Chapter 4.

Combining analysis of the statistical patterning of variables in relation to well-known and well-established EB IV types, the typology is both objective and accessible for comparison with other sites. The basic form types are: cooking pots, holemouth jars, spouted vessels ("teapots"), storejars, jugs, bowls, platter bowls, cups, and lamps. The specific types combine basic form types with rim and other variables. As a chapter in a volume, the presentation below favors an approach somewhat more synthetic that that of Bâb adh-Dhrâ' in discussing the basic form code and specific EB IV types. Striving for equivalent presentations, the methodology and outline used here is the same as that found in Chapter 4, with the proviso cited earlier.

The primary intent of this chapter, as with Chapter 4, is to present the specific types (sometimes in combined sizes) along with any significant quantitative observations from Chapter 5. When data are available, there will be mention of wares and fabrics; however, storage of virtually the entire cemetery corpus in Jordan has militated against a systematic technological analysis at this time. Also, unlike the analysis in Chapter 4, there is less concern here for chronology (but see the proposed seriation in Ch. 5).

The secondary goal of the cemetery study is to highlight comparisons and contrasts with the

Khirbat Iskandar tell assemblage and with the Bâb adh-Dhrâ' cemetery corpus (Tombs A52 and A54). Numerous references will also be made to the collection of whole vessels discovered in the Area B "storeroom" at Khirbat Iskandar (Richard 2000). As indicated in the study of Area C, there is a considerable overlap of forms with the assemblage in the cemeteries, suggestive of shared domestic customs in both. For a discussion of this phenomenon, see conclusions in Chapter 16 and Richard (2009).

Whereas the major focus of the Bâb adh-Dhrâ' tomb volume, as with the town, was a comparative study of the ceramic traditions in the cemeteries throughout the Early Bronze Age, obviously, the concern here is the EB IV period at Khirbat Iskandar and the several objectives outlined above. The format followed in this chapter is similar to that used in the Bâb adh-Dhrâ' volumes so as to enhance comparative analysis. To avoid undue citations, specific page references to materials at Bâb adh-Dhrâ' are limited (see Schaub and Rast 1989: 473–503 for details); likewise limited are specific references to the Area C tell corpus (see Ch. 4 for details).

EB IV BASIC CEMETERY FORMS

There are 46 basic EB IV forms in the tomb assemblage, a much larger assortment than the 37 basic forms found in Tombs A52 /A54 at Bâb adh-Dhrâ'. Although regional variations exist, the basic forms at both sites are comparable: spouted vessels ("teapots"), wide necked jars of various sizes, wide mouth jugs and pitchers, deep bowls, platter bowls, small bowls and cups, and lamps. Of the notable differences, there are specialized vessels at Bâb adh-Dhrâ' not attested at Khirbat Iskandar. They are the following: tetrafoil rim jugs (4250 series) and narrow necked jars (4300 series), as well as straight-sided bowls (4780 series) and votive cups (4790 series). As for the Khirbat Iskandar tomb vessels not found at Bâb adh-Dhrâ', there are only three, the holemouth storage jar and cooking pot (restricted 4020 series), as well as a miscellaneous form (4900). The remaining discrepancies are primarily matters of size, for example, the larger size

range in the following categories were missing at Bâb adh-Dhrâ': spouted vessels (4030 series), jars (4100 series), deep wide bowls (4500 series), and cups (4700/4705 series). Overall, though, the basic tomb forms at both sites parallel well (Ch. 5). With few exceptions (below), the basic tomb and tell forms at Khirbat Iskandar likewise parallel well.

Function of EB IV Cemetery Forms

The distribution analysis of basic forms from the Bâb adh-Dhrâ' EB I–EB IV tombs offers comparative detail in terms of shifts of vessel forms and thus function over time. At Khirbat Iskandar, the distribution of basic forms in the tombs in comparison with the tell provides an opportunity to distinguish EB IV ceramic functions between the living and the dead. As the quantitative analysis in Chapter 5 makes clear, the similarity of tomb and tell forms suggests that tomb rituals and everyday rituals of the living were relatively indistinguishable. Apart from the absence of necked cooking pots and holemouth bowls (spouted vats/basins and cooking pots)—not expected in tombs in any case—as well as functional ledge handles in the tombs, the major differences with the tell appear to be size and frequency. Although not expected also, examples of the holemouth storejar and cooking pot categories are extant but few. Likewise few in number are the large to medium deep bowls. Regarding size, most notable is the absence of necked storejars in the large to pithoi size (probably explaining the lack of functional ledge handles), and the "teapots" appears to be less than "life-size." Conversely, the tombs have many more lamps, necked jars, pitchers, jugs and juglets, especially in the smaller to miniature ranges. There is virtually nothing in the tombs that is not found on the tell, even if it is the rare lamp or miniature vessel. Yet, there is a distinctive character to the small jars at Khirbat Iskandar and Bâb adh-Dhrâ', as at other EB IV cemetery sites.

EB IV Wares, Fabrics, Surface Treatment, Plastic Applications

From an analysis of ware colors, it appears that the Khirbat Iskandar corpus, like that of Bâb adh-Dhrâ', shows continuity of the Early Bronze tradition of reddish or reddish-yellow wares. However, as in Area C, pinkish wares appear to be the dominant ware type in the tombs as well. There is also a small number of vessels of other types of ware colors. Thin-section analysis identified six fabric types at Khirbat Iskandar, an analysis that included samples from the tombs (Ch. 6). At this stage, there is no reason to suspect that the tomb pottery is not of the same manufacture and type of fabric as Area C (see discussion in Ch. 4), even though color distributions vary between the two. As is typical of Area C pottery, the tomb corpus is handmade with striations on the necks and upper body, which, along with the rilled and combed decoration, gives every indication of the use of a tournette.

The surface treatment of tomb vessels at Khirbat Iskandar compares favorably with that at Bâb adh-Dhrâ', where four types have been noted: slip, slip and burnish, pattern combing, and untreated surfaces. There is, however, a fifth type present at Khirbat Iskandar—molding, including thumb-indented and piecrust examples. Also at Khirbat Iskandar, the pattern combing repertoire breaks down into rills (deep incisions), band combing, wavy band combing, zigzag combing, single line combing, stabs, and herringbone stab design. A perusal of Tombs A52 and A54 reveals a type of overall body pattern combing (e.g., figs. 274:1–3, 11; 281:1–2, 4), not discerned in the Khirbat Iskandar tombs.

As at Bâb adh-Dhrâ', the tomb repertoire includes numerous (23) examples of knobs ("dots") on "teapots" and necked jars, with six of the latter exhibiting two parallel knobs. The placement of knobs on jars is often suggestive typologically of a handle, although they could be merely decorative. Clearly reminiscent of the well-known EB IV ledge-handled bowl, however, are the five bowls with slightly larger knobs (the knob-ledge). The two bowls with double knob-ledges would seem to affirm the link. Envelope ledge-handles are absent, as mentioned earlier, but there are three

clear examples of vestigial handles on "teapots," one with an envelope (pinch lapped profile), the other two with scalloped edge. More typical of Bâb adh-Dhrâ' Tombs A52/A54 is the slashed appliquéd band of clay added to "teapots," only two examples of which are attested in the Khirbat Iskandar tombs. The open-channel spout on several "teapots" at Bâb adh-Dhrâ' (fig. 282:4) is unique. There are lug-handled "teapots" at both sites, but only at Khirbat Iskandar is there a "teacup" with lug handle. There were only four lug handles in the tombs. There remain the loop handles (10) ranging from attachment at or below the rim of jugs, but mostly attached to mid neck (6). In section they appear to be elliptical or round, but there is a clear strap handle among the group.

SPECIFIC EB IV TOMB TYPES

Figures 12.1–4 illustrate virtually all the basic form types that, when combined with rim, present the specific EB IV type series identified from the tombs at Khirbat Iskandar. The relevant data for each appears in the facing descriptive page. The benefit of parsing the corpus into such quantifiable size/form and size/form/rim types is to grasp the overall distribution of major and minor vessel groups in the tombs for comparison between tomb and tell and with other sites. Those who wish to analyze the pottery by tomb have access to all the pottery utilized in the quantitative study (see Chs. 10–11).

The outline presents the classification in the following manner: EB IV functional types (e.g., spouted vessels) are subsumed under the primary form (Restricted, Necked Jar, and Bowl) and size (Very large, Large, Medium, Small) categories, further broken down according to contour (e.g., squat or global), base type, and/or rim types. More precision is possible with whole vessels, of course allowing for elaboration of the form into distinctive vessel shapes (contour/base). After each rim type, the number of examples is listed in parentheses followed by the specific code for the rim. Generally, the four-digit form code is included after size.

As an example, within the Restricted (essentially "holemouth") category, there are three main form/functional types in the tombs: storejars, cooking pots, and spouted vessels. These break down into distinctive vessel shapes, involving primarily morphological criteria, as within the spouted vessel category there are squat and global types. Finally, there is a breakdown according to rim type. Thus, within the Restricted (Holemouth Jar) category, there are three Large (4036) Spouted Vessels of the mid-low tangent (squat) type. One has a direct rim (I[1].C.1.a.i) with rim type 11, and three have a turned-up rim (I[1].C.1.a.ii) with rim types 41, 42. For comparative purposes with Chapter 4, major categories unattested in the tombs are listed in the outline. For a complete list of the specific types in this chapter (and Ch. 4), see the corpus in Appendix I. All of the code descriptions used for Khirbat Iskandar vessels are detailed in Appendices D and E.

I(1). Restricted (Holemouth Jar) Forms

A. Storejars (1 ex.)
    1.   Medium (4020) storejars with bulbous direct rim (1 ex.): 18
B. Cooking Pots (2 ex.)
    1.   Medium (4020) cooking pots with direct rim (2 ex.): 10, 11
C. Spouted Vessels ("teapots") (17 ex.)
    1.   Mid-low tangent (squat) spouted vessels (14 ex.)
        a.   large (4036) spouted vessels
            i.   direct rim (1 ex.): 11
            ii.   turned-up rim (3 ex.): 41, 42
        b.   medium (4066) spouted vessels
            i.   direct rim (4 ex.): 11
            ii.   turned-up rim (5 ex.): 41, 42
            iii.   flared (1 ex.): 61
    2.   Mid-range tangent (global) spouted vessels (3 ex.)
        a.   medium-small (4071) spouted vessels
            i.   direct rim (1 ex): 11
            ii.   turned-up rim (2 ex.): 41

Holemouth Jars

Basic Forms: Paralleling the Area C assemblage, there are three major categories of holemouth jars: cooking pots, storejars, and spouted vessels.

Likewise, although other sizes (4 examples of large, 3 of medium–small) are present, in all three categories the preferred size is medium. Notably, as with several other types, the quantitative study found a predilection for smaller sizes in the tombs. There were no storejars or cooking pots in the Bâb adh-Dhrâ' tombs. Based on ware and temper (soot, calcite, blackened), the two holemouths were distinguishable as cooking pots.

A. Storejar

Specific Types: Within the holemouth category, one medium-sized storejar with thumb-indented bulbous rim was found in Tomb D9 (fig. 12.1:7). Such a storage container—rare in tombs in any case—is attested in the town, of course, but only one example there has a bulbous rim and none had molding. The two holemouth vessels found at Umm al-Bighal could be storejars or cooking pots (Helms and McCreery 1988: fig. 7:11–12).

B. Cooking pots

Specific Types: The two holemouth cooking pots with direct rim represent one type (fig. 12.1:6). Both from Tomb E10 (see the other in fig. 11.7:12), they provide evidence for cooking in connection with burial ritual. Although cooking pots are found elsewhere, for example, in the Qedesh caves (Tadmor 1978), they are not a typical grave offering. These medium direct rim vessels correlate with the most popular-sized cooking pots on the tell, where both direct and bulbous rims are well attested. The discovery in Tomb D3 of a mass of crumbly, reddish-black fragments resembling tabun ware could, in retrospect, have been a cooking pot.

C. Spouted vessels ("teapots")

Specific Types: The "teapots" are of two types, the characteristic EB IV wide flat-based (squat) type (fig. 12.1:3) and a round (global) variety (fig. 12.1:4). Whether the global shape is unique to the tombs or also found in Area C is difficult to know. The closest example from the tell (Area B) is a much larger vessel with high neck (Richard 2000: fig.

2.13). Shared characteristics include a mid-range tangent and roughly equivalent base and mouth diameter. In any case, the global "teapots" in the tombs only appear in the medium–small range and are relatively rare (3/17). Two-thirds of all the vessels are slipped (half of them have red slip and burnish), and virtually all have multiple rilling at the neck. Unfortunately, many of the "teapots" are partial vessels whose classifications are not definitive; however, both Khirbat Iskandar and Bâb adh-Dhrâʿ share a preference for the squat type. The global type seems to be missing from the latter site, while an unusual high-tangent vessel appearing there (Schaub and Rast 1989: fig. 275:2) is absent in the Khirbat Iskandar tombs. According to the seriation results, spouted vessels are not part of the tomb tradition in late EB IV (see Ch. 5).

Of the 17 examples of "teapots," nine have an appendage of some sort (knob or vestigial ledge handle) which, along with the exclusive use of two rim types (turned-up and direct), combines to link with similar characteristics at Bâb adh-Dhrâʿ. With few exceptions, the Khirbat Iskandar spouts generally have straight upper and lower walls, whereas the tendency for a flaring lower wall was noted at Bâb adh-Dhrâʿ. One noticeable disparity between the tomb corpora from the two sites is the presence of a large-size category at Khirbat Iskandar. Although none is complete, a height of close to 25–30 cm can be estimated on the basis of several examples. This is a size approaching the range of the large "teapots" found in the Area B "storeroom" (Richard 2000: fig. 2:7).

Except for the absence of a "taller rim flared teapot" type, and a preference for limited rim types (direct and slightly upturned), the tomb types are comparable to Area C, even though a comparison of rim diameters between the two is difficult. A study of rim diameters among the "teapots" in the tombs shows that there are limits to using diameter to determine vessel size, as the 9.1 cm diameter of the medium-small (4071) vessel in Tomb D2 (fig. 10.8:1) and the 9.5 cm diameter of the large (4036) vessel in Tomb D3 (fig. 10.13:14) illustrate. Even with this proviso, however, the tomb "teapots" (like the necked jars) seem to be less than "life-size" in contrast to those on the tell. For a discussion of

the latter and an interesting pairing of small and large spouted vessels in both the tombs and in the rooms of Area C, see Chapter 5.

No Restricted Holemouth Bowl forms are present in the tombs.

II. Necked Vessels

A. Storejars with wide flaring necks (36 ex.)
   1. Storejars (23 ex.)
      a. Low-tangent (squat) storejars (16 ex.)
         i. medium-large (4142)
           1. direct rim (1 ex): 11
           2. flared rim (2 ex.): 60
         ii. medium (4220/4222/4225/4232)
           1. direct rim (4 ex.): 10, 11, 12
           2. flared rim (8 ex.): 60, 61, 62
         iii. medium (4211) amphoriskos with direct rim (1 ex.): 11
      b. Mid-range tangent (global) storejars (7 ex.)
         i. medium-large (4141) with flared rim (3 ex.): 61, 62
         ii. medium (4221/4231) with flared rim (3 ex.): 60, 61
         iii. medium (4230) with direct rim (1 ex.): 11
   2. Miniature jars/bottles (13 ex.)
      a. Low-tangent (squat) (4262/4272) jars
         i. direct rim (3 ex.): 10, 11
         ii. flared rim (6 ex.): 61, 62
      b. Mid-range tangent (global) (4271/4281) jars
         i. direct rim (1 ex.): 12
         ii. flared rim (3 ex.): 61
B. Cooking pots: none
C. One-handled jugs and pitchers (11 ex.)
   1. Jugs (4 ex.)
      a. Medium-large (4421)
         i. direct rim (1 ex.): 12
         ii. flared rim (3 ex.): 61
   2. Flask-pitchers (7 ex.)
      a. medium-large (4422), low-tangent
         i. direct rim (1 ex.): 11
         ii. flared rim (5 ex.): 60, 61, 62

FIG. 12.1 *Cemetery specific type series: Restricted (holemouth) and necked vessels.*

#	Form	Tomb	Type	FormHaRiBa	Size	Description	Ref
1	Necked Jar	D02	Handleless Storejar	4142.54.11.13	Medium Large	Storejar, squat, with direct (rounded) rim; 2 knobs	fig. 10.7:14
2	Holemouth Jar	D02	Spouted Vessel	4036.00.41.00	Large	"Teapot," squat, with turned-up rim	fig. 10.8:4
3	Holemouth Jar	D03	Spouted Vessel	4066.17b.11.13	Medium	"Teapot," squat, with direct (rounded) rim; vestigial ledge handle	fig. 10.13:12
4	Holemouth Jar	D03	Spouted Vessel	4071.54.11.13	Medium Small	"Teapot," global, with direct (rounded) rim; 1 knob	fig. 10.13:11
5	Necked Jar	D02	Handleless Storejar	4141.54.62.13	Medium Large	Storejar, global, with flared (tapered) rim; 1 knob	fig. 10.7:20
6	Holemouth Jar	E10	Cooking Pot	4020C.00.11.00	Medium	Cooking pot with direct (rounded) rim	fig. 11.7:13
7	Holemouth Jar	D09	Storejar	4020.00.18.00	Medium	Storejar with direct (bulbous) rim; molding	fig. 10.23:20
8	Necked Jar	D10	Handleless Storejar	4221.54.61.13	Medium	Storejar, global, with flared (rounded) rim; 2 knobs	fig. 10.26:5
9	Necked Jar	D02	Handleless Storejar	4222.00.60.13	Medium	Storejar, squat, with flared (squared) rim; band combing	fig. 10.7:13
10	Necked Jar	E14	Handleless Storejar	4225.00.61.30	Medium	Storejar, squat, with flared (rounded) rim; herringbone	fig. 11.9:4
11	Necked Jar	D03	Handleless Storejar	4231.54.60.13	Medium	Storejar, global, with flared (squared) rim; 2 knobs	fig. 10.13:9
12	Necked Jar	D03	Handleless Storejar	4232.54.12.13	Medium	Storejar, ovaloid, with direct (tapered) rim; 2 knobs	fig. 10.13:8
13	Necked Jar	D02	Handleless Storejar	4262.54.61.13	Small	Storejar, ovaloid, with flared (rounded) rim; 1 knob	fig. 10.7:7
14	Necked Jar	D03	Handleless Jar	4271.54.61.13	Small	Storejar, ovaloid, with flared (rounded) rim; 1 knob	fig. 10.13:6
15	Necked Jar	D02	Handleless Storejar	4272.00.00.11	Small	Storejar, ovaloid, with flared rim	fig. 10.7:4
16	Necked Jar	D02	Handleless Storejar	4281.54.61.13	Small	Storejar, ovaloid, with flared (rounded) rim; 2 knobs	fig. 10.7:2

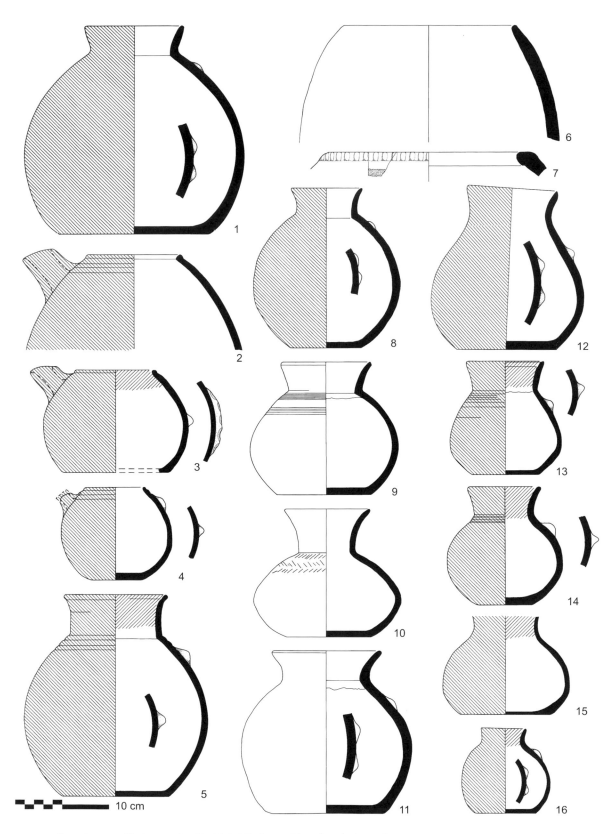

FIG. 12.1 *Cemetery specific type series: Restricted (holemouth) and necked vessels.*

b.   medium (4443), global, with flared
rim (1 ex.): 61

Necked Vessels

Basic Forms: Necked vessels in the tombs fall into
two major categories: handleless storejars of various sizes (fig. 12.1:1, 5, 8–16) and one-handled pitchers or jugs/juglets (fig. 12.2:1–3). The one outlier in
the handleless storejar category in the tombs is a
rare example of a squat amphriskos with wide flat
base from Tomb D10 (fig. 10:26.4). The popular
necked cooking pots found on the tell are missing
in the tombs. Absent the one holemouth storage
jar (above), the preferred ritual vessel for storage
is, typically, the necked jar. Indeed, necked jars are
the second largest category of tomb offerings (after
bowls). Also, the popular envelope ledge handle
jars from the site (pls. 21–22: passim; see Richard
2000: fig. 3:8–11) are totally absent in the tombs,
where only the vestigial ledge handle is attested.
Given the proposed seriation of the tombs, this
absence is presumably a functional rather than
chronological variant and relates to the absence
of large storage jars in the tombs.

More than half of the jars have slip and/or burnish, with 11 having both slip and combing. Another
11 vessels have combing only. As mentioned earlier,
the pithoi and large-size storejars found in Area C
are missing, but there is a medium–large class (not
at Bâb adh-Dhrâ‘). The quantitative study revealed
a consistency or standardization of size, shape,
and rim in necked jar tomb offerings: the uniform
size ranges are medium–large, medium, and small
(miniature), the shape is either squat or global, and
rims are direct or, more commonly, flared.

As noted in the discussion of necked vessels in
Chapter 4, although the terminology for describing
necks differs somewhat between tomb and tell, the
correlation between the two assemblages derives
from the type of neck, either inflected (curved-out)
or everted (corner point), along with rim type. In
contrast to Area C, overall it appears that necked
vessels in the tombs are smaller than "life-size;" that
is, the mean rim diameter in the former is 14.2 cm,
while it is 8.8 cm. in the latter. The seriation showed
that necked jars increase in size from early to late,

and the global form does not appear until nearly
the end, a possible forerunner of the subsequent
Middle Bronze Age tradition.

1. Handleless jars with wide flaring necks

Specific Types – Medium–large and medium storejar:
The tendency noted for two distinct "teapot" types
(squat and global) is evident in the storejar category
as well. The rounded or global form (fig. 12.1:5, 8, 11)
is not characteristic of southern sites; large rounded
storejars discovered in the Area B "storeroom" were
posited as northern imports (Richard 2000: fig. 3:
9, 10). In fact, it is the squat form in the southern
style that predominates in both medium–large and
medium examples (fig. 12.1:1, 9–10, 12). Unlike the
tell assemblage, the majority of these necked vessels
have red slip, burnish and rilling, or band combing,
and one shows an interesting herringbone design
(fig. 12.1:10). The flared rims divide evenly between
corner point and inflected necks, and only two rim
types are attested, the flared or less popular direct
rim examples.

Except for the lack of medium–large vessels at
Bâb adh-Dhrâ‘, the necked vessels at both sites
correlate well, including the popularity of knob
appendages. An exception is Bâb adh-Dhrâ‘ form
4282 (Schaub and Rast 1989: fig. 275:9)—the "squat,
low tangent jar with short, angled neck"—which
is missing from Khirbat Iskandar. Across the size
ranges, there are 18 necked vessels with knobs, six
of which have two contiguous knobs. There are,
however, no examples of four knobs per vessel,
as seen at Bâb adh-Dhrâ‘ (fig. 281: 9), where the
tradition of single and multiple knob appendages stretches back to EB I, indicating a probable
Transjordanian regional feature. Nine non-slipped,
usually band-combed jars with flaring square-cut
(fig. 12.1:9) or slightly tapered (fig. 10.17:14) rims are
attested in the tombs, five of which were in Tomb
D2. Several of these rims approach the sharply
everted (#63) rims that taper down or end in a
slight flange that were found on the tell.

Specific Types – Small/miniature storejar: The most
distinctive of the three standardized sizes illuminated by the quantified study are the small/minia-

ture storejars called bottles or flasks by Dever (1975: 22*). Paralleling the form of the "teapots" and large storejars, this category likewise exhibits a global (fig. 12.1:14, 16) and a squat form (fig. 12.1:13, 15). At Bâb adh-Dhrâ', all jar forms are described as squat or ovaloid (Schaub and Rast 1989: table 29). Examples at both sites tend to have a constriction and deep groove or band-combing around the neck, plus one to two knobs. The well-known Jericho/Central Hills/Jerusalem tomb bottles are cylindrical (Kenyon 1965: fig. 47), while at 'Ain-Sâmiya, cylindrical and squat types overlap (Dever 1972: fig. 2:7–10). In Khirbat Iskandar Tomb D4, two vessels approach the cylindrical form (fig. 10.17:10–11), the former (termed miscellaneous) is possibly a short-necked version similar to bottles found at Dhahr Mirzbâneh (Lapp 1966, fig. 35:2, 4). Ranging from 9–12.6 cm in height and virtually all red slipped, the Khirbat Iskandar miniatures evince a regional type somewhat different from the "hourglass" flasks in the Bâb adh-Dhrâ' tombs (Schaub and Rast 1989: figs. 274:16–17; 281: 9–10). Several of the Area C small storejars seem comparable to the tomb types, in size and shape of neck and either slightly flared or direct rim (especially fig. 4.2:16), and miniature and small storejars were part of the Area B "storeroom" collection (Richard 2000: fig. 2). Nonetheless, the tomb vessels do have a certain distinctiveness, possibly indicative of specialized tomb offerings.

2. Amphoriskos with wide flaring neck

Specific Types: There is only one exemplar of a storejar with handles and it is a squat amphoriskos with two lug handles on the shoulders (fig. 10.26:4). There are no parallels as yet for this type of vessel on the tell, where the preference appears to be for the bottle amphoriskos (Richard 2000: fig. 1:8, 13–14). The type seems to be lacking in both the tombs and in the town at Bâb adh-Dhrâ', but appears at Iktanu and northern sites (Prag 1973: fig. 5:11, 18).

3. One-handled jugs and pitchers (fig. 12.2)

Specific Types: As for wide-mouthed one-handled vessels, two major types are apparent, both of which are attested on the tell: the one-handled jug and the distinctive flask-pitcher. At Bâb adh-Dhrâ', where they are considered one category of medium–large "loop-handled jugs," parallels for both types occur (Rast and Schaub 1989: figs. 274:3–5, 7–10; 281:5–8). Out of a total of 11 examples at Khirbat Iskandar, all but four have red slip and burnish surface treatment. Handle attachments lie typically just below the rim or at mid-neck, although one is at the rim. Several of the one-handled jugs at Khirbat Iskandar (e.g., fig. 12.2:1) match examples in the 21–30 cm range found in the Area B "storeroom" (Richard 2000: fig. 1:11, 14–15), suggesting a larger size range at the site. The straight neck of fig. 12.2:1 does not meet the criterion of inflected neck with flared rim either. Both variables may be reason for distinguishing another specific type in the future.

As for the distinctive flask-pitcher, the type occurs in two varieties distinguished by shape and size: the medium–large squat version (fig. 12.2:2) as also found at Bâb adh-Dhrâ' (figs. 274:9–10; 281:6, 8), and a small global type (fig. 12.2:3) unattested at the latter site. Generally, even the medium–large category at Khirbat Iskandar fits the lower range of 10–17 cm, pointing to some differences with Bâb adh-Dhrâ'. The flask-pitcher usually has a characteristic "hour-glass shape" at both sites. For the smaller, global flask-pitcher a new form code was created (4443). With the qualifications mentioned for flask-pitchers and one-handled jugs, and the notable absence of the unique tetrafoil jug, the Khirbat Iskandar vessels compare favorably to the "Loop-handled Jugs" at Bâb adh-Dhrâ'.

III. Bowls, Platters, Cups, Lamps

Basic Forms: Of the three broad form categories, Restricted, Necked, and Bowl, it is the Bowl form that comprises the greatest range of distinct classes of vessel types. Thus, it seemed appropriate to situate this general section before, not after the outline, as was the practice in the Restricted and Necked categories. Additionally, here the outline is presented in three parts, followed by discussion. In this general Bowl category, the major specific types are deep bowls, platters, medium–small bowls, cups, and lamps. The parallels between tomb and tell are close, including closed/open forms, rim types, sur-

FIG. 12.2 *Cemetery specific type series: Jugs, deep bowls, and platter bowls.*

#	Form	Tomb	Type	FormHaRiBa	Size	Description	Ref
1	Jug	J01	Jug	4421.21.61.13	Medium Large	One-handled Jug with straight neck	fig. 10.30:2
2	Jug	J01	Flask Pitcher	4422.23.61.13	Medium Large	Flask-pitcher with flared (rounded) rim	fig. 10.30:1
3	Jug	D03	Flask Pitcher	4443.22.61.15	Small	Flask-pitcher with flared (rounded) rim	fig. 10.13:1
4	Deep Bowl	D04	Lightly closed	4503.00.76.00	Large	Carinated bowl with direct (beveled) rim	fig. 10.17:9
5	Deep Bowl	D02	Open	4531.00.75.00	Large	Bowl with thickened (turned-down) rim	fig. 10.6:9
6	Deep Bowl	D03	Lightly closed	4568.00.11.13	Medium	Incurved (carinated) bowl with direct (rounded) rim	fig. 10.12:8
7	Deep Bowl	D02	Lightly closed	4518.00.13.13	Medium Large	Carinated bowl with direct (beveled) rim; zigzag line	fig. 10.6:8
8	Deep Bowl	D03	Open	4538.00.73.13	Medium Large	Bowl with thickened (rolled) rim	fig. 10.12:10
9	Platter Bowl	D03	Lightly closed	4603.00.74.13	Very Large	Shouldered platter bowl with thickened (rolled) rim	fig. 10.11:8
10	Platter Bowl	D03	Lightly closed	4602.00.13.00	Very Large	Shouldered platter bowl with direct (beveled) rim	fig. 10.11:9
11	Platter Bowl	E09	Open	4605.00.75.13	Very Large	Platter bowl with thickened (turned-down) rim	fig. 11.5:7

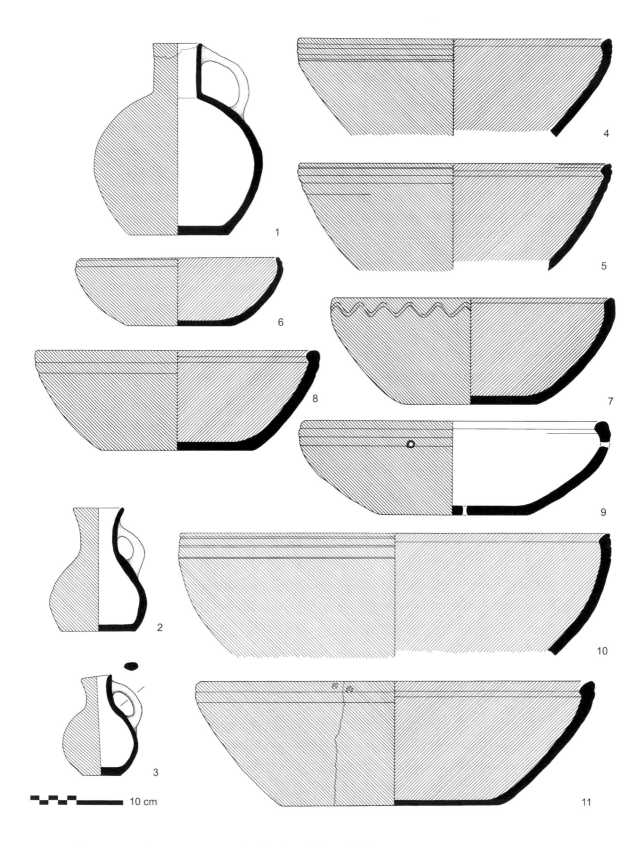

FIG. 12.2 *Cemetery specific type series: Jugs, deep bowls, and platter bowls.*

FIG. 12.3 *Cemetery specific type series: Platter bowls.*

#	Form	Tomb	Type	FormHaRiBa	Size	Description	Ref
1	Platter Bowl	D04	Open	4606.00.75.13	Very Large	Platter bowl with thickened (turned-down) rim	fig. 10.17:4
2	Platter Bowl	D02	Open	4612.00.75.10	Very Large	Platter bowl with thickened (turned-down) rim	fig. 10.4:4
3	Platter Bowl	D10	Open	4625.00.75.13	Large	Platter bowl with thickened (turned-down) rim	fig. 10.26:2
4	Platter Bowl	D02	Open	4645.00.74.13	Medium Large	Platter bowl with thickened (rolled) rim	fig. 10.3:15
5	Platter Bowl	D02	Open	4626.00.75.13	Large	Platter bowl with thickened (turned-down) rim	fig. 10.3:19
6	Platter Bowl	D05	Lightly closed	4628.51.12.13	Large	Carinated platter bowl with direct (tapered) rim	fig. 10.20:2
7	Platter Bowl	D03	Lightly closed	4623.00.72.13	Large	Platter bowl with thickened (flat) rim	fig. 10.11:1
8	Platter Bowl	D02	Lightly closed	4623.00.72.10	Large	Platter bowl with thickened (flat) rim	fig. 10.3:18
9	Platter Bowl	D02	Lightly closed	4659.00.11.13	Medium Large	Platter bowl with direct (rounded) rim	fig. 10.3:12
10	Platter Bowl	D02	Open	4667.00.10.30	Medium Large	Curved wall platter bowl with direct (squared) rim	fig. 10.3:10
11	Platter Bowl	E14	Lightly closed	4669.00.10.13	Medium	Carinated platter bowl with direct (squared) rim	fig. 11.9:2
12	Platter Bowl	D02	Open	4665.00.74.13	Medium	Platter bowl with thickened (rolled) rim	fig. 10.3:9
13	Platter Bowl	D02	Open	4666.51.73.13	Medium	Platter bowl with thickened (rolled) rim; knob	fig. 10.3:8
14	Platter Bowl	D02	Lightly closed	4659.00.19.13	Medium Large	Platter-bowl with direct (thinned) rim	fig. 10.3:11
15	Platter Bowl	D04	Lightly closed	4668.51.10.13	Medium	Carinated platter bowl with direct (squared) rim; knob	fig. 10.17:1
16	Platter Bowl	D04	Lightly closed	4659.00.10.30	Medium Large	Carinated platter bowl with direct (squared) rim	fig. 10.17:2

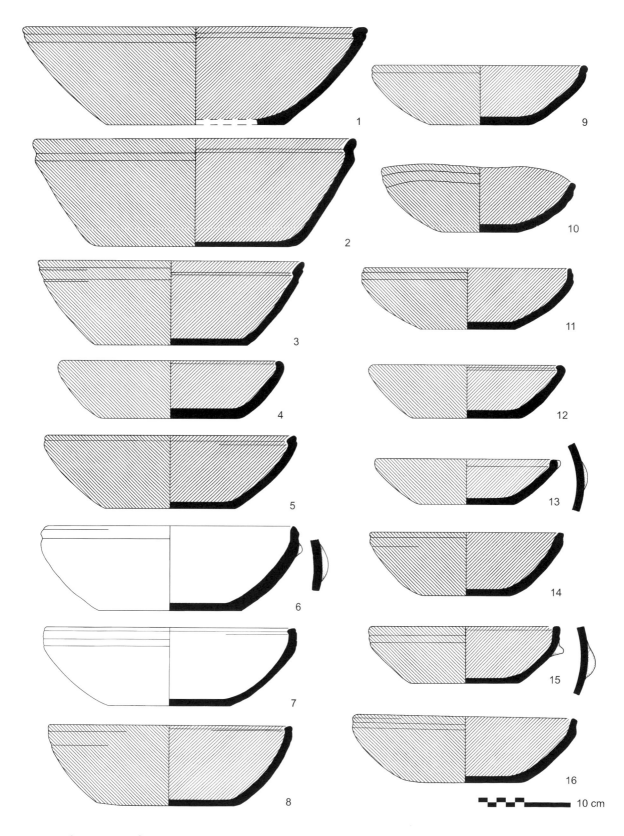

FIG. 12.3 *Cemetery specific type series: Platter bowls.*

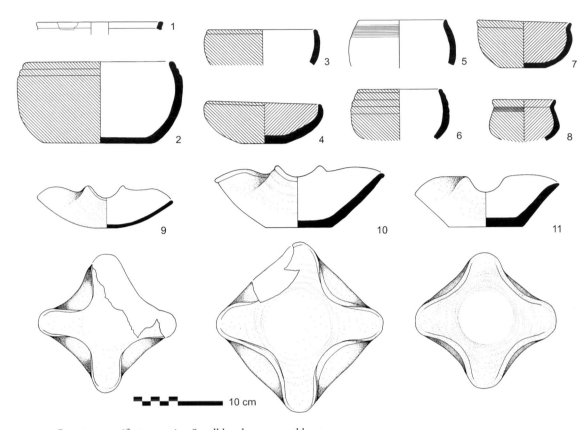

FIG. 12.4 *Cemetery specific type series: Small bowls, cups, and lamps.*

#	FORM	TOMB	TYPE	FORMHARIBA	SIZE	DESCRIPTION	REF
1	Deep Bowl	E03	Open Cup Bowl	4730.00.62.00	Medium Small to Small	Cup-bowl with flared rim	fig. 11.2:4
2	Deep Bowl	E03	Closed Cup Bowl	4705.00.11.13	Medium Small to Small	Cup-bowl with direct (rounded) rim	fig. 11.2:1
3	Deep Bowl	D02	Open Cup Bowl	4740.00.11.00	Medium Small	Cup-bowl with direct (rounded) rim	fig. 10.3:6
4	Deep Bowl	D02	Open Cup Bowl	4749.00.12.13	Medium Small	Cup-bowl with direct (tapered) rim	fig. 10.3:7
5	Deep Bowl	E10	Closed Cup	4764.00.62.00	Small	Cyma-profiled cup with flared (tapered); band combing	fig. 11.7:3
6	Deep Bowl	D02	Closed Cup	4766.00.11.00	Small	Cup-bowl with direct (rounded) rim	fig. 10.3:4
7	Deep Bowl	D02	Closed Cup	4765.00.60.13	Small	Cyma-profiled cup with flared (squared) rim	fig. 10.3:3
8	Deep Bowl	D02	Closed Cup	4762.00.41.00	Small	Cyma-profiled cup with everted rim	fig. 10.3:2
9	Shallow Bowl	D03	Lamp, round base	4851.00.11.20	Small	Four-spouted lamp with direct (rounded) rim	fig. 10.14:11
10	Shallow Bowl	D03	Lamp, flat base	4856.00.62.13	Small	Four-spouted lamp with flared rim	fig. 10.15:5
11	Shallow Bowl	D02	Lamp, flat base	4857.00.61.11	Small	Four-spouted lamp with flared rim	fig. 10.9:2

in EB IV, given the occurrence of both types in the same context (Richard 2000). The sequence from EB I through EB IV, however, does exhibit an observable development of small bowl with incipient spout to the characteristic fully flanged EB IV type. As is typical elsewhere in the EB IV period, the lamp category is a popular tomb gift, although at Bâb adh-Dhrâ' only two were found, both flat-based and in Tomb A54 (Schaub and Rast 1989: fig. 282:15–16).

COMPARISON OF TOMBS AND TELL

As shown in figures 12.5–6 and Table 12.1, the correspondences between tell and tomb ceramic corpora are immediately apparent. Even with the rare cooking pot and holemouth storejar removed from the tombs (fig. 12.5:1, 3), the two assemblages are remarkably similar. Virtually every type in the tombs occurs on the tell, even the miniature vessel and lamp, although much less popular (fig. 12.6:6, 25). As confirmation of these observations, the quantitative study revealed significant correspondences between tell and tombs in all but a few categories. There were correspondences in spouted vessels, medium and small necked storejars, pitchers and jugs, open and closed deep bowls and platter bowls, medium and small bowls, cups, and lamps (see Ch. 5).

Yet, there are distinctions to note that may provide us with some insight into particular customs associated with burial ritual. The tombs lack holemouth bowls (including basins), pithoi, and large necked storejars, all of which occur in Area C (fig. 12.6:7–8, 13–14). The tombs lack the functional ledge handles and piecrust rim decoration of Area C (fig 12.6:7, 15, 20). However, both are attributable to the lack of large storejars, basins, and necked cooking pots in the tombs. Other than these, the remaining differences appear to be examples of distribution. That is, the platter bowls have a smaller rim diameter range than on the tell (fig. 12.5:9, 12, 16), the large–medium deep bowls are fewer (fig. 12.5:14), there are many more lamps (fig. 12.5:18), more medium to small to miniature necked jars (fig. 12.5:8, 11), as well as pitcher/juglets (fig. 12.5:5, 7).

TABLE 12.1 *Comparison of tell and tomb assemblages at Khirbat Iskandar.*

	CEMETERIES		AREA C	
	No.	%	No.	%
holemouth bowl	2	1%	19	6%
holemouth jar	1	0%	11	3%
lamp	26	10%	4	1%
L-M bowl	13	5%	35	11%
M-S bowl	17	7%	23	7%
necked jar	58	23%	41	13%
spouted vessel	17	7%	33	10%
pitcher/juglet	12	5%	7	2%
platter bowl	102	41%	145	46%
TOTAL	248	100%	318	100%

Summarily, as noted in Chapter 5, the distinctiveness of the tomb assemblage (that is its differences with Area C) appears to be primarily a lack of long-term storage vessels and equipment needed for the preparation or processing of food, or perhaps even olive oil manufacturing. Whether the lack of such vessels—primarily larger vessels—relates to the constrained space in the tombs or reflects burial customs that did not consider them appropriate grave goods, these distinctions provide a lens through which to pursue further studies on the burial rituals of EB IV sedentary peoples. For a discussion of the ramifications of these similarities between tell and tombs, as well as the distinctions between Cemeteries E and D, see the conclusions in Chapter 16.

FIG. 12.5 *Selection of cemetery ceramics.*

#	FORM	TYPE	SIZE	DESCRIPTION	REF
1	Holemouth Jar	Cooking Pot	Medium	Cooking pot with direct (rounded) rim	fig. 11.7:13
2	Holemouth Jar	Spouted Vessel	Medium	"Teapot," squat, with direct (rounded) rim; vestigial ledge handle	fig. 10.13:12
3	Holemouth Jar	Storejar	Medium	Storejar with direct (bulbous) rim; molding	fig. 10.23:20
4	Deep Bowl	Closed Cup	Small	Cup-bowl with direct (rounded) rim	fig. 10.3:4
5	Jug	Flask Pitcher	Medium Large	Flask-pitcher with flared (rounded) rim	fig. 10.30:1
6	Necked Jar	Handleless Storejar	Medium Large	Storejar, global, with flared (tapered) rim; 1 knob	fig. 10.7:20
7	Jug	Jug	Medium Large	One-handled Jug with straight neck	fig. 10.30:2
8	Necked Jar	Handleless Storejar	Small	Storejar, ovaloid, with flared (rounded) rim; 1 knob	fig. 10.7:7
9	Platter Bowl	Lightly closed	Medium	Carinated platter bowl with direct (squared) rim	fig. 11.9:2
10	Necked Jar	Handleless Storejar	Medium Large	Storejar, squat, with flared (squared) rim; band combing	fig. 10.7:17
11	Necked Jar	Handleless Storejar	Medium	Storejar, squat, with flared (squared) rim; band combing	fig. 10.7:13
12	Platter Bowl	Open	Medium Large	Platter bowl with thickened (rolled) rim	fig. 10.3:15
13	Necked Jar	Handleless Storejar	Medium	Storejar, squat, with flared (squared) rim	fig. 10.17:14
14	Deep Bowl	Lightly closed	Medium Large	Carinated bowl with direct (beveled) rim; zigzag line	fig. 10.6:8
15	Deep Bowl	Closed Cup	Small	Cyma-profiled cup with everted rim	fig. 10.3:2
16	Platter Bowl	Open	Large	Platter bowl with thickened (turned-down) rim	fig. 10.3:20
17	Deep Bowl	Closed Cup	Small	Cyma-profiled cup with everted rim; lug handle	fig. 10.3.1
18	Shallow Bowl	Lamp, flat base	Small	Four-spouted lamp with direct (tapered) rim	fig. 10.8:16

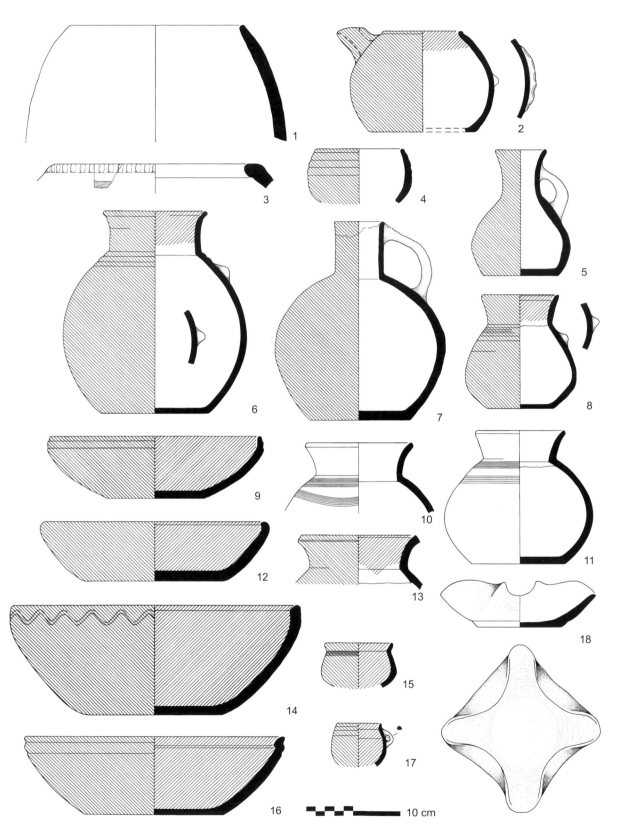

FIG. 12.5 *Selection of cemetery ceramics.*

FIG. 12.6 *Selection of Area C ceramics.*

#	FORM	TYPE	SIZE	DESCRIPTION	REF
1	Cooking Pot	Cooking Pot	Medium	Cooking pot with direct (bulbous) rim	pl. 13:9
2	Holemouth Jar	Spouted Vessel	Medium	"Teapot" with direct (squared) rim	pl. 4:20
3	Holemouth Jar	Storejar	Large	Storejar with direct (interior lip) rim	pl. 6:3
4	Holemouth Jar	Storejar	Medium	Storejar with direct (rounded) rim	pl. 3:14
5	Deep Bowl	Lightly closed Cup	Small	Incurved cup with direct (rounded) rim	pl. 5:4
6	Necked Jar	Necked Storejar	Small	Storejar with lightly flared (rounded) rim	pl. 5:19
7	Necked Jar	Cooking Pot	Pithoi	Cooking pot with lightly flared (squared) piecrust rim	pl. 11:11
8	Jug	Jug	Large	One-Handled Jug with lightly flared (rounded) rim	pl. 15:17
9	Necked Jar	Necked Storejar	Medium Small	Storejar with lightly flared (rounded) rim	pl. 18:6
10	Necked Jar	Necked Storejar	Large	Storejar with sharply flared (squared) rim; band combing	pl. 20:3
11	Necked Jar	Necked Storejar	Medium Small	Storejar with lightly flared (rounded) rim	pl. 15:20
12				Envelope ledge handle with folded/overlapping flaps	pl. 21:1
13	Deep Bowl	Basin	Very Large	Basin with thickened (flat) piecrust rim	pl. 3:11
14	Holemouth Bowl	Spouted Vessel	Large	Spouted basin with thickened (flat) rim	pl. 11:16
15				Vestigial ledge handle, envelope/pinch-lapped profile	pl. 21:11
16	Deep Bowl	Lightly closed Cup-Bowl	Medium Small	Cup-bowl with direct (rounded) rim; knob	pl. 12:12
17	Deep Bowl	Lightly closed Cup-Bowl	Medium Small	Cyma-profiled bowl with everted rim	pl. 4:7
18	Deep Bowl	Lightly closed	Medium	Carinated bowl with direct (rounded) rim	pl. 17:4
19	Deep Bowl	Lightly closed Cup	Small	Cyma-profiled cup with flared rim	pl. 20:1
20				Envelope ledge handle with spaced flaps (clear pinching)	pl. 21:14
21	Platter Bowl	Open	Medium	Platter Bowl with thickened (rolled) rim	pl. 2:13
22	Deep Bowl	Lightly closed	Large	Carinated bowl with thickened (beveled) rim	pl. 17:6
23	Platter Bowl	Lightly closed	Large	Platter bowl with thickened (beveled) rim	pl. 15:16
24	Platter Bowl	Open	Large	Platter bowl with thickened (turned-down) rim	pl. 10:19
25	Bowl	Lamp	Small	Four-spouted lamp with direct (rounded) rim	pl. 17:17

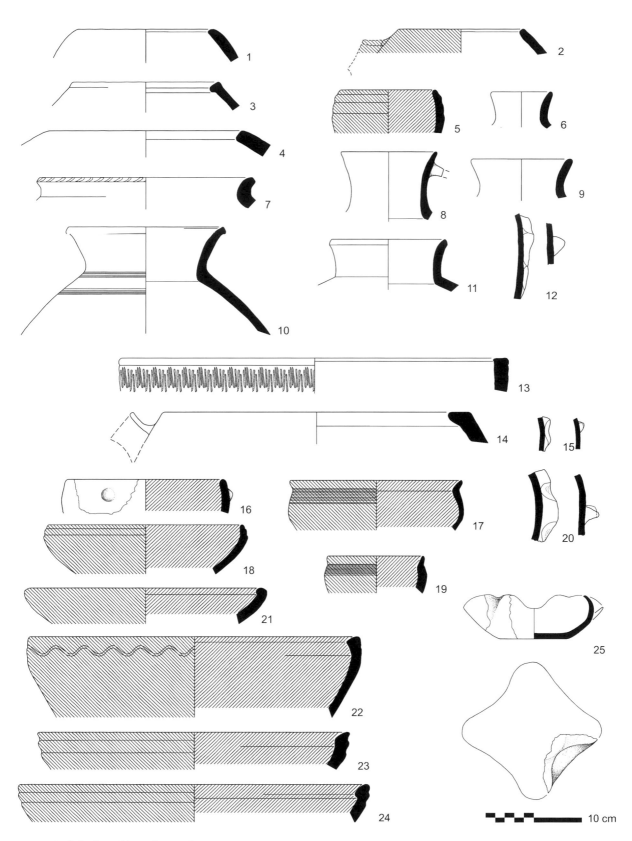

FIG. 12.6 *Selection of Area C ceramics.*

FIG. 13.8 *Photo Metal Dagger with four rivets A268.*

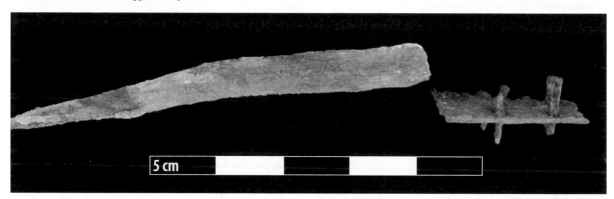

FIG. 13.9 *Photo Metal Dagger with four rivets A268.*

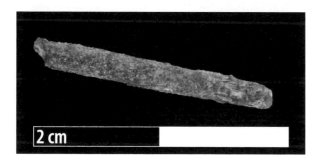

FIG. 13.10 *Photo Metal Pin shaft A269.*

FIG. 13.11 *Photo Metal Pin shaft A270.*

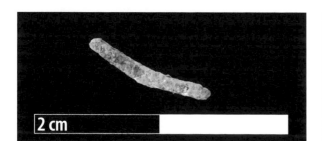

FIG. 13.12 *Photo Metal Pin shaft A271.*

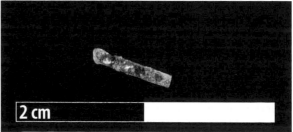

FIG. 13.13 *Photo Metal Pin shaft A272.*

Table 14.1 *Demographic breakdown of skeletal remains by cemetery area.*

	Area D	Area E	Area H	Area J	Total
Infant (<1 year)	0	0	0	0	0
Juvenile (1–12 years)	2	2	0	2	6
Adolescent (12–20 years)	1	1	0	0	2
Young Adult (20–40 years)	3	0	0	0	3
Older Adult (40+ years)	2	0	0	0	2
Adult Unknown Age	6	4	1	0	11
Total	14	7	1	2	24

varied between the different tombs, from only two percent of the bone fragments in tomb E14 to 100 percent of the material from D4 displaying a heavy buildup of carbonates. This problem was generally more pronounced in the tombs from Area D, compared to those from Area E. In particular, tombs D4 and D9 seem to have been most severely affected by this problem. It seems likely that these deposits were the result of water percolation into the tombs through the limestone formations into which the Area D tombs were cut.

Furthermore, the bones were fragmented, with very few identifiable pieces and a high proportion of unidentifiable scrap with fragments less than 1 cm in maximum dimension. The majority of the material was only identifiable very generally to skeletal element (for example: cranial fragments, long bone shaft fragments, etc.), while very little could be specifically identified to particular elements. The proportion of identifiable elements varied from a low of 1.7 percent in tomb E14 to a high of 14 percent of bone fragments in tomb D9. None of the tombs in areas D or E displayed percentages of identifiable fragments higher than 15 percent. While the fragmentation of the remains can be partially attributed to the collapse of several of the roofs of the shaft tombs, it seems likely that the fragmentation may have also been partially the result of repeated flash flooding in the tombs. The repeated rapid soaking and drying likely resulted in increased fragmentation of the bones. It also likely contributed to the soft, powdery, chalk-like consistency of much of the skeletal material. The softness of the bone caused a heavy degree of wear on most fragments, preventing refitting of the material in many cases.

The taphonomic changes observed in this collection provide evidence that a significant amount of disturbance may have been caused by flooding in the tombs in areas D and E. Given the condition of the skeletal material, it seems unlikely that the positions in which the remains were found during excavation represent the original deposition context of the bodies placed in these tombs. Rather, it seems that the skeletal material was dispersed and redeposited during flooding episodes.

DISCUSSION

A grand total (at a minimum) of 24 individuals were identified in the tombs excavated from areas D, E, H and J (Table 14.1). No infants (<1 year) were identified in the sample, but six juveniles (1–12 years), two adolescents (12–20 years), and 16 adults (>20 years) were identified. In no cases could the sex of any of these adults be determined, due to the poor condition of the bones. In a few cases, it was possible to determine with greater accuracy the ages of some of the adults present. Due to the preservation of the skeletal material, these estimations were primarily based on dental wear. Of the adults present, there were three younger adults (20–40 years), two older adults (>40 years), and 11 adults of unknown age.

It is not unusual for infants to be under-represented in archaeological skeletal samples, and this may be due to several factors, including differences in burial practices (i.e., infants were not buried, or were buried in different locations than other juveniles and adults), and differential preservation of infant skeletal remains, which are much more fragile than adult osteological material. Considering the state of preservation of the adult skeletal material, the latter seems like a reasonable explanation for the lack of infant remains. Similar to the patterns seen at sites like Jebel Qaʿaqir, but in contrast to Dhahr Mirzbâneh, juveniles of a variety of ages (ranging from 2 years to 12 years) were found interred in these tombs (Smith 1982; Lapp 1966). These juveniles were interred both in the presence of adults and in tombs where no evidence of adult remains were found.

Of the 24 individuals at Khirbat Iskandar, 14 originated from tombs from Area D, and seven from Area E. Areas H and J, both of which had only one excavated tomb, produced one and two individuals respectively. The small sample sizes preclude any conclusions about differences in the demographic composition of the cemeteries in Areas D and E, although it is worth noting that both areas produced the remains of juvenile and adolescent individuals, in addition to adult material.

None of the tombs in Areas D or E provide any evidence of primary articulation of the skeletal remains. Rather, the evidence provided by the skeletal material suggests that in none of the tombs were the human remains found *in situ*, but rather that there was a great deal of post-depositional disturbance. This disturbance was the result of a number of factors, such as roof collapse and possible repeated flooding. As a result, it is impossible to reconstruct the patterns of deposition that occurred in the EB IV tombs at Khirbat Iskandar. However, the tombs themselves, as well as the general pattern of a combination of single and multiple interments of small groups of individuals, is consistent with other EB IV cemeteries at sites in the Southern Levant. The number of individuals found in the tombs at Khirbat Iskandar ranged from one to four; no tombs provide any evidence for the interment of more than four individuals.

The typical pattern of burial in the EB IV consists of secondary, disarticulated remains of small numbers of individuals, as seen at Jebel Qaʿaqir (Smith 1982). The EB IV tombs at Jericho contain primarily single interments, while the EB IV shaft tombs at Bâb adh-Dhrâʿ contain multiple individuals, limited to between four and seven individuals (Kenyon 1960; 1965; Chesson 1999). Many EB IV cemeteries display a pattern of primary interment followed by secondary reorganization of the remains during the deposition of subsequent individuals. While post-depositional disturbance prevents a firm conclusion, it seems reasonable to believe that the burial practices at Khirbat Iskandar may fit this pattern.

Chapter 15

Comparison of EB IV Radiocarbon Results from Khirbat Iskandar and Bâb adh-Dhrâ'

by Paul S. Holdorf

In this chapter the results of two Area C radiocarbon analyses are set forth and compared with five Bâb adh-Dhrâ' results from EB IV Stratum I. The objectives are to determine whether the Area C determinations 1) are consistent with EB IV dates, and 2) can corroborate the phase-to-phase correlations seen in the pottery (see Ch. 5).

In 2003, two Khirbat Iskandar Area C carbon samples, numbers 1 and 2 on Table 15.1, were analyzed by the NSF-Arizona AMS Laboratory and the University of Tübingen, respectively. Both had been collected from Square 2, the first in 1987 and the second in 1984, and kept in plastic bags, sealed in aluminum, until submission for testing. One is charcoal from an unknown wood, possibly from one of the charred timbers found in its locus. The second is from an ash pocket of olive wood. The first is from a Phase 3 locus that appears to be mixed with Phase 2 destruction debris. The second is from a Phase 2 surface. It is not known whether the wood from either sample was new, old, or when last used in its context.

Table 15.1 provides the basic information on the two results in the same format as used by James Weinstein (Rast and Schaub 2003: 639–40), together with the two "new" (4 and 6), and three "old" (3, 5, and 7) results from Bâb adh-Dhrâ'. All of the radiocarbon dates have been calibrated using a more current version 4.0.5 of the OxCal software package (Christopher Bronk Ramsey 2007)[1]. Because the proportion of radiocarbon in the atmosphere is variable, OxCal calibrations are adjusted periodically. As a result, the previously published Bâb adh-Dhrâ' date ranges have shifted somewhat, but typically not by more than 20 years. Not included are the two Bâb adh-Dhrâ' EB IVA results (SI-2869 and SI-2870) that Weinstein deemed to be outliers, far too early for EB IV (Rast and Schaub 2003: 638, table 22.2).

Radiocarbon dates are inexact; they must depend on imprecise measurements both of old, long-lived tree rings and on the samples analyzed. In addition, atmospheric radiocarbon concentration has varied over time. This is illustrated graphically in figure 15.1 (for Area C sample AA50178). The most likely (one-*sigma*) date range spans 109 years, from 2571 to 2462 BCE. This is a relatively high date for EB IV, but a reasonably possible (two-*sigma*) date range (see table 15.1) brings it to as late as 2344 BCE, a date that is consistent with EB IV dating. Since this sample is from no earlier than Phase 2 of Area C, it does appear to be early.

TABLE 15.1 *Carbon 14 samples from Khirbat Iskandar and Bâb adh-Dhrâ'.*

#	SAMPLE	ARCH. DATE	MATERIAL	P.	CONTEXT	13 C/12C RATIO	14 C AGE BP	CALIBRATED DATE B.C.	PROB. OF RANGE
1	AA50178	EB IV	Charcoal	3	Area C, L. 2043, Compact layer…with clumps of plaster, some mudbrick, and charred timber; appears to be mixed with Phase 2 destruction debris.	-23.5 o/oo	3975 +/- 43	2571–2513 (1σ) 2503–2462 2618–2610 (2σ) 2581–2344	38.9% 29.3% 0.7% 94.7%
2		EB IV	Ash Pocket Olive Wood	2	Area C, L. 2030, Debris layer…with ash pits, patches of burnt mud-brick, and numerous sherds.		3930 +- 60	2519 2399 (1σ) 2490–2336 2324–2307 2576–2277 (2σ) 2253–2228 2223–2209	2.3% 60.5% 4.8% 91.7% 2.5% 1.2%
3	SI–2872	EB IVA	Charcoal	IC	Field X.3 Locus 49 Brick fall Gray soil layer below Locus 48		3805 +-60	2342–2141 (1σ) 2462–2128 (2σ) 2088–2046	68.2% 90.2% 5.2%
4	134016	EB IVA	Charcoal	I	Field XVI.4 Locus 7 Mud–brick debris with ash pockets	–25.0 o/oo	3800 +– 60	2341–2139 (1σ) 2461–2124 (2σ) 2091–2043	68.2% 88.9% 6.5%
5	P–2573	EB IVA	Olive stones	IA	Field X.1 Locus 23 Similar to ash pile Locus 22		3770+–60	2290–2131 (1σ) 2086–2051 2457–2419 (2σ) 2407–2376 2351–2026	58.8% 9.4% 2.6% 2.6% 90.1%
6	134017	EB IVA	Charcoal	IB	Field XVI.I Locus 12 Gray bricky soil, below Locus 7	–24.2 o/oo	3690 +– 60	2195–2175 (1σ) 2145–2013 1999–1978 2279–2250 (2σ) 2230–2220 2211–1915	6.2% 55.4% 6.6% 2.6% 0.7% 92.1%
7	SI–2875	EB IVA	Charcoal	IC	Field X.3 Locus 60 Ashy living surfaces, as many a three in succession, each with flat–lying pottery, below Locus 59		3595+–70	2116–2099 (1σ) 2039–1879 1839–1829 1791–1786 2139–1753 (2σ)	3.9% 61.0% 2.3% 1.0% 95.4%

The date ranges shown in figure 15.2 for the other Area C sample (olive wood) are even broader: a total of 242 years in the one *sigma* ranges, to as late as 2307 BCE, and a total of 367 years in the two *sigma* ranges, to as late as 2209 BCE (see table 15.1).

Figure 15.3 is a multi-plot chart that shows the two Area C and five Bâb adh-Dhrâʿ results together, generally from early to late. The first three Bâb adh-Dhrâʿ results (3–5) fit quite comfortably within EB IV dating. But the one-*sigma* date range for #7 (SI-2875) extends to 1786 BCE. The position of SI-2872 (#3), from Field X Phase C Locus 49, makes sense, since that phase is the earliest in Stratum I. But SI-2875 (#7) is also from a Field X Phase C Locus (60) and it is the third locus *below* Locus 49 (with Loci 59 and 58 in between).[2] The samples do not have overlapping one-*sigma* ranges. The only olive stone, and Phase A, sample, #5 (P-2573), should be later than Phase B #6 (134017), but does overlap it comfortably at the one-*sigma* level.

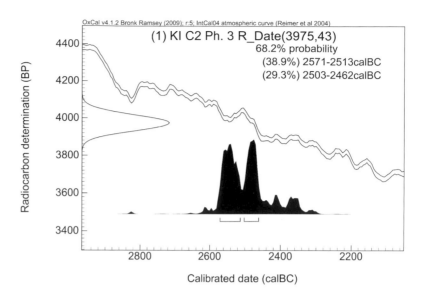

FIG. 15.1   *Area C radiocarbon sample AA50178.*

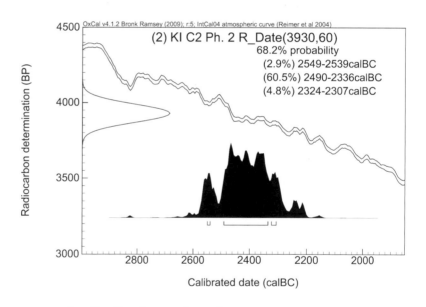

FIG. 15.2   *Area C radiocarbon sample wood.*

Wood used in construction is vulnerable to the "old wood" issue, not just because it was many years old when the tree was harvested, but also because it may have been used in a structure for many years, and then reused in a newer structure. Although olive wood is unlikely to have been used in construction, furniture, serving implements, or bowls carved from it can be used for a long time, perhaps as legacy pieces. Moreover, the life expectancy of an olive tree is 300–600 years.[3] It can be hundreds of years old before it is harvested and the carving begins; or it can be only a couple years old if it consists merely of twigs from a recent trimming. Accordingly, it is perilous at best to try to correlate EB IV phases using charcoal samples.

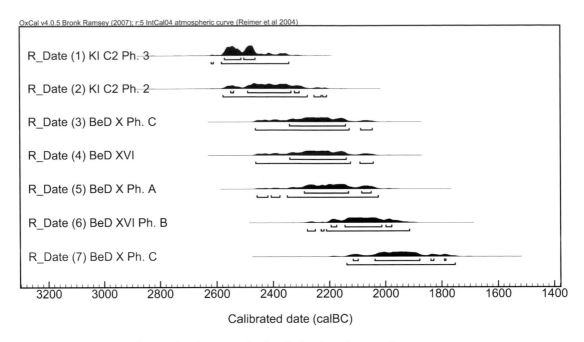

OxCal v4.0.5 Bronk Ramsey (2007); r:5 IntCal04 atmospheric curve (Reimer et al 2004)

FIG. 15.3 *Comparison Khirbat Iskandar and Bâb adh-Dhrâ' radiocarbon samples.*

In all events, the Bâb adh-Dhrâ' sequence demonstrates that using C14 samples that are or may be from wood is unlikely to be helpful in correlating phases of a 400-year age, either within a site or between sites. About all that can be said for the EB IV results to date is that they are consistent with commonly accepted time intervals for this period.

NOTES

1 Figures 15.1–2 were re-done using the format of OxCal version 4.1.2, but this did not change any date ranges or probabilities.

2 Rast and Schaub 2003: 417–18.

3 http://www.sfakia-crete.com/sfakia-crete/olive. html, last accessed 4/2/07.

Chapter 16

Summary and Conclusions

by Suzanne Richard and Jesse C. Long, Jr.

This attempt at summary and synthesis concentrates on highlighting the major contributions and conclusions of this volume. The authors believe that the wealth of excavated data presented here provides an opportunity to offer a tentative interpretation of the site of Khirbat Iskandar in the EB IV period. This interpretation is a critical analytical tool, for it will be a hypothesis to test against the EB IV stratigraphic and ceramic record in Areas A and B, and, ultimately, against the antecedent Early Bronze Age occupation on the mound. The view reconstructed here situates Khirbat Iskandar in its eco-environmental setting, illuminates its occupational history and burial customs, and presents a well-stratified and quantified typo-chronological ceramic sequence. The view also reconstructs a sequence comparison with the southern Dead Sea Plain site of Bâb adh-Dhrâʿ, anchored by means of the same classification system and quantification method. Moreover, as the only available fully published stratified EB IV site in Transjordan, Bâb adh-Dhrâʿ has necessarily been the focus of our comparative study, followed by other Transjordanian sites with stratified occupational and ceramic sequences. Moving beyond single site comparisons, the discussion below broadens

the perspective to situate Khirbat Iskandar in its regional setting of the Central Plateau, specifically in relation to the Madaba Plains at the north end, and to the south, the neighboring Karak Plateau.

Given the as yet unique gate complex in Area C, the comparative analysis draws general architectural parallels with the excavated settlement sites of Transjordan. There will be a brief overview of the ceramic studies, but for a ceramic comparanda, see Chapters 4 and 12. Ultimately, it is Khirbat Iskandar set against the background of its particular landscape that, we think, provides the most insight on its inhabitants in EB IV. The authors also offer a glimpse of the site and cemeteries in light of ongoing work and investigation of the megalithic structures in the vicinity and possible symbolic interrelations between the peoples and their landscape.

ENVIRONMENT AND SUBSISTENCE

Paleoclimatic records show that the time spanning the Chalcolithic period and Early Bronze Age witnessed high variability and sudden change. It appears that the earlier periods were wet, but the EB III period saw some fluctuations in precipitation and some colluvial accumulation on flood-plains. In the EB IV period, there seems to have been a decline in precipitation. Locally, it appears that this dry event relates to the abandonment of Khirbat Iskandar at the end of EB IV, ca. 2000 BCE. Once the fertile floodplain soils were eroded, the wâdi became unattractive as a place of settlement. Whether or not this idiosyncratic site history offers an explanation for urban collapse at the end of EB III and widespread cultural change in the southern Levant is conjectural; however, much comparative and diverse paleoclimatic and geoarchaeological data from the southern Levant generally suggest that climate change was a major factor. Obviously, other factors as detailed in Chapter 2, such as deterioration of catchment areas by human activities and possible tectonic activity, etc., all played a role in the dramatic changes occurring at Khirbat Iskandar at the end of the third millennium BCE.

A major contribution of the geoarchaeological study is the discovery of a large floodplain near the site in the Early Bronze Age, based on the alluvial deposits of the Wâdi al-Wâla. Pollen analysis suggests that cereals, in particular wheat and barley, were cultivated on the floodplain and that the numbers of olive tree pollen are considerable, even compared with today's numbers. The latter suggests that olive cultivation was probably the main agricultural activity in the floodplain. Moreover, the extraordinary amount of olive wood samples from the site, as well as olive-stone remains, supports the view that settled agriculturalists cultivated the fertile soils in the vicinity of Khirbat Iskandar in the EB IV period. Further confirmation of the cultivation of the floodplain near the site comes from palaeobotanical remains, from which preliminary analysis indicates the following cultivated plants: olive (*Olea europaea*), six-row barley (*Hordeum vulgare*), lentil (*Lens culinaris*), as well as chick pea (*Cicer arietinum*), pea (*Pisum sativum*), grape (*Vitis vinifera*), and fig (*Ficus carica*). It is not certain whether fig was cultivated or gathered; apparently pistachio nuts were gathered in the wild. Thus the evidence from Khirbat Iskandar, along with that from sites such as Khirbat Zaraqun, Bâb adh-Dhrâ', and Numayra, demonstrates the development of olive culture in Jordan in the Early Bronze Age (see Neef 1990).

These conclusions concerning agricultural activity at the site are mirrored by the paleozoological study conducted on the faunal remains from Area C. The study indicates a developing complexity in animal husbandry over time, as seen by the addition of cattle and pigs to the subsistence patterns in Phases 2–3. The faunal deposition suggests that the Khirbat Iskandar husbandry strategy was based on maximizing sheep/goat herd security while maintaining protein offtake. In general, the faunal remains in Area C point to a successful agricultural system that supported the community. These conclusions will, of course, serve as a hypothesis for study of the far greater numbers of botanical and faunal remains found in Areas A and B; however, the floral, faunal, and pollen studies, along with geomorphological study, all affirm what the stratified profile in Area C epitomizes: Khirbat Iskandar was a permanent, continuously occupied, sedentary community throughout the EB IV period.

THREE PHASES OF EB IV SETTLEMENT IN AREA C

The two major stratigraphical conclusions drawn from the Area C excavations are that there were three phases of continuous occupation in EB IV, and that the area was transformed into a "gateway" complex in the latest phase.

Regarding the first, the superposition of architecture, realignment of structures, the associated surfaces, and quantitative ceramic study all contribute to the conclusion that three separate EB IV occupational phases existed at Khirbat Iskandar. Reuse of Phase 2 Wall 5013 in the Phase 3 "gateway" shows that immediate rebuilding occurred even following the destruction of the broadroom house structure (R521/R221). The similarities and continuities in the Phases 1–3 ceramic assemblages likewise affirm continuous occupation, the major change occurring between Phases 1–2. The "fossil type" EB IV platter bowl with turned-down rilled rim becomes dominant in Phase 2. This observation agrees with the stratified evidence to suggest that the Phase 1 settlement may be early, possibly a transitional EB III/EB IV occupational phase. Adding support to this view is Phase 1 Wall 8018B, which is a rebuild of pre-EB IV Wall 1818A. There are indications of a transitional phase at other sites, for example, Tall Abu an-Niʿaj (Falconer and Magness-Gardiner 1989), Tall Umm Hammad (Helms 1986), Khirbat Hamra Ifdan (Adams 2000), and Bâb adh-Dhrâʿ (Rast and Schaub 2003). At Bâb adh-Dhrâʿ the statistical study showed the "fossil type" rilled-rim platter bowl to be virtually a null value in the earliest EBIV phase, but to dominate thereafter, just as is the case at Khirbat Iskandar (Rast and Schaub 2003; Richard 2003). These data support the view that there was cultural continuity between EB III/IV, especially in Transjordan.

Regarding the second conclusion, following the destruction of the Phase 2 broad-room structure, a transformation of settlement plan occurred in Area C. The former domestic area was reconfigured into a public area evidenced by a "gateway" and benches for communal activities. Moreover, there were features and material culture to suggest that specialized activities, like agricultural processing/ long-term storage and a chipped-stone workshop were a primary focus in the "gateway" complex. Interestingly, Phase 3 shared a ceramic assemblage that, generally, exhibited a range of ceramic types similar to those found in the earlier domestic phases. A similar phenomenon was noted at Tall al-Hayyât, where public temple ceramics and domestic assemblages were likewise similar (Falconer et al. 2006: 106).

Though not a "gateway" *per se*, that is, an opening in an outer fortification curtain wall, this unique complex nevertheless witnesses to the only ingress into the upper site within a series of interconnected walls and structures running east–west along the crest of the mound. The interpretation of Area C hinges to a certain extent on excavations across the mound, as well as on important observations about the defenses made by Nelson Glueck. All of these data suggest a "gateway" context for the Area C complex (and see figs. 1:2; 1:6–7).

The several lines of evidence that provide this context are: 1) Glueck's observations that the defenses of the site included an outer perimeter wall with square towers, an intermediary wall bisecting the site east–west, and interval towers; 2) continuous interconnecting wall running east–west from Area C to Area A; 3) a stratigraphic link between the east–west wall and tower discovered in 2007 in Area A; and 4) definitive evidence for EB IV walls abutting the outer western perimeter wall (Richard, Long, and Libby 2007). This confirmation of a link to the perimeter wall clarifies earlier probes and excavations west of the Area A tower and to the east of Area C (Richard 1990), which were suggestive, but not conclusive, of a link-up with the outer perimeter wall.

Thus, extrapolating from excavations across the mound, our working hypothesis concerning the Area C complex is that the Phase 3 population built a type of east–west boundary at the crest of the mound, which linked to and reused the earlier eastern and western perimeter walls on the site. This boundary wall connects to a tower in Area A; its only break is in Area C, where there is a passageway into the upper site. The best evidence for the "gateway" is in the latest phase (Phase 3B), when benches and stairs were erected on the plastered entryway and against the blocked walls of the two juxtaposed rooms. Architectural evidence, along with sub phases within the gate complex suggest that in the original construction of the gate (Phase 3A) two pylons served as roof supports. The above two conclusions derive from a wealth of data, the most critical stratigraphic elements of which are summarized at the end of Chapter 3, along with a brief synopsis of rooms and room assemblages.

COMPARATIVE ANALYSIS

Settlement Plan

The rectangular buildings in Area C may be compared generally with the stone and/or mudbrick structures found at a number of EB IV sites, such as Bâb adh-Dhrâʿ (Rast and Schaub 2003: figs. 12:8, 13), Iktanu (Prag 1971: fig. 11), Nahal Refaim (Eisenberg 1993a: 1277–80), Shaʿar Ha-Golan (Eisenberg 1993b: 1340–43), Khirbat al-Batrawy (Nigro 2006: fig. 3.33), Tall Abu an-Niʿaj (Falconer and Magness-Gardiner 1989), Tall al-ʿUmayri (Mitchel 1989: fig. 18.2), Jericho (Nigro 2003), ʿEin el-Helu (Covello-Paran 2009), and even Har Yeruham (Kochavi 1967). Both longroom and broadroom houses are found in EB IV, as they are in earlier periods. Good examples of both are attested in Area B at Khirbat Iskandar (Richard 1990; Richard and Long 2006). As for specific plan, there are no EB IV parallels to the settlement plan in Area C in Phase 3; however, the general tendency for the construction of rooms with shared walls is evident where settlement plans are available, such as at Sha'ar Ha-Golan, Rephaim, Tall Umm Hammad, and Iktanu. What is not evident from the Area C architecture (or elsewhere on the mound, for that matter) is the "block house" architectural style uncovered at Tall Umm Hammad (later stages 6–8; Helms 1986) or Iktanu (Prag 1971: fig. 13). The Tall Umm Hammad plan shows a block of 14 rooms framing a central courtyard. EB IV architecture generally appears to reflect its local Early Bronze Age antecedents, although recently Prag has suggested that certain "urban-like" traditions, such as architectural styles, may have derived from Syrian tradition (2009: 87).

Further insight into the nature of the Area C complex derives from a comparison with an extensive domestic neighborhood in Area B (Phase A), where a considerable assemblage of domestic equipment came to light (Richard and Boraas 1984; 1988; Richard 1990). The contrasts with Area B are apparent: in Area C there are no tabuns, virtually no grinding slabs, few handstones and associated food preparation equipment, a limited number of cooking vessels, few spindle whorls and bone objects, with limited faunal, floral, and ceramic materials generally. The contrast between these two neighborhoods highlights variability at the site and strongly suggests that, despite similarities with earlier domestic assemblages (see above), the Area C Phase 3 settlement was not a domestic residential area like the uppermost (Phase A) settlement in Area B. Rather, it was primarily a public area, where apparently a variety of communal activities took place, attested by evidence for specialized processing and/or storage facilities, a workshop, and the bench-lined passageway itself, which probably witnessed pedestrian traffic into and out of the upper site, as well as communal gatherings.

Gateways

The direct-access gate of Khirbat Iskandar, unlike more monumental gate structures in the Early and Middle Bronze Ages, is a passageway in a type of boundary line. Due to its stairway at both ends, plastered surface, and benches, the complex is not simply a doorway into a room or series of rooms, as appears to be the case in Area H at Iktanu (Prag 1990: 125–26). Thus, there still do not exist contemporary parallels for the Area C complex, and it remains unique for the period in the southern Levant. Nonetheless, there is a tradition of simple, direct-access gates that one can trace back as early as the Chalcolithic period, as seen at 'En Gedi (Ushishkin 1980). There, a bench-lined rectangular building served as a type of gateway or gatehouse in a *temenos* surrounding the sanctuary and courtyard. It is a single-entry, direct-access gate with double piers and steps at each end. A similar gate, apparently a simple postern with steps, provided access from the east. Another parallel is the EB I gate (LG1) at Tall Jawa. This is a double-chambered direct-entry gate connected to a type of casemate wall (Helms 1981: fig. 9c). In addition, there are also interesting parallels in early village sites, which show a band of interconnected houses in a defensive posture, with few passages or breaks, somewhat reminiscent of the Khirbat Iskandar plan. For parallels at Tulaylât al-Ghassûl IV and other early sites, see, conveniently, Helms (1981: 111–14). There are also numerous Early Bronze Age gates for which parallels can be cited, such as the EB I–II gate at Tel el-Far'ah with its multi-roomed flanking bastions (see Kempinsky 1992: 68–80).

A newly excavated gate at Tall Rukeis, in the Hauran, offers yet another parallel for the Area C gate structure (McLaren 2003; fig. 48a–g). The gate at Tall Rukeis deserves some consideration, both for its chronological proximity (MB I–II) as well as for its stylistic similarities. The simple direct-entry gate structure, of the double-chambered variety, has a cobbled passage and guardrooms with benches; however, it is a monumental gate and connected to an outer defensive curtain wall, unlike the Area C gate. McLaren posits that the Tall Rukeis and Khirbat Iskandar (Phase 3A) gates evince continuity of Early Bronze Age architectural traditions and transitional Middle Bronze Age characteristics. In the latter period, the triple-entryway gate becomes the standard (2003: 40–41).

McLaren's thesis that Tall Rukeis, located in the Hauran in geographic proximity to southern Syria, was a desert frontier military establishment has merit. His suggestion that Khirbat Iskandar may have been a frontier settlement in EB IV is questionable, since the site's long history of settlement in the Early Bronze Age, as well as its location on the King's Highway and its environmental context (see Ch. 2), contradicts this view. Combined with transitional Middle Bronze Age ceramic and bronze types, the Area C gate suggests continuity at the EB IV/MB IIA nexus. The role that the rural villages played in the reemergence of sociopolitical complexity in the Middle Bronze Age is evident at the site of Tall al-Hayyat (see Falconer et al. 2006).

THE CERAMIC STUDIES

The major conclusions drawn from the quantitative ceramic studies are that 1) there were three typo-chronological phases at Khirbat Iskandar in EB IV, and 2) typo-chronological linkages exist between Khirbat Iskandar and Bâb adh-Dhrâ'. For a summary of the tell/tomb results, see below.

As detailed in Chapters 4–5, statistical typo-chronological diagnostics were discernible in the Area C assemblage. The best evidence comes from a comparison of the platter bowls: Phase 1 flat rim platters die out in Phase 2, while rolled and rolled pointed rim platters become increasingly rare, virtually dying out in Phase 3. Although a few examples of the turned-down rilled-rim platter bowl—the EB IV "fossil type"—occur in Phase 1, it is in Phase 2 that the type dominates and supersedes earlier forms. This dominance continues in Phase 3, along with the appearance of the beveled rim bowl and the straight-sided cooking pot. There were numerous statistically significant diagnostics (e.g., the Phase 3 straight-sided cooking pot with steam holes), including size differences and changes in richness, which support the three-phase sequence.

A major contribution of these studies is the typo-chronological link proposed between the central and southern Transjordanian regions in EB IV, based on the quantitative study comparing Khirbat Iskandar and Bâb adh-Dhrâ'. This is a first step in developing interregional ceramic cross-phasing in a period where one-period sites, cemeteries, and regionalization are the norm. It is hoped that the diagnostics and correlations with Bâb adh-Dhrâ' will offer some chronological datums for other sites in the period.

The petrographic study that indicated a predominantly locally produced corpus of pottery at Khirbat Iskandar is not surprising for the EB IV period. Tthe study, however, also revealed connections with the Rift Valley and Dead Sea basin. Although the Fabric E holemouth vessels could derive from the 'Uvda Valley, a provenience in Central or Southern Transjordan is likewise possible. Connections with the region south of the Dead Sea, especially the Faynan, is not indicated. The links are northern, for example the area of the Wâdi az-Zarqa', as well as an import from the Beth Shean region (Ch. 6). Excavation at the site has also uncovered data supporting evidences for trade and or gifts (metals, zoomorphic figurines, and apparent imports from the A-Z family as detailed in Richard 2000; 2006).

CEMETERIES

Despite the disturbed condition of the tombs, the cemeteries at Khirbat Iskandar appear to reflect the well-known EB IV tradition of shaft chamber tombs with multiple secondary burials, although the Tomb E9 interments are suggestive of primary burial (see Ch. 14). Nonetheless, the burial traditions at Khirbat Iskandar appear to contrast with the primary burial custom found, for example, at Bâb adh-Dhrâ'. On the basis of tomb types and a quantified ceramic study comparing tell and tomb, as well as comparing tombs within separate cemeteries, there were three major discoveries: 1) the cemeteries were in use contemporaneously with Area C; 2) ceramic traditions of the "living" were remarkably similar to those of the "dead" at Khirbat Iskandar; and 3) patterning and variations in the cemeteries indicated distinctions between Cemeteries D and E.

The close correspondence between tell and tomb assemblages throughout the three phases in Area C strengthens the inference that those buried in the cemeteries were sedentists from the site, rather than outside populations. A comparison of tell/tomb assemblages demonstrates strong linkage between the two (see figs. 12.5–6). Along with the domestic character of the cemetery repertoire, there was domestic equipment recovered from the tombs: ground stone artifacts probably related to food preparation, flint blades related to agricultural, and a bone needle perhaps used in basketry or weaving.

The differences between the two highlight customs associated with burial. The tombs lack holemouth bowls (including basins) and pithoi, the platter bowls have a smaller size range, the large–medium deep bowls are fewer, and there were no envelope handles in the tombs. Moreover, there were more medium-to-small to miniature necked jars, pitcher/juglets, and lamps in the tombs. The lack of long-term storage, food preparation, or processing/industrial equipment (for example for olive oil manufacturing) in the tombs, as well as the general lack of large sizes, may relate to the constrained space within the tomb. Alternatively, those items were not considered appropriate grave goods.

Major questions posed in the ceramic study were: Why is there such a close correspondence between the "living" and the "dead" at Khirbat Iskandar (also at Bâb adh-Dhrâʿ), and why is the burial repertoire more limited and specialized at central hills locations, as at Dhahr Mirzbâneh (Lapp 1966: figs. 1–40: *passim*) and Gibeon (Pritchard 1963: fig. 62:34–40: *passim)*, where we see the ubiquitous small jars or "milk bottles" and little else? The answer may be as simple as that at Khirbat Iskandar we have cemeteries serving the needs of the sedentary occupants of the site, whereas isolated cemeteries probably do represent the interments of seasonal peoples who make or purchase few specialized vessels as grave gifts. The different assemblages probably reflect sedentary vs. pastoral burial custom distinctions. Other permanent sites and associated cemeteries

also seem to reflect a similar tomb/tell repertoire, for example Bâb adh-Dhrâʿ (Schaub and Rast 1989) and Jericho (Nigro 2003).

As to comparisons between Cemeteries D and E, distinctions in these cemeteries are represented by variability in burial assemblages, differences in tomb type, and cemetery location (next to the site or across the wâdi). The quantitative study showed Cemetery E to include, proportionately, many more medium–small bowls, fewer (and smaller) platter bowls, and more well-fired pottery. These and other characteristics are comparable to the assemblage in Field XVI (the cultic area) at Bâb adh-Dhrâʿ. In contrast, Cemetery D contained evidence for reuse, extraordinary numbers of vessels, and was located across the wâdi to the south in what was probably the major burial ground for the population. Along with ceramic distinctions and the presence of architectural elements in Cemetery E, the aboveground megalithic markers and the proximity to the tell combine to suggest some social distinctiveness of those interred there in contrast to those interred in the large cemetery of reused shaft tombs in Area D. Even so, the variability found within Cemetery D itself is also suggestive of social distinctions. For a discussion of social stratification in EB IV tombs, see Palumbo (1987) and Baxevani (1995).

KHIRBAT ISKANDAR AND THE CENTRAL PLATEAU

To date, there are few known EB IV occupational and ceramic sequences on the Central Plateau. At the northern edge, the Madaba Plains site of Tall al-ʿUmayri has revealed two stratified phases thought to be early EB IV or transitional EB III/EB IV (Herr 2002: 14–15). The house remains in the earlier Stratum 18 and more ephemeral remains in Stratum 17, above, are important because they directly supersede well-preserved EB III houses and thus are indicative of continuity with the preceding period (Mitchel 1989). Based on its late EB IV cemetery pottery corpus (Waheeb and Palumbo 1993), Tall al-ʿUmayri appears to be in the greater Amman cultural orbit. That pottery—hybrid jugs with ledge handles and pot-marked strap handles—is so characteristic of the Amman-Zarqaʾ

area that it was identified as a new regional family, A-Z (Palumbo and Peterman 1993). On the basis of A-Z vessels in Area B at Khirbat Iskandar (Palumbo and Peterman 1993: fig. 3; Richard 2000: fig. 3:8)—the southernmost examples attested—it is evident that exchange networks were operative between the two areas. The results of the petrographic study (Ch. 6), where contacts with the Beth-Shean area came to light, add weight to this inference of northern contacts.

Future comparative study of pre-EB IV strata at Khirbat Iskandar will undoubtedly show additional linkages with other EB II/III fortified sites in the Madaba Plains area, such as Tall al-'Umayri, Jalul, and Tall Madaba (Harrison 1997). Both Tall al-'Umayri and Khirbat Iskandar also evidence EB IB tombs, both of which contained 15–20 interments with similar EB IB pottery (Dubis and Dabrowski 2002; and see preliminarily Richard 1990).

Elsewhere on this northern half of the Central Plateau, evidence for EB IV occupation comes from surface survey and/or isolated cemetery sites. Despite a paucity of excavated EB IV settlement sites, survey data has revealed a significant degree of continuity between EB III and EB IV (Palumbo 1990: 60–61). This phenomenon also describes the Karak Plateau (see below). These data enhance the view argued in this volume that it is continuity of Early Bronze Age tradition that explains the quite remarkable level of prosperity as well as sociopolitical and economic complexity at Khirbat Iskandar. On present evidence, it seems reasonable to infer that Khirbat Iskandar was the major EB IV settlement in this part of the Central Plateau.

On the more southern part of the Central Plateau—the Karak Plateau region—'Ara'ir and Adir are well-known in the EB IV literature. That they were major sites in the period is clear from their architectural remains, multiple-phased occupation, and important ceramic sequences (Olávarri 1969; Cleveland 1960). As the ceramic comparisons illustrate (fig. 4.11), the closest parallels to the Khirbat Iskandar assemblage are with the primarily red-slipped and rilled pottery from the southern areas (including Bâb adh-Dhrâ', located below the Karak Plateau on the southern Dead Sea Plain). Moreover, as the petrographic analysis suggests

(Ch. 6), connections with the Rift Valley included the Dead Sea basin, but probably did not extend southward toward the Wadi Faynan.

As is the case further north, information about the EB IV settlement patterns on the Karak Plateau derives primarily from survey. From the published statistics of the original JADIS database of Early Bronze Age sites (Palumbo 1990), it was already clear that there was more evidence for EB III/IV continuity on the Central Plateau and, in particular, on the Karak Plateau, than anywhere else in the southern Levant. Recent test excavations (Chesson et al. 2005: 33–37) have uncovered EB III/IV occupation layers at the large (5.5 ha) site of Khirbet el-Minsahlat, which, combined with Adir and 'Ara'ir, witnesses to substantial sedentary occupation in the EB IV period, again significant correlative evidence for the substantial nature of the settlement at Khirbat Iskandar.

KHIRBAT ISKANDAR AND NORTHERN TRANSJORDAN

Moving beyond the Central Plateau, we encounter apparent regional differences with Khirbat Iskandar. The Amman-Zarqa' (A-Z) family and its characteristic corpus of jugs has already been mentioned. The Jordan Valley, with its painted pottery tradition, is a distinct region in comparison with Khirbat Iskandar, the notable exception being Iktanu, at the southernmost tip of the region. That site's cultural connections link to Dever's "TJ" family, which includes the Central Plateau and southern Transjordan (and see the comparative study in Ch. 4). Sites in the Jordan Valley more typically have mudbrick architecture, lack the tradition of red-slipped and rilled vessels, especially the platter bowl, and include trickle-painted pottery. That permanent agricultural settlements existed is clear from the multi-phased sites of Tall Abu an-Ni'aj and Tall Umm Hammad (above). The overlap of regional ceramic styles, however, is well-attested, pointing to contact among the various regions. The Khirbat Iskandar Area B "storeroom" has an amalgam of features (Richard 2000; and note the trickle-painted sherd in Area C, pl. 21:2) as noted by Helms at Tall Umm Hammad (1986) and, likewise, by Falconer and Magness-Gardiner at Tall al-Hayyât (1984). Thus, on a site-by-site level, one notes some good parallels with the north (see fig. 4.11), but when those assemblages are understood holistically, the differences perhaps outweigh the similarities. In one interesting link with Tall al-Hayyât (Falconer et al. 2006), Khirbat Iskandar exhibits some continuity with MBIIA traditions in terms of transitional pottery, the gate structure, and the evidence for a tin-bronze spearhead (Richard 2006).

Further north, to Syria, the parallels drop off, as one encounters the highly sophisticated wheel-made corrugated and painted ware known as the "caliciform" ceramic tradition. Aside from well-known imports in the southern Levant (Dever 1980: fig. 5) indicating close contacts with Syria, the EB IV corpus generally reflects a hybrid quality, combining the local EB III and the widely popular Syrian "caliciform" tradition ("teapots," cups, necked cooking pots, etc.), as noted in the study of the Area C ceramics (Ch. 4). The sources of Syrian influence remain debated in the scholarly literature, as discussed elsewhere.

KHIRBAT ISKANDAR IN THE EB IV PERIOD

The stratified three-phase occupational profile at Khirbat Iskandar, like the evidence for multi-phase occupation at other sites in Transjordan, affirms a significant permanently settled population in the EB IV period. Excavated sites, such as Tall Umm Hammad (Helms 1986), Iktanu and Tall al-Hammad (Prag 1991), Abu en-Niʿaj and Dhahrat Umm al-Marar (Falconer, Fall, and Jones 2007), Tall al-Hayyât (Falconer et al. 2006), Bâb adh-Dhrâʿ (Rast and Schaub 2003), ʿAraʿir (Olávarri 1969), Adir (Cleveland 1960), Khirbat al-Batrawy (Nigro 2006), and Khirbat Hamra Ifdan (Adams 2000), document the settled element in what was, undoubtedly, some variant of a symbiotic relationship with pastoral nomads. What the data from Khirbat Iskandar show, further, is that strong continuities with Early Bronze tradition characterized the EB IV period in Transjordan, including some evidences for social stratification.

Khirbat Iskandar is an excellent example of a site whose three superimposed EB IV settlements correlate well with the paradigm of recovery (Phase 1), reorganization (Phase 2), and growth (Phase 3) following the collapse of urban communities in the EB III period (see Richard and Long 2009). The ceramic assemblage, as it evolves from Phases 1–3, affirms these developmental stages. It is in Phase 2 that the well-built broad-room structure, along with the hybrid local Early Bronze Age and Syrian "caliciform" (for example, turned down rilled-rim platter bowl) tradition, marks the beginning of a period of change, innovation, and reorganization that continues through Phase 3, as epitomized in the "gateway" complex. There was a revitalization of occupation at the site of Khirbat Iskandar in the EB IV period. As mentioned above, it is likely that other sites exhibit a transitional phase prior to reorganization in the period. Although abandoned at the end of the EB IV period, Khirbat Iskandar is an exemplar of the role that the EB IV permanent agricultural communities played in the reemergence of town life in the Middle Bronze Age.

Excavation and survey of the present expedition affirms observations made by Nelson Glueck about the area east of the site. Glueck commented (1939: 128) on the numerous circles-of-stone, menhirs, and rectangular structures (open-air sanctuaries) across the ridge as probably indicating a "tremendous ancient cemetery." Indeed, our excavations have uncovered remains of that cemetery, as well as numerous features visible at the time of Glueck's visit. The remaining features at Khirbat Iskandar in the EB IV period are the vestiges of what originally must have been a visually captivating landscape of not inconsiderable symbolic significance mirroring connections between the living and the dead.

Adding to this landscape is the recent discovery of a "high place" on the summit of Umm al-Idhâm(Richard, Long, and Libby 2005), overlooking the site from the north and completing the virtual 360-degree cultic ring encircling the tell (and the living). Although this apparent ring could merely be utilitarian and/or fortuitous, it is far more likely that it was a purposeful and planned symbolic manipulation of the ecocultural landscape and is reflective of a religious ideology, a sociopolitical ideology, or both. Along with the close connections between tell and tomb noted in the ceramic assemblages, this landscape suggests a symbolism of close ties between the living and the dead (Parker Pearson 1999: 124–41). Such strong ties are particularly obvious in the EB II–III charnel houses at Bâb adh-Dhrâ', houses of the dead that are identical to houses of the living (see Chesson 1999).

As tomb and tell assemblages evoke the close ties between the living and the dead, the 360-degree cultic/mortuary landscape may reflect the watchful eyes of the ancestors over the site and the living. As Parker Pearson notes: "Placing the dead is one of the most visible activities through which human societies map out and express their relationships to ancestors, land and the living (1999: 141)." If our interpretation of the distinctions between Cemeteries D and E has merit, then, at a deeper symbolic level, the megalithic aboveground features in that area may validate an ideology of inequality in the social organization of the site. For a discussion of archaeological correlates to complexity at the site, see Richard (2006; 2009) and Richard and Long (2006; 2009).

The megalithic structures at Khirbat Iskandar are part of a tradition of stone monuments that includes dolmens, menhirs, cairns, circles-of-stone, and rectangular open sanctuaries. These date primarily to the EB I and IV periods, although there are examples from other periods. Scholars have surmised that megalithic structures (especially dolmens) may represent territorial markers of pastoral societies, symbolic landscape markers between agriculturalists and pastoralists, or, at least, a border where the nomads and sedentists came into contact and maybe conflict (Zohar 1989: 27; Prag 1995), or, recently, that they were the burial place of EB II–III populations (Vinitzky 1992). Although the megalithic structures at Khirbat Iskandar could originate earlier in the Early Bronze Age, as future publication will show, excavation has revealed sealed EB IV pottery in one of the megalithic structures, and, as detailed in this volume, usage of the cemetery was in EB IV. From the vantage point of a well-established permanent Early Bronze Age settlement like Khirbat Iskandar, it is difficult to conclude that the megalithic structures represent territorial markers of a pastoral-nomadic society. More likely, they reflect a sacred landscape. Whether the symbolism evoked is an ideology associated with the ancestors and/or the social structure at the site, or whether it reasserts traditional hierarchies of the past, it seems clearly to reflect the close ties between the living and the dead in the EB IV at Khirbat Iskandar (for a development of the evidence, see Richard 2009).

Appendix A

Area C Ceramic Corpus

PL. 1   *Pottery of Square 1, Area C.*

#	LOCUS	REG	PH	FORMHARIBA	M	FORM	DESCRIPTION
1	C01010	C01.10.01	3	4620.00.75.00	38	Platter	5YR8/4 pink; 2.5YR6/6 light red; burnished ext. and int.; black inclusions.
2	C01010	C01.10.02	3	4119C.00.65.00	25	Jar	2.5YR5/6 red; 5YR7/4 pink; gray inclusions.
3	C01015	C01.18.03	3	4770.00.19.00	10	Bowl	5YR6/2 pinkish gray; 5YR7/4 pink; burnished ext. and int.; black inclusions.
4	C01015	C01.18.02	3	4620.00.75.00	38	Platter	10R6/6 light red; 7.5YR7/2 pinkish gray; white inclusions.
5	C01015	C01.18.01	3	4620.00.75.00	38	Platter	5YR7/4 pink; 10R6/6 light red; burnished ext. and int.; black inclusions.
6	C01015	C01.14.03	3	4520.00.91.00	45	Bowl	5YR6/2 pinkish gray; 5YR6/4 light reddish brown; black inclusions.
7	C01016	C01.17.04	2	4660.00.32.00	28	Platter	5YR7/6 reddish yellow; 10R5/6 red; burnished ext. and int.; gray inclusions.
8	C01016	C01.22.01	2	4620.00.73.00	30	Platter	5YR6/2 pinkish gray; 2.5YR6/6 light red; burnished ext. and int.; black inclusions. Local to KI.
9	C01016	C01.17.01	2	4620.00.75.00	31	Platter	7.5YR7/4 pink; 10R6/6 light red; burnished ext. and int.; black inclusions.
10	C01016	C01.17.06	2	4620.00.75.00	34	Platter	7.5YR7/4 pink; 10R6/8 light red; burnished ext. and int.; black inclusions.
11	C01016	C01.22.05	2	4570.00.11.00	20	Bowl	5YR7/4 pink; 2.5YR6/8 light red; burnished ext.; black inclusions.
12	C01016	C01.22.04	2	4050.00.12.00	15	Bowl	5YR7/4 pink; 10R5/6 red; burnished ext. and int.; black inclusions.
13	C01016	C01.22.02	2	4050.00.12.00	18	Bowl	2.5YR6/6 light red; 10R5/6 red; burnished ext.; black inclusions. Local to KI.
14	C01016	C01.17.02	2	4080.00.71.00	37	Bowl	5YR7/4 pink; 7.5YR7/4 pink; black inclusions.
15	C01018	C01.23.03	2	4770.00.11.00	12	Bowl	5YR5/2 reddish gray; 5YR7/3 pink; burnished int.; black inclusions.
16	C01018	C01.23.09	2	4660.00.33.00	23	Platter	5YR7/3 pink; 5YR7/4 pink; black inclusions.
17	C01018	C01.23.04	2	4546.00.11.00	25	Bowl	10R5/8 red; 2.5YR6/6 light red; burnished ext. and int.; black inclusions.
18	C01018	C01.23.02	2	4139C.00.61.00	20	Jar	2.5YR5/6 red; 2.5YR6/6 light red; white inclusions.
19	C01018	C01.23.01	2	4600.00.74.00	43	Platter	2.5YR6/6 light red; 2.5YR6/6 light red; burnished ext. and int.; black inclusions.

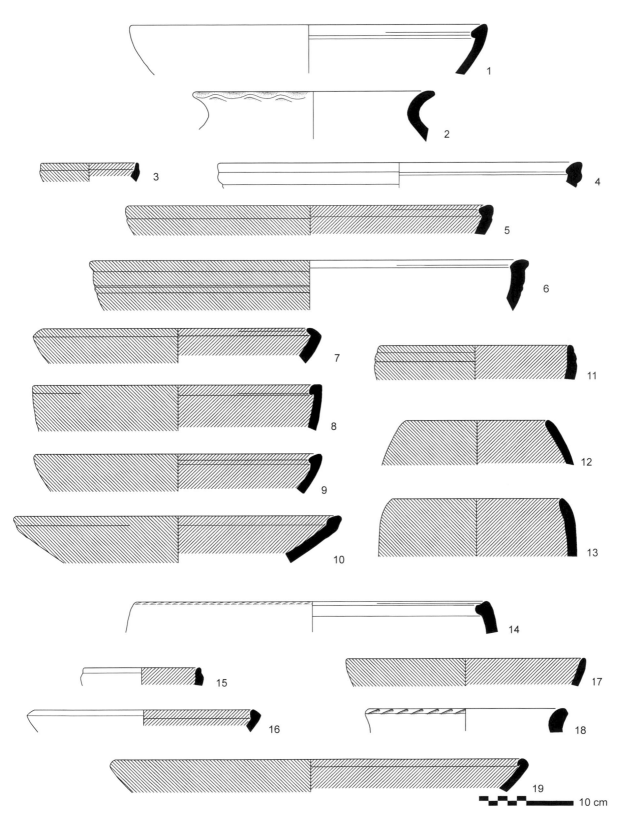

PL. 1 *Pottery of Square 1, Area C.*

PL. 2 *Pottery of Square 1, Area C.*

#	LOCUS	REG	PH	FORMHARIBA	M	FORM	DESCRIPTION
1	C01019	C01.21.08	1	4620.00.73.00	33	Platter	10R 6/6 light red; 10R 6/6 light red; burnished ext. and int.; black inclusions.
2	C01019	C01.20.02	1	4620.00.74.00	33	Platter	5YR7/4 pink; 2.5YR6/6 light red; burnished ext. and int.; black inclusions. Local to KI.
3	C01019	C01.20.01	1	4067.44.41.00	11	Teapot	5YR7/4 pink; 2.5YR6/6 light red; black inclusions.
4	C01021	C01.24.03	1	4660.00.12.00	22	Platter	5YR7/4 pink; 10R5/6 red; burnished int.; black inclusions.
5	C01021	C01.24.01	1	4620.00.75.00	31	Platter	5YR6/3 light reddish brown; 10R6/6 light red; burnished ext. and int.; black inclusions.
6	C01021	C01.24.08–09	1	4139C.00.60.00	21	Jar	2.5YR6/8 light red; 5YR6/4 light reddish brown; black inclusions.
7	C01021	C01.24.07	1	4020C.00.18.00	16	Jar	2.5YR5/4 reddish brown; 2.5YR6/6 light red; crystalline inclusions.
8	C01021	C01.24.04a	1	4020C.00.11.00	18	Jar	5YR6/4 light reddish brown; many sm.–med. limestone, gravel; some calcite inclusions.
9	C01021	C01.24.04	1	4020C.00.11.00	18	Jar	5YR6/1 gray; 5YR6/2 pinkish gray; crystalline inclusions.
10	C01021	C01.30.02	1	4149.00.61.00	14	Jar	5YR7/3 pink; 5YR7/3 pink; black inclusions.
11	C01026	C01.31.01	1	4530.00.71.00	30	Bowl	5YR6/1 gray; 5YR7/3 pink; gray inclusions.
12	C01031	C01.34.01	3	4620.00.75.00	34	Platter	5YR7/3 pink; 10R5/6 red; burnished ext. and int.; black inclusions.
13	C01036	C01.41.20	2	4660.00.73.00	24	Platter	10R5/8 red; 10R6/6 light red; burnished ext. and int.; gray inclusions.
14	C01036	C01.41.02	2	4660.00.11.00	26	Platter	5YR7/3 pink; 2.5YR6/6 light red; burnished ext. and int.; black inclusions.
15	C01036	C01.40.07	2	4660.00.74.00	26	Platter	2.5YR5/6 red; 5YR7/4 pink; black inclusions.
16	C01036	C01.41.06	2	4660.00.73.00	28	Platter	5YR5/2 reddish gray; 5YR5/6 yellowish red; burnished ext. and int.; black inclusions.
17	C01036	C01.40.09	2	4660.00.73.00	28	Platter	5YR6/4 light reddish brown; 10R6/6 light red; burnished ext. and int.; black inclusions.
18	C01036	C01.40.05	2	4620.00.52.00	30	Platter	5YR6/2 pinkish gray; 7.5YR7/2 pinkish gray; black inclusions.
19	C01036	C01.41.05	2	4620.00.74.00	32	Platter	5YR6/4 light reddish brown; 2.5YR6/6 light red; burnished ext. and int.; black inclusions.
20	C01036	C01.41.11	2	4620.00.75.00	32	Platter	5YR6/1 gray; 5YR5/2 reddish gray; burnished ext. and int.; black inclusions.
21	C01036	C01.41.10	2	4620.00.75.00	34	Platter	2.5YR6/2 pale red; 2.5YR6/6 light red; burnished ext. and int.; black inclusions.

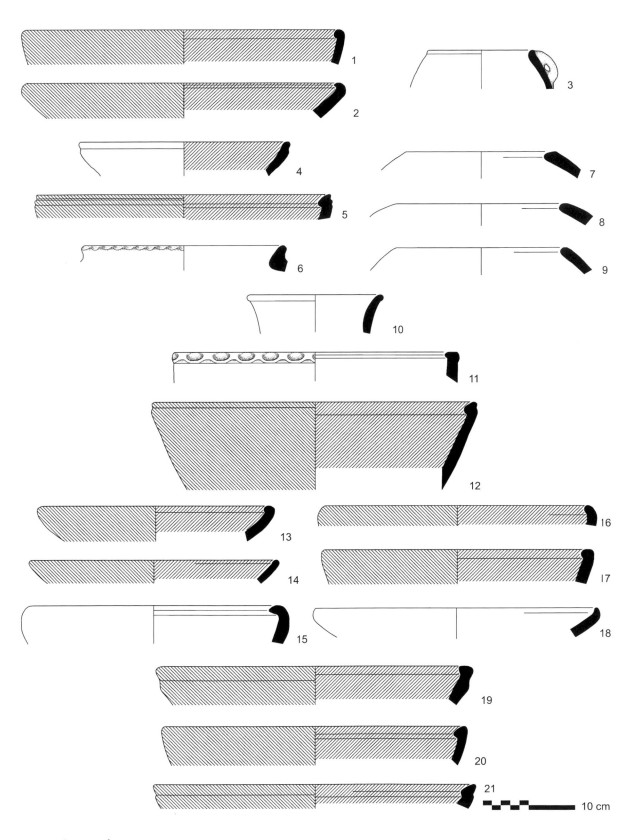

PL. 2   *Pottery of Square 1, Area C.*

PL. 3   *Pottery of Square 1, Area C.*

#	LOCUS	REG	PH	FORMHARIBA	M	FORM	DESCRIPTION
1	C01036	C01.41.07	2	4620.00.74.00	37	Platter	10R6/6 light red; 7.5YR7/4 pink; white inclusions.
2	C01036	C01.41.15	2	4560.00.11.00	22	Bowl	5YR7/6 reddish yellow; 2.5YR6/4 light reddish brown; burnished ext. and int.; black inclusions.
3	C01036	C01.40.06	2	4530.00.11.00	24	Bowl	5YR7/3 pink; 2.5YR6/4 light reddish brown; burnished ext.; black inclusions.
4	C01036	C01.41.13	2	4530.00.71.00	28	Bowl	7.5YR7/4 pink; 2.5YR6/4 light reddish brown; black inclusions.
5	C01036	C01.40.01	2	4264.00.61.00	8	Jar	2.5YR6/6 light red; 5YR7/6 reddish yellow; black inclusions.
6	C01036	C01.40.03	2	4139C.00.61.00	20	Jar	2.5YR4/6 red; 2.5YR6/4 light reddish brown; black inclusions.
7	C01036	C01.41.14	2	4119C.00.60.00	22	Jar	5YR5/6 yellowish red; 5YR7/4 pink; gray inclusions.
8	C01036	C01.41.01	2	4520.00.75.00	40	Bowl	5YR7/3 pink; 2.5YR6/4 light reddish brown; black inclusions.
9	C01036	C01.41.12	2	4520.00.71.00	50	Bowl	5YR6/2 pinkish gray; 10R6/6 light red; black inclusions.
10	C01036	C01.40.02	2	4080.00.71.00	30	Bowl	5YR7/2 pinkish gray; 5YR7/4 pink; black inclusions.
11	C01036	C01.41.03	2	4080.00.70.00	40	Bowl	5YR7/3 pink; 2.5YR6/6 light red; black inclusions.
12	C01036	C01.41.04	2	4080.00.10.00	50	Bowl	2.5YR4/6 red; 7.5YR5/2 brown; gray inclusions.
13	C01036	C01.41.19	2	4020.00.10.00	18	Jar	5YR5/6 yellowish red; 5YR7/3 pink; black inclusions.
14	C01036	C01.41.18	2	4020.00.10.00	20	Jar	2.5YR6/4 light reddish brown; 5YR7/4 pink; crystalline inclusions.
15	C01038	C01.43.01	1	4020C.00.18b.00	16	Jar	2.5YR6/6 light red; 5YR7/6 reddish yellow; crystalline inclusions.

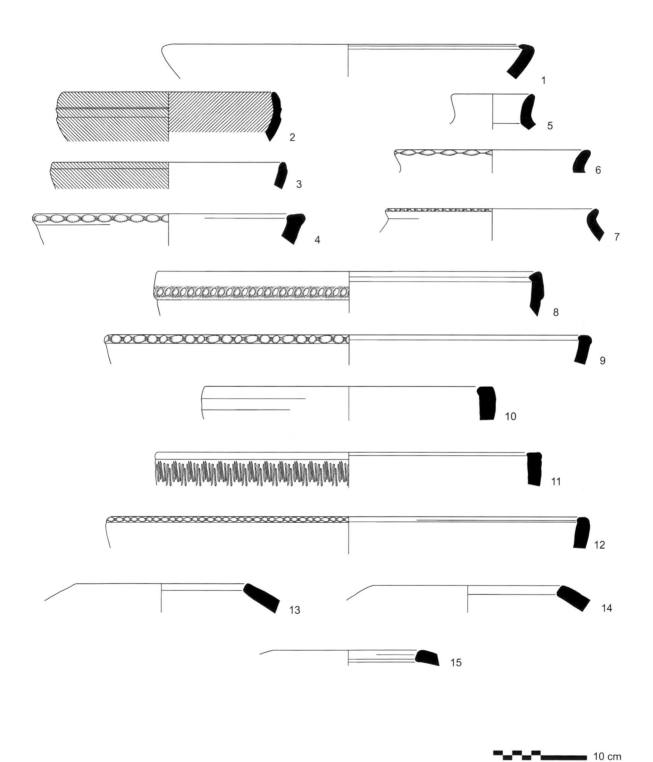

10 cm

PL. 3   *Pottery of Square 1, Area C.*

PL. 4   *Pottery of Square 2, Area C.*

#	Locus	Reg	Ph	FormHaRiBa	M	Form	Description
1	C02008	C02.36.04	3	4660.00.75.00	24	Platter	5YR7/4 pink; 10R6/6 light red; burnished ext. and int.; black inclusions.
2	C02018	C02.23.11	3	4620.00.75.00	33	Platter	5YR6/1 gray; 10R5/6 red; black inclusions.
3	C02018	C02.23.05	3	4060.00.17.00	16	Teapot	7.5R 4/0 dark gray; 2.5YR6/6 light red; white inclusions. Southeastern Jordan Valley.
4	C02018	C02.23.04	3	4040C.00.11.00	40	Bowl	5YR4/2 dark reddish gray; 5YR7/6 reddish yellow; black inclusions.
5	C02018	C02.23.06	3	4020.00.18d.00	16	Jar	
6	C02018	C02.23.01	3	4010C.00.17.00	21	Jar	5YR4/1 dark gray; 5YR6/4 light reddish brown; crystalline inclusions.
7	C02022	C02.25.02	3	4730.00.42.00	18	Bowl	5YR6/4 light reddish brown; 5YR6/6 reddish yellow; white inclusions.
8	C02022	C02.28.01	3	4620.00.75.00	32	Platter	7.5YR7/4 pink; 7.5YR7/4 pink; white inclusions.
9	C02022	C02.28.03	3	4600.00.75.00	43	Platter	2.5YR6/4 light reddish brown; 10R6/6 light red; burnished ext. and int.; black inclusions.
10	C02022	C02.25.01	3	4510.00.13.00	28	Bowl	5YR7/3 pink; 2.5YR6/6 light red; burnished ext. and int.; black inclusions.
11	C02022	C02.25.05	3	4114.00.63.00	22	Jar	7.5YR5/2 brown; 5YR6/3 light reddish brown; gray inclusions.
12	C02023	C02.27.05	3	4221.00.11.00	12	Jar	5YR6/4 light reddish brown; 5YR7/6 reddish yellow; black inclusions.
13	C02023	C02.27.02	3	4060.00.18d.00	22	Teapot	5YR7/4 pink; 5YR7/3 pink; burnished ext.; gray inclusions.
14	C02025	C02.33.03	3	4660.00.13.00	22	Platter	5YR7/4 pink; 5YR7/4 pink; black inclusions. Local to KI.
15	C02025	C02.32.01	3	4620.00.75.00	34	Platter	5YR7/3 pink; 10R5/6 red; burnished ext. and int.; gray inclusions.
16	C02025	C02.31.01	3	4620.00.73.00	35	Platter	2.5YR6/6 light red; 5YR7/3 pink; gray inclusions.
17	C02025	C02.33.02	3	4620.00.75.00	35	Platter	5YR7/4 pink; 2.5YR6/8 light red; burnished ext. and int.; black inclusions.
18	C02025	C02.32.03	3	4620.00.76.00	36	Platter	2.5YR5/2 weak red; 5YR5/1 gray; gray inclusions.
19	C02025	C02.32.02	3	4120.00.62.00	16	Jar	5YR6/6 reddish yellow; 5YR6/4 light reddish brown; gray inclusions.
20	C02025	C02.32.04	3	4067.00.10.00	13	Teapot	5YR7/6 reddish yellow; 2.5YR6/4 light reddish brown; burnished ext.; black inclusions.

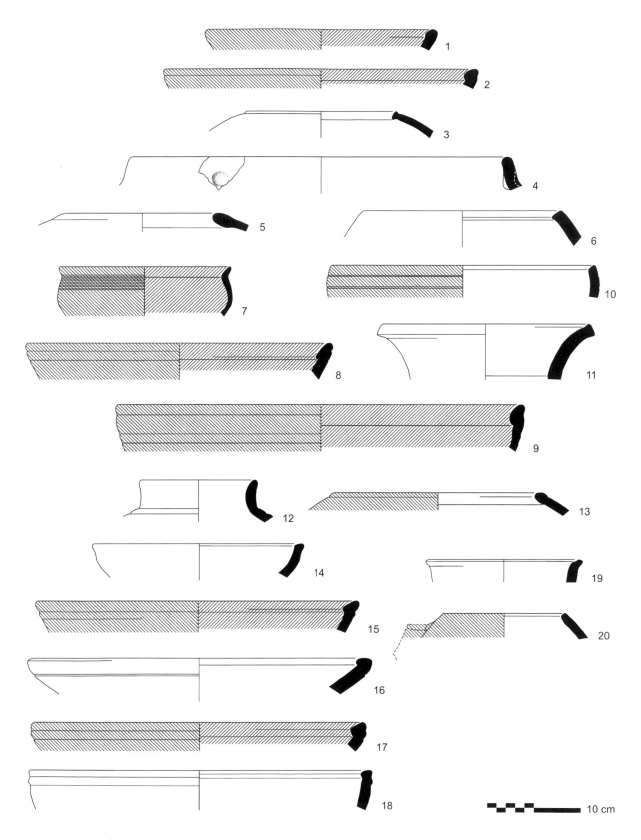

PL. 6　　*Pottery of Square 2, Area C.*

#	Locus	Reg	Ph	FormHaRiBa	M	Form	Description
1	C02030	C02.46.21	2	4020.00.11.00	14	Jar	5YR7/4 pink; 5YR7/4 pink; gray inclusions. Undetermined.
2	C02030	C02.46.16	2	4020.00.17.00	20	Jar	5YR7/3 pink; 7.5YR8/2 pinkish white; gray inclusions. Local to KI.
3	C02030	C02.43.25	2	4010.00.17.00	15	Jar	2.5YR6/4 light reddish brown; 2.5YR6/6 light red; black inclusions.
4	C02030	C02.46.08	2	4080.00.91.00	54	Bowl	5YR5/1 gray; 5YR7/3 pink; black inclusions. Local to KI.
5	C02033	C02.49.05	3	4620.00.75.00	34	Platter	5YR7/4 pink; 10R6/6 light red; burnished ext. and int.; black inclusions.
6	C02033	C02.49.03	3	4422.00.61.00	8	Jug	2.5YR6/6 light red; 2.5YR6/6 light red; white inclusions.
7	C02033	C02.49.06	3	4122.00.61.00	16	Jar	2.5YR6/4 light reddish brown; 10YR8/3 very pale brown; black inclusions.
8	C02033	C02.49.04	3	4060.00.10.00	18	Teapot	5YR7/3 pink; 2.5YR6/6 light red; burnished ext. and int.; black inclusions.
9	C02033	C02.48.05	3	4060.00.41.00	22	Teapot	2.5YR5/6 red; 2.5YR6/6 light red; gray inclusions.
10	C02034	C02.51.04	3	4660.00.91.00	28	Platter	5YR6/2 pinkish gray; 2.5YR5/6 red; burnished ext. and int.; black inclusions.
11	C02034	C02.51.02	3	4620.00.75.00	30	Platter	7.5YR7/4 pink; 10R6/8 light red; burnished ext. and int.; gray inclusions.
12	C02034	C02.51.03	3	4620.00.75.00	34	Platter	5YR7/3 pink; 10R6/6 light red; burnished ext. and int.; white inclusions.
13	C02034	C02.50.01	3	4620.00.75.00	34	Platter	5YR5/1 gray; 10R6/6 light red; black inclusions.
14	C02034	C02.51.07	3	4422.00.11.00	6	Jug	5YR5/2 reddish gray; 5YR4/1 dark gray; black inclusions.
15	C02034	C02.51.05	3	4020C.00.17.00	14	Jar	2.5YR6/6 light red; 10R5/6 red; gray inclusions.
16	C02037	C02.63.03	2	4660.00.10.00	28	Platter	5YR7/4 pink; 10R6/6 light red; burnished ext. and int.; white inclusions.
17	C02037	C02.76.04	2	4620.00.73.00	34	Platter	7.5YR8/4 pink; 10R5/6 red; burnished ext. and int.; gray inclusions.
18	C02037	C02.76.02	2	4620.00.73.00	34	Platter	7.5YR7/4 pink; 2.5YR6/6 light red; burnished ext. and int.; black inclusions.
19	C02037	C02.65.05	2	4620.00.75.00	36	Platter	5YR7/3 pink; 10R5/6 red; burnished ext. and int.; black inclusions.
20	C02037	C02.65.01	2	4520.00.70.00	42	Bowl	2.5YR5/4 reddish brown; 5YR7/4 pink; gray inclusions.

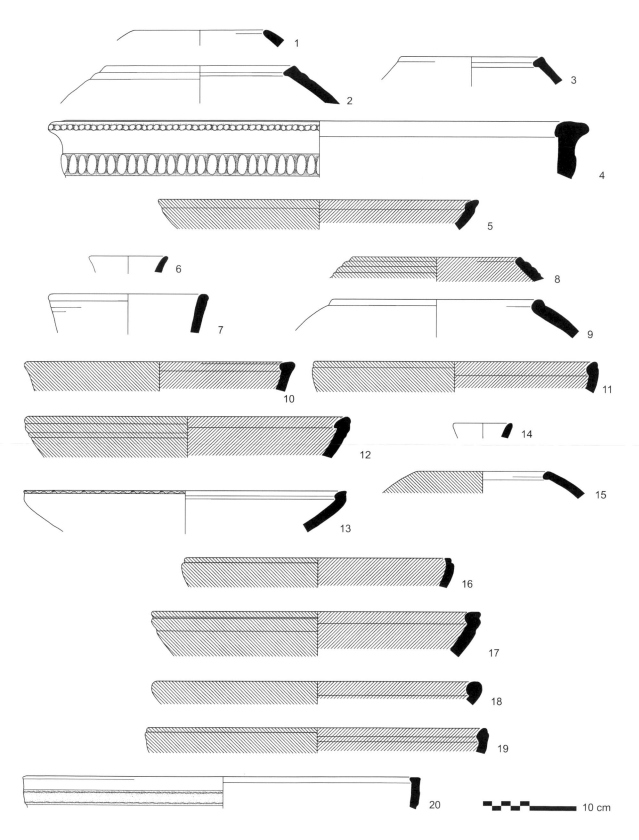

PL. 8   *Pottery of Square 3, Area C.*

#	LOCUS	REG	PH	FORMHARIBA	M	FORM	DESCRIPTION
1	C03015	C03.60.16	3	4620.00.75.00	32	Platter	7.5YR5/2 brown; 10R5/8 red; burnished ext. and int.; black inclusions. Local to KI.
2	C03016	C03.63.01	3	4620.00.75.00	36	Platter	10R6/4 pale red; 10R6/6 light red; burnished ext. and int.; gray inclusions.
3	C03016	C03.63.05	3	4620.00.73.00	36	Platter	7.5YR7/4 pink; 10R 5/6 red; burnished ext. and int.; gray inclusions.
4	C03016	C03.62.01	3	4120.00.62.00	20	Jar	5YR7/3 pink; 5YR7/3 pink; black inclusions.
5	C03016	C03.61.10	3	4050C.00.11.00	18	Bowl	10R 5/1 reddish gray; 5YR7/4 pink; black inclusions.
6	C03016	C03.61.07	3	4000.00.10.00	28	Jar	Undetermined.
7	C03017	C03.44.03	3	4620.00.76.00	38	Platter	5YR7/3 pink; 2.5YR6/6 light red; black inclusions.
8	C03017	C03.44.01	3	4620.00.75.00	38	Platter	2.5YR6/6 light red; 10YR6/6 brownish yellow; burnished ext. and int.; gray inclusions. Local to KI.
9	C03017	C03.44.02	3	4530.00.10.00	22	Bowl	7.5YR6/0 gray; 10R 6/6 light red; burnished ext. and int.; black inclusions. Local to KI.
10	C03021	C03.49.01	3	4660.00.75.00	24	Platter	5YR7/4 pink; 10YR6/6 brownish yellow; burnished ext. and int.; black inclusions.

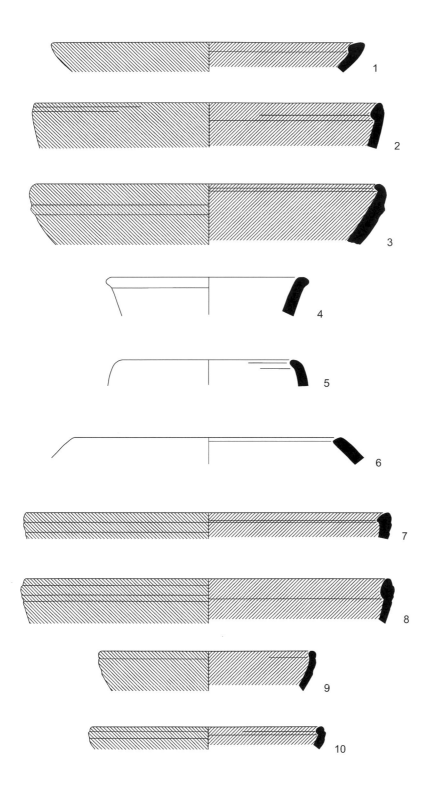

10 cm

PL. 10   *Pottery of Square 5, Area C.*

#	Locus	Reg	Ph	FormHaRiBa	M	Form	Description
1	C05010	C05.17.02	3	4660.00.91.00	28	Platter	5YR7/4 pink; 2.5YR6/6 light red; black inclusions.
2	C05010	C05.16.03	3	4620.00.73.00	30	Platter	7.5YR7/4 pink; 10R6/6 light red; burnished ext. and int.; black inclusions.
3	C05010	C05.17.08	3	4620.00.75.00	32	Platter	2.5YR6/6 light red; 5YR7/4 pink; white inclusions.
4	C05010	C05.17.03a	3	4620.00.75.00	32	Platter	5YR7/3 pink; 7.5YR7/4 pink; burnished ext. and int.; gray inclusions.
5	C05010	C05.16.04	3	4600.00.75.00	44	Platter	5YR6/4 light reddish brown; 7.5YR5/6 strong brown; burnished ext. and int.; black inclusions.
6	C05010	C05.17.07	3	4080.00.10.00	30	Bowl	7.5YR6/2 pinkish gray; 7.5YR6/2 pinkish gray; black inclusions.
7	C05010	C05.17.03	3	4224.00.63.00	12	Jar	2.5YR6/6 light red; 2.5YR6/6 light red; black inclusions.
8	C05010	C05.16.01	3	4224.00.61.00	12	Jar	10R5/6 red; 2.5YR6/6 light red; gray inclusions.
9	C05010	C05.17.05	3	4067.00.13.00	12	Teapot	7.5YR7/4 pink; 2.5YR6/6 light red; burnished ext. and int.; black inclusions.
10	C05010	C05.16.05	3	4067.00.41.00	12	Teapot	10 YR4/3 dark brown; many small limestone (also calcite) inclusions.
11	C05010	C05.16.06	3	4060.00.42.00	16	Teapot	
12	C05010	C05.16.09	3	4020C.00.10.00	16	Jar	2.5YR5/6 red; 5YR5/2 reddish gray; crystalline inclusions.
13	C05010	C05.16.03a	3	4020C.00.11.00	16	Jar	10YR8/3 very pale brown; 10R6/6 light red; many sm. gravel inclusions.
14	C05010	C05.16.02	3	4020C.00.17.00	17	Jar	2.5YR5/2 weak red; 7.5YR6/4 light brown; crystalline inclusions.
15	C05010	C05.17.01	3	4020C.00.11.00	18	Jar	2.5YR4/4 reddish brown; 5YR6/4 light reddish brown; crystalline inclusions.
16	C05011	C05.72.01	3	4080.00.91.00	30	Bowl	5YR7/4 pink; 5YR7/4 pink; black inclusions.
17	C05014	C05.18.03	2	4620.00.73.00	30	Platter	10R5/8 red; 10R6/6 light red; burnished ext. and int.; gray inclusions.
18	C05014	C05.19.03	2	4620.00.73.00	34	Platter	5YR7/6 reddish yellow; 5YR7/4 pink; black inclusions.
19	C05014	C05.21.06	2	4620.00.75.00	36	Platter	5YR6/1 gray; 10R6/6 light red; burnished ext. and int.; gray inclusions.
20	C05014	C05.21.02	2	4620.00.75.00	38	Platter	2.5YR4/0 dark gray; 2.5YR6/6 light red; burnished ext.; gray inclusions.

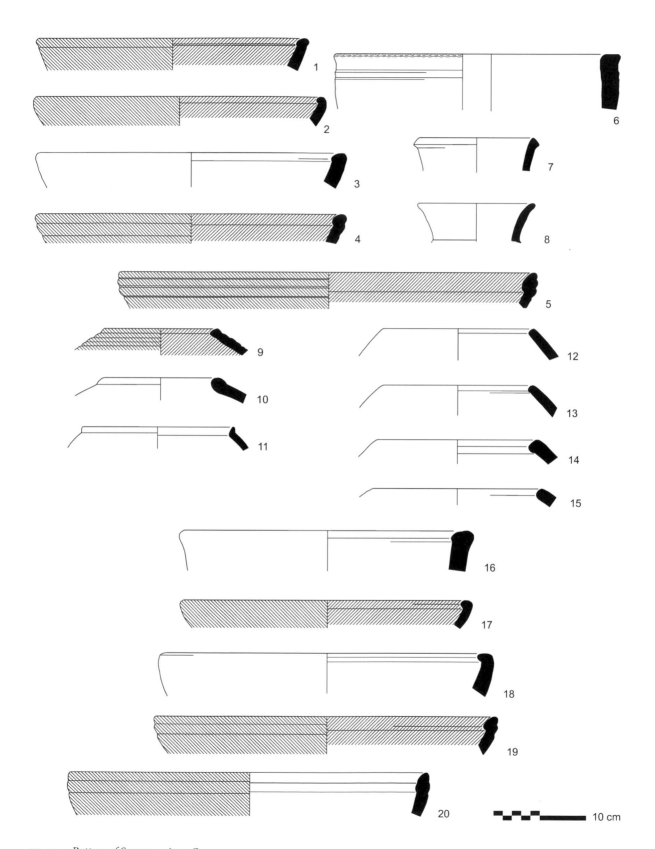

PL. 10 *Pottery of Square 5, Area C.*

PL. 11   *Pottery of Square 5, Area C.*

#	Locus	Reg	Ph	FormHaRiBa	M	Form	Description
1	C05014	C05.18.02	2	4620.00.75.00	38	Platter	7.5YR6/4 light brown; 2.5YR6/6 light red; burnished ext. and int.; black inclusions.
2	C05014	C05.21.01	2	4600.00.75.00	42	Platter	2.5YR6/6 light red; 10R5/8 red; burnished ext. and int.; gray inclusions.
3	C05014	C05.18.01	2	4600.00.75.00	44	Platter	7.5YR5/2 brown; 5YR7/4 pink; black inclusions.
4	C05014	C05.19.04	2	4520.00.71.00	40	Bowl	7.5YR4/0 dark gray; 2.5YR4/4 reddish brown; gray inclusions.
5	C05014	C05.21.07	2	4510.00.10.00	20	Bowl	2.5YR6/6 light red; 2.5YR6/6 light red; gray inclusions.
6	C05014	C05.21.08	2	4422.00.61.00	6	Jug	7.5YR7/4 pink; 5YR7/6 reddish yellow; black inclusions.
7	C05014	C05.19.07	2	4422.00.60.00	8	Jug	5YR4/2 dark reddish gray; 2.5YR5/6 red; gray inclusions.
8	C05014	C05.21.03	2	4261.00.12.00	8	Jar	10R6/4 pale red; 5YR7/3 pink; white inclusions.
9	C05014	C05.19.06	2	4221.00.11.00	12	Jar	5YR6/2 pinkish gray; 5YR7/4 pink; white inclusions.
10	C05014	C05.20.01	2	4139C.00.62.00	16	Jar	5YR5/4 reddish brown; 5YR7/3 pink; black inclusions.
11	C05014	C05.21.04	2	4119C.00.60.00	22	Jar	5YR5/3 reddish brown; 5YR7/4 pink; gray inclusions.
12	C05014	C05.18.04	2	4080.00.73.00	50	Bowl	
13	C05014	C05.19.05	2	4067.00.41.00	10	Teapot	2.5YR6/6 light red; 2.5YR6/6 light red; burnished ext.; gray inclusions.
14	C05014	C05.21.05	2	4067.00.42.00	12	Teapot	5YR7/3 pink; 5YR8/3 pink; black inclusions.
15	C05014	C05.19.01	2	4060.00.10.00	22	Teapot	5YR7/3 pink; 5YR8/4 pink; black inclusions.
16	C05014	C05.18.02a	2	4040.00.71.00	32	Bowl	5YR4/1 dark gray; 7.5YR7/2 pinkish gray; black inclusions.

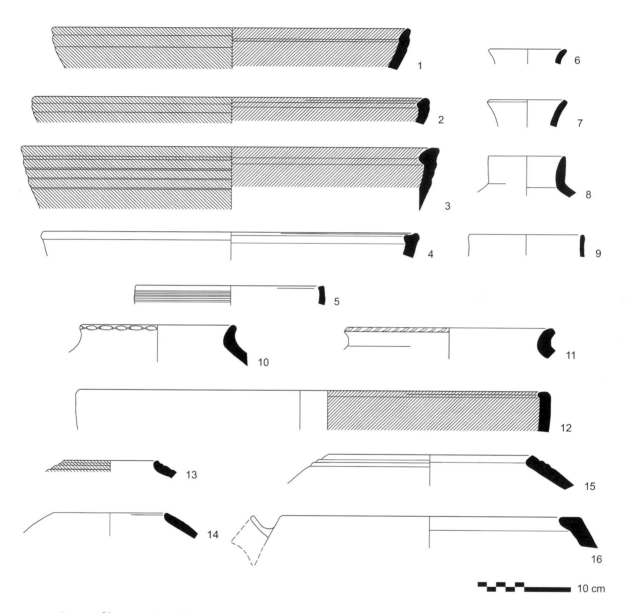

PL. 11 *Pottery of Square 5, Area C.*

PL. 12 *Pottery of Square 6, Area C.*

#	Locus	Reg	Ph	FormHaRiBa	M	Form	Description
1	C06012	C06.31.02	2	4700.00.11.00	16	Bowl	5YR7/4 pink; 5YR7/3 pink; burnished ext.; black inclusions.
2	C06016	C06.32.05	2	4710.00.11.00	14	Bowl	2.5YR6/6 light red; 10R5/6 red; burnished ext. and int.; black inclusions.
3	C06016	C06.28.01	2	4124.00.62.00	18	Jar	5YR7/3 pink; 5YR7/3 pink; white inclusions. Local to KI.
4	C06016	C06.43.01	2	4080.00.10.00	34	Bowl	2.5YR6/6 light red; 10R6/6 light red; gray incl.
5	C06016	C06.32.02	2	4072.00.11.00	6	Teapot	5YR7/4 pink; 10R6/6 light red; burnished int.; black inclusions.
6	C06016	C06.32.01	2	4020C.00.18d.00	15	Jar	5YR4/1 dark gray; 5YR6/4 light reddish brown; crystalline inclusions.
7	C06016	C06.32.04	2	4020.00.10.00	20	Jar	5YR6/1 gray; 5YR7/3 pink; gray inclusions.
8	C06018	C06.50.04	2	4740.00.11.00	12	Bowl	7.5YR6/2 pinkish gray; 10R6/6 light red; burnished ext. and int.; white inclusions.
9	C06018	C06.50.05	2	4620.00.51.00	34	Platter	2.5YR6/4 light reddish brown; 10R5/6 red; burnished ext. and int.; gray inclusions.
10	C06018	C06.40.04	2	4020C.00.17.00	14	Jar	2.5YR5/4 reddish brown; 5YR6/2 pinkish gray; crystalline inclusions.
11	C06018	C06.40.09	2	4020C.00.10.00	14	Jar	2.5YR6/4 light reddish brown; 5YR6/3 light reddish brown; crystalline inclusions.
12	C06019	C06.51.14	2	4700.00.11.00	16	Bowl	5YR7/4 pink; 5YR7/4 pink; burnished int.; gray incl.
13	C06019	C06.46.01	2	4660.00.74.00	24	Platter	5YR8/3 pink; 5YR7/4 pink; burnished ext. and int.; gray inclusions.
14	C06019	C06.51.10	2	4660.00.75.00	28	Platter	5YR7/4 pink; 10R6/6 light red; burnished ext. and int.; black inclusions.
15	C06019	C06.51.11	2	4620.00.70.00	36	Platter	5YR7/3 pink; 2.5YR5/6 red; burnished ext. and int.; black inclusions.
16	C06019	C06.51.05	2	4620.00.75.00	38	Platter	5YR7/4 pink; 10YR5/6 yellowish brown; burnished ext. and int.; black inclusions.
17	C06019	C06.46.03	2	4520.00.71.00	40	Bowl	5YR7/4 pink; 10R6/6 light red; black inclusions.
18	C06019	C06.51.02	2	4224.00.63.00	12	Jar	2.5YR6/4 light reddish brown; 10YR7/3 very pale gray; black inclusions.
19	C06019	C06.35.05	2	4139C.00.61.00	18	Jar	2.5YR5/4 reddish brown; 2.5YR6/4 light reddish brown; gray inclusions.
20	C06019	C06.51.07	2	4067.00.42.00	12	Teapot	burnished ext. and int.
21	C06019	C06.37.08	2	4060.00.11.00	17	Teapot	2.5YR6/6 light red; 2.5YR6/6 light red; burnished ext.; gray inclusions.
22	C06019	C06.51.09	2	4020C.00.18d.00	14	Jar	5YR3/1 very dark gray; 2.5YR4/2 weak red; crystalline inclusions. Undetermined.
23	C06019	C06.37.15	2	4020.00.12.00	16	Jar	

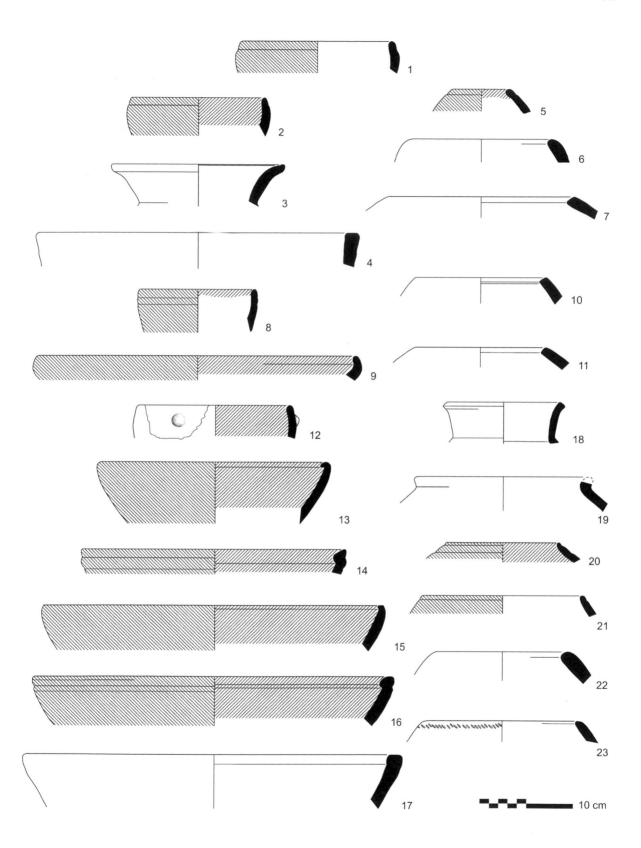

PL. 13   *Pottery of Square 6, Area C.*

#	LOCUS	REG	PH	FORMHARIBA	M	FORM	DESCRIPTION
1	C06021	C06.36.18	3	4660.00.75.00	28	Platter	2.5YR6/4 light reddish brown; 10R5/6 red; burnished ext. and int.; gray inclusions.
2	C06021	C06.36.11	3	4620.00.75.00	30	Platter	5YR7/3 pink; 2.5YR6/6 light red; burnished ext. and int.; black inclusions.
3	C06021	C06.36.13	3	4020C.00.17.00	20	Jar	
4	C06029	C06.55.07	1	4756.00.11.00	6	Bowl	5YR7/4 pink; 2.5YR5/6 red; burnished ext.; gray incl.
5	C06029	C06.56.09	1	4756.00.11.00	10	Bowl	7.5YR7/2 pinkish gray; 7.5YR7/2 pinkish gray; burnished ext. and int.; black inclusions. Southeastern Jordan Valley(?)
6	C06029	C06.52.07/15	1	4570.00.11.00	18	Bowl	7.5YR7/4 pink; 10R6/6 light red; burnished ext.; gray inclusions.
7	C06029	C06.52.14	1	4067.00.42.00	14	Teapot	2.5YR6/4 light reddish brown; 5YR4/1 dark gray; burnished ext. and int.; gray inclusions.
8	C06029	C06.56.04	1	4260.00.11.00	8	Jar	5YR7/3 pink; 5YR7/3 pink; gray inclusions.
9	C06029	C06.55.01,2,3	1	4020C.00.11.00	14	Jar	2.5YR6/4 light reddish brown; 5YR7/3 pink; gray incl.
10	C06029	C06.52.02/04	1	4020C.00.11.00	17	Jar	2.5YR5/6 red; 5YR5/2 reddish gray; crystalline incl.
11	C06029	C06.56.05	1	4020C.00.18d.00	18	Jar	2.5YR5/6 red; 5YR5/2 reddish gray; gray inclusions.
12	C06029	C06.56.06	1	4020C.00.18d.00	18	Jar	2.5YR5/6 red; 5YR5/2 reddish gray; crystalline incl.
13	C06029	C06.52.12	1	4020C.00.10.00	20	Jar	5YR5/3 reddish brown; 5YR7/4 pink; gray incl.
14	C06029	C06.55.08	1	4010C.00.18d.00	24	Jar	2.5YR4/6 red; 5YR4/1 dark gray; crystalline incl.
15	C06029	C06.52.08	1	4520.00.10.00	42	Bowl	2.5YR4/6 red; 5YR7/4 pink; black inclusions.
16	C06030	C06.57.26	1	4660.00.73.00	22	Platter	5YR7/3 pink; 10R6/6 light red; burnished ext. and int.; black inclusions.
17	C06030	C06.57.19	1	4660.00.70.00	22	Platter	10YR5/1 gray; 2.5YR5/4 reddish brown; burnished ext. and int.; black inclusions.
18	C06030	C06.57.13	1	4660.00.73.00	24	Platter	5YR6/2 pinkish gray; 2.5YR5/4 reddish brown; burnished ext. and int.; black inclusions.
19	C06030	C06.57.10	1	4660.00.75.00	24	Platter	5YR7/3 pink; 5YR6/6 reddish yellow; burnished ext. and int.; sm. wadi gravel inclusions.
20	C06030	C06.53.19	1	4660.00.74.00	25	Platter	5YR7/4 pink; 5YR7/3 pink; burnished ext.; white incl.
21	C06030	C06.57.25	1	4660.00.70.00	26	Platter	5YR7/3 pink; 10R5/6 red; burnished ext. and int.; black inclusions.
22	C06030	C06.57.30	1	4660.00.70.00	26	Platter	burnished ext. and int.
23	C06030	C06.57.25a	1	4660.00.73.00	28	Platter	burnished ext. and int.
24	C06030	C06.57.11	1	4660.00.74.00	28	Platter	10R5/6 red; 10R6/6 light red; burnished ext. and int.; gray inclusions.
25	C06030	C06.57.24	1	4620.00.73.00	34	Platter	5YR7/4 pink; 2.5YR6/4 light reddish brown; burnished ext. and int.; black inclusions.
26	C06030	C06.57.02	1	4620.00.75.00	38	Platter	burnished int.
27	C06030	C06.53.01	1	4570.00.11.00	18	Bowl	burnished ext.
28	C06030	C06.57.23	1	4530.00.11.00	24	Bowl	7.5YR7/2 pinkish gray; 10R5/6 red; burnished ext. and int.; black inclusions.

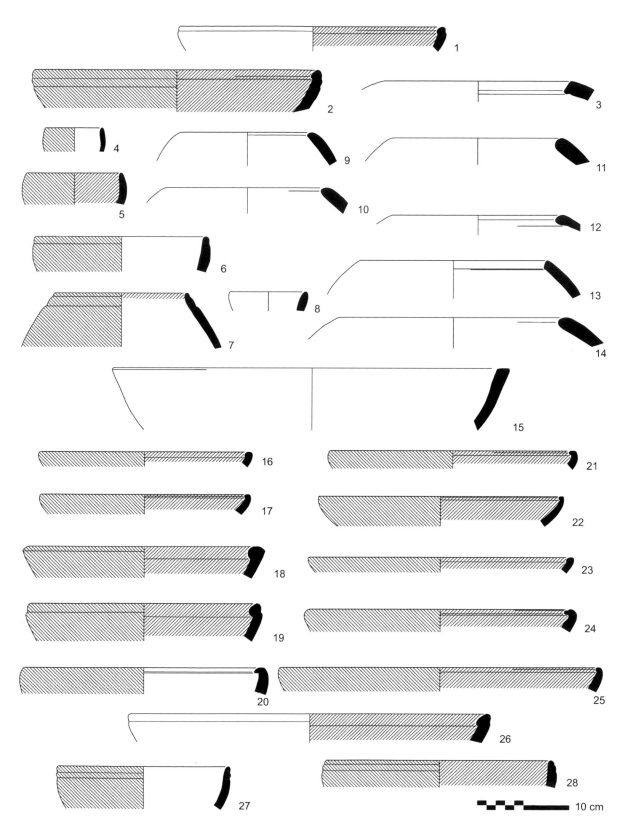

PL. 14   *Pottery of Square 6, Area C.*

#	Locus	Reg	Ph	FormHaRiBa	M	Form	Description
1	C06030	C06.57.29	1	4224.00.62.00	10	Jar	5YR7/3 pink; 5YR7/3 pink; black inclusions.
2	C06030	C06.57.01	1	4149.00.61.00	14	Jar	5YR6/4 light reddish brown; 5YR7/3 pink; gray inclusions.
3	C06030	C06.57.39	1	4139C.00.60.00	16	Jar	5YR3/1 very dark gray; 5YR5/2 reddish gray; gray inclusions.
4	C06030	C06.57.20	1	4020C.00.17.00	16	Jar	5YR7/3 pink; 7.5YR7/2 pinkish gray; crystalline inclusions.
5	C06030	C06.57.03	1	4080.00.91.00	50	Bowl	5YR7/3 pink; 7.5YR7/4 pink; gray inclusions.
6	C06030	C06.57.36	1	3110.00.65.00	22	Jar	5YR7/4 pink; 2.5YR6/6 light red; gray inclusions
7	C06030	C06.57.04	1	3110.00.64.00	24	Jar	5YR7/6 reddish yellow; 10R6/6 light red; gray incl.
8	C06031	C06.54.07	2	4660.17a.73.00	24	Platter	2.5YR6/4 light reddish brown; 2.5YR6/6 light red; burnished ext. and int.; black inclusions.
9	C06031	C06.54.02	2	4660.00.91.00	28	Platter	5YR7/3 pink; 2.5YR5/6 red; burnished ext. and int.; black inclusions.
10	C06031	C06.54.08	2	4221.00.11.00	10	Jar	7.5YR7/4 pink; 5YR7/3 pink; black inclusions.
11	C06031	C06.54.10	2	4140.00.60.00	14	Jar	10YR5/1 gray; 10YR5/1 gray; gray inclusions.
12	C06031	C06.54.09	2	4020C.00.17.00	14	Jar	7.5YR7/4 pink; 5YR5/1 gray; crystalline inclusions.
13	C06032	C06.58.06	1	4620.00.73.00	30	Platter	5YR7/3 pink; 10R6/6 light red; burnished ext. and int.; black inclusions.
14	C06032	C06.58.03	1	4510.00.13.00	28	Bowl	2.5YR5/4 reddish brown; 10R5/6 red; burnished ext.; black inclusions.
15	C06032	C06.65.01	1	4010C.00.18d.00	22	Jar	2.5YR4/6 red; 2.5YR5/2 weak red; crystalline incl.
16	C06032	C06.58.05	1	4050.00.12.00	12	Bowl	5YR7/3 pink; 5YR7/4 pink; burnished ext. and int.; black inclusions.
17	C06033	C06.59.03	1	4620.00.91.00	37	Platter	5YR7/4 pink; 2.5YR6/6 light red; burnished ext. and int.; white inclusions.
18	C06033	C06.59.04	1	4030.00.17.00	10	Jar	2.5YR5/6 red; 2.5YR6/6 light red; gray inclusions. Southern Negev/Jordan.
19	C06033	C06.59.06	1	4020C.00.10.00	14	Jar	5YR7/3 pink; 5YR7/4 pink; black inclusions.
20	C06033	C06.59.05	1	4020C.00.11.00	16	Jar	2.5YR5/6 red; 2.5YR6/6 light red; white inclusions.
21	C06033	C06.59.02	1	4020C.00.18d.00	16	Jar	5YR6/3 light reddish brown; 5YR7/3 pink; gray inclusions. Southern Negev/Jordan.
22	C06033	C06.59.07	1	4020C.00.18d.00	18	Jar	2.5YR5/6 red; 5YR5/2 reddish gray; gray inclusions.
23	C06035	C06.62.02	1	4620.00.73.00	36	Platter	5YR7/4 pink; 5YR7/4 pink; black inclusions. Local to KI.
24	C06035	C06.62.05	1	4281.00.61.00	8	Jar	5YR7/6 reddish yellow; 5YR6/3 light reddish brown; gray inclusions. Local to KI.
25	C06038	C06.63.02	1	4660.00.71.00	26	Platter	burnished ext. and int.
26	C06038	C06.63.03	1	4020C.00.12.00	14	Jar	

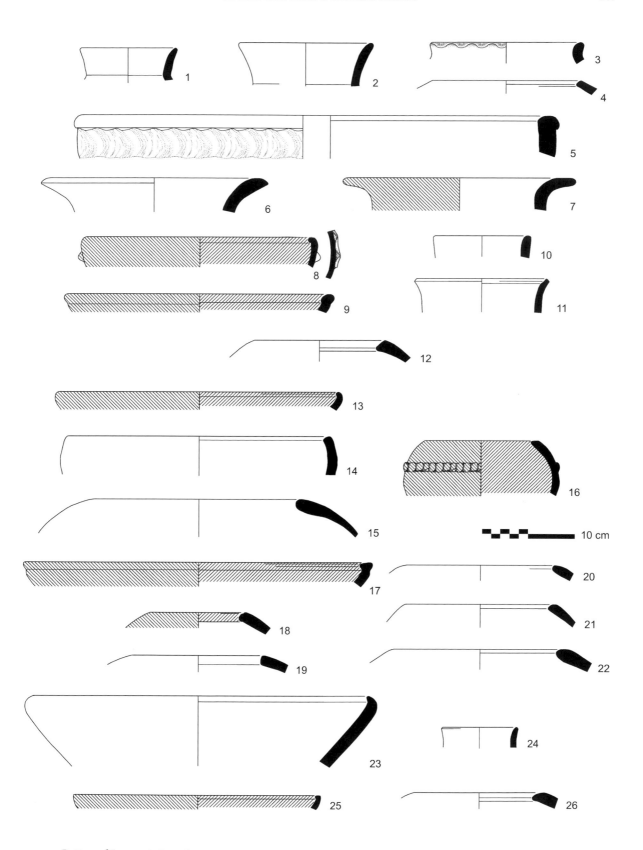

PL. 14 *Pottery of Square 6, Area C.*

PL. 15   *Pottery of Square 7, Area C.*

#	LOCUS	REG	PH	FORMHARIBA	M	FORM	DESCRIPTION
1	C07015	C07.20.21	3	4760.00.62.00	10	Bowl	7.5YR7/4 pink; 2.5YR6/6 light red; burnished ext. and int.; gray inclusions. Local to KI.
2	C07015	C07.20.13	3	4760.00.62.00	10	Bowl	5YR7/4 pink; 5YR8/3 pink; black inclusions.
3	C07015	C07.21.24	3	4730.00.42.00	14	Bowl	7.5YR7/2 pinkish gray; 5YR7/4 pink; burnished ext. and int.; black inclusions. Local to KI.
4	C07015	C07.21.52	3	4710.00.10.00	16	Bowl	5YR7/4 pink; 2.5YR6/6 light red; burnished ext.; black inclusions.
5	C07015	C07.21.57	3	4660.00.13.00	22	Platter	7.5YR7/4 pink; 5YR7/6 reddish yellow; burnished ext. and int.; gray inclusions.
6	C07015	C07.20.15	3	4660.00.75.00	28	Platter	5YR7/4 pink; 10R6/6 light red; burnished ext. and int.; black inclusions.
7	C07015	C07.21.56	3	4660.00.13.00	28	Platter	2.5YR6/4 light reddish brown; 10R5/6 red; burnished ext. and int.; black inclusions.
8	C07015	C07.20.08	3	4620.00.75.00	30	Platter	5YR7/4 pink; 5YR7/6 reddish yellow; burnished ext. and int.; black inclusions.
9	C07015	C07.21.17	3	4620.00.75.00	30	Platter	5YR6/3 light reddish brown; 7.5YR8/2 pinkish white; white inclusions.
10	C07015	C07.25.03	3	4620.00.75.00	30	Platter	5YR7/3 pink; 10R6/6 light red; burnished ext. and int.; black inclusions.
11	C07015	C07.25.08	3	4620.00.75.00	30	Platter	5YR5/1 gray; 7.5YR7/2 pinkish gray; burnished ext.; black inclusions.
12	C07015	C07.25.12	3	4620.00.75.00	30	Platter	5YR6/3 light reddish brown; 10R5/6 red; burnished ext. and int.; black inclusions.
13	C07015	C07.26.07	3	4620.00.73.00	30	Platter	5YR7/4 pink; 10R6/6 light red; burnished ext. and int.; black inclusions.
14	C07015	C07.20.04	3	4620.00.76.00	32	Platter	10R6/6 light red; 5YR7/3 pink; white inclusions.
15	C07015	C07.20.11	3	4620.00.75.00	32	Platter	5YR7/4 pink; 10R6/6 light red; burnished ext. and int.; gray inclusions.
16	C07015	C07.21.37	3	4620.00.76.00	32	Platter	5YR5/2 reddish gray; 2.5YR6/4 light reddish brown; burnished ext. and int.; gray inclusions.
17	C07015	C07.25.07	3	4400.22.61.00	10	Jug	2.5YR3/0 very dark gray; 5Y 2.5/1 black; white inclusions. Southeastern Jordan Valley.
18	C07015	C07.20.03	3	4264.00.61.00	8	Jar	5YR6/3 light reddish brown; 10YR7/3 very pale gray; white inclusions. Local to KI.
19	C07015	C07.25.04	3	4224.00.61.00	10	Jar	5YR5/1 gray; 10YR7/1 light gray; black inclusions.
20	C07015	C07.25.09	3	4224.00.61.00	12	Jar	2.5YR6/2 pale red; 7.5YR7/2 pinkish gray; white inclusions.
21	C07015	C07.20.02	3	4221.00.62.00	12	Jar	5YR6/2 pinkish gray; 5YR7/4 pink; burnished ext.; black inclusions.
22	C07015	C07.20.05	3	4140.00.62.00	14	Jar	10YR6/1 gray; 2.5YR6/6 light red; white incl.
23	C07015	C07.21.117	3	4730.00.62.00	16	Bowl	2.5YR6/6 light red; 5YR7/4 pink; black inclusions.
24	C07015	C07.19.45	3	4129C.00.41.00	20	Jar	2.5YR4/4 reddish brown; 2.5YR6/6 light red; gray inclusions. Local to KI.
25	C07015	C07.19.09/08/27	3	4114.00.63.00	22	Jar	10R6/6 light red; 7.5YR8/4 pink; gray inclusions. Local to KI.

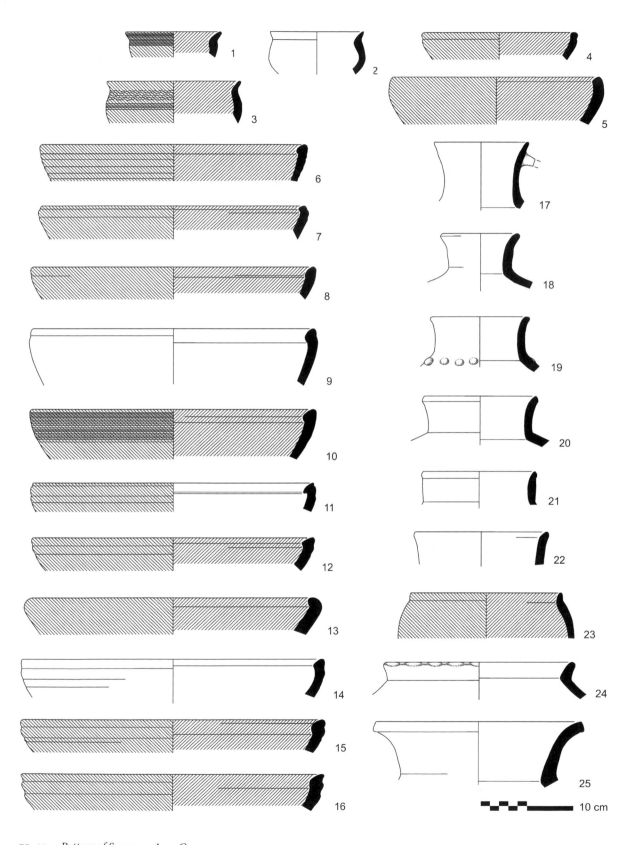

PL. 15   *Pottery of Square 7, Area C.*

PL. 16   *Pottery of Square 7, Area C.*

#	Locus	Reg	Ph	FormHaRiBa	M	Form	Description
1	C07015	C07.29.01	3	4620.00.76.00	32	Platter	2.5YR5/6 red; 2.5YR6/6 light red; burnished ext. and int.; black inclusions.
2	C07015	C07.25.06	3	4620.00.76.00	36	Platter	5YR6/1 gray; 2.5YR6/4 light reddish brown; burnished ext. and int.; gray inclusions.
3	C07015	C07.26.03	3	4620.00.75.00	36	Platter	2.5YR5/6 red; 2.5YR6/6 light red; burnished ext. and int.; black inclusions.
4	C07015	C07.19.04	3	4620.00.76.00	38	Platter	5YR7/2 pinkish gray; 2.5YR6/6 light red; burnished ext. and int.; black inclusions.
5	C07015	C07.20.01	3	4620.00.75.00	38	Platter	2.5YR5/4 reddish brown; 2.5YR6/6 light red; burnished ext. and int.; black inclusions.
6	C07015	C07.25.11	3	4620.00.75.00	38	Platter	5YR5/1 gray; 2.5YR6/4 light reddish brown; burnished ext. and int.; black inclusions.
7	C07015	C07.29.06	3	4620.00.75.00	38	Platter	5YR6/4 light reddish brown; 5YR7/4 pink; burnished ext. and int.; black inclusions.
8	C07015	C07.29.09	3	4620.00.75.00	38	Platter	5YR7/4 pink; 2.5YR6/4 light reddish brown; burnished ext. and int.; white inclusions.
9	C07015	C07.19.34	3	4600.00.75.00	40	Platter	7.5YR7/4 pink; 2.5YR6/6 light red; burnished ext. and int.; black inclusions.
10	C07015	C07.20.06	3	4600.00.75.00	40	Platter	5YR6/4 light reddish brown; 5YR6/6 reddish yellow; burnished ext. and int.; black inclusions.
11	C07015	C07.29.03	3	4600.00.75.00	40	Platter	5YR6/4 light reddish brown; 2.5YR6/6 light red; burnished ext. and int.; black inclusions.
12	C07015	C07.20.09	3	4600.00.75.00	42	Platter	5YR6/4 light reddish brown; 2.5YR6/6 light red; burnished ext. and int.; black inclusions.
13	C07015	C07.21.27	3	4600.00.75.00	42	Platter	5YR7/4 pink; 10R6/6 light red; burnished ext. and int.; black inclusions.

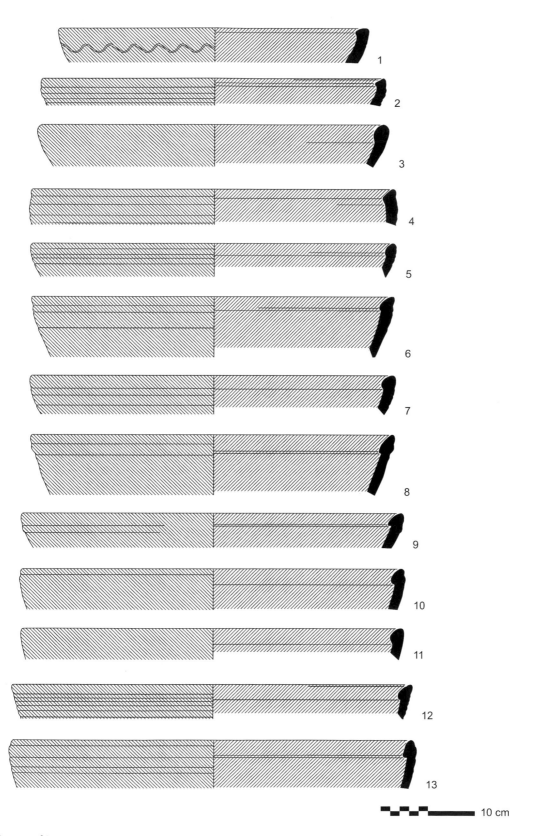

PL. 16 *Pottery of Square 7, Area C.*

PL. 17   *Pottery of Square 7, Area C.*

#	LOCUS	REG	PH	FORMHARIBA	M	FORM	DESCRIPTION
1	C07015	C07.19.23	3	4570.00.19.00	17	Bowl	2.5YR6/4 light reddish brown; 5YR7/4 pink; burnished ext. and int.; black inclusions.
2	C07015	C07.26.01	3	4570.00.10.00	20	Bowl	7.5YR6/2 pinkish gray; 7.5YR6/2 pinkish gray; burnished ext. and int.; black inclusions.
3	C07015	C07.29.04	3	4570.00.11.00	20	Bowl	5YR6/1 gray; 10R6/8 light red; burnished ext. and int.; black inclusions.
4	C07015	C07.26.02	3	4560.00.11.00	20	Bowl	5YR7/4 pink; 10R6/6 light red; burnished ext. and int.; gray inclusions.
5	C07015	C07.21.42	3	4500.00.76.00	32	Bowl	10R6/1 reddish gray; 2.5YR6/4 light reddish brown; burnished ext. and int.; white inclusions.
6	C07015	C07.20.16	3	4500.00.76.00	34	Bowl	2.5YR6/6 light red; 5YR7/4 pink; burnished int.; black inclusions.
7	C07015	C07.21.26	3	4500.00.76.00	36	Bowl	10R6/1 reddish gray; 5YR7/4 pink; burnished ext. and int.; black inclusions.
8	C07015	C07.19.74	3	4500.00.76.00	36	Bowl	2.5YR5/6 red; 2.5YR6/6 light red; burnished ext. and int.; gray inclusions.
9	C07015	C07.21.46	3	4520.00.71.00	44	Bowl	5YR6/4 light reddish brown; 10R6/6 light red; white inclusions.
10	C07015	C07.19.50	3	4080.00.10.00	50	Bowl	5YR6/3 light reddish brown; 5YR7/4 pink; black inclusions. Local to KI.
11	C07015	C07.19.65	3	4080.00.73.00	50	Bowl	7.5YR7/4 pink; 5YR7/4 pink; burnished ext.; gray inclusions.
12	C07015	C07.20.12	3	4080.00.73.00	50	Bowl	7.5YR7/4 pink; 5YR7/4 pink; black inclusions.
13	C07015	C07.19.31	3	4067.00.13.00	12	Teapot	7.5YR7/4 pink; 10R6/6 light red; burnished ext. and int.; black inclusions. Local to KI.
14	C07015	C07.25.02	3	4060.00.65.00	22	Teapot	5YR6/3 light reddish brown; 5YR7/4 pink; black inclusions.
15	C07015	C07.21.86	3	4010C.00.10.00	24	Jar	light grey core; 7.5YR7/4 pink sm.–med. limestone; wadi gravel sm. inclusions.
16	C07015	C07.21.129	3	4040C.00.12.00	40	Bowl	10R6/6 light red; 10R6/6 light red; black inclusions. Southeastern Jordan Valley.
17	C07015	C07.25.01	3	4855.00.12.13	15	Lamp	

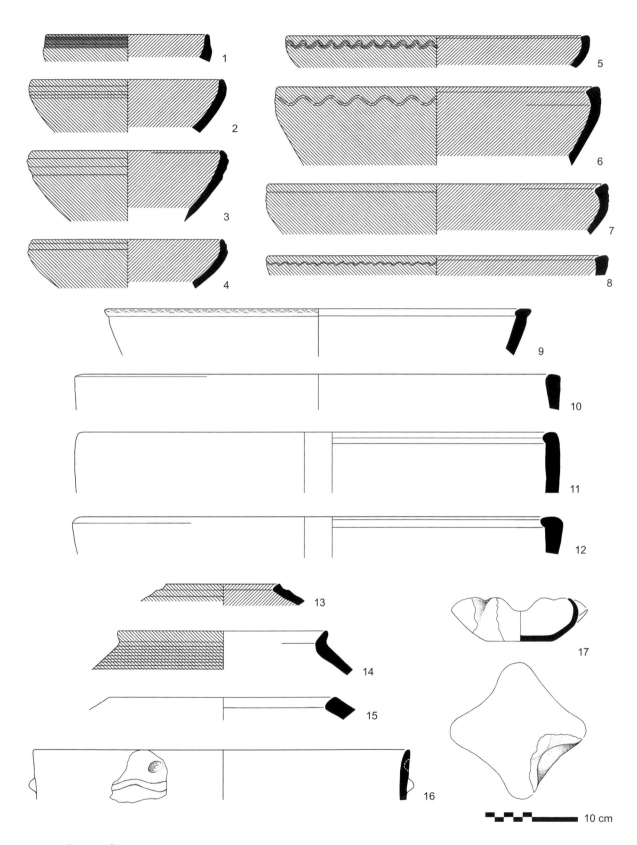

PL. 18   *Pottery of Square 7, Area C.*

#	LOCUS	REG	PH	FORMHARIBA	M	FORM	DESCRIPTION
1	C07017	C07.18.06	3	4175C.00.41.00	14	Jar	2.5YR4/4 reddish brown; 2.5YR6/6 light red; gray inclusions.
2	C07017	C07.18.01	3	4139C.00.61.00	16	Jar	2.5YR4/2 weak red; 5YR6/4 light reddish brown; black inclusions.
3	C07020	C07.31.07	3	4660.00.75.00	28	Platter	5YR7/4 pink; 10R6/6 light red; burnished ext. and int.; black inclusions.
4	C07020	C07.31.15	3	4600.00.71.00	42	Platter	2.5YR5/4 reddish brown; 5YR7/4 pink; gray inclusions.
5	C07020	C07.31.06	3	4060.00.41.00	17	Teapot	5YR7/3 pink; 2.5YR6/6 light red; burnished ext.; black inclusions.
6	C07020	C07.31.19	3	4232.00.61.00	10	Jar	7.5YR8/4 pink; 2.5YR7/2 ; black inclusions.

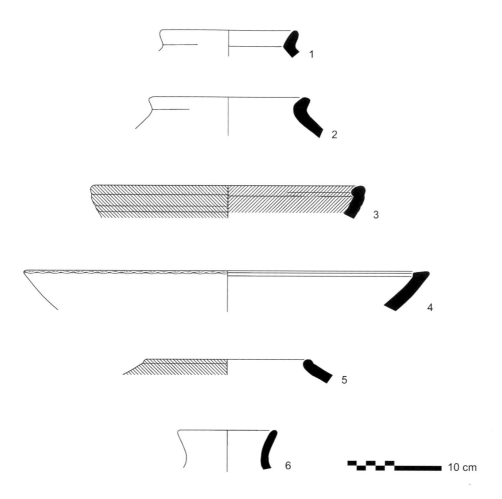

PL. 18 *Pottery of Square 7, Area C.*

PL. 20   *Pottery of Square 9, Area C.*

#	Locus	Reg	Ph	FormHaRiBa	M	Form	Description
1	C09001	C09.09.28	2	4760.00.62.00	10	Bowl	5YR7/4 pink; 5YR7/4 pink; burnished ext. and int.; black inclusions. Local to KI.
2	C09001	C09.09.37/38	2	4600.00.75.00	50	Platter	5YR7/4 pink; 2.5YR6/6 light red; burnished ext. and int.; black inclusions.
3	C09001	C09.09.92	2	4124.00.63.00	16	Jar	2.5YR6/4 light reddish brown; 2.5YR6/6 light red; black inclusions.
4	C09001	C09.09.50	2	4124.00.60.00	20	Jar	5YR5/1 gray; 5YR7/4 pink; gray inclusions.
5	C09001	C09.09.24/133/5	2	4124.00.81.00	20	Jar	5YR7/6 reddish yellow; 5YR7/6 reddish yellow; gray inclusions.
6	C09001	C09.09.107	2	4122.00.11.00	16	Jar	5YR6/2 pinkish gray; 5YR7/4 pink; black inclusions.
7	C09001	C09.09.08	2	4119.00.10.00	24	Jar	
8	C09001	C09.07.01	2	4067.00.65.00	14	Teapot	5YR7/1 light gray; 2.5YR6/8 light red; burnished ext. and int.; black inclusions.
9	C09001	C09.09.86/88/137	2	4060.00.61.00	18	Teapot	5YR7/4 pink; 5YR6/3 light reddish brown; burnished ext. and int.; white inclusions.
10	C09007	C09.08.08	3	4620.00.76.00	32	Platter	5YR7/4 pink; 5YR7/4 pink; burnished int.; black inclusions. Local to KI.
11	C09007	C09.08.02	3	4620.00.75.00	32	Platter	2.5YR5/6 red; 2.5YR6/4 light reddish brown; gray inclusions.
12	C09007	C09.08.11	3	4620.00.73.00	36	Platter	2.5YR6/6 light red; 10R6/6 light red; burnished ext. and int.; gray inclusions.
13	C09007	C09.08.18	3	4067.00.42.00	14	Teapot	5YR7/3 pink; 5YR5/3 reddish brown; burnished ext. and int.; black inclusions.

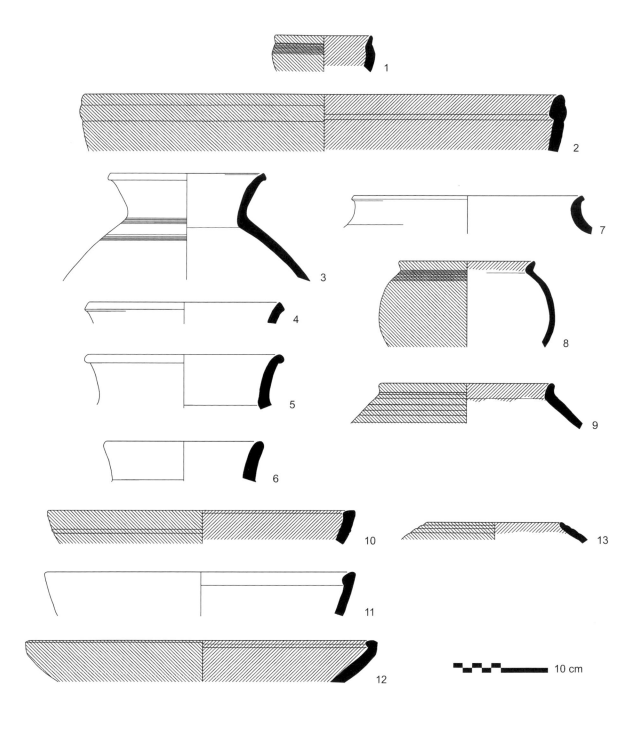

PL. 20   *Pottery of Square 9, Area C.*

PL. 22   *Area C appendages.*

#	Locus	Reg	Ph	Code	Description
1	C03024	C03.52.03	2	14	wavy ledge handle
2	C03024	C03.52.16	2	16a	envelope ledge handle with spaced flaps
3	C05014	C05.18.01a	2	40a	lug and ear handle, functional lug
4	C05014	C05.20.02	2	17a	vestigial ledge handle, envelope/pinch-lapped profile
5	C06012	C06.36.04	2	40b	lug and ear handle, pierced ear
6	C06019	C06.37.01	2	16a	envelope ledge handle with spaced flaps
7	C06028	C06.52.05	3	17a	vestigial ledge handle, envelope/pinch-lapped profile
8	C06028	C06.52.13	3	17a	vestigial ledge handle, envelope/pinch-lapped profile
9	C06029	C06.56.02	1	20b	loop-round handle
10	C06030	C06.53.16	1	16c	envelope ledge handle with folded/overlapping flaps
11	C06031	C06.54.05	2	40b	lug and ear handle, pierced ear
12	C07015	C07.16.04	3	20a	loop-strap handle
13	C07015	C07.16.03	3	40b	lug and ear handle, pierced ear
14	C07015	C07.19.13	3	16a	envelope ledge handle with spaced flaps
15	C07015	C07.21.115	3	100b	spout - long
16	C07015	C07.25.10	3	16a	envelope ledge handle with spaced flaps
17	C08008	C08.12.18	3	100a	spout - short
18	C08009	C08.15.01	3	16b	envelope ledge handle with spaced flaps (clear pinching)
19	C08011	C08.19.01	3	40a	lug and ear handle, functional lug

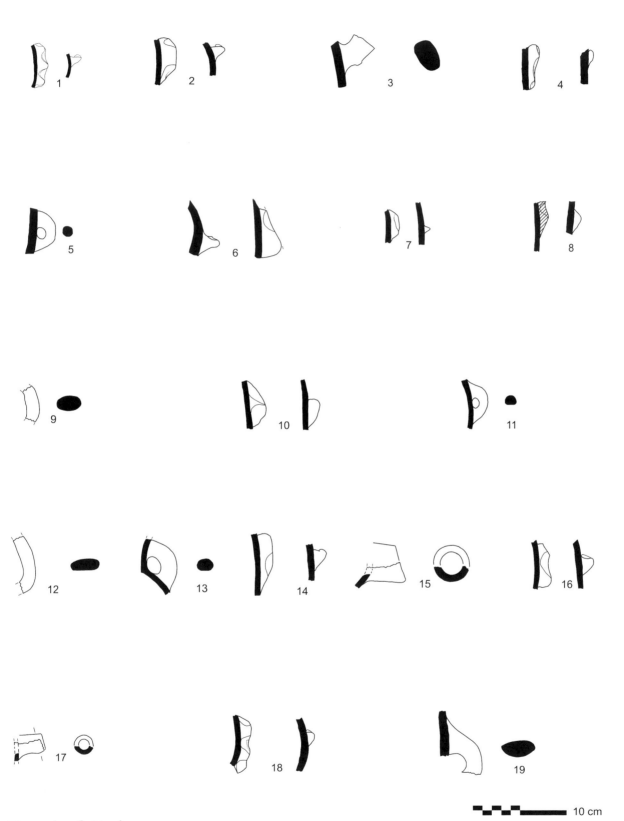

PL. 22 *Area C appendages.*

10 cm

LOCUS	BUCKETS	PH	ROOM	DESCRIPTION	REG. OBJECT(S)
C01013	12	Srfc.		Collapsed into Locus 1000.	
C01014	13	4		Collapsed into Locus 1001.	
C01015	14, 18	3	131	Ashy layer of buildup E of Wall 1004 and S of Wall 5013 overlying founding surface 1018a; probably represents use of Room 131 subsequent to construction.	#045, flint Canaanean sickle blade (1)
C01016	17, 22	2	522	Compact beaten-earth surface underlying Phase 3 Surface 1010; dimensions: 1.50 × 3.00 m; contemporary with Phase 2 Surfaces 2037 and 1034.	
C01017	16, 25	3A		Surface just N of Threshold 1033 that equals Surface 5011 to the N.	
C01018	23	2	522	Beaten-earth surface in NE sector of square, apparently cut by the construction of Phase 3 Wall 1004; dimensions: 1.00 × 1.00 m; contemporary with Surface with 1016.	
C01019	20–21	1	111	Earthen surface underlying and sealed by Phase 2 Surface 1016, probably a Phase 1 surface; dimensions: 1.10 × 1.00 m.	
C01020		2	522	Loose soil layer in NE sector of square underlying Surface 1018; dimensions: 1.00 × 1.00 m; contemporary with Phase 2 Surface 1016.	
C01021	24, 30	1	111	Surface in NE sector of square underlying Soil Layer 1020; dimensions: 1.00 × 1.00 m; probably a Phase 1 surface contemporary with Surface 1019.	
C01022		3A		Cobbled threshold in association with Stairway 1033 at S end of Entryway 231; contemporary with Surface 5011.	
C01023	26, 29	2B		Layer of fill deposited on Surface 2037; dimensions: 0.80 × 0.80 m exposed; appears to be contemporary with Fill Layers 3025, 3027, 3028, 3032 and 8005.	
C01024	28	2	522	Surface underlying Fill 1023; dimensions: 0.80 × 0.80 m; contemporary with Phase 2 Surface 2037.	
C01025		1		Collapsed into Locus 1035.	
C01026	31	1		Collapsed into Locus 1035.	
C01027		3A		N/S wall that with Wall 2024 forms the E boundary of Room 131, abutted by Wall 1004; two rows (ca. 0.80 m), five courses preserved; constructed in Phase 2 and reused in Phase 3.	
C01028		2		Soil layer to the N of Phase 1 Wall 1035; appears to be fill.	
C01029	32a, 32–33, 35–36	Misc.		Balk removal.	#290–291, #319 flint flakes debitage (31); #327, flint worked flakes (6)
C01030		3A		Surface in S sector of square that equals Surface 5011.	
C01031	34	3	131	Collapsed into Locus 1015.	#299, flint flakes debitage (10)

LOCUS	BUCKETS	PH	ROOM	DESCRIPTION	REG. OBJECT(S)
C01032	37	Misc.		Balk removal.	#358, flint flakes debitage (2)
C01033		3A		Stairway at S end of Phase 3 Entryway (Room 231) beyond S boundary of the building, consisting of two rows of stones, at different levels; stairway stones on the E have been removed; contemporary with Threshold 1022 and Surface 5011.	
C01034	38	Misc.		Balk removal.	
C01035		1		N/S wall that corners with Wall 2045 to form what remains from Phase 1 Room 111, two rows (ca. 0.50 m), two courses preserved.	
C01036	40–41	2	131	Soil layer in the SE corner of square, underlying Phase 3 Build-Up Layer 1015; dimensions: 1.50 × 1.50 m; contemporary with Surface 2037.	#460, limestone unfinished hammerstone/pounder
C01037	42	2		Soil layer below SE corner of Room 131; underlying Phase 2 Soil Layer 1036 S of Wall 2045; dimensions: 1.50 × 0.75 m.	
C01038	43	1	131	Soil layer in the SE corner of Room 111, adjacent to Wall 2045 on the S, underlying Soil Layer 1037; dimensions: 1.00 × 0.25 m; probably represents Phase 1 deposition.	
C02000	1	Misc.		Ground surface covering square.	#021, flint retouched flake (11); #022, flint flake (1)
C02001		Misc.		Collapsed into Locus 2000.	
C02002	2–3, 6, 24	4		Post-occupational wall collapse and debris layer underlying ground surface.	#017, flint frags. (3); #034, ceramic frag. spindle whorl; #064, flint retouched blade (1); #065, flint retouched flake (1); #066, flint worked flake (1)
C02003	7–8	Misc.		Ground surface covering square.	
C02004	4–5, 9, 11	4		Post-occupational wall collapse and debris layer underlying ground surface.	#043, flint triangular blade; #044, flint frag. (1)
C02005		3A		Central pylon forming part of the W boundary of Room 232; Block 2026 was added to the north later, to form a solid wall; dimensions: ca. 1.20 × 1.40 m.	
C02006		3A		E/W wall forming the N boundary of Room 231; two rows (ca. 1.00 m), two courses preserved; associated with Surfaces 2018 and 2029a.	
C02007	10, 12	4		Collapsed into Locus 2002.	#047, #048, flint worked frags. (2)
C02008	36	3A		Collapsed into Surface 5011.	
C02009		3A		E/W wall extension of Wall C05013 in Phase 3; two rows (ca. 0.50), three courses preserved; associated with Surface 2018.	
C02010		3B		N/S bench lining the W face of Pylon 2005 and Block 2026 in Room 231; dimensions: 4.00 × 0.30–0.45 m; associated with Entryway Surface 5011.	
C02011	13, 67, 73	4		Collapsed into Locus 2002.	#332, #457, flint flakes debitage (47)

LOCUS	BUCKETS	PH	ROOM	DESCRIPTION	REG. OBJECT(S)
C02012		3A	232	Collapsed into Locus 2038.	
C02013	14	4		Collapsed into Locus 2002.	
C02014	15–16	Misc.		Collapsed into Locus 2000.	
C02015		3B		Appears to be late N/S squatter wall or block to the entrance to Room 131; two rows (0.70–0.80 m), one course preserved; associated with Surface 2016.	
C02016		3B	131	Collapsed into Locus 2018.	
C02017	18	Misc.		Collapsed into Locus 2000.	#076, flint hammerstone/pounder; #077, hammerstone/pounder
C02018	19, 23	3B	231	Plaster surface E of Pylon 2005 in Room 231 & 131; with granules of charcoal and olive sized bits of flint; dimensions: ca. 4.2 × 2.75 m exposed; second phase of E "guardroom."	#083, flint frag. hammerstone/pounder
C02019	20	Misc.		Collapsed into Locus 2000.	
C02020	22	Misc.		Collapsed into Locus 2000.	#075, stone pierced stone
C02021		3A		Collapsed into Wall 2006.	
C02022	25, 28	3		Make-up layer for Surface 2018; dimensions: ca. 4.20–2.75 m. exposed.	
C02023	26–27	3		Collapsed into Locus 2022.	
C02024		3A		N-S wall in E balk; abuts Wall 8002 to the N and Wall 1027 to the S; abutted by Wall 2006; two rows (ca. 0.80 m), at least seven courses preserved; constructed in Phase 2 and reused in Phase 3.	
C02025	31–33	3	231	Rock layer and debris in Room 231; below latest use Surface 2018 and above first use Surface 2029a; destruction layer of first phase (3A) of "guardroom."	
C02026		3B		Block in opening created by Wall 2006 and Pylon 2005 in the W boundary of Room 231; associated with Surface 2018.	
C02027	34	3		Collapsed into Locus 2025.	
C02028		3A		Collapsed into Locus 2038.	
C02029	37a	3A		Destruction debris layer above the first phase of Room 231; dimensions: ca. 2.75 × 2.75 m. exposed.	
C02029a	37–39, 41	3A	231	Plaster surface that was the first-use floor of Room 231; dimensions: ca. 2.75 × 2.75 m. exposed.	#139, lithic frag (1)
C02030	40, 42–46	2B	221	Debris layer for last phase of Room 221; with ash pits, patches of burnt mudbrick, and numerous sherds; in NE corner, a heavy rock accumulation (ping pong/tennis ball size) and much burnt mudbrick; dimensions: ca. 2.75 × 2.75 m. exposed.	#148, limestone spindle whorl
C02031		2B	221	Collapsed into Locus 2030.	

Locus	Buckets	Ph	Room	Description	Reg. Object(s)
C02032	47	2B	221	Latest use surface of Room 221; strewn with pottery; with patches of mudbrick; probe dimensions: 1.00 × 1.00 m.; equals Surface 2040.	
C02033	48–49	3A		E/W strip/soil layer along S sector of square; S of Wall 2009; appears to be below Surface 2018; dimensions: 0.50 × 5.00 exposed; included bone frags, pottery, and mudbrick.	#155, flint frags. blade (2)
C02034	50–51	3A		E/W strip/soil layer along S sector of square; S of Wall 2009; underlying Soil Layer 2033; dimensions: 0.50 × 5.00 exposed; included bone frags, pottery, and mudbrick.	
C02035	57–60	Misc.		Balk removal.	#284, flint frag. blade (1); #289, limestone spindle whorl
C02036	62, 64	Misc.		Balk removal.	#368, #394, flint flakes debitage (15)
C02037	63, 65–66, 76	2A		Compacted Surface in SW corner of square; underlying Fill 1023; surface on which Wall 5013 was constructed; dimensions: ca. 1.00 × 4.00 m exposed; equals Surface 1024.	#393, flint flakes debitage (14); #458, flint flake (1)
C02038	68–69, 71, 74	3A	232	Makeup for Entryway Surface 5011; N of Wall 5013 in Room 231; appears to be mixed with Phase 2 destruction debris; dimensions: ca. 1.00 × 4.00 m exposed.	#414, #433, #435, flint flakes debitage (36); #416, flint flake (1)
C02039		2A		N/S stone wall below Phase 3 "gateway;" E boundary of Room 521; with overlying Stone Facing & Mudbrick Layer 2041; both wall and stone facing with mudbrick underlie Makeup 2038; two rows (ca. 0.50 m); one course exposed; constructed in Phase 2A, reused in Phase 2B.	
C02040	70	2B	221	Unexcavated surface underlying Makeup 2038; appears to be latest use surface in Room 521; dimensions: 0.25 × 1.0 m exposed; associated with exposed course of Wall 2039; contemporary with Surface 2032.	
C02041		2B		Stone facing and mudbrick atop wall C02039; dimensions: 0.20 × 2.00 m exposed; represents reuse of Wall 2039 in Phase 2B.	
C02042		2B		Collapsed into Locus 2041.	
C02043	75, 82	3A	232	Compact layer W of Wall 2039 and above Surface 2040; with clumps of plaster, some mudbrick, and charred timber; appears to be mixed with Phase 2 destruction debris; dimensions: 1.00 × 2.00 m exposed; equals Phase 3 Makeup 2038 for Surface 5011.	
C02044		3A		Collapsed into Stairway 5012.	
C02045		1		E/W wall that corners with Wall 1035 to form what remains from Phase 1 Room 111; two rows (ca. 0.50 m), two courses preserved.	
C02046	77	3	232	Compacted soil layer between Stairway 2044 and Wall 3013.	

LOCUS	BUCKETS	PH	ROOM	DESCRIPTION	REG. OBJECT(S)
C02047	78, 80	3	232	Collapsed into Locus 2046.	#455, #463, flint flakes debitage (13)
C02048	79	2		Loose soil layer N of Wall 2045; dimensions: 3.75 × 0.25 m; contemporary with Soil Layer 1037.	
C02049		2B		Mudbrick layer above Stone Facing & Mudbrick 2041 (atop wall C02039); underlying Soil Layer 2046; dimensions: 0.30 × 0.30.	
C02050	81	3A	232	Collapsed into Locus 2038.	
C02051	83	2		Soil layer (probably fill) S of Wall 3013; identified in a 0.50 × 0.50 m probe to determine the relationship between Wall 2039 and Wall 3013; contemporary with Fill Layers 2025, 2027, 2028, & 3032.	#472, flint flakes debitage (6)
C02052		2A	321	Unexcavated surface identified in a 0.50 × 0.50 m probe in the corner formed by Walls 3013 and 2039; surface on which the walls of the Phase 2A building were constructed; equals Surface 3033.	
C03000	1–2	Misc.		Ground surface covering square.	#166, flint frag. (1)
C03001		4		Post-occupational wall collapse and debris layer underlying ground surface.	
C03002	3–4	4		Collapsed into Locus 3001.	#081, ceramic frag. spindle whorl; #164, flint frag; #170, sandstone flake
C03003		2A	321	Collapsed into Wall 3013.	
C03004		Misc.		Back-fill from 1982.	
C03005	4a, 7–10	4		Post-occupational wall collapse and debris layer underlying ground surface.	
C03006		3A		N/S wall in NE sector of square; forms a corner with E/W Wall 8002 of Room 831; two rows (0.75–0.85 m), six courses exposed.	
C03007	11–13, 25, 27–28, 31, 34, 38	4		Collapsed into Locus 3001.	#190, ceramic burnishing tool
C03008	14–17, 20–23, 32, 36	4		Collapsed into Locus 3001.	
C03009	18–19, 30	4		Collapsed into Locus 3001.	#154, flint flake
C03010	24, 26, 29	4		Collapsed into Locus 3001.	#176, limestone frag. worked?; #201, sedimentary worked object?
C03011	33, 35	4		Collapsed into Locus 3001.	
C03012		3A		Collapsed into Wall 8002.	

Locus	Buckets	Ph	Room	Description	Reg. Object(s)
C03013		2A	321	E/W wall along S balk; N boundary of Phase 2 central broad room (Room 521); two rows (ca. 0.50 m), seven courses preserved; constructed in Phase 2A, reused in 2B; appears to have been cut on the E when the entryway was constructed in Phase 3A.	
C03014	43	Misc.		Balk removal.	
C03015	57, 60	3A	331	Cobbled pavement in SE sector of square; adjacent to Surface 3016 to the E; extends south to Wall 2006; dimensions: 2.60 × 1.50 m exposed; equals Cobbled Pavement 3021; contemporary with Surfaces 3016 & 7020.	
C03016	61–64	3A	331	Hard-packed surface in SE sector of square; adjacent to Cobbled Surface 3015 to the W; extends south to Wall 3021; dimensions: 2.60 × 1.50 m exposed; contemporary with Cobbled Pavements 3015 & 3021 and Surface 7020.	
C03017	44	3B	331	Hard-packed surface in W sector of square; with small pebbles and flat lying sherds; dimensions: 2.9 × 1.5 m exposed; equals Phase 3B Courtyard Surface 7015.	
C03018	45	3B		Loosely packed makeup layer for Surface 3017; dimensions: 2.9 × 1.5 m.	
C03019	46, 48	3B		Fill that serves as foundation/makeup for Surface 3017; underlying Makeup Layer 3018; dimensions: 2.9 × 1.5 m exposed.	
C03020	42, 47	Misc.		Back fill.	#437, flint flake (1)
C03021	49	3A	331	Cobbled pavement in SE sector of square; underlying Makeup Layer 3019; dimensions: 1.50 × 2.00 m exposed; equals Cobbled Pavement 3015; contemporary with Surfaces 3016 & 7020.	
C03022	50	3A		Ashy layer underlying Cobbled Surface 3021 (and also rises above 3021); appears to be fill/makeup for this Phase 3A surface; ash may represent Phase 2 destruction debris; dimensions: 4.5 × 1.5 m exposed.	
C03023	51	3A		Loosely packed soil layer mixed with cobbles, pottery, and faunal remains; underlying Ash Layer 3022 and Cobbled Surface 3021; represents foundation/makeup for Surface 3021; dimensions: 2.00 × 1.50 m exposed.	#432, flint flakes debitage (5)
C03024	52	2B	521	Plaster Surface underlying Makeup Layer 3023; represents Phase 2B occupational surface; dimensions: 2.00 × 1.50 m exposed; equals Plaster Surface 3026.	
C03025	53, 56	2B		Layer of fill underlying Plaster Surface 3024; dimensions: 1.50 × 1.50 m exposed; contemporary with Fill Layers 2027, 2028, 2051, & 3032.	
C03026		2B	321	Plaster surface in SW sector of square; underlying Cobbled Surface 3015; slopes up to Wall 2021 to the S; appears to be eroded to the N and E; dimensions: 1.05 × 2.00 m exposed; equals Plaster Surface 3024.	

LOCUS	BUCKETS	PH	ROOM	DESCRIPTION	REG. OBJECT(S)
C03027	54	2B		Layer of fill underlying Plaster Surface 3024; dimensions: 1.50 × 0.60 m exposed; contemporary with Fill Layers 2025, 2028, 2051, & 3032.	
C03028	58	2B		Finger-like layer of fill sandwiched within Fill Layer 3027 (see C3 W Balk); dimensions: 0.50 × 1.50 m exposed; contemporary with Fill Layers 2025, 2027, 2051, & 3032.	
C03029	55	Misc.		Back fill.	
C03030		3		Collapsed into Locus 2046.	
C03031	59	2B		Collapsed into Locus 3032.	
C03032		2B		Layer of fill in S sector of square; underlying Surfaces 3016 and 3026; dimensions: 2.50 × 1.00 m exposed; contemporary with Fill Layers 2025, 2027, 2028, and 2051.	
C03033		2A	321	Unexcavated, hard-packed clay surface in S sector of square; underlying Fill Layer 3032; dimensions: 3.50 × 1.25 m exposed; equals Surface 3034.	
C03034	41	2A	321	Unexcavated, hard-packed clay surface in SE sector of square; underlying Fill Layers 2025 and 3027; dimensions: 2.10 × 1.50 m exposed; surface upon which Wall 3013 was constructed; equals Surface 3033.	
C04000	1–3, 6	Misc.		Ground surface covering square.	#163, flint frag. blade; #172, flint frag. slingstone?; #182, flint frag. with bulb of percussion
C04001		4		Post-occupational wall collapse and debris layer underlying ground surface.	
C04002	4–5, 7	4		Layer of hardened silt with limestone frags and sherds, underlying Wall Collapse 4001.	
C04003	8–9	4		Collapsed into Locus 4002.	
C04004		3A		E/W wall that in Phase 3 forms S boundary of Room 531, the W "guardroom"; continues the line of the wall that N. Glueck observed bisecting the mound (see Locus 9002); two rows (ca. 1.0 m), ? courses preserved.	
C04005		2		N/S wall underlying Phase 3 Wall 4004; two rows (ca. 0.82–0.94 m), one course exposed; appears to be contemporary with Wall 4006.	
C04006		2		N/S wall in the W balk underlying Phase 3 Wall 4004; two rows, one course exposed; appears to be contemporary with Wall 4005.	
C04007		3A		N/S wall forming the E boundary of Room 531; extending beyond E/W Wall 4004 to the S; unusual bipartite construction (see top plan) may represent subphasing; width ca. 0.79–0.86 m, three courses preserved.	
C04008		3A		Collapsed into Locus 1022.	

Locus	Buckets	Ph	Room	Description	Reg. Object(s)
C04009		3B	531	Cobbled pavement in S half of Room 531; a Phase 3B extension of Pavement 5009 in N half of room; cobbles in Pavement 4009 are larger than cobbles in Phase 3A Pavement 5009; cobble dimensions average 0.37 × 0.28 m.	
C04010		3A		Surface just W of Stairway 1033; equals Exterior "Gateway" Surface 1030; contemporary with Surface 5011 of Room 231.	
C05000	1–4, 14–15, 40	Misc.		Ground surface covering square.	#140, ceramic leg of bowl; #165, flint frag. (1)
C05001		Misc.		Collapsed into Locus 5000.	
C05002		3A		Central pylon forming the E boundary of Room 531; blocks 5002a and 5002b were added later to form a solid wall; dimensions: ca. 1.50 × 1.50 m; associated with Cobbled Pavement 5009.	
C05002a		3B		Block in opening created by Wall 5004 and Pylon 5002 in the E boundary of Room 531; associated with Pavement 5009.	
C05002b		3B		Block in opening created by Wall 4007 and Pylon 5002 in the E boundary of Room 531; associated with Pavement 5009.	
C05003	5–6, 9	4		Post-occupation wall collapse and debris layer underlying ground surface.	#143, glass beads from late Bedouin burial; #144, glass frag. bead from late Bedouin burial
C05004		3A		E/W wall forming the N boundary of Room 531; two rows (ca. 0.80 m), three courses preserved; associated with Cobbled Pavement 5009.	
C05005		3A		N/S wall in the W balk forming the E boundary of Room 1031 and the W boundary of Room 531; two rows, three courses preserved; associated with Cobbled Pavements 5009 and 4009 in Room 531.	
C05006	7	Misc.		Post EB IV (modern) cist burial.	#145, glass beads from late Bedouin burial
C05007	8	4		Collapsed into Locus 5003.	
C05008	10–12, 17a	4		Collapsed into Locus 5003.	#149, flint blade with ventral retouch
C05009		3A	531	Cobbled pavement in N half of Room 531; extended in Phase 3B when Cobbled Pavement 4009 was constructed; cobbles in Pavement 5009 are smaller than cobbles in Phase 3B Pavement 4009; cobble dimensions average 0.22 × 0.25 m.	
C05010	13, 16–17	3B		N/S bench lining the E face of Pylon 5002 and Blocks 5002a and 5002b in Room 231; dimensions: 5.00 × 0.30–0.45 m; associated with Entryway Surface 5011.	
C05011	61, 67, 72–73	3A	231	Plaster surface covering Phase 3 Entryway 231; associated with Benches 5010 and 2010; contemporary with Exterior Entryway Surface 1030.	#431, flint flakes debitage (21)

LOCUS	BUCKETS	PH	ROOM	DESCRIPTION	REG. OBJECT(S)
C05012		3A		Stairway at N end of Phase 3 Entryway 231; consisting of two rows, at different levels, of three aligned stones spanning the width of the entryway (2.85 m); steps lie N of parallel E/W "Guardroom" Walls 5004 and 2021; contemporary with Surface 5011.	
C05013		2A		E/W wall forming the S boundary of the Phase 2 Broadroom House 32; underlying Phase 3 Plaster Surface 5011; dimensions: 2 rows (0.50–0.60 m), one course exposed; associated with Founding Surface 2037.	
C05014	18–21	2		Soil layer beneath Cobble Pavements 4005 and 5009; exposed in a probe of the SE sector of the square.	#353, flint flakes, one a partial worked blade (2)
C05015		2A		N/S wall fragment discovered in a probe in the SE sector of square, two rows (ca. 0.60 m), one course exposed; bonds with Phase 2 E/W Wall 5013; Wall 5015 runs to the N beneath Phase 3 structures and appears to equal Wall 5016, with which it must form the W boundary of Phase 2 Room 521.	
C05016		2A		N/S wall in N balk that forms a corner and bonds with Phase 2 E/W Wall 3013; two rows (ca. .60 m), one course exposed; Wall 5016 runs to the S beneath Phase 3 structures and appears to equal Wall 5015, with which it must form the W boundary of Phase 2 Room 521.	
C06000	1–4	Misc.		Ground surface covering square.	#189, flint frag. retouched blade
C06001		4		Post-occupational wall collapse and debris layer underlying ground surface.	
C06002	5–9, 11, 13–14, 16, 18, 21, 23	4		Collapsed into Locus 6001.	#162, flint lithic; #177, flint frag. hammerstone/pounder; #197, limestone mortar
C06003	10, 12	Misc.		Collapsed into Locus 6000.	
C06004		3A		E/W wall that forms the S boundary of Corner Bin 632; two rows (ca. 0.60–0.70 m), six courses preserved; associated with Flagstone Surface 6022, Surface 6021, and Step 6015/6015a.	
C06005		3A		N/S pillared wall along E balk (Room 631); with three stacked pillars; of uneven construction, four courses preserved; added in Phase 3A reorientation of area; blocks (6005a) added in Phase 3B to form a solid wall.	
C06006	15, 17, 19, 22, 24, 26	4		Collapsed into Locus 6001.	
C06007	20	4		Collapsed into Locus 6001.	
C06008	25	4		Collapsed into Locus 6001.	
C06009		3A		E/W well-constructed wall along N balk; abuts Wall 2024 on the W, abutted by Wall 6005 on the E; forms N wall of Bin 612 in Phase 3; two rows (ca. 0.45–0.70 m), seven courses preserved; associated in Phase 3 with Surfaces 6021, 6022, and 6027.	

Locus	Buckets	Ph	Room	Description	Reg. Object(s)
C06010	26a	3a		N/S wall that forms the E boundary of Corner Bin 612; two rows (ca. 0.60–0.80 m), six courses preserved; associated with Flagstone Surface 6022 and Surface 6021.	
C06011		4		Collapsed into Locus 6001.	
C06012	27a, 31, 34	2b		Work table in S half of square, E of Work Table 6013; constructed of stone and mudbrick; dimensions: 1.00 × 0.67 m; associated with Surfaces 6016 and 6018, in which were significant quantities of flint debitage.	#302, #315, flint flakes debitage (76)
C06013		2b		Work table S half of square, W of Work Table 6012; constructed of stone and mudbrick; dimensions: 1.28 × 0.92 m; mudbrick "collar" on W measures 0.15 m; associated with Surfaces 6016 and 6018, in which were significant quantities of flint debitage.	
C06014		3a		Stone bench in the SW corner of Room 631; constructed in the Phase 3 reorientation of Room 631; contemporary with Surface 6027.	
C06015		3a		Rock step in Bin 632, in the N corner formed by Walls 2024 and 6004; bonded to Wall 6004; top stone of step appears to be the same as the top stone of Step 6015a; dimensions: 0.50 × 0.50 m, ca. 0.30 m high; associated with Surface 6022.	
C06015a		3a		Rock step outside Bin 632, in the S corner formed by Walls 2024 and 6004; bonded to 6004; top stone of step appears to be the same as the top stone of Step 6015; dimensions: 0.50 × 0.50 m, ca. 0.30 m high.	
C06016	28, 28a, 29, 29a, 30, 32, 38–39, 43–44	2b	621	Surface identified in the SE sector of square (Room 621); below Surface Buildup 6016a; above Surface 6018; use surface in Phase 2 industrial phase; with significant quantities of flint debitage; associated with Work Tables 6012 and 6013.	#293, #295, #317, #333, #346, flint flakes debitage (153); #305, flint frag. hammerstone/pounder; #306, flint handstone, discoidal (Type B); #307, ceramic oval lid
C06016a		2b	621	Surface buildup in SE sector of square (Room 621); above Surface 6016; associated with Work Tables 6012 and 6013.	
C06017	33	2b		Collapsed into Locus 6012.	#301, flint flakes worked (2)
C06018	40, 45, 50	2b	621	Surface identified in the SE sector of square (Room 621); below Surface 6016; above Phase 2a Surface 1019; Phase 2b industrial features constructed in this surface; associated with Work Tables 6012 and 6013.	#334, #369, flint flakes debitage (12); #337, basalt handstone (Type C)
C06019	35, 37, 42, 46, 51	2a	621	Surface identified in the SE sector of square (Room 621); below Surface 6018; first identified above Phase 1 Wall 6025; seals Phase 1 architecture and fill.	#311, limestone pierced stone (Type B); #312, #318, #321, #347, #374, flint flakes debitage (54)

LOCUS	BUCKETS	PH	ROOM	DESCRIPTION	REG. OBJECT(S)
C06020		3A		E/W wall in S balk; S boundary of Rooms 621 and 631; bonded to N/S Wall 1027; abutted by Wall 2024; overlying Phase 1 Wall 6026; two rows (ca. 0.70–0.88 m), six courses preserved; contemporary with Surface 6019.	
C06021	36	3B	632	Surface buildup/layer of accumulation within Bin 632; over Flagstone Surface 6022.	
C06022		3A	632	Flagstone surface in Bin 632; below Surface Buildup 6021; contemporary with Surface 6027.	
C06023		2B		Soil layer beneath Flagstone Surface 6022; exposed by probe in NW corner of Bin 632.	
C06024	41	2A		Soil layer beneath Work Table 6013; above Phase 1 Wall 6025.	#344, flint flakes (1); #395, flint flakes debitage (46)
C06025	48	1		N/S wall in the SW sector of square; bonded to Wall 6026; below Surface 6019; resting on Surface 6033; two rows (ca. 0.60–0.66 m), three courses preserved.	
C06026		1		E/W wall in S balk; bonded to Wall 6025; below Surface 6019; resting on Surface 6033; two rows, four courses preserved.	
C06027	47, 49	3A	631	Plaster surface identified in NE sector of square, Room 631.	#350, basalt handstone, discoidal (Type B); #351, basalt hammerstone/pounder; #360, basalt pestle
C06028		3A		Stone table overlying Surface 6027; dimensions: 1.50 × 0.40 × 0.20 m; Work Stones A350 and A351 lie on this surface. Associated features: 6028a: stone bench to the north of the table, 0.41 × 0.19 m; 6028b: stone bench to the west of the table at the northern end, 0.24 × 0.17 m; 6028c: stone bench to the west of the table at the southern end, 0.44 × 0.21 m.	
C06029	52, 55–56	1		Layer of fill in S sector of square; overlying Phase 1 Surface 6033; sealed by Phase 2A Surface 6019; corresponds with Fill 6030 and 6032.	#387, #388, #399, flint flakes debitage (28)
C06030	53, 57	1		Layer of fill in SE sector of Square; overlying Phase 1 Surface 6035; sealed by Phase 2A Surface 6019; corresponds with Fill 6029 and 6032.	#389, #398, flint flakes debitage (40)
C06031	54	2		Soil layer below Bench 6014, above Surface 6018.	#386, flint flakes debitage (15); #404, carnelian lotus-shaped pendant
C06032	58, 64–65	1		Layer of fill W of Phase 1 Wall 6025; sealed by Phase 2A Surface 6019; corresponds with Fill 6029 and 6030.	#412, #456, flint flakes debitage (14)
C06033	59	1	611	Compact plaster surface in S sector of square; on which the Phase 1 building was constructed.	
C06034		1		N/S wall in the SE sector of square; constructed on Surfaces 6033 and 6035; two rows (ca. 0.64–0.70 m), three courses preserved.	

LOCUS	BUCKETS	PH	ROOM	DESCRIPTION	REG. OBJECT(S)
C06035	60, 62	1	612	Surface E of Wall 6034; underlying Fill 6030; contemporary with Surface 6033.	
C06036	61	2B	621	Soil layer below Step 6015; overlying Surface 6019.	#424, ceramic frag. spindle whorl
C06037	66	1		N/S wall in the SW sector of square; underlying Wall 2024; constructed on Surface 6033.	
C06038	63	1	611	Hard-packed surface in S sector of square; underlying Surface 6033; with some charcoal and patches of plaster; earliest surface in Area C.	#434, flint flakes debitage (10)
C06039		2A		N/S wall in E sector of square; overlying Wall 6034; underlying Wall 6005; two rows (ca. 0.60 m), two courses preserved; contemporary with Surface 6019.	
C06040				beginning locus excavation–Probe	
C06041				possible surface	
C06042				surface	
C06043				30 cm down continuing excavation in probe	
C07000	1–2, 5–6	Misc.		Ground surface covering square.	#292, flint flakes debitage (2)
C07001		4		Post-occupational wall collapse and debris layer underlying ground surface.	
C07002	3–4	4		Collapsed into Locus 7001.	
C07003		3A		N/S wall in W. balk, SW sector of square; appears to form a corner with Wall 11001 of Room 1031; two rows wide (ca. 0.75 m), preserved to four courses; contemporary with Room 732.	
C07004		4		Ashy layer in SW sector of square, underlying Rubble Layer 7001, overlying Rubble Layer 7006; 1.00 × 1.25 m; may represent post-EB IV activity area; no ceramics.	
C07005		3A	732	N/S wall on E side of square; abutted by Wall 7007a; two rows (0.60–0.70 m); contemporary with Wall 7003 and Room 1031.	
C07006	8, 10, 15, 24	4		Post-occupational wall collapse and debris layer underlying ground surface.	#326, flint flakes debitage (7); #329, basalt frag. mortar; #339, basalt frag. pierced stone (Type A); #372, flint flake (1)
C07007		3A	732	N/S wall that with Walls 7007a, 7012, and 7005 forms Room 732; two rows wide (0.35–0.40 m), five courses preserved; contemporary with Wall 7003 of Room 1031.	
C07007a		3A	732	N/S wall that with Walls 7007, 7012, and 7005 forms Room 732; two rows wide (0.35–0.40 m), five courses preserved; contemporary with Wall 7003 of Room 1031.	

LOCUS	BUCKETS	PH	ROOM	DESCRIPTION	REG. OBJECT(S)
C07008		3A	732	E/W wall that bonds with Wall 7007 as part of Room 732; two rows (ca. 0.35–0.40 m), five courses preserved; contemporary with Wall 7003 of Room 1031.	
C07009	7, 11, 14	4		Collapsed into Locus 7001.	#405, metal lump of slag
C07010	9, 13, 17	4		Collapsed into Locus 7001.	
C07011		2A	321	Collapsed into Wall 3013.	
C07012		3A		E/W wall that forms a corner with Wall 7007 as part of Room 732; two rows (ca. 0.35–0.40 m), five courses preserved; contemporary with Wall 7003 of Room 1031.	
C07012a	3B			Block in the entrance to Room 732, formed by Walls 7012 and 7005.	
C07013	12	4		Collapsed into Locus 7001.	
C07014		2	1121	N/S wall in W balk; abuts Wall 11001/7003 to the S; 2.5 courses exposed.	
C07015	16, 19–21, 25–26, 29	3B	731	Hard-packed plaster surface covering most of square; with flat-lying sherds; significant amount of pottery outside Room 732 at its SW corner; associated with Rooms 732, 231, and 1031.	#342, #357, #377, flint flakes debitage (46); #361, basalt frag. handstone (Type A); #378, flint frag. handstone/pounder; #379, flint disc.
C07016		3A	732	Cobbled pavement covering the S third of Room 732; dimensions: 0.75 × 1.35 m.	
C07017	18	3A	732	Hard-packed plaster surface covering N two-thirds of Room 732; dimensions: 1.5 × 1.5 m.	
C07018	22	Misc.		Balk removal.	
C07019	23	Misc.		Balk removal.	
C07020	30–31	3A	731	Hard-packed plaster-like surface covering most of square; underlying Surface 7015; with pottery on surface; associated with Rooms 732, 231, and 1031.	
C07021	27	Misc.		Balk removal.	#400, basalt grooved stone grinding slab
C07022	28	Misc.		Balk removal.	
C08000	1, 2A, 5–7, 21	Misc.		Ground surface covering square.	#331, basalt frag. pierced stone (Type B)
C08001		4		Post-occupational wall collapse and debris layer underlying ground surface.	
C08002	2	3A		E/W wall forming a corner with N/S Wall 3006; two rows (ca. 0.85), eight courses exposed; associated with Wall 8003 and Room 831.	#206, metal frag. (copper?) pin
C08003	3A, 18	3A		N/S wall in NE sector of excavated portion of square; with Walls 3006 and 8002 forming Room 831; two rows (ca. 0.70 m), ?courses preserved.	#410, flint flakes debitage (14); #425, flint frag. hammerstone; #426, flint frag. hammerstone/pounder

LOCUS	BUCKETS	PH	ROOM	DESCRIPTION	REG. OBJECT(S)
C08004	4	3A		Collapsed into Locus 8002.	
C08005		3A		Layer of fill S of Wall 8002; underlying Surface 8005a; mixed with ceramics and lithics throughout; contemporary with Fill Layers 3025, 3027, 3028, and 3032.	
C08005a	9–10	3A	832	Exterior surface S of Wall 8002; overlying Fill 8005; covering exposed area of Room 832.	#359, flint flakes debitage (21)
C08006		4		Post-occupational wall collapse and debris layer underlying ground surface; located in the NW sector of the square, N of Wall 8002.	
C08007		3A		Collapsed into Wall 2024.	
C08008	8, 12–13	3B	831	Surface with plaster inclusions N of Wall 8002, in Room 831; overlying Surface 8011; associated with Block 8013.	#343, #371, #390, flint flakes debitage (249)
C08009	11, 15–17	3A	832	Hard-packed surface S of Wall 8002; overlying Surface 8010; with significant quantities of flint debitage; covering exposed area of Room 832; associated with Pillar Base 8012.	#367, basalt frag. grinding slab; #373, #392, #397, #411, flint flakes debitage (261)
C08010	86–87	3A	832	Plaster surface S of Wall 8002; underlying Surface 8009; covering exposed area of Room 832; surface on which Pillar Base 8012 was set.	
C08011	14, 19	3A	831	Plaster surface N of Wall 8002, in Room 831; underlying Surface 8008.	#391, flint flakes debitage (25)
C08012		3A		Stone pillar base, in Room 832; set on Surface 8010; sealed by Surface 8005a; dimensions: 0.73 × 0.71 × 0.36 m.; associated with Surfaces 8009 and 8010.	
C08013		3B	831	Block for doorway formed by Walls 8002 and 8003; associated with Surface 8008 of Room 831.	
C08014	22–23, 27, 42, 55–56, 58, 89, 91	Misc.		Cleanup of backfill from 1987 season.	#715, stone gaming piece?; #816, #826, #828, flint flakes debitage (72)
C08015	24–25, 29, 43, 57, 59, 60–61, 93	3A	832	Earth layer below 8014, with small to medium flat lying boulders in the north; makeup for Surface 8010, covering square.	#808, flint flakes debitage (4)
C08016	26, 28, 30, 32–35, 44–45, 62–67, 70–71, 94–95, 97	3A		Fill laid for the construction of Phase 3 building, covering square; with two medium to large flat lying boulders embedded in the north, covering square.	#769, ceramic half spindle whorl; #834, flint flakes debitage (1)
C08017	31, 46, 68	3A		Ashy layer within Fill 8016, located in southern part of the square just north of Wall 6009 (.90 × 1.40 m).	
C08018a		Prev.		Lower courses of Wall 8018, which represent Pre-EBIV construction in Area C.	
C08018b		1		SW to NE running wall (1.5 × .63 m), apparently cornering with Wall 8031 to the north.	

LOCUS	BUCKETS	PH	ROOM	DESCRIPTION	REG. OBJECT(S)
C08019	36, 47	1	811	Ashy layer extending from Wall 6009 1.5 m north to subsidiary balk running EW across the square; layer of destruction material covering Phase 1 Layer 8020.	
C08020	39, 73, 84	1	811	Surface buildup/destruction material, above Surface 8022; with a large amount of ash to the east.	
C08021	38	1		Rock fall associated with Wall 8018B, falling to the west on 8020; fill (8016) above Wall 8018B with rock fall directly west suggests that an upper course of 8018B was removed at the construction of Wall 6009.	
C08022	40	1	811	Stone-paved surface, with small to medium boulders, associated with Phase 1 Wall 8018B; running 1.5 m north to subsidiary balk running EW across the square.	
C08023	72	2		NS running wall (1.48 × .56 m) just inside the west balk.	
C08024		3B		NS running wall exposed by erosion in the C8 east balk.	
C08025	48–50	Misc.		Balk trim.	#812, flint flakes debitage (3)
C08026	49, 54	Misc.		Cleanup of backfill from 2004 season.	#810, #815, flint flakes debitage (3)
C08027		1		Dark brown soil with flat boulders below 8022; two layers of stone in the SW and three layers in NE; may represent surface below or makeup for 8022.	
C08028	53	1		Flat boulders jutting out of subsidiary balk running EW across the square; equals 8020, above 8022.	
C08029		3A	832	Collapsed into Locus 8015.	
C08030	105	3A		Collapsed into Locus 8016.	
C08031		1		EW wall (1.5 × ca. .5 m) to the north in the C8 Probe, running under Phase 2 Wall 8023 to the west and apparently cornering with Phase 1 Wall 8018B to the east; south face preserved, north face appears to have been robbed, perhaps when Pit 8035 was cut.	
C08032	69	Misc.		Probe between 8023 and 8030.	
C08033	74, 78	1		Soil surrounding stones in Locus 8028.	
C08034	75	1	811	Collapsed into Locus 8022.	
C08035	76	3		Pit cut into the NW corner of the probe, below 8015.	
C08036	77	3		Collapsed into Locus 8035.	
C08037	80	3		Collapsed into Locus 8035.	
C08038	82–83, 88, 106	Prev.		Layer of yellowish brown soil (10YRS/4) with cobbles, identified in a 1.20 by .85 m probe west of Wall 8018A.	#853, basalt grinding slab

LOCUS	BUCKETS	PH	ROOM	DESCRIPTION	REG. OBJECT(S)
C08039	92, 99, 100	Prev.		Collapsed into Locus 8038.	
C08040	98	Prev.		Collapsed into Locus 8038.	
C08041	102	Prev.		Collapsed into Locus 8038.	
C08942		Prev.		Surface on which Wall 8018A was constructed (476.00-476.05 m).	
C09000	1, 4, 5–6	Misc.		Ground surface covering square.	#442, basalt frag. hammerstone/ pounder
C09001	2, 7, 9	2	921	Surface in S sector of square upon which Wall 9002 was constructed; underlying Ground Surface 9000 and Surfaces 9007 & 9008.	
C09002	3	3A		E/W wall in N sector of the square; continues line of the wall that N. Glueck observed bisecting the site; two rows (ca. 0.90 m), three courses preserved.	
C09003		2	921	Corner fragment S of Wall 9002; two rows (ca. 0.50 m), two courses preserved; apparently constructed in Phase 2, reused in Phase 3; associated with Surfaces 9007 and 9008.	
C09004		3	931	N/S wall frag abutting Wall 9002 to the N; one row (ca. 0.25 m), one course preserved; associated with Surfaces 9005 & 9006.	
C09005		3	931	Cobbled surface N of Wall 9002 and E of Wall 9004; dimensions: 1.40 × 0.70 m; associated with Wall 9004.	
C09006		3	931	Surface N of Wall 9002 and W of Wall 9004; dimensions: 0.60 × 0.40 m; associated with Wall 9004.	
C09007	8, 10	3	932	Surface S of Wall 9002 and N of Corner Fragment 9003; dimensions: 1.50 × 2.50 m; associated with Wall 9002 and the reuse of Corner Fragment 9003.	
C09008		2	921	Plaster floor within Corner Fragment 9003; dimensions: 1.08 × 0.60 m; associated with the reuse of Phase 2 Wall 9003.	
C10000	1–3	Misc.		Ground surface covering square.	#443, limestone mortar
C10001		3A		E/W wall forming the S boundary of Room 1031; two rows (ca. 0.75 m), three courses exposed; associated with Plaster Surface 10002.	
C10001A		3B		Block for doorway formed by Walls 10001 & 10003.	
C10002		3	1031	Plaster surface N of Wall 10001; dimensions: 1.90 × 1.70 m; associated with Walls 10001 and 10003 of Room 1031.	
C10003		3		N/S wall forming W boundary of Room 1031; two rows (ca. 0.90 m), two courses exposed; associated with Plaster Surface 10002.	

LOCUS	BUCKETS	PH	ROOM	DESCRIPTION	REG. OBJECT(S)
C10004	4	4		Post-occupational wall collapse and debris layer underlying ground surface.	
C10005		4		Collapsed into Locus 10004.	
C10006	6	2		Phase 2 rubble layer; sealed by Phase 3 Surface 10002.	#450, flint flakes debitage (2)
C11000	1, 3	Misc.		Ground surface covering square.	
C11001		3A		E/W wall in S sector of square; corners with Phase 3 N/S Wall 7003 in Square 7; two rows (ca. 0.80 m), five courses preserved; associated with Rooms 1132 and 1031.	
C11002		3		Collapsed into Wall 10003.	
C11002a		3B		Block for doorway formed by Walls 11001 and 11002.	
C11003	2, 7–8	4		Post-occupational wall collapse and debris layer underlying ground surface.	
C11004	4, 6	4		Post-occupational wall collapse and debris layer underlying ground surface.	
C11005	5, 9, 11	4		Post-occupational wall collapse and debris layer underlying ground surface.	
C11006	10	2		E/W wall in N sector of square; two rows (ca. 0.75 m), two courses exposed; associated with Room 1121.	
C11007		3	1031	Beaten earth surface with some cobbles in NW corner of Room 1031; dimensions: 1.30 × 0.80 m; associated with Walls 11001 and 11002.	
C11008		2		N/S wall in the W balk running underneath Phase 3 Wall 11001; two courses exposed; probably associated with Phase 2 Wall 11006 and Room 1121.	
C11009		4		Collapsed into Locus 11003.	
C11010	12	4		Post-occupational wall collapse and debris layer underlying ground surface.	
C11011		2		N/S wall in the W balk that abuts Wall 11006 on the N; two courses exposed; associated with Room 1121.	
C11012	13	4		Post-occupational wall collapse and debris layer underlying ground surface.	
C11013		3A	1131	Beaten-earth surface S of Wall 11006; probably covered Wall 11006; dimensions: 0.38 × 0.50 m; contemporary with Phase 3 Surfaces 11014 and 7020.	
C11014		3A	1131	Beaten-earth surface N of Wall 11006; probably covered Wall 11006; dimensions: 1.56 × 1.40 m; contemporary with Phase 3 Surfaces 11013 and 7020.	

Appendix C

Inventory of Faunal Remains

Registration	Locus	Spe	SP	Elem	Ph	Side	Age
C1.10.1010	C01010	o/c	Metac	distal	3	L/R	Imm
C1.10.1010	C01010	o/c	Mand		3	R	
C1.14.1015	C01015	o/c	Inn	a+p	3		unknown
C1.14.1015	C01015	o/c	Inn	isch	3	L	unknown
C1.14.1015	C01015	o/c	Tibia	d.diaph	3	L	Imm
C1.12.1016	C01016	o/c	Astrag		2	R	
C1.17.1016	C01016	o/c	Inn	a+il	2	L	Imm
C1.17.1016	C01016	o/c	Metac	distal	2	L	unknown
C1.17.1016	C01016	o/c	Fem	distal	2	R	Mat
C1.17.1016	C01016	o/c	Fem	p.diaph	2	R	Imm
C1.17.1016	C01016	o/c	Fem	proximal	2	R	Mat
C1.17.1016	C01016	o/c	Fem	distal	2	R	Mat
C1.17.1016	C01016	o/c	Inn	a+is	2	L	unknown
C1.17.1016	C01016	o/c	Metac	distal	2	L	Mat
C1.17.1016	C01016	o/c	Inn	il	2	R	unknown
C1.17.1016	C01016	o/c	Phalange	1	2	b	Mat
C1.17.1016	C01016	Ovis	Inn	a+il	2	L	unknown
C1.17.1016	C01016	o/c	Inn	a+is	2	R	Mat
C1.17.1016	C01016	Ovis	Calc		2	R	Mat
C1.17.1016	C01016	o/c	Inn	a+il	2	R	Mat
C1.17.1016	C01016	o/c	Phalange	1	2	a	Mat
C1.17.1016	C01016	Bos	Phalange	1	2	b	Mat
C1.17.1016	C01016	o/c	Phalange	1	2	b	Mat
C1.17.1016	C01016	o/c	Phalange	1	2	b	Imm

REGISTRATION	LOCUS	SPE	SP	ELEM	PH	SIDE	AGE
C1.17.1016	C01016	Bos	Phalange	1	2	b	Mat
C1.17.1016	C01016	o/c	Astrag		2	R	
C1.17.1016	C01016	o/c	Calc		2	R	Mat
C1.17.1016	C01016	o/c	Maxilla		2	R	
C1.17.1016	C01016	o/c	skull	Hcore	2	R	
C1.17.1016	C01016	o/c	skull	Hcore	2	L	
C1.17.1016	C01016	o/c	skull	Hcore	2	L	
C1.17.1016	C01016	o/c	skull	Malar	2	R	
C1.17.1016	C01016	Bos	Phalange	1	2	b	Imm
C1.17.1016	C01016	o/c	skull	Malar	2	L	
C1.17.1016	C01016	o/c	Inn	a+il	2	L	unknown
C1.17.1016	C01016	o/c	Maxilla		2		
C1.17.1016	C01016	o/c	Mand		2	L	
C1.17.1016	C01016	o/c	Maxilla	M1/M2	2	L	ABC
C1.17.1016	C01016	o/c	Hum	distal	2	L	Mat
C1.17.1016	C01016	o/c	Rad	distal	2	L	Imm
C1.17.1016	C01016	o/c	Maxilla		2	R	
C1.17.1016	C01016	Capra	Hum	distal	2	L	Mat
C1.17.1016	C01016	o/c	Mand	Condyle	2	R	
C1.17.1016	C01016	o/c	Hum	distal	2	R	Mat
C1.17.1016	C01016	o/c	Hum	distal	2	R	Mat
C1.17.1016	C01016	Ovis	Hum	distal	2	R	Mat
C1.17.1016	C01016	o/c	Scap	prox	2	L	Mat
C1.17.1016	C01016	o/c	Rad	proximal	2	R	Mat
C1.17.1016	C01016	o/c	Phalange	1	2	a	Mat
C1.17.1016	C01016	oc	sk	malar	2	R	
C1.17.1016	C01016	oc	sk	malar	2	L	
C1.17.1016	C01016	oc	sk	hc	2	R	
C1.17.1016	C01016	oc	sk	hc	2	L	
C1.17.1016	C01016	oc	sk	hc	2	L	
C1.19.1016	C01016	o/c	Tibia	diaph	2	L/R	unknown
C1.20.1010	C01016	o/c	Metat	d.diaph	2	R	unknown
C1.20.1016	C01016	Capra	Calc		2	R	Mat
C1.20.1016	C01016	o/c	Phalange	1	2	a	Mat
C1.25.1017	C01017	o/c	Astrag		3	L	
C1.25.1017	C01017	o/c	Astrag		3	L	
C1.20.1019	C01019	o/c	Inn	a+p	1	L	unknown
C1.20.1019	C01019	o/c	Metat	complete	1	L	Mat

Registration	Locus	Spe	SP	Elem	Ph	Side	Age
C1.20.1019	C01019	o/c	Metat	complete	1	L	Mat
C1.20.1019	C01019	o/c	Phalange	1	1	a	Mat
C1.23.1020	C01020	o/c	Metac	proximal	2	R	Mat
C1.23.1020	C01020	Bos	Fem	distal	2	L	Mat
C1.23.1020	C01020	Bos	Metac	proximal	2	R	unknown
C1.23.1020	C01020	o/c	Metac	p	2	R	unknown
C1.24.1021	C01021	Ovis	Inn	a+p	1	R	unknown
C1.24.1021	C01021	o/c	Inn	a+is	1	L	Mat
C1.35.1023	C01023	o/c	Phalange	1	2	a	Mat
C1.34.1031	C01031	o/c	Max	P3/P4	3	L	
C1.34.1031	C01031	o/c	Hum	d	3	R	Mat
C1.34.1031	C01031	o/c	Hum	d	3	L	Mat
C1.34.1031	C01031	oc	sk	malar	3	R	
C1.40.1036	C01036	o/c	Scap		2	R	Mat
C1.41.1036	C01036	o/c	Scap		2	L	Mat
C1.41.1036	C01036	o/c	Rad	p	2	L	Mat
C1.41.1036	C01036	o/c	Inn	a/i/i/	2	R	Mat
C1.41.1036	C01036	o/c	Inn	il	2	L	unknown
C1.41.1036	C01036	o/c	Inn	a+is	2	R	unknown
C1.41.1036	C01036	oc	sk	hc	2	R	
C1.41.1036	C01036	Bos	Phal	2	2	B	Mat
C1.41.1036	C01036	Bos	Phal	3	2	B	
C2.10.8005	C02005	Equid	Phalange	2	3	L	Mat
C2.26.3010	C02010	o/c	Tibia	distal	3	L	Mat
C2.23.2018	C02018	o/c	Scap	prox	3	L	unknown
C2.23.2018	C02018	o/c	Scap	prox	3	L	unknown
C2.23.2018	C02018	o/c	Scap		3	L	unknown
C2.32.2025	C02025	o/c	Hum	proximal	3	L/R	Imm
C2.32.2025	C02025	o/c	Maxilla	M3	3	R	
C2.33.2025	C02025	o/c	Max	M3	3	R	G
C2.27.2029	C02029	o/c	Metat	distal	3	R	unknown
C2.27.2029	C02029	o/c	Metat	p	3	R	unknown
C2.38.2029	C02029	o/c	Calc		3	L	Mat
C2.38.2029	C02029	o/c	Astrag		3	L	
C2.42.2030	C02030	o/c	Fem	diaph	2	L	unknown
C2.43.2030	C02030	o/c	Metac	p	2	L	unknown
C2.44.2030	C02030	o/c	Hum	distal	2	R	unknown
C2.44.2030	C02030	o/c	Hum	distal	2	L	Mat

Registration	Locus	Spe	SP	Elem	Ph	Side	Age
C2.46.2031	C02031	Ovis	Phalange	1	2	a	Mat
C2.46.2031	C02031	Bos	Carp	nav-cub	2	R	
C2.46.2031	C02031	Bos	Carp	Rad	2	R	
C2.48.2033	C02033	o/c	Hum	distal	3	L	Mat
C2.49.2033	C02033	Sus	Inn	a+p	3	R	unknown
C2.49.2033	C02033	o/c	Inn	a+il	3	R	unknown
C2.49.2033	C02033	o/c	Tibia	distal	3	L	Mat
C2.49.2033	C02033	o/c	Inn	a+il	3	L	unknown
C2.49.2033	C02033	o/c	Rad	proximal	3	L	Mat
C2.49.2033	C02033	o/c	Rad	diaph	3	L/R	unknown
C2.49.2033	C02033	o/c	skull	Para P	3	L	
C2.49.2033	C02033	o/c	Mand	Condyle	3	R	
C2.49.2033	C02033	o/c	Inn	a+il	3	L	unknown
C2.49.2033	C02033	o/c	Tibia	d	3	L	Mat
C2.49.2033	C02033	o/c	sk	Para Proc	3	L	
C2.49.2033	C02033	Sus	Inn	Pub	3	R	unknown
C2.59.2033	C02033	Eq	Metac	P	3		unknown
C2.50.2034	C02034	o/c	Tibia	diaph	3	L/R	unknown
C2.50.2034	C02034	o/c	Tibia	distal	3	R	Mat
C2.50.2034	C02034	o/c	Metac	d.diaph	3	R	unknown
C2.65.2037	C02037	o/c	Phal	1	3	b	Mat
C2.65.2037	C02037	o/c	Mand	M1/M2	2	R	DEFG
C2.66.2037	C02037	o/c	Metac	P	2	L	unknown
C2.66.2037	C02037	o/c	Metac	complete	2	L	Imm
C2.66.2037	C02037	Bos	Fem	d	2	R	Mat
C2.66.2037	C02037	Bos	Carp	Int	2	R	
C2.66.2037	C02037	Sus	Mand		2	R	
C2.76.2037	C02037	o/c	Phal	1	2	a	Mat
C2.76.2037	C02037	o/c	Scap		2	L	Mat
C2.76.2037	C02037	o/c	Hum	d	2	R	Mat
C2.76.2037	C02037	o/c	Rad	p	2	R	Imm
C2.76.2037	C02037	o/c	Inn	1/2 inn	2	R	Mat
C2.76.2037	C02037	o/c	Inn	il	2	L	unknown
C2.76.2037	C02037	o/c	Metac	d	2	L	Mat
C2.76.2037	C02037	oc	sk	hc	2	L	
C2.76.2037	C02037	Bos	Ulna		2	R	unknown
C2.69.2038	C02038	o/c	Tib	d	3	R	Mat
C2.69.2038	C02038	o/c	Phal	1	3	a	Mat

Registration	Locus	Spe	SP	Elem	Ph	Side	Age
C2.74.2038	C02038	o/c	Inn	a+is	3	R	imm
C2.82.2043	C02043	o/c	Scap		3	L	Mat
C2.79.2046	C02046	o/c	Inn	i+is	3	L	unknown
C2.79.2048	C02048	o/c	Max	M3	2	L	F
C2.79.2048	C02048	o/c	Mand	M1/M2	2	R	CD
C2.79.2048	C02048	o/c	Hum	d	2	R	Mat
C2.79.2048	C02048	o/c	Scap		2	R	Mat
C2.83.2051	C02051	o/c	Max	M3	2	R	E
C2.83.2051	C02051	o/c	Fem	d	2	L	Imm
C3.11.3003	C03003	Bos	Maxilla	M1/M2	2	L	
C3.42.3034	C03034	o/c	Scap		2	L	unknown
C3.42.3034	C03034	o/c	Rad	diaph	2	L	unknown
C3.42.3034	C03034	o/c	Mand		2	L	DE
C3.61.3016	C03016	o/c	Tibia	diaph	3	L/R	unknown
C3.62.3016	C03016	o/c	Metat	p	3	R	unknown
C3.46.3019	C03019	o/c	Inn	a+i+i	3	R	Mat
C3.48.3019	C03019	o/c	Scap		3	L	unknown
C3.48.3019	C03019	oc	Inn	il	3	R	unknown
C3.48.3019	C03019	o/c	Scap		3	L	Mat
C3.48.3019	C03019	o/c	Hum	d	3	R	Mat
C3.48.3019	C03019	Bos	Sk	Occupit	3		
C3.48.3019	C03019	Bos	Calc		3	R	unknown
C3.49.3021	C03021	o/c	Mand		3	R	I
C3.49.3021	C03021	o/c	sk	Occup	3		
C3.50.3022	C03022	o/c	Hum	p	3	R	Mat
C1.51.3023	C03023	o/c	Mand	Ant	3	R	
C3.51.3023	C03023	o/c	Mand	Condyle	3	L	
C3.51.3023	C03023	o/c	Mand	Cond	3	R	
C3.51.3023	C03023	o/c	Max	M1/M2	3	L	CD
C3.51.3023	C03023	o/c	Maxilla		3	R	DEF
C3.51.3023	C03023	o/c	Mand		3	R	DEF
C3.51.3023	C03023	o/c	Scap		3	R	Mat
C3.51.3023	C03023	o/c	Scap		3	R	unknown
C3.51.3023	C03023	o/c	Inn	a+p	3	R	unknown
C3.51.3023	C03023	o/c	Inn	a+is	3	R	I
C3.51.3023	C03023	o/c	Inn	a+is	3	L	Mat
C3.51.3023	C03023	o/c	Inn	a+il	3	L	unknown
C3.51.3023	C03023	o/c	Fem	p	3	L	Mat

REGISTRATION	LOCUS	SPE	SP	ELEM	PH	SIDE	AGE
C3.51.3023	C03023	o/c	Carp	uln	3	R	
C3.51.3023	C03023	oc	sk	occ cond	3	L	
C3.51.3023	C03023	oc	sk	occ cond	3	R	
C3.51.3023	C03023	o/c	Rad	d	3	L	Mat
C3.51.3023	C03023	o/c	Fem	d	3	L	Imm
C3.51.3023	C03023	Bos	Sk	Horn core	3	R	unknown
C3.51.3023	C03023	Bos	Fem	p	3	L	Mat
C3.51.3023	C03023	Bos	Metat	p	3	L/R	unknown
C3.51.3023	C03023	Bos	Carp	Nav cub	3	R	
C3.53.3023	C03023	o/c	Inn	isch	3	L	unknown
C3.52.3024	C03024	o/c	Scap		2	R	Mat
C3.52.3024	C03024	o/c	Hum	d	2	R	Mat
C3.52.3024	C03024	o/c	Hum	p	2	L	I
C3.52.3024	C03024	o/c	Rad	p	2	R	Mat
C3.52.3024	C03024	o/c	Mand		2	R	DE
C3.52.3024	C03024	Sus	Inn	Pub	2	L	Imm
C3.53.3025	C03025	o/c	Inn	a+il	2	R	unknown
C3.53.3025	C03025	o/c	Ulna	p	2	L	I
C3.53.3025	C03025	o/c	Ulna	p	2	R	unknown
C3.54.3027	C03027	o/c	Max	M1/M2	2	R	
C3.56.3028	C03028	o/c	Maxilla		2	L	C
C3.56.3028	C03028	o/c	Mand	M3	2	R	E
C3.56.3028	C03028	o/c	Rad	p	2	L	I
C3.56.3028	C03028	o/c	Ulna	p	2	L	unknown
C3.56.3028	C03028	Bos	Scap		2	L/R	unknown
C3.63.3032	C03032	o/c	Tibia	diaph	2	L/R	unknown
C5.17.5010	C05010	o/c	Metat	p	3	L	unknown
C5.21.5012	C05012	o/c	Astrag		3	L	
C5.21.5012	C05012	o/c	Calc		3	R	Mat
C5.16.5014	C05014	o/c	Vert	Cerv	2		Mat
C6.50.6010	C06010	o/c	Tibia	diaph	3	L/R	unknown
C6.31.6012	C06012	o/c	Maxilla	M1/M2	2	L	CDE
C6.31.6012	C06012	o/c	Inn	a+Il	2	R	unknown
C6.35.6015	C06015	o/c	Fem	p	2	R	Imm
C6.30.6016	C06016	Capra	Phalange	1	2	b	Mat
C6.30.6016	C06016	o/c	Phalange	1	2	b	Mat
C6.30.6016	C06016	o/c	Metap	d1/2	2	L/R	Mat
C6.36.6016	C06016	o/c	Rad	proximal	2	R	Mat

Registration	Locus	Spe	SP	Elem	Ph	Side	Age
C6.38.6016	C06016	Capra	Astrag		2	R	
C6.38.6016	C06016	o/c	Calc		2	R	Mat
C6.38.6016	C06016	o/c	Ulna	proximal	2	L	Imm
C6.38.6016	C06016	o/c	Astrag		2	R	
C6.38.6016	C06016	o/c	Calc		2	R	Mat
C6.39.6016	C06016	o/c	Tibia	d	2	R	Mat
C6.43.6016	C06016	o/c	Mand	Cond	2	R	
C6.44.6016	C06016	Bos	Innom	II	2	R	Imm
C9.39.6016	C06016	o/c	Tibia	distal	2	R	Mat
C6.35.6018	C06018	o/c	Ulna	proximal	2	L/R	unknown
C6.40.6018	C06018	o/c	Phalange	1	2	b	Mat
C6.40.6018	C06018	o/c	Mand	c+c	2	L	
C6.40.6018	C06018	o/c	Metac	compl	2	L	Imm
C6.40.6018	C06018	o/c	Mand		2	R	GHI
C6.45.6018	C06018	o/c	Tibia	diaph	2	R	unknown
C6.20.6019	C06019	o/c	Maxilla	dp3	2	L	
C6.35.6019	C06019	o/c	Mand		2	R	DEF
C6.35.6019	C06019	o/c	Ulna	proximal	2	L	Imm
C6.35.6019	C06019	o/c	Maxilla	M3	2	L	F
C6.35.6019	C06019	o/c	Mand	Cond	2	R	
C6.35.6019	C06019	o/c	Hum	distal	2	L	Mat
C6.35.6019	C06019	o/c	Maxilla		2	R	
C6.35.6019	C06019	Capra	Hum	distal	2	L	Mat
C6.35.6019	C06019	o/c	Mand	Incisor	2	L	
C6.35.6019	C06019	o/c	Ulna	p	2	L	I
C6.37.6019	C06019	o/c	Hum	distal	2	R	Imm
C6.51.6019	C06019	o/c	Mand		2	L	EFG
C6.36.6021	C06021	o/c	Metat	d.diaph	3	R	unknown
C6.36.6021	C06021	o/c	Hum	distal	3	L	Mat
C6.36.6021	C06021	o/c	Metat	p	3	R	unknown
C6.52.6028	C06028	o/c	Scap		3	L	
C6.52.6028	C06028	o/c	Inn	a+p	3	L	unknown
C6.52.6028	C06028	o/c	Tibia	p	3	R	Mat
C6.55.6029	C06029	o/c	Tibia	diaph	1	L/R	unknown
C6.56.6029	C06029	o/c	Max	M1/M2	1	L	CD
C6.56.6029	C06029	o/c	Max	P3/P4	1	L	
C6.56.6029	C06029	o/c	sk	hc	1	R	
C2.57.6030	C06030	Sus			1	L	

Registration	Locus	Spe	SP	Elem	Ph	Side	Age
C6.53.6030	C06030	o/c	Rad	p	1	R	Imm
C6.53.6030	C06030	o/c	Metac	p	1	L	unknown
C6.53.6030	C06030	Bos	Metat	P	1	L	unknown
C6.57.6030	C06030	o/c	Phalange	1	1	a	Mat
C6.57.6030	C06030	o/c	Max	dp4	1	R	
C6.57.6030	C06030	o/c	Rad	p	1	L	Mat
C6.57.6030	C06030	o/c	Inn	a+il	1	L	Imm
C6.57.6030	C06030	o/c	Fem	d	1	R	Imm
C6.57.6030	C06030	o/c	Fem	p	1	L	Mat
C6.57.6030	C06030	o/c	Fem	p	1	R	I
C6.57.6030	C06030	o/c	Phalange	1	1	B	Mat
C6.57.6030	C06030	o/c	Phalange	1	1	b	Mat
C6.54.6031	C06031	o/c	Astrag		2	R	
C6.54.6031	C06031	o/c	Astrag		2	R	
C6.58.6032	C06032	o/c	Tibia	d	1	L	Imm
C6.58.6032	C06032	o/c	Tars	Os C	1	R	
C6.64.6032	C06032	o/c	Fem	d	1	R	Imm
C6.64.6032	C06032	o/c	Metac	p	1	L	unknown
C6.62.6035	C06035	o/c	Max	P2	1	L	
C6.57.6037	C06037	o/c	Mand	M1/M2	1	L	
C6.63.6038	C06038	o/c	Fem	d	1	R	Imm
C6.63.6038	C06038	o/c	Carp	rad	1	R	
C6.63.6038	C06038	o/c	Phalange	1	1	A	Mat
C1.21.7015	C07015	oc	sk	malar	3	L	
C7.16.7015	C07015	Ovis	Hum	distal	3	R	Mat
C7.18.7017	C07015	o/c	Tibia	d	3	L	Imm
C7.19.7015	C07015	o/c	Scap		3	R	unknown
C7.21.7015	C07015	o/c	Calc		3	L	Mat
C7.21.7015	C07015	o/c	Scap		3	R	Mat
C7.21.7015	C07015	o/c	Scap		3	L	Mat
C7.21.7015	C07015	o/c	Hum	d	3	R	Mat
C7.21.7015	C07015	o/c	Astr		3	L	
C7.21.7015	C07015	o/c	Calc		3	R	Mat
C7.21.7015	C07015	o/c	Rad	d	3	R	Imm
C7.21.7015	C07015	o/c	Inn	il	3	L	unknown
C7.21.7015	C07015	Sus	Scap		3	L/R	unknown
C7.25.7015	C07015	o/c	Scap		3	L	unknown
C7.26.7015	C07015	o/c	Vert	Atlas	3		

Registration	Locus	Spe	SP	Elem	Ph	Side	Age
C7.26.7015	C07015	o/c	Tibia	d	3	R	Mat
C7.26.7015	C07015	Bos	Sk	Occ Con	3	R	unknown
C7.26.7015	C07015	Bos	Sk	Occ Con	3	L	unknown
C7.7015	C07015	o/c	Mand		3	L	E
C7.7015	C07015	o/c	Mand		3	L	C
C7.7015	C07015	o/c	Tibia	d	3	R	Imm
C7.7015	C07015	o/c	Sk	occ cond	3	R	
C7.7015	C07015	o/c	Sk	occ cond	3	L	
C7.7015	C07015	o/c	Sk	occ cond	3	L	
C7.7015	C07015	o/c	Max	M3	3	R	F
C7.7015	C07015	o/c	Scap		3	L	Mat
C7.7015	C07015	o/c	Hum	d	3	L	Mat
C7.7015	C07015	o/c	Inn	a+p	3	L	unknown
C7.7015	C07015	o/c	Inn	a+i+i	3	L	Mat
C7.7015	C07015	o/c	Inn	a+il	3	L	unknown
C7.18.7017	C07017	o/c	Astrag		3	L	
C7.30.7020	C07020	o/c	Max	M1/M2	3	L	DEFG
C7.31.7020	C07020	o/c	Rad	p	3	L	Mat
C7.31.7020	C07020	o/c	Fem	d	3	R	Imm
C7.31.7020	C07020	o/c	Tibia	d	3	R	Imm
C8.18.8003	C08003	o/c	Metac	p	3	L	unknown
C8.18.8003	C08003	o/c	Scap		3	L	Imm
C8.18.8003	C08003	o/c	Hum	d	3	R	Mat
C2.10.8005	C08005	Eq	Phal	2	3	a/b	
C8.10.8005	C08005	o/c	Calc		3	L	Mat
C8.12.8008	C08008	o/c	Scap	prox	3	R	unknown
C8.12.8008	C08008	o/c	Mand	Coronoid	3	L/R	
C8.13.8008	C08008	o/c	Mand	M1/M2	3	R	
C8.13.8008	C08008	o/c	Mand	Condyle	3	L	
C8.13.8008	C08008	o/c	Calc		3	L	unknown
C8.13.8008	C08008	o/c	Calc		3	L	unknown
C8.10.8009	C08009	o/c	Maxilla		3	L	
C8.10.8009	C08009	o/c	Calc		3	L	Imm
C8.11.8009	C08009	Columba	Ulna		3	R	
C8.11.8009	C08009	Capra	Phalange	1	3	b	Mat
C8.11.8009	C08009	o/c	Phalange	1	3	b	Mat
C8.16.8009	C08009	o/c	Mand	Cond	3	R	
C8.16.8009	C08009	o/c	sk	hc	3	L	

REGISTRATION	LOCUS	SPE	SP	ELEM	PH	SIDE	AGE
C8.17.8009	C08009	o/c	Max	M1/M2	3	R	DEFG
C10.6.10006	C10006	o/c	Maxilla	M3	2	R	
C10.6.10006	C10006	o/c	Mand	M3	2	L	G
C11.7.11006	C11006	o/c	Mand	M1/M2	2	L	

Appendix D

Basic Form Classifications
for Area C and the Cemeteries

TELL FORMS

Code	Description	#
3010	holemouth jar: L (21+) (EB III)	1
3110	necked jar: pithoi (30–22) general, diameter only (EB III)	2
3749	bowl: S (11–6) neutral to open	1
4000	holemouth jar: unclassified	2
4010	holemouth jar: L (21+)	1
4010C	holemouth jar cooking pot: L (21+)	4
4020	holemouth jar: M (20–14)	7
4020C	holemouth jar cooking pot: M (20–14)	30
4030	holemouth jar: S (13–10)	1
4030C	holemouth jar cooking pot: S (13–10)	2
4040	holemouth bowl: L (28+)	1
4040C	holemouth bowl cooking pot: L (28+)	2
4046	holemouth bowl: M (24–20)	1
4050	holemouth bowl: M S (18–12)	3
4050C	holemouth bowl cooking pot: M S (18–12)	1
4060	teapot: L (15+)	11

CODE	DESCRIPTION	#
4067	teapot: M (14–10)	17
4072	teapot: S (9–)	3
4080	holemouth bowl: deep basin	14
4114	necked jar: pithoi (30–22) tall neck, curved out (everted)	2
4119	necked jar: pithoi (30–22) short neck, curved out (flared)	2
4119C	necked jar cooking pot: pithoi (30–22) short neck, curved out (flared)	3
4120	necked jar: L (21–16) general, diameter only	2
4122	necked jar: L (21–16) tall neck, corner point, angled out	2
4124	necked jar: L (21–16) tall neck, corner point (everted)	5
4129C	necked jar cooking pot: L (21–16) short neck, corner point, curved out (everted)	2
4139C	necked jar cooking pot: L (21–16) short neck, inflected, curved out	8
4140	necked jar: M/L (15–12) general, diameter only	2
4149	necked jar: M/L (15–12) tall neck, corner point, curved out (everted)	3
4175C	necked jar cooking pot: M/L (15–11) short neck, corner point, curved out (everted)	1
4221	necked jar: M/S (12–9) tall, wide neck, corner point, cylindrical neck	4
4224	necked jar: M/S (12–9) tall, wide neck, corner point, curved out (everted)	8
4232	necked jar: M/S (12–9) tall, wide neck, inflected curve	1
4260	necked jar: S (8–7) general, diameter only	1
4261	necked jar: S (8–7) tall neck, corner point, cylindrical	1
4264	necked jar: S (8–7) tall neck, corner point (everted)	3
4272	necked jar: S (8–7) tall neck, inflected point, curved out	1
4281	necked jar: S (8–7) short, wide neck	1
4400	wide mouth pitcher/juglet: L, tall neck	1
4420	wide mouth pitcher/juglet: M/L, tall neck	1
4422	wide mouth pitcher/juglet: M/L, tall, cylindrical neck, inflected point	4
4500	deep bowl: L (32+) lightly closed	4
4510	deep bowl: M/L (31–22) lightly closed	5
4520	deep bowl: L (32+) lightly curved, neutral to open	10
4530	deep bowl: M/L (31–22) lightly curved, neutral to open	6
4546	deep bowl: M/L (31–22) angled to splaying walls	1
4560	deep bowl: M (21–17) lightly closed	2
4570	deep bowl: M (21–17) lightly curved, neutral to open	7
4600	platter bowl: VL, wide (40+) shallow, flat base	14

CODE	DESCRIPTION	#
4620	platter bowl: L (39–30) shallow, flat base	88
4660	platter bowl: M (29–17) shallow, flat base	43
4700	bowl: M/S (16–6) deep cut lightly closed	2
4710	bowl: M/S (16–6) deep cut neutral to open	2
4730	bowl: M/S (18–10) medium depth carinated walls	5
4740	bowl: M/S (18–10) medium depth neutral to open	1
4756	bowl: S (11–6) lightly closed	3
4760	bowl: S (11–6) medium depth carinated walls	4
4770	bowl: S (11–6) neutral to open	5
4855	lamp: S (16–) lamp, flat base	1

TOMB FORMS

CODE	VESSEL	WIDTH	HEIGHT	SIZE	B/M	H/M	DESCRIPTION	KI	BED
4020	Holemouth jar			M				1	
4020C	Holemouth bowl cooking pot			M				2	
4036	Spouted vessel	21+		L	1.00+		mid to low tangent (added)	4	
4066	Spouted vessel	20–15		M	1.00+		mid to low tangent	10	8
4071	Spouted vessel	14–11		M/S	0.60–0.99		mid to low tangent (interpolated)	3	
4140	Necked jar		21+	M/L 1800+			tall, wide neck, corner point, General	2	
4141	Necked jar		21+	M/L 1800+			tall, wide neck, corner point, wide, flat base, mid–range tangent, global to rounded	3	
4142	Necked jar		21+	M/L 1800+			tall, wide neck, corner point, wide, flat base, low tangent, ovaloid (interpolated)	5	
4211	Necked jar		15–20	M 1799–712			short, wide neck, corner point, wide, flat base, squat, low tangent – added	1	
4220	Necked jar		15–20	M 1799–712			tall, wide neck, corner point, General	12	
4221	Necked jar		15–20	M 1799–712			tall, wide neck, corner point, wide, flat base, mid–range tangent, global to rounded	1	
4222	Necked jar		15–20	M 1799–712			tall, wide neck, corner point, wide, flat base, low tangent, ovaloid	11	1

CODE	VESSEL	WIDTH	HEIGHT	SIZE	B/M	H/M	DESCRIPTION	KI	BeD
4740	M–S bowl	16–12		M/S		0.35+	open, curved walls, General, EB III: w. 16–9	1	1
4749	M–S bowl	16–12		M/S	0.27–0.43	0.44–0.35	open, curved walls, EB III: w. 16–9	1	
4762	M–S bowl	11–7		S	0.44+	0.67+	carinated walls (added)	6	
4764	M–S bowl	11–7		S	0.44+	0.66–0.56	carinated walls (added)	1	
4765	M–S bowl	11–7		S	0.44+	0.55–0.45	carinated walls (added)	2	
4766	M–S bowl	11–7		S	0.44+	0.66–0.56	closed, curved walls	1	1
4850	Lamp	–16		S		0.34–	lamp forms, General	3	
4851	Lamp	–16		S		0.34–	lamp forms, round base	1	
4856	Lamp	–16		S	0.27–0.43	0.34–	lamp forms, flat base (interpolated)	7	
4857	Lamp	–16		S	0.44+	0.34–	lamp forms, flat base	15	1
4960	Funnel							1	

Appendix E

Basic Rim / Handle / Base Classifications
for Area C and the Cemeteries

RIM FORMS

Code	Description	Tell	Tombs
10	simple-direct: squared	25	11
11	simple-direct: rounded	39	30
12	simple-direct: tapered	12	22
13	simple-direct: beveled, inside	11	3
14	simple-direct: beveled, outside		1
17	simple-direct: interior lip	14	
18	simple-direct: bulbous	2	1
18a	simple-direct: folded, thickened -- beveled	2	
18b	simple-direct: folded, thickened -- slanted sharply down and in	1	
18d	simple-direct: folded, thickened -- rounded bulbous	11	
19	simple-direct: thinned, with exterior groove	2	2
31	inverted: rounded, same thickness	1	
32	inverted: tapered, same thickness	2	
33	inverted: triangular, short	1	
41	everted/angled: slight angle, rounded	13	8
42	everted/angled: slight angle, tapered	9	6
45	everted/angled: sharp angle, tapered	1	
51	curved-in or upright: rounded	1	
52	curved-in or upright: tapered	1	
60	curved-out: lightly flared, squared	9	8
61	curved-out: lightly flared, rounded	21	23

Appendix F

List of Registered Objects
from Area C and the Cemeteries

Custodian (Cu): Gannon University (GU); Department of Antiquities, Jordan (AN)

AREA C

REG	LOCUS	BUCKET	PHASE	MATERIAL	DESCRIPTION	FLINT#	CU	REF
A017	C02002	C02.02	4	flint	frags.	3	GU	
A019	C01000	C01.01	Srfc.	limestone	pierced stone (Type A); L: 17.1, W: 11.9; T: 8.1 cm		GU	fig. 8.17
A021	C02000	C02.01	Misc.	flint	retouched flake	11	GU	
A023	C02002	C02.02	4	glass	discard		DR	
A026	C01000	C01.01	Srfc.	flint	retouched flakes, probable borer or perforator	2	GU	
A034	C02002	C02.06	4	ceramic	frag. spindle whorl; Dia. 2.1, T: 1 cm		GU	fig. 8.25
A043	C02004	C02.11	4	flint	triangular blade; L: 6, W: 3, T: 0.75 cm		AN	
A044	C02004	C02.11	4	flint	frag.	1	GU	
A045	C01015	C01.18	3	flint	Canaanean sickle blade; L: 64, W: 29, T: 7 mm.	1	GU	
A047	C02007	C02.10	4	flint	worked frag	1	GU	
A048	C02007	C02.10	4	flint	worked frag	1	GU	
A058	C01000	C01.01	Srfc.	flint	worked flake	1	GU	
A064	C02002	C02.02	4	flint	retouched blade 51 x 22 x 7 mm	1	GU	
A065	C02002	C02.02	4	flint	retouched flake	1	GU	
A066	C02002	C02.02	4	flint	worked flake	1	GU	
A075	C02020	C02.22	Misc.	stone	pierced stone (Type C); L: 5.2, W: 4.8 cm		GU	fig. 8.20

REG	LOCUS	BUCKET	PHASE	MATERIAL	DESCRIPTION	FLINT#	CU	REF
A076	C02017	C02.18	Misc.	flint	hammerstone/pounder; Dia. 6.0 cm	1	GU	fig. 8.7
A077	C02017	C02.18	Misc.	flint	hammerstone/pounder; Dia. 6.3–6.8 cm.	1	GU	fig. 8.7
A081	C023002	C03.04	4	ceramic	frag. spindle whorl; Dia. 2.3, T: 1.1 cm		GU	fig. 8.7
A083	C02018	C02.23	3	flint	frag. hammerstone/pounder		AN	
A139	C02029a	C02.38	3	lithic	frag. L: 3, W: 5, T: 1 cm	1	GU	
A140	C05000	C05.03	Misc.	ceramic	leg of bowl; L: 7.4, W: 4.1, T: 3 cm		AN	fig. 8.28
A143	C05003	C05.05	4	glass	beads from late Bedouin burial; Dia: 0.2–0.5 cm		AN	fig. 8.32
A144	C05003	C05.05	4	glass	frag. bead from late Bedouin burial		GU	
A145	C05006	C05.07	Misc.	glass	bead from late Bedouin burial; Dia. 0.2–0.5 cm		GU	fig. 8.33
A148	C02030	C02.43	2	limestone	spindle whorl. L: Dia. 3.4, T: 0.8 cm		GU	fig. 8.23
A149	C05008	C05.11	4	flint	blade with ventral retouch; L: 8, W: 2, T: 1 cm	1	AN	
A154	C03009	C03.19	4	flint	flake. L: 5.5, W: 3.5, T: 3 cm		GU	
A155	C02033	C02.49	3	flint	frags. bladel L: 3 &1, W: 2.5 & 0.7 cm	2	GU	
A156	Cxxxxx	xxx.xx		limestone	frag. macehead; L: 5.5, W: 3, T: 3 cm		AN	fig. 8.21
A162	C06002	C06.11	4	flint	lithic		GU	
A163	C04000	C04.01	Misc.	flint	frag. blade. L: 4.5, W: 3, T: 1.5 cm	1	AN	
A164	C03002	C03.03	4	flint	frag. L: 3, W: 2, T: 1 cm	1	AN	
A165	C05000	C05.01	Misc.	flint	frag.	1	GU	
A166	C03000	C03.01	Misc.	flint	frag. L: 3, W: 2.5, T: 1 cm	1	AN	
A170	C03002	C03.03	4	sandstone	flake. L: 11, W: 8 cm		GU	
A172	C04000	C04.02	Misc.	flint	1/2 nodule; slingstone? L: 34, W: 6.5 cm	1	AN	
A176	C03010	C03.26	4	limestone	frag. worked?		GU	
A177	C06002	C06.16	4	flint	frag. hammerstone/pounder; Dia: 6.2–7.1 cm	1	AN	fig. 8.8
A182	C04000	C04.03	Misc.	flint	frag. with bulb of percussion; L: 6, W: 3.5 cm	1	AN	
A189	C06000	C06.01	Misc.	flint	frag. retouched blade; L: 2, W: 2.5, T: 1 cm	1	AN	
A190	C03007	C03.34	4	ceramic	burnishing tool; L: 2.4, W: 2.1, T: 1.1 cm		GU	
A197	C06002	C06.08	4	limestone	mortar; L: 5.6, W: 3.6, T: 3.1 cm		GU	fig. 8.12
A201	C03010	C03.26	4	sedimentary	worked object?		GU	

REG	LOCUS	BUCKET	PHASE	MATERIAL	DESCRIPTION	FLINT#	CU	REF
A206	C08002	C08.02	3	metal	frag. (copper?) pin; L: 2.6, Dia. 0.4 cm		GU	fig. 8.30
A284	C02035	C02.58	Misc.	flint	frag. blade. L: 6.8, W: 5.1, T: 2 cm	1	AN	
A289	C02035	C02.60	Misc.	limestone	spindle whorl; Dia. 3, T: 1.3 cm		GU	fig. 8.24
A290	C01029	C01.32	Misc.	flint	flakes debitage	2	AN	
A291	C01029	C01.33	Misc.	flint	flakes debitage	3	AN	
A292	C07000	C07.02	Misc.	flint	flakes debitage	2	AN	
A293	C06016	C06.30	2	flint	flakes debitage	104	AN	
A295	C06016	C06.32	2	flint	flakes debitage	3	AN	
A299	C01031	C01.34	3	flint	flakes debitage	10	AN	
A301	C06017	C06.33	2	flint	flakes worked	2	AN	
A302	C06012	C06.31	2	flint	flakes debitage	64	AN	
A305	C06016	C06.38	2	flint	frag. hammerstone/pounder; Dia. 7.3 cm	1	AN	fig. 8.9
A306	C06016	C06.38	2	flint	handstone, discoidal (Type B); L: 6.6, W: 4.9, T: 4.9 cm		AN	fig. 8.5
A307	C06016	C06.38	2	ceramic	oval lid; L: 11.1, W: 9.9, T: 1.5 cm		AN	fig. 8.29
A311	C06019	C06.35	2	limestone	pierced stone (Type B); Dia. 11.6, T: 3.8 cm		AN	
A312	C06019	C06.35	2	flint	flakes debitage	12	GU	
A315	C06012	C06.34	2	flint	flakes debitage	12	AN	
A317	C06016	C06.38	2	flint	flakes debitage	38	AN	
A318	C06019	C06.37	2	flint	flakes debitage	29	GU	
A319	C01029	C01.35	Misc.	flint	flakes debitage	26	AN	
A321	C06019	C06.35	2	flint	flakes debitage	5	AN	
A326	C07006	C07.08	4	flint	flakes debitage	7	GU	
A327	C01029	C01.36	Misc.	flint	worked flakes	6	AN	
A329	C07006	C07.08	4	basalt	frag. mortar; L: 12.8, W: 7.1, T: 4.8 cm		AN	fig. 8.13
A331	C08000	C08.07	Misc.	basalt	frag. pierced stone (Type B); Dia. 7.6, T: 4.3 cm		AN	fig. 8.19
A332	C02011	C02.67	4	flint	flakes debitage	34	AN	
A333	C06016	C06.39	2	flint	flakes debitage	5	AN	
A334	C06018	C06.40	2	flint	flakes debitage	4	AN	
A337	C06018	C06.40	2	basalt	handstone (Type C); L: 2.2, W: 4.5, Dia. 4.5 cm		GU	

Reg	Locus	Bucket	Phase	Material	Description	Flint#	Cu	Ref
A339	C07006	C07.10	4	basalt	frag. pierced stone (Type A); L: 10.8, W: 8.1, T: 5 cm		AN	fig. 8.18
A342	C07015	C07.16	3	flint	flakes debitage	8	GU	
A343	C08008	C08.08	3	flint	flakes debitage	25	AN	
A344	C06024	C06.41	2	flint	flakes	1	GU	
A346	C06016	C06.44	2	flint	flakes debitage	3	AN	
A347	C06019	C06.46	2	flint	flakes debitage	2	AN	
A350	C06027	C06.47	3	basalt	handstone, discoidal (Type B); L: 8.9, W: 7.2, T: 5.4 cm		GU	fig. 8.6
A351	C06027	C06.47	3	basalt	hammerstone/pounder? L: 8.5, W: 4.2, T: 4.5 cm		AN	
A353	C05014	C05.21	2	flint	flakes, one a partial worked blade 9.5 cm long.	2	AN	
A357	C07015	C07.19	3	flint	flakes debitage	36	AN	
A358	C01032	C01.37	Misc.	flint	flakes debitage	2	AN	
A359	C08005a	C08.10	3	flint	flakes debitage	21	AN	
A360	C06027	C06.49	3	basalt	pestle; L: 7, Dia. 4.4 cm		AN	fig. 8.15
A361	C07015	C07.19	3	basalt	frag. handstone (Type A); L: 13.7, W: 11.9, T: 3 cm		AN	fig. 8.4
A367	C08009	C08.11	3	basalt	frag. grinding slab; L: 13, W: 10.5, T: 4 cm		AN	fig. 8.3
A368	C02036	C02.62	Misc.	flint	flakes debitage	4	AN	
A369	C06018	C06.50	2	flint	flakes debitage	8	AN	
A371	C08008	C08.12	3	flint	flakes debitage	156	AN	
A372	C07006	C07.15	4	flint	flake. L: 6, W: 4.2, T: 2 cm	1	AN	
A373	C08009	C08.11	3	flint	flakes debitage	38	AN	
A374	C06019	C06.51	2	flint	flakes debitage	6	AN	
A377	C07015	C07.21	3	flint	flakes debitage	2	GU	
A378	C07015	C07.21	3	flint	frag. handstone/pounder; Dia. 7.6 cm		AN	fig. 8.10
A379	C07015	C07.25	3	flint	disc. L: 4.8, W: 9.7, T: 1.7 cm	1	AN	
A386	C06031	C06.54	2	flint	flakes debitage	15	AN	
A387	C06029	C06.52	1	flint	flakes debitage	7	AN	
A388	C06029	C06.55	1	flint	flakes debitage	8	GU	
A389	C06030	C06.53	1	flint	flakes debitage	28	AN	
A390	C08008	C08.13	3	flint	flakes debitage	68	AN	

Reg	Locus	Bucket	Phase	Material	Description	Flint#	Cu	Ref
A391	C08011	C08.14	3	flint	flakes debitage	25	AN	
A392	C08009	C08.15	3	flint	flakes debitage	42	AN	
A393	C02037	C02.65	2	flint	flakes debitage	14	AN	
A394	C02036	C02.64	Misc.	flint	flakes debitage	11	AN	
A395	C06024	C06.41	2	flint	flakes debitage	46	AN	
A397	C08009	C08.16	3	flint	flakes debitage	111	AN	
A398	C06030	C06.57	1	flint	flakes debitage	12	AN	
A399	C06029	C06.56	1	flint	flakes debitage	13	AN	
A400	C07021	C07.27	Misc.	basalt	grooved stone grinding slab; L: 9.8, W: 7.9, T: 7.5 cm		AN	fig. 8.16
A404	C06031	C06.54	2	carnelian	lotus-shaped pendant; L: 1.5, W: 0.5 cm		GU	fig. 8.22
A405	C07009	C07.07	4	metal	lump of slag; L: 1.7, W: 1.2 cm		GU	fig. 8.31
A410	C08003	C08.18	3	flint	flakes debitage	14	AN	
A411	C08009	C08.17	3	flint	flakes debitage	70	AN	
A412	C06032	C06.58	1	flint	flakes debitage	4	AN	
A414	C02038	C02.69	3	flint	flakes debitage	23	AN	
A416	C02038	C02.68	3	flint	flake	1	AN	
A424	C06036	C06.61	2	ceramic	frag. spindle whorl; Dia. 4.3, T: 1.4 cm		GU	fig. 8.27
A425	C08003	C08.18	3	flint	frag. hammerstone. L: 3.6, W: 7.6, Dia. 7.3 cm		GU	
A426	C08003	C08.18	3	flint	frag. hammerstone/pounder; Dia. 6.6-6.8 cm		AN	fig. 8.11
A431	C05011	C05.72	3	flint	flakes debitage	21	AN	
A432	C03023	C03.51	3	flint	flakes debitage	5	AN	
A433	C02038	C02.71	3	flint	flakes debitage	5	AN	
A434	C06038	C06.63	1	flint	flakes debitage	10	AN	
A435	C02038	C02.74	3	flint	flakes debitage	8	AN	
A437	C03020	C03.47	Misc.	flint	flake	1	AN	
A442	C09000	C09.04	Misc.	basalt	frag. hammerstone/pounder? L: 15, W: 10.6, T: 8.2 cm		AN	
A443	C10000	C10.01	Misc.	limestone	mortar; L: 24.6, W: 13.3, T: 7.7 cm		AN	fig. 8.14
A450	C10006	C10.06	2	flint	flakes debitage	2	AN	
A455	C02047	C02.78	3	flint	flakes debitage	4	AN	
A456	C06032	C06.64	1	flint	flakes debitage	10	AN	

REG	LOCUS	BUCKET	PHASE	MATERIAL	DESCRIPTION	FLINT#	CU	REF
A457	C02011	C02.73	4	flint	flakes debitage	13	AN	
A458	C02037	C02.76	2	flint	flake	1	AN	
A460	C01036	C01.41	2	limestone	unfinished hammerstone/pounder? L: 14, W: 11.5, T: 5.9 cm		AN	
A463	C02047	C02.80	3	flint	flakes debitage	9	AN	
A472	C02051	C02.83	2	flint	flakes debitage	6	AN	
A715	C08014	C08.022	Misc.	stone	gaming piece? L: 1.5, W: 1.5, T: 0.5 cm		GU	
A769	C08016	C08.062	3	ceramic	half spindle whorl?		GU	
A808	C08015	C08.057	3	flint	flakes debitage	4	GU	
A810	C08026	C08.049	Misc.	flint	flakes debitage	2	GU	
A812	C08025	C08.048	Misc.	flint	flakes debitage	3	GU	
A815	C08026	C08.054	Misc.	flint	flakes debitage	1	GU	
A816	C08014	C08.058	Misc.	flint	flakes debitage	16	GU	
A826	C08014	C08.056	Misc.	flint	flakes debitage	23	GU	
A828	C08014	C08.055	Misc.	flint	flakes debitage	33	GU	
A834	C08016	C08.067	3	flint	flakes debitage	1	GU	
A853	C08038	C08.106	Prev.	basalt	grinding slab		GU	

TOMBS

REG	LOCUS	BUCKET	MATERIAL	DESCRIPTION	CU	REF
A137	D01001	D01.01	basalt	frag. grinding slab; L: 10, W: 8, T: 3 cm.	AN	fig. 13.3
A270	D02010	D02.10	metal	frag. (copper?) pin shaft; L: 2.5 cm.	AN	fig. 13.11
A268	D02013	D02.19	metal	(copper?) dagger with four of six rivets left; L: 17, W: 4 cm.	AN	figs. 13.8–9
A269	D02013	D02.24	metal	frag. (copper?) pin shaft; L: 5, W: 1 cm.	AN	fig. 13.10
A271	D02014	D02.14	metal	frag. (copper?) pin shaft; L: 2 cm.	AN	fig. 13.12
A285	D03001	D03.01	flint	frag. blade, one ridge, bulb of percussion; L: 4, W: 2.5 cm.	AN	fig. 13.7
A272	D03018	D03.23	metal	frag. (copper?) pin shaft; L: 1.3 cm.	AN	fig. 13.13
A273A	D04.02	D04.02, near entrance	metal	frag. (copper?) pin shaft; L: 2.5, W: 0.25 cm.	AN	
A273	D04002	D04.02	metal	frag. (copper?) pin shaft; L: 2.3 cm.	AN	fig. 13.14
A286	D07001	D07.01	bone/shell	cylinder spacer bead; L: 4.5, W: 1, T: 0.75 cm.	GU	
A328	D09006	D09.09	flint	probable pendant; L: 2, W: 1.5, T: 0.5 cm	AN	fig. 13.24

Reg	Locus	Bucket	Material	Description	Cu	Ref
A355	D09007	D09.24	carnelian	short cylinder bead; L: 0.5, D: 0.5 cm	GU	figs. 13.15; 13.19
A354	D10001	D10.01	carnelian	cylinder disc bead; L: 0.2, D: 0.5 cm	GU	fig. 13.18
A401	D10003	D10.02	stone	long cylinder bead; L: 2.3, Dia: 0.7 cm.	GU	fig. 13.16
A402	D10003	D10.02	stone	black short cylinder bead; L: 0.9, Dia: 0.7 cm.	GU	fig. 13.23
A403	D10003	D10.04	stone	frags. short cylinder bead; L: 0.75, Dia: 1.0 cm.	GU	
A407	D10003	D10.07	stone	long barrel bead; L: 0.9, Dia: 0.5 cm.	GU	fig. 13.17
A408	D10003	D10.07	carnelian	short cylinder bead; L: 0.2, Dia: 0.4 cm.	GU	fig. 13.20
A409	D10003	D10.07	carnelian	short barrel bead; L: 0.5, Dis: 0.5 cm.	GU	fig. 13.21
A175	E01001	E01.01	flint	frag. blade; L: 2.5, W: 1 cm.	GU	fig. 13.5
A171	E03003	E03.04	flint	frags.	GU	
A178	E03003	E03.01	flint	frag.	GU	
A185	E03005	E03.01	flint	frag. blade, bulb of percussion; L: 2.5, W: 1.5 cm.	AN	fig. 13.6
A205A	E09002	E09.01	flint	frag. blade, trapezoidal; L: 6, W: 2.5, T: 1 cm.	AN	
A247	E09007	E09.05	basalt	frag. handstone; L: 11, W: 10, T: 5.5 cm.	AN	
A246	E09008	E09.10	metal	frag. (copper?) pin shaft; L: 2.2, W: 3 cm.	GU	
A445	E09XXX	EX	bone	frag. needle; L: 4.5, W: 0.07, T: 0.5 cm.	GU	fig. 13.26
A406	E10004	E10.03	limestone	frag. handstone; L: 11, W: 9.9, T: 7.5 cm.	AN	fig. 13.4
A294	H03004	H03.03	shell	probable pendant; L: 28, D: 2.5, W: 0.6 cm.	GU	fig. 13.25
A366a	J01001	J01.01	stone	black pendant bead; L: 1.4, W: 0.3-0.8 cm.	GU	fig. 13.22
A366b	J01001	J01.01	stone	black pendant bead; L: 1.2, W: 0.3-0.8 cm.	GU	fig. 13.22

ID	ELEMENT	SIDE	SEGMENT	COMPLETE-NESS	MNI	COUNT	AGE	COMMENTS
KI.87.D9.11.1	Scrap	Unknown	Scrap	Fragment	1	37	Adult	
KI.87.D9.11.10	Humerus	Unknown	Shaft	Fragment	1	1	Adult	
KI.87.D9.11.11	Os Coxa	Unknown	Unknown	Fragment	1	1	Adult	
KI.87.D9.11.12	Talus	Unknown		Fragment	1	1	Adult	Side UD.
KI.87.D9.11.2	Rib	Unknown	Shaft	Fragment	1	1	Adult	
KI.87.D9.11.3	Cranial Fragment	Unknown	Vault	Fragment	1	1	Adult	
KI.87.D9.11.4	Metacarpal	Unknown	Shaft	Fragment	1	1	Adult	Possible MC4 or MC5
KI.87.D9.11.5	Long Bone	Unknown	Shaft	Fragment	1	2	Adult	
KI.87.D9.11.6	Non-human	Unknown			1	1	Adult	Non-human rib fragment, SM?
KI.87.D9.11.7	Long Bone	Unknown	Shaft	Fragment	1	29	Adult	
KI.87.D9.11.8	Femur	Unknown	Shaft	Fragment	1	6	Adult	All mend together.
KI.87.D9.11.9	Tibia	Unknown	Shaft	Fragment	1	2	Adult	Mend with each other.
KI.87.D9.8.1	Radius	Unknown	Shaft	Fragment	1	1	Adult	
KI.87.D9.8.2	Tibia	Unknown	Shaft	Fragment	1	1	Adult	
KI.87.D9.8.3	Scrap	Unknown	Scrap	Fragment	1	9	Adult	All chunks cancellous bone
KI.87.D9.8.4	Scrap	Unknown	Scrap	Fragment	1	2	Adult	Non-cancellous
KI.87.D9.8.5	Long Bone	Unknown	Shaft	Fragment	1	15	Adult	
KI.87.D9.8.6	Long Bone	Unknown	Shaft	Fragment	1	2	Adult	Mend with each other.
KI.87.D9.8.7	Femur	Unknown	Shaft	Fragment	1	1	Adult	
KI.87.D9.8.8	Mandible	Unknown		Fragment	1	1	Adult	Coronoid process.
KI.87.D9.9.1	Long Bone	Unknown	Shaft	Fragment	1	2	Adult	
KI.87.D9.9.2	Non-human	Unknown			1	1	Adult	Non-human, vertebra, SM?

TOMB D9 TEETH

ID	PERMANENT/DECIDUOUS	TOOTH TYPE	TOOTH POSITION	SIDE	MAXILLARY MANDIBULAR	DEVELOP-MENT	WEAR	COMMENTS
KI.87.D9.11.11	Permanent	Molar	1	Left	Mandibular	0	M4	
KI.87.D9.11.12	Permanent	Molar	1	Right	Mandibular	0	M9	
KI.87.D9.11.13	Permanent	Premolar	4	Unknown	Maxillary	0	P4	
KI.87.D9.11.14	Permanent	Premolar	4	Left	Mandibular	0	P4	

ID	PERMANENT/ DECIDUOUS	TOOTH TYPE	TOOTH POSITION	SIDE	MAXILLARY MANDIBULAR	DEVELOP-MENT	WEAR	COMMENTS
KI.87.D9.11.15	Permanent	Molar	2	Unknown	Mandibular	0	M8	
KI.87.D9.11.16	Permanent	Molar	3	Unknown	Maxillary	10		Root 1/2
KI.87.D9.11.17	Permanent	Premolar	4	Right	Mandibular	0	P4	
KI.87.D9.11.18	Unknown	Unknown	Unknown	Unknown	Unknown	0		Tooth root.
KI.87.D9.11.19	Permanent	Canine	1	Right	Mandibular	0	M2	
KI.87.D9.11.20	Permanent	Incisor	1	Left	Maxillary	0	IC3	Wear stage 3-4
KI.87.D9.11.21	Permanent	Molar	1	Left	Mandibular	0	M4	
KI.87.D9.11.22	Permanent	Premolar	4	Left	Mandibular	0	P4	

TOMB D10 BONE

ID	ELEMENT	SIDE	SEGMENT	COMPLETE-NESS	MNI	COUNT	AGE	COMMENTS
KI.87.D10.1.1	Cranial Fragments	Unknown	Vault	Fragment	1	28	Adult	1 identifiable as occipital, rest UD vault fragments
KI.87.D10.1.10	Scrap	Unknown	Scrap	Fragment	1	244	Adult	All cancellous
KI.87.D10.1.11	Sacrum	L	Proximal	Fragment	1	1	Adult	Superior body, L superior articular facet
KI.87.D10.1.12	Talus	Unknown	Proximal	Fragment	1	1	Adult	Superior articular facet, side UD, some evidence of DJD, grooving
KI.87.D10.1.13	Navicular	Unknown		Fragment	1	1	Adult	
KI.87.D10.1.14	Os Coxa			Fragment	1	1	Adult	
KI.87.D10.1.2	Humerus/ Femur	Unknown	Head	Fragment	1	4	Adult	
KI.87.D10.1.3	Humerus	L	Distal	Almost Complete	1	1	Adult	
KI.87.D10.1.4	Os Coxa	Unknown	Acetabulum	Fragment	1	1	Adult	
KI.87.D10.1.5	Patella	Unknown		1/3	1	1	Adult	Eburnation/grooving visible on posterior surface
KI.87.D10.1.6	Talus	L		Almost Complete	1	1	Adult	
KI.87.D10.1.7	Proximal Phalanx-Hand	Unknown	Proximal		1	1	Adult	

ID	Element	Side	Segment	Complete-ness	MNI	Count	Age	Comments
KI.87.D10.1.8	Tarsal	Unknown		1/2	1	1	Adult	Cuneiform, probably intermediate
KI.87.D10.1.9	Scaphoid	Unknown		Almost Complete	1	1	Adult	Very worn
KI.87.D10.2.1	Humerus	R	Shaft	Fragment	1	1	Adult	Partial olecranon fossa
KI.87.D10.2.10	Femur	Unknown	Head	Fragment	1	1	Adult	With fovea capitis
KI.87.D10.2.11	Humerus	Unknown	Head	Fragment	1	1	Adult	
KI.87.D10.2.12	Humerus	Unknown	Trochlea	Fragment	1	1	Adult	Doesn't mend with #2 from this bag
KI.87.D10.2.13	Scrap	Unknown	Scrap	Fragment	1	5	Adult	
KI.87.D10.2.14	Non-human	Unknown			1	2	Adult	Non-human: rodent? Proximal humerus & proximal ulna
KI.87.D10.2.15	Long Bone	Unknown	Shaft	Fragment	1	102	Adult	
KI.87.D10.2.16	Tibia	Unknown	Shaft	Fragment	1	1	Adult	
KI.87.D10.2.17	Humerus	Unknown	Shaft	Fragment	1	1	Adult	
KI.87.D10.2.18	Femur	Unknown	Shaft	Fragment	1	1	Adult	
KI.87.D10.2.19	Radius/Ulna	Unknown	Shaft	Fragment	1	2	Adult	
KI.87.D10.2.2	Humerus	R	Distal	Fragment	1	1	Adult	Trochlea
KI.87.D10.2.20	Scrap	Unknown	Scrap	Fragment	1	503	Adult	
KI.87.D10.2.3	Cranial Fragmen	Unknown	Vault	Fragment	1	19	Adult	One with thickened bone and surface porosity
KI.87.D10.2.4	Occipital	Unknown	Vault	Fragment	1	1	Adult	
KI.87.D10.2.5	MT2	L	Proximal	Fragment	1	1	Adult	
KI.87.D10.2.6	Navicular	Unknown		Fragment	1	1	Adult	
KI.87.D10.2.7	Ulna	Unknown	Proximal	Fragment	1	1	Adult	
KI.87.D10.2.8	Os Coxa	Unknown		Fragment	1	1	Adult	
KI.87.D10.2.9	Frontal	Unknown		Fragment	1	1	Adult	Zygomatic process/ superciliary arch
KI.87.D10.3.1	Ulna	Unknown	Proximal	Fragment	1	1	Adult	Worn
KI.87.D10.3.10	Radius	Unknown	Shaft	Fragment	1	1	Adult	
KI.87.D10.3.11	Humerus/ Femur	Unknown	Shaft	Fragment	1	1	Adult	
KI.87.D10.3.12	Non-human	Unknown			1	2	Adult	Non-human: MM (sheep/goat), rib frags
KI.87.D10.3.13	Mandible	L	Coronoid	Fragment	1	1	Possible juvenile	Coronoid process

ID	Element	Side	Segment	Complete-ness	MNI	Count	Age	Comments
KI.87.D10.3.19	Fibula	Unknown	Shaft	Fragment	1	1	Adult	<25% shaft, ca 25% circumference.
KI.87.D10.3.2	Middle Phalanx-Hand	Unknown	Complete	Complete	1	1	Adult	Slightly worn
KI.87.D10.3.20	Mandible	Unknown		Fragment	1	1	Adult	
KI.87.D10.3.3	Radius	Unknown	Proximal	Fragment	1	1	Adult	Proximal shaft with partial tubercle
KI.87.D10.3.4	Cranial Fragment	Unknown	Vault	Fragment	1	26	Adult	
KI.87.D10.3.5	Occipital	Unknown	Vault	Fragment	1	1	Adult	
KI.87.D10.3.6	Cranial Fragment	Unknown	Vault	Fragment	1	1	Possible juvenile	
KI.87.D10.3.7	Long Bone	Unknown	Shaft	Fragment	1	65	Adult	
KI.87.D10.3.8	Scrap	Unknown	Scrap	Fragment	1	117	Adult	
KI.87.D10.3.9	Tibia	Unknown	Shaft	Fragment	1	1	Adult	

TOMB D10 TEETH

ID	Permanent/ Deciduous	Tooth Type	Tooth Position	Side	Maxillary Mandibular	Develop-ment	Wear	Comments
KI.87.D10.2.21	Permanent	Molar	1	Right	Maxillary	7	0	Dev stage 7–8, possibly left. 2 fragm. of molar crown.
KI.87.D10.2.22	Deciduous	Canine	1	Right	Mandibular	0	IC1	
KI.87.D10.3.14	Permanent	Premolar	4	Unknown	Maxillary	0	P3	Crown only.
KI.87.D10.3.15	Permanent	Molar	2	Right	Maxillary	0	M1	Crown only.
KI.87.D10.3.16	Permanent	Molar	1	Right	Mandibular	6		Partial crown. Formation stage 6–7
KI.87.D10.3.17	Unknown	Unknown	Unknown	Unknown	Unknown	0		2x roots, teeth uncertain
KI.87.D10.3.18	Unknown	Unknown	Unknown	Unknown	Unknown	0		1 unknown tooth frag. Crown frag. Possibly canine?

TOMB E3 BONE

ID	ELEMENT	SIDE	SEGMENT	COMPLETE-NESS	MNI	COUNT	AGE	COMMENTS
E3	Parietal	L		Almost Complete	1	1	Juvenile	
E3	Parietal	R		1/2	1	1	Juvenile	
E3	Occipital	Unknown		Fragments	1	??	Juvenile	
E3	Temporal	L	Squama and Petrous	Almost Complete	1	1	Juvenile	
E3	Maxilla	L		Fragments	1	??	Juvenile	
E3	Zygomatic	L		Fragments	1	??	Juvenile	
E3	Mandible			Almost Complete	1	1	Juvenile	M2s root 1/4 complete.Decidous M2s and permanent M1s present.
E3	Maxilla	L		Almost Complete	1	??	Juvenile	Deciduous M2 and C, permanent M1 and I2 present. Permanent M2 root 1/4 complete. Permanent P1 root 1/2 complete.
E3	Maxilla			Almost Complete	1	1	Juvenile	Decidous I1s,I2s,Cs, M2s present. Permanent M1 crown 3/4 complete. I2 crown complete, C crown 3/4 complete.
E3	Mandible			Almost Complete	1	1	Juvenile	Decidous Cs, M2s present. Permanent M1s present.
E3	CV			Fragments	1	??	Juvenile	
E3	Distal Phalanx			Fragments	1	??	Juvenile	
E3	Scapula	L		Fragment	1	1	Juvenile	
E3	Rib			Fragments	1	??	Juvenile	Various rib shaft fragments
E3	Temporal	R	Petrous	Fragment	1	1	Juvenile	
E3	Metatarsal			Fragments	1	3	Juvenile	No fusion
E3	Metacarpal			Fragments	1	1	Juvenile	No fusion
E3	Proximal Phalanx-Hand			Fragments	1	3	Juvenile	No fusion
E3	Middle Phalanx-Hand			Fragments	1	1	Juvenile	No fusion
E3	Distal Phalanx-Hand			Fragments	1	3	Juvenile	No fusion

ID	ELEMENT	SIDE	SEGMENT	COMPLETE-NESS	MNI	COUNT	AGE	COMMENTS
E3	Femur	L		Almost Complete	1	1	Juvenile	Unfused
E3	Humerus	L		Almost Complete	1	1	Juvenile	Unfused.
E3	Clavicle	L	Distal	1/2	1	1	Juvenile	
E3	Vertebrae		Arch	Fragments	1	8	Juvenile	Including 1 C1, arch halves unfused.
E3	Ulna			Partial	1	1	Juvenile	Ends missing.
E3	Ilium			Fragments	1	3	Juvenile	
E3	Long Bone	Unknown	Shaft	Fragments	1	??	Juvenile	Various long bone shaft fragments
E3	Manubrium			Fragment	1	1	Juvenile	
E3	Talus			Fragment	1	1	Juvenile	
E3	MT1			Almost Complete	1	1	Juvenile	Proximal epiphysis unfused. Distal just fusing, line of fusion visible.
E3	Proximal Phalanx-Hand			Almost Complete	1	1	Juvenile	
E3	Tibia	Unknown	Shaft	Fragment	1	1	Juvenile	

TOMB E9 BONE

ID	ELEMENT	SIDE	SEGMENT	COMPLETE-NESS	MNI	COUNT	AGE	COMMENTS
KI.84.E9.47.1	Rib	Unknown	Shaft	Fragment	1	19	Adult	
KI.84.E9.47.2	Scrap	Unknown	Scrap	Fragment	1	4	Adult	Cancellous scrap
KI.84.E9.47.3	Scrap	Unknown	Scrap	Fragment	1	69	Adult	
KI.84.E9.48.1	Os Coxa	Unknown	Acetabulum	Fragment	1	9	Adult	
KI.84.E9.48.2	Os Coxa	Unknown		Fragment	1	25	Adult	Without acetabulum
KI.84.E9.48.3	Scrap	Unknown	Scrap	Fragment	1	41	Adult	
KI.84.E9.49.1	Clavicle	R	Shaft	3/4	1	1	Adult	All except ends
KI.84.E9.49.2	Clavicle	L	Lateral	<1/4	1	1	Adult	<25% from lateral edge
KI.84.E9.50.1	TV	Midline	Arch	Fragment	1	1	Adult	Single body surface articular facet, poss 10TV (11?), superior articular facet
KI.84.E9.50.10	CV	Midline	Body	Fragment	1	1	Adult	Osteoarthritic lipping present
KI.84.E9.50.11	LV	Midline	Arch	Fragment	1	2	Adult	Inferior articular facet

ID	Element	Side	Segment	Complete-ness	MNI	Count	Age	Comments
KI.84.E9.50.12	Vertebral Fragment	Midline	Body	Fragment	2	15	Adult	3 reasonably complete but worn, unobservable for degenerative changes.Rest very fragmentary
KI.84.E9.50.13	LV	Midline	Arch	Fragment	1	1	Adult	Superior articular facet
KI.84.E9.50.14	LV	Midline	Arch	Fragment	1	2	Adult	Inferior articular facet
KI.84.E9.50.15	Vertebral Fragment	Midline		Fragment	1	12	Adult	
KI.84.E9.50.16	Scrap	Unknown	Scrap	Fragment	1	37	Adult	
KI.84.E9.50.2	LV	Midline	Arch	Fragment	1	1	Adult	LV arch frag, with inferior articular facets
KI.84.E9.50.3	LV	Midline	Arch	Fragment	1	1	Adult	LV arch frag, with superior articular facets
KI.84.E9.50.4	LV	Midline	Arch	Fragment	1	1	Adult	LV arch frag, transverse process
KI.84.E9.50.5	LV	Midline	Arch	Fragment	1	1	Adult	LV arch frag with superior articular facets
KI.84.E9.50.6	TV	Midline	Arch	Fragment	1	1	Adult	TV arch frag, with superior articular facet, part of transverse process
KI.84.E9.50.7	LV	Midline	Arch	Fragment	1	1	Adult	LV arch frag, superior articular facet
KI.84.E9.50.8	Vertebral Fragment	Midline	Arch	Fragment	1	9	Adult	
KI.84.E9.50.9	LV	Midline	Body	Fragment	1	3	Adult	Osteoarthritic lipping present in all
KI.84.E9.51.1	Clavicle	Unknown	Shaft	Fragment	1	1	Adult	No mend with piece in Bag #1. No ends
KI.84.E9.51.2	Scapula	Unknown	Body	Fragment	1	1	Adult	Lateral border below glenoid.
KI.84.E9.51.3	Rib	Unknown	Shaft	Fragment	1	1	Adult	
KI.84.E9.51.4	Sacrum	Unknown		Fragment	1	2	Adult	
KI.84.E9.51.5	Os Coxa	Unknown		Fragment	1	2	Adult	
KI.84.E9.51.6	Os Coxa	Unknown		Fragment	1	2	Adult	Mendable.
KI.84.E9.51.7	Clavicle	Unknown	Lateral	Fragment	1	1	Adult	
KI.84.E9.51.8	Scrap	Unknown	Scrap	Fragment	1	31	Adult	
KI.87.E9.14.1	Long Bone	Unknown	Shaft	Fragment	1	295	Adult	
KI.87.E9.14.10	Humerus	Unknown	Shaft	Fragment	1	2	Adult	ca 50% circumference, <25% shaft.

ID	Element	Side	Segment	Complete-ness	MNI	Count	Age	Comments
KI.87.E9.14.11	Humerus	Unknown	Shaft	Fragment	1	1	Adult	Distal end, leading into coronoid fossa
KI.87.E9.14.12	Femur	Unknown	Shaft	Fragment	1	3	Adult	<25% circumference, <25% shaft.
KI.87.E9.14.13	Femur	Unknown	Shaft	Fragment	1	1	Adult	ca. 50% circumference, 25% shaft.
KI.87.E9.14.14	Femur	Unknown	Shaft	Fragment	1	2	Adult	Mendable. ca. 25% circumference, 25% shaft. Very pronounced linea aspera.
KI.87.E9.14.15	Cranial Fragment	Unknown	Vault	Fragment	1	9	Adult	Very small vault pieces.
KI.87.E9.14.16	Rib	Unknown	Shaft	Fragment	1	13	Adult	1L, 1R, rest UD.
KI.87.E9.14.17	Clavicle	Unknown	Shaft	Fragment	1	1	Adult	No ends, side UD, quite small.
KI.87.E9.14.18	Radius	Unknown	Shaft	Fragment	1	5	Adult	One mend. All ca. 25% circumference, <25% shaft.
KI.87.E9.14.19	Maxilla	Unknown		Fragment	1	1	Adult	With dentary (tooth crypt), very small piece of palate.
KI.87.E9.14.2	Ulna	Unknown	Shaft	Fragment	1	1	Adult	100% circumference, 50% shaft.
KI.87.E9.14.20	Lumbar Vertebra	Unknown	Inferior	Fragment	1	2	Adult	Inferior articular facets of LV
KI.87.E9.14.21	Metacarpal/Metatarsal	Unknown	Shaft	Fragment	1	2	Adult	100% circumference, ca. 50% shaft.
KI.87.E9.14.22	Metacarpal/Metatarsal	Unknown	Proximal	Fragment	1	2	Adult	Proximal portion, ca 50% circumference, # UD, side UD
KI.87.E9.14.23	Long Bone	Unknown	Shaft	Fragment	1	3	Adult	Very little weathering, ancient breaks.
KI.87.E9.14.24	Mandible	Unknown	Body	Fragment	1	2	Adult	
KI.87.E9.14.25	Vertebral Fragment	Unknown	Body	Fragment	1	3	Adult	Vertebral body fragments.
KI.87.E9.14.26	Vertebral Fragment	Unknown	Inferior	Fragment	1	2	Adult	Inferior articular facets, vertebral type UD
KI.87.E9.14.27	Ulna	Unknown	Proximal	Fragment	1	1	Adult	Very small portion of trochlear notch.
KI.87.E9.14.28	Os Coxa	Unknown	Acetabulum	Fragment	1	1	Adult	
KI.87.E9.14.29	Os Coxa	Unknown		Fragment	1	2	Adult	UD pelvis frags.
KI.87.E9.14.3	Fibula	Unknown	Shaft	Fragment	1	1	Adult	100% circumference, <25% shaft.
KI.87.E9.14.30	Temporal	Unknown	Mastoid	Fragment	1	1	Adult	Mastoid process.

ID	ELEMENT	SIDE	SEGMENT	COMPLETE-NESS	MNI	COUNT	AGE	COMMENTS
KI.87.E9.14.31	Scrap	Unknown	Scrap	Fragment	1	1	Adult	Scrap, cancellous bone, with very clear cylindrical hole.
KI.87.E9.14.32	Cervical Vertebra	Unknown		Fragment	1	2	Adult	
KI.87.E9.14.33	Cervical Vertebra	Unknown	Arch	Fragment	1	1	Adult	1 CV arch frag.
KI.87.E9.14.34	Non-human			Fragment	1	1	Adult	Non-human. RSF. SM.
KI.87.E9.14.35	Tibia	Unknown	Shaft	Fragment	1	1	Adult	50% circumference, <25% shaft, just below tibial tuberosity.
KI.87.E9.14.36	Humerus/ Femur	Unknown	Head	Fragment	1	2	Adult	
KI.87.E9.14.37	Pelvis/ Scapula	Unknown		Fragment	1	3	Adult	Glenoid/acetabulum frags.
KI.87.E9.14.38	Phalanx	Unknown		Fragment	1	3	Adult	Probable phalanx frags.
KI.87.E9.14.39	Scrap	Unknown	Scrap	Fragment	1	1561	Adult	
KI.87.E9.14.4	Ulna	Unknown	Shaft	Fragment	1	3	Adult	100% circumference, <25% shaft.
KI.87.E9.14.40	Non-human	Unknown		Fragment	1	1	Adult	Non-human. SM. Proximal femur.
KI.87.E9.14.41	Distal Phalanx-Hand	Unknown	Distal	Fragment	1	1	Adult	Distal portion of distal phalanx 1 of hand.
KI.87.E9.14.5	Fibula	Unknown	Shaft	Fragment	1	2	Adult	<25% circumference, <25% shaft.
KI.87.E9.14.6	Fibula	Unknown	Shaft	Fragment	1	3	Adult	ca. 50% circumference, <25% shaft.
KI.87.E9.14.7	Tibia	Unknown	Shaft	Fragment	1	9	Adult	<25% circumference, <25% shaft.
KI.87.E9.14.8	Tibia	Unknown	Shaft	Fragment	1	4	Adult	ca 50% circumference, <25% shaft.
KI.87.E9.14.9	Tibia	L	Shaft	Fragment	1	1	Adult	Posterior, nutrient foramen, popliteal line.
KI.87.E9.15.1	Talus	R	Complete	Almost Complete	2	2	Adult	
KI.87.E9.15.10	Distal Phalanx-Hand	Unknown	Distal	Fragment	1	1	Adult	
KI.87.E9.15.11	Patella	R	Complete	Complete	3	3	Adult	
KI.87.E9.15.12	Patella	L	Complete	Complete	1	1	Adult	
KI.87.E9.15.13	MT5	R	Proximal	Fragment	1	1	Adult	

ID	ELEMENT	SIDE	SEGMENT	COMPLETE-NESS	MNI	COUNT	AGE	COMMENTS
KI.87.E9.15.14	MT5	L	Proximal	Fragment	1	1	Adult	
KI.87.E9.15.15	MT2	R	Proximal	Fragment	2	2	Adult	Both proximal only
KI.87.E9.15.16	MT4	L	Complete	Complete	1	1	Adult	
KI.87.E9.15.17	MC4	R	Proximal	Fragment	1	1	Adult	
KI.87.E9.15.18	MC2	R	Distal	Fragment	1	1	Adult	
KI.87.E9.15.19	MC2	Unknown	Proximal	Fragment	1	1	Adult	
KI.87.E9.15.2	Talus	L	Complete	Almost Complete	2	2	Adult	
KI.87.E9.15.20	MC3	R	Proximal	Fragment	1	1	Adult	
KI.87.E9.15.21	MC4	L	Proximal	Fragment	1	1	Adult	
KI.87.E9.15.22	MT3	L	Proximal	Fragment	1	1	Adult	
KI.87.E9.15.23	Metacarpal/ Metatarsal	Unknown	Shaft	Fragment	1	15	Adult	
KI.87.E9.15.24	MC3	R	Proximal	Fragment	1	1	Adult	
KI.87.E9.15.25	MT3	L	Proximal	Fragment	1	1	Adult	
KI.87.E9.15.26	Metacarpal/ Metatarsal	Unknown	Proximal	Fragment	1	3	Adult	
KI.87.E9.15.27	Capitate	L	Complete	Almost Complete	1	1	Adult	
KI.87.E9.15.28	Calcaneus	L		Fragment	1	1	Adult	
KI.87.E9.15.29	Navicular	Unknown		Fragment	1	1	Adult	
KI.87.E9.15.3	Calcaneus	R	Complete	Almost Complete	1	1	Adult	
KI.87.E9.15.30	Talus	Unknown		Fragment	1	1	Adult	Can't mend with any others above.
KI.87.E9.15.31	Tarsal	Unknown		Fragment	1	8	Adult	
KI.87.E9.15.32	Hamate	L	Complete	Almost Complete	1	1	Adult	
KI.87.E9.15.33	Calcaneus	Unknown		Fragment	1	3	Adult	
KI.87.E9.15.34	Proximal Phalanx-Foot	Unknown	Complete	Almost Complete	1	5	Adult	2–5
KI.87.E9.15.35	Proximal Phalanx-Foot	R	Proximal	Fragment	1	1	Adult	Proximal Phalanx 1
KI.87.E9.15.36	Proximal Phalanx-Hand	Unknown	Proximal	Fragment	1	1	Adult	Proximal phalanx 1
KI.87.E9.15.37	Middle Phalanx-Hand	Unknown	Complete	Almost Complete	1	4	Adult	2-5

ID	Element	Side	Segment	Complete-ness	MNI	Count	Age	Comments
KI.87.E9.15.38	Proximal Phalanx-Hand	Unknown	Distal	Fragment	1	4	Adult	2-5
KI.87.E9.15.39	Phalanx-Hand	Unknown	Proximal	Fragment	1	12	Adult	
KI.87.E9.15.4	Calcaneus	L	Complete	Almost Complete	1	1	Adult	Markedly difference size from above. Two different individuals.
KI.87.E9.15.40	Proximal Phalanx-Hand	Unknown	Complete	Almost Complete	1	2	Adult	Proximal phalanx 1
KI.87.E9.15.41	Os Coxa	Unknown		Fragment	1	1	Adult	
KI.87.E9.15.42	Scrap	Unknown	Squama	Fragment	1	54	Adult	Likely pieces of MCs/MTs/Phals
KI.87.E9.15.5	Cuboid	R	Complete	Almost Complete	1	1	Adult	
KI.87.E9.15.6	Lateral Cuneiform	L	Complete	Almost Complete	1	1	Adult	
KI.87.E9.15.7	Proximal Phalanx-Foot	R	Complete	Almost Complete	2	2	Adult	Proximal phalanx 1.
KI.87.E9.15.8	Proximal Phalanx-Foot	L	Complete	Almost Complete	1	1	Adult	Proximal phalanx 1.
KI.87.E9.15.9	Proximal Phalanx-Foot	L	Proximal	Fragment	1	1	Adult	Proximal phalanx 1. Proximal portion only
KI.87.E9.4.1	Humerus	Unknown	Distal	3/4	1	3	Adult	3 mendable fragments, distal 75% of humerus, 100% circumference, broken at coronoid fossa, has septal aperture.
KI.87.E9.4.10	Ulna	Unknown	Shaft	Fragment	1	4	Adult	<25% shaft each, all 100% circumference
KI.87.E9.4.11	Ulna	Unknown	Shaft	Fragment	1	1	Adult	<25% shaft each, 50% circumference.
KI.87.E9.4.12	Radius	Unknown	Shaft	Fragment	1	1	Adult	25-50% shaft, 100% circumference
KI.87.E9.4.13	Ulna	R	Shaft	Fragment	1	1	Adult	Shaft frag with bottom piece of trochlear notch (doesn't seem to mend with any of the other pieces), ca. 25-50% shaft, 100% circumference
KI.87.E9.4.14	Humerus	Unknown	Head	Fragment	1	1	Adult	
KI.87.E9.4.15	Long Bone	Unknown	Shaft	Fragment	1	103	Adult	

ID	Element	Side	Segment	Complete-ness	MNI	Count	Age	Comments
KI.87.E9.4.16	Scrap	Unknown	Scrap	Fragment	1	230	Adult	
KI.87.E9.4.2	Ulna	R	Proximal	Almost Complete	2	2	Adult	2 R proximal ulnas, with trochlear notch. Heavily worn.
KI.87.E9.4.3	Ulna	L	Proximal	Almost Complete	2	2	Adult	2 L proximal ulnas, with trochlear notch. Heavily worn.
KI.87.E9.4.4	Ulna	Unknown	Proximal	Almost Complete	1	1	Adult	1 side unknown, proximal ulna, with trochlear notch. Heavily worn.
KI.87.E9.4.5	Fibula	Unknown	Shaft	Fragment	1	3	Adult	
KI.87.E9.4.6	Radius	Unknown	Shaft	Fragment	1	1	Adult	125% shaft, 100% circumference.
KI.87.E9.4.7	Ulna	Unknown	Shaft	Fragment	1	1	Adult	Piece of ulna shaft, bottom part of trochlear notch with radial articular surface, no evidence it mends with any of the others in bag.
KI.87.E9.4.8	Radius	Unknown	Shaft	Fragment	1	1	Adult	Not mendable with #4, 50% shaft, 100% circumference.
KI.87.E9.4.9	Radius	Unknown	Distal	Fragment	1	1	Adult	
KI.87.E9.45.1	Cranial Fragment	Unknown	Vault	Fragment	1	112	Adult	
KI.87.E9.45.2	Mandible	Unknown	Unknown	Fragment	1	3	Adult	
KI.87.E9.45.3	Cranial Scrap	Unknown	Unknown	Fragment	1	102	Adult	
KI.87.E9.45.4	Mandible/ Maxilla	Unknown	Dentary	Fragment	1	3	Adult	
KI.87.E9.45.5	Temporal	Unknown	Mastoid	Fragment	1	1	Adult	
KI.87.E9.53.1	Sacrum	Unknown		Fragment	1	1	Adult	Large sacrum fragment.
KI.87.E9.53.2	Sacrum	Unknown	Body	Fragment	1	1	Adult	Proximal sacrum fragment, proximal portion, body.
KI.87.E9.53.3	Sacrum	Unknown	Arch	Fragment	1	1	Adult	Arch?
KI.87.E9.53.4	Sacrum	Unknown		Fragment	1	5	Adult	Possible sacrum fragments.
KI.87.E9.53.5	Sacrum	Unknown		Fragment	1	1	Adult	Proximal articular facet.
KI.87.E9.53.6	Unknown	Unknown		Fragment	1	2	Adult	Could be sacrum or pelvis frags.
KI.87.E9.53.7	Scrap	Unknown	Scrap	Fragment	1	56	Adult	
KI.87.E9.54.1	Femur	Unknown	Shaft	Fragment	1	1	Adult	100% circumference, <25% shaft. Just under trochanter. Posterior surface, possible red ochre traces.

ID	Element	Side	Segment	Complete-ness	MNI	Count	Age	Comments
KI.87.E9.54.10	Long Bone	Unknown	Shaft	Fragment	1	35	Adult	
KI.87.E9.54.11	Fibula	Unknown	Shaft	Fragment	1	2	Adult	Probable fibula shaft fragments, 100% circumference, <25% shaft, but could possibly be ulna
KI.87.E9.54.12	Fibula	Unknown	Shaft	Fragment	1	1	Adult	25% circumference, <25% shaft.
KI.87.E9.54.13	Fibula	Unknown	Shaft	Fragment	1	2	Adult	100% circumference, ca 25% shaft.
KI.87.E9.54.14	Tibia	Unknown	Shaft	Fragment	1	2	Adult	Probable tibial tuberosity.
KI.87.E9.54.15	Tibia	Unknown	Proximal	Fragment	2–3	8	Adult	8 proximal tibia fragments, with 1 mend only visible, making 5 half-size portions of the proximal tibia. 3 tibiae minimum, but since no mends, could be higher than 2 MNI. 4 medial portions (1 UD, 2 L, 1 R), 3 lateral portions (1UD, 1L, 1R), 1 UD portion.
KI.87.E9.54.16	Tibia	Unknown	Distal	Fragment	1	1	Adult	Just distal articular surface, side UD, medial portion.
KI.87.E9.54.17	Tibia	L	Distal	Fragment	1	1	Adult	Medial malleolus.
KI.87.E9.54.18	Tibia	R	Distal	Fragment	1	1	Adult	Antero-lateral corner of distal articular surface.
KI.87.E9.54.19	Tibia	Unknown	Distal	Fragment	1	1	Adult	Not articular portion.
KI.87.E9.54.2	Tibia	Unknown	Shaft	Fragment	1	2	Adult	Mendable. 100% circumference, 50–75% shaft.
KI.87.E9.54.20	Tibia	Unknown	Shaft	Fragment	1	1	Adult	Proximal shaft portion, just below tibial plateau.
KI.87.E9.54.21	Scapula	Unknown	Scrap	Fragment	1	2	Adult	2 chunks cancellous bone, could be portions of proximal or distal tibia, but unknown.
KI.87.E9.54.22	Scrap	Unknown	Scrap	Fragment	1	144	Adult	
KI.87.E9.54.3	Tibia	Unknown	Shaft	Fragment	1	2	Adult	Mendable. 100% circumference, <25% shaft.
KI.87.E9.54.4	Tibia	Unknown	Shaft	Fragment	1	1	Adult	100% circumference, <25% shaft.
KI.87.E9.54.5	Tibia	Unknown	Shaft	Fragment	1	2	Adult	<25% circumference, <25% shaft, but possibly very distal end of shaft.

ID	ELEMENT	SIDE	SEGMENT	COMPLETE-NESS	MNI	COUNT	AGE	COMMENTS
KI.87.E9.54.6	Tibia	L	Shaft	Fragment	1	1	Adult	25–50% circumference, <25% shaft, posterior portion (nutrient foramen visible), probably L
KI.87.E9.54.7	Tibia	Unknown	Shaft	Fragment	1	9	Adult	All <10% circumference, <25% shaft, anterior portion (anterior crest)
KI.87.E9.54.8	Tibia	Unknown	Shaft	Fragment	1	1	Adult	Posterior poriton (popliteal line), ca. 25% shaft, <25% circumference
KI.87.E9.54.9	Tibia	Unknown	Shaft	Fragment	1	2	Adult	Probable tibia shaft fragments, < 25% circumference, <25% shaft.

TOMB E9 TEETH

ID	PERMANENT/ DECIDUOUS	TOOTH TYPE	TOOTH POSITION	SIDE	MAXILLARY MANDIBULAR	DEVELOP-MENT	WEAR	COMMENTS
KI.87.E9.45.6	Unknown	Unknown	Unknown	Unknown	Unknown	0		3 x UD root frags.
KI.87.E9.45.7	Permanent	Incisor	1	Left	Maxillary	0	IC2	
KI.87.E9.45.8	Permanent	Canine	1	Left	Maxillary	0	IC3	

TOMB E10 BONE

ID	ELEMENT	SIDE	SEGMENT	COMPLETE-NESS	MNI	COUNT	AGE	COMMENTS
E10	Cranial Fragments	Unknown	Vault	Fragments	1	??	Adolescent	
E10	Mandible	L		Incomplete	1	??	Adolescent	L 3rd molar unerupted
E10	Clavicle	L	Midshaft	Fragments	1	1	Adolescent	
E10	Scapula	L	Glenoid	Fragments	1	??	Adolescent	
E10	Humerus	R	Proximal	Almost Complete	1	??	Adolescent	Epiphysis not fused
E10	Humerus	L	Midshaft	Fragments	1	??	Adolescent	
E10	Humerus	R	Distal	Almost Complete	1	1	Adolescent	Epiphysis not fused
E10	Humerus	L	Distal	Almost Complete	1	1	Adolescent	Epiphysis not fused

ID	ELEMENT	SIDE	SEGMENT	COMPLETE-NESS	MNI	COUNT	AGE	COMMENTS
E10	Ulna	R	Proximal	Almost Complete	1	1	Adolescent	Epiphysis fusion 1/2 complete
E10	Radius	R	Proximal	Almost Complete	1	1	Adolescent	Epiphysis not fused
E10	Radius	R	Distal	Almost Complete	1	1	Adolescent	
E10	Carpals	Unknown		Almost Complete	1	??	Adolescent	Various
E10	MC3	R		Almost Complete	1	1	Adolescent	Distal epiphysis not fused
E10	Os Coxa	R	Acetabulum/ Ilium	Incomplete	1	1	Adolescent	
E10	Femur	R	Proximal	Almost Complete	1	1	Adolescent	Epiphysis not fused
E10	Femur	Unknown	Shaft	Fragments	1	??	Adolescent	
E10	Femur	R	Distal Epiphysis	Almost Complete	1	1	Adolescent	Epiphysis not fused
E10	Femur	L	Distal Epiphysis	Almost Complete	1	1	Adolescent	Epiphysis not fused
E10	Tibia	R	Proximal Epiphysis	Almost Complete	1	1	Adolescent	Epiphysis not fused
E10	Tibia	Unknown	Shaft	Fragments	1	??	Adolescent	
E10	Patella	L		Fragments	1	1	Adolescent	
E10	Patella	R		Fragments	1	1	Adolescent	

TOMB E11 BONE

ID	ELEMENT	SIDE	SEGMENT	COMPLETENESS	MNI	COUNT	AGE	COMMENTS
E11	Parietal	Unknown		Fragments	1	??	Adult	

TOMB E14 BONE

ID	ELEMENT	SIDE	SEGMENT	COMPLETE-NESS	MNI	COUNT	AGE	COMMENTS
KI.87.E14.5.1	Cranial Fragment	Unknown	Vault	Fragment	1	38	Adult	
KI.87.E14.5.2	Radius	Unknown	Shaft	Fragment	1	2	Adult	100% circumference, 25–50% shaft

ID	Element	Side	Segment	Complete-ness	MNI	Count	Age	Comments
KI.87.E14.5.3	Ulna	Unknown	Shaft	Fragment	1	1	Adult	100% circumference, ca 25% shaft
KI.87.E14.5.4	Long Bone	Unknown	Shaft	Fragment	1	37	Adult	
KI.87.E14.5.5	Metacarpal/ Metatarsal	Unknown	Shaft	Fragment	1	1	Adult	
KI.87.E14.5.6	Cranial Fragment	Unknown	Scrap	Fragment	1	127	Adult	
KI.87.E14.6.1	Long Bone	Unknown	Shaft	Fragment	1	1	Adult	
KI.87.E14.6.2	Scrap	Unknown	Scrap	Fragment	1	1	Adult	
KI.87.E14.7.1	Phalanx-Hand	Unknown	Shaft	Fragment	1	1	Adult	
KI.87.E14.7.2	Long Bone	Unknown	Shaft	Fragment	1	4	Adult	
KI.87.E14.7.3	Scrap	Unknown	Scrap	Fragment	1	25	Adult	

TOMB E14 TEETH

ID	Permanent/ Deciduous	Tooth Type	Tooth Position	Side	Maxillary Mandibular	Development	Wear	Comments
KI.87.E14.5.7	Permanent	Premolar	4	Left	Mandibular	0		P4
KI.87.E14.5.8	Permanent	Canine	1	Right	Mandibular	0		IC4
KI.87.E14.5.9	Permanent	Incisor	1	Left	Maxillary	0		IC5

TOMB H3 BONE

ID	Element	Side	Segment	Complete-ness	MNI	Count	Age	Comments
H3	Long Bone	Unknown	Shaft	Fragments	1	?	Adult	Numerous long bone shaft fragments
H3	Tibia	Unknown	Distal	Fragments	1	1	Adult	
H3	Middle Phalanx-Hand	Unknown		Almost Complete	1	1	Adult	
H3	MC5	L		Almost Complete	1	1	Adult	

TOMB J1 BONE

ID	ELEMENT	SIDE	SEGMENT	COMPLETE-NESS	MNI	COUNT	AGE	COMMENTS
J1	Long Bone	Unknown	Shaft	Fragments	1	??	Juvenile	Various long bone shaft fragments
J1	Rib	Unknown	Shaft	Fragments	1	??	Juvenile	Various rib shaft fragments
J1	Vertebra	Unknown	Unknown	Fragments	1	??	Juvenile	Various vertebral fragments. Vertebrae are unfused to bodies
J1	Phalanges	Unknown	Unknown	Fragments	1	??	Juvenile	Various phalanges. Unfused.

TOMB J1 TEETH

ID	PERMANENT/ DECIDUOUS	TOOTH TYPE	TOOTH POSITION	SIDE	MAXILLARY MANDIBULAR	DEVELOP-MENT	BUWear	COMMENTS
J1	Permanent	Incisor	1	R	Maxillary			Root complete
J1	Permanent	Incisor	1	L	Maxillary			Root complete
J1	Permanent	Canine	1	Unknown	Maxillary			Root complete
J1	Permanent	Incisor	1	R	Mandibular			Root complete
J1	Permanent	Incisor	1	L	Mandibular			Root complete
J1	Permanent	Canine	1	L	Mandibular			Root fragment, root complete.
J1	Permanent	Canine	1	R	Mandibular			Root complete
J1	Permanent	Premolar	2	R	Mandibular			Root 3/4
J1	Permanent	Premolar	1	L	Mandibular			Root complete
J1	Permanent	Molar	1	R	Mandibular			Root complete
J1	Permanent	Molar	1	L	Mandibular			Root complete
J1	Permanent	Molar	2	R	Mandibular			Root 1/2
J1	Permanent	Molar	2	L	Mandibular			Root 1/2
J1	Permanent	Molar	3	R	Mandibular			Root initiated
J1	Deciduous	Incisor	1	R	Maxillary			
J1	Deciduous	Incisor	2	R	Maxillary			
J1	Deciduous	Canine	1	R	Maxillary			
J1	Deciduous	Molar	1	R	Maxillary			

ID	Permanent/ Deciduous	Tooth Type	Tooth Position	Side	Maxillary Mandibular	Develop- ment	BUWear	Comments
J1	Deciduous	Incisor	2	L	Maxillary			
J1	Deciduous	Canine	1	L	Maxillary			
J1	Deciduous	Molar	1	L	Maxillary			
J1	Deciduous	Incisor	1	R	Mandibular			
J1	Deciduous	Incisor	2	R	Mandibular			
J1	Deciduous	Molar	1	R	Mandibular			
J1	Deciduous	Incisor	1	L	Mandibular			
J1	Deciduous	Canine	1	L	Mandibular			
J1	Permanent	Incisor	2	R	Maxillary			
J1	Permanent	Canine	1	R	Maxillary			Root initiated
J1	Permanent	Premolar	1	R	Maxillary			Crown complete.
J1	Permanent	Canine	1	L	Maxillary			Root initiated
J1	Permanent	Incisor	2	R	Mandibular			
J1	Permanent	Premolar	2	R	Mandibular			Crown complete
J1	Permanent	Molar	1	R	Mandibular			Root 1/2
J1	Permanent	Molar	2	R	Mandibular			Crown 3/4
J1	Permanent	Incisor	1	L	Mandibular			Root 1/4-1/2
J1	Permanent	Incisor	2	L	Mandibular			
J1	Permanent	Molar	1	L	Mandibular			Root 1/2

Appendix I

Specific Types Corpora
for Area C and the Cemeteries

AREA C

Code	Form	Form Description	Rim	Rim Description	Pl	#
I.1.A.1	4000	holemouth jar: unclassified	10	simple-direct: squared	8	6
I.1.A.1	4000	holemouth jar: unclassified	10	simple-direct: squared	9	20
I.1.A.2	3010	holemouth jar: L (21+) (EB III)	18d	simple-direct: folded, thickened – rounded bulbous	19	19
I.1.A.3	4010	holemouth jar: L (21+)	17	simple-direct: interior lip	6	3
I.1.A.4.a	4020	holemouth jar: M (20–14)	10	simple-direct: squared	3	13
I.1.A.4.a	4020	holemouth jar: M (20–14)	10	simple-direct: squared	3	14
I.1.A.4.a	4020	holemouth jar: M (20–14)	10	simple-direct: squared	12	7
I.1.A.4.a	4020	holemouth jar: M (20–14)	11	simple-direct: rounded	6	1
I.1.A.4.a	4020	holemouth jar: M (20–14)	12	simple-direct: tapered	12	23
I.1.A.4.b	4020	holemouth jar: M (20–14)	17	simple-direct: interior lip	6	2
I.1.A.4.c	4020	holemouth jar: M (20–14)	18d	simple-direct: folded, thickened – rounded bulbous	4	5
I.1.A.5	4030	holemouth jar: S (13–10)	17	simple-direct: interior lip	14	18
I.1.B.1.a	4010C	holemouth jar cooking pot: L (21+)	10	simple-direct: squared	17	15
I.1.B.1.b	4010C	holemouth jar cooking pot: L (21+)	17	simple-direct: interior lip	4	6
I.1.B.1.c	4010C	holemouth jar cooking pot: L (21+)	18d	simple-direct: folded, thickened – rounded bulbous	13	14
I.1.B.1.c	4010C	holemouth jar cooking pot: L (21+)	18d	simple-direct: folded, thickened – rounded bulbous	14	15
I.1.B.2.a	4020C	holemouth jar cooking pot: M (20–14)	10	simple-direct: squared	9	13
I.1.B.2.a	4020C	holemouth jar cooking pot: M (20–14)	10	simple-direct: squared	10	12

CODE	FORM	FORM DESCRIPTION	RIM	RIM DESCRIPTION	PL	#
I.1.B.2.a	4020C	holemouth jar cooking pot: M (20–14)	10	simple-direct: squared	12	11
I.1.B.2.a	4020C	holemouth jar cooking pot: M (20–14)	10	simple-direct: squared	13	13
I.1.B.2.a	4020C	holemouth jar cooking pot: M (20–14)	10	simple-direct: squared	14	19
I.1.B.2.a	4020C	holemouth jar cooking pot: M (20–14)	11	simple-direct: rounded	2	8
I.1.B.2.a	4020C	holemouth jar cooking pot: M (20–14)	11	simple-direct: rounded	2	9
I.1.B.2.a	4020C	holemouth jar cooking pot: M (20–14)	11	simple-direct: rounded	10	13
I.1.B.2.a	4020C	holemouth jar cooking pot: M (20–14)	11	simple-direct: rounded	10	15
I.1.B.2.a	4020C	holemouth jar cooking pot: M (20–14)	11	simple-direct: rounded	13	9
I.1.B.2.a	4020C	holemouth jar cooking pot: M (20–14)	11	simple-direct: rounded	13	10
I.1.B.2.a	4020C	holemouth jar cooking pot: M (20–14)	11	simple-direct: rounded	14	20
I.1.B.2.a	4020C	holemouth jar cooking pot: M (20–14)	11	simple-direct: rounded	19	18
I.1.B.2.a	4020C	holemouth jar cooking pot: M (20–14)	12	simple-direct: tapered	14	26
I.1.B.2.b	4020C	holemouth jar cooking pot: M (20–14)	17	simple-direct: interior lip	6	15
I.1.B.2.b	4020C	holemouth jar cooking pot: M (20–14)	17	simple-direct: interior lip	9	12
I.1.B.2.b	4020C	holemouth jar cooking pot: M (20–14)	17	simple-direct: interior lip	10	14
I.1.B.2.b	4020C	holemouth jar cooking pot: M (20–14)	17	simple-direct: interior lip	12	10
I.1.B.2.b	4020C	holemouth jar cooking pot: M (20–14)	17	simple-direct: interior lip	13	3
I.1.B.2.b	4020C	holemouth jar cooking pot: M (20–14)	17	simple-direct: interior lip	14	4
I.1.B.2.b	4020C	holemouth jar cooking pot: M (20–14)	17	simple-direct: interior lip	14	12
I.1.B.2.c	4020C	holemouth jar cooking pot: M (20–14)	18	simple-direct: bulbous	2	7
I.1.B.2.c	4020C	holemouth jar cooking pot: M (20–14)	18	simple-direct: bulbous	19	21
I.1.B.2.c	4020C	holemouth jar cooking pot: M (20–14)	18b	simple-direct: folded, thickened – slanted sharply down and in	3	15
I.1.B.2.c	4020C	holemouth jar cooking pot: M (20–14)	18d	simple-direct: folded, thickened – rounded bulbous	12	6
I.1.B.2.c	4020C	holemouth jar cooking pot: M (20–14)	18d	simple-direct: folded, thickened – rounded bulbous	12	22
I.1.B.2.c	4020C	holemouth jar cooking pot: M (20–14)	18d	simple-direct: folded, thickened – rounded bulbous	13	11
I.1.B.2.c	4020C	holemouth jar cooking pot: M (20–14)	18d	simple-direct: folded, thickened – rounded bulbous	13	12
I.1.B.2.c	4020C	holemouth jar cooking pot: M (20–14)	18d	simple-direct: folded, thickened – rounded bulbous	14	21
I.1.B.2.c	4020C	holemouth jar cooking pot: M (20–14)	18d	simple-direct: folded, thickened – rounded bulbous	14	22

Code	Form	Form Description	Rim	Rim Description	Pl	#
I.1.B.3	4030C	holemouth jar cooking pot: S (13–10)	17	simple-direct: interior lip	7	4
I.1.B.3	4030C	holemouth jar cooking pot: S (13–10)	17	simple-direct: interior lip	9	14
I.1.C.1.a	4060	teapot: L (15+)	10	simple-direct: squared	6	8
I.1.C.1.a	4060	teapot: L (15+)	10	simple-direct: squared	11	15
I.1.C.1.a	4060	teapot: L (15+)	11	simple-direct: rounded	12	21
I.1.C.1.b	4060	teapot: L (15+)	17	simple-direct: interior lip	4	3
I.1.C.1.c	4060	teapot: L (15+)	18a	simple-direct: folded, thickened – beveled	5	25
I.1.C.1.c	4060	teapot: L (15+)	18d	simple-direct: folded, thickened – rounded bulbous	4	13
I.1.C.1.d	4060	teapot: L (15+)	41	everted/angled: slight angle, rounded	6	9
I.1.C.1.d	4060	teapot: L (15+)	41	everted/angled: slight angle, rounded	18	5
I.1.C.1.d	4060	teapot: L (15+)	42	everted/angled: slight angle, tapered	10	11
I.1.C.1.e	4060	teapot: L (15+)	61	curved-out: lightly flared, rounded	20	9
I.1.C.1.e	4060	teapot: L (15+)	65	curved-out: sharply flared, tapered	17	14
I.1.C.2.a	4067	teapot: M (14–10)	10	simple-direct: squared	4	20
I.1.C.2.a	4067	teapot: M (14–10)	11	simple-direct: rounded	19	20
I.1.C.2.b	4067	teapot: M (14–10)	13	simple-direct: beveled, inside	10	9
I.1.C.2.b	4067	teapot: M (14–10)	13	simple-direct: beveled, inside	17	13
I.1.C.2.c	4067	teapot: M (14–10)	41	everted/angled: slight angle, rounded	2	3
I.1.C.2.c	4067	teapot: M (14–10)	41	everted/angled: slight angle, rounded	5	24
I.1.C.2.c	4067	teapot: M (14–10)	41	everted/angled: slight angle, rounded	9	18
I.1.C.2.c	4067	teapot: M (14–10)	41	everted/angled: slight angle, rounded	9	19
I.1.C.2.c	4067	teapot: M (14–10)	41	everted/angled: slight angle, rounded	10	10
I.1.C.2.c	4067	teapot: M (14–10)	41	everted/angled: slight angle, rounded	11	13
I.1.C.2.c	4067	teapot: M (14–10)	41	everted/angled: slight angle, rounded	19	8
I.1.C.2.c	4067	teapot: M (14–10)	41	everted/angled: slight angle, rounded	19	9
I.1.C.2.c	4067	teapot: M (14–10)	42	everted/angled: slight angle, tapered	11	14
I.1.C.2.c	4067	teapot: M (14–10)	42	everted/angled: slight angle, tapered	12	20
I.1.C.2.c	4067	teapot: M (14–10)	42	everted/angled: slight angle, tapered	13	7
I.1.C.2.c	4067	teapot: M (14–10)	42	everted/angled: slight angle, tapered	20	13
I.1.C.2.d	4067	teapot: M (14–10)	65	curved-out: sharply flared, tapered	20	8
I.1.C.3.a	4072	teapot: S (9–)	11	simple-direct: rounded	12	5
I.1.C.3.b	4072	teapot: S (9–)	41	everted/angled: slight angle, rounded	5	23

CODE	FORM	FORM DESCRIPTION	RIM	RIM DESCRIPTION	PL	#
I.1.C.3.b	4072	teapot: S (9–)	45	everted/angled: sharp angle, tapered	9	11
I.2.A.1	4046	holemouth bowl: M (24–20)	18a	simple-direct: folded, thickened – beveled	7	3
I.2.A.2	4050	holemouth bowl: M S (18–12)	12	simple-direct: tapered	1	12
I.2.A.2	4050	holemouth bowl: M S (18–12)	12	simple-direct: tapered	1	13
I.2.A.2	4050	holemouth bowl: M S (18–12)	12	simple-direct: tapered	14	16
I.2.B.1	4040C	holemouth bowl cooking pot: L (28+)	11	simple-direct: rounded	4	4
I.2.B.1	4040C	holemouth bowl cooking pot: L (28+)	12	simple-direct: tapered	17	16
I.2.B.2	4050C	holemouth bowl cooking pot: M S (18–12)	11	simple-direct: rounded	0	5
I.2.C.1	4040	holemouth bowl: L (28+)	71	thickened inside: flat, thick	11	16
I.2.D.1.a	4080	holemouth bowl: deep basin	70	thickened inside: flat, thin	3	11
I.2.D.1.a	4080	holemouth bowl: deep basin	71	thickened inside: flat, thick	1	14
I.2.D.1.a	4080	holemouth bowl: deep basin	71	thickened inside: flat, thick	3	10
I.2.D.1.a	4080	holemouth bowl: deep basin	71	thickened inside: flat, thick	7	2
I.2.D.1.b	4080	holemouth bowl: deep basin	73	thickened inside: rolled	11	12
I.2.D.1.b	4080	holemouth bowl: deep basin	73	thickened inside: rolled	17	11
I.2.D.1.b	4080	holemouth bowl: deep basin	73	thickened inside: rolled	17	12
I.2.D.1.c	4080	holemouth bowl: deep basin	91	thickened, in and out: rounded-knob	6	4
I.2.D.1.c	4080	holemouth bowl: deep basin	91	thickened, in and out: rounded-knob	10	16
I.2.D.1.c	4080	holemouth bowl: deep basin	91	thickened, in and out: rounded-knob	14	5
I.2.D.2	4080	holemouth bowl: deep basin	10	simple-direct: squared	3	12
I.2.D.2	4080	holemouth bowl: deep basin	10	simple-direct: squared	10	6
I.2.D.2	4080	holemouth bowl: deep basin	10	simple-direct: squared	12	4
I.2.D.2	4080	holemouth bowl: deep basin	10	simple-direct: squared	17	10
II.A.1.a	3110	necked jar: pithoi (30–22) general, diameter only (EB III)	64	curved-out: sharply flared, rounded	14	7
II.A.1.a	3110	necked jar: pithoi (30–22) general, diameter only (EB III)	65	curved-out: sharply flared, tapered	14	6
II.A.1.b	4114	necked jar: pithoi (30–22) tall neck, curved out (everted)	63	curved-out: sharply flared, squared	4	11
II.A.1.b	4114	necked jar: pithoi (30–22) tall neck, curved out (everted)	63	curved-out: sharply flared, squared	15	25
II.A.1.c.1	4119	necked jar: pithoi (30–22) short neck, curved out (flared)	10	simple-direct: squared	20	7

Code	Form	Form Description	Rim	Rim Description	Pl	#
II.A.1.c.2	4119	necked jar: pithoi (30–22) short neck, curved out (flared)	63	curved-out: sharply flared, squared	5	22
II.A.2.a.1	4122	necked jar: L (21–16) tall neck, corner point, angled out	11	simple-direct: rounded	20	6
II.A.2.a.2	4122	necked jar: L (21–16) tall neck, corner point, angled out	61	curved-out: lightly flared, rounded	6	7
II.A.2.b.1	4120	necked jar: L (21–16) general, diameter only	62	curved-out: lightly flared, tapered	4	19
II.A.2.b.1	4120	necked jar: L (21–16) general, diameter only	62	curved-out: lightly flared, tapered	8	4
II.A.2.b.1	4124	necked jar: L (21–16) tall neck, corner point (everted)	60	curved-out: lightly flared, squared	20	4
II.A.2.b.1	4124	necked jar: L (21–16) tall neck, corner point (everted)	62	curved-out: lightly flared, tapered	12	3
II.A.2.b.1	4124	necked jar: L (21–16) tall neck, corner point (everted)	63	curved-out: sharply flared, squared	5	21
II.A.2.b.1	4124	necked jar: L (21–16) tall neck, corner point (everted)	63	curved-out: sharply flared, squared	20	3
II.A.2.b.1	4140	necked jar: M/L (15–12) general, diameter only	60	curved-out: lightly flared, squared	14	11
II.A.2.b.1	4140	necked jar: M/L (15–12) general, diameter only	62	curved-out: lightly flared, tapered	15	22
II.A.2.b.1	4149	necked jar: M/L (15–12) tall neck, corner point, curved out (everted)	60	curved-out: lightly flared, squared	19	17
II.A.2.b.1	4149	necked jar: M/L (15–12) tall neck, corner point, curved out (everted)	61	curved-out: lightly flared, rounded	2	10
II.A.2.b.1	4149	necked jar: M/L (15–12) tall neck, corner point, curved out (everted)	61	curved-out: lightly flared, rounded	14	2
II.A.2.b.2	4124	necked jar: L (21–16) tall neck, corner point (everted)	81	thickened outside: rounded	20	5
II.A.3.a.1	4221	necked jar: M/S (12–9) tall, wide neck, corner point, cylindrical neck	11	simple-direct: rounded	4	12
II.A.3.a.1	4221	necked jar: M/S (12–9) tall, wide neck, corner point, cylindrical neck	11	simple-direct: rounded	11	9
II.A.3.a.1	4221	necked jar: M/S (12–9) tall, wide neck, corner point, cylindrical neck	11	simple-direct: rounded	14	10
II.A.3.a.2	4221	necked jar: M/S (12–9) tall, wide neck, corner point, cylindrical neck	62	curved-out: lightly flared, tapered	15	21
II.A.3.b	4224	necked jar: M/S (12–9) tall, wide neck, orner point, curved out (everted)	61	curved-out: lightly flared, rounded	9	9
II.A.3.b	4224	necked jar: M/S (12–9) tall, wide neck, corner point, curved out (everted)	61	curved-out: lightly flared, rounded	10	8
II.A.3.b	4224	necked jar: M/S (12–9) tall, wide neck, corner point, curved out (everted)	61	curved-out: lightly flared, rounded	15	19

Code	Form	Form Description	Rim	Rim Description	Pl	#
II.A.3.b	4224	necked jar: M/S (12–9) tall, wide neck, corner point, curved out (everted)	61	curved-out: lightly flared, rounded	15	20
II.A.3.b	4224	necked jar: M/S (12–9) tall, wide neck, corner point, curved out (everted)	62	curved-out: lightly flared, tapered	9	10
II.A.3.b	4224	necked jar: M/S (12–9) tall, wide neck, corner point, curved out (everted)	62	curved-out: lightly flared, tapered	14	1
II.A.3.b	4224	necked jar: M/S (12–9) tall, wide neck, corner point, curved out (everted)	63	curved-out: sharply flared, squared	10	7
II.A.3.b	4224	necked jar: M/S (12–9) tall, wide neck, corner point, curved out (everted)	63	curved-out: sharply flared, squared	12	18
II.A.3.c	4232	necked jar: M/S (12–9) tall, wide neck, inflected curve	61	curved-out: lightly flared, rounded	10	6
II.A.4.a	4260	necked jar: S (8–7) general, diameter only	11	simple-direct: rounded	13	8
II.A.4.a	4261	necked jar: S (8–7) tall neck, corner point, cylindrical	12	simple-direct: tapered	11	8
II.A.4.b	4264	necked jar: S (8–7) tall neck, corner point (everted)	61	curved-out: lightly flared, rounded	3	5
II.A.4.b	4264	necked jar: S (8–7) tall neck, corner point (everted)	61	curved-out: lightly flared, rounded	15	18
II.A.4.b	4264	necked jar: S (8–7) tall neck, c orner point (everted)	62	curved-out: lightly flared, tapered	7	5
II.A.4.c	4272	necked jar: S (8–7) tall neck, inflected point, curved out	61	curved-out: lightly flared, rounded	5	19
II.A.4.d	4281	necked jar: S (8–7) short, wide neck	61	curved-out: lightly flared, rounded	14	24
II.B.1	4119C	necked jar cooking pot: pithoi (30–22) short neck, curved out (flared)	60	curved-out: lightly flared, squared	3	7
II.B.1	4119C	necked jar cooking pot: pithoi (30–22) short neck, curved out (flared)	60	curved-out: lightly flared, squared	11	11
II.B.1	4119C	necked jar cooking pot: pithoi (30–22) short neck, curved out (flared)	65	curved-out: sharply flared, tapered	1	2
II.B.2.a.1	4129C	necked jar cooking pot: L (21–16) short neck, corner point, curved out (everted)	41	everted/angled: slight angle, rounded	15	24
II.B.2.a.1	4139C	necked jar cooking pot: L (21–16) short neck, inflected, curved out	62	curved-out: lightly flared, tapered	11	10
II.B.2.a.2	4129C	necked jar cooking pot: L (21–16) short neck, corner point, curved out (everted)	61	curved-out: lightly flared, rounded	5	20
II.B.2.b.1	4139C	necked jar cooking pot: L (21–16) short neck, inflected, curved out	60	curved-out: lightly flared, squared	2	6
II.B.2.b.1	4139C	necked jar cooking pot: L (21–16) short neck, inflected, curved out	60	curved-out: lightly flared, squared	14	3
II.B.2.b.1	4139C	necked jar cooking pot: L (21–16) short neck, inflected, curved out	60	curved-out: lightly flared, squared	19	7

Code	Form	Form Description	Rim	Rim Description	Pl	#
II.B.2.b.1	4139C	necked jar cooking pot: L (21–16) short neck, inflected, curved out	61	curved-out: lightly flared, rounded	1	18
II.B.2.b.1	4139C	necked jar cooking pot: L (21–16) short neck, inflected, curved out	61	curved-out: lightly flared, rounded	3	6
II.B.2.b.2	4139C	necked jar cooking pot: L (21–16) short neck, inflected, curved out	61	curved-out: lightly flared, rounded	12	19
II.B.2.b.2	4139C	necked jar cooking pot: L (21–16) short neck, inflected, curved out	61	curved-out: lightly flared, rounded	18	2
II.B.3	4175C	necked jar cooking pot: M/L (15–11) short neck, corner point, curved out (everted)	41	everted/angled: slight angle, rounded	18	1
II.C.1	4400	wide mouth pitcher/juglet: L, tall neck	61	curved-out: lightly flared, rounded	15	17
II.C.2	4420	wide mouth pitcher/juglet: M/L, tall neck	62	curved-out: lightly flared, tapered	19	2
II.C.3.a	4422	wide mouth pitcher/juglet: M/L, tall, cylindrical neck, inflected point	60	curved-out: lightly flared, squared	11	7
II.C.3.a	4422	wide mouth pitcher/juglet: M/L, tall, cylindrical neck, inflected point	61	curved-out: lightly flared, rounded	6	6
II.C.3.a	4422	wide mouth pitcher/juglet: M/L, tall, cylindrical neck, inflected point	61	curved-out: lightly flared, rounded	11	6
II.C.3.b	4422	wide mouth pitcher/juglet: M/L, tall, cylindrical neck, inflected point	11	simple-direct: rounded	6	14
III.A.1.a.1.a	4520	deep bowl: L (32+) lightly curved, neutral to open	70	thickened inside: flat, thin	6	20
III.A.1.a.1.a	4520	deep bowl: L (32+) lightly curved, neutral to open	71	thickened inside: flat, thick	3	9
III.A.1.a.1.a	4520	deep bowl: L (32+) lightly curved, neutral to open	71	thickened inside: flat, thick	5	17
III.A.1.a.1.a	4520	deep bowl: L (32+) lightly curved, neutral to open	71	thickened inside: flat, thick	5	18
III.A.1.a.1.a	4520	deep bowl: L (32+) lightly curved, neutral to open	71	thickened inside: flat, thick	11	4
III.A.1.a.1.a	4520	deep bowl: L (32+) lightly curved, neutral to open	71	thickened inside: flat, thick	12	17
III.A.1.a.1.a	4520	deep bowl: L (32+) lightly curved, neutral to open	71	thickened inside: flat, thick	17	9
III.A.1.a.1.a	4530	deep bowl: M/L (31–22) lightly curved, neutral to open	71	thickened inside: flat, thick	2	11
III.A.1.a.1.a	4530	deep bowl: M/L (31–22) lightly curved, neutral to open	71	thickened inside: flat, thick	3	4
III.A.1.a.1.b	4520	deep bowl: L (32+) lightly curved, neutral to open	75	thickened inside: turned down	3	8
III.A.1.a.1.b	4530	deep bowl: M/L (31–22) lightly curved, neutral to open	75	thickened inside: turned down	5	16

Code	Form	Form Description	Rim	Rim Description	Pl	#
III.A.1.a.1.c	4520	deep bowl: L (32+) lightly curved, neutral to open	91	thickened, in and out: rounded-knob	1	6
III.A.1.a.2	4520	deep bowl: L (32+) lightly curved, neutral to open	10	simple-direct: squared	13	15
III.A.1.b	4530	deep bowl: M/L (31–22) lightly curved, neutral to open	10	simple-direct: squared	8	9
III.A.1.b	4530	deep bowl: M/L (31–22) lightly curved, neutral to open	11	simple-direct: rounded	3	3
III.A.1.b	4530	deep bowl: M/L (31–22) lightly curved, neutral to open	11	simple-direct: rounded	13	28
III.A.1.b	4570	deep bowl: M (21–17) lightly curved, neutral to open	10	simple-direct: squared	17	2
III.A.1.b	4570	deep bowl: M (21–17) lightly curved, neutral to open	11	simple-direct: rounded	1	11
III.A.1.b	4570	deep bowl: M (21–17) lightly curved, neutral to open	11	simple-direct: rounded	5	15
III.A.1.b	4570	deep bowl: M (21–17) lightly curved, neutral to open	11	simple-direct: rounded	13	6
III.A.1.b	4570	deep bowl: M (21–17) lightly curved, neutral to open	11	simple-direct: rounded	13	27
III.A.1.b	4570	deep bowl: M (21–17) lightly curved, neutral to open	11	simple-direct: rounded	17	3
III.A.1.b	4570	deep bowl: M (21–17) lightly curved, neutral to open	19	simple-direct: thinned, with exterior groove	17	1
III.A.1.c	4546	deep bowl: M/L (31–22) angled to splaying walls	11	simple-direct: rounded	1	17
III.A.2.a	4500	deep bowl: L (32+) lightly closed	76	thickened inside: beveled	17	5
III.A.2.a	4500	deep bowl: L (32+) lightly closed	76	thickened inside: beveled	17	6
III.A.2.a	4500	deep bowl: L (32+) lightly closed	76	thickened inside: beveled	17	7
III.A.2.a	4500	deep bowl: L (32+) lightly closed	76	thickened inside: beveled	17	8
III.A.2.b	4510	deep bowl: M/L (31–22) lightly closed	10	simple-direct: squared	11	5
III.A.2.b	4510	deep bowl: M/L (31–22) lightly closed	13	simple-direct: beveled, inside	4	10
III.A.2.b	4510	deep bowl: M/L (31–22) lightly closed	13	simple-direct: beveled, inside	7	1
III.A.2.b	4510	deep bowl: M/L (31–22) lightly closed	13	simple-direct: beveled, inside	9	8
III.A.2.b	4510	deep bowl: M/L (31–22) lightly closed	13	simple-direct: beveled, inside	14	14
III.A.2.c	4560	deep bowl: M (21–17) lightly closed	11	simple-direct: rounded	3	2
III.A.2.c	4560	deep bowl: M (21–17) lightly closed	11	simple-direct: rounded	17	4
III.B.1.a	4600	platter bowl: VL, wide (40+) shallow, flat base	75	thickened inside: turned down	4	9
III.B.1.a	4600	platter bowl: VL, wide (40+) shallow, flat base	75	thickened inside: turned down	10	5

Code	Form	Form Description	Rim	Rim Description	Pl	#
III.B.1.a	4600	platter bowl: VL, wide (40+) shallow, flat base	75	thickened inside: turned down	11	2
III.B.1.a	4600	platter bowl: VL, wide (40+) shallow, flat base	75	thickened inside: turned down	11	3
III.B.1.a	4600	platter bowl: VL, wide (40+) shallow, flat base	75	thickened inside: turned down	16	9
III.B.1.a	4600	platter bowl: VL, wide (40+) shallow, flat base	75	thickened inside: turned down	16	10
III.B.1.a	4600	platter bowl: VL, wide (40+) shallow, flat base	75	thickened inside: turned down	16	11
III.B.1.a	4600	platter bowl: VL, wide (40+) shallow, flat base	75	thickened inside: turned down	16	12
III.B.1.a	4600	platter bowl: VL, wide (40+) shallow, flat base	75	thickened inside: turned down	16	13
III.B.1.a	4600	platter bowl: VL, wide (40+) shallow, flat base	75	thickened inside: turned down	20	2
III.B.1.b	4600	platter bowl: VL, wide (40+) shallow, flat base	73	thickened inside: rolled	19	6
III.B.1.b	4600	platter bowl: VL, wide (40+) shallow, flat base	74	thickened inside: rolled and pointed	1	19
III.B.1.c	4600	platter bowl: VL, wide (40+) shallow, flat base	91	thickened, in and out: rounded-knob	5	14
III.B.1.d	4600	platter bowl: VL, wide (40+) shallow, flat base	71	thickened inside: flat, thick	18	4
III.B.2.a	4620	platter bowl: L (39–30) shallow, flat base	75	thickened inside: turned down	1	1
III.B.2.a	4620	platter bowl: L (39–30) shallow, flat base	75	thickened inside: turned down	1	4
III.B.2.a	4620	platter bowl: L (39–30) shallow, flat base	75	thickened inside: turned down	1	5
III.B.2.a	4620	platter bowl: L (39–30) shallow, flat base	75	thickened inside: turned down	1	9
III.B.2.a	4620	platter bowl: L (39–30) shallow, flat base	75	thickened inside: turned down	1	10
III.B.2.a	4620	platter bowl: L (39–30) shallow, flat base	75	thickened inside: turned down	2	5
III.B.2.a	4620	platter bowl: L (39–30) shallow, flat base	75	thickened inside: turned down	2	12
III.B.2.a	4620	platter bowl: L (39–30) shallow, flat base	75	thickened inside: turned down	2	20
III.B.2.a	4620	platter bowl: L (39–30) shallow, flat base	75	thickened inside: turned down	2	21
III.B.2.a	4620	platter bowl: L (39–30) shallow, flat base	75	thickened inside: turned down	4	2
III.B.2.a	4620	platter bowl: L (39–30) shallow, flat base	75	thickened inside: turned down	4	8
III.B.2.a	4620	platter bowl: L (39–30) shallow, flat base	75	thickened inside: turned down	4	15
III.B.2.a	4620	platter bowl: L (39–30) shallow, flat base	75	thickened inside: turned down	4	17
III.B.2.a	4620	platter bowl: L (39–30) shallow, flat base	75	thickened inside: turned down	5	2
III.B.2.a	4620	platter bowl: L (39–30) shallow, flat base	75	thickened inside: turned down	5	6
III.B.2.a	4620	platter bowl: L (39–30) shallow, flat base	75	thickened inside: turned down	5	8
III.B.2.a	4620	platter bowl: L (39–30) shallow, flat base	75	thickened inside: turned down	5	9
III.B.2.a	4620	platter bowl: L (39–30) shallow, flat base	75	thickened inside: turned down	5	11
III.B.2.a	4620	platter bowl: L (39–30) shallow, flat base	75	thickened inside: turned down	5	12
III.B.2.a	4620	platter bowl: L (39–30) shallow, flat base	75	thickened inside: turned down	5	13

Code	Form	Form Description	Rim	Rim Description	Pl	#
III.B.2.a	4620	platter bowl: L (39–30) shallow, flat base	75	thickened inside: turned down	6	5
III.B.2.a	4620	platter bowl: L (39–30) shallow, flat base	75	thickened inside: turned down	6	11
III.B.2.a	4620	platter bowl: L (39–30) shallow, flat base	75	thickened inside: turned down	6	12
III.B.2.a	4620	platter bowl: L (39–30) shallow, flat base	75	thickened inside: turned down	6	13
III.B.2.a	4620	platter bowl: L (39–30) shallow, flat base	75	thickened inside: turned down	6	19
III.B.2.a	4620	platter bowl: L (39–30) shallow, flat base	75	thickened inside: turned down	7	6
III.B.2.a	4620	platter bowl: L (39–30) shallow, flat base	75	thickened inside: turned down	8	1
III.B.2.a	4620	platter bowl: L (39–30) shallow, flat base	75	thickened inside: turned down	8	2
III.B.2.a	4620	platter bowl: L (39–30) shallow, flat base	75	thickened inside: turned down	8	8
III.B.2.a	4620	platter bowl: L (39–30) shallow, flat base	75	thickened inside: turned down	9	5
III.B.2.a	4620	platter bowl: L (39–30) shallow, flat base	75	thickened inside: turned down	9	16
III.B.2.a	4620	platter bowl: L (39–30) shallow, flat base	75	thickened inside: turned down	10	3
III.B.2.a	4620	platter bowl: L (39–30) shallow, flat base	75	thickened inside: turned down	10	4
III.B.2.a	4620	platter bowl: L (39–30) shallow, flat base	75	thickened inside: turned down	10	19
III.B.2.a	4620	platter bowl: L (39–30) shallow, flat base	75	thickened inside: turned down	10	20
III.B.2.a	4620	platter bowl: L (39–30) shallow, flat base	75	thickened inside: turned down	11	1
III.B.2.a	4620	platter bowl: L (39–30) shallow, flat base	75	thickened inside: turned down	12	16
III.B.2.a	4620	platter bowl: L (39–30) shallow, flat base	75	thickened inside: turned down	13	2
III.B.2.a	4620	platter bowl: L (39–30) shallow, flat base	75	thickened inside: turned down	13	26
III.B.2.a	4620	platter bowl: L (39–30) shallow, flat base	75	thickened inside: turned down	15	8
III.B.2.a	4620	platter bowl: L (39–30) shallow, flat base	75	thickened inside: turned down	15	9
III.B.2.a	4620	platter bowl: L (39–30) shallow, flat base	75	thickened inside: turned down	15	10
III.B.2.a	4620	platter bowl: L (39–30) shallow, flat base	75	thickened inside: turned down	15	11
III.B.2.a	4620	platter bowl: L (39–30) shallow, flat base	75	thickened inside: turned down	15	12
III.B.2.a	4620	platter bowl: L (39–30) shallow, flat base	75	thickened inside: turned down	15	15
III.B.2.a	4620	platter bowl: L (39–30) shallow, flat base	75	thickened inside: turned down	16	3
III.B.2.a	4620	platter bowl: L (39–30) shallow, flat base	75	thickened inside: turned down	16	5
III.B.2.a	4620	platter bowl: L (39–30) shallow, flat base	75	thickened inside: turned down	16	6
III.B.2.a	4620	platter bowl: L (39–30) shallow, flat base	75	thickened inside: turned down	16	7
III.B.2.a	4620	platter bowl: L (39–30) shallow, flat base	75	thickened inside: turned down	16	8
III.B.2.a	4620	platter bowl: L (39–30) shallow, flat base	75	thickened inside: turned down	19	4
III.B.2.a	4620	platter bowl: L (39–30) shallow, flat base	75	thickened inside: turned down	20	11

Code	Form	Form Description	Rim	Rim Description	Pl	#
III.B.2.b	4620	platter bowl: L (39–30) shallow, flat base	73	thickened inside: rolled	1	8
III.B.2.b	4620	platter bowl: L (39–30) shallow, flat base	73	thickened inside: rolled	2	1
III.B.2.b	4620	platter bowl: L (39–30) shallow, flat base	73	thickened inside: rolled	4	16
III.B.2.b	4620	platter bowl: L (39–30) shallow, flat base	73	thickened inside: rolled	5	10
III.B.2.b	4620	platter bowl: L (39–30) shallow, flat base	73	thickened inside: rolled	6	17
III.B.2.b	4620	platter bowl: L (39–30) shallow, flat base	73	thickened inside: rolled	6	18
III.B.2.b	4620	platter bowl: L (39–30) shallow, flat base	73	thickened inside: rolled	8	3
III.B.2.b	4620	platter bowl: L (39–30) shallow, flat base	73	thickened inside: rolled	9	7
III.B.2.b	4620	platter bowl: L (39–30) shallow, flat base	73	thickened inside: rolled	10	2
III.B.2.b	4620	platter bowl: L (39–30) shallow, flat base	73	thickened inside: rolled	10	17
III.B.2.b	4620	platter bowl: L (39–30) shallow, flat base	73	thickened inside: rolled	10	18
III.B.2.b	4620	platter bowl: L (39–30) shallow, flat base	73	thickened inside: rolled	13	25
III.B.2.b	4620	platter bowl: L (39–30) shallow, flat base	73	thickened inside: rolled	14	13
III.B.2.b	4620	platter bowl: L (39–30) shallow, flat base	73	thickened inside: rolled	14	23
III.B.2.b	4620	platter bowl: L (39–30) shallow, flat base	73	thickened inside: rolled	15	13
III.B.2.b	4620	platter bowl: L (39–30) shallow, flat base	73	thickened inside: rolled	19	5
III.B.2.b	4620	platter bowl: L (39–30) shallow, flat base	73	thickened inside: rolled	20	12
III.B.2.b	4620	platter bowl: L (39–30) shallow, flat base	74	thickened inside: rolled and pointed	2	2
III.B.2.b	4620	platter bowl: L (39–30) shallow, flat base	74	thickened inside: rolled and pointed	2	19
III.B.2.b	4620	platter bowl: L (39–30) shallow, flat base	74	thickened inside: rolled and pointed	3	1
III.B.2.b	4620	platter bowl: L (39–30) shallow, flat base	74	thickened inside: rolled and pointed	5	7
III.B.2.c	4620	platter bowl: L (39–30) shallow, flat base	91	thickened, in and out: rounded-knob	14	17
III.B.2.d	4620	platter bowl: L (39–30) shallow, flat base	70	thickened inside: flat, thin	9	6
III.B.2.d	4620	platter bowl: L (39–30) shallow, flat base	70	thickened inside: flat, thin	12	15
III.B.2.d	4620	platter bowl: L (39–30) shallow, flat base	70	thickened inside: flat, thin	19	16
III.B.2.e	4620	platter bowl: L (39–30) shallow, flat base	31	inverted: rounded, same thickness	9	17
III.B.2.e	4620	platter bowl: L (39–30) shallow, flat base	51	curved-in or upright: rounded	12	9
III.B.2.e	4620	platter bowl: L (39–30) shallow, flat base	52	curved-in or upright: tapered	2	18
III.B.3	4620	platter bowl: L (39–30) shallow, flat base	76	thickened inside: beveled	4	18
III.B.3	4620	platter bowl: L (39–30) shallow, flat base	76	thickened inside: beveled	8	7
III.B.3	4620	platter bowl: L (39–30) shallow, flat base	76	thickened inside: beveled	15	14
III.B.3	4620	platter bowl: L (39–30) shallow, flat base	76	thickened inside: beveled	15	16

CODE	FORM	FORM DESCRIPTION	RIM	RIM DESCRIPTION	PL	#
III.B.3	4620	platter bowl: L (39–30) shallow, flat base	76	thickened inside: beveled	16	1
III.B.3	4620	platter bowl: L (39–30) shallow, flat base	76	thickened inside: beveled	16	2
III.B.3	4620	platter bowl: L (39–30) shallow, flat base	76	thickened inside: beveled	16	4
III.B.3	4620	platter bowl: L (39–30) shallow, flat base	76	thickened inside: beveled	20	10
III.B.4.a	4660	platter bowl: M (29–17) shallow, flat base	75	thickened inside: turned down	4	1
III.B.4.a	4660	platter bowl: M (29–17) shallow, flat base	75	thickened inside: turned down	8	10
III.B.4.a	4660	platter bowl: M (29–17) shallow, flat base	75	thickened inside: turned down	9	1
III.B.4.a	4660	platter bowl: M (29–17) shallow, flat base	75	thickened inside: turned down	9	2
III.B.4.a	4660	platter bowl: M (29–17) shallow, flat base	75	thickened inside: turned down	12	14
III.B.4.a	4660	platter bowl: M (29–17) shallow, flat base	75	thickened inside: turned down	13	1
III.B.4.a	4660	platter bowl: M (29–17) shallow, flat base	75	thickened inside: turned down	13	19
III.B.4.a	4660	platter bowl: M (29–17) shallow, flat base	75	thickened inside: turned down	15	6
III.B.4.a	4660	platter bowl: M (29–17) shallow, flat base	75	thickened inside: turned down	18	3
III.B.4.a	4660	platter bowl: M (29–17) shallow, flat base	75	thickened inside: turned down	19	12
III.B.4.a	4660	platter bowl: M (29–17) shallow, flat base	75	thickened inside: turned down	19	14
III.B.4.a	4660	platter bowl: M (29–17) shallow, flat base	75	thickened inside: turned down	19	15
III.B.4.b	4660	platter bowl: M (29–17) shallow, flat base	73	thickened inside: rolled	2	13
III.B.4.b	4660	platter bowl: M (29–17) shallow, flat base	73	thickened inside: rolled	2	16
III.B.4.b	4660	platter bowl: M (29–17) shallow, flat base	73	thickened inside: rolled	2	17
III.B.4.b	4660	platter bowl: M (29–17) shallow, flat base	73	thickened inside: rolled	5	1
III.B.4.b	4660	platter bowl: M (29–17) shallow, flat base	73	thickened inside: rolled	9	4
III.B.4.b	4660	platter bowl: M (29–17) shallow, flat base	73	thickened inside: rolled	13	16
III.B.4.b	4660	platter bowl: M (29–17) shallow, flat base	73	thickened inside: rolled	13	18
III.B.4.b	4660	platter bowl: M (29–17) shallow, flat base	73	thickened inside: rolled	13	23
III.B.4.b	4660	platter bowl: M (29–17) shallow, flat base	73	thickened inside: rolled	14	8
III.B.4.b	4660	platter bowl: M (29–17) shallow, flat base	74	thickened inside: rolled and pointed	2	15
III.B.4.b	4660	platter bowl: M (29–17) shallow, flat base	74	thickened inside: rolled and pointed	12	13
III.B.4.b	4660	platter bowl: M (29–17) shallow, flat base	74	thickened inside: rolled and pointed	13	20
III.B.4.b	4660	platter bowl: M (29–17) shallow, flat base	74	thickened inside: rolled and pointed	13	24
III.B.4.c	4660	platter bowl: M (29–17) shallow, flat base	91	thickened, in and out: rounded-knob	6	10
III.B.4.c	4660	platter bowl: M (29–17) shallow, flat base	91	thickened, in and out: rounded-knob	10	1
III.B.4.c	4660	platter bowl: M (29–17) shallow, flat base	91	thickened, in and out: rounded-knob	14	9

Code	Form	Form Description	Rim	Rim Description	Pl	#
III.B.4.d	4660	platter bowl: M (29–17) shallow, flat base	70	thickened inside: flat, thin	9	3
III.B.4.d	4660	platter bowl: M (29–17) shallow, flat base	70	thickened inside: flat, thin	13	17
III.B.4.d	4660	platter bowl: M (29–17) shallow, flat base	70	thickened inside: flat, thin	13	21
III.B.4.d	4660	platter bowl: M (29–17) shallow, flat base	70	thickened inside: flat, thin	13	22
III.B.4.d	4660	platter bowl: M (29–17) shallow, flat base	71	thickened inside: flat, thick	14	25
III.B.4.e	4660	platter bowl: M (29–17) shallow, flat base	11	simple-direct: rounded	2	14
III.B.4.e	4660	platter bowl: M (29–17) shallow, flat base	32	inverted: tapered, same thickness	1	7
III.B.4.e	4660	platter bowl: M (29–17) shallow, flat base	33	inverted: triangular, short	1	16
III.B.5.a	4660	platter bowl: M (29–17) shallow, flat base	13	simple-direct: beveled, inside	4	14
III.B.5.a	4660	platter bowl: M (29–17) shallow, flat base	13	simple-direct: beveled, inside	9	15
III.B.5.a	4660	platter bowl: M (29–17) shallow, flat base	13	simple-direct: beveled, inside	15	5
III.B.5.a	4660	platter bowl: M (29–17) shallow, flat base	13	simple-direct: beveled, inside	15	7
III.B.5.a	4660	platter bowl: M (29–17) shallow, flat base	13	simple-direct: beveled, inside	19	13
III.B.5.b	4660	platter bowl: M (29–17) shallow, flat base	10	simple-direct: squared	6	16
III.B.5.b	4660	platter bowl: M (29–17) shallow, flat base	12	simple-direct: tapered	2	4
III.C.1.a.1	4710	bowl: M/S (16–6) deep cut neutral to open	10	simple-direct: squared	15	4
III.C.1.a.1	4710	bowl: M/S (16–6) deep cut neutral to open	11	simple-direct: rounded	12	2
III.C.1.a.2	4740	bowl: M/S (18–10) medium depth neutral to open	11	simple-direct: rounded	12	8
III.C.1.b.1	4700	bowl: M/S (16–6) deep cut lightly closed	11	simple-direct: rounded	12	1
III.C.1.b.1	4700	bowl: M/S (16–6) deep cut lightly closed	11	simple-direct: rounded	12	12
III.C.1.b.2	4730	bowl: M/S (18–10) medium depth carinated walls	42	everted/angled: slight angle, tapered	4	7
III.C.1.b.2	4730	bowl: M/S (18–10) medium depth carinated walls	42	everted/angled: slight angle, tapered	5	5
III.C.1.b.2	4730	bowl: M/S (18–10) medium depth carinated walls	42	everted/angled: slight angle, tapered	15	3
III.C.1.b.2	4730	bowl: M/S (18–10) medium depth carinated walls	42	everted/angled: slight angle, tapered	19	1
III.C.1.b.2	4730	bowl: M/S (18–10) medium depth carinated walls	62	curved-out: lightly flared, tapered	15	23
III.C.2.a.1	4770	bowl: S (11–6) neutral to open	11	simple-direct: rounded	1	15
III.C.2.a.1	4770	bowl: S (11–6) neutral to open	12	simple-direct: tapered	5	3
III.C.2.a.1	4770	bowl: S (11–6) neutral to open	12	simple-direct: tapered	19	3
III.C.2.a.1	4770	bowl: S (11–6) neutral to open	12	simple-direct: tapered	19	10
III.C.2.a.1	4770	bowl: S (11–6) neutral to open	19	simple-direct: thinned, with exterior groove	1	3

CODE	FORM	FORM DESCRIPTION	RIM	RIM DESCRIPTION	PL	#
III.C.2.a.2	3749	bowl: S (11–6) neutral to open	32	inverted: tapered, same thickness	19	22
III.C.2.b.1	4756	bowl: S (11–6) lightly closed	11	simple-direct: rounded	5	4
III.C.2.b.1	4756	bowl: S (11–6) lightly closed	11	simple-direct: rounded	13	4
III.C.2.b.1	4756	bowl: S (11–6) lightly closed	11	simple-direct: rounded	13	5
III.C.2.b.2	4760	bowl: S (11–6) medium depth carinated walls	62	curved-out: lightly flared, tapered	15	1
III.C.2.b.2	4760	bowl: S (11–6) medium depth carinated walls	62	curved-out: lightly flared, tapered	15	2
III.C.2.b.2	4760	bowl: S (11–6) medium depth carinated walls	62	curved-out: lightly flared, tapered	19	11
III.C.2.b.2	4760	bowl: S (11–6) medium depth carinated walls	62	curved-out: lightly flared, tapered	20	1
III.C.3.a	4855	lamp: S (16–) lamp, flat base	12	simple-direct: tapered	17	17

CEMETERIES

CODE	FORM	VESSEL	SIZE	DESCRIPTION	RIM	RIM DESCRIPTION	FIG	#
I.1.A.1	4020	Holemouth jar	M		18	simple-direct: bulbous	10.23	20
I.1.B.1	4020C	Holemouth bowl cooking pot	M		10	simple-direct: squared	11.7	12
I.1.B.1	4020C	Holemouth bowl cooking pot	M		11	simple-direct: rounded	11.7	13
I.1.C.1.a.1	4036	Spouted vessel	L	mid to low tangent (added)	11	simple-direct: rounded	10.8	6
I.1.C.1.a.2	4036	Spouted vessel	L	mid to low tangent (added)	41	everted/angled: slight angle, rounded	10.8	4
I.1.C.1.a.2	4036	Spouted vessel	L	mid to low tangent (added)	42	everted/angled: slight angle, tapered	10.13	14
I.1.C.1.a.2	4036	Spouted vessel	L	mid to low tangent (added)	42	everted/angled: slight angle, tapered	10.8	5
I.1.C.1.b.1	4066	Spouted vessel	M	mid to low tangent	11	simple-direct: rounded	10.13	12
I.1.C.1.b.1	4066	Spouted vessel	M	mid to low tangent	11	simple-direct: rounded	10.18	2
I.1.C.1.b.1	4066	Spouted vessel	M	mid to low tangent	11	simple-direct: rounded	10.8	3
I.1.C.1.b.1	4066	Spouted vessel	M	mid to low tangent	11	simple-direct: rounded	11.7	11
I.1.C.1.b.2	4066	Spouted vessel	M	mid to low tangent	41	everted/angled: slight angle, rounded	10.18	1

Code	Form	Vessel	Size	Description	Rim	Rim Description	Fig	#
I.1.C.1.b.2	4066	Spouted vessel	M	mid to low tangent	41	everted/angled: slight angle, rounded	10.23	19
I.1.C.1.b.2	4066	Spouted vessel	M	mid to low tangent	41	everted/angled: slight angle, rounded	10.8	2
I.1.C.1.b.2	4066	Spouted vessel	M	mid to low tangent	41	everted/angled: slight angle, rounded	11.2	6
I.1.C.1.b.2	4066	Spouted vessel	M	mid to low tangent	42	everted/angled: slight angle, tapered	10.13	13
I.1.C.1.b.3	4066	Spouted vessel	M	mid to low tangent	61	curved-out: lightly flared, rounded	11.5	8
I.1.C.2.a.1	4071	Spouted vessel	M/S	mid to low tangent (interpolated)	11	simple-direct: rounded	10.13	11
I.1.C.2.a.2	4071	Spouted vessel	M/S	mid to low tangent (interpolated)	41	everted/angled: slight angle, rounded	10.23	18
I.1.C.2.a.2	4071	Spouted vessel	M/S	mid to low tangent (interpolated)	41	everted/angled: slight angle, rounded	10.8	1
II.A.1.a.1.1	4142	Necked jar	M/L 1800+	tall, wide neck, corner point, wide, flat base, low tangent, ovaloid (interpolated)	11	simple-direct: rounded	10.7	14
II.A.1.a.1.2	4142	Necked jar	M/L 1800+	tall, wide neck, corner point, wide, flat base, low tangent, ovaloid (interpolated)	60	curved-out: lightly flared, squared	10.13	10
II.A.1.a.1.2	4142	Necked jar	M/L 1800+	tall, wide neck, corner point, wide, flat base, low tangent, ovaloid (interpolated)	60	curved-out: lightly flared, squared	10.7	17
II.A.1.a.2.1	4220	Necked jar	M 1799–712	tall, wide neck, corner point, General	10	simple-direct: squared	11.9	5
II.A.1.a.2.1	4222	Necked jar	M 1799–712	tall, wide neck, corner point, wide, flat base, low tangent, ovaloid	11	simple-direct: rounded	10.17	15
II.A.1.a.2.1	4222	Necked jar	M 1799–712	tall, wide neck, corner point, wide, flat base, low tangent, ovaloid	11	simple-direct: rounded	10.7	11
II.A.1.a.2.1	4232	Necked jar	M 1799–712	tall, wide neck, inflected curve, wide, flat base, low tangent, ovaloid	12	simple-direct: tapered	10.13	8
II.A.1.a.2.2	4220	Necked jar	M 1799–712	tall, wide neck, corner point, General	62	curved-out: lightly flared, tapered	10.23	17
II.A.1.a.2.2	4222	Necked jar	M 1799–712	tall, wide neck, corner point, wide, flat base, low tangent, ovaloid	60	curved-out: lightly flared, squared	10.17	14
II.A.1.a.2.2	4222	Necked jar	M 1799–712	tall, wide neck, corner point, wide, flat base, low tangent, ovaloid	60	curved-out: lightly flared, squared	10.7	13

Code	Form	Vessel	Size	Description	Rim	Rim Description	Fig	#
II.A.1.a.2.2	4222	Necked jar	M 1799–712	tall, wide neck, corner point, wide, flat base, low tangent, ovaloid	61	curved-out: lightly flared, rounded	10.17	12
II.A.1.a.2.2	4222	Necked jar	M 1799–712	tall, wide neck, corner point, wide, flat base, low tangent, ovaloid	61	curved-out: lightly flared, rounded	10.7	10
II.A.1.a.2.2	4222	Necked jar	M 1799–712	tall, wide neck, corner point, wide, flat base, low tangent, ovaloid	62	curved-out: lightly flared, tapered	10.17	13
II.A.1.a.2.2	4222	Necked jar	M 1799–712	tall, wide neck, corner point, wide, flat base, low tangent, ovaloid	62	curved-out: lightly flared, tapered	10.7	15
II.A.1.a.2.2	4225	Necked jar	M 1799–712	tall, wide neck, corner point, round to flattened base, low tangent, ovaloid	61	curved-out: lightly flared, rounded	11.9	4
II.A.1.a.3	4211	Necked jar	M 1799–712	short, wide neck, corner point, wide, flat base, squat, low tangent - added	11	simple-direct: rounded	10.26	4
II.A.1.b.1	4141	Necked jar	M/L 1800+	tall, wide neck, corner point, wide, flat base, mid-range tangent, global to rounded	61	curved-out: lightly flared, rounded	10.7	19
II.A.1.b.1	4141	Necked jar	M/L 1800+	tall, wide neck, corner point, wide, flat base, mid-range tangent, global to rounded	61	curved-out: lightly flared, rounded	11.9	6
II.A.1.b.1	4141	Necked jar	M/L 1800+	tall, wide neck, corner point, wide, flat base, mid-range tangent, global to rounded	62	curved-out: lightly flared, tapered	10.7	20
II.A.1.b.2	4221	Necked jar	M 1799–712	tall, wide neck, corner point, wide, flat base, mid-range tangent, global to rounded	61	curved-out: lightly flared, rounded	10.26	5
II.A.1.b.2	4231	Necked jar	M 1799–712	tall, wide neck, inflected curve, wide, flat base, mid-range tangent, global to rounded	60	curved-out: lightly flared, squared	10.13	9
II.A.1.b.2	4231	Necked jar	M 1799–712	tall, wide neck, inflected curve, wide, flat base, mid-range tangent, global to rounded	60	curved-out: lightly flared, squared	10.7	9
II.A.1.b.3	4230	Necked jar	M 1799–712	tall, wide neck, inflected curve, General (interpolated)	11	simple-direct: rounded	10.29	3
II.A.2.a.1	4272	Necked jar	S–711	tall, wide neck, inflected point, wide, flat base, low tangent, ovaloid	10	simple-direct: squared	10.7	3

Code	Form	Vessel	Size	Description	Rim	Rim Description	Fig	#
II.A.2.a.1	4272	Necked jar	S–711	tall, wide neck, inflected point, wide, flat base, low tangent, ovaloid	11	simple-direct: rounded	10.13	4
II.A.2.a.1	4272	Necked jar	S–711	tall, wide neck, inflected point, wide, flat base, low tangent, ovaloid	11	simple-direct: rounded	11.7	9
II.A.2.a.2	4262	Necked jar	S–711	tall, wide neck, corner point, wide, flat base, low tangent, ovaloid	61	curved-out: lightly flared, rounded	10.23	16
II.A.2.a.2	4262	Necked jar	S–711	tall, wide neck, corner point, wide, flat base, low tangent, ovaloid	61	curved-out: lightly flared, rounded	10.7	5
II.A.2.a.2	4262	Necked jar	S–711	tall, wide neck, corner point, wide, flat base, low tangent, ovaloid	61	curved-out: lightly flared, rounded	10.7	6
II.A.2.a.2	4262	Necked jar	S–711	tall, wide neck, corner point, wide, flat base, low tangent, ovaloid	61	curved-out: lightly flared, rounded	10.7	7
II.A.2.a.2	4262	Necked jar	S–711	tall, wide neck, corner point, wide, flat base, low tangent, ovaloid	62	curved-out: lightly flared, tapered	10.17	11
II.A.2.a.2	4272	Necked jar	S–711	tall, wide neck, inflected point, wide, flat base, low tangent, ovaloid	61	curved-out: lightly flared, rounded	11.7	8
II.A.2.b.1	4281	Necked jar	S–711	short, wide neck, wide, flat base, mid-range tangent, global to rounded	12	simple-direct: tapered	10.7	1
II.A.2.b.2	4271	Necked jar	S–711	tall, wide neck, inflected point, wide, flat base, mid-range tangent, global to rounded	61	curved-out: lightly flared, rounded	10.13	5
II.A.2.b.2	4271	Necked jar	S–711	tall, wide neck, inflected point, wide, flat base, mid-range tangent, global to rounded	61	curved-out: lightly flared, rounded	10.13	6
II.A.2.b.2	4281	Necked jar	S–711	short, wide neck, wide, flat base, mid-range tangent, global to rounded	61	curved-out: lightly flared, rounded	10.7	2
II.C.1.a.1	4421	Wide Mouth Jar//Jug/let	M/L	tall neck, inflected point, cylindrical neck, flat base, mid-range tangent	12	simple-direct: tapered	10.23	15
II.C.1.a.2	4421	Wide Mouth Jar//Jug/let	M/L	tall neck, inflected point, cylindrical neck, flat base, mid-range tangent	61	curved-out: lightly flared, rounded	10.13	3

Code	Form	Vessel	Size	Description	Rim	Rim Description	Fig	#
II.C.1.a.2	4421	Wide Mouth Jar//Jug/let	M/L	tall neck, inflected point, cylindrical neck, flat base, mid-range tangent	61	curved-out: lightly flared, rounded	10.30	2
II.C.1.a.2	4421	Wide Mouth Jar//Jug/let	M/L	tall neck, inflected point, cylindrical neck, flat base, mid-range tangent	61	curved-out: lightly flared, rounded	10.6	12
II.C.2.a.1	4422	Wide Mouth Jar//Jug/let	M/L	tall neck, inflected point, cylindrical neck, flat base, low tangent	11	simple-direct: rounded	10.20	4
II.C.2.a.2	4422	Wide Mouth Jar//Jug/let	M/L	tall neck, inflected point, cylindrical neck, flat base, low tangent	60	curved-out: lightly flared, squared	10.6	11
II.C.2.a.2	4422	Wide Mouth Jar//Jug/let	M/L	tall neck, inflected point, cylindrical neck, flat base, low tangent	61	curved-out: lightly flared, rounded	10.23	14
II.C.2.a.2	4422	Wide Mouth Jar//Jug/let	M/L	tall neck, inflected point, cylindrical neck, flat base, low tangent	61	curved-out: lightly flared, rounded	10.30	1
II.C.2.a.2	4422	Wide Mouth Jar//Jug/let	M/L	tall neck, inflected point, cylindrical neck, flat base, low tangent	61	curved-out: lightly flared, rounded	10.6	10
II.C.2.a.2	4422	Wide Mouth Jar//Jug/let	M/L	tall neck, inflected point, cylindrical neck, flat base, low tangent	62	curved-out: lightly flared, tapered	11.2	5
II.C.2.b	4443	Juglet	M 270+	tall neck, corner point, round body, wide base, low tangent, EB III: round body, flat base, mid-tangent, high tangent	61	curved-out: lightly flared, rounded	10.13	1
III.A.1.a	4531	L–M bowl	M–L	neutral to open (interpolated)	75	thickened inside: turned down	10.6	9
III.A.1.a	4570	L–M bowl	M	neutral to open, General	75	thickened inside: turned down	10.29	2
III.A.1.b	4538	L–M bowl	M–L	neutral to open	73	thickened inside: rolled	10.12	10
III.A.1.b	4538	L–M bowl	M–L	neutral to open	73	thickened inside: rolled	10.6	7
III.A.1.b	4538	L–M bowl	M–L	neutral to open	73	thickened inside: rolled	11.9	3
III.A.2.a	4503	L–M bowl	L	lightly closed	76	thickened inside: beveled	10.17	9
III.A.2.a	4518	L–M bowl	M–L	lightly closed (interpolated)	13	simple-direct: beveled, inside	10.6	8
III.A.2.b	4568	L–M bowl	M	lightly closed	10	simple-direct: squared	10.12	9
III.A.2.b	4568	L–M bowl	M	lightly closed	11	simple-direct: rounded	10.12	8
III.A.2.b	4568	L–M bowl	M	lightly closed	11	simple-direct: rounded	10.6	6
III.A.2.c	4560	L–M bowl	M	lightly closed, General	75	thickened inside: turned down	10.23	13

Code	Form	Vessel	Size	Description	Rim	Rim Description	Fig	#
III.B.1.a.1	4600	Platter bowl	VL 3200+	shallow, flat base, General	75	thickened inside: turned down	10.12	1
III.B.1.a.1	4600	Platter bowl	VL 3200+	shallow, flat base, General	75	thickened inside: turned down	10.12	2
III.B.1.a.1	4600	Platter bowl	VL 3200+	shallow, flat base, General	75	thickened inside: turned down	10.12	3
III.B.1.a.1	4600	Platter bowl	VL 3200+	shallow, flat base, General	75	thickened inside: turned down	10.12	4
III.B.1.a.1	4600	Platter bowl	VL 3200+	shallow, flat base, General	75	thickened inside: turned down	10.12	5
III.B.1.a.1	4600	Platter bowl	VL 3200+	shallow, flat base, General	75	thickened inside: turned down	10.12	6
III.B.1.a.1	4600	Platter bowl	VL 3200+	shallow, flat base, General	75	thickened inside: turned down	10.12	7
III.B.1.a.1	4600	Platter bowl	VL 3200+	shallow, flat base, General	75	thickened inside: turned down	10.17	6
III.B.1.a.1	4600	Platter bowl	VL 3200+	shallow, flat base, General	75	thickened inside: turned down	10.17	7
III.B.1.a.1	4600	Platter bowl	VL 3200+	shallow, flat base, General	75	thickened inside: turned down	10.17	8
III.B.1.a.1	4600	Platter bowl	VL 3200+	shallow, flat base, General	75	thickened inside: turned down	10.21	2
III.B.1.a.1	4600	Platter bowl	VL 3200+	shallow, flat base, General	75	thickened inside: turned down	10.21	3
III.B.1.a.1	4600	Platter bowl	VL 3200+	shallow, flat base, General	75	thickened inside: turned down	10.23	10
III.B.1.a.1	4600	Platter bowl	VL 3200+	shallow, flat base, General	75	thickened inside: turned down	10.23	11
III.B.1.a.1	4600	Platter bowl	VL 3200+	shallow, flat base, General	75	thickened inside: turned down	10.23	12
III.B.1.a.1	4600	Platter bowl	VL 3200+	shallow, flat base, General	75	thickened inside: turned down	10.29	1
III.B.1.a.1	4600	Platter bowl	VL 3200+	shallow, flat base, General	75	thickened inside: turned down	10.5	4
III.B.1.a.1	4600	Platter bowl	VL 3200+	shallow, flat base, General	75	thickened inside: turned down	10.5	5
III.B.1.a.1	4600	Platter bowl	VL 3200+	shallow, flat base, General	75	thickened inside: turned down	10.5	6
III.B.1.a.1	4600	Platter bowl	VL 3200+	shallow, flat base, General	75	thickened inside: turned down	10.5	7
III.B.1.a.1	4600	Platter bowl	VL 3200+	shallow, flat base, General	75	thickened inside: turned down	10.5	8
III.B.1.a.1	4600	Platter bowl	VL 3200+	shallow, flat base, General	75	thickened inside: turned down	10.6	1

Code	Form	Vessel	Size	Description	Rim	Rim Description	Fig	#
III.B.1.a.1	4600	Platter bowl	VL 3200+	shallow, flat base, General	75	thickened inside: turned down	10.6	3
III.B.1.a.1	4600	Platter bowl	VL 3200+	shallow, flat base, General	75	thickened inside: turned down	10.6	4
III.B.1.a.1	4600	Platter bowl	VL 3200+	shallow, flat base, General	75	thickened inside: turned down	10.6	5
III.B.1.a.1	4600	Platter bowl	VL 3200+	shallow, flat base, General	75	thickened inside: turned down	11.7	7
III.B.1.a.1	4605	Platter bowl	VL 3200+	shallow, flat base, walls straight to lightly curved, open	75	thickened inside: turned down	10.11	4
III.B.1.a.1	4605	Platter bowl	VL 3200+	shallow, flat base, walls straight to lightly curved, open	75	thickened inside: turned down	10.11	5
III.B.1.a.1	4605	Platter bowl	VL 3200+	shallow, flat base, walls straight to lightly curved, open	75	thickened inside: turned down	10.11	6
III.B.1.a.1	4605	Platter bowl	VL 3200+	shallow, flat base, walls straight to lightly curved, open	75	thickened inside: turned down	10.11	7
III.B.1.a.1	4605	Platter bowl	VL 3200+	shallow, flat base, walls straight to lightly curved, open	75	thickened inside: turned down	10.20	3
III.B.1.a.1	4605	Platter bowl	VL 3200+	shallow, flat base, walls straight to lightly curved, open	75	thickened inside: turned down	10.4	7
III.B.1.a.1	4605	Platter bowl	VL 3200+	shallow, flat base, walls straight to lightly curved, open	75	thickened inside: turned down	10.4	8
III.B.1.a.1	4605	Platter bowl	VL 3200+	shallow, flat base, walls straight to lightly curved, open	75	thickened inside: turned down	10.4	9
III.B.1.a.1	4605	Platter bowl	VL 3200+	shallow, flat base, walls straight to lightly curved, open	75	thickened inside: turned down	10.4	10
III.B.1.a.1	4605	Platter bowl	VL 3200+	shallow, flat base, walls straight to lightly curved, open	75	thickened inside: turned down	10.5	1
III.B.1.a.1	4605	Platter bowl	VL 3200+	shallow, flat base, walls straight to lightly curved, open	75	thickened inside: turned down	10.5	2
III.B.1.a.1	4605	Platter bowl	VL 3200+	shallow, flat base, walls straight to lightly curved, open	75	thickened inside: turned down	11.5	7
III.B.1.a.1	4606	Platter bowl	VL 3200+	shallow, flat base, walls straight to lightly curved, open	75	thickened inside: turned down	10.11	3
III.B.1.a.1	4606	Platter bowl	VL 3200+	shallow, flat base, walls straight to lightly curved, open	75	thickened inside: turned down	10.17	4
III.B.1.a.1	4606	Platter bowl	VL 3200+	shallow, flat base, walls straight to lightly curved, open	75	thickened inside: turned down	10.4	5
III.B.1.a.1	4606	Platter bowl	VL 3200+	shallow, flat base, walls straight to lightly curved, open	75	thickened inside: turned down	10.4	6

CODE	FORM	VESSEL	SIZE	DESCRIPTION	RIM	RIM DESCRIPTION	FIG	#
III.B.1.a.1	4612	Platter bowl	VL 3200+	platter bowl, flattened to rounded base, walls straight to lightly curved	75	thickened inside: turned down	10.17	5
III.B.1.a.1	4612	Platter bowl	VL 3200+	platter bowl, flattened to rounded base, walls straight to lightly curved	75	thickened inside: turned down	10.4	4
III.B.1.a.2	4600	Platter bowl	VL 3200+	shallow, flat base, General	73	thickened inside: rolled	10.26	3
III.B.1.a.3	4600	Platter bowl	VL 3200+	shallow, flat base, General	11	simple-direct: rounded	10.6	2
III.B.1.b.1	4620	Platter bowl	L 2900–1800	shallow, flat base, General	75	thickened inside: turned down	10.23	8
III.B.1.b.1	4620	Platter bowl	L 2900–1800	shallow, flat base, General	75	thickened inside: turned down	10.23	9
III.B.1.b.1	4620	Platter bowl	L 2900–1800	shallow, flat base, General	75	thickened inside: turned down	10.4	3
III.B.1.b.1	4625	Platter bowl	L 2900–1800	shallow, flat base, walls straight to lightly curved, open	75	thickened inside: turned down	10.26	1
III.B.1.b.1	4625	Platter bowl	L 2900–1800	shallow, flat base, walls straight to lightly curved, open	75	thickened inside: turned down	10.26	2
III.B.1.b.1	4625	Platter bowl	L 2900–1800	shallow, flat base, walls straight to lightly curved, open	75	thickened inside: turned down	10.3	21
III.B.1.b.1	4626	Platter bowl	L 2900–1800	shallow, flat base, walls straight to lightly curved, open	75	thickened inside: turned down	10.3	19
III.B.1.b.1	4626	Platter bowl	L 2900–1800	shallow, flat base, walls straight to lightly curved, open	75	thickened inside: turned down	10.3	20
III.B.1.b.2	4620	Platter bowl	L 2900–1800	shallow, flat base, General	73	thickened inside: rolled	11.7	6
III.B.1.b.2	4620	Platter bowl	L 2900–1800	shallow, flat base, General	74	thickened inside: rolled and pointed	10.4	2
III.B.1.b.2	4625	Platter bowl	L 2900–1800	shallow, flat base, walls straight to lightly curved, open	73	thickened inside: rolled	10.17	3
III.B.1.b.3	4620	Platter bowl	L 2900–1800	shallow, flat base, General	76	thickened inside: beveled	10.4	1
III.B.1.b.4	4620	Platter bowl	L 2900–1800	shallow, flat base, General	11	simple-direct: rounded	10.27	1
III.B.1.b.4	4620	Platter bowl	L 2900–1800	shallow, flat base, General	11	simple-direct: rounded	10.3	22
III.B.1.b.5	4620	Platter bowl	L 2900–1800	shallow, flat base, General	14	simple-direct: beveled, outside	10.11	2
III.B.1.c.1	4640	Platter bowl	M/L 1799–1000	shallow, flat base, General	75	thickened inside: turned down	11.7	5

CODE	FORM	VESSEL	SIZE	DESCRIPTION	RIM	RIM DESCRIPTION	FIG	#
III.B.1.c.1	4645	Platter bowl	M/L 1799–1000	shallow, flat base, walls straight to lightly curved, open	75	thickened inside: turned down	10.23	7
III.B.1.c.1	4660	Platter bowl	M 900–300	shallow, flat base, General	75	thickened inside: turned down	10.28	1
III.B.1.c.1	4660	Platter bowl	M 900–300	shallow, flat base, General	75	thickened inside: turned down	11.5	4
III.B.1.c.1	4660	Platter bowl	M 900–300	shallow, flat base, General	75	thickened inside: turned down	11.5	5
III.B.1.c.1	4666	Platter bowl	M 900–300	shallow, flat base, walls straight to lightly curved, open	75	thickened inside: turned down	11.5	6
III.B.1.c.1	4667	Platter bowl	M 900–300	shallow, flat base, walls straight to lightly curved, open (interpolated)	75	thickened inside: turned down	11.2	2
III.B.1.c.2	4645	Platter bowl	M/L 1799–1000	shallow, flat base, walls straight to lightly curved, open	73	thickened inside: rolled	10.23	6
III.B.1.c.2	4645	Platter bowl	M/L 1799–1000	shallow, flat base, walls straight to lightly curved, open	74	thickened inside: rolled and pointed	10.3	15
III.B.1.c.2	4665	Platter bowl	M 900–300	shallow, flat base, walls straight to lightly curved, open	73	thickened inside: rolled	10.20	1
III.B.1.c.2	4665	Platter bowl	M 900–300	shallow, flat base, walls straight to lightly curved, open	73	thickened inside: rolled	10.23	2
III.B.1.c.2	4665	Platter bowl	M 900–300	shallow, flat base, walls straight to lightly curved, open	73	thickened inside: rolled	10.23	5
III.B.1.c.2	4665	Platter bowl	M 900–300	shallow, flat base, walls straight to lightly curved, open	74	thickened inside: rolled and pointed	10.3	9
III.B.1.c.2	4666	Platter bowl	M 900–300	shallow, flat base, walls straight to lightly curved, open	73	thickened inside: rolled	10.3	8
III.B.1.c.2	4666	Platter bowl	M 900–300	shallow, flat base, walls straight to lightly curved, open	73	thickened inside: rolled	10.3	13
III.B.1.c.3	4640	Platter bowl	M/L 1799–1000	shallow, flat base, General	76	thickened inside: beveled	11.7	4
III.B.1.c.4	4664	Platter bowl	M 900–300	shallow, flat base, walls straight to lightly curved, open	71	thickened inside: flat, thick	10.23	4
III.B.1.c.5	4640	Platter bowl	M/L 1799–1000	shallow, flat base, General	10	simple-direct: squared	10.21	1
III.B.1.c.5	4640	Platter bowl	M/L 1799–1000	shallow, flat base, General	10	simple-direct: squared	10.3	17

CODE	FORM	VESSEL	SIZE	DESCRIPTION	RIM	RIM DESCRIPTION	FIG	#
III.B.1.c.5	4645	Platter bowl	M/L 1799–1000	shallow, flat base, walls straight to lightly curved, open	42	everted/angled: slight angle, tapered	10.3	14
III.B.1.c.5	4660	Platter bowl	M 900–300	shallow, flat base, General	11	simple-direct: rounded	10.3	16
III.B.1.c.5	4665	Platter bowl	M 900–300	shallow, flat base, walls straight to lightly curved, open	11	simple-direct: rounded	10.23	3
III.B.1.c.5	4666	Platter bowl	M 900–300	shallow, flat base, walls straight to lightly curved, open	19	simple-direct: thinned, with exterior groove	11.2	3
III.B.1.c.5	4667	Platter bowl	M 900–300	shallow, flat base, walls straight to lightly curved, open (interpolated)	10	simple-direct: squared	10.3	10
III.B.2.a.1	4603	Platter bowl	VL 3200+	shallow, flat base, walls curved upright (interpolated)	74	thickened inside: rolled and pointed	10.11	8
III.B.2.a.2	4623	Platter bowl	L 2900–1800	shallow, flat base, walls curved upright	72	thickened inside: flat, pointed	10.11	1
III.B.2.a.2	4623	Platter bowl	L 2900–1800	shallow, flat base, walls curved upright	72	thickened inside: flat, pointed	10.3	18
III.B.2.a.3	4602	Platter bowl	VL 3200+	shallow, flat base, walls curved upright	13	simple-direct: beveled, inside	10.11	9
III.B.2.a.3	4602	Platter bowl	VL 3200+	shallow, flat base, walls curved upright	13	simple-direct: beveled, inside	10.5	3
III.B.2.b	4628	Platter bowl	L 2900–1800	shallow, flat base, walls turned upright (carinated)	12	simple-direct: tapered	10.20	2
III.B.2.b	4659	Platter bowl	M/L 1799–1000	shallow, flat base, walls turned upright (carinated) (interpolated)	10	simple-direct: squared	10.17	2
III.B.2.b	4659	Platter bowl	M/L 1799–1000	shallow, flat base, walls turned upright (carinated) (interpolated)	11	simple-direct: rounded	10.3	12
III.B.2.b	4659	Platter bowl	M/L 1799–1000	shallow, flat base, walls turned upright (carinated) (interpolated)	19	simple-direct: thinned, with exterior groove	10.3	11
III.B.2.b	4668	Platter bowl	M 900–300	shallow, flat base, walls turned upright (carinated) (interpolated)	10	simple-direct: squared	10.17	1
III.B.2.b	4669	Platter bowl	M 900–300	shallow, flat base, walls turned upright (carinated) (interpolated)	10	simple-direct: squared	11.9	2
III.C.1.a	4740	M–S bowl	M/S	open, curved walls, General, EB III: w. 16–9	11	simple-direct: rounded	10.3	6
III.C.1.a	4749	M–S bowl	M/S	open, curved walls, EB III: w. 16–9	12	simple-direct: tapered	10.3	7

CODE	FORM	VESSEL	SIZE	DESCRIPTION	RIM	RIM DESCRIPTION	FIG	#
III.C.1.b	4730	M–S bowl	M/S to S	carinated walls, General	62	curved-out: lightly flared, tapered	11.2	4
III.C.2	4705	M–S bowl	M/S to S	closed, incurved walls, high tangent, EB III: closed, un-curved walls, high tangent	11	simple-direct: rounded	11.2	1
III.D.1	4766	M–S bowl	S	closed, curved walls	10	simple-direct: squared	10.3	5
III.D.1	4766	M–S bowl	S	closed, curved walls	11	simple-direct: rounded	10.3	4
III.D.1	4766	M–S bowl	S	closed, curved walls	12	simple-direct: tapered	11.5	1
III.D.1	4766	M–S bowl	S	closed, curved walls	12	simple-direct: tapered	11.7	2
III.D.2	4762	M–S bowl	S	carinated walls (added)	41	everted/angled: slight angle, rounded	10.3	2
III.D.2	4762	M–S bowl	S	carinated walls (added)	42	everted/angled: slight angle, tapered	10.3	1
III.D.2	4762	M–S bowl	S	carinated walls (added)	62	curved-out: lightly flared, tapered	10.23	1
III.D.2	4762	M–S bowl	S	carinated walls (added)	62	curved-out: lightly flared, tapered	11.5	2
III.D.2	4762	M–S bowl	S	carinated walls (added)	62	curved-out: lightly flared, tapered	11.7	1
III.D.2	4762	M–S bowl	S	carinated walls (added)	62	curved-out: lightly flared, tapered	11.9	1
III.D.2	4764	M–S bowl	S	carinated walls (added)	62	curved-out: lightly flared, tapered	11.7	3
III.D.2	4765	M–S bowl	S	carinated walls (added)	42	everted/angled: slight angle, tapered	11.5	3
III.D.2	4765	M–S bowl	S	carinated walls (added)	60	curved-out: lightly flared, squared	10.3	3
III.E.1	4851	Lamp	S	lamp forms, round base	11	simple-direct: rounded	10.14	11
III.E.2.a	4856	Lamp	S	lamp forms, flat base (interpolated)	12	simple-direct: tapered	10.15	1
III.E.2.a	4856	Lamp	S	lamp forms, flat base (interpolated)	12	simple-direct: tapered	10.15	3
III.E.2.a	4856	Lamp	S	lamp forms, flat base (interpolated)	12	simple-direct: tapered	10.9	3
III.E.2.a	4856	Lamp	S	lamp forms, flat base (interpolated)	12	simple-direct: tapered	11.9	9
III.E.2.a	4857	Lamp	S	lamp forms, flat base	11	simple-direct: rounded	10.8	17
III.E.2.a	4857	Lamp	S	lamp forms, flat base	11	simple-direct: rounded	10.9	1
III.E.2.a	4857	Lamp	S	lamp forms, flat base	11	simple-direct: rounded	11.5	12
III.E.2.a	4857	Lamp	S	lamp forms, flat base	12	simple-direct: tapered	10.1	1

Code	Form	Vessel	Size	Description	Rim	Rim Description	Fig	#
III.E.2.a	4857	Lamp	S	lamp forms, flat base	12	simple-direct: tapered	10.14	12
III.E.2.a	4857	Lamp	S	lamp forms, flat base	12	simple-direct: tapered	10.14	13
III.E.2.a	4857	Lamp	S	lamp forms, flat base	12	simple-direct: tapered	10.15	2
III.E.2.a	4857	Lamp	S	lamp forms, flat base	12	simple-direct: tapered	10.15	4
III.E.2.a	4857	Lamp	S	lamp forms, flat base	12	simple-direct: tapered	10.26	6
III.E.2.a	4857	Lamp	S	lamp forms, flat base	12	simple-direct: tapered	10.26	7
III.E.2.a	4857	Lamp	S	lamp forms, flat base	12	simple-direct: tapered	10.26	8
III.E.2.a	4857	Lamp	S	lamp forms, flat base	12	simple-direct: tapered	10.8	15
III.E.2.a	4857	Lamp	S	lamp forms, flat base	12	simple-direct: tapered	10.8	16
III.E.2.a	4857	Lamp	S	lamp forms, flat base	12	simple-direct: tapered	11.5	13
III.E.2.b	4856	Lamp	S	lamp forms, flat base (interpolated)	62	curved-out: lightly flared, tapered	10.15	5
III.E.2.b	4857	Lamp	S	lamp forms, flat base	61	curved-out: lightly flared, rounded	10.9	2

References

Adams, J. L.
2002   *Ground Stone Analysis: A Technological Approach*. Salt Lake City, UT: The University of Utah.

Adams, R. B.
2000   The Early Bronze Age III–IV Transition in southern Jordan: Evidence from Khirbet Hamra Ifdan. Pp. 379–401 in *Ceramics and Change in the Early Bronze Age of the Southern Levant,* eds. G. Philip and D. Baird. Sheffield: Sheffield Academic.
2003   External influences at Faynan during the Early Bronze Age: A Re-analysis of Building 1 at Barqa el-Hetiye, Jordan. *Palestine Exploration Quarterly* 135: 6–21.

Adavasio, J.; Andrews, R. L.; and J. S. Illingworth; with Pappas, C. A., and Oliver, E. A.
2003   Basketry Impressions and Weaving Accoutrements from the Bâb edh-Dhrâ', Town Site. Pp. 599–621 in *Bâb edh-Dhrâ': Excavations at the Town Site (1975–1981),* eds. W. E. Rast and R. T. Schaub. Winona Lake, IN: Eisenbrauns.

Aharoni, Y.
1979   *The Land of the Bible: A Historical Geography*, rev., and enl., Trans. A. F. Rainey. Philadelphia, PA: Westminster.

Albright, W. F.
1924   The Archaeological Results of an Expedition to Moab and the Dead Sea. *Bulletin of the American Schools of Oriental Research* 14: 2–12.
1925   The Jordan Valley in the Bronze Age. *Annual of the American Schools of Oriental Research* 6: 13–74.
1949   *The Archaeology of Palestine*. London: Penguin.
1962   The Chronology of Middle Bronze I (Early Bronze–Middle Bronze). *Bulletin of the American Schools of Oriental Research* 168: 36–42.

Al-Eisawi, D. M.
1985   Vegetation in Jordan. Pp. 45–57 in *Studies in the History and Archaeology of Jordan* 2, ed. A. Hadadi. New York, NY: Kegan Paul.

Al-Hunjul, N. G.
1985   The *Geology of Madaba Area: Map Sheet (3153-II), Geological Mapping Series, Geology Bulletin 31*. Amman: Geology Directorate, Geological Map Division, Natural Resources Authority.

Alon, D., and Yekutieli, Y.
1995   The Tel Halif Terrace "Silo Site" and Its Implications for the Early Bronze Age I. *'Atiqot* 26: 149–89.

Amiran, D. H. K, et al., Board of Editors
1970   *Atlas of Israel*. 2nd ed. Amsterdam: Elsevier.

Amiran, R.
1960   The pottery of the Middle Bronze Age I in Palestine. *Israel Exploration Journal* 10: 204–25.
1969   Ancient Pottery of the Holy Land. New Brunswick, NJ: Rutgers University

1970 The Beginnings of Urbanization in Canaan. Pp. 83–100 in *Near Eastern Archaeology in the Twentieth Century: Essays in Honor of Nelson Glueck,* edited by J. A. Sanders. Garden City, NY: Doubleday.

Amiran, R., and Ilan, O
1996 *Early Arad II: The Chalcolithic and Early Bronze IB Settlements and the Early Bronze II City: Architecture and Town Planning.* Jerusalem: The Israel Museum/The Israel Exploration Society.

Amiran, R.; Paran, U.; Shiloh, Y.; Brown, R.; Tsafrir, Y.; and Ben-Tor, A.
1978 *Early Arad I. The Chalcolithic Settlement and Early Bronze Age City. I–V Seasons of Exavations (1962–1966).* Jerusalem: The Israel Exploration Society.

Angel, J. L., and Bisel, S.
1986 Health and Stress in an Early Bronze Age Population. Pp 12–30 in *Ancient Anatolia: Aspects of Change and Cultural Development – Essays in Honor of Machteld J. Mellink,* eds. J. Canby, E. Porada, B. Ridgway, and T. Stech. Madison, WI: University of Wisconsin.

Ashbel, D.
1967 *Rainfall Maps and Tables of the Dead Sea and Jordan Valley Catchment Area.* Jerusalem: Hebrew University.

Baly, D.
1974 *The Geography of the Bible,* rev. ed. New York, NY: Harper and Row.
1985 The Nature of Environment, with special relation to the Country of Jordan. Pp. 19–24 in *Studies in the History and Archaeology of Jordan* 2, ed. A. Hadidi. New York, NY: Kegan Paul.

Barjous, M. O.
1992 *The Geology of the Ash Shawbak Area (Map Sheet No. 3151 III).* Amman.

Bar-Matthews, M.; Ayalon, A.; and Kaufman, A.
1998 Middle to Late Holocene (6500 years period) Paleoclimate in the Eastern Mediterranean from Isotopic Composition of Speleothems from Soreq Cave, Israel. Pp. 203–14 in *Water, Environment and Society in Times of Climate Change,* eds. A. Issar and N. Brown. Dodrecht: Kluwer Academic.

Baruch, U.
1990 Palynological Evidence of Human Impact on the Vegetation as recorded in Late Holocene Lake Sediments in Israel. Pp. 283–93 in *Man's Role in the Shaping of the Eastern Mediterranean Landscape,* eds. S. Bottema, G. Entjes-Nieborg, and W. van Zeist. Rotterdam: Balkema.

Baruch, U., and Bottema, S.
1999 A New Pollen Diagram from Lake Hula. Vegetational, Climatic, and Anthropogenic Implications. Pp. 75–86 in *Ancient Lakes: Their Cultural and Biological Diversity,* eds. H. Kawanabe, G. W. Coulter, and A. C. Roosevelt. Ghent: Kenobi.

Baxevani, E.
1995 The Complex Nomads: Death and Social Stratification in EB IV Southern Levant. Pp. 85–95 in *The Archaeology of Death in the Ancient Near East,* eds. S. Campbell and A. Green. Oxbow Monograph 51. Oxford: Oxbow.

Beaumont, P.
1985 Man-induced Erosion in Northern Jordan. Pp. 291–96 in *Studies in the History and Archaeology of Jordan* 2, ed. A. Hadidi. New York, NY: Kegan Paul.

Beck, H. C.
1928 Classification and Nomenclature of Beads and Pendants. *Archaeologia* 11: 1–76 (Reprinted as a book in 1981 by George Shumway, York, PA).

Bender, F.
1974 *Geology of Jordan.* Contributions to the Regional Geology of the Earth. Supplementary ed. of vol. 7 in English with minor revisions. Trans. Moh'd Kamal Khdeir. Berlin: Gebrüder Borntraeger.
1975 *Geology of the Arabian Peninsula: Jordan.* Geological Survey Professional Paper 560–I. Washington, DC: U.S. Government Printing Office.

1992   The Early Bronze Age. Pp. 81–125 in *The Archaeology of Ancient Israel*, ed. A. Ben-Tor. New Haven, CT: Yale University.

Betts, A. V. G.
1991   The Jawa Area in Prehistory. Pp. 181–90 in *Excavations at Jawa 1972–1986. Stratigraphy, Pottery and Other Finds*, ed. A. V. G. Betts. Edinburgh: Edinburgh University.

Beynon, D. E.; Donahue, J.; Schaub, R. T.; and Johnston, R. A.
1986   Tempering Types and Sources for Early Bronze Age Ceramics from Bâb edh-Dhrâ' and Numeira, Jordan. *Journal of Field Archaeology* 13: 297–305.

Braemer, F., and Echallier, J.-C.
2000   Summary Statement on the EBA Ceramics from southern Syria, and the Relationship of this Material with that of Neighbouring Regions. Pp. 403–10 in *Ceramics and Change in the Early Bronze Age of the Southern Levant,* eds. R. Adams and Y. Goren. London: Sheffield.

Braun, E.
1985   *En Shadud Salvage Excavations at a Farming Community in the Jezreel Valley, Israel.* BAR International Series 249. Oxford: British Archaeological Reports.

Brice, W.
1978   Introduction. Pp. 1–2 in *The Environmental History of the Near and Middle East since the Last Ice Age*, ed. W. C. Brice. London: Academic.

Broeder, N. H., and Skinner, H. C. W.
1992   Beads from the 1986 Season. Pp. 135–53 in *The Southern Ghors and Northeast 'Arabah Archaeological Survey*, ed. B. MacDonald. Sheffield Archaeological Monographs 5. Sheffield: Collis.
2003   Jewelry and Ornaments. Pp. 566–98 in *Bâb edh-Dhrâ': Excavations at the Town Site (1975–1981)*, eds. W. E. Rast and R. T. Schaub. Winona Lake, IN: Eisenbrauns.

Bronitsky, G., and Hamer, R.
1986   Experiments in Ceramic Technology: The Effects of Various Tempering Materials on Impact and Thermal-shock Resistance. *American Antiquity* 51: 89–101.

Bronk Ramsey, C.
2005   OxCal Program Version 3.10. Oxford Radiocarbon Accelerator Unit, University of Oxford. Http://www.rlaha.ox.ac.uk/orau/calibration.

Brothwell, D.
1965   The Palaeopathology of the E.B.–M.B., and Middle Bronze Age Remains from Jericho (1957–1958 Excavations). Pp. 685–93 in *Excavations at Jericho, Vol. II,* ed. K. Kenyon. London: British School of Archaeology in Jerusalem.

Brünnow, R. E., and von Domazewski, A.
1904   *Die Provincia Arabia*. Vol. 1. Strassbourg: Trübner.

Bunimovitz, S., and Greenberg, R.
2004   Revealed in Their Cups: Syrian Drinking Customs in Intermediate Bronze Age Canaan. *Bulletin of the American Schools of Oriental Research* 334: 19–31.
2006   Of Pots and Paradigms: Interpreting the Intermediate Bronze Age in Israel/Palestine. Pp. 21–31 in *Confronting the Past: Archaeological and Historical Essays on Ancient Israel in Honor of William G. Dever,* eds. S. Gitin, J. E. Wright, and J. P. Dessel. Winona Lake, IN: Eisenbrauns.

Burdon, D. J.
1959   *Handbook of the Geology of Jordan*. Amman: Government of the Hashemite Kingdom of Jordan

Burckhardt, J. L.
1822   *Travels in Syria and the Holy Land*. London: Murray.

Butzer, K. W.
[1975] 1981   Patterns of Environmental Change in the Near East during Late Pleistocene and Early Holocene Times. Pp. 389–410 in *Problems in Prehistory: North Africa and the*

Levant, eds. F. Wendorf and A. E. Marks. Dallas, TX: Southern Methodist University; reprint ed., Ann Arbor: University Microfilms.

1996   Sociopolitical Discontinuity in the Near East c. 2200 B.C.E.: Scenarios from Palestine and Egypt. Pp. 245–96 in *Third Millennium BC Climate Change; and Old World Collapse,* eds. H. N. Dalfes, G. Kukla, and H. Weiss. Berlin: Springer.

Callaway, J.
1980   *Early Bronze Age Citadel and Lower City at Ai (et-Tell): A Report of the Joint Archaeological Expedition to Ai (et-Tell). 2.* American Schools of Oriental Research Excavation Reports. Cambridge, MA: American Schools of Oriental Research.

Chesson, M. S.
1999   Libraries of the Dead: Early Bronze Age Charnel Houses and Social Identity at Urban Bâb edh-Dhrâʿ, Jordan. *Journal of Anthropological Archaeology* 18: 137–64.

Chesson, M.S.; Makarewicz, C.; Kuijt, I.; and Whiting, C.
2005   Results of the 2001 Kerak Plateau Early Bronze Age Survey. Pp. 3–62 in *Annual of the American Schools of Oriental Research* 59. Boston, MA: American Schools of Oriental Research.

Christopherson, G. L., and Guertin, D. P.
1995   Soil Erosion, Agricultural Intensification, and Iron Age Settlement in the Region of Tell el-Umeiri, Jordan. Annual Meeting of the American Schools of Oriental Research. Philadelphia, PA: Unpublished Manuscript.

Clason, A. T., and Clutton-Brock, J.
1982   The Impact of Domestic Animals on the Vegetation during the First Phases of Animal Husbandry in the Mediterranean and Near East. Pp. 145–48 in *Palaeoclimates, Palaeoenvironments and Human Communities in the Eastern Mediterranean Region in Later Prehistory,* Part I, eds. J. L. Bintliff and W. van Zeist. BAR International Series 112. Oxford: British Archaeological Reports.

Cleveland, R. L.
1960   The Excavation of the Conway High Place (Petra) and the Soundings at Khirbet Ader. Pp. 79–97 in *Annual of the American Schools of Oriental Research* 34–35. New Haven, CT: American Schools of Oriental Research.

Climatic Atlas of Jordan
1971   *Climatic Atlas of Jordan.* Amman: The Hashemite Kingdom of Jordan, Ministry of Transport, Meteorological Department.

Cohen, R.
1986   *The Settlement of The Central Negev in the Light of Archaeology and Literary Sources During the 4th–1st Millennia B.C.E.* Unpublished Ph.D. dissertation. Jerusalem: The Hebrew University of Jerusalem. (Hebrew).
1992   The Nomadic or Semi Nomadic Middle Bronze Age I Settlements in the Central Negev. Pp. 105–31 in *Pastoralism in the Levant: Archaeological Materials in Anthropological Perspectives,* eds. O. Bar-Yosef and A. Khazanov. Madison, WI: Prehistory.

Cohen, R., and Dever, W. G.
1979   Preliminary Report of the Second Season of the Central Negev Highlands Project. *Bulletin of the American Schools of Oriental Research* 236: 41–60.
1981   Preliminary Report of the Third and Final Season of the "Central Negev Highlands Project." *Bulletin of the American Schools of Oriental Research* 243: 57–77.

Cole, D. P.
1984   *Shechem I: The Middle Bronze IIB Pottery.* Winona Lake, IN: Eisenbrauns/American Schools of Oriental Research.

Cordova, C. E.
1999a   Geoarchaeology of Alluvial Deposits and Soils in the Wâdi Systems of Northern Moab. Archaeology in Jordan, eds. P. M. Bikai and V. Egan. *American Journal of Archaeology* 103: 488–89.
1999b   Landscape Transformation in the Mediterranean-steppe Transition Zone of Jordan: A Geoarchaeological Approach. *The Arab World Geographer* 2: 188–201.

2000 Geomorphological Evidence of Intense Soil Erosion in the Highlands of Central Jordan. *Physical Geography* 21 (6): 538–67.

2007 *Geoarchaeology and Cultural Ecology of Millennial Landscape Change in Jordan.* Tucson, AZ: University of Arizona.

Cordova, C. E.; Foley, C.; Nowell, A.; and Bisson, M.

2005 Landforms, Sediments, Soil Development and Prehistoric Site Settings in the Madaba-Dhiban Plateau, Jordan. *Geoarchaeology* 20: 29–56.

Covello-Paran, K.

1999 The Rural Aspect of the Jezreel Valley during the Intermediate Bronze Age in Light of the Excavations at ʿEin Helu (Migdal Ha ʿEmeq). Unpublished M.A. thesis. Tel Aviv University.

2009 Socio-Economic Aspects of an Intermediate Bronze Age Village in the Jezreel Valley. Pp. 9–20 in *The Levant in Transition,* ed. P. J. Parr. Palestine Exploration Fund Annual 9. London: Maney.

Currid, J. D.

1984 The Deforestations of the Foothills of Palestine. *Palestine Exploration Quarterly* 116: 1–11.

Dalfes, H. N.; Kukla, G.; and Weiss, H.

1997 *Third Millennium BC Climate Change and Old World Collapse.* Berlin: Springer.

Danin, A.

1985 Palaeoclimates in Israel: Evidence from Weathering Patterns on Stones in and near Archaeological Sites. *Bulletin of the American Schools of Oriental Research* 259: 33–43.

Daviau, P. M. M.

1993 *Houses and their Furnishings in Bronze Age Palestine.* Sheffield: Sheffield Academic.

Vaux, R. de

1971 Palestine in the Early Bronze Age. Pp. 208–37 in *Cambridge Ancient History,* third revised edition, volume 1, part 2. Cambridge: Cambridge University.

Dever, W. G.

1970 The 'Middle Bronze I Period' in Syria-Palestine. Pp. 132–63 in *Near Eastern Archaeology in the Twentieth Century: Essays in Honor of Nelson Glueck,* ed. J. A. Sanders. Garden City, NY: Doubleday.

1971 The Peoples of Palestine in the Middle Bronze I Period. *Harvard Theological Review* 64: 197–226.

1972 A Middle Bronze I Site on the West Bank of the Jordan. *Archaeology* 25: 231–33.

1973 EBIV–MBI Horizon in Transjordan and Southern Palestine. *Bulletin of the American Schools of Oriental Research* 210: 37–63.

1974 The Middle Bronze Occupation and Pottery of ʿArâq en-Naʿsâneh (Cave II). Pp. 33–48 in *Discoveries in the Wâdï ed-Dâliyeh,* eds. P. W. Lapp and N. L. Lapp. Annual of the American Schools of Oriental Research 41. Cambridge, MA: American Schools of Oriental Research.

1975 A Middle Bronze I Cemetery at Khirbet el-Kirmil. *Eretz Israel* 12: 18*–3*.

1980 New Vistas on the EB IV (MBI) Horizon in Syria-Palestine. *Bulletin of the American Schools of Oriental Research* 237: 35–64.

1985a From the End of the Early Bronze Age to the Beginning of the Middle Bronze. Pp. 113–35 in *Biblical Archaeology Today: Proceedings of the International Congress on Biblical Archaeology,* ed. J. Amitai. Jerusalem: Israel Exploration Society.

1985b Village planning at Beʿer Resisim and Socio-economic Structure in Early Bronze Age IV Palestine. *Eretz-Israel* 18: 18–28.

1989 The Collapse of the Urban Early Bronze Age in Palestine: Toward a Systemic Analysis. Pp. 225–46 in *Lʾurbanisation de la Palestine a lʾâge du Bronze ancien,* Part ii, ed. P de Miroschedji. BAR International Series 527. Oxford: British Archaeological Reports.

1992 Pastoralism and the End of the Urban Early Bronze Age in Palestine. Pp. 83–92 in *Pastoralism in the Levant: Archaeological Materials in Anthropological Perspectives,* eds. O. Bar-Yosef and A. Khazanov. Monographs in World Archaeology 10. Madison, WI: Prehistory.

1995 Social Structure in the Early Bronze IV Period in Palestine. Pp. 282–96 in *The Archaeology of Society in the Holy Land*, ed. T. E. Levy. London: Leicester University.

2003 An EB IV Tomb Group from Tell Beit Mirsim. *Eretz-Israel* 27 (Tadmor Volume): 29*–36*.

Dever, W. G., and Lance, H. D. (eds.)
1978 *A Manual of Field Excavation: Handbook for Field Archaeologists*. Cincinnati, OH: Hebrew Union College/Jewish Institute of Religion.

Donahue, J.
1985 Hydrologic and Topographic Change during and after Early Bronze Occupation at Bâb edh-Dhrâʿ and Numeira. Pp. 131–40 in *Studies in the History and Archaeology of Jordan 2*, ed. A. Hadidi. New York, NY: Kegan Paul.
1988 Geologic History of Wadi el-Hasa Survey Area. Pp. 26–39 in *The Wadi el-Hasa Archaeological Survey, 1979–1983, West-Central Jordan*, ed. B. MacDonald. Waterloo, ON: Wilfrid Laurier University.

Donahue, J.; Peer, B.; and Schaub, R. T.
1997 The Southeastern Dead Sea Plain: Changing Shorelines and their Impact on Settlement Patterns through Historical Periods. Pp. 127–36 in *Studies in the History and Archaeology of Jordan 4*, eds. G. Bisheh, M. Zaghlouo, and I. Kehrberg. Amman: Department of Antiquities of Jordan.

Dorrell, P.
1983 Appendix A: Stone Vessels, Tools and Objects. Pp. 485–75 in *Excavations at Jericho* V, eds. K. Kenyon and T. A. Holland. London: British School of Archaeology in Jerusalem.

Drennan, R. D.
1966 Statistics for Archaeologists: A Common Sense Approach. New York, NY: Plenum.

Dubis, E., and Dabrowski, B.
2002 The Dolmen and Other Features on the South Slopes of Tall al-ʿUmayri. Pp. 171–77

in *Madaba Plains Project 5: The 1994 Season at Tall al-ʿUmayri and Subsequent Studies*, eds. L. G. Herr, D. R. Clark, L. T. Geraty, R. W. Younker, and Ø S. LaBianca. Berrien Springs, MI: Andrews University.

Eisenberg, E.
1993a Nahal Rephaim. Pp. 1277–80 in *The New Encyclopedia of Archaeological Excavations in the Holy Land*, eds. E. Stern, A. Lewinson-Gilbow, and J. Aviram. Jerusalem: Israel Exploration Society.
1993b Shaʿar Ha Golan. Pp. 1340–43 in *The New Encyclopedia of Archaeological Excavations In the Holy Land*, eds. E. Stern, A. Lewinson-Gilbow, and J. Aviram. Jerusalem: Israel Exploration Society.

Eliot, C.
1983 Kissonerga Mylouthkia: An Outline of the Ground Stone Industry. *Levant* 15: 11–37.

Ellis, S.
2006 Area AA Report, Excavation of Abila of the Decapolis. Unpublished manuscript.

Epstein, C.
1998 *The Chalcolithic Culture of the Golan*. Israel Antiquities Authority Reports 4. Jerusalem: Israel Antiquities Authority.

Falconer, S. E.
1987 Village Pottery Production and Exchange: A Jordan Valley Perspective. Pp. 251–59 in *Studies in the History and Archaeology of Jordan III*, ed. A. Hadidi. New York, NY: Kegan Paul.

Falconer, S. E, and Fall, P. L.;
with Berelov, I., and Metzger, M. C.
2006 *Bronze Age Rural Ecology and Village Life at Tell el-Hayyat, Jordan*. BAR International Series 1586. Oxford: Archaeopress.

Falconer, S. E.; Fall, P. L.; and Jones, J. E.
1998 Winter 1996/97 Excavations in the Northern Jordan Valley: The Jordan Valley Village Project. *American Journal of Archaeology* 102: 588–89.
2007 Life at the Foundation of Bronze Age Civilization: Agrarian Villages in the Jordan

Valley. Pp. 261–68 in *Crossing Jordan: North American Contributions to the Archaeology of Jordan,* eds. T. E. Levy, P. M. M. Daviau, R. W. Younker, and M. Shaer. London: Equinox.

Falconer, S. E., and Magness-Gardiner, B.
1989   Bronze Age Village Life in the Jordan Valley: Archaeological Investigations at Tell el-Hayyat and Tell Abu en-Niʿaj, 2000. *American Journal of Archaeology* 105: 438–39.

Fall, P.; Lines, L.; and Falconer, S. E.
1998   Seeds of Civilization: Bronze Age Rural Economy and Ecology in the Southern Levant. *Annals of the Association of American Geographers* 88: 107–25.

Fargo, V. M.
1979   Settlement in Southern Palestine during Early Bronze III. Unpublished Ph.D. dissertation. University of Chicago.

Feinbrun, N., and Zohary, M.
1955   A Geobotanical Survey of Trasjordan. *Bulletin of the Research Council of Israel* 5: 7–12.

Ferguson, K., and Hudson, T.
1986   Climate of Tell Hesban and Area. Pp. 7–22 in *Hesban 2: Environmental Foundations: Studies of Climatical, Geological, Hydrological, and Phytological Conditions in Hesban and Vicinity,* eds. Ø. S. LaBianca and L. Lacelle. Berrien Springs, MI: Andrews University.

Finkelstein, I.
1991   The Central Hill Country in the Intermediate Bronze Age. *Israel Exploration Journal* 41: 19–45.
1995   *Living on the Fringe.* Sheffield: Sheffield Academic.

Finnegan, M.
1978   Faunal Remains from Bâb edh-Dhrâʿ, 1975. Pp. 51–54 in *Preliminary Excavation Reports: Bâb edh-Dhrâʿ, Sardis, Meiron, Tell el-Hesi, Carthage (Punic),* ed. D. N. Freedman. Annual of the American Schools of Oriental Research 43. Cambridge, MA: American Schools of Oriental Research.
1981   Faunal Remains from Bâb Edh-Dhrâʿ and Numeira. Pp. 177–80 in *The Southeastern*

Dead Sea Plain Expedition: An Interim Report of the 1977 Season, ed. J. A. Callaway. Annual of the American Schools of Oriental Research 46. Cambridge, MA: American Schools of Oriental Research.

Food and Agriculture Organization
of the United Nations
[1974] 1990   Soil Map of the World. *World Soil Resources Report.* Reprint. Rome.

Frunkin, A. M., and Elitzur, Y.
2000   Historic Dead Sea Level Fluctuations Calibrated with Geological and Archaeological Evidence. *Quaternary Research* 57: 334–42.

Frumkin, A. M.; Magaritz, I.; Carmi, I.; and Zak, I.
1991   The Holocene Climatic Record of the Salt Caves in Mount Sedom, Israel. T*he Holocene* 1: 191–200.

Gilead, I.
1995   *Grar: A Chalcolithic Site in the Northern Negev.* Negev: Ben-Gurion University.

Gitin, S.
1975   Middle Bronze I "Domestic Pottery" at Jebel Qaʿaqir, A Ceramic Inventory of Cave G23. *Eretz Israel* 12: 46*–62*.

Glueck, N.
1939   *Explorations in Eastern Palestine, III.* Annual of the American Schools of Oriental Research 18–19. New Haven, CT: American Schools of Oriental Research.

Goldberg, P., and Bar-Yosef, O.
1982   Environmental and Archaeological Evidence for Climatic Change in the Southern Levant. Pp. 399–414 in *Palaeoclimates, Palaeoenvironments and Human Communities in the Eastern Mediterranean Region in Later Prehistory,* Part 2, eds. J. L. Bintliff and W. van Zeist. BAR International Series 133(ii). London: British Archaeological Reports.

Gophna, R.; Liphschitz, N.; and Lev-Yadun, S.
1986   Man's Impact on the Natural Vegetation of the Central Coastal Plain of Israel during the Chalcolithic Period and the Bronze Age. *Tel Aviv* 13: 71–84.

Goren, Y.

1991a The Beginnings of Pottery Production in Israel, Technology and Typology of Proto-Historic Ceramic Assemblages in Eretz-Israel (6th–4th Millennia B.C.E.). Unpublished Ph.D. dissertation. Hebrew University of Jerusalem. (Hebrew.)

1991b Petrographic Examination of the Ceramic Assemblage from Tel 'Amal. *'Atiqot 20*: 129–30.

1992 Petrographic Study of the Pottery Assemblage from Munhata. Pp. 329–60 in *The Pottery Assemblage of the Sha'ar Hagolan and Rabah Stages of Munhata (Israel)*, ed. Y. Garfinkel. Paris: Paléorient.

1996 The Southern Levant during the Early Bronze Age IV: The Petrographic Perspective. *Bulletin of the American Schools of Oriental Research* 303: 33–72.

Goren, Y.; Finkelstein,I.; and Na'aman, N.

2004 *Inscribed in Clay, Provenance Study of the Amarna Tablets and Other Near Eastern Texts*. Tel Aviv:

Goren, Y., and Fischer, P.

1999 Petrographic Study of Ceramic Assemblages as a Regional Project: The Early and Late Bronze Ages in the Central Jordan Valley. Pp. 143–46 in *Practical Impact of Science on Near Eastern & Aegean Archaeology*, eds. S. Pike and S. Gitin. London: James and James.

Greenberg, R.

2002 *Early Urbanizations in the Levant: A Regional Narrative*. London: Leicester.

Guy, P. L. O., and Engberg, R.

1938 *Megiddo Tombs*. Chicago, IL: University of Chicago.

Harlan, J. R.

1981 Natural Resources of the Southern Ghor. Pp. 155–64 in *The Southeastern Dead Sea Plain Expedition: An Interim Report of the 1977 Season*, eds. W. E. Rast and R. T. Schaub. Annual of the American Schools of Oriental Research 46. Cambridge, MA: American Schools of Oriental Research.

1985 The Early Bronze Age Environment of the Southern Ghor and the Moab Plateau. Pp. 125–29 in *Studies in the History and Archaeology of Jordan* 2, ed. A. Hadidi. New York, NY: Kegan Paul.

Harrison, T. P.

1997 Shifting Patterns of Settlement in the Highlands of Central Jordan during the Early Bronze Age. *Bulletin of the American Schools of Oriental Research* 306: 1–37.

Hauptmann, A.

2007 *The Archaeometallurgy of Copper: Evidence from Faynan, Jordan*. Natural Science in Archaeology, eds. B. Herrmann and G. A. Wagner. Berlin: Springer.

Helms, S. W.

1981 *Jawa: Lost City of the Black Desert*. Ithaca, NY: Cornell University.

1986 Excavations at Tell Umm Hammad, 1984. *Levant 18*: 25–50.

1989 An EB IV Pottery Repertoire at Amman, Jordan. *Bulletin of the American Schools of Oriental Research* 273: 17–36.

1991 Other Finds. Pp. 155–67 in *Excavations at Jawa 1972–1986 Stratigraphy, Pottery and Other Finds*, ed. A. V. G. Betts. Edinburgh: Edinburgh University.

Helms, S. W., and McCreery, D. W.

1988 Rescue Excavations at Umm el-Bighal: The Pottery. *Annual of the Department of Antiquities of Jordan* 32: 319–47.

Hennessy, J. B.

1967 *The Foreign Relations of Palestine During the Early Bronze Age*. Colt Archaeological Institute Publications. London: Quaritch

Herr, L. G.

1989 The Pottery. Pp. 299–353 in *Madaba Plains Project 5: The 1984 Season at Tell el-'Umeiri and Subsequent Studies*, eds., L. T. Geraty, L. G. Herr, Ø. S. LaBianca, and R. W. Younker. Berrien Springs, MI: Andrews University.

2002 Excavation and Cumulative Results. Pp. 8-22 in *Madaba Plains Project 5: The 1994 Season at Tall al-'Umayri and Subsequent*

Studies, eds. L. G. Herr, D. R. Clark, L. T. Geraty, R. W. Younker, and Ø S. LaBianca. Berrien Springs, MI: Andrews University.

Herr, L. G., and Christopherson, G. L.
1998   *Excavation Manual Madaba Plains Project* (rev. ed.). Berrien Springs, MI: Andrews University.

Herr, L. G.; Geraty, L. T.; LaBianca, Ø. S.; Younker, R. W.; and Clark, D. R. (eds.)
2002   *Madaba Plains Project 5: The 1994 Season at Tall al-ʿUmayri and Subsequent Studies.* Berrien Springs, MI: Andrews University.

Honça, D., and Algaze, G.
1998   Preliminary Report on the Human Skeletal Remains at Titriş Höyük: 1991–1996 Seasons. *Anatolica 24*: 101–41.

Hopkins, D. C.
1985   *The Highlands of Canaan: Agricultural Life in the Early Iron Age.* Sheffield: Almond.

Horwitz, L.
1989   Diachronic Changes in Rural Husbandry Practices in Bronze Age Settlements from the Refaim Valley, Israel. *Palestine Exploration Quarterly* 121: 44–54.

Hovers, E.
1996   Groundstone Industry. Pp. 171–203 in *Excavations at the City of David 1978–1985*, Vol. IV, eds. D. T. Ariel and A. De Groot. Jerusalem: Israel Exploration Society.

Ibrahim, M., and Qadi, N.
1995   El-Musheirfeh "Shnellar" Tombs: An Intermediate Bronze Age Cemetery. Pp. 81–102 in *Trade, Contact, and the Movement of Peoples in the Eastern Mediterranean: Studies in Honour of J. Basil Hennessy*, eds. S. Bourke and J.-P. Descœudres. Mediterranean Archaeology Supplement 3. Sydney: Australian Archaeological Institute at Athens.

Ionides, M. G.
1939   *Government of Transjordan: Report on the Water Resources of Transjordan and their Development.* Incorporating a Report on Geology, Soils and Minerals, and Hydro-

Geological Correlations by G. S. Blake. London: Published on the behalf of the Government of Transjordan by the Crown Agents for the Colonies.

Irby, C., and Mangles, J.
1823   *Travels in Egypt and Nubia, Syria, and Asia Minor; during the years 1817 & 1818.* London: Darf.

Issar, A. S.
2003   *Climate Changes during the Holocene and their Impact on Hydrological Systems.* International Hydrological Series. Cambridge: Cambridge University.

Isserlin, B. S. J.
1955   Ancient Forests in Palestine: Some Archaeological Indications. *Palestine Exploration Quarterly* 87: 87–88.

Joffe, A. H.
1993   *Settlement and Society in the Early Bronze I and II Southern Levant: Complementarity and Contradiction in Small-Scale Complex Society.* Sheffield: Sheffield Academic.

Kaufman, D.
1998   Measuring Archaeological Diversity: An Application of the Jackknife Technique. *American Antiquity* 63: 73–85.

Kempinsky, A.
1978   *The Rise of an Urban Culture: The Urbanization of Palestine in the Early Bronze Age.* Jerusalem: Israel Ethnographic Society.
1992   Fortifications, Public Buildings and Town Planning in the Early Bronze Age. Pp. 68–80 in *The Architecture of Ancient Israel from the Prehistoric to the Persian Periods*, eds. A. Kempinski and R. Reich. Jerusalem: Israel Exploration Society.

Kenyon, K.
1960   *Excavations at Jericho, vol. 1: The Tombs Excavated in 1952–54.* London: British School of Archaeology in Jerusalem.
1965   *Excavations at Jericho, vol. 2: The Tombs Excavated in 1955–58.* London: British School of Archaeology in Jerusalem.

1979   *Archaeology of the Holy Land.* 4th ed. New York, NY: Norton.

Kenyon, K.; Bottéro J.; and Posener, G.

1971   Syria and Palestine c. 2160-1780 B.C. Pp. 532–94 in *Cambridge Ancient History,* 3rd rev. ed. Vol. 1, Part 2. Cambridge: Cambridge University.

Kochavi, M.

1967   The Settlement of the Negev in the Middle Bronze (Canaanite) I Age. Unpublished Ph.D. dissertation. The Hebrew University of Jerusalem. (Hebrew.)

Koucky, F.

1982   Consultation with Khirbet Iskander Excavations.

Lacelle, L.

1986   Bedrock Geology, Surficial Geology, and Soils. Pp. 23–58 in *Hesban 2: Environmental Foundations: Studies of Climatical, Geological, Hydrological, and Phytological Conditions in Hesban and Vicinity*, eds. Ø. S. LaBianca and L. Lacelle. Berrien Springs, MI: Andrews University.

Lapp, P. W.

1966   *The Dhahr Mirzbâneh Tombs.* New Haven, CT: American Schools of Oriental Research.

1970   Palestine in the Early Bronze Age. Pp. 101–31 in *Near Eastern Archaeology in the Twentieth Century: Essays in Honor of Nelson Glueck,* edited by J. A. Sanders. Garden City, NY: Doubleday.

Lee, J. R.

1973   Chalcolithic Ghassul: New Aspects and Master Typology. Unpublished Ph.D. dissertation. The Hebrew University of Jerusalem.

2003   Worked Stones. Pp. 622–37 in *Bâb edh-Dhrâ': Excavation at the Town Site (1975–81)*, eds. W. E. Rast and R. T. Schaub. Reports of the Expedition to the Dead Sea Plain, Jordan 2. Winona Lake, IN: Eisenbrauns.

Lemau, H.

1978   Faunal Remains, Strata I–III. Pp 83–113 in *Early Arad: The Chalcolithic Settlement and Early Bronze City,* vol. I, ed. R. Amiran. Jerusalem: Israel Exploration Society.

Levy, T. E., and Adams, R. B.

2001   Khirbet Hamra Ifdan. Pp. 216–17 in *Archaeological Encyclopedia of the Holy Land.* New Revised Edition, eds. A. Negev and S. Gibson. Nashville, TN: Nelson.

Levy, T. E.; Adams, R. B.; Hauptmann, A.; Prange, M.; Schmitt-Strecker, S.; and Najjar, M.

2002   Early Bronze Age Metallurgy: A Newly Discovered Copper Manufactory in Southern Jordan. *Antiquity* 76: 425–37

Levy, T. E.; Adams, R. B.; and Najjar, M.

2001   Jabal Hamrat Fidan. *American Journal of Archaeology* 105: 442–45.

Levy, T. E.; Adams, R. B.; Witten, A. J.; Anderson, J.; Arbel, Y.; Kuah, S.; Moreno, J.; Lo, A.; and Wagoner, M.

2001   Early Metallurgy, Interaction, and Social Change: The Jabal Hamrat Fidan Archaeological Project Research Design and 1998 Survey. *Annual of the Department of Antiquities, Jordan* 45: 45–76.

London, G. A.

1985   Decoding Designs: The Late Third Millennium B.C. Pottery from Jebel Qa'aqir. Unpublished Ph.D. dissertation. The University of Arizona.

Long, J. C., Jr.

1988   Early Bronze IV at Khirbet Iskander and the Excavated Sites of Palestine-Transjordan: Analysis of Sedentary Adaptation at the End of the Third Millennium, B.C. Unpublished Ph.D. dissertation. Drew University.

2003   Theory in Archaeology: Culture change at the End of the Early Bronze Age. Pp. 308–318 in *Near Eastern Archaeology: A Reader,* ed. S. Richard. Winona Lake, IN: Eisenbrauns.

Long, J. C., Jr., and Libby, B.

1999   Khirbet Iskander. Archaeology in Jordan, eds. V. Egan and P. M. Bikai. *American Journal of Archaeology* 103: 498–99.

Long, J. C., Jr., and Richard, S.
2007 Expedition 2007 to Khirbet Iskander, Jordan. Paper delivered at the Annual Meeting of the American Schools of Oriental Research, San Diego, CA.

Mabry, J. B.
1989 Investigations at Tell el-Handaquq, Jordan (1987-88). *Annual of the Department of Antiquities of Jordan* 33: 59–95
1992 Alluvial Cycles and Early Agricultural Settlement Phases in the Jordan Valley. Unpublished Ph.D. dissertation. University of Arizona.

MacDonald, B.
1992 *The Southern Ghors and Northeast 'Arabah Archaeological Survey.* Sheffield Archaeological Monographs 5. Sheffield:Collis.

Maddin, R., Muhly, J. D., and Stech, T.
2003 Metallurgical Studies on Copper Artefacts from Bâb edh-Dhrâ'. Pp. 513–21 in *Bâb edh-Dhrâ': Excavations at the Town Site (1975–1981),* eds. W. E. Rast and R. T. Schaub. Winona Lake, IN.: Eisenbrauns.

Magness-Gardiner, B., and Falconer, S. E.
1994 Community, Polity and Temple in a Middle Bronze Age Village. *Journal of Mediterranean Archaeology* 7: 127–64.

Mattingly, G. L.
1980 A Reconstruction of Early Bronze Age Cultural Patterns in Central Moab. Unpublished Ph.D. dissertation. Southern Baptist Theological Seminary.

Mazzoni, S.
1985 Elements of the Culture of Early Syrian Ebla in Comparison with Syro-Palestinian EB IV. *Bulletin of the American Schools of Oriental Research* 257: 1–18.

McConaughy, M. A.
2003 Chipped Stone Tools at Bâb edh-Dhrâ'.Pp. 473–512 in *Bâb edh-Dhrâ': Excavation at the Town Site (1975–81),* eds. W. E. Rast and R. T. Schaub. Reports of the Expedition to the Dead Sea Plain, Jordan 2. Winona Lake, IN: Eisenbrauns.

McCreery, D. W.
1980 The Nature and Cultural Implications of Early Bronze Age Agriculture in the Southern Ghor of Jordan: An Archaeological Reconstruction. Unpublished Ph.D. dissertation. University of Pittsburgh.

McDonald, M., Sir, and Partners
1965 *East Bank Jordan Water Resources: Diversion of the Wâdi Walâ.* Amman: Hashemite Kingdom of Jordan, Central Water Authority.

McLaren, P. B.
2003 *The Military Architecture of Jordan During the Middle Bronze Age: New Evidence from Pella and Rukeis.* BAR International Series 1202. Oxford: Archaeopress.

Miller, N. F.
1991 The Near East. Pp. 133–60 in *Progress in Old Worked Paleoethnobotany: A Retrospective View on the Occasion of 20 Years of the International Work Group for Paleoethnobotany,* eds. W. Van Zeist, K. Wasylikova, and K. E. Behre. Rotterdam: Balkema.

Mitchel, L.
1989 Field D: The Lower Southern Terrace. Pp. 282–95 in *Madaba Plains Project 1: The 1984 Season at Tell el-'Umeiri and Vicinity and Subsequent Studies,* eds. L. T. Geraty, L. G. Herr, Ø S. LaBianca, and R. W. Younker. Berrien Springs, MI: Andrews University.

Moorman, E.
1959 *The Soils of East Jordan: Report to the Government of Jordan. Expanded Technical Assistance Program,* No. 1132. Rome: Food and Agriculture Organization (FAL).

Musil, A.
1907 *Arabia Petraea I.* Vienna: Holder.

Naval Intelligence Division
1943 *Palestine and Transjordan.* B.R. 14 Geographical Handbook Series. London: Oxford and Cambridge University for the Naval Intelligence Division of the Admiralty.

Neef, R.
1990   Introduction, Development and Environmental Implications of Olive Culture: The Evidence from Jordan. Pp. 295–306 in *Man's Role in the Shaping of the Eastern Mediterranean Landscape,* eds. S. Bottema, G. Enties-Nieborg, and W. van Zeist. Rotterdam: Balkema.

Nigro, L.
2003   Tell es-Sultan in the Early Bronze Age IV (2300–2000 BC.): Settlement vs. Necropolis– A Stratigraphic Periodization. *Contributi e Materiali di Archeologia Orientale 9:* 121–58.
2006   *Khirbet al-Batrawy: An Early Bronze Age Fortified Town in North-Central Jordan: Preliminary Report of the First Season of Excavations* (2005). Studies on the Archaeology of Palestine and Transjordan 3. Rome: Università di Roma "La Sapienza".

NSMLUP
        National Soil Map and Land Use Project (1989-1995). The Ministry of Agriculture (MOA), the Royal Jordanian Geographic Centre and Huntings Technical Service (UK).

Olávarri, E.
1965   Sondages à l'Aro'er sur l'Arnon. *Revue Biblique* 2: 77–94.
1969   Fouilles à l'Aro'er sur l'Arnon. *Revue Biblique* 76: 230–59.

Oren,E. D., and Yekutieli, Y.
1990   North Sinai during the MBI Period–Pastoral Nomadism and Sedentary Settlement. *Eretz-Israel* 21: 6–22

Orni, E., and Efrat, E.
1971   *Geography of Israel.* 3rd rev. ed. Jerusalem: Israel Universities.

Orthmann, W.
1981   *Halawa 1977–1979.* Bonn: Habelt.

Ortner, D.
1981   A Preliminary Report on the Human Remains from the Bâb edh-Dhrâ'. Cemetery. *Annual of the American Schools of Oriental Research* 46: 119–32

O'Tool, N.
1991   Other finds. Pp. 132–35 in *Excavations at Tell Um Hammad 1982–1984,* ed. A. D. G.Betts. Edinburgh: Edinburgh University.

Palumbo, G.
1987   "Egalitarian" or "Stratified" Society? Some Notes on Mortuary Practices and Social Structure at Jericho in EB IV. *Bulletin of the American Schools of Oriental Research* 267: 43–59.
1990   *The Early Bronze IV in the Southern Levant: Settlement Patterns, Economy, and Material Culture of a "Dark Age."* Contributi e Materiali di Archeologia Orientale III. Roma: Università di Roma "La Sapienza".
1994   *Jordan Antiquities Database and Informations System: A Summary of the Data.* Amman: Department of Antiquities of Jordan and American Center of Oriental Research.
2008   Early Bronze Age IV. Pp. 227–62 in *Jordan: An Archaeological Reader,* ed. R. B. Adams. London: Equinox.

Palumbo, G.; Mabry, J.; and Kuijt, I.
1990   The Wadi el-Yabis Survey: Report on the 1989 Field Season. *Annual of the Department of Antiquities of Jordan* 34: 95–118.

Palumbo, G.; Munzi, M.; Collins, S.; Hourani, F.; Peruzzetto, A.; and Wilson, M. D.
1996   The Wadi az-Zarqa/Wadi ad-Dulayil Excavations and Survey Project: Report on the October–November 1993 Fieldwork Season. *Annual of the Department of Antiquities of Jordan* 40: 375–427.

Palumbo, G., and Peterman, G.
1993   Early Bronze Age IV Ceramic Regionalism in Central Jordan. *Bulletin of the American Schools of Oriental Research* 289: 23–32.

Parker-Pearson, M.
1999   *The Archaeology of Death and Burial.* College Station, TX: Texas A & M University.

Parr, P. J.
1956   Khirbet Iskander. Excavations in Jordan, 1953–1954. *Annual of the Department of Antiquities of Jordan* 3: 81.

1960 Excavations at Khirbet Iskander. *Annual of the Department of Antiquities of Jordan* 4–6: 128–33.

2009 Afterword. Pp. in 118–21 in *The Levant in Transition*, ed. P. J. Parr. Palestine Exploration Fund Annual 9. London: Maney.

Parsche, F.; Ziegelmayer,G.;
and Behm-Blancke, M.

1984 Hassek Höyük: Vorläufiger Bericht über die Grabungen den Jahren 1981–1983. *Istanbuler Mitteilungen* 34: 31–149.

1992 *Hassek Höyük: Naturwissenschaftliche Untersuchungen und Lithische Industrie.* Tübingen: Wasmuth.

Payne, S.

1973 Kill-off Patterns in Sheep and Goats: the Mandibles from Aşvan-Kale. *Anatolian Studies* 23: 281–304.

Peretz, B., and Smith, P.

2004 Dental Morphology and Pathology of Middle Bronze Age Populations in Israel: Sasa and Jebel Qaʻaqir. *ʻAtiqot* 46: 45–49.

Perrot, J.

1961 Une Tombe Ossuaires du IVe Millénaire à Azor près de Tel Aviv. *ʻAtiqot* 111: 1–83.

Philip, G.

1989 *Metal Weapons of the Early and Middle Bronze Age in Syria-Palestine.* BAR International Series 526. Oxford: British Archaeological Reports.

2001 The Early Bronze I–III Ages. Pp. 163–232 in *The Archaeology of Jordan*, eds. B. MacDonald, R. Adams, and P. Bienkowski. Sheffield: Sheffield University.

2008 The Early Bronze Age I–III. Pp. 161–226 in *Jordan: An Archaeological Reader*, ed. R. B. Adams. London: Equinox.

Platt, E. E.

2000 The Objects. Pp. 201–214 in *Madaba Plains Project 4: The 1992 Season at Tall al-ʻUmayri and Subsequent Studies*, eds. L. G. Herr, D. R. Clark, L. T. Geraty, R. W. Younker, and Ø. S. LaBianca. Berrien Springs, MI: Andrews University.

Porat, N.

1984 Petrography and Mineralogy of Pottery from Archaeological Sites from Southern Israel. Unpublished MSc. thesis. Hebrew University of Jerusalem. (Hebrew.)

1989a Petrography of Pottery from Southern Israel and Sinai. Pp. 169–88 in *L'urbanisation de la Palestine a l'âge du Bronze ancien, bilan et perspectives des recherches actuelles* I, ed. P. de Miroschedji. BAR International Series 527. London: British Archaeological Reports.

1989b Composition of Pottery - Application to the Study of the Interrelations between Canaan and Egypt during the 3rd Millennium B.C. Unpublished Ph.D. dissertation. Hebrew University of Jerusalem.

Prag, K.

1971 A Study of the Intermediate Early Bronze— Bronze Age in Transjordan, Syria and Lebanon. Unpublished Ph.D dissertation. St. Hugh's College, University of Oxford.

1974 The Intermediate Early Bronze–Middle Bronze Age: An Interpretation of the Evidence from Transjordan, Syria, and Lebanon. *Levant* 6: 69–116.

1986 The Intermediate Early Bronze–Middle Bronze Age Sequences at Jericho and Tell Iktanu Reviewed. *Bulletin of the American Schools of Oriental Research* 264: 61-72.

1988 Kilns of the Intermediate Early Bronze–Middle Bronze Age Sequences at Tell Iktanu: Preliminary Report, 1987 Season. *Annual of the Departmenet of Antiquities of Jordan* 32: 59–72.

1990 Preliminary Report on the Excavations at Tell Iktanu, Jordan, 1989. *Annual of the Department of Antiquities of Jordan* 34: 119–30.

1991 Preliminary Report on the Excavations at Tell Iktanu and Tell al-Hammam, Jordan *Levant* 23: 55–66.

1995 The Dead Sea Dolmens: Death and the Landscape. Pp. 75–84 in *The Archaeology of Death,* eds. S. Campbell and A. Green. Oxbow Monograph 51. Oxford: Oxbow.

2001　The Third Millennium in Jordan: A Perspective, Past and Future. Pp. 179–190 in *Studies in the History and Archaeology of Jordan VII*. Amman: Department of Antiquities, Jordan.

2009　The Late Third millennium in the Levant: A Reappraisal of the North–South Divide. Pp. 80–89 in *The Levant in Transition*, ed. P. J. Parr. Palestine Exploration Fund Annual 9. London: Maney.

Pritchard, J. B.

1963　*The Bronze Age Cemetery at Gibeon*. Philadelphia, PA: The University Museum, University of Pennsylvania.

Quennell, A. M.

1955　Geological Map of Jordan (East of the Rift Valley) 1:250,000; Sheet Kerak. Amman: Hashemite Kingdom.

Rainfall in Jordan: Water Years 1976–1980

1980　Technical Paper No. 50. Amman: The Hashemite Kingdom of Jordan, Water Authority, Water Resources Department.

Rast, W. E.

1980　Palestine in the Third Millennium: Evidence for Interconnections. *Scripta Mediterranea* 1: 5–20.

Rast, W. E., and Schaub, R. T.

1978　Preliminary Report of Excavations at Bâb edh-Dhrâʿ, 1975. Pp. 1–31 in *Preliminary Excavation Reports: Bâb edh-Dhrâʿ, Sardis, Meiron, Tell el-Hesi, Carthage (Punic)*, ed. D. N. Freedman. Annual of the American Schools of Oriental Research 43. Cambridge, MA: American Schools of Oriental Research.

2003　*Bab edh-Dhra': Excavations at the Town Site (1975–1981)*. Parts 1–2. Reports of the Expedition to the Dead Sea Plain, Jordan 2. Winona Lake, IN: Eisenbrauns

Redding, R.

1981　Decision-Making in Subsistence Herding of Sheep and Goats in the Middle East. Unpublished Ph.D. dissertation. University of Michigan

Rice, P. M.

1987　*Pottery Analysis: A Sourcebook*. Chicago, IL: University of Chicago.

Richard, S.

1978　End of the Early Bronze Age in Palestine-Transjordan: A Study of the Post-EB III Cultural Complex. Unpublished Ph.D. dissertation. The Johns Hopkins University.

1980　Toward a Consensus of Opinion on the End of the Early Bronze Age in Palestine-Transjordan. *Bulletin of the American Schools of Oriental Research* 237: 5–34.

1982　Report of the 1981 Season of Survey and Soundings at Khirbet Iskander. *Annual of the Department of Antiquities of Jordan* 26: 289–99.

1983　Report on the Expedition to Khirbet Iskander and its Vicinity, 1982. *Annual of the Department of Antiquities of Jordan* 27: 45–53.

1987a　The Early Bronze Age: The Rise and Collapse of Urbanism. *Biblical Archaeologist* 50: 22–43.

1987b　Questions of Nomadic Incursions at the End of the 3rd Millennium B.C. Pp.241–46 in *Studies in the History ad Archaeology of Jordan* 3, ed. A. Hadidi. Amman: Department of Antiquities.

1988　Four Seasons of Excavations at the Early Bronze IV Site of Khirbet Iskander. *Liber Annuus* 37: 40–44.

1989　Khirbet Iskander. Pp. 301–9 in *Archaeology of Jordan II: Field Reports*, eds. J. B. Hennessy and D. Homès-Fredericq. Assyriological Foundation Georges Dossin. Brussels: Peeters.

1990　Expedition to Khirbet Iskander and its Vicinity. Fourth Preliminary Report. Pp. 33–58 in *Bulletin of the American Schools of Oriental Research Supplement* 26, ed. W. E. Rast. Baltimore: Johns Hopkins University for the American Schools of Oriental Research.

1991　Khirbet Iskander. Archaeology in Jordan, ed. B. De Vries. *American Journal of Archaeology* 95: 262–64.

2000 Chronology vs. Regionalism in the Early Bronze IV Period: An Assemblage of Whole and Restored Vessels from the Public Building at Khirbet Iskander. Pp. 399–417 in *The Archaeology of Jordan and Beyond: Essays in Honor of James A. Sauer,* eds. L. E. Stager, J. A. Greene, and M. D. Coogan. Winona Lake, IN: Eisenbrauns.

2002 2000 Season of Excavations at Khirbet Iskander, Jordan. Pp. 105–14 in *Proceedings, Eastern Great Lakes and Midwest Biblical Societies, Vol. 21,* ed. B. Fiore. Buffalo, NY: Canisius College.

2003 The Early Bronze Age in the Southern Levant. Pp. 286–302 in *Near Eastern Archaeology: A Reader,* ed. S. Richard. Winona Lake: IN: Eisenbrauns.

2006 Early Bronze IV Transitions: An Archaeometallurgical Study. Pp.119–32 in *Confronting the Past: Archaeological and Historical Essays on Ancient Israel in honor of William G. Dever,* eds. S. Gitin, J. E. Wright, and J. P. Dessel. Winona Lake, IN: Eisenbrauns.

n.d.a Early Bronze Age of Jordan. In *Oxford Handbook of the Levant,* eds. A. Killebrew and M. Steiner. Oxford: Oxford University.

2009 Early Bronze IV Peoples: Connections between the Living and the Dead at Khirbat Iskander. Pp. 61–701 in *Studies in the History and Archaeology of Jordan X,* ed. F. al-Khraysheh. Amman: Department of Antiquities.

Richard, S., and Boraas, R. S.

1984 Preliminary Report of the 1981–82 Seasons of the Expedition to Khirbet Iskander and Its Vicinity. *Bulletin of the American Schools of Oriental Research* 254: 63–87.

1988 The Early Bronze IV Fortified Site of Khirbet Iskander, Jordan: Third Preliminary Report, 1984 Season. Pp. 107–30 in *Bulletin of the American Schools of Oriental Research Supplement* 25, ed. W. E. Rast. Baltimore, MD: Johns Hopkins University for the American Schools of Oriental Research.

Richard, S., and Holdorf, P. S.

2000 An Overall Assessment of the EB IV Ceramic Tradition at Khirbet Iskander with a Chronotypological Comparison to Bâb edh-Dhrâ'. Paper delivered at the Annual Meeting of the American Schools of Oriental Research, Nashville, TN.

Richard, S., and Long, J. C., Jr.

1995a Archaeological Expedition to Khirbat Iskandar and its Vicinity, 1994. *Annual of the Department of Antiquities of Jordan* 39: 81–92.

1995b Khirbet Iskander. Archaeology in Jordan, eds. P. M. Bikai, and D. Kooring. *American Journal of Archaeology* 99: 512–14.

1998 Khirbet Iskander. Archaeology in Jordan, eds. V. Egan and P. M. Bikai. *American Journal of Archaeology* 102: 587–88.

2000 Khirbet Iskander. *ACOR Newsletter* 12.1 (Summer): 7–8.

2006 Three Seasons of Excavations at Khirbet Iskander, Jordan: 1997, 2000, 2004. *Annual of the Department of Antiquities of Jordan* 49: 261–76.

2007a Social Institutions at Khirbet Iskander: An Argument for Elites in EB IV. Pp. 71–81 in *Studies in the History and Archaeology of Jordan IX,* ed. F. al-Khraysheh. Amman: Department of Antiquities.

2007b Khirbet Iskander: A City in Collapse at the end of the Early Bronze Age. Pp. 269–76 in *Crossing Jordan– North American Contributions to the Archaeology of Jordan.* Eds. T. E. Levy, P. M. M. Daviau, R. W. Younker and M. Shaer. London: Equinox.

2009 Khirbet Iskander, Jordan and Early Bronze IV Studies: A View from a Tell. Pp. 90–100 in *The Levant in Transition,* ed. P. J. Parr. Palestine Exploration Fund Annual 9. London: Maney.

Richard, S.; Long, J.; and Libby, B

2001 Khirbet Iskander. Archaeology in Jordan 2001, eds. S. A. Savage, K. A. Zamora, and D. R. Keller. *American Journal of Archaeology* 105:3: 440–41.

2004   Khirbet Iskander. *ACOR Newsletter* 16.2
        (Winter): 4–5.
2005   Khirbet Iskander. Archaeology in Jordan,
        2004, eds. S. A. Savage, K. A. Zamora, and D.
        R. Keller. *American Journal of Archaeology*
        108: 541–42.
2007   Khirbet Iskander. *ACOR Newsletter* 19.2
        (Winter): 7–8.
2008   Khirbet Iskander. Archaeology in Jordan
        2007, eds. S. A. Savage, C. Tuttle, and D. R.
        Keller. *American Journal of Archaeology* 112:
        521–22.

Robinson, E. G. D.
1995   Basil Hennessy and the Nicholson Museum:
        Two Early Bronze Age IV Tomb Groups
        from Jericho. Pp. 62–80 in *Trade, Contact,
        and the Movement of Peoples in the Eastern
        Mediterranean: Studies in Honour of J. Basil
        Hennessy,* eds. S. Bourke and J.-P. Descœu-
        dres. Mediterranean Archaeology Supple-
        ment 3. Sydney: Australian Archaeological
        Institute at Athens.

Rosen, A. M.
1986a   *Cities of Clay: The Geoarchaeology of Tells.*
        Prehistoric Archaeology and Ecology Se-
        ries, eds. K. W. Butzer and L. G. Freeman.
        Chicago, IL: University of Chicago.
1986b   Environmental Change a Settlement at Tell
        Lachish, Israel. *Bulletin of the American
        Schools of Oriental Research* 263: 55–60.
1989   Environmental Change at the End of
        Early Bronze Age Palestine. Pp. 247–55
        in *L'urbanisation de la Palestine à l'âge du
        Bronze ancient: Bilan et perspectives des
        recherces actuelles,* Part 2, ed. P. de Miro-
        schedji. BAR International Series 527. Ox-
        ford: British Archaeological Reports.
1991   Early Bronze Age Tel Eraini: An Environ-
        mental Perspective. *Tel Aviv* 18: 192–204.
1995   Preliminary Analysis of Phytoliths from
        Prehistoric Sites in Southern Jordan. Pp.
        399–403 in *Prehistoric Cultural Ecology and
        Evolution: Insights from Southern Jordan,* ed.
        D. O. Henry. New York: Plenum.

Rosen, S. T.
1997   *Lithics After the Stone Age: A Handbook of
        Stone Tools from the Levant.* Walnut Creek,
        CA: Altamira.

Ross, J. F.
1980   The Early Bronze Age in Palestine. Pp. 147–
        70 in *Historical Essays in Honor of Kenneth
        R. Rossman,* edited by K. Newmyer. Crete,
        NE: Doane College.

Roux, V.
1985   *Materiel de broyage: étude ethnoarchéologi-
        que à Tichitt (R.I. Mauritanie).* Mémoire 58.
        Paris: Éditions Recherche sur les Civilisa-
        tions.

Rowan, Y. M.
2003   The Ground Stone Assemblage. Pp. 183–202
        in *Salvage Excavations at the Early Bronze
        Age Site of Qiryat 'Ata,* ed. A. Golani. Israel
        Antiquity Authority Reports 18. Jerusalem:
        Israel Antiquity Authority.
2005   The Groundstone Assemblages. Pp. 113–39
        in *Shoham (North): Late Chalcolithic Burial
        Caves in the Lod Valley, Israel,* eds. E. C. M.
        van den Brink and R. Gophna. Israel Antiq-
        uity Authority Reports 27. Jerusalem: Israel
        Antiquity Authority.
2006   The Ground Stone Assemblage. Pp. 211–50
        in *'En Esur ('Ein Assawir) I. Excavations at
        a Protohistoric Site in the Coastal Plain of Is-
        rael,* ed. E. Yannai. Israel Antiquity Author-
        ity Reports 31. Jerusalem: Israel Antiquity
        Authority.

Rowan, Y. M., and Ebling, J. R.
2008   The Potential of Ground Stone Studies. Pp.
        1–15 in *New Approaches to Old Stones: Re-
        cent Studies of Ground Stone Artifacts,* eds.
        Y. M. Rowan and J. R. Ebeling. London:
        Equinox.

Rowan, Y.; Levy, T. E.; Goren, Y.; and Alon, D.
2006   Gilat's Grinding Stone Assemblage: Stone
        Fenestrated Stands, Bowls, Palettes, and Re-
        lated Artifacts. Pp. 575–684 in *Archaeology,
        Anthropology and Cult: The Sanctuary at
        Gilat,* eds. D. Alon and T. E. Levy. Leicester:
        Leicester University.

Rowton, M.
1967   The Woodlands of Ancient Western Asia. *Journal of Near Eastern Studies* 26: 261–77.

Runnels, C.
1981   A Diachronic Study and Economic Analysis of Millstones from the Argolid. Ph.D. dissertation. Indiana University, Bloomington.

Sass, B.
2000   Finds. Pp. 349–423 in *Megiddo III: 1992–1996 Seasons. Vol. II*, eds. I. Finkelstein, D. Ussishkin, and B. Halpern. Tel Aviv: Tel Aviv University.

Sauders, R. R.
2001   A Technological Analysis of the EB IV Pottery at Khirbet Iskander. Unpublished M.A. thesis. American University.

Savage, S. H.; Falconer, S. E.; and Harrison, T. P.
2007   The Early Bronze Age City-States of the Southern Levant: Neither Cities nor States. Pp. 285–97 in *Crossing Jordan: North American Contributions to the Archaeology of Jordan*, eds. T. E. Levy, P. M. M. Daviau, R. W. Younker, and M. Shaer. London: Equinox.

Schaub, R. T.
2000   Ceramic Corpus of the EB IV village of Bâb edh-Dhrâ' with suggested Correlations to the EB IV pottery of Khirbet Iskander. Paper delivered at the Annual Meeting of the American Schools of Oriental Research, Nashville, TN.
2009   The Southern Ghors and the Kerak Plateau in EB IV. Pp. 101–10 in *The Levant in Tradition,* ed. P. J. Parr. Palestine Exploration Fund Quarterly 9. London: Maney.

Schaub, R. T., and W. E. Rast
1989   *Bâb edh-Dhrâ': Excavations in the Cemetery Directed by Paul W. Lapp (1965–67).* Reports of the Expedition to the Dead Sea Plain, Jordan 1. Winona Lake, IN: Eisenbrauns.

Schick, C.
1879   Journey into Moab. *Palestine Exploration Fund Quarterly Statement*: 187–92.

Schneider, J.
1993   Milling Implements: Biases and Problems in their use as Indicators of Prehistoric Behavior and Paleoenvironment. *Pacific Coast Archaeological Society Quarterly* 29: 5–21.

Schwab, M. J.; Newmann, F.; Litt, T.; Negendank, J. F. W.; and Stein, M.
2004   Holocene Palaeoecology of the Golan Heights (Near East): Investigation of Lacustrine Sediments from Birkat Ram Crater Lake. *Quaternary Science Reviews 23*: 1723–31.

Shamir, O.
1966a   A Spindle Whorl. P. 22 in Salvage Excavations in the Early Bronze Age Site of Me'ona. Final Report. '*Atiqot* 28: 1–39.
1966b   Loomweights and Whorls. Pp. 135–70 in *Excavations at the City of David 1978–1985, Vol. IV,* eds. D. T. Ariel and A. De Groot. Jerusalem: Israel Exploration Society.
1999   A Spindle Whorl. P. 32 in *Salvage Excavations at the Early Bronze Age IA Settlement at Azor*, eds. A. Golani and E. C. M. van den Brink. '*Atiqot* 38.

Shehadeh, N.
1985   The Climate of Jordan in the Past and Present. Pp 25–37 in *Studies in the History and Archaeology of Jordan* 2, ed. A. Hadidi. New York, NY: Kegan Paul.

Shinaq, R., and Bandel, K.
1998   Lithostratigraphy of the Belqa Group (Late Cretaceous) in Northern Jordan. *Mitteilungen des Geologisch-Paläontologischen Instituts, Universität Hamburg* 81: 163–84.

Shinaq, R.; Shereideh, S.; and Saifuldin, N.
2006   Microfacies and Depositional Environment of Upper Cretaceous Phosphorites in Northern Jordan. *Paläontologie, Stratigraphie, Fazies* 14, Freiberger Forschungshefte, C 511: 43–56. Freiberg: Technische Universität.

Silver, I. A.
1969   The Aging of Domestic Animals. Pp 283–302 in *Science in Archaeology*, eds. D. R. Brothwell and E. S. Higgs. New York, NY: Praeger.

Sinopoli, C. M.

1991 *Approaches to Archaeological Ceramics*. New York, NY: Plenum.

Smith, G. A.

[1933] 1966 *The Historical Geography of the Holy Land*. 25th ed. Reprint, with an introduction by H. H. Rowley. New York, NY: Harper & Row.

Smith, P.

1982 The Physical Characteristics and Biological Affinities of the Skeletal Remains from Jabel Qaʿaqir. *Bulletin of the American Schools of Oriental Research* 245: 65–73.

1984 The Skeletal Biology and Paleopathology of Early Bronze Age Populations in the Levant. Pp. 297–313 in *L'Urbanisation de la Palestine à l'age du Bronze ancien: Bilan et perspectives des recherces actuelles*, Part 2, ed. P. de Miroschedji. BAR International Series 527. Oxford: British Archaeological Reports.

Smith, R. H., and Hennessy, J. B.

1992 The Early Bronze Age. Pp. 29-34 in *Pella in Jordan 2: The Second Interim Report of the Joint University of Sydney and College of Wooster Excavations at Pella, 1982–1985*, eds. A. W. McNicoll, P. C. Edwards, J. Hanbury-Tenison, J. B. Hennessy, T. F. Potts, R. H. Smith, A. Walmsley, and P. Watson. Mediterranean Archaeology Supplement 2. Sydney: Australian Archaeological Institute at Athens.

Soil Survey Staff

1975 *Soil Taxonomy, A Basic System of Soil Classification for Making and Interpreting Soils*. Soil Conservation Service, United States Department of Agriculture, Agricultural Handbook No. 436.

Steele, C. S.

1989 Early Bronze Age Socio-Political Organization in Southwestern Jordan. *Zeitschrift des Deutschen Palästina-Vereins* 105: 1–33.

Tadmor, M.

1978 A Cult Cave of the Middle Bronze Age I Near Qedesh. *Israel Exploration Journal* 28: 1–30.

Tubb, J. N.

1990 *Excavations at the Early Bronze Age Cemetery of Tiwal esh-Sharqi*. London: British Museum.

Ullinger, J.

2006 Daily Activity and Its Skeletal Impact at Bâb edh-Dhrâʿ. Paper delivered at the Annual Meeting of the American Schools of Oriental Research, Philadelphia, PA.

Ushishkin, D.

1980 The Ghassulian Shrine at En-Gedi. *Tel Aviv* 7: 1–44.

Vinitzky, L.

1992 The Date of the Dolmens in the Golan and the Galilee: A Reassessment. *Tel Aviv* 19: 100–12.

Waheeb, M., and Palumbo, G.

1993 Salvage Excavations at a Bronze Age Cemetery near Tell el-Umeiri. *Annual of the Department of Antiquities of Jordan* 337: 147–63.

Weinstein, J. M.

2003 A New Set of Radiocarbon Dates from the Town Site. Pp. 638–48 in *Bâb edh-Dhrâʿ: Excavations at the Town Site (1975–1981)*, eds. W. E. Rast and R. T. Schaub. Winona Lake, IN.: Eisenbrauns.

Weiss, H.

2000 Beyond the Younger Dryas: Collapse as Adaptation to Abrupt Climate Change in Ancient West Asia and the Eastern Mediterranean. Pp. 75–98 in *Confronting Natural Disaster: Engaging the Past to Understand the Future*, eds. G. Bawden and R. Reycraft. Albuquerque, NM: University of New Mexico.

Western, A. C.

1971 The Ecological Interpretation of Ancient Charcoals from Jericho. *Levant* 3: 31–40.

Wightman, G. J.

1988 An EB IV Cemetery in the North Jordan Valley. *Levant* 20: 139–59.

Wilkinson, A.
1989a Objects from the Early Bronze I Tombs: Jewelry Beads. Pp. 302–16 in *Bâb edh-Dhrâʿ: Excavations in the Cemetery Directed by Paul W. Lapp (1965–67)*. Reports of the Expedition to the Dead Sea Plain, Jordan 1. Winona Lake, IN.: Eisenbrauns for the American Schools of Oriental Research.
1989b Objects from the Early Bronze II and III Tombs. Pp. 444–70 in *Bâb edh-Dhrâʿ: Excavations in the Cemetery Directed by Paul W. Lapp (1965-67)*. Reports of the Expedition to the Dead Sea Plain, Jordan 1. Winona Lake, IN: Eisenbrauns for the American Schools of Oriental Research.

Wilcox, G. H.
1974 A History of Deforestation as Indicated by Charcoal Analysis of Four Sites in Eastern Anatolia. *Anatolian Studies* 24: 117–23.

Wright, G. E.
1937 *The Pottery of Palestine from the Earliest Times to the End of the Early Bronze Age*. New Haven, CT: American Schools of Oriental Research.
1971 Archaeology of Palestine from the Neolithic Through the Middle Bronze Age. *Journal of the American Oriental Society* 91: 276–93.

Wright, K. I.
1991 The Origins and Development of Ground Stone Assemblages in Late Pleistocene Southwest Asia. *Paleorient* 17: 19–45.
1992a Ground Stone Assemblage Variations and Subsistence Strategies in the Levant, 22,000-5,500 B.P. Unpublished Ph.D. dissertation. Yale University
1992b A Classification System for Ground Stone Tools from the Prehistoric Levant. *Paléorient* 18: 53–81.

1993 Early Holocene Ground Stone Assemblages in the Levant. *Levant* 25: 93–111.

Zayadine, F.
1978 An EB–MB Bilobate Tomb at Amman. Pp. 59–66 in *Archaeology in the Levant: Essays in Honor of Kathleen M. Kenyon*, eds. P. R. S. Moorey and P. J. Parr. Warminster: Aris & Philips.

Zeist, W. van
1985 Past and Present Environments of the Jordan Valley. Pp 199–204 in *Studies in the History and Archaeology of Jordan* 2, ed. A. Hadidi. New York, NY: Kegan Paul.

Zeist, W. van, and Bottema, S.
1982 Vegetational History of the Eastern Mediterranean and the Near East during the last 20,000 years. Pp. 277–321 in *Palaeoclimates, Palaeoenvironments and Human Communities in the Eastern Mediterranean Region in Later Prehistory*, Pt. 2, eds. J. L. Bintliff and W. van Zeist. BAR International Series 133. Oxford: British Archaeological Reports.

Zohar, M.
1989 Rogem Hiri: A Megalithic Monument in the Golan. *Israel Exploration Journal* 39: 18–31.

Zohary, M.
1962 *Plant Life of Palestine: Israel and Jordan*. New York, NY: Ronald.
1966 *Flora Palestina, Vol 1, Part 1, Text: Equisetacea to Moringaceae*. Jerusalem: Israel Academy of Sciences and Humanities.
1973 *Geobotanical Foundations of the Middle East*, Vol. 1. Stuttgart: Fischer.

Geographical Index

Names of Sites, Places, Regions/Zones, and Geographic Features